Brittany

M. Renaudeau/HOA QUI

*... these granite crosses rise up everywhere on the
advanced cliffs of this mariners' land, as if beseeching
mercy; as if seeking to appease the great,
moving mysterious thing, which lures men and does not
give them back ... One could see, outlined into the far
distance, one beyond the other, all the indentations
of the coast; the land of Brittany ended in
denticulated points which stretched out into the
tranquil emptiness of the waters.*

Pierre Loti
Pêcheur d'Islande

Travel Publications

38 Clarendon Road – WATFORD Herts WD1 1 SX – U.K.
Tel. (01923) 415 000
www.michelin-travel.com
TheGreenGuide-uk@uk.michelin.com

Manufacture française des pneumatiques Michelin

Société en commandite par actions au capital de 2 000 000 000 de francs
Place des Carmes-Déchaux – 63 Clermont-Ferrand (France)
R.C.S. Clermont-Fd B 855 200 507

Dépôt légal Août 2000 – ISBN 2-06-000060-2 – ISSN 0763-1383
Printed in France – 03-01/5.2

Typesetting: NORD COMPO à Villeneuve-d'Ascq
Printing and binding: I.F.C.-ASKRÉA à St-Germain-du-Puy

Cover design: Carré Noir, Paris 17ᵉ arr.

THE GREEN GUIDE:
The Spirit of Discovery

*The exhilaration of new horizons,
the fun of seeing the world,
the excitement of discovery: this is
what we seek to share with you.
To help you make the most of your
travel experience, we offer first-hand
knowledge and turn a discerning eye
on places to visit.
This wealth of information gives
you the expertise to plan your own
enriching adventure. With THE
GREEN GUIDE showing you the way,
you can explore new destinations
with confidence or rediscover old
ones.
Leisure time spent with THE GREEN
GUIDE is also a time for refreshing
your spirit, enjoying yourself, and
taking advantage of our selection
of fine restaurants, hotels and other
places for relaxing.
So turn the page and open a window
on the world. Join THE GREEN
GUIDE in the spirit of discovery.*

Contents

Calvary in Gurunhuel,
typical of Breton religious expression

H. Gyssels/DIAF

Embroidery on vestments used for
a traditional procession in Locronan

J.-M. Roignant/HOA QUI

Practical information

Colourful sails catch the wind
off the coast of Port–Blanc

Place des Lices
in Vannes

Maps
and plans

ROAD MAPS
FOR THIS REGION

Motorists who plan ahead will always have the appropriate maps at hand. Michelin products are complementary: for each of the sights listed in The Green Guide, map references are indicated which help you find your location on our range of maps. The image below shows the maps to use for each geographic area covered in this guide.

To travel the roads in this region, you may use any of the following:

• the **regional map** at a scale of 1:200 000 no 230, which covers the main roads and secondary roads, and includes useful indications for finding tourist attractions. This is a good map to choose for travelling in a wide area. At a quick glance, you can locate and identify the main sights to see. In addition to identifying the nature of the road ways, the maps show castles, churches and other religious edifices, scenic view points, megalithic monuments, swimming beaches on the coast, lakes and rivers, swimming pools, golf courses, race tracks, air fields, and more.

• the **detailed maps** are based on the regional map data, but with a reduced format (about half a region), which makes them easier to consult and fold. These maps are recommended for tourists who plan to stay within a limited area, without travelling far. For Brittany, use maps 56, 59 and 63.

• **departmental maps** (at a scale of 1:150 000, an enlargement of the 1:200 000 maps). These maps are very easy to read, and make it easy to travel on all of the roads in the following departments: Côtes-d'Armor (4022), Finistère (4029), Ille-et-Villaine (4035), Morbihan (4056). They come with a complete index of place names and include a plan of the towns which serve as administrative seats (préfectures).

And remember to travel with the latest edition of the **map of France** no **989**, which gives an overall view of the region of Brittany, and the main access roads which connect it to the rest of France. The entire country is mapped at A 1:1 000 000 scale and clearly shows the main road network.

Michelin is pleased to offer a route-planning service on the Internet: **www.michelin-travel.com**. Choose the shortest route, a route without tolls, or the Michelin recommended route to your destination; you can also access information about hotels and restaurants from The Red Guide, and tourists sites from The Green Guide. *Bon voyage!*

There are a number of useful maps and plans in the guide, listed here:

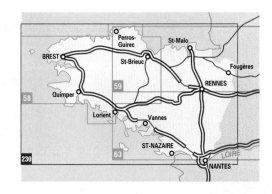

Using this guide

● The summary maps on the following pages are designed to assist you in planning your trip: the **Map of principal sights** identifies major sights and attractions, the **Touring programmes** propose regional driving itineraries and the **Places to stay map** points out pleasant holiday spots.

● We recommend that you read the **Introduction** before setting out on your trip. The background information it contains on history, the arts and traditional culture will prove most instructive and make your visit more meaningful.

● The main towns and attractions are presented in alphabetical order in the **Sights** section. In order to ensure quick, easy identification, original place names have been used throughout the guide. The clock symbol ⊙, placed after monuments or other sights, refers to the **Admission times and charges** section at the end of the guide, in which the names appear in the same order as in the Sights section.

● The **Practical information** section offers useful addresses for planning your trip, seeking accommodation, indulging in outdoor activities and more; opening hours and admission prices for monuments, museums and other tourist attractions; festival and carnival dates; suggestions for thematic tours on scenic railways and through nature reserves etc. We have selected **hotels and restaurants**, and other places for **entertainment and going out** for many of the towns in this guide. Turn to the pages bordered in blue.

● The **Index** lists attractions, famous people and events, and other subjects covered in the guide.

Let us hear from you. We are interested in your reaction to our guide, in any ideas you have to offer or good addresses you would like to share. Send your comments to Michelin Travel Publications, 38 Clarendon Road, Watford, Herts WD 1 1SX, U.K. or by e-mail to thegreenguide-uk@uk.michelin.com.

R. Mattès

Key

	Sight	Seaside Resort	Winter Sports Resort	Spa
Worth a journey	★★★	≌≌≌	✸✸✸	‡‡‡
Worth a detour	★★	≌≌	✸✸	‡‡
Interesting	★	≌	✸	‡

Tourism

ⓥ	Admission Times and Charges listed at the end of the guide	►►	Visit if time permits
◉ ⟶	Sightseeing route with departure point indicated	**AZ B**	Map co-ordinates locating sights
🛉 🛉 🛉 🛉	Ecclesiastical building	🄸	Tourist information
🕎 ☪	Synagogue – Mosque	⊶ ⁂	Historic house, castle – Ruins
▨	Building (with main entrance)	⌣ ☼	Dam – Factory or power station
▪	Statue, small building	☆ ⋒	Fort – Cave
⊥	Wayside cross	⛏	Prehistoric site
◎	Fountain	▼ Ⱎ	Viewing table – View
—●—■—►■—	Fortified walls – Tower – Gate	▲	Miscellaneous sight

Recreation

🏇	Racecourse	🏃	Waymarked footpath
⛸	Skating rink	◊	Outdoor leisure park/centre
≋ ▨	Outdoor, indoor swimming pool	🎢	Theme/Amusement park
⟠	Marina, moorings	⩜	Wildlife/Safari park, zoo
⬠	Mountain refuge hut	✸	Gardens, park, arboretum
▫▪▫▪▫	Overhead cable-car	◉	Aviary, bird sanctuary
🚂	Tourist or steam railway		

Additional symbols

══ ══	Motorway (unclassified)	⊠ ⊚	Post office – Telephone centre
❶ ❶	Junction: complete, limited	⊠	Covered market
▭▭ ══	Pedestrian street	⋅×⋅	Barracks
ɪ ⩵⩵⩵ ɪ	Unsuitable for traffic, street subject to restrictions	△	Swing bridge
▦▦▦ ⸱⸱⸱⸱	Steps – Footpath	⌣ ✕	Quarry – Mine
🚆 🚌	Railway – Coach station	B F	Ferry (river and lake crossings)
▫+++++▫	Funicular – Rack-railway	🛥	Ferry services: Passengers and cars
—•— ◉	Tram – Metro, Underground	⇌	Foot passengers only
Bert (R.)...	Main shopping street	③	Access route number common to MICHELIN maps and town plans

Abbreviations and special symbols

A	Agricultural office (Chambre d'agriculture)	**P**	Local authority offices (Préfecture, sous-préfecture)
C	Chamber of commerce (Chambre de commerce)	**POL.**	Police station (Police)
H	Town hall (Hôtel de ville)	▣	Police station (Gendarmerie)
J	Law courts (Palais de justice)	**T**	Theatre (Théâtre)
M	Museum (Musée)	**U**	University (Université)
		❶	Hotel

Principal sights

Ile de Batz
Roscoff
Primel-Tré
St-Pol-de-Léon
Carantec
Brignogan-Plages
Kérouzéré
Cairn de
Barnenez
Plouescat
I' Ile Vierge
Dunes de Ste-Marguerite
Goulven
l'Aber-Wrac'h
Berven
Trémazan
Lesneven
Kerjean
Lambader
le Folgoët
St-Thégonnec
Ile d'Ouessant
ABERS
la Roche-Maurice
Landivisiau
réac'h
Gouesnou
Landerneau
la Martyre
Guimiliau
Trézien
BREST
Pencran
Lampaul-Guimiliau
En
Pont
de l'Iroise
le Conquet
Plougastel-Daoulas
Sizun
Roc Tré
Presqu'île
de Plougastel
Daoulas
Pointe de St-Mathieu
Montagne
St-Michel
Pointe des Espagnols
Landévennec
Rumengol
St-F
Camaret
le Faou
Forêt
du Cranou
POINTE DE PENHIR
Crozon
Quimerch
MONTS D'ARRÉE
Pointe de Dinan
MÉNEZ HOM
29
Pleyben
PRESQU'ILE DE CROZON
Morgat
N 164
Ste-Marie
Roche du Feu
Cap de la Chèvre
Châteaulin
Trévarez
Not
Pointe de Leydé
du
Réserve du
Ste-Anne-la-Palud
Laz
Pointe de Brézellec
Cap Sizun
Pointe du Van
Odet
Ile de Sein
Locronan
POINTE DU RAZ
Douarnenez
Quilinen
Pont-Croix
Site du Stangala
St-Tugen
Audierne
CORNOUAILLE
Plozévet
QUIMPER
Kerdévot
Languivoa
Bords
Rosporden
de l'Odet
Fouesnant
Cap-Coz
N.-D. de Tronoën
Pont-l'Abbé
Concarneau
Kérazan
Bénodet
Pont-Aven
Penmarch
Loctudy
Beg-Meil
Eckmühl
Port-Manech

Iles de Glénan

OCÉAN

ATLANTIQ

The names of towns or sights described
in the guide appear in black
on the maps throughout.
See the index for page number.

Seaside resorts are
classified using criteria specific
to the nature of the resort.

Worth a journey ★★★	
Worth a detour ★★	
Interesting ★	

29 Nº and limit of administrative region.

0   20 km

WHERE TO GO...

For coastal scenery

Abers*
Corniche de l'Armorique**
Corniche Bretonne **
Cornouaille**
Presqu'île de Crozon***
Côte d'Émeraude***
Presqu'île de Guérande*
Golfe du Morbihan**
Presqu'île de Quiberon*

For islands

Belle-Ile-en-Mer**
Bréhat**
Groix*
Ouessant (Ushant)**

For natural scenery inland

Parc natural regional d'Armorique
Monts d'Arrée**
Parc naturel régional de Brière*
Lac de Guerlédan**
Ménez-Hom***
Montagnes Noires**
Forêt de Paimpont*

For a taste of Brittany's past

Mégalithes de Carnac**
Mont Dol*
Cairn de Gavrinis**
Mégalithes de Locmariaquer**
Calvaire de Notre-Dame-de-Tronoën**
Enclos paroissiaux (Parish Closes)**

Touring programmes

TOUR: ═══════

Lannion - Roscoff - Brest
(550km - 342 miles)

TOUR: ═══════

Lorient - Quimper - Pleyben
(750km - 446 miles)

TOUR: ═══════

Mont-St-Michel -
Perros-Guirec - Pontivy
(850km - 528 miles)

TOUR: ═══════

Rennes - Vannes - Nantes
(950km - 590 miles)

The current **Michelin Red Guide France** offers a selection of quiet, pleasant and well-situated hotels. Each entry includes the facilities provided (gardens, tennis courts, swimming pool and equipped beach) and annual closure dates. Also included is a selection of establishments recommended for their cuisine: well-prepared meals at a moderate price, stars for good cooking.

The current **Michelin Guide Camping Caravaning France** indicates the facilities and recreational amenities offered by each individual site. Shops, bars, laundries, games room, tennis courts, miniature golf, children's play area, paddling pool, swimming pool, etc.

Places to stay

This map illustrates a selection of holiday destinations which are particularly to be recommended for the accommodation and leisure facilities they offer, and for their pleasant setting.

Accommodation

Consult the Michelin publication **The Red Guide France** for hotels and restaurants and the **Michelin Guide Camping Caravaning France** for camp sites. Both are compiled with the help of regular on-the-spot visits and enquiries. Hotels and camp sites are classified according to the degree of comfort and range of amenities they offer.

Tourist offices *(syndicats d'initiative)* offer different types of accommodation (country cottages, guest rooms etc) as well as providing information on local open-air activities, cultural or traditional events, and sports. The address and telephone numbers of the larger tourist offices are given in the **Admission times and charges** section at the end of the guide.

Michelin maps at a scale of 1:200 000 help you to see at a glance the sort of surroundings in which your holiday destination is located and indicate not only road information but also places where you can swim, or play golf, or go to the races etc.

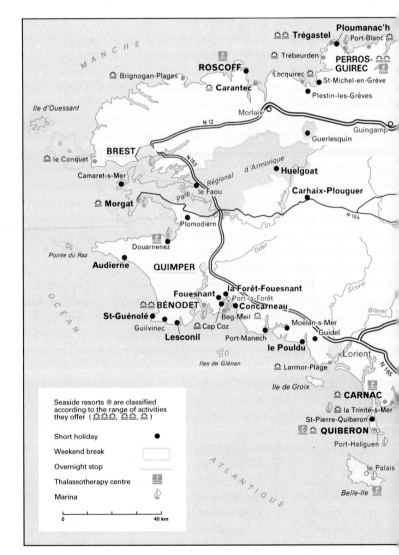

Choosing where to stay

The Places to stay map shows **overnight stops**, fairly large towns which should be visited and which have good accommodation facilities. Besides **seaside resorts**, of which there are many, the map indicates traditional destinations for a **short break**, which combine accommodation, charm and a peaceful setting. As far as Rennes, Vannes, Nantes and St-Malo are concerned, the influence they exert in the region and the wealth of monuments, museums and other sights to which they are home make them the ideal setting for a **weekend break**.

Finally the map mentions **marinas** and **thalassotherapy centres**. Brittany is excellently endowed with facilities of this type, which are all located where the beauty of their setting best combines with the health- and pleasure-giving properties of the sea.

Presqu'île de Crozon

Introduction

Landscape

Formation of the land

The relief of Brittany is the result of an evolutionary process which has taken place over millions of centuries. The planet earth, a fiery globe, is thought to have detached itself from the sun over 4 000 million years ago. This period is divided into eras.

Folded areas of the Tertiary Era

Regions submerged during the Secondary Era

Primary massifs (Hercynian folds)

Primary Era – This began about 600 million years ago. Water covered the entire area of what is now France. It was in this era that the earth's crust underwent a tremendous upheaval; this upheaval or folding movement, known as the "Hercynian fold", whose V-shaped appearance is shown by dotted lines on the map opposite, resulted in the emergence of a number of high mountainous areas (the Armorican and Central Massifs, the Vosges and the Ardennes). These mountains of impermeable, crystalline rock – granite, gneiss and mica-schist mixed with volcanic rock such as porphyry – appeared in Brittany as two massive chains stretching from east to west and separated by a central furrow.

Secondary Era – This began about 200 million years ago. From the beginning of this era, the Hercynian relief was levelled by erosion forming the Armorican peneplain. Erosion, or the constant destruction of the soil by alternating rain, sun, frost and the action of running water, wore away rocks as hard as granite or sandstone.

Tertiary Era – This began about 60 million years ago. The altitude of the Armorican Massif rose only slightly. The highest point is the Toussaines Beacon – Tuchenn Gador – in the Monts d'Arrée (alt 384m/1 288ft). The deep cuts into the coastline were formed by rocking movements of the earth.

Quaternary Era – This, the present era, began about 2 million years ago. It is the age during which the evolution of man has taken place.

Changes in the sea level, due to the waters freezing over during the Ice Age followed by a rise in water level as the ice melted, brought about the flooding of valleys, thus forming the deep estuaries known in Breton as **abers**. The inland mountains became steep cliffs (Cap Fréhel, Pointe du Penhir, Pointe du Raz) and the hills turned into islands (Batz, Ouessant, Sein, Groix, Belle-Île etc).

THE LAND, THE SEA AND THEIR HARVEST

The Armor

The name **Armor**, which means "country near the sea", was given to the coastal region by the Gauls; the interior was Argoat, "country of the wood" *(see below)*.

The Breton coast is extraordinarily indented; this makes it 1 200km/750mi long whereas it would be half that without its saw-teeth. The jagged nature of this coastline with its islands, islets and reefs is due only in part to the action of the sea and is one of the characteristics of Brittany.

The most typical seascapes are to be found at the western tip of the peninsula. Sombre cliffs, rugged capes 50-70m/160-224ft high, islands, rocks and reefs give the coastline a grimness which is reflected in sinister local names: the Channel of Fear (Fromveur), the Bay of the Dead (Baie des Trépassés), the Hell of Plogoff (Enfer de Plogoff).

There are many other impressive features, too: piles of enormous blocks of pink granite sometimes rising as much as 20m/64ft as at Ploumanach and Trégastel; the red-sandstone promontory of Cap Fréhel standing 57m/182ft above the sea; the brightly coloured caves of Morgat. The Brest roadstead, the bay of Douarnenez, the Golfe du Morbihan and its islands are unforgettable. The successive estuaries between the Rance and the Loire offer magnificent views at high tide as one crosses the impressive bridges that span them (Pont Albert-Louppe and Pont de Térénez).

Some low-lying sections of the coast contrast with the more usual rocks. In the north, Mont-St-Michel Bay is bordered by a plain reclaimed from the sea; in the south, the inhospitable bay of Audierne, the coast between Port-Louis and the base of the Presqu'île de Quiberon, and the beach at La Baule give a foretaste of the great expanses of sand which predominate south of the Loire.

22

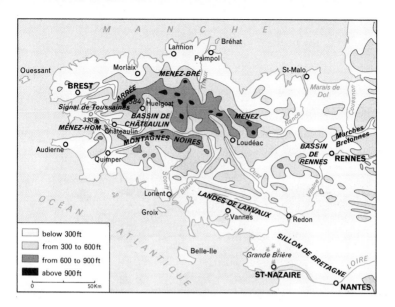

Wherever the coast is directly open to the sea winds, it is completely barren. This is so on the points and on the summits of the cliffs; the salt with which the winds are impregnated destroys the vegetation. But in sheltered spots there are magnificent profusely flowering shrubs. Arum lilies, camellias, hydrangeas and rhododendrons, which would be the pride of many a skilled gardener, grace the smallest gardens.

The climate is so mild that plants which grow in hot countries flourish in the open, eg mimosa, agave, pomegranate, palm, eucalyptus, myrtle, oleander and fig trees.

The tides – Visitors should first learn the rhythm of the tides, a division of time as regular as that of the sun. Twice every 24hr the sea advances on the coast – this is the rising tide. It reaches high water mark, where it stays for a while, and then drops back – this is the falling or ebb tide – until it reaches low water mark. It remains at this low level for a while, and then the cycle begins again.

The timetables for the tides are displayed in hotels, on quays and in local papers. Look at them before planning a trip, as they may affect the timing of your programme. It is at high tide that the coast of Brittany is most beautiful. The waves advance on the coast, break on the rocky outspurs and surge in parallel crests into the bays; a shining liquid carpet fills the estuaries. This is the time when a journey along a coast road or a walk to the harbour is the most rewarding. At low tide the uncovered rocks, stained with algae and seaweed, are often dirty and can be disappointing. At the mouths of the great coastal rivers there is only a poor thread of water winding between mudflats. The greater the tide and the gentler the slope, the greater is the expanse of shore uncovered; in Mont-St-Michel Bay the sea retreats 15-20km/9-12mi. On the other hand, low tide is the joy of anyone fishing for crab, shrimp, clams, mussels etc.

On the north coast, the tide sweeps in, in exceptional cases to a height of 13.50m/43ft in the bay of St-Malo and 15m/49ft in Mont-St-Michel Bay. When the wind blows, the battering-ram effect of the sea is tremendous. Sometimes the shocks given to the rocks off Penmarch are felt as far off as Quimper, 30km/18mi away. Attacking the softest parts of the cliffs, the sea makes fissures and brings down slabs of rock. In this way, caves (Morgat), tunnels and arches (Dinan "Château") are formed. Peninsulas joined to the mainland by strips of softer material are turned gradually into islands.

The waves do not only destroy; they also have a constructive effect. The sand they carry, added to the alluvial deposits brought down by the rivers, forms beaches, gradually silts up the bays (Mont-St-Michel Bay is a striking example), and connects islands with the mainland; this is the case at Quiberon and it will also be the same, in due course, at Bréhat.

A people of the sea – The Bretons, if one is to believe a well-known proverb, "are born with the waters of the sea flowing round their hearts". Whether they are engaged in coastal or deep-sea fishing, fishing for cod or crustaceans, they have kept pace with the latest techniques. Lorient and Concarneau are the two most important fishing ports in France after Boulogne, and consequently Brittany is the greatest fishing region, both in monetary value and size of the catch.

Coastal fishing – All along the coast there is inshore fishing. Boats which sail and return with the tide bring in fresh fish such as sole, mullet, turbot, skate, bass, seabream, mackerel, crustaceans, scallops etc. Even so the catch is not nearly enough for local needs, and a town like St-Brieuc on the north side of the peninsula receives supplementary supplies from Lorient in the south.

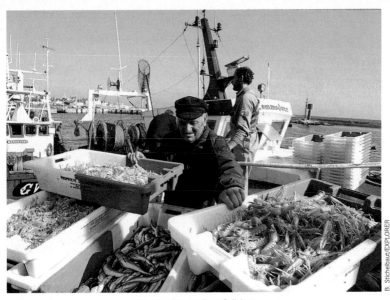

Unloading the catch at Guilvinec

On the Atlantic coast, the season for sardine fishing lasts from June to September. In winter the sardine boats are used for trawling, lobster or crab fishing.

Deep-sea fishing – Trawlers operating in the bay of Biscay, the Irish Sea and off the coasts of Iceland bring in most of the fresh fish, especially the kinds of fish in great demand. Trawling is the main activity of big ports like Lorient, Concarneau and Douarnenez.

For **tuna** fishing both live bait and nets are used in the bay of Biscay and seine nets along the African coasts. The white tuna is fished from June to October: starting somewhere between Portugal and the Azores, the season ends in the bay of Biscay. Tropical or albacore tuna is the quarry of a fleet of some 30 boats with refrigerated holds, equipped at Concarneau and operating from the ports of West Africa during the season.

Crustaceans – Most crustacean fishing takes place along the rocky coasts using lobster pots and traps, but long-distance fishing using modern equipment is also common. Lobster boats with refrigeration plants leave from Camaret, Audierne and Douarnenez for the coast of Mauritania for several months at a time. The boats are equipped with tanks as well as freezing plants. When the boats return to harbour, part of the catch is put into storage beds. These are situated at many points round the coast, the most important lying between Primel and Audierne.

Oysters and shellfish – Conchyliculture – or oyster and mussel breeding – has become commercially important. Brittany, which has long been the great production region for flat oysters *(belons)*, has also developed its Portuguese oyster beds (sold as *Creuses de Bretagne* or *Fines de Bretagne*). There are considered to be a dozen different excellent types of Breton oyster. The biggest maturing beds lie between Cancale and the Abers passing by Paimpol, Morlaix Bay, Peuzé and Brest river estuaries; on the Atlantic coast from Audierne to Le Croisic, mainly in the River Étel and River Pénerf, Quiberon Bay and Golfe du Morbihan. Brittany's annual oyster production amounts, in 9 000ha/22 500 acres of breeding pools, to 30 000t of *creuses* and 2 000t of *plates*, which is a quarter of France's national production.

Mussel breeding on poles known as "*bouchots*" is carried out along the coast from Mont-St-Michel Bay to St-Brieuc Bay and in the Vilaine estuary. Mussel farms are found all along the southern coast.

Fish processing – Sardines, mackerel, white and albacore tunny are all canned in the factories round the coast, particularly in the Penmarch region, at Douarnenez, Concarneau, Étel and Nantes. Brittany produces two-thirds of the national total.

Algae and algae-processing – Harvested and used as fertiliser for many years, then as raw materials for the chemical industry (soda from the 18C, iodine in the 19C, discovery of gelling properties in the early 20C), the various types of algae are as likely nowadays to be found in bathrooms as on restaurant tables or in thalassotherapy centres. Both sea wrack and seaweed found on the shore used to be collected and used for fertiliser, however harvesting is now subject to regulations.

The Bretons also use shelly sand from beaches, sea mud and maërl (sand from banks containing calcified algae, found around Paimpol) to improve the soil. According to a local saying, these sands change "gorse to clover and rye grass to wheat"; they can be used either in their natural form or as a processed product.

Morbihan *sinago*
(oyster fishing boat)

Île de Groix tunny boat

Quimper coasting lugger

Légué lugger

Camaret Dundee lobster boat

Brest schooner

Dahouët *chaloupe*
(lugger)

Paimpol schooner

Vast plants (the largest is at Pleubian) process seaweed and alginates which are found in a diverse range of products such as foodstuffs (biscuits), cosmetics and plastics. Other plants along the coast manufacture iodine and soda, refine maërl and process fish offal for use in fertilisers, animal feed and pharmaceutical products.

Naval dockyards – Half of all the ships built in France come from the Breton yards: the Atlantic Dockyards at St-Nazaire for merchant vessels and battleships and Brest and Lorient Dockyards for ships for the French Navy. The Atlantic Dockyards, capable of dealing with ships of up to 500 000t, began the year 2000 with news of the award to build the largest ocean-liner ever, the Queen Mary II.

The Golden Belt – In addition to the sea-related activities, market gardening in the sheltered, rich alluvial coastal area between St-Malo and the Loire, which is known as the Golden Belt *(Ceinture Dorée)*, makes an essential contribution to the Breton economy. Potatoes, cauliflower, artichokes, peas, French beans, carrots, cabbage, onions and garlic are all grown in the open fields. Part of the production supplies the large consumer markets, notably the Paris region, and the rest is sent to the local canneries and exported to Great Britain and Germany.

The Argoat

Inland Brittany, the Argoat, has its own beauty and appeals strongly to those who enjoy the bucolic charms of the countryside.

The plateaux – Plains cover most of the country, although you must not expect to find great expanses extending without a break to far horizons. Instead you cross a series of rises without any clear idea of their general direction. Between these uplands flow deeply sunken rivers with brown, rushing waters. The land is usually cut up into a chequerboard pattern by banks and dry-stone walls which form the boundaries of fields and pastures. Pollarded oaks grow on most of the banks and it is these which make the countryside, seen from a distance, seem heavily wooded.

The mountains – Mountains! The word rather overpowers the Breton hills. But this is what the coast dwellers call the central part of Brittany. It must be said that in many places the barrenness and loneliness of the heights, the saw-toothed crests contrasting with the undulating plains that they overshadow and the strong wind give an impression of high altitude.
In clear weather a vast expanse can be seen from the Roc Trévezel (384m/1 229ft), the Ménez-Hom (330m/1 056ft) and the Menez Bré (302m/966ft).

Forests and moors – Brittany once had immense forests of oak and beech. Successive generations since the Romans have wielded the axe in these woods, and there are now only scattered strips of woodland: the forests of Paimpont, Loudéac, Huelgoat, Quénécan etc. These woodlands are very hilly and intersected by gorges, ravines and tumbled rocks. A perfect example of this type of country is to be seen at Huelgoat. Unfortunately most of the woodlands would appear to be neglected and brushwood predominates. The fine forests are rare and these Breton woodlands owe their picturesque quality more to their relief than to their trees.
Untilled moors succeeded the forests. Near the summits they still form great empty stretches whose gloom is relieved for a time only when the gorse wears its golden cloak and the heather spreads a purple carpet on the hills. Elsewhere, moors have yielded to the efforts of the peasants and have become tilled fields. Such are the Landes de Lanvaux, where the visitor, misled by the name and expecting rough ground, finds reclaimed land, rich in promise for the future.

Agriculture – For a long time the Argoat was essentially an agricultural and stock-rearing region, but more recently industrial development has been encouraged by local authorities.
Nearly one-third of the land under cultivation is given over to cereal production together with fodder crops (mainly corn) reserved as cattle feed.
There are still many apple orchards in Ille-et-Vilaine and in the south of the Finistère but a certain decline is noticeable in Morbihan. The apples are used to make cider, apple juice and concentrate.
The Argoat has a reputation for its dairy cattle, which produce about 20 % of French dairy products. Large dairies are located throughout the region. Pig rearing has been industrialised and represents half of France's production. It supplies national markets and the many firms which produce fresh, canned or salted pork products.

Historical table and notes

Events in italics indicate milestones in history.

Ancient Armor

6C BC	The Celts arrive in the peninsula and name it Armor (country of the sea). A little-known people who set up many megaliths were there before them.
56 AD	Caesar destroys the fleet of the Veneti, the most powerful tribe in Armor *(see Golfe du Morbihan)*, and conquers the whole country.
	For four centuries Roman civilization does its work. Then the barbarian invasions wreck Armor, which returns almost to savagery.

Armor becomes Brittany

460	Arrival of the Celts from Britain, driven out by the Angles and Saxons. Immigration continues for two centuries. These colonists revive and convert Armor and give it a new name, Little Britain, later shortened to Brittany. The Breton people make saints of their religious leaders, who become the patrons of many towns in the peninsula.
	The political state, made up of innumerable parishes, remains anarchic.
799	Charlemagne subjugates all Brittany.

The Duchy of Brittany

826	Louis the Pious makes Nominoé, a noble of Vannes, Duke of Brittany.
845	Nominoé throws off Frankish suzerainty by defeating Charles the Bald, near Redon. He brings all of Brittany under his authority and founds an independent ducal dynasty which lasts for more than a century.
851	Erispoë, son of Nominoé, takes the title, King of Brittany. He is later assassinated by his cousin Salomon who reigns from 857.
874	Salomon (the Great, or St Salomon) assassinated. During his reign the Kingdom of Brittany reached its zenith, embracing Anjou and Cotentin.
919	Great invasion of Norsemen. Violent robbery and pillage.
939	King Alain Barbe-Torte drives out the last Norsemen.
952	Death of Alain, the last King of Brittany. In the fortresses built all over the country to resist the Norsemen, the nobles defy the successors of Barbe-Torte. There follows a period of disorder and poverty which lasts until nearly the end of the 14C.
1066	*William the Conqueror lands in England.*
1215	*Magna Carta.*
1337	Start of the Hundred Years War ending in 1453.
1341	The War of Succession begins on the death of Duke Jean III. His niece, Jeanne de Penthièvre, wife of Charles of Blois, supported by the French, fights her brother Jean of Montfort, ally of the English, for the duchy.
1351	Battle of the Thirty.
1364	Charles of Blois, though aided by Du Guesclin, is defeated and killed at Auray. Brittany emerges ruined from this war.

The Montforts

1364-1468	The dukes of the House of Montfort restore the country. This is the most brilliant period of its history. The arts reach their highest development. The dukes are the real sovereigns and pay homage only in theory to the king of France. Constable de Richemont *(see Vannes)*, the companion-in-arms of Joan of Arc, succeeds his brother in 1457 as Duke of Brittany.
1488	Duke François II, who has entered into the federal coalition against the Regent of France, Anne of Beaujeu, is defeated at St-Aubin-du-Cormier and dies. His daughter, Anne of Brittany, succeeds him.

Reunion of Brittany with France

1491	Anne of Brittany marries Charles VIII *(see Rennes)* but remains Duchess and sovereign of Brittany.
1492	*Christopher Columbus discovers America on 12 October.*
1498	Charles VIII dies accidentally. Anne returns to her duchy.
1499	Anne again becomes Queen of France by marrying Louis XII, who had hastily repudiated his first wife. The duchy remains distinct from the Crown *(see Vannes)*.

| 1514 | Anne of Brittany dies. Her daughter, Claude of France, inherits the duchy. She marries François of Angoulême, the future François I. |
| 1532 | Claude cedes her duchy to the Crown. François I has this permanent reunion of Brittany with France ratified by the Parliament at Vannes. |

Anne of Brittany

French Brittany

1534	Jacques Cartier discovers the St Lawrence estuary *(see St-Malo)*.
1588	Brittany rebels against its governor, the Duke of Mercœur, who wants to profit from the troubles of the League to seize the province. Bandits like the famous La Fontenelle ravage the country *(see Douarnenez)*.
1598	By the Edict of Nantes, Henri IV puts an end to religious strife *(see Nantes)*.
1675	The "Stamped Paper" Revolt *(see Pont-L'Abbé)* develops into a peasants' rising.
1711	Duguay-Trouin takes Rio de Janeiro.
1764	The Rennes Parliament and its Public Prosecutor, La Chalotais, oppose Governor Aiguillon. The authority of the Crown is much weakened. The Revolution is near.
1765	Arrival on Belle-Île of many Acadian families of French origin from Nova Scotia.
1773	Birth of Surcouf, the Breton pirate.
1776	*American Declaration of Independence.*
1789	The Bretons welcome the Revolution with enthusiasm.

Surcouf

1793	Carrier has thousands drowned in the Loire near Nantes.
1793-1804	The Laws against the priests and the mass levies give rise to the *Chouannerie* (revolt of Breton Royalists).
1795	A landing by Royalist exiles is defeated at Quiberon.
1804	Cadoudal, who tried to revive the *Chouannerie*, is executed.
1826	René Laënnec, the great physician, dies.
1832	Another attempted revolt, organised by the Duchess of Berry, fails. This is the last uprising.
1861	*Start of the American Civil War.*
1909	Strikes and riots among the Concarneau cannery workers.
1914-8	Brittany pays a heavy toll in loss of life during the First World War.

Brittany today

1927-8	The Morbihan aviator Le Brix, accompanied by Costes, is the first to fly round the world.
1940	The islanders of Sein are the first to rally to General de Gaulle's call.
1942	An Anglo-Canadian commando raids the St-Nazaire submarine base.
1944-5	The end of the German Occupation leaves in its wake a trail of destruction, especially at Brest, Lorient and St-Nazaire.
1951	Formation of the organisation Comité d'Études et de Liaison des Intérêts Bretons (CELIB), to safeguard Breton interests, is an initial step towards the rejuvenation of the local economy.
1962	First transatlantic transmission by satellite of a television programme by the station at Pleumeur-Bodou.
1966	The opening of the Rance tidal power scheme and the Monts d'Arrée nuclear station near Brennilis.

1967	The *Torrey Canyon* disaster off the English coast causes great oil slicks to contaminate the beaches of Brittany.
1969	Creation of the Parc naturel régional d'Armorique.
1970	Creation of the Parc naturel régional de Brière.
1975	First search for oil in the Iroise Sea off the Finistère coast.
1978	Establishment of a charter and council to safeguard the Breton cultural heritage. *Amoco Cadiz* oil spill on Brittany beaches.
1985	Introduction of bilingual road signs in French and Breton.
1994	The Law Courts at Rennes, home to the Breton Parliament, are burned to the ground by rioting French farmers. The opening of the Pont de l'Iroise spanning the Eloen.
1996	Inauguration of the La Roche-Bernard bridge.
2000	The *Erica* founders in a storm, once again, "black tides" damage the shore and wildlife. St Nazaire receives a commission to build the *Queen Mary II*, the world's largest ocean liner.

Traditions and folklore

A LAND OF LEGENDS

The Breton soul has always been inclined to the dreamy, the fantastic and the supernatural. This explains the astonishing abundance and persistence of legends in the Armor country.

The Round Table – After the death of Christ, Joseph of Arimathea, one of His disciples, left Palestine, carrying away a few drops of the divine blood in the cup from which the Redeemer drank during the Last Supper. He landed in Britain according to some legends, in Brittany according to others, where he lived for some time in the Forest of Brocéliande (now the Forêt de Paimpont) before vanishing without trace. In the 6C King Arthur and 50 knights set out to find this precious cup. For them it was the Holy Grail, which only a warrior whose heart was pure could win. Percival (Wagner's Parsifal) was such a man. In the Middle Ages the search for the Grail gave rise to the endless stories of adventure which formed the Cycle of the Round Table. The most famous versions of the tale in English are, of course, Sir Thomas Malory's *Morte d'Arthur* (1471) and Alfred Lord Tennyson's *Idylls of the King* (1859).

Merlin and Viviane – One of King Arthur's companions, Merlin the sorcerer, came to the Forest of Brocéliande to live in seclusion. But he met the fairy Viviane, and love inflamed them both. To make sure of keeping Merlin, Viviane enclosed him in a magic circle. It would have been easy for him to escape, but he joyfully accepted this romantic captivity for ever.

Pardon at Ste-Anne-la-Palud

Tristan and Isolde – Tristan, Prince of Lyonesse, was sent to Ireland by his Uncle Mark, King of Cornouaille, to bring back Isolde, whom Mark was to marry. On board their ship, Tristan and Isolde accidentally drank a philtre which was intended to bind Isolde to her husband in eternal love. Passion stronger than duty sprang up in both their hearts. There are several versions of the end: sometimes Tristan is slain by Mark, furious at his betrayal; sometimes he marries and dies in his castle in Brittany. But Isolde always follows him to the grave. Wagner's opera has made the love story famous.

The town of Is – At the time of good **King Gradlon**, about the 6C, Is was the capital of Cornouaille; finds in Trépassés and Douarnenez Bays and off the Presqu'île de Penmarch are said to have come from Is. The town was protected from the sea by a dike, opened by locks to which the King always carried the golden key.

The King had a beautiful but dissolute daughter, **Dahut**, also known as Ahès, who was seduced by the Devil in the form of an attractive young man. To test her love he asked her to open the sea gate. Dahut stole the key while the King was asleep, and soon the sea was rushing into the town.

King Gradlon fled on horseback, with his daughter on the crupper. But the waves pursued him and were about to swallow him up. At this moment a celestial voice ordered him, if he would be saved, to throw the demon who was riding behind him into the sea. With an aching heart the King obeyed, and the sea withdrew at once, but Is was destroyed.

For his new capital Gradlon chose Quimper; this is why his statue stands between the two towers of the cathedral. He ended his days in the odour of sanctity, guided and sustained by St Corentine. As for Dahut, she turned into a mermaid, who is known as **Marie-Morgane** and whose beauty still lures sailors to the bottom of the sea. This state of affairs will persist until the Good Friday when Mass is celebrated in one of the churches of the drowned city. Then Is will cease to be accursed, and Marie-Morgane will no longer be a siren.

THE PARDONS

The Breton *pardons* are above all a manifestation of popular religious fervour. They take place in the churches and chapels which may be consecrated by the tradition of a thousand years. There the faithful come to seek forgiveness, fulfil a vow or beg for grace. The great *pardons* are most impressive, while the smaller events, though they may be less spectacular, are often more fervent. It is well worth tourists' while to arrange their trip so that they may be present at one of them *(see Calendar of events)*. It is also one of the rare occasions when they will see the old costumes, perhaps slightly modernised.

THE SAINTS OF BRITTANY

Brittany, with its magicians, spirits, fairies and demons – both male and female – has also claimed more haloes than any other part of France. Its saints number in hundreds and are represented by painted wooden statues adorning chapels and churches. Truth

---

The "Tro Breiz"

Until the 16C, tradition demanded that every Breton should make a pilgrimage at least once in his or her lifetime to the seven cathedrals of Brittany. The **"Tro Breiz"**, or "Tour of Brittany", as it was known, drew people in the thousands during the 12C to the 16C, with its popularity reaching a peak in the 14C; estimates suggest that crowds numbering up to 30 000 to 40 000 pilgrims were taking to the roads! The tour covered nearly 700km/435mi, and it enabled the faithful to pay homage to the holy relics of the founding saints of Brittany: St Brieuc and St Malo at the town of those names, St Samson at Dol-de-Bretagne, St Patern at Vannes, St Corentine at Quimper, St Paul the Aurelian at St-Pol-de-Léon and St Tugdual at Tréguier. Whoever failed to carry out this duty was supposed to have to undertake the pilgrimage after death, advancing by one coffin-length every seven years.

Nowadays, ever increasing numbers of individuals continue to make this journey, in groups or alone, retracing the steps of the earlier pilgrims.

For further details, contact: "Les Chemins du Tro Breiz", Maison Prébendale, 29250 St-Pol-de-Léon, ☎ 02 98 69 16 53.

to tell, those who were canonised by the Vatican authorities (St Yves for example) can be counted on one's fingers. The most "official" among them were simply recognised by the bishops; the people themselves adopted others. Their fame goes no further than the borders of the province, or even the limits of the villages where they are venerated. (For the purposes of this guide, the names of saints revered in a particular region have been left in their local form).

Patrons of towns – The Celtic religious leaders who landed from the British Isles in the 5C *(see Celtic Exodus)* were adopted as the patron saints of the seven former bishoprics: St-Malo, St-Brieuc, (St Brioch), St-Pol-de-Léon (St Paul the Aurelian), Dol (St Samson), Tréguier (St Tugdual), Quimper (St Corentine) and Vannes (St Patern). This applies to many other localities: St-Efflam, St-Lunaire, St-Briac, St-Gildas etc.

The "healing saints" – The Bretons have always been on trusting, friendly and even familiar terms with their saints.
There are saints who are invoked on all occasions. Innumerable others are invoked against specified aliments: rheumatism, baldness etc. For centuries they took the place of doctors. Horses and oxen also have their appointed saints (St Cornely and St Herbot).

COSTUMES AND HEADDRESSES

Costumes – Brittany possesses costumes of surprising richness and variety. The fine clothes passed down from one generation to another were to be seen at every family festivity. It was customary for a girl at her marriage to acquire a costly and magnificent outfit that would last many years. Nowadays the traditional costumes are brought out only on great occasions such as *pardons*, and sometimes High Mass on feast days. In spite of attempts to modernise the dress, and the efforts of regional societies over the last few years – and they have had some success – to make the young appreciate the old finery, the tourist who travels quickly through Brittany is not likely to see many of the elaborate traditional dresses made familiar by picture postcards and books on the subject.
The most striking and attractive feature of the women's traditional costumes is their aprons which reveal how well off the family is by the abundance of their decoration. The aprons, of every size and shape, are made of satin or velvet and are brocaded, embroidered or edged with lace: at Quimper they have no bib, at Pont-Aven they have a small one, while at Lorient the bib reaches to the shoulders. Ceremonial dresses are usually black and are often ornamented with bands of velvet. The finest examples are those of Quimper which are adorned with multi-coloured embroidery. The men's traditional costume includes a felt hat with ribbons and an embroidered waistcoat.

Headdresses – The most original feature of the Breton costume is the **coiffe** or headdress, once worn mainly in the Finistère and Morbihan.
One of the most attractive is the headdress of **Pont-Aven** which has, as an accessory, a great starched lace collar.
The **Bigouden** headdress from the **Pont-l'Abbé** area is one of the most curious; it used to be quite small but since 1930 has become very tall.
In **Quimper** the headdress is much smaller and is worn on the crown of the head; in **Plougastel**, where tradition is still strong, it has a medieval appearance with ribbons tied on the side.

H. Oyssels/DIAF

Baud headdresses

P. Somelet /DIAF

A. Le Bot/DIAF

Pont-Aven headdress

Bigouden headdresses

In **Tréguier** the plainest of materials is allied with the most original of shapes. The **Douarnenez** headdress is small and fits tightly round the bun on the back of the head, that of **Auray** shades the forehead and that of **Huelgoat** is almost like a lace hair net.

In order to get a complete picture of the richness and variety of Breton costume, the tourist should visit the museums of Quimper, Guérande, Rennes, Nantes, Dinan, Pont-l'Abbé etc all of which have fine collections of traditional dress.

Language and culture

THE BRETON LANGUAGE

Modern Breton *(brezhoneg)*, derived from Brythonic, belongs to the Celtic languages and manifests itself in four main dialects: *cornouaillais* (south Finistère), *léonard* (north Finistère), *trégorrois* (Tréguier and the bay of St-Brieuc) and *vannetais* (Vannes and the Golfe du Morbihan). *Vannetais* distinguishes itself from the other three, which are closely related, for example by replacing "z" with "h"; thus *Breiz (Brittany)* becomes Breih. In an attempt to overcome such differences, the use of "zh" has been introduced for the relevant words, thus *Breizh*.

Place names – In Brittany, as in other French provinces, the meaning of place names is often easy to find. Most names are formed from a root to which the name of a saint or local character has been added.

The original term **ploue**, from the Latin *plebs* (people), came to mean "church" in the Middle Ages and, by extension, "parish". **Pleu, plou, plo** and **pl** are all derived from **ploue** and, combined with suffixes, give rise to names like: Ploudaniel (parish of St Daniel), Plogoff (parish of St Cof), Ploërmel (parish of St Armel), Plounevez (new parish), Pleumeur (large parish), Pleubian (bishop's parish), Ploudiry (oak parish) etc.

Tré, trèv or **tref**, meaning "parish subdivision", give rise to: Tréboul (place of the pool), Trégastel (place of the castle), Trémeur (large place) etc.

Loc (holy place) gives: Locmaria (place of Mary Mother of God), Locronan (place of St Ronan), Locminé (place of monks) etc.

Lann or **lan** (sanctuary or church) give: Lannion (church of St Yon), Lampaul (church of St Paul), Landerneau (church of St Ternoc) etc.

Ker, kear, car, cré, quer, all unique to Breton (meaning village or house), often appear in the names of places off the beaten track: Kermaria (Mary's village), Kermeur (big house), Kerfeunteun (village of the fountain) etc.

Gwik, from the Latin *vicus*, then **gui** (hamlet) give: Guimiliau (town of St Méliau), Guisseny (town of St Seny) etc.

Bleiz, bleid, blaid, blaye (wolf): although wolves disappeared from Brittany more than a century ago, names such as Boblaye (wolf's lair), Kerbleiz (wolf's village), Poulbleizi (wolves' pool) etc bear witness to their passage.

Traon, traou, tro (valley) give: Tromelin (valley of the mill), Tromeur (great valley) etc.

Koad, coat, goat, goët, hoet (wood) appears in Huelgoat (tall wood), Penhoët (end of the wood), Toulgoët (clearing in the wood) etc.

Double toponymy – Place names appear on road signs in both French and Breton eg Châteauneuf-du-Faou/Kastel-Nevez-Ar-Faou, Guérande/Gwenrann, Lorient/An Oriant, Morlaix/Montroulez, Nantes/Naoned, Pontivy/Pondivi, Port-Launay/Meilh-ar-Wern, Quimper/Kemper, Rennes/Roazhon, St-Brieuc/Sant-Brieg, St-Paul-de-Léon/ Kastell-Paol, Tréguier/Landreger, Vannes/Gwened.

Family names – Many are formed from Ker (house) followed by a variation of a Christian name: Kerber (house of Peter), Kerbol (house of Paul) etc.
Other names indicate professions: Le Barazer (cooper), Le Goff (blacksmith), Le Quéméneur (tailor), Le Tocquer (hatter) etc and others reflect nicknames: Le Bihan (little), Le Braz (big), Le Bail (marked on the forehead), Le Fur (wise), Gallouédec (powerful), Le Moigne (one-armed), Le Troadec (big feet), Le Guen (white), Le Dantec (toothy), Pennec (stubborn) etc.

Common Christian names include: Alan, Anna, Aziliz, Arzhel or Armel, Edern, Erwan or Iwan, Fañch, Goulven, Gweltaz, Gwenn, Gwenole, Jakez, Jezequel, Kaourintin, Loeiz, Maloù, Marzhin, Per and Tangi.

The Breton variations for "grenouille" *(frog) have given rise to some memorable place names, such as Poulrian (Frog Pond) and Riantec (The Froggery) – from rian/réan – or, more simply Glesquer (Frog) from* glesker *– or Le Grand Signan (The Big Frog) – from* chignan.

EVOLUTION AND REGIONALISM

The **two Brittanies** – The map below delimits **Upper Brittany** (Haute-Bretagne), or the "Gallo" country, and **Lower Brittany** (Basse-Bretagne), or the Breton-speaking country.
French is spoken in the first, French and Breton in the second. Lower Brittany has four regions, each of which has its customs and brings shades of diversity to the Breton language – the district of Tréguier or Trégorrois, the district of Léon, the district of Cornouaille and the district of Vannes or Vannetais.

THE BRETON LANGUAGE
- - - Culmination (9C)
—— Recession (present day)

Apart from the language, these limits conform with tradition. It is in Lower Brittany that one is more likely to find the old customs; in Upper Brittany they have hardly left a trace. And the delimitation has not remained fixed.

The Breton language – From the ethnic and linguistic point of view, the Bretons are nearer to the Irish and Welsh than to the French.
This is because from the 4C to the 7C, Armorica (present day Brittany) offered asylum to Britons driven from Britain (present-day Great Britain) by the Anglo-Saxon invasion. Brittany was founded, and the Breton language opposed the French language, derived from Low Latin.
In the 9C, the dynasty of Nominoé marked the apogee of the Breton nation and the furthest advance of its language. The Viking invasions that followed and feudal rule harmed the unity of Brittany.
The annexation of the province to France in the 15C and the French Revolution enhanced the trend in favour of French.
An association called UDB (Union for the Defence of the Breton Language), after a vigorous campaign for the optional teaching of Breton in Lower Brittany, secured this in the secondary and teachers' training schools.

Brittany's rapid development – Brittany changed more in the first half of the 20C than in the two previous centuries. Contacts of Breton soldiers with men from other provinces, and especially the return to their homeland of men who had held administrative or executive posts in the navy, the civil service, commerce and industry, hastened the evolution started by the tourists.
The distinctive character of customs, dress and furniture has faded away. Villages no longer keep alive a mass of traditional customs and traditional beliefs. Less than half the population still know their own language.

Regionalism and Celtic Clubs – Brittany cultivates regionalism. There are more than 250 Celtic Clubs, which revive and bring fame to all that is Breton – dances, music, and costume. The traditional bagpipe *(cornemuse écossaise)* and bombard *(biniou)* players, for example, are in great demand at parties, festivals etc.

A. Dauzat

The Breton flag – The current flag is called Gwenn ha du (white and black) and was designed by Morvan Marchal in 1925. The five black stripes represent the five original bishoprics of Upper Brittany (Rennes, Nantes, Dol, St-Malo and St-Brieuc); the four white stripes represent those of Lower Brittany (Léon, Cornouaille, Vannes and Tréguier); the field of ermine evokes the Duchy of Brittany.

The Triskell – This ornament takes the form of a revolving cross with three arms or vortexes symbolising earth, fire and water. It is Celtic in origin, and has been found on Celtic coins, in the British Isles, Denmark, even in South and North America.

CULTURE

The Middle Ages and the Renaissance – Learning was centred in the monasteries; the language used was Latin; the subjects studied were concerned, for the most part, with the history of the Church or of Brittany, moral philosophy and the lives of the saints. A life of St Guénolé was written by Wurdistein, Abbot of Landévennec, in the 9C, and a life of St Pol by Wromonoc, a monk from the same abbey.

Authors are rarely known by name, but there are some exceptions such as, in the 12C: the philosopher **Pierre Abélard**, one of the most brilliant figures of the Middle Ages, who was born at Le Pallet near Nantes and became Abbot of St-Gildas-de-Rhuys. **Étienne de Fougères**, who was named Bishop of Rennes in 1168, wrote *Livre des manières*, a Book of Manners, which gave him free rein to lecture his contemporaries on moral issues. **Guillaume Le Breton** was poet and historian at the court of Philippe-Auguste, whose reign he patriotically eulogised.

Students from Brittany first went to Paris University, and then to Nantes when that establishment was founded in the 15C. Schools were established to supplement the teaching provided by the churches and monasteries in out of the way parishes. However, it was not until the 15C and 16C that one began hearing of names such as those of the historians Pierre Le Baud, Alain Bouchard and Bertrand d'Argentré, of the poet Meschinot from Nantes who wrote a series of ballads entitled *Les Lunettes des princes* (The Princes' Spectacles), which became well known in his own time, of Noël du Fail, Councillor of the Rennes Parliament, who depicted the world around him so well, and of the Dominican Albert Legrand, who wrote *Vie des Saints de la Bretagne armoricaine* (Life of the Saints of Armorican Brittany).

17C and 18C – The best-known figures of the 17C and 18C are **Mme de Sévigné** – Breton by marriage – who addressed many of her letters from her residence, the Rochers-Sévigné Château and wrote vivid descriptions of Rennes, Vitré, Vannes and Port-Louis, **Lesage**, the witty author of *Gil Blas* who came from Vannes, and Duclos, moralist and historian, who was Mayor of Dinan. There was also **Élie Fréron**, who became known only through his disputes with Voltaire and who was the director of a literary journal published in Paris and, finally, the Benedictines Dom Lobineau and Dom Morice, historians of Brittany.

The Romantics and contemporary writers – Three figures dominated literature in the 19C in Brittany: **François-René de Chateaubriand**, who had an immense influence on French literature. The effect he had over his contemporaries arose from his sensitivity, his passionate eloquence, his fertile imagination, all of which were displayed with brilliant and powerful style; in his *Mémoires D'Outre-Tombe* (Beyond the Tomb), he recounts his childhood at St-Malo and his youth at Combourg Castle;

Celtic music at Perros-Guirrec

G. Guittot/DIAF

Lamennais, fervent apologist of theocracy who became a convinced democrat, reflected in his philosophical works the evolution of his thought;

Ernest Renan, philologist, historian and philosopher, was a thinker who maintained that he had faith only in science. He wrote many books in an easy and brilliant prose and in one, *Souvenirs d'enfance et de jeunesse* (Recollections of Childhood and Youth), described his native Brittany.

Others who came from Brittany and should be noted though they did not write in praise of their native province are: the Symbolist poet **Villiers-de-l'Isle-Adam**; **Jules Verne** (1828-1905), precursor of modern scientific discoveries; **Louis Hémon** who became known through his *Maria Chapdelaine*, and finally **Pierre Loti** with his *Pêcheur d'Islande* and *Mon frère Yves*.

Henri Queffélec (1910-92) is one of the contemporary authors who has most lauded Brittany in *Le Recteur de l'île de Sein*, *Un homme d'Ouessant*, *Au bout du monde*, *Franche et secrète Bretagne* and *Promenades en Bretagne*. Another contemporary author, **Pierre-Jakez Hélias** (b 1917), recounts vividly in *Cheval d'orgueil* the traditions of the Pont-l'Abbé region (Claude Chabrol made a memorable film from the work). Unfortunately, few Breton authors have been translated into English.

ABC of architecture

RELIGIOUS ARCHITECTURE

St-BRIEUC – Ground plan of the Cathédrale St-Étienne (13C and 14C)

Bay: a section of the nave between two pillars

Arm of the transept

Ambulatory: The side aisles extend around the chancel so that the faithful can pass before the relics.

Lady Chapel or **Axial chapel**

Chevet: the eastern end of the church (outside). Inside the church, this area is called the **Apse.**

Nave

Side aisle

Radiating chapel or **apsidial chapel**

Chancel: usually facing east

Transept crossing

Side doorway

ST-POL-DE-LÉON – Cross-section of the first two bays on the northern side of the cathedral nave (13C and 14C)

Clerestory window

Grand arcade: separates the nave from the side aisles

Lancet: raised, pointed arch, in the form of a lance

Clustered slender columns

Mullion

Public gallery

Triforium gallery: public gallery which is contained in the thickness of the wall (in late Gothic architecture, this becomes decorative arcading)

DINAN – Porch with three arches on the Basilique St-Sauveur (12C)

Mandorla

Semicircular barrel arch

Capital

Column shaft

Coving: concentric arches covering the opening of a bay; together this forms the archivolt.

Baldaquin: embellished with decorative elements and set above a statue or an altar.

Cabled column

Upright archshafts: vertical members which support the arches

Lintel

Tympanium: shows scenes with human figures

Stylophorus lion (bears the column)

Twisted column

Column with twisted fluting

R. Corbel

36

QUIMPER – Cathédrale St-Corentin (13C to 19C)

Crockets

Symmetrical façade
with two towers

Finial

Spire

Pinnacle

Waterspout:
protruding from the
building, drains off
rain water

English-style
clerestory
window

Pinnacle: an
upright member
ending in a small
spire which gives
weight to a
buttress
or angle pier

Twin bays

Flamboyant window:
stone tracery
divides the
opening of the
bay

Flying
buttress

Gallery

Open-work railing

Gable: a decorative
element used above
certain doorways

Buttress: supports the wall from the outside, protrudes
from the wall to which it is bonded

Main doorway

R. Corbel

TRÉGUIER – Interior of the Cathédrale St-Tugdal (15C)

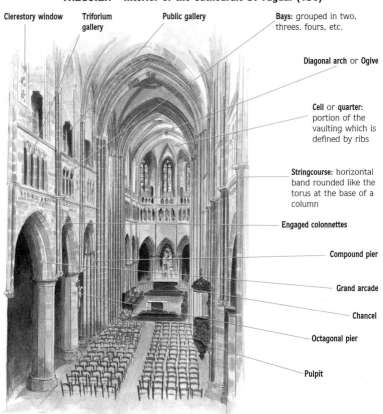

Clerestory window

Triforium gallery

Public gallery

Bays: grouped in two, threes, fours, etc.

Diagonal arch or **Ogive**

Cell or **quarter:** portion of the vaulting which is defined by ribs

Stringcourse: horizontal band rounded like the torus at the base of a column

Engaged colonnettes

Compound pier

Grand arcade

Chancel

Octagonal pier

Pulpit

COMMANA – Église St-Derrien – St-Anne Altarpiece

Placed behind and above the altar, this altarpiece is a jewel of Baroque art in Brittany

God the Father, in **Majesty**, presents the **Crucified Christ**

Niche

Entablature: protruding crown, made up of the **architrave**, the **frieze** and the **cornice**

Twisted column, embellished with a vine motif

Fluted column: the shaft is decorated with garlands

Attic: surmounts the entablature

Console

Sculpture in relief

Medallion: sculpted portrait or other subject in a circular or round frame

Tabernacle

Predella: lower section of the altarpiece

Antependium: decorative panel on the front of the altar

Altar table

R. Corbel

38

PLOUGASTEL-DAOULAS – Calvary (17C)

The words of the Evangelists are here written in stone; scenes from the life of Christ are sculpted on these imposing monuments, typical of religious expression in the region.

Crossbar

Capital placed atop a shaft, upon which rests the cross.

Crosspiece

Pieta: statuary group representing the Virgin holding the body of Christ.

The shaft is sculpted to resemble a branch from which the smaller branches have been removed.

Altar for offerings: stone altar dedicated to one or more saints.

Free-standing column: separate from the wall behind it.

Crucifix

Tau cross (in the shape of the Greek letter "Tau")

The two thieves: the good thief was on Christ's right hand, the bad thief on the left.

Shaft

Console

ST-THÉGONNEC – Triumphal gateway to the Parish Close (17C)

The "Gateway of the Dead", an ornately worked entranceway, marks the separation between the sacred and the profane; it was used for religious processions and funerals corteges.

End-ornament

Lantern

Rounded pediment

Round end-ornament with gadroon notching

Triangular pediment

Attic: horizontal crown surmounting the entablature

Gargoyle

Shell-shaped niche

Cornice: a set of horizontal, protruding mouldings, overlapping each other.

Entablature

Frieze

Agrafe: decorative element placed on the keystone of a bay

Semicircular arch

Foundation

Pier: a pillar embedded in the wall

R. Corbel

FORT LA LATTE – Fortified castle (14C)

More than 60m/200ft above the sea, this 14C fort was modified in the 17C and restored in the 20C, but remains medieval in appearance.

Bartizan: a small overhanging lodge; the floor has openings for defensive fire.

Crenel: the open space between the **merlons** of a battlement

Loophole: used for shooting arrows

Bartizan: small overhanging construction used as a lookout

Donjon or **keep**

Curtain wall: the portion of the wall between two towers

Watch path

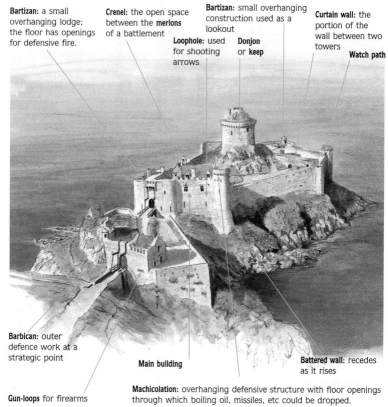

Barbican: outer defence work at a strategic point

Main building

Battered wall: recedes as it rises

Gun-loops for firearms

Machicolation: overhanging defensive structure with floor openings through which boiling oil, missiles, etc could be dropped.

BELLE-ÎLE-EN-MER – Vauban Citadel (17C)

Built in the 16C, the citadel was entirely redesigned by Vauban in the 17C. It is in exceptionally good condition, and a remarkable illustration of military architecture.

Cavalier: raised area used for artillery

Escarpment: a steep slope in front of the fortification to impede the approach of the enemy

Protruding angle: on the outwork; the angle formed by two walls which point outward; the inward-pointing angle is a **reentrant angle.**

Parade field

Barracks

Powder magazine

Redoubt: a fortification detached from the site, here at a lower level.

Ravelin or **demilune:** an outwork with two sides forming a sharp angle, set in front of the curtain wall.

Curtain wall

Bastion: a pentagonal design projects from the fortified inner walls.

R. Corbel

40

JOSSELIN – Interior façade of the château (1490-1510)

Erected at the beginning of the 16C; this magnificent façade facing the courtyard illustrates the exuberance, the imagination and the abundance of sculpted dormer windows typical of the Renaissance.

Pinnacle: an upright member, which is a small, ornate spire rising from a square or polygonal base.

Finial

Crocket

Dormer window: two storeys, extending out from the façade.

Attic space

Polygonal roof

Gable

Ornate crockets

Mullion window: the **mullion** is the vertical bar; the horizontal crossbar is the **transom**.

Mullion window with two crosspieces

Ogee arch

Ashlar laid in a large course

Open-work railing: supported by imitation gargoyles (the water is drained through ordinary gutters).

R. Corbel

41

RENNES – Hôtel de ville (1730-1742)

Built by the architect Jacques Gabriel; the belfry is set off by the concave form of the building, a typically Baroque touch of the spectacular.

Onion-shaped dome

Flaming urn finial: decorative element with a distinctive design.

Bull's-eye window

Triangular pediment

Belfry

Segment-arched window

Bas-relief sculpture (slightly protruding)

Stylobate: the base upon which the column is set

Central block of the building, set out in front of the other parts.

Brace with **boss-work:** rough-finished stone projects beyond the mortar joints.

Wing

JOSSELIN – Maison "Lovys Piechel" (1624)

Hipped roof or **gambrel roof**

Dormer window

Foundation sill: a long, wide horizontal beam placed atop a thick wall, serving as a support for the other pieces of the frame.

Half-timbering

"St-Andrew's cross" load bearing beam pattern

Corbelling creates an overhang

Ground floor in stone (green schist)

Small beam

R. Corbel

BRETON ART

Prehistoric monuments

The megaliths or "great stones" – More than 3 000 "great stones" are still to be found in the Carnac district alone. These monuments were set up between 5000 and 2000 BC by the little-known race who preceded the Gauls. They must have had a certain degree of civilization to be able to move and set upright stones which weigh up to 350t. To give a simple comparison, the Luxor obelisk in the Place de la Concorde in Paris weighs only 220t.

The **menhir**, or single stone, was set up at a spring, near a tomb and more often on a slope. It must have had a symbolic meaning. In Brittany there are about twenty menhirs over 7m/23ft high; the biggest is at Locmariaquer.

The **alignments** or lines of menhirs are probably the remains of religious monuments associated with the worship of the sun or moon. Most are formed by only a few menhirs set in line (many of the menhirs now isolated are the remains of more complicated groups). There are, however, especially in the Carnac area *(see Carnac: Megalithic Monuments)*, fields of menhirs arranged in parallel lines running from east to west and ending in a semicircle or **cromlech**. In the Lagatjar area the lines intersect. The lines of the menhirs appear also to be astronomically set, with an error of a few degrees, either by the cardinal points of the compass, or in line with sunrise and sunset at the solstices, from which it has been concluded that sun worship had something to do with the purpose of the monuments. As for the **dolmens** (the best-known is the Table des Marchands at Locmariaquer), these are considered to have been burial chambers. Some are preceded by an ante-chamber or corridor. Originally all were buried under mounds of earth or dry stones called tumuli but most of them have been uncovered and now stand in the open air. The round **tumuli** found in the interior are of more recent date than the tumuli with closed chambers like the one of St Michel at Carnac and the former were probably built up to 1000 BC. **Cairns** are tumuli composed entirely of stones such as the ones at Barnenez, which dates back to over 5000 BC and at Gavrinis, which is not so old. Some tumuli without burial chambers probably served as boundary markers. In northern Brittany **gallery graves** or **covered alleyways** are formed of a double row of upright stones with flat slabs laid on them, sometimes engraved.

Although the tumuli have never been fully excavated, some have been found to contain beautiful artefacts: polished axes made of rare stone (jadeite), or jewellery and marvellous necklaces made of *callaïs*. The museums at Carnac and Vannes contain particularly good collections of these early works of art.

Mystical tradition – For many centuries the menhirs were connected with the mystic life of the people of Brittany. The Romans adapted some to their rites, carving pictures of their gods upon them. When the Christian religion became established, it acknowledged many raised stones that people still venerated by crowning them with a cross or cutting symbols on them.

Churches and chapels

Nine cathedrals or former cathedrals, about 20 large churches and thousands of country churches and chapels make up an array of religious buildings altogether worthy of mystical Brittany.

Société Polymathique du Morbihan, Vannes

"Callaïs" necklace (variscite) – Musée archéologique de Vannes

Chapelle St-Fiacre

The edifices were built by the people and designed by artists who transmitted to them an inspired faith. This faith appeared in a richness that was sometimes excessive – the exaggeratedly decorated altarpieces are an example – and a realism that was at times almost a caricature – as, for instance, the carvings on certain capitals and many purlins. Only affected in part by outside influences, the artists always preserved their individuality and remained faithful to their own traditions.

Cathedrals – These are inspired by the great buildings in Normandy and Ile-de-France, although they do not rival their prototypes either in size or ornamentation. The small towns that built them had limited means. Moreover, their erection was influenced by the use of granite, a hard stone, difficult to work. The builders had to be content with rather low vaulting and simplified decoration. Financial difficulties dragged out the work for three to five centuries. As a result, every phase of Gothic architecture is found in the buildings, from the bare and simple arch of early times to the wild exuberance of the Flamboyant style; the Renaissance often added the finishing touches.

The most interesting cathedrals are those of St-Pol-de-Léon, Tréguier, Quimper, Nantes and Dol-de-Bretagne.

The corresponding Gothic period in England lasted until the end of the 13C and included in whole or in part the cathedrals of Wells (1174), Lincoln (chancel and transept: 1186), Salisbury (1220-58), Westminster Abbey (c 1250) and Durham (1242).

Country churches and chapels – In the Romanesque period (11C and 12C) Brittany was miserably poor. Buildings were few and small. Most of them were destroyed or transformed in the following centuries.

It was during the Gothic and the Renaissance periods, under the dukes and after the union with France, that the countryside saw the growth of churches and chapels.

Buildings constructed before the 16C are usually rectangular, though one also frequently sees the disconcerting T-plan in which the nave, usually without side aisles, ends in a chancel flanked by often disproportionately large chapels. The chevet is flat; there are no side windows – light comes through openings pierced right at the east end of the church.

Stone vaulting is rare and is nearly always replaced by wooden panelling, often painted, whose crocodile headed tie-beams (cross-beams dividing the roof timbers), wooden cornices at the base of the vaulting and hammerbeams are frequently carved and painted. When there is no transept, a great stone arch separates the chancel from the nave.

From the 16C onwards there was a complete transformation in architectural design; it became necessary to include a transept which, inevitably, gave rise to the Latin Cross outline. The central arch disappeared; the east end became three-sided; the nave was lit by windows in the aisles.

Belfries – The Bretons take great pride in their belfries. The towers did not serve only to hold bells; they were also symbolic of both religious and civic life. In olden days the people prized them greatly, and it was a terrible punishment for them when an angry king had them laid low.

The belfries are usually square in outline and their position on the building varies considerably.

Small churches and chapels were often given the lighter and less costly gable tower in preference to a belfry. The tower was placed either on the west front gable or on the roof itself, at the intersection of the chancel and the nave. It is reached by outside steps or by stairs in the turrets that flank it and are linked to it by a gallery.

Sometimes these little belfries become so reduced as only to be walls in gable form, pierced by arcades. This form of architecture, while fairly widespread in southwest France, is somewhat rare in Brittany.

Porches – Breton churches have a large porch on the south side.

For a long period the porch was used as a meeting place for the parish notables, who were seated on stone benches along the walls.

A double row of Apostles often decorates the porch. They can be recognised by their attributes: St Peter holds the key of Heaven; St Paul, a book or a sword; St John, a chalice; St Thomas, a set square; St James the Elder, a pilgrim's staff. Others carry the instruments of their martyrdom: St Matthew, a hatchet; St Simon, a saw; St Andrew, a cross; St Bartholomew, a knife.

Religious furnishings

Sculpture – From the 15C to the 18C an army of Breton sculptors working in stone and more particularly in wood supplied the churches with countless examples of religious furnishings: pulpits, organ casings, baptisteries and fonts, choir screens, rood screens, rood beams, altarpieces, triptychs, confessionals, niches with panels, Holy Sepulchres, statues etc.

These works are, as a general rule, more highly developed than the figures carved on the Calvaries, since it is much easier to work in oak, chestnut or alabaster than in granite. Visits to the churches and chapels of Guimiliau, Lampaul-Guimiliau, St-Thégonnec, St-Fiacre near Le Faouët and Tréguier Cathedral (stalls) will give a good general idea of Breton religious furnishings.

The many **rood screens** *(jubés)* to be found in the churches of Brittany are often of unparalleled richness. Some are cut in granite, as in the church at Le Folgoët, but most are carved in wood which makes them peculiar to Brittany.

Their decoration is very varied and is different on both sides.

The rood screen serves two purposes: it separates the chancel from the part of the church reserved for worshippers and completes the side enclosures of the chancel; the upper gallery may also be used for preaching and reading prayers. (The name derives from the first word of a prayer sung from the gallery.) The screen is usually surmounted by a large Crucifix flanked by statues of the Virgin and St John the Divine facing the congregation.

The **rood beam** or *tref*, which supported the main arch of the church, was the origin of the rood screen.

To prevent the beam from bowing it had to be supported by posts which were eventually replaced by a screen carved to a greater or lesser degree. It is to be seen mostly in the small chapels and churches where it serves as a symbolic boundary for the chancel; it is usually decorated with scenes from the Passion and always carries a group of Jesus Christ, the Virgin and St John.

Renaissance works are numerous and very elaborate. **Fonts** and **pulpits** are developed into richly decorated monuments.

Altarpieces, or retables, show an interesting development which can be traced through many stages in Breton churches. Originally the altar was simply a table: as the result of decoration it gradually lost its simplicity and reached a surprising size. In the 12C and 14C altars were furnished with a low step and altarpiece, the same length as the altar. Sculptors took possession of the feature and added groups of figures in scenes drawn from the Passion. From the 15C onwards, the altarpiece became a pretext for twisted columns, pediments, niches containing statues and sculpted panels, which reached their highest expression in the 17C.

Finally the main subject was lost in decoration consisting of angels, garlands etc and the altarpiece occupied the whole of the chapel reserved for the altar, and sometimes even, joined to the retables of side altars, decorating the whole wall of the apse as is the case at Ste-Marie-de-Ménez-Hom.

Of less importance but equally numerous are the niches which, when the two panels are open, reveal a **Tree of Jesse**. Jesse, who was a member of the tribe of Judah, had a son, David, from whom the Virgin Mary was

Holy Trinity (15C)
(Musée départemental breton, Quimper)

Musée départemental breton, Quimper

45

Rood screen, Chapelle St-Fiacre

descended. Jesse is usually depicted lying on his side; from his heart and his body spring the roots of the tree whose branches bear the figures, in chronological order, of the kings and prophets who were Christ's forebearers. In the centre the Virgin is portrayed representing the branch which bears the flower: Jesus Christ.

Among the many statues ornamenting the churches, such as the Trinity of St Anne and the Virgin and Child, portraits of real people and items of great importance in the study of the history of costume in Brittany are often to be found. Such representation, seen frequently in Central Europe, is rare in France.

Stained-glass windows – Whereas the altarpieces, friezes and statues were often coloured, paintings and frescoes, as such, were rare; almost the only exception are those at Kernascléden. In contrast there are a great many stained-glass windows, often Italian or Flemish inspired, but always made in Brittany. Some are really fine: the cathedral at Dol has a beautiful 13C window.

The workshops at Rennes, Tréguier and Quimper produced stained glass between the 14C and 16C which should be seen; the most remarkable windows from these workshops are in the churches of Notre-Dame-du-Crann, La Roche and St-Fiacre near Le Faouët.

In the 20C, the restoration and building of numerous churches and chapels has offered the possibility of decorating these edifices with colourful non-figurative stained-glass windows. The cathedral at St-Malo is a good example.

Gold and silver church plate – In spite of considerable losses, Brittany still possesses many wonderful pieces of gold and silver church plate. This was made by local craftsmen, most of them from Morlaix. Though fine chalices and shrines may be hidden away for security, magnificent reliquaries, chalices, richly decorated patens and superb processional crosses may be seen at Carantec, St-Jean-du-Doigt, St-Gildas-de-Rhuys, Paimpont and Locarn.

Parish closes

The parish close *(enclos paroissial)* is the most typical monumental grouping in Breton communities.

The tourist should not leave Brittany without having seen a few examples, and we therefore describe a tour of parish closes taking in the most interesting.

The centre of the close was the cemetery which was very small and with gravestones of uniform size. Nowadays this is tending to disappear. Around the cemetery, which is often reached through a **triumphal arch**, are grouped the **church** with its small square *(placître)*, the **Calvary**, and the **charnel house** or ossuary. Thus the spiritual life of the parish is closely linked with the community of the dead. Death, *Ankou*, was a familiar idea to the Bretons who often depicted it *(illustration see La Roche-Maurice)*.

The extraordinary rivalry between neighbouring villages explains the richness of the closes which were built in Lower Brittany at the time of the Renaissance and in the 17C. Competition between Guimiliau and St-Thégonnec went on for two centuries: a Calvary answered a triumphal arch, a charnel house a porch, a tower replied to a belfry, a pulpit to a font, an organ loft to a set of confessionals, an Entombment to chancel woodwork. The two finest closes in Brittany sprang from this rivalry.

Triumphal arch – The entrance to a cemetery is often ornamented with a monumental gateway. This is treated as a triumphal arch to symbolise the accession of the Just to immortality.

Some arches built during the Renaissance, like those of Sizun and Berven, are surprisingly reminiscent of the triumphal arches of antiquity.

Charnel house or ossuary – In the tiny Breton cemeteries of olden days, bodies had to be exhumed to make room for new dead. The bones were piled in small shelters with ventilation openings, built against the church or cemetery wall. The skulls were placed there separately in special "skull caskets". Then these charnel houses became separate buildings, larger and more carefully built and finally reliquaries, which could be used as funerary chapels.

Calvary – This is the name of the hill, also known as Golgotha, where Christ was crucified; its name was inspired by its skull-like shape (Skull: *calvaria* in Latin). Breton Calvaries representing scenes from the Passion and Crucifixion are not to be confused with wayside crosses often erected at crossroads or near churches to mark the site of a pilgrimage or procession.

The unique Breton monuments illustrate episodes of the Passion, represented around Christ on the Cross. Many of them were built to ward off, as in 1598, a plague epidemic, or to give thanks after it ended. The priest preached from the dais, pointing out with a wand the scenes which he described to his congregation.

The distant forerunners of the Calvaries were Christianised menhirs, which were still fairly common, and their immediate predecessors were the crosses, plain or ornate. Crosses along roads in this countryside are countless, certainly numbering tens of thousands at one time. In the 16C a Bishop of Léon boasted that he alone had had 5 000 put up. The oldest remaining Calvary is that of Tronoën, which dates from the end of the 15C. They were being erected as late as the end of the 17C. The most famous are those of Guimiliau with 200 figures, Plougastel-Daoulas with 180 and Pleyben.

The sculpture is rough and naive – the work of a village stonemason – but it shows a great deal of observation and is often strikingly lifelike and expressive. Many figures, notably soldiers, wear the costumes of the 16C and 17C.

Guimiliau Calvary (detail)

Castles and fortresses

Breton granite is somewhat daunting to the tourist coming to Brittany for the first time. Clean cut and hard, it does not age or weather and it would, therefore, not be possible to give a date to the grey buildings that blend perfectly into the landscape were it not for the architectural design and methods employed in construction. With the exception of the fortresses, most of which stood guard on the eastern border in fear of the kings of France or along the coast to ward off the raids of English invaders, there are few great castles in Brittany. This lack conveys perfectly the Breton character that turned all its artistic endeavour to the service of religion.

Nevertheless, it is easy to imagine Brittany in the Middle Ages. Few regions, in fact, had such fortresses and though many were destroyed or have fallen into ruin, a number are still standing. Before these walls the problems of war in the Middle Ages can be imagined. Although some fortresses fell at once to a surprise attack, it was not unusual for a siege to go on for several months. The attacker then sapped the ramparts, brought up machines which could hurl stones weighing over 100kg/200lb, and tried to smash the gates with battering rams before launching the final assault.

47

Vitré – Entrance gateway of the castle

In the mid 15C, artillery brought about new methods of attack and changes in military architecture.

At St-Malo and at Guérande, the stone walls that encircled these towns can be seen in their entirety. Remains of ramparts of varying extent can be seen in many other places. Vannes, Concarneau and Port-Louis have ramparts that are almost complete. There are many fortresses: those of Fougères and Vitré are among the finest in France. Dinan and Combourg have fortified castles still standing; Suscinio, Tonquédec etc have impressive ruins; La Hunaudaye, of lesser importance, the towers of Elven, Oudon and Châteaugiron still stand proudly upright. Fort la Latte, standing like a sentinel, boasts a magnificent site.

Buildings, half fortress and half palace, like Kerjean, Josselin and the Château des Ducs de Bretagne at Nantes, are interesting to see, but there are few of them. The fact is that the Breton nobility, except for the duke and a few great families, were poor. They included many country gentlemen who lived in very simple manors, which nevertheless retained their watchtower defences. They cultivated their own land, like the peasants, but they did not give up their rank and they continued to wear the sword. In some places these manor farms add a great deal of character to the Breton countryside. This is the case in Léon where they are numerous and where Kergonadéac'h, Kerouzéré, Kergroadès and Traonjoly together form a background setting to Kerjean, pride of the province. Certain other châteaux, such as Rocher-Portail, were built later, and lack all appearance of being fortresses, but impress by their simplicity of outline and the grouping of the buildings; at such places as Lanrigan and La Bourbansais, on the other hand, it is the detail that charms the visitor. Landal is one of those that gain enormously from their surroundings; others take great pride in a well laid-out garden or a fine park – these include Bonne-Fontaine, Caradeuc and Rosanbo.

Modern towns

It is difficult to find any basis of comparison between the old towns with their historical associations and the modern towns. Nonetheless, while Dinan, Locronan, Vitré, Morlaix and Quimper, to name but a few, as well as the marvellously reconstructed St-Malo, have an undeniable appeal, it is impossible not to be struck also by the planning and grouping of buildings in such towns as Brest and Lorient. The wide streets and huge, airy squares are elegant and have obviously been built to achieve harmony and unity. Visitors may well be surprised by certain buildings, but they will find something to admire in the upward sweep of a tall bell-tower, the simple lines of a concrete façade, the successful decorative effect of stone and cement combined. Above all, if they have some slight appreciation of colour harmony and go inside any building, they will be struck by the contemporary artist's skill in lighting.

Breton food and drink

Breton cooking is characterised by the high quality and freshness of the ingredients used, many of which will have been plucked from land or sea and brought almost directly to table after the briefest of interventions in the kitchen.

Seafood, crustaceans and fish – Shellfish, crustaceans and fish are all excellent. Particularly outstanding are the spiny lobsters, grilled or stuffed clams, scallops, shrimp, crisp batter-covered fried fish morsels and crab pasties.
Belon oysters, Armorican oysters from Concarneau, La Forêt and Île-Tudy, and Cancale oysters are all well known in France, but are not at their best until the end of the tourist season.

Lobster is served grilled or with cream and especially in a *coulis*, the rich hot sauce which makes the dish called *Armoricaine* or *à l'Américaine* (the latter name is due to a mistake made in a Paris restaurant).

Try also *cotriade* (a Breton fish soup like *bouillabaisse*), conger-eel stew, the Aulne or Élorn salmon, trout from the Monts d'Arrée and the Montagnes Noires, or pike and shad served with "white butter" in the district near the Loire. This is a sauce made from slightly salted butter, vinegar and shallots, and its preparation requires real skill. Finally, there are *civelles* (elvers), which are a speciality of Nantes.

Meat, vegetables and fruit – The salt pasture sheep *(prés-salés)* of the coast are famous. Breton leg of mutton (with white beans) is part of the great French gastronomic heritage. Grey partridges and heath hares are tasty as are the chickens from Rennes and Nantais ducks. Pork butchers' meat is highly flavoured: Morlaix ham, bacon, black pudding, smoked sausage from Guéméné-sur-Scorff and chitterlings from Quimperlé. Potatoes, artichokes, cauliflowers and green peas are the glory of the Golden Belt. There are also strawberries and melons from Plougastel, cherries from Fouesnant and many other fruits.

Crêpes, cakes and sweetmeats – Most towns have *crêperies* (pancake shops) where these very flat pancakes, called *crêpes*, made either of wheat or buckwheat, are served with cider or yoghurt. In some of the smaller, picturesque shops, often decorated with Breton furnishings, you may see them being made. Crêpes are served plain or with jam, cheese, eggs, ham etc. The buckwheat pancake *(crêpe de sarrasin)* is salted and often served as a starter while the wheat pancake *(crêpe de froment)* is sweet and served at dessert.

Also worth tasting are the Quimper wafer biscuits *(crêpes-dentelles)*, Pont-Aven butter cookies *(galettes)*, Nantes biscuits, Quintin oatmeal porridge and the *far* and *kouign amann* cakes. Among the sweets are the pralines from Rennes and berlingots (sweet drops) from Nantes.

Cider and wine – The local drink is cider *(cidre)*, of special note are the ciders from Fouesnant, Beg-Meil, and Pleudihen-sur-Rance.

The only Breton wine is **Muscadet**, which in 1936, was granted the *appellation d'origine contrôlée* (A.O.C.), literally "controlled place of origin". The people of Nantes guard it jealously and have founded a brotherhood, the Ordre des Chevaliers Bretvins, after *la petite brette* (little rapier), the nickname given to Anne of Brittany.

The grape, the *Melon de Bretagne*, has been cultivated since the early 17C, and gives a dry and fruity white wine which complements fish and seafood particularly well. Muscadet is produced in three distinct geographical areas, each with its own *appellation*: Muscadet, produced in the Grand-Lieu region; Muscadet de Sèvre et Maine, produced south of Nantes; and Muscadet des Coteaux de la Loire, produced in the Ancenis region *(for more information on local wines see The Green Guide Châteaux of the Loire).*

Vines still grow on the Presqu'île de Rhuys, but the wine drawn from them is a subject of Breton humour. "To drink it", the Bretons say, "you need four men and a wall: one man to pour it out, one to drink, two to hold him up and the wall to stop him from falling backwards." Distilled, on the other hand, it produces an excellent brandy.

Other Breton drinks worth tasting are mead, also called hydromel *(chouchen)*, strawberry liqueur *(liqueur de fraises)*, an orange-flavoured apéritif, and even a Breton whisky.

Seafood extravaganza

J. D. Sudres/SCOPE

SOME RECIPES

Galettes de sarrasin – This traditional recipe for savoury buckwheat pancakes allows for infinite variety depending on your choice of filling. You will need: 500g/1lb 2oz buckwheat flour, 100g/3.5oz salted butter, 2 eggs, 500ml/16fl oz cider. Make a well in the flour, break the eggs into it, add the cider and a little water, then mix in the melted butter and beat until you get a smooth, but not runny, batter. Leave this at room temperature for a few hours, then cook the pancakes over a hot flame for a couple of minutes in a heavy frying pan lightly greased with lard. Flip them over, butter them and garnish with sausages, bacon, onions, cheese etc.

Cotriade – Named after the Breton word "Koateriad" meaning the contents of a cauldron, this is a Breton variation of the Provençal fish dish, *bouillabaisse*. For six to eight people you will need: 500g/1lb 2oz conger eel (head end, chopped into 2cm/1in chunks), 500g sea pike (in 8cm/4in chunks), 500g mackerel and 500g whiting (cut each fish into 3), 400g/14oz pollack (in chunks), half a dozen sardines, 200g/6oz lard or butter, 5 or 6 large onions, 2 cloves, 2kg/4lb 8oz potatoes, 20g/1tsp mustard, 5cl/1tbsp cider vinegar, bouquet garni, salt, pepper, croutons (cubes of bread fried in butter until golden). The secret of this dish lies in the order in which it is cooked: in a large casserole, fry the onions and cloves in the lard until soft; add salt, pepper, bouquet garni, potatoes and chunks of conger, cover with about 5cm/2in water and boil vigorously for 15min; add the sea pike, mackerel and pollack and cook for a further 5min; finally, add the whiting and the sardines and cook for 5min. Strain the stock and set aside over a gentle heat. Set aside and keep warm some potatoes, the sardines and some chunks of mackerel. Put the rest of the fish and vegetables in a blender for a couple of minutes (the traditional Breton method is to pound them in an enormous pestle and mortar), then stir them into the stock. Serve the reserved fish and potatoes on separate plates, with the fish broth garnished with the croutons in bowls by the side.

Kig-ha-farz – This is a Breton version of the traditional French stew (pot-au-feu) and needs quite a lot of preparation time. For eight people you will need 500g/1lb 2oz buckwheat flour, 750g/1lb 11oz salt pork (soaked overnight), 500g blade bone of beef, 200g/6oz salted butter, 2 dessert spoons of thick cream, 4 eggs (beaten), 200g raisins, 200g dried fruit, 500ml/16fl oz milk, 4 onions, 2 cloves, 1 white cabbage, 6 turnips, 4 large carrots, the white of a leek, a stick of celery, bouquet garni, 2 dessert spoons of sugar, salt, an old linen tea towel folded in half and sewn into a bag and soaked for 10min. In a very large casserole, bring to the boil 7l/just under 12pt of water, adding the vegetables (except the cabbage) and the bouquet garni. Once the water is boiling, add the meat, season lightly and simmer for 2hr. When 1hr has passed make the farz by working together the flour, 200ml/7fl oz of the stock, the milk, the eggs, 125g/4oz of melted butter, salt, dried fruit and sugar to get a smooth dough. Leave to rest until the second hour is up; then pour into the tea-towel-bag, tie the neck firmly, plunge into the simmering pot and cook for a further 1hr 30min. Half an hour before cooking time is up, roughly chop the cabbage and blanch it in salted boiling water for 5min. Empty out the water, add the rest of the butter and 200ml/7fl oz of the stock and heat gently with a lid on until the stew is ready. Take out the bag of farz and leave to strain in a colander for 5min. Arrange the meat on a warmed serving dish. Once the *farz* has cooled a little, roll the bag around on a pastry board until the contents have broken up into a granular consistency. Open the bag and arrange its contents around the meat. Decorate with the vegetables and cabbage and serve with the stock as a sauce on the side.

Kouign-amann – This Breton sweetmeat is made from 500g/1lb 2oz flour, 250g/9 oz butter, 200g/7oz sugar, 10g/1tsp baking powder, pinch of salt and an egg yolk. Work the flour, baking powder and salt into a dough with a little water and leave to rise for 30min. Form the dough into a large flat pancake about 30cm/12in in diameter, spread half the butter on this, taking care not to go right up the edge, and sprinkle on about a third of the sugar. Fold the pancake into four, pressing the outer edges firmly together, and leave for 10min. Flatten the dough into a large pancake and cover with butter and sugar as before. Fold into four and leave for 10min. Flatten out to form a pancake of 25-30cm/10-12in in diametre and about 1-2cm/1in thick. Paint with the egg yolk and sprinkle with the rest of the sugar. Cook in a very hot oven for 30min. If the butter oozes out, use it to baste the kouign-amann until it has finished cooking.

Vieille Lighthouse, Pointe du Raz

51

Port de Sauzon à Belle-Île-en-Mer

Sights

Les ABERS ☖☖

Michelin map 58 folds 3 and 4 or 230 folds 2 and 3 – Finistère (29).

The low and rocky northwest coast of Finistère, still known as the Coast of Legends, offers a magnificent sight. The coastline stretching from the Pointe St-Mathieu to Brignogan-Plages is particularly wild and rugged, and is broken up by estuaries called *abers* (Aber-Wrac'h, Aber-Benoît, Aber-Ildut). The Finistère residents have a hard life, and the enormous anchor of the Amoco Cadiz reminds them of the violence the elements can inflict on their coastal region.

Visitors who enjoy manicured beaches will be disappointed here. On the other hand, those who enjoy romantic vistas, solitary coastal paths, and the smell of seaweed will feel right at home.

THE "COAST OF LEGENDS"

195km/121mi – allow one day

This tour offers the visitor the opportunity to go off the beaten track and to enjoy nature in its unspoiled state.

Leave Brest by north road towards Roscoff.

Gouesnou – The 17C Gothic and Renaissance **church** ⊘ has a polygonal chevet (1615) surmounted by three pediments. To the west, below the church, is a fine Renaissance fountain with an altar adorned with a statue of St Gouesnou.

Take the road towards Lannilis and at Bourg-Blanc, turn right.

Chapelle St-Jaoua ⊘ – Standing in the centre of a shady parish close is a charming early-16C chapel which contains the tomb and effigy of St Jaoua.

Plouvien – In the **parish church** is a tomb in Kersanton granite dating from 1555. The recumbent figure rests on 16 little monks depicted at prayer, reading or meditating.

Leave Plouvien to the east by the Lesneven road.

St-Jean-Balanant – The 15C **chapel** ⊘ was founded by the Order of St John of Jerusalem and was a dependant of the La Feuillée Commandery in the Monts d'Arrée.

Continue towards Lesneven and at the fourth junction turn right towards Locmaria.

Chapelle de Locmaria – In front of the 16C-17C chapel with its square belfry-porch, there is a fine **cross★** with two crossbars adorned with figures.

Go to Le Drennec and take the road on the left to Le Folgoët.

★★**Le Folgoët** – *See Le FOLGOËT.*

Take the road towards Lannilis and at Croas-Kerzu, bear right towards Plouguerneau.

Plouguerneau – The village **church** hosts an interesting collection of 17C wooden statuettes called the little saints which can be found near the baptistery on the left on entering. Formerly carried in processions, these statuettes are the result of a wish made by villagers who had miraculously escaped the plague.

Take the D 32 towards St-Michel.

At the exit to the village, on the right, is a small **museum of maritime traditions** which explains the techniques of seaweed-gathering through the ages.

Ruines d'Iliz Koz ⊘ – These ruins of the church and the presbytery, which have been silted up since the early 18C, provide an excellent example of Breton funerary art at the end of the Middle Ages. A sign-posted route enables visitors to discover the most important elements of the site. Pay special attention to the tombs' ornamental motifs which describe the function of the tomb's occupant (knight, clerk or commoner).

Near the ruins is a good sheltered beach of fine sand in a rocky cove.

Phare de l'Île Vierge ⊘ – This is the tallest lighthouse in France (82.5m/270ft). From the top (397 steps) the **panorama★** extends over the Finistère coast.

Return to Plouguerneau and take D 113 towards Lannilis.

Only 2km/1mi further on, the old road has become a lookout point (small Calvary) affording a good **view★** of l'Aber-Wrac'h.

Turn right at Lannilis.

L'Aber-Wrac'h – With its important sailing centre, l'Aber-Wrac'h is a very popular pleasure port. Its sailing school overlooks the village, and also livens up this seaside stay. The corniche road runs along the Baie des Anges; past the ruins of the 16C convent of Notre-Dame-des-Anges.

Bear right towards Ste-Marguerite Dunes, then right again towards Cézon Fort.

From the platform by the roadside, there is an interesting **view** of l'Aber-Wrac'h estuary, the ruins of Cézon Fort on an island commanding the approach to the estuary, and the lighthouse on the Île Vierge.

Turn back and after Poulloc, bear right for the dunes.

Dunes de Ste-Marguerite – ◪ The footpaths through the dunes afford good views. Seaweed is left to dry on the dunes for two to three days and then is sent to the processing factories.

Make for the Chapelle de Brouënnou and turn left towards Passage St-Pabu. Go to Lannilis via Landéda and then take the Ploudalmézeau road.

Aber-Benoît – The road crosses the *aber* and runs along it for a while giving good views of the pretty setting.

After 5km/3mi, turn right for St-Pabu and after St-Pabu follow the signposts for the camp site to reach the Corn-ar-Gazel Dunes.

Dunes de Corn-ar-Gazel – Beautiful **view** of Ste-Marguerite Peninsula, Aber-Benoît and its islets.

Turn round and follow the scenic road winding through the dunes and affording glimpses of the coast.

Lampaul-Ploudalmézeau – The **church** has a Renaissance north door and a magnificent **belfry-porch★** crowned by a dome with three lanterns.

Portsall ⊘ – This small harbour is located in a bay sheltered by a chain of reefs called the Roches de Portsall, the rocks on which the oil tanker, Amoco Cadiz, ran aground in 1978. One of its two enormous anchors (20t) is fixed to the harbour breakwater in memory of the shipwreck, on which a legal settlement was not reached until 1992.

Kersaint – Beyond the village, towards Argenton, are the ruins of the 13C **Château de Trémazan**. Be careful! These ruins are very dangerous. However a lookout point allows one to admire the majesty of the site.

Trémazan – From the large car park past the village, the **view★** extends over the Île Verte, the Roches de Portsall and Corn Carhai Lighthouse.

★Scenic road *(Route touristique)* – The corniche road follows a wild coast studded with rocks; note the curious jagged **Pointe de Landunvez**. The road runs through several small resorts, Argenton, **Porspoder** – where St Budoc, Bishop of Dol-de-Bretagne is said to have landed in the 6C – and Melon.

The Aber-Ildut inlet, Lanildut

B. Kaufmann

Turn right at the entrance of Lanildut.

Lanildut – This is Europe's foremost seaweed port. The Rumorvan quarter hosts several beautiful captain's houses from the 17C and 18C.

Rocher du Crapaud – It offers good views of the harbour and the *aber*, a picturesque estuary accessible to boats regardless of the tides. The northern bank is wooded, the southern bank has dunes and beaches.

After Lanildut, the road follows the aber as far as Brélès.

Château de Kergroadès ⊘ – The main courtyard of this early-17C castle is closed by a crenellated gallery and is surrounded by an austere main building flanked by two round towers.

Return to Brélès and take the direction of Plouarzel and turn right after Lampaul-Plouarzel. The road then runs along Porspol Bay with Ségal Island in the distance, and through Trézien.

Phare de Trézien – The lighthouse (37m/121ft high) has an average range of 35km/22mi.

Continue towards Porsmoguer Beach (Grève de Porsmoguer) and after some houses turn right.

The road passes by the Corsen Maritime Station (Station de Corsen) and leads to a ruined house on the cliff.

Eating Out

BUDGET

Relais du Vieux Port – *1 quai du Drellac'h, 29217 Le Conquet* – ☎ *02 98 89 15 91 – closed Jan – 40/140F*. The restaurant serves crêpes and seafood in a maritime decor of stone and wood. Its five hotel rooms, each named after a Breton island, offers harbour views. Here you will awaken to the sound of sea-gulls.

Hotels

BUDGET

Pointe Ste-Barbe – *29217 Le Conquet* – ☎ *02 98 89 00 26 – closed 12 Nov-17 Dec* – ▣ – *49 rooms 201/658F – breakfast 40F – restaurant 102/474F*. Clinging to the rocky coast, this modern hotel offers spectacular views over the ocean and the islands. The rooms with panoramic views are far superior to those which look onto the port. Which accounts for the considerable differences in price.

OUR SELECTION

Hôtel Baie des Anges – *29214 Landéda, at l'Aber-Wrac'h* – ☎ *02 98 04 90 04 – closed 5 Jan-5 Feb* – ▣ – *20 rooms 320/520F – breakfast 55F*. Run by a local family, this hotel with sea views has been entirely renovated. Two buildings house its fairly spacious rooms; decorated in pale colours, they are light and pleasant.

Discovering the Sea

Sailing station at l'Aber-Wrac'h – Offers sailing trips to sea accompanied by a skipper. *At the Landéda port –* ☎ *02 98 04 90 64.*

Boat with views underwater – *L'Aquafaune, port du Conquet* – ☎ *02 98 89 17 66.* Offers trips in a specially equipped boat that lets you see underwater and discover the world of sea animals.

Pointe de Corsen – This 50m/160ft cliff is the most westerly point in continental France. There is a fine **view** of the coast and islands.

Go to Ploumoguer passing through Porsmoguer Beach, then turn towards Le Conquet. After 5km/3mi, bear right for the Pointe de Kermorvan.

Pointe de Kermorvan – Its central part is an isthmus which gives a pretty view on the right of Blancs Sablons Beach and on the left of the **site**★ of Le Conquet. The Groaë footbridge gives pedestrians access to the point; at the very tip, to the left of the entrance to the lighthouse, the rocky chaos makes a marvellous lookout point.

⌂ **Le Conquet** – This town occupies a pretty **site**★, and affords a superb view of the Pointe de Kermorvan. This small fishing port is the departure point for the islands of Ouessant and Molène.

🚶 The harbour corniche road, the coastal footpaths and especially the Pointe de Kermorvan are pleasant walks offering good views of the port, the Four Channel, the Ouessant archipelago and its many lighthouses in the distance.

The road from Le Conquet to Brest is described in the opposite direction under BREST: Excursions.

Use the Map of Principal Sights to plan an itinerary.

Monts d'ARRÉE ⌂⌂

Michelin map 58 folds 5 and 6 and 15 and 16 or 230 folds 18 and 19 – Finistère (29)

Dividing the Cornouaille and the Léon, the Arrée Mountains are the highest in Brittany, yet their topmost point is less than 400m/1 200ft. Solitary, barren, covered in heaths, often wet, these sharp crests of quartz have been incorporated into the **Parc national régional d'Armorique** to better preserve their wild nature. In the midst of the park, the different sites which make up the **Écomusée des Monts d'Arrée** illustrate the rural way of life of times past.

The mountain chain is wooded in parts, especially towards the east, but the summits are usually quite desolate. There is not a tree on them; the heath is pierced by rocky scarps; here and there are clumps of gorse with golden flowers in spring and purple heather in September.

*Map labels:*
LANDIVISIAU · LANDIVISIAU · MORLAIX

Sizun · ★★ ◆Roc Trévezel · 384 · D 764 · la Feuillée

D 18 · St-Cadou · D 342 · D 785 · D 36 · D 14 · PARC D'ARMORIQUE

Domaine de Menez-Meur · RÉGIONAL · Réservoir de St-Michel · ★★ Huelgoat

PARC · 210 · St-Rivoal · 380 · Brennilis

★Pen-ar-Hoat · D 42 · ★Montagne St-Michel

Forêt du Cranou ★ · ★Maison des Artisans · 227 · St-Herbot ★

★Rumemgol · D 42 · Loqueffret · Roc'h Begheor · D 764

Quimerch ★ · Brasparts · D 21 · Grd Pont · D 14 · Elez

le Faou · N 165 · D 770 · Lannédern

Doufine · D 14

Pont-de-Buis-lès-Quimerch · D 785 · D 36

St-Sébastien · Port-Launay · † Pleyben★★

Châteaulin · N 164 · N 164

D 887

BREST · CROZON · CARHAIX-PLOUGER · RENNES

QUIMPER · CHÂTEAUNEUF-DU-FAOU

ROUND TOUR CROSSING LA MONTAGNE PELÉE

122km/76mi – allow one day

In nice weather, a good way to appreciate the beauty of Brittany's interior.
Leave Huelgoat south in the direction of Pleyben.

★St-Herbot – The **church★** with its square tower, stands surrounded by trees. It is mainly in the Flamboyant Gothic style. A small Renaissance ossuary abuts on the south porch. There is a fine Crucifix-Calvary in Kersanton granite (1571) in front of the building.

Inside, the **chancel** is surrounded by a remarkable **screen★★** in carved oak topped by a Crucifixion. Against this screen, on the nave side, are two stone tables for the tufts of hair from the tails of oxen and cows, which the peasants offer on the *pardon* to obtain the protection of St Herbot, the patron saint of horned cattle. Note also the richly decorated stalls (lift the seats) against the screen.

Roc'h Begheor – *15min on foot. Car park to the right of the road.* A good **view★** over the Monts d'Arrée and the Montagnes Noires.

Lannédern – In the **parish close** is a Cross decorated with figures; note St Edern riding a stag. Inside the **church** ⊘ the saint's tomb (14C) and six polychrome low-relief sculptures (17C) illustrating his life are of interest.

Continue towards Pleyben and turn right after 1.5km/1mi.

Brasparts – Perched atop a hill, this village has an interesting 16C **parish close**. Inside the church, by the nave (on the right) stands a splendid **Virgin of Pity★** (16C)

🚶 For ramblers, from the town, follow the trails marked Du Méné (11km/5.5mi) and De Gorre (16km/8mi).

Make for Pleyben.

★★Pleyben – *See PLEYBEN.*

A house near Brasparts

D'après photo Christiane Olivier

Châteaulin – Standing on a bend of the Aulne, in the green and deep valley through which the canalized river flows, this little town is a centre for freshwater fisherman. In fact, the tide does not reach Châteaulin but dies out a little way downstream at Port-Launay which harbours numerous pleasure boats.

Salmon Fishing

Châteaulin is the salmon-fishing centre in the Aulne Valley; the salmon has always appeared on the town's coat of arms. Less often than in the past, the salmon come up the river to spawn, trying to leap the small waterfalls formed by the overflows from the locks. Angling (bait casting, spin casting) is done below the locks over a distance of some 100m, especially in March and April.

Chapelle Notre-Dame – *Access via rue Graveran and a road to the left, opposite the cemetery.* The castle's former chapel stands in an enclosure near some 17C houses. Pass through the triumphal arch, there is a 15C Calvary cross presenting a rather unusual Last Judgement. Modified in the 17C and 18C, and extensively restored in 1991, the chapel retains some vestiges of the 13C (columns, capitals), and some 17C altarpieces.

Follow the south bank of the Aulne.

Port-Launay – This is the port of Châteaulin, on the Aulne. The long quay makes for pleasant walks.

Leave the Brest road on the right and continue along the Aulne, pass under the railway viaduct, bear right at the roundabout and 100m/110yd further on, turn left.

Chapelle St-Sébastien – In the 16C **parish close** stand a triumphal arch surmounted by St Sebastian between two archers, and a fine Calvary with figures including the saint pierced by arrows.

Follow the small road over the railway line and the Quimper-Brest motorway and turn left towards Brest.

Pont-de-Buis-lès-Quimerch – On leaving the village, below the road, on the left, can be seen a 300-year-old explosives factory.

★**Quimerch** – *Viewing table.* The **view** extends from Ménez-Hom to the Forêt du Cranou taking in the Brest roadstead and the Presqu'île de Plougastel.

Laandéerennec/Le Faou –*From Le Faou, take the small road to Rumengol.*

Rumengol – Rumengol dates from the time of King Gradlon who built a chapel here in the 5C, just after the town of Ys disappeared. The **church** is 16C as shown by the south porch and the magnificent west front in Kersanton granite but significant alterations were made in the 17C and 18C. The two **altarpieces**★ and altars date from 1686. In the centre of the village, near the church apse, is a sacred fountain (1792), an object of devotion on *pardon* days.

★**Forêt du Cranou** – The road, hilly and winding, runs through the state forest of Cranou, which covers over 600ha/1 483 acres and consists mostly of oaks and beeches. Picnic areas.

On leaving the Forêt du Cranou, bear right towards St-Rivoal; at the entrance to Kerancuru, turn left for Pen-ar-Hoat-ar-Gorré. In the hamlet (schist houses), turn left towards Hanvec and again left onto an uphill road.

★**Pen-ar-Hoat** – *Alt 217m/712ft.* 🏃 *45min on foot there and back.* Walk round the farm and bear left towards the line of heights; after passing between low walls, the climb ends among gorse bushes. The **panorama** extends over the heath-clad hills: to the north are the hills bordering the left bank of the Elorn, to the east the nearer heights of the Arrée, to the south Cranou Forest and in the distance the Montagnes Noires and the Ménez-Hom, and lastly, to the west, the Brest roadstead.

Return to Kerancuru and bear left; 3.5km/2mi further on, left again.

Domaine de Menez-Meur ⊘ – The estate sprawls over 400ha/988 acres in an undulating countryside. The Tourist Information Centre (Maison du Parc) presents exhibitions devoted to the Parc naturel régional d'Armorique.

🏃 A nature trail *(about 1hr 30min)*, accompanied by panels giving information on the region's flora, winds through the large enclosures where ponies, sheep, deer, wild boar, horses etc roam.

Go to St-Rivoal, passing through St-Cadou.

St-Rivoal – After the village, below the Le Faou road, to the left, is the **Maison Cornec** ⏱, a small farm dating from 1702. It is one of the many exhibits dispersed throughout the Parc d'Armorique, which makes up the open-air museum devoted to the different styles of Breton architecture. The little house, built of schist and with a fine external covered stairway going up to the hayloft, comprises a large room with the living quarters for the farmer and his family round the great chimney and the domestic animals at the other end.

Take the road in the direction of Brasparts.

The road winds through a countryside of hills, and of green and wooded valleys whose freshness contrasts with the bare rocky summits.

After 5.5km/3mi, bear left towards Morlaix.

Maison des Artisans ⏱ – *North of Brasparts.* Part of the regional nature park, the centre is housed in St-Michel farmhouse; it displays the creations of over 200 Breton craftspeople.

Continue towards Morlaix; take the road which branches off to the left.

★**Montagne St-Michel** – From the top of the rise (alt 380m/1 246 ft) where there is a small chapel which reaches an altitude of 391m/1 282ft at its summit, there is a **panorama** of the Monts d'Arrée and the Montagnes Noires. From the foot of the hill, a great peat bog called the Yeun Elez extends towards the east. In the winter mists, the place is so grim that Breton legend says it contains the Youdig, a gulf forming the entrance to Hell. Beyond it may be seen St-Michel reservoir which supplies the Monts d'Arrée thermal power station at Brennilis. Note the megalithic alignment on the rocky point to the right of the lake.

Fine views of the countryside, the mountains and Brennilis basin from the road passing by the Toussaines Signal Station (Signal de Toussaines, alt 384m/1 260ft).

★★**Roc Trévezel** – This rocky escarpment, which juts up on the skyline (384m/1 260ft), is in a remarkably picturesque spot in a truly mountainous setting.

🚶 *Take the path (30min on foot there and back) near a signpost. Go towards the left, cross a small heath, bearing to the right, and make for the most distant rocky point.* From here the **panorama**★★ is immense. To the north, the Léon Plateau appears, bristling with spires; in clear weather you can see the Kreisker spire at St-Pol-de-Léon and to the east Lannion Bay; to the west, the end of the Brest roadstead; to the south, the St-Michel Mountain and, beyond it, the dark line of trees on the Montagnes Noires.

By the Roc-Tredudon pylon turn right towards Huelgoat and after 6km/4mi, bear right to Brennilis.

Brennilis – This village has a 15C **church** ⏱ topped by a delicate pierced belfry. Inside, seven polychrome panels (17C) at the high altar and a stained-glass window (16C) in the chancel illustrate scenes from the life of the Virgin.

Return to the entrance to Brennilis and turn right, 90m/100yd further to the right, a signposted path leads to a covered alleyway partly hidden by a tumulus. Continue on the secondary road to Huelgoat.

The length of time given in this guide
– for touring allows time to enjoy the views and the scenery;
– for sightseeing is the average time required for a visit.

AURAY★

Population 10 323
Michelin map 6 fold 2 or 20 fold 36 – Local map see Golfe du MORBIHAN

This ancient town, built on the banks of the Loch or River Auray, is one of the eight Breton towns honoured with the title *"ville d'art et d'histoire"*. Many visitors come to enjoy its attractive harbour, its old St-Goustan Quarter, and its proximity to the marvellous **Golfe du Morbihan**.

The Battle of Auray (14C) – The town is famous in Breton history for the battle that was fought under its walls in 1364 ending the War of Succession. The troops of Charles of Blois, backed by Du Guesclin, held a bad position on a marshy plain north of Auray. Jean de Montfort, Charles's cousin, Olivier de Clisson, and the English, commanded by Chandos, were in a dominating position. Against Du Guesclin's advice, Charles attacked but was soundly defeated, before being slain by one of De Montfort's Breton soldiers.

AURAY

0   200 m

Barré (R. J.-M.)	3	Franklin (Quai B.)	15	St-Goustan (Pont de)	30
Clemenceau (R. Georges)	12	Gaulle (Av. du Gén.-de)	16	St-Julien (R.)	31
République (Pl. de la)	28	Joffre (Pl. du Maréchal)	18	St-René (R.)	32
		Lait (R. du)	19	St-Sauveur (Pl.)	34
Abbé-Martin (R.)	2	Neuve (R.)	22	St-Sauveur (R.)	36
Briand (R. Aristide)	5	Notre-Dame (Pl.)	23		
Cadoudal (R. G.)	9	Penher (R. du)	24		
Château (R. du)	10	Père-Éternel (R. du)	25	**M** Goélette St-Sauveur	
Église-St-Goustan (R. de l')	14	Petit-Port (R. du)	26		

Georges Cadoudal – A farmer's son from around Auray, he was 22 years old when the **Chouannerie**, a Breton Royalist revolt, broke out in 1793. He threw himself wholeheartedly into the cause. When the men of the Vendée were beaten, he carried on the struggle in Morbihan. He was captured, imprisoned at Brest but escaped, and took part in the action at Quiberon. He came away unhurt, submitted to Hoche in 1796 and reopened the campaign in 1799. Bonaparte offered the rebel a pardon and the rank of general, without success. The struggle ended only in 1804; Cadoudal had gone to Paris to try to kidnap Napoleon; he was arrested, sentenced to death and executed.

★**Église St-Gildas** – This 17C church, with its Renaissance porch, contains a very fine stone and marble **altarpiece**★ (1664) attributed to Olivier Martinet. Note the 18C woodwork in the side chapels and elegant organ loft (1761) by the Auray organ-builder Waltrin.

★**Promenade du Loch** – There is a good **view** over the port, St-Goustan Quarter and Auray River, crossed by an attractive old stone bridge with cutwaters.

Moored in the loch is a schooner, the **Goélette St-Sauveur** ⊙ (**M**), which has been painstakingly reconstructed from an old hull. It contains information on the way of life in St-Goustan port during the last century, including slide shows with soundtracks. A display of tools belonging to maritime carpenters evokes the construction techniques which were once used.

St-Goustan

Near the old bridge note the En-Bas Pavilion, an attractive 16C house.

★**Quartier St-Goustan** – This little port, particularly lively in the evening, still has some beautiful 15C houses and other pretty dwellings in place St-Sauveur (**34**) and up some of the steep, in places even stepped, little lanes leading off the square. The quay to the left of the square is named after Benjamin Franklin (**15**). In 1776, during the War of Independence, the famous American diplomat and statesman sailed from Philadelphia to negotiate a treaty with France and landed at Auray instead of Nantes due to the unfavourable weather conditions. The house (no 8) where he stayed bears a plaque.

LE PAYS ALRÉEN

Round tour of 23km/14mi – 3hr. Leave Auray on avenue du Général-de-Gaulle.

Chartreuse d'Auray ⊘ – On the battlefield where he defeated Charles of Blois, Jean de Montfort (who became Duke Jean IV) built a chapel and a collegiate church, which was later transformed into a Carthusian monastery (from 1482-1790).

The funeral chapel was built in the early 19C to hold the bones of exiles and Chouans who were shot on the Champ des Martyrs in 1795; in the centre, the black and white marble mausoleum bears the names of 953 exiles.

Champ des Martyrs – The exiles and Chouans were shot in this enclosure during the Royalist insurrection (1793-1804). The Duchess of Angoulême had a chapel built in the style of a Greek temple on the site where they were executed and buried, before the remains were transferred to the Carthusian Monastery.

Follow the road to Ste-Anne-d'Auray.

The road skirts the Kerzo Bog (on the right) where the Battle of Auray was fought on 29 September 1364.

After 500m/550yd bear left in the direction of St-Degan.

St-Degan – Overlooking the deep valley of the Loch, the hamlet hosts the **écomusée** ⊘ (open-air museum), which contains restored thatched-roof buildings, and furniture of the Bas-Vannetais, thus rediscovering its 17C look.

Go to Brech and turn right.

Eating out

BUDGET

Crêperie la Frégate – *11 rue du Petit-Port (at the port of St-Goustan)* – ☎ *02 97 50 71 95 – closed 2 weeks in Jan and 2 weeks in Oct.* After dropping anchor in the old harbour, go up the narrow street to reach this half-timbered house where you can enjoy your fill of crêpes in front of the fireplace. The second-hand shop next door has some interesting items.

OUR SELECTION

Closerie de Kerdrain – *20 rue L-Billet* – ☎ *02 97 56 61 27 – closed 1-14 Mar, 15 Nov-1 Dec, Feb school holidays and Mon – 180/450F.* This manor house located in a garden is quite popular with the locals. The restaurant's delightful summer terrace and very comfortable salons contribute much to the success of the restaurant and its classic French cuisine.

Hotels

OUR SELECTION

Les Chaumières de Cahire – *Hameau de Cahire, 7km/4.5mi on the route de Vannes, exit at Plougoumelen then follow the directions of Cahire* – ☎ *02 97 57 91 18 – closed 1 Jan-10 Feb, and Thur off-season – credit cards not accepted – 4 rooms 290/400F.* Located in a hamlet listed as a *"monument historique"*, the calm and comfort of these three thatched cottages will surely seduce you. One of the cottages formerly housed the old bread oven. Breakfast is served in the pretty kitchen in front of the fireplace.

Boat Trip

Le golfe du Morbihan boat trip – This pleasant excursion takes one up the River Auray to Bono and around the gulf. A marvellous way to discover what you can't possibly see by car. From mid-May to mid-Sept. Contact NAVIX. ☎ *02 97 46 60 00.*

★Ste-Anne-d'Auray – Ste-Anne is the outstanding Breton place of pilgrimage. The first *pardon* takes place on 7 March; then, from Easter until Rosary (the first Sunday in October); there are parish pilgrimages (especially Wednesdays and Sundays from the end of April to the end of September). The *pardon* of St Anne on 26 July is the most frequented, together with the those on 15 August and of the Rosary.

In 1623 St Anne appeared to a ploughman, Yves Nicolazic, and asked him to rebuild a chapel which had been previously dedicated to her in one of his fields. On 7 March 1625, Yves unearthed, at the spot she had indicated, an old statue of St Anne. A church was built there the same year. The present basilica, in the Renaissance style, took its place in the late 19C.

Basilica (Basilique) – Built from 1866-72, it took the place of the 17C chapel.

★Treasury (Trésor) ⊘ – Located in the cloister, it contains objects devoted to St Anne, notably a relic of St Anne presented by Anne of Austria in thanks for the birth of Louis XIV. There are also gold and silver plates and the cloak of the old statue, and, in a glass case in the centre, ornaments given by Anne of Austria. A Breton art gallery contains 15C-19C statues.

Scala Sancta – Old doorway from the square with a double staircase which pilgrims climb on their knees.

Fontaine miraculeuse – The fountain consists of a basin and a column adorned with smaller basins and surmounted by a statue of St Anne.

Monument aux morts – The war memorial was raised by public sub-

L'Auberge – *56400 Ste-Anne-d'Auray,* ☎ *02 97 57 61 55 – closed 15 Nov-5 Dec, Feb school holidays, Tues (except in summer months and noon from Easter-Oct) and Wed – 90/350F.* Behind the flower-be-decked façade, this inn serves generous dishes of local cuisine. The young couple who manage the inn are very friendly, and they also offer several rooms for guests. This place gives you value for your money. Children's menu available.

scription all over Brittany to the 250 000 Breton soldiers and sailors who died in the First World War. It has become the memorial to all dead during the wars which have occurred in the 20C.

Not far away, on the other side of the road, a Franco-Belgian cemetery contains the graves of 1 338 soldiers.

Historial de Sainte Anne ⊘ – This retrospective exhibit presents the life of Yves Nicolazic and the origins of the annual pilgrimage.

Musée du Costume breton ⊘ – *To the right of the war memorial.*
A fine collection of old dolls in Breton costume and two small boats offered as ex-votos.

Maison de Nicolazic ⊘ – It was in this house that St Anne appeared to the pious peasant. Inside are a chapel and some 17C furniture.

Monument du comte de Chambord – *Towards Brech, on the left about 500m/1 500ft from the town.* This monument was erected in 1891. Each year, for St Michael's day, followers and friends made the pilgrimage to Ste-Anne. Representations of Bayard, Du Guesclin, St Geneviève and St Jeanne d'Arc frame the statue of Charles X's grandson.

Pluneret – In the cemetery, alongside the central alley, on the right, are the tombs of Sophie Rostopchine, the Countess de Ségur, the well-known author of children's books and of her son, Mgr Louis-Gaston de Ségur.
Proceed towards Bono and after 2km/1mi turn left for Ste-Avoye.

Ste-Avoye – Among picturesque cottages, near a fountain, stands a pretty Renaissance **chapel** ⊘ with a fine keel-shaped **roof★**.
Turn back in the direction of Ste-Anne-d'Auray and bear left to Auray.

Michelin's famous star ratings are allocated for various categories:
regions of scenic beauty with dramatic natural features
cities with an exceptional cultural heritage
elegant resorts and charming villages
ancient monuments and fine architecture
museums and galleries.

La BAULE⚘⚘⚘

Population 14 845
Michelin map 6 fold 14 or 20 folds 51 and 52 – Local map see Presqu'île de GUÉRANDE.

La Baule's long beach of fine sand, which boasts the title of "Europe's most beautiful beach," stretches along south Brittany. Water sports, tennis, casino and golf make this one of the most popular seaside resorts on the Atlantic coast.

★**Seafront** – Sheltered from the winds, this elegant promenade lined with modern buildings stretches for about 7km/4mi between Pornichet and Le Pouliguen. Unfortunately, the turn-of-the-century villas which were once the heart of the resort, have since fallen prey to developers.

⚘⚘LA BAULE-LES-PINS

La Baule is extended eastwards by this resort, which was built in 1930, in an area of pine forests. The attractive Allée Cavalière leads to the Escoublac Forest. Near the place des Palmiers is the **Parc des Dryades**★, a lovely park landscaped with trees of many varieties and colourful flower beds.

⚘**Pornichet** – Originally a salt-marsh workers' village, Pornichet became a fashionable seaside resort in 1860. The town was a popular rendezvous for Parisian

Eating out

BUDGET

Crêperie La Galette de Plonéour – *66 avenue du Gén.-de-Gaulle – closed Oct-Easter, except during school holidays and on weekends – 40/80F.* What a pleasure it is to discover this typically Breton old-style crêperie in La Baule's main shopping street. You can watch crêpes being prepared. Good prices.

Les Halles – *194 avenue du Mar.-de-Lattre-de-Tassigny – ☎ 02 40 60 23 02 – closed 2-8 Jan, Wed evening and Thur off-season – 95/180F.* After strolling around the market, take a table in this bar with a seafaring theme to savour a few oysters or a shellfish platter, accompanied by a glass of chilled Muscadet. In the summer, the secluded terrace behind the house is quite popular.

OUR SELECTION

La Croisette – *31 place du Mar.-Leclerc – ☎ 02 40 60 73 00 – 120/220F.* You'll almost believe you are in Cannes on the Mediterranean in this restaurant with its beautiful woodwork and nautical furnishings. Boasts an extensive menu of salads, seafood, grilled meat, pasta and pizzas. Serves drinks and ice cream in the afternoons. Pleasant terrace.

Le Garde Côte – *1 jetée du Port, in Pouliguen – ☎ 02 40 42 31 20 – 120/165F.* From its location at the end of the harbour's jetty, you can enjoy a spectacular view of La Baule's bay. The restaurant's unusual architecture is modelled after the two after-decks of a cruise liner.

Hotels

OUR SELECTION

Hôtel la Closerie – *173 avenue du Mar.-de-Lattre-de-Tassigny – ☎ 02 51 75 17 00 – closed 1-15 Dec and 6 Jan-14 Feb – ▣ – 15 rooms 270/400F – breakfast 40F.* On the road to Croisic, in a residential area, this modern house decorated with flowers hides a swimming pool. Frequented by a regular clientele who appreciate its familial and tidy atmosphere, it is a pleasant stopping place.

Hôtel Marini – *22 avenue G.-Clemenceau – ☎ 02 40 60 23 29 – 33 rooms 326/385F – breakfast 42F – restaurant 108F.* This hotel is located in a small half-timbered building near the train station, and has been decorated with care and character. The rooms are neat and tidy, and the small interior swimming pool is a plus. The restaurant is reserved for hotel guests.

Villa Flornoy – *7 avenue Flornoy, in Pornichet (near the town hall) – ☎ 02 40 11 60 00 – closed end-Oct to mid-Feb – 21 rooms 390/530F – breakfast 42F – restaurant 120/145F.* With its amusing 1920's façade, this hotel has retained its by-gone charm, despite being entirely renovated inside. The antique furnishings add a personal touch to the rooms, and the pretty garden also enhances this peaceful villa.

Hôtel Beau Rivage – *11 rue J.-Benoit, in Pouliguen – ☎ 02 40 42 31 61 – closed 2 Nov to mid-Feb – ▣ – 65 rooms 350/420F – breakfast 42F – restaurant 120/250F.* The modern hotel is right on the beach. The dining room's bay windows open right onto the sand and the sea. The rooms in the main building are preferable; their bamboo furnishings give them a light and modern look.

64

publishers, among whom was Camille Flammarion. The town is composed of two distinct districts: Old Pornichet, to the southeast, which is busy all the year round, and Pornichet-les-Pins to the northwest, whose large villas surrounded by greenery are livelier in the summer. Also in the summer, horse races are held in the Côte d'Amour's racecourse. And finally the **Boulevard des Océanides** runs along the beach and leads to the pleasure boat harbour which can take over 1 000 boats.

Le Pouliguen – Separated from La Baule by a channel *(étier)*, this village with its narrow streets became a fashionable resort in 1854, made popular by men of letters such as Louis Veuillot and Jules Sandeau. A sheltered beach and a pleasant 6ha/15 acre wood make Le Pouliguen a very pleasant place to stop.

Chapelle Ste-Anne-et-St-Julien ⊘ – *Place Mgr-Freppel*. Standing near a Calvary, this Gothic chapel has a 16C **statue of St Anne** and a stained-glass window representing St Julian (in the chancel). At the west end, on either side of the porch are two interesting **bas-relief sculptures** depicting the Coronation of the Virgin and the Adoration of the Magi.

★ La Côte Sauvage – This stretch of coast starts from the Pointe de Penchâteau. Skirted by a road and footpaths, the coastline alternates rocky parts with great sandy bays and has numerous caves which are accessible only at low tide, in particular the cave of the Korrigans, little elves of Breton legends. Geographical Brittany begins here.

TREAT YOURSELF!

Castel Marie-Louise – *1 rue Andrieu – ☎ 02 40 11 48 38 – closed 3 Jan-11 Feb – ▱ – 31 rooms from 1 300F – breakfast 105F – restaurant 240/480F*. This is one of La Baule's most charming spots: in an old private home, the luxurious rooms are decorated in floral patterns, and their windows open onto a peaceful park. Close to the sea, this hotel is also a starred stopover. Tennis.

Saint Christophe – *Place Notre-Dame – ☎ 02 40 60 35 35 – ▱ – 32 rooms from 510F – breakfast 45F – restaurant 125/190F*. Three pretty villas dating from 1900 in a residential area. The restaurant is decorated in bright colours, paintings and bay-windows. In the rooms, tapestries, antiques and rare curios create a soft and refined atmosphere. Attractive off-season prices.

Night-life

Le Bidule – *122 avenue Mazy, in Pornichet*. Lovers of sea and wind sports meet here. In the summer, after a day spent at sea, they crowd around the barrels that serve as tables to enjoy a glass (or several) of Banyuls, and animated conversation.

Le Bar'ouf – *3 allée des Houx – ☎ 02 40 60 52 81 – during school holidays, daily 10pm-4am; outside school holidays, Fri-Sat 10pm-4am*. This fashionable bar, with restrained and modern decor, belongs to the actor Gérard Lanvin. Young professionals come here to amuse themselves in earnest, and to dance to an eclectic music collection. Varied Menu.

Ship-Inn – *18 avenue du Général-de-Gaulle – ☎ 02 51 75 04 82*. This chic bar, with metallic design decor and avant-garde tendencies, belongs to the Lucien Barrière group, which also owns the casino, the Heritage, the Thalassotherapy Centre and the Tennis Country Club.

Casino – *Esplanade Lucien-Barrière – ☎ 02 40 11 48 28* – Sun-Thur 10pm-3am, Fri-Sat 10pm-4am. This casino has 200 slot machines, a room for traditional gaming, a bar, a restaurant and a discothèque. Also often hosts organized evening parties.

Recreation

The beach – In La Baule alone, there are 20 beach clubs. If you wish to rent a beach cabin (by day, by week, or by month), or simply a lounge chair, contact the concessionaire whose office is off avenue De-Gaulle. Sand sailing is prohibited from 15 May to 15 Sept and during school holidays.

Club Holywind – *Esplanade François-André – ☎ 02 40 60 51 96 – Apr-Oct, daily 9am-6pm*. This nautical centre offers sailing lessons, and rents out small boats, catamarans, surfboards, sand sailors and kayaks.

Forum Voile Pajot – *Boulevard des Océanides, in Pornichet – ☎ 02 40 61 44 44 – Feb-Nov, outside of school holidays, Wed-Sun 10am-7pm; during school holidays, every day 10am-7pm*. One of the region's principal nautical centres. Lessons and rentals of small boats, sailboards, sand sailors (except in July and August) and kayaks.

Municipal swimming pool – *5 avenue Honoré-de-Balzac – ☎ 02 40 60 09 70 – indoor pool daily 1.15pm-7pm except Tues and Fri 8pm-10pm – outdoor pool daily 9am-7pm, except Tues and Fri 8pm-10pm – diving and wading areas 10am-7pm*. The Aquabaule is an aquatic complex containing an outdoor salt-water pool (50m/165ft), an indoor pool (25m/82ft), a diving area, and a covered slide that is 126m/413ft long.

Bicycle rental – Available from Michel Chaillou, *3 place de la Victoire* (opposite the tourist office) or from Grand Bi, *237 avenue du Mar.-de-Lattre-de-Tassigny* (near the market).

Horseback riding – Manège des Platanes, *23 avenue Louis*, ☎ *02 40 60 37 37*, and *Centre Équestre, 5 avenue Rosières*, ☎ *02 40 60 02 80*. You may ride on the beach from sunrise until 9am, and from 8pm until sunset (1 Oct-31 May, anytime).

Aéroclub de la Côte d'Amour – *Aérodrome d'Escoublac* – ☎ *02 40 60 23 84* – *open year round*. This club organizes outings in planes, ULM(ultrra-light flyers) and helicopters. The Club house has a comfortable, convivial bar.

Golf international de La Baule – *In St-Denac, near St-André-des-Eaux* – ☎ *02 40 60 46 18*. Very chic. Its 27-hole golf course is quite renowned. Regularly hosts high-level competitions.

Regional specialty

Confiserie Manuel – *2-4 avenue du Général-de-Gaulle* – ☎ *02 48 60 28 66* – *Feb to mid-Nov, daily 9.30am-12.30pm, 2.30pm-7.30pm*. Manuel is the confectioner who invented the famous *niniche*, a sort of soft lollypop that comes in 21 flavours. It's a local institution! The best part is the sweets are prepared before your eyes.

BÉCHEREL

Population 599
Michelin map 59 fold 16 or 20 fold 25

Bécherel, perched on a hill (alt 176m/577ft), was once a seigneurial stronghold; only a few ruins and old granite houses still stand. In former times, flax was cultivated and the purest linen thread was produced here. Now the town is known for its book market, held on the first Sunday of the month and which attracts 40 000 visitors annually. Bécherel is also among the 19 towns honoured for their typical Breton character. From Thabor Gardens the view extends as far as Dol, Dinan and Combourg.

Château de Caradeuc ⊙ – *1km/0.6mi*. This château, the former home of a famous attorney-general, Louis-René, Marquis de Caradeuc de la Chalotais (1701-85), has a very fine **park★** dotted with statues and other monuments inspired by history and mythology. It has been nicknamed the "Breton Versailles".

EXCURSIONS

8km/4mi north on D 68, then left onto D 26, and left again onto D 39, then follow Le Quiou.

Château de Hac ⊙ – This large manor house, a 14C seigneurial residence, has survived without any major alterations. The large rooms open to visitors house Gothic and Renaissance furniture; in particular an interesting collection of chests, for the most part Breton.

7km/3.5mi southwest on D 27.

★**Église des Iffs** – Inside are nine lovely 16C **stained-glass windows★** inspired by the Dutch and Italian Schools (16C): scenes of the Passion (in the chancel), Christ's childhood (in the north chapel), the Story of Susannah and the Two Elders (in the south chapel).

800m/875yd north of Les Iffs.

★**Château de Montmuran** – A drawbridge across the moat leads to the narrow portcullised gateway framed by two massive round machicolated towers. Behind the entrance fort an external staircase goes to the chapel where Du Guesclin was knighted in 1354 after a skirmish with the English in the neighbourhood. He later married, as his second wife, Jeanne de Laval.

Tinténiac – *8km/5mi east of Bécherel on D 279*. The trades and tools museum, **Musée de l'Outil et des Métiers** ⊙, is located in a wood building near the canal. Old trades are brought back to life.

Hédé – *5km/3mi south of Tinténiac in the tiny village of La Madeleine. After the bridge over the canal, bear left to the car park by the lock keeper's house*. There are eleven locks, the **Onze Écluses**, three before and eight after the bridge, to negotiate a drop of 27m/89ft on the Ille-et-Rance Canal. Pleasant walk in a pretty setting along the towpath.

BELLE-ÎLE★★★

Population 4 489
Michelin map 63 folds 11 and 12 or 230 folds 48 and 49

This, the largest of the Breton islands, is a schist plateau measuring about 84km²/32sq mi; 17km/11mi long and 5-10km/3-6mi wide. Its name alone is enticing. Once there though, its beauty surpasses expectations. Numerous valleys cut deeply into the high rocks and finish up as beaches or harbours, wheat fields alternate with patches of gorse, and whitewashed houses stand in lush fields. Belle-Île is for lovers of long walks and horseback riding.

Fouquet, Marquis of Belle-Île – Superintendent Fouquet bought Belle-Île in 1658, completed the fortifications and added 50 cannons. His immense wealth even enabled him to keep his own fleet, of which the flagship was the *Grand Écureuil*. This daring behaviour, added to the swindles and slights which he practised on Louis XIV, was his undoing. The final act was played out at Nantes, where the Court was visiting in 1661. D'Artagnan and the Musketeers seized Fouquet as he came out of the castle and put him into a coach which took him to Vincennes.

A fortified rock – Being the sole island between the Channel and the Mediterranean with fresh water in abundance, Belle-Île was attacked many times by British and Dutch fleets. The British captured the island twice – in 1572 and 1761 – and occupied it until the *Treaty of Paris* (1763) returned it to the French. The island has conserved its defensive system: in addition to Le Palais citadel, fortified by the military architect Vauban, there are several 18C and 19C isolated outworks (redoubts) around the coast.

Acadians and Bretons – In 1766, 78 Acadian families came to live on the island; they brought with them the potato many years before Parmentier introduced it to France. These Acadians were descendants of the French who had lived in Canada since the beginning of the 17C and had refused to submit to the English who had held Nova Scotia from the time of the *Treaty of Utrecht*, 1713. The Acadian families were moved to New England and then, after the *Treaty of Paris*, were moved by Louis XV to Belle-Île.

LE PALAIS

Citadelle (R. de la) 2
Église (R. de l') 3
Ferry (Av. Jules) 5
Gambetta (Quai) 8
Simon (R. J.) 9
Verdun (R. de) 12

B	Casemate	**F**	Bastion du Dauphin
D	Poudrière circulaire	**M**	Musée historique
E	Arsenal		

SIGHTS

LE PALAIS *2hr*

The island's capital and main town is where most of the facilities are to be found. Inhabitants simply call it "Palais".

★Citadelle Vauban ⊙ – *Cross the mobile footbridge over the lock, go through Bourg gate and follow the path along the* **huge moat**, *cut from the rock itself, as far as Donjon gate. A signposted tour takes visitors past all the sights of the citadel.*
Built in 1549, the citadel was enlarged by the Duke Gondi de Retz and Fouquet. Its double ramparts, powerful corner bastions and outward appearance show the influence of Vauban, who resided here in 1683, 1687 and 1689. Besieged at the end of the Seven Years War, it fell into the hands of the English, who occupied it until the signing of the Treaty of Paris (1763). It was subsequently abandoned by the army and sold in 1960.
The most remarkable buildings include: the **historical museum** (**M**), set up in the Louis-Philippe blockhouses featuring "maple leaf" vaulting and displaying a host of documents on the history of Belle-Île and its illustrious visitors (Arletty, Claude Monet, Sarah Bernhardt); the **round powder magazine** (**D**) and its strange acoustics; the large

arsenal (**E**) with superb oak timbering; the Louis XIII **storerooms**; the **blockhouse** (**B**) which contains the map room; finally the military prison and the cells. The belvederes overlooking the sea and the **Bastion du Dauphin** (**F**) afford remarkable **views**★ of Le Palais, the north coast and its harbour, the Île de Houat and the Île d'Hœdic.

TOURS

★★★**1** Côte sauvage *Round tour of 49km/30mi – about 3hr 30min*

Leave Le Palais on Quai Gambetta and Promenade Boulogne and turn right towards the citadel. Near the coast, bear left and then right.

Pointe de Taillefer – Near the signal station there is a fine **view** over Le Palais roadstead, the Pointe de Kerdonis, Hœdic and Houat Islands and Quiberon.

Turn round and make for Sauzon.

Getting there

Daily boat service from Quiberon to Le Palais (45min, 5 to 12 round trips per day, depending on the season). 105F return (Jan-May and Oct-Dec), 110F return (June-Sept). Société morbihannaise et nantaise de navigation. ☎ 02 97 31 80 01.

Going Out

Bar du Castel Clara – *Rue du Port-Goulphar* – ☎ *02 97 31 84 21* – *mid-Feb to mid-Nov, daily 8am-noon.* This prestigious bar – a favourite of François Mitterrand – offers a beautiful view of the natural harbour of Goulphar.

L'Étoile du Port – *9 quai Vauban* – ☎ *02 97 31 80 25* – *Sept-June, Mon-Sat 6.30am-8pm, Sun 8.30am-1pm; July-Aug, Mon-Sat until 1am.* Easy to spot, this bar (and PMU) is full of fisherman who stop in to knock back a glassful between tides. They readily offer their opinion that Le Goéland (the bar opposite) is better left to the Parisians. Concerts of Breton music.

Le Goéland – *3 quai Vauban* – ☎ *02 97 31 81 26* – *daily noon-4pm, 6pm-2am.* This is Belle-Île's only nightclub, and is very popular with some of the locals. Paradoxically, it is run by a Parisian! Blues, jazz and rock concerts every night in the summer.

Eating Out

BUDGET

Le Comptoir – *Quai Gerveur, 56360 Sauzon* – ☎ *02 97 31 62 81* – *closed Jan, Mar, 11 Nov-20 Dec* – *85/120F.* After a long walk, replenish your energy by savouring mussels and oysters at any hour inside this pretty seaside bistro or on its terrace which looks out onto the docks. For a more elaborate meal, go next door to its mother restaurant, the Café de la Cale.

Crêperie chez Renée – *Route de Port-Kérel, behind the church* – ☎ *02 97 31 52 87* – *closed Jan and weekdays Oct-Easter, except during school holidays* – *40/70F.* Off in the fields, this former farm looks like a doll's house with its two vividly coloured dining rooms and its charming little shaded terrace. It's best to reserve, since its crêpes have had an excellent reputation ever since it opened … 20 years ago!

Le Perroquet Vert – *Route de Bangor, 1km/0.6mi, 56360 Le Palais* – ☎ *02 97 31 32 50* – *closed Dec to mid-Jan, Wed except during school holidays, and Sun* – *100/140F.* Wonderful savoury pies, salads, daily specials and fresh desserts. This brightly coloured restaurant is a real treat. In addition to the small bistro dining room, there is a space where children can play, and a summer terrace. Take-away service too.

La Saline – *Route de Port-Coton* – ☎ *02 97 31 84 70* – *closed weekdays off-season, except during school holidays* – *94/198F.* Stop in this white and blue fisherman's house for a simple lunch in one of its small dining rooms with nautical accents. In season, the roof terrace overlooks a small garden.

OUR SELECTION

Roz Avel – *Behind the church, 56360 Sauzon* – ☎ *02 97 31 61 48* – *closed 5 Jan-29 Feb and Wed* – *105F.* Behind the church, this historic house is quite charming, and it opens its terrace as soon as the weather warms up. Its small dining room is very popular with the local islanders, so it is wise to reserve.

Nearby is **Port-Fouque** with a pretty, sheltered beach.

★**Sauzon** – This small port with its busy marina lies in a pretty **setting**★ on the east bank of the River Sauzon's estuary.

🚶 A pleasant excursion *(1hr 30min on foot there and back)* starting from the port, takes you round the **Pointe du Cardinal** and affords views over the approach to the port, the Pointe de Taillefer, the Presqu'île de Quiberon and the Pointe des Poulains.

★★🚶 **Pointe des Poulains** – *30min on foot there and back.* From the car park, on the left is Fort Sarah Bernhardt, which is near the estate where the actress spent her summers. Make your way down the slip to the sandy isthmus which connects the island with the Pointe des Poulains on which stands a lighthouse and which is completely cut off at spring tide. From the point there is a vast **panorama**★.

Hotels

OUR SELECTION

Apothicairerie – *56360 L'Apothicairerie* – ☎ *02 97 31 62 62* – 🅿 – *38 rooms 350/630F* – *breakfast 55F* – *restaurant 84/180F.* This modern hotel may not be known for its aesthetic qualities, however, it is admirably situated, perched on the cliff of the Roche Percée. Its light rooms and pale wood furniture let you enjoy the remarkable calm and tranquillity of the site.

TREAT YOURSELF!

Désirade – *In Bangor, route de Port-Goulphar, 56360 Le Palais* – ☎ *02 97 31 70 70* – *closed 16 Nov-31 Jan, except Christmas and New Year's Day* – 🅿 – *24 rooms 680F* – *breakfast 70F* – *restaurant 200F.* Its quaint pink houses with blue shutters are set around the swimming pool. The rooms are large and comfortable. You can enjoy the island's pleasant atmosphere from the restaurant's beautiful terrace in the evenings. The restaurant only serves dinner.

Chambres d'hôte Hostellerie La Touline – *Rue de Port Vihan, 56360 Sauzon* – ☎ *02 97 31 69 69* – *5 rooms 550F.* You are assured of a pleasant stay in this fisherman's house. Behind its pink façade, the pretty rooms have evocative names (Bretagne, Capitaine, Zanzibar ...) and are attractively decorated with antiques and curios. A veranda looks onto the small garden.

Regional Specialties

La Poterie de Kerledan – *Village of Kerledan* – ☎ *02 97 31 67 41* – *Mon, Wed, Thur, Sat and Sun 9am-1pm, 6pm-8pm, Tues and Fri 6pm-8pm.* This traditional potter exhibits and sells his creations at the Palais market every Tuesday and Friday morning.

Le Grenier de Manon – *8 place de l'Hôtel-de-Ville* – ☎ *06 83 15 14 24* – *mid-Apr to mid-Sept, daily 10am-1pm, 4pm-7.30pm.* This boutique's proprietor is assisted by three women with amazingly nimble fingers who create lace tablecloths, napkins, clothing ... before your eyes.

La Maison du Pêcheur – *9 rue de l'Église* – ☎ *02 97 31 58 15* – *Apr-Sept, Mon-Sat 9.30am-12.30pm, 4pm-7pm, Sun 9.30am-12.30pm.* This refreshingly simple small boutique sells numerous seafood products in preserves (sardines, tuna, fish soup and the rare "velouté de pouce-pieds" (goose barnacles)).

Les Niniches – *5 rue de la Citadelle* – ☎ *02 97 31 42 33* – *Apr-Oct, daily 10am-12.30pm, 3pm-7pm; July-Aug 9am-11pm.* For three generations this confectionery has been making caramels (Salidou) and lollypops (les niniches).

Pâtisserie-confiserie Pétrel – *Place de l'Hôtel-de-Ville* – ☎ *02 97 31 85 12* – *year round, Thur-Tues 8.30am-7pm.* This pastry chef and confectioner makes several local specialities: caramels, Citadelle shortbread and rock-shaped sweets.

Boat Trips

Le golfe du Morbihan, Houat et Hoedic – ☎ *02 97 31 59 37* – *perso.club-internet.fr/belleile.* On board the catamaran La Sterne.

Recreation

Aéroclub – Aérodrome – ☎ *02 97 31 53 19* – *Sept-June 2.30pm-6.30pm; July-Aug 10am-7pm.* Belle-Île-en-Mer's flying-club organizes small plane outings during which you will be treated to a unique view of the island and its landscape.

Rambling and cycling – The tourist office sells a guide to coastal hiking trails (15F), and another guide to hiking and biking trails (45F).

★Stêr-Vraz and Stêr-Ouen – These *abers* cutting deeply into the coastline are at the foot of the **birdlife reserve** on the Pointe du Vieux-Château.

On Kerlédan Moor stand the menhirs **Jean and Jeanne**, said to be young fiancés punished because they wanted to meet before their wedding day.

★★Port-Donnant – *30min on foot there and back; car park.* The setting is superb: a fine sandy beach and a rolling sea enclosed between high cliffs. Bathing is dangerous.

Grand Phare ⊘ – The lighthouse opened near Goulphar in 1836 is 46m/150ft high and has a beam which carries 44.5km/26mi. From the balcony there is a fine **view★★** of Belle-Île, the neighbouring islands and the coast as far as the Presqu'île de Rhuys.

★Port-Goulphar –This is one of the most charming sites on the island. After Goulphar manor house take a steep road downhill *(15min on foot there and back)* to the port, a long, narrow channel at the foot of picturesque cliffs. A group of islets marks its entrance. From the cliff is the best **view★** of this curious mass of rocks.

★★Aiguilles de Port-Coton – Port-Coton is called so because the sea there seems to boil and builds up a great mass of foam like cotton wool. At the end of the road loom the **Needles**.

Aiguilles de Port-Coton

Bangor –The most primitive sites on the island are found in this village. It takes its name from the Bangor Abbey (Northern Ireland), which was one of the most well-known in Western Christianity, and from which came the first Celtic monks to settle on the island in the 6C.

In a rocky setting lies **Port-Kérel,** the most popular beach on the island.

Return to Le Palais.

★ ② **Pointe de Kerdonis** *Round tour of 33km/20mi – about 2hr*

Leave Le Palais by avenue Carnot and rue Villaumez on the left.

The first part of this tour is devoted to seeing different beaches. Backing onto the point of the same name is the **Plage de Ramonette**; this is Le Palais' beach.

At the entrance to Port-Salio, turn left, then 250m/274yd further, turn left again to reach **La Belle Fontaine**. This reservoir was created under Vauban's orders, to supply fresh water to high-ranking ships.

The **Plage de Bordardoué** is a fine sheltered, sandy beach.

Turn round and bear left twice.

The road descends towards **Port-Yorc'h** closed in by the Pointe du Bugul to the right and the Pointe du Gros Rocher to the left, which is extended by an islet on which stands an old fort. The road from Port-Yorck to the Pointe de Kerdonis commands superb **views**★★ over Houat and Le Palais roadstead.

Les Grands Sables – This, the largest beach on Belle-Île, has traces of fortifications erected in 1747, as in the 17C and 18C British and Dutch forces made several attempts to land on the island.

Pointe de Kerdonis – At the southern tip of the island stands a lighthouse which commands the sea lane between Hœdic and Belle-Île. Nearby is **Port-An-Dro**, a sandy beach off a small valley where the English forces landed in 1761.

Locmaria – The village is reputed among the islanders as a place where sorcery occurs. A downhill road to the right of the church leads to **Port-Maria**, a deep cleft in the rocks which offers a fine sandy beach at low tide. Slightly farther south, the cliffs of Arzic Point overlook the small cove of **Port-Blanc**.

Pointe du Skeul – *Unsurfaced road after Skeul hamlet.* A semicircle of jagged rocks in a wild setting.

Return to the main road and Le Pailais, but make a slight detour to see the Acadian village, Grand-Cosquet.

BELLE-ISLE-EN-TERRE

Population 1 067
Michelin map 58 folds 7 and 8 or 20 south of fold 7

As this old township's name indicates, it is perfect example of inland Brittany's beauty, a picturesque region of forests, hills and ravines, favorable for walking, fishing, canoeing or kayaking.

EXCURSIONS

★ **Menez-Bré** – *9km/5.5mi northeast. Take D 116, the Guingamp road. 2.5km/1.5mi after Louargat, turn left onto the steep uphill road.*

The Menez-Bré, a lonely hill with an altitude of 302m/991ft, and its Chapelle de St-Hervé at the summit commands a wide **panorama**★ over the Trégorrois Plateau: to the north, the plateau slopes gently towards the sea, to the south over the maze of hills and valleys of Cornouaille; and to the southwest towards the Monts d'Arrée.

Loc-Envel – *4km/2.5mi south. Leave on the Callac road, D 33, and turn right fairly soon onto a winding and picturesque road.*

The Flamboyant Gothic style **church** of Loc-Envel rises from the top of a mound and dominates the village. To the left of

M. Cambazard/EXPLORER

Loc-Envel – Hanging keystones
in the church

the belfry-porch, note three small semicircular openings through which the lepers followed the services. Particularly striking features, on entering, are the Flamboyant **rood screen**★ and the rich decoration of the wood-panelled **vaulting**★: carved purlins and tie-beams, polychrome hammerbeams with the Evangelists and the two hanging keystones.

Gurunhuel – *9km/5.5mi southeast on D 22.*
Near the 16C church stands a Calvary of the same period. From the base rise three columns: the central one bears a Crucifixion with Christ between the Virgin Mary and St John on one side and a Virgin of Pity on the other. The other two crosses show the robbers; their souls are being received by an angel in the case of the good robber, and a demon in the case of the bad robber.

BÉNODET ⚏⚏

Population 2 436
Michelin map 58 fold 15 or 230 fold 32
Local map see QUIMPER: Excursion

This charming seaside resort lies in a pretty, verdant setting at the mouth of the Odet estuary. Bénodet offers all the summer pleasures: a small harbour, fine beaches of pale sand, open-air sports, sailing, a casino, and a new film festival.

Hotels

OUR SELECTION

Hôtel Ker Moor – *Corniche de la Plage* – ☎ *02 98 57 04 48 – closed 1 Nov-31 March –* 🅿 *– 60 rooms 400/600F – breakfast 45F – restaurant 120/320F.* Close to the fine sand beach, this grand hotel from the 1930's offers you an oasis of calm in its pretty park. Its rooms have been gradually renovated, and are of standard comfort. Swimming pool, tennis and squash courts.

Hôtel Minaret – *Corniche de l'Estuaire* – ☎ *02 98 57 03 13 – closed 4 Nov-1Apr –* 🅿 *– 20 rooms 430/500F – breakfast 45F – restaurant 90/230F.* A surprising Moorish villa, built in 1925 on the banks of the estuary. Those who enjoy a Moroccan atmosphere will be delighted here; the hotel is entirely decorated with Moorish pottery and mosaics, and the exotic gardens inspired by the Alhambra are spectacular. Choose the rooms with sea views.

Eating Out

OUR SELECTION

Ferme du Letty – *At Letty, southeast, 2km by D 44 and smaller road –* ☎ *02 98 57 01 27 – closed end of Nov-beginning of Feb, Tues Sept-June, Thur lunch in summer and Wed – 155/540F.* A former farm, this restaurant has retained its rustic atmosphere of old stone walls and beautiful wooden ceiling beams, and several agricultural implements displayed. But one really comes here to enjoy the inventive cuisine which honours many regional products, such as abalone and pork dishes.

Going Out

L'Alhambra – *Corniche de l'Estuaire* – ☎ *02 98 57 03 13 – Apr-Sept, Sun-Thur 11am-midnight, Fri-Sat 11am-1am.* This old bar of the Minaret formerly belonged to a Moorish hotel built by a king of Morocco. Today, the Alhambra is an independent establishment, but the refined decor from its previous life has remained intact. It provides a very pleasant spot to dally over a cocktail or an ice cream, either in its beautiful sunlit octagonal room, or on its terrace facing the sea.

La Chaumière – *Chemin des Douaniers at Ste-Marine* – ☎ *02 98 56 49 28 – Sept-June, Fri-Sat; July and Aug, daily.* The region's most popular discotheque.

Recreation

Yacht races – Le Yacht Club (☎ 02 98 57 26 09) organises regattas, one of which, called "Pieds Gelés" ("Frozen Feet") is held at the end of December.

Film Festival "Les Chercheurs d'âme" – First held in 1999, this film festival takes place at the Complexe Cinémarine (enter through the casino) during the last two weeks of June: for information call ☎ 02 98 95 20 20 (agence Co-pilote).

Casino – *Corniche de la Plage* – ☎ *02 98 57 04 16 – open 3pm-3am.*

Sea fishing – ☎ *02 98 66 23 46.* Each morning in the summer, the *Picot II* embarks up to 20 people for bass-fishing at sea; in the afternoons, children can learn how to fish for mackerel.

THE ODET

★★ **Boat Trip Up the River Odet** ⏱ – *1hr 30min departing from Bénodet.*

View over the Odet (**E**) – *Access by avenue de Kercréven.* This viewpoint affords a fine view of the river and the pleasure boat harbour.

Pont de Cornouaille – *1km/0.6mi northwest on D 44.*
This elegant bridge is 610m/2.001ft long, and affords a good **view**★ of the port Ste-Marine, the estuary and the Odet, up-river.

EXCURSIONS

From Bénodet to Concarneau on the coast road – *40km/25mi – about 3hr.*
Leave Bénodet east by D 44 towards Fouesnant and after 2km/1mi turn right.

Le Letty – A large lake sheltered by a dune provides the perfect place for sailing schools.
Return to the road to Fouesnant.

Le Perguet – An unusual stone staircase on the roof of the Chapelle of Ste-Brigitte leads to the pierced bell tower. *After 2.5km/1mi, a fork to the right goes to the Pointe de Mousterlin. Turn round. After 2km/1mi bear right and 4.5km/2.75mi further on turn right.*

⌂ **Beg-Meil and Fouesnant** – The road runs along Kerleven Beach, a long beach of fine sand, at the bottom of La Forêt Bay, then after a steep descent (15% or 1:7), along St-Laurent Cove and crosses St-Jean Bay to Concarneau. Beautiful **sites**★ especially at high tide. *Also see FOUESNANT.*

BLAIN

Population 7 434
Michelin map 6 fold 16 or 20 fold 54

An old Roman crossroads, Blain plays an important commercial role between Nantes, Redon and the Anjou. The Nantes-Brest Canal separates the town from its castle (whose first construction dates from 1104).

Musée de la Fève et de la Crèche – located in the old presidial of the dukes of Rohan, this museum revives the past of the Blain area. Two rooms are devoted to popular Christmas traditions: one room displays thousands of bean kings (lucky trinkets hidden in Twelfth Night cakes), the other about 100 Nativity cribs from all over the world.

Château – This fortress originally belonged to Olivier de Clisson, and later became Rohan family property. Despite the fact that in 1628 Richelieu razed the ramparts, impressive ruins still stand. Since 1995, the Château has housed the Centre de la Fresque (Workshop for the painting technique *a fresco*).

★TOUR OF THE FORÊT DU GÂVRE

Round tour of 13km/8mi northwest on D 15, the road to Guéméné-Penfao.

The road crosses the stands of oak interspersed with beeches and pines, which cover 4 400ha/10 900 acres, to reach the Belle Étoile crossroads, the meeting point of 10 converging avenues.
Turn right towards Le Gâvre and at La Maillardais turn left.

Chapelle de la Magdeleine – This modest 12C chapel has a charming 15C polychrome Virgin, Notre-Dame-de-Grâce (Our Lady of Grace).
Return to La Maillardais and continue straight on to Le Gâvre.

Le Gâvre – **Maison Benoist** ⏱ is a 17C home with a corner turret. The ground floor exhibit is concerned with the Forêt du Gâvre: its flora, forestry, fauna (stuffed animals).
Not far from the school *(école)*, the **wooden shoemaker's home** shows the life of the shoemaker who lived and worked in his workshop.
Return to Blain.

The most recent additions to **The Green Guide** *collection include:*
Pacific Northwest – USA East – USA West – Budapest and Hungary – Scandinavia and Finland – Venice – Wales – The West Country – Tuscany – Prague

VALLÉE DU BLAVET★

Michelin A28 map 230, folds 22, 35 and 36

The River Blavet, which originates in the Côtes-d'Armor, is 140km/70mi long. Canalised as of the Guerlédan Lake, it crosses pleasant, lush, bucolic countryside before joining the Scorff which flows into the Atlantic.

SIGHTS

Pontivy – The old capital of the Rohan owes its name to a monastery founded in the 7C by St Ivy. The old town, with its narrow, winding streets, contrasts with the geometrical town plan laid out by Napoleon.

Napoléonville – Pontivy was a prosperous town and in 1790 declared wholeheartedly for the Republic. Napoleon, who was Consul at the time had a barracks, town hall, court and school built and, to ensure communication with the sea, he had the Blavet canalised. During the wars of the First Empire, coastal navigation between Brest and Nantes was very dangerous because of British cruisers in the Channel. Napoleon, therefore, decided to build a canal linking the two ports and to turn Pontivy into the military and strategic centre of Brittany.

From 1806 the straight roads of the new town could be seen as they were dug out of the ground. The grateful townspeople called the city "Napoléonville". By the fall of the Empire, Napoléonville became Pontivy once more. It changed again under the Second Empire to Napoléonville but in due course reverted again.

★**Old houses** (Y) – To admire the old half-timbered and corbelled houses of the 16C and 17C, walk along **rue du Fil**, place du Martray, the centre of old Pontivy, rue du Pont and re du Docteur-Guépin. At the corner of rue Lorois and rue Général-de-Gaulle, note the turreted house (1578), which is presumed to be the hunting pavilion of the Rohan family, and at place Anne-de-Bretagne, the elegant 18C buildings.

Château ⊘ (Y) – The castle was built in the 15C by Jean II de Rohan. The façade is flanked by two large machicolated towers with pepper-pot roofs, all that remains of the four towers of the perimeter wall. The main building, remodelled in the 18C, is adorned with cusped pediments and a spiral staircase.

Église Notre-Dame-de-Joie (Y) – The 16C church, built in the Flamboyant style, has in the north chapel, a statue of Notre-Dame-de-Joie, venerated by the local people since 1696 when an epidemic decimated the town.

PONTIVY

Eating Out

OUR SELECTION

Pommeraie – 17 quai du Couvent, in Pontivy – ☎ 02 97 25 60 09 – closed 15-30 Sept, 15-31 Jan, Sun evening and Mon – 130/220F. Located in a nice area near the old part of the city, and owned by a young couple, this restaurant is a very pleasant place to stop. Those who enjoy originality in cooking will be delighted to savour the dishes in these two quaint dining rooms … Good prices too.

Hotels

TREAT YOURSELF!

Château de Locguénolé – 4km/1.8mi south of Hennebont, route de Port-Louis via D 781 – ☎ 02 97 76 76 – closed 2 Jan-11 Feb – �P – 18 rooms from 820F – breakfast 85F – restaurant 190/520F. You'll be treated to the high life in a chateau the minute you enter this beautiful residence: in a resplendent park on the banks of a river, you'll delight in the holiday of your dreams. The rooms are spacious and beautifully furnished, its restaurant is starred, and the site is truly exceptional.

Boat Trips

Boat trips on the Blavet River – Cruises and dinner-cruises on the *Étoile du Blavet* leave from Inzinzac-Lochrist: reservations ☎ 02 97 65 60 93.

FROM PONTIVY TO HENNEBONT

90km/45mi. About 4hr. Leave Pontivy on rue Albert-de-Mun, in the direction of Auray and turn right at Talvern-Nenez.

Chapelle St-Nicodème – This 16C chapel is preceded by a massive tower with a granite steeple. A Renaissance doorway leading to a 16C staircase opens at the base of the tower.

To the left of the chapel, a Gothic fountain empties into three piscinas in front of three niches surmounted by richly carved gables. *Pardon* on the first Sunday in August.

Turn right after the chapel.

St-Nicolas-des-Eaux – The little town is built on the side of a hill. With its chapel above the town, surrounded by thatch-roofed houses, St-Nicolas-des-Eaux is certainly unusual.

★**Site de Castennec** – This Celtic site became an oppidum and then a fortified Roman camp; it offers a magnificent view of the valley of the Blavet.

Turn left after Castennec.

Bieuzy – To the left of the **church** ⏱, note two Renaissance houses with bread oven and well. Inside the church, the stained-glass windows, the woodwork and beams are also worth looking at.

Many farms in the area have graceful 17C-18C wells which are of interest.

Go to Melrand passing through La Paule.

Melrand – The **Ferme archéologique** (Archeological Farm) ⏱ consists of an excavated village, Lann Gouh (meaning old heath), dating back to c 1000 and a reconstituted farm. It illustrates rural Medieval architecture and the daily life of the inhabitants who shared quarters with their animals.

Return to Melrand. Behind the church, take D 142 in the direction of St-Barthélémy where you turn right towards St-Adrien.

Chapelle St-Adrien – The 15C chapel stands below the road, between two fountains; the one on the right is surmounted by a Calvary. Inside there is a simple rood screen, carved on the nave side and painted on the other.

The road (D 327) follows the valley of the Blavet through delightful countryside. Turn left towards Baud (D 3).

Baud – 3km/6mi from the sea, the Baud region offers many pretty walks which show the more traditional side of Brittany. In the lower town, below the Locminé road, at the far end of the large car park, is the **Fontaine Notre-Dame-de-la-Clarté.**

Venus de Quinipily ⏱ – *2km/1mi southwest. Leave Baud by the road to Hennebont. At Coët Vin bear left; 500m/550yd further on leave your car (car park on right).*

Venus de Quinipily

From the other side of a wooden gate, a steep path leads up to the Venus, placed above a fountain, set in the park of the restored Château de Quinipily. The origins of the statue are uncertain. It has been taken for a Roman idol or an Egyptian Isis. As it was the object of almost pagan worship, it was thrown into the Blavet several times by order of the ecclesiastical authorities; the Count of Lannion installed it here in 1696.

Return to Baud and go towards Poul Fetan.

★Poul Fetan, a typical Breton village of the past
🕐 – Overhanging the Blavet Valley, a quaint little 16C hamlet has been painstakingly reconstituted from ruins abandoned during the 1970s. Among the charming thatched cottages, note the Maison du Minour (The Chef's House), the Inn (Auberge), where you may be served a typical Breton meal, the former bakery and the Museum of Man and the Environment (écomusée). In the summer, craftsmen attired in regional costume demonstrate trades from typical peasant life of yesteryear: washerwomen rub the steaming linen, a baker is busy at his oven; one farmer is making millet porridge while another churns butter. A pottery workshop illustrates traditional sculpting and firing techniques. The various farm animals include the "black magpie," a small cow typical of the Breton region.

Make a U-turn, turn left onto D 159, then take the road to Hennebont.

Hennebont Hennebont is a former fortified town on the steep banks of the Blavet (good fishing).
The 16C basilica, **Basilique Notre-Dame-de-Paradis** has a big **bell-tower★** and is surmounted by a steeple 65m/213ft high. At the base of the tower is a fine Flamboyant porch ornamented with niches leading into the nave, which is lit by stained-glass windows by Max Ingrand.

Porte Broërec'h and ramparts – This restored gateway, a vestige of the 13C fortifications, was once used as a prison. *Go through the gate and take a stairway on the left up to the wall walk.* The 15C ramparts completely encircled the old fortified town. Gardens are laid out along the walls.

Parc de Kerbihan – *Access by rue Nationale and rue Léo-Lagrange (the latter reserved for pedestrians).* The botanical park, bordered by the St-Gilles stream, is planted with species (all labelled) from the five continents.

Écomusée industriel de Inzinzac-Lochrist 🕐 – The open-air museum occupies the site of the Hennebont Ironworks, one of Brittany's most important companies, which operated from 1860-1966.

Musée des Métallurgistes des Forges d'Hennebont – Located on the River Blavet's north bank in the old research laboratory, the museum concentrates on the heart of the iron and steel industry of Brittany (technology, social conditions and family life, the rise of trade unions and the strikes that resulted etc).

Maison de l'Eau et de l'Hydraulique – Near the dam, in the Hennebont Ironworks caretaker's house, is an exhibit devoted to the canalisation of the River Blavet.

Île de BRÉHAT★★

Population 461
Michelin map 59 fold 2 or 20 fold 8

Bréhat is a much-frequented holiday resort. Its pink rocks stand out against the sea. Cars are not allowed; however tractors are used for transportation.

GEOGRAPHICAL AND HISTORICAL NOTES

A mild climate – Bréhat, which is about 3.5km/2mi long and 1.5km/1mi wide, consists of two islands joined in the 18C by a bridge built by Vauban. The coast, very broken and indented, is surrounded by 86 islets and reefs. Thanks to its mild climate (winter average 6°C/43°F), mimosa, eucalyptus and fig trees grow out in the open and the façades are bedecked with geraniums. There is little rain, the clouds generally passing over the flat island to condense over the mainland. The island's interior is a labyrinth of paths lined with honeysuckle or flower-bedecked dry stone walls, low houses with masses of hydrangea bushes, villas with vast gardens, a couple of cows in a tiny field or sheep on the heath. Its southern part is more welcoming than the rugged north. This colourful island has attracted such personalities as Prosper Mérimée, Ernest Renan and Louis Pasteur.

A varied history – Bréhat owes its name (Breiz Coat: Brittany of the Woods) to an Irish monk, St Budoc, who landed on Lavrec Island in AD 470. A medieval fortress facing this island was destroyed by the English in 1409 and local people were hanged on the sails on Crec'h ar Pot mill (moulin) on North Island. La Corderie Bay, on the west coast, was used as anchorage. According to local tradition, it was a sea captain from Morlaix, Coatanlem, living in Lisbon, who revealed the existence of the New World to Christopher Columbus in 1484 – eight years before its official discovery – and showed him the course taken by the island's fishermen already familiar with Newfoundland waters. During the Wars of Religion, in 1591, Crec'h Tarek mill on South Island served as a place of execution. In 1598, Henri IV ordered the castle to be razed. In the 19C the island was frequented by privateers and during the last war, it was occupied by German troops until 4 August 1944.

Hotels

OUR SELECTION

Hôtel Bellevue – *Port-Clos* – ☎ *02 96 20 00 05* – *closed 14-30 Nov, 3 Jan-8 Feb* – *17 rooms 440/540F* – *breakfast 57F* – *restaurant 125/190F*. You can enjoy the view of the port either from the large terrace or from the dining room's veranda of this gay and attractive hotel. Its old façade hides modern rooms. Well-known and appreciated by the locals.

Vieille Auberge – *In town* – ☎ *02 96 20 00 24* – *closed 2 Nov-Easter* – *14 rooms 400/500F* – *breakfast 45F* – *restaurant 90/250F*. In a lovely old house with beautiful old stone walls, this immaculate hotel-restaurant is run by a local family. With a little luck, you'll be able to bask in the sun in its charming flowered courtyard.

TOUR ⏱ *allow half a day*

The island is crisscrossed by paths with arrows at ground level showing the way.

Le Bourg – The houses of the island's capital are grouped around a small square lined with plane trees.

In the 12C and 18C church, which has an unusual bell-tower, the high altar and the font grille are 17C and the lectern is 18C.

Bois de la Citadelle – Planted with conifers, the woods overlook the cliff. From the lifeboat shelter below, there is a good **view★** of Kerpont Channel, which is impressive at low tide when the mass of rocks is visible, and of the Île Béniguet.

La Corderie – Bounded by Ar Prat Bridge (Pont Vauban) this vast bay between the two islands is the main harbour. Beautiful villas.

Grève du Guerzido – Petit and Grand Guerzido are beaches of pink shingle.

Croix de Maudez – Erected in 1788 amid the heather and facing the ocean, the cross evokes the memory of a monk named Maudez who founded a monastery in AD 570, on a neighbouring island. There is a fine **view★** of the islands of Béniguet to the left and Maudez to the right and the reefs.

★**Phare du Paon** – *On the tip of North Island.* The paved platform at the foot of the lighthouse affords a remarkable **view** of the rugged coastline, the chasm, the pink rocks and the shingles. This is the wildest part of the island.

Port-Clos – This is a landing point for the boat service.

Phare du Rosédo – Dating from 1862, it stands inland.

Chapelle St-Michel – High on a mound (26m/85ft; 39 steps), this chapel serves as a landmark for ships.

There is an extensive **view★** over the Île Sud the Kerpont channel and the Île Béniguet, Birlot Pool overlooked by the ruins of a once tide-operated mill, La Corderie Bay and the Île Nord and, in the distance, Talbert Spit (Sillon de Talbert).

BOAT TRIPS ⏱

★★**Tour of the island** – *1hr.* The tour allows the visitor to admire the changing aspects of the coast: the beauty of the northern rocks and cliffs, the Mediterranean charm of the eastern shore and the ever-changing colour of the sea, which is often a deep blue.

★**Estuaire de Trieux** – This pleasant excursion along the Trieux Estuary, whose banks are in turn sheer, rocky and wooded and at times low-lying and under cultivation, offers views of the pretty site of Lézardrieux with its suspension bridge. The river flows at the foot of Château de la Roche-Jagu, which can be reached by a fairly steep path through woodlands.

Celtic Exodus from the British Isles

Celtic monks and hermits who played a part in evangelising Brittany in the 5C-7C include:

St Budoc, who is thought to have been born in a cask in which his mother had been cast into the sea off Brest and which eventually landed both of them safe and sound in Ireland, from where the saint returned to Bréhat Island; St Goustan, a Cornish hermit who lived for a while on Hœdic Island, where there is now a church named after him; St Harvey (Hervé to the French), a wandering minstrel hermit (thought to be the son of a bard) who became Abbot of Plouvier before settling in Lanhourneau, and who is widely revered throughout Brittany; St Hernin, who gave his name to the place where he settled; St Mewan (St Méen to the French), who followed St Samson from Wales to Brittany, where he evangelised the Brocéliande region and founded the abbey of St-Méen-le-Grand; St Quay, who gave his name to St-Quay-Portrieux; St-Ronan, who gave his name to Locronan; St Winwaloe (Guénolé to the French), who founded the great monastery at Landévennec in the Cornouaille region.

After the full-scale destruction of the town during the Second World War, the centre of Brest was rebuilt on a geometrical (grid) layout. The main artery linking the naval base to the enormous place de la Liberté is the wide **rue de Siam**, once a tiny street. Running at right angles to this artery are roads leading to the River Penfeld or the Cours Dajot, from which there are good views of the magnificent roadstead, which, nowhere less than 10m/33ft deep, is almost an inland sea in itself.

For several years now, Brest has ranked as Brittany's second university town. The Arts Centre and Congress Hall (Palais des Arts et Congrès, or Quartz) are witness to this cultural expansion. On the shore of Ste-Anne-du-Portzic, the Centre Océanographique de Bretagne and the Océanopolis offer opportunities for scientific research.

Poop of the schooner *La Recouvrance*

Pambour/CAMPAGNE/CAMPAGNE

HISTORICAL NOTES

The English set foot in Brest (14C) – During the War of Succession which began in 1341, Montfort, ally of the English, was rash enough to let them guard the town. When he became Duke of Brittany, he tried in vain to drive out the intruders. The king of France had just as little success in his turn. At last, in 1397, Charles VI persuaded the King of England, Richard II, who had married Charles's eldest daughter, Isabella, to restore Brest to the Duke.

The "Belle Cordelière" – On 10 August 1513, St Laurence's Day, the English fleet of Henry VIII set out to attack Brest. The Breton fleet hurriedly set sail to meet it; however, under its panic-stricken commander it fled back to the Brest channel. The *Belle Cordelière*, the gift of Anne of Brittany to her Duchy and on which 300 guests were dancing when the order came to weigh anchor, covered the commander's retreat and bore the brunt of the attack. Fire broke out on board the *Cordelière* as she was fighting gun to gun with an English ship. The commander, Hervé de Portzmoguer, or as he was known in France, Primauguet, knowing that his ship was lost, exhorted his crew and his guests to die bravely with the words: "We will now celebrate the Feast of St Laurence who died by fire!" The two ships blew up together.

The work of Colbert (17C) – Colbert, the greatest minister the French Navy ever had, completed the task begun by Richelieu, making Brest the maritime capital of the kingdom. To obtain good crews he set up the *Inscription Maritime* (marine record and administrative office), which still exists today. After completing their military service, fishermen between the ages of 18 and 48 are placed on the French Naval reserve; the *Inscription Maritime* looks after them and their families throughout their lives.

Colbert also founded at Brest a school of gunnery, a college of marine guards, a school of hydrography and a school for marine engineers. From this enormous effort a magnificent fleet developed. Ships reached a tonnage of 5 000 and carried up to 120 cannons; their prows and sterns were carved by such artists as Coysevox.

Duquesne improved the naval dockyard, built ramparts round the town and organised the defence of the channel (Le Goulet). Vauban, the military architect, completed the projects. Tourville improved mooring facilities in the roadstead laying down buoys to which ships could moor instead of dropping anchor.

Brest for Tourists

Urban transport – By bus. Individual tickets (6F) can be bought from the bus driver, and are valid for 1hr. Day tickets (18F) can also be bought from the bus driver or from the Bibus stand at place de la Liberté.

Regional information in the media – Current entertainment and cultural events can be found in the newspapers: *Le Télégramme de Brest* (Wednesday edition) and *Ouest-France* (Brest edition), or by listening to Radio-France Bretagne Ouest 101.4 Mhz.

Festivities – Les "Jeudis du Port" – From late July to the end of August, the commercial port hosts free concerts Thursday evenings from 7.30pm until midnight.

Eating Out

BUDGET

Amour de Pomme de Terre – *Behind les-Halles-St-Louis* – ☎ *02 98 43 48 51 – 90/160F*. The samba? For this small, convivial and often crowded restaurant, it designates a kind of potato. If your napkin has a hole in it, ask the owner to tell you the story behind it!

Crêperie Moderne – *34 rue d'Algésiras* – ☎ *02 98 44 44 36 – closed Sun lunch; 40/80F*. If longevity is a test of quality, this restaurant takes the cake! Founded in 1922, it continues to attract the locals who remain devoted to it. They don't come for the decor, but rather to admire the dexterity of the crêpe-makers at work.

OUR SELECTION

Fleur de Sel – *15 bis rue de Lyon* – ☎ *02 98 44 38 65 – closed 2-23 Aug, 23-28 Dec, Sat lunch and Sun – 138F*. In a pretty dining room decorated in blond woodwork and yellow walls, long banquettes welcome the gourmets who come here to enjoy the up-to-date cuisine served by smiling and attentive servers. Quality food at reasonable prices.

Ma Petite Folie – *Moulin-Blanc Marina* – ☎ *02 98 42 44 42 – closed 23 Dec-8 Jan, 8-28 Aug and Sun – 110F*. Eating on a lobster boat without getting seasick? Inconceivable … except if the boat is in a dry dock on the sand! One can enjoy seafood here of course, in the hull, or on the upper deck in nice weather. What a port of call!

Hotels

OUR SELECTION

Hôtel du Belvédère – *7km/4.2mi west of Brest via D 789 and a country lane, 29200 Ste-Anne-du-Portiz* – ☎ *02 98 31 86 00* – 🅿 – *30 rooms 365/680F – breakfast 50F – restaurant 118/215F*. Standing alone on the beach, this modern hotel overlooks the roadstead's entrance to Brest. All the spacious and functional rooms look out onto the sea. You can also enjoy the view from its rotunda restaurant with large bay windows.

Going Out

Tara Inn – *1 rue Blaveau* – ☎ *02 98 80 36 07 – Mon-Fri 11am-1am, Sat and Sun from 3pm*. This is one of the rare pubs to be owned by real Irish people. It is located in the trendy commercial port area. The original atmosphere hosts stained-glass windows that bathe the room in soft light. Concert once a month.

Le Thalassa – *6 rue de Siam* – ☎ *02 98 44 13 71 – Mon-Fri 10am-1am, Sat and Sun from 11am*. This is one of the most beautiful pubs in Brest. The decor is nautical with diver's helmets and ship rudders displayed. An immense terrace looks out onto the mobile bridge of the Recouvrance.

Conti – *22 rue de Lyon* – ☎ *02 98 80 50 40 – daily, 24hr*. This chic bar, located in the Mercure-Continental Hotel, has a very pretty turn-of-the-century decor, and offers a wide selection of whiskies and cocktails.

The "Belle Poule" – In 1778, during the American War of Independence, the frigate *La Belle Poule* encountered the British Arethusa and forced her to retreat. This victory was very popular at court and all the ladies wore a new hairstyle *La Belle Poule*, which included, perched on their tresses, a model ship in full sail.

The "Surveillante" – In 1779 a British captain, George Farmer, wagered that no French frigate could destroy his *Québec*. Du Couëdic, who commanded the frigate *Surveillante*, challenged the wager – a furious sea duel ensued.
After a spirited battle, north of Ushant, both ships were dismasted. The sails of the *Québec* fell across its guns, setting the ship on fire. Du Couëdic ordered rescue action.

Aux Quatre Vents – *18 quai de la Douane* – ☎ *02 98 44 42 84* – *Mon-Fri 9am-1am, Sat from 10am, Sun from 2pm*. This charming bar-restaurant is a local institution. Sailors and other residents of Brest gather there for lunch or to have a beer in the evening. Small terrace facing the cranes in the commercial port.

Dubliners – *28 rue Matthieu-Donnard* – ☎ *02 98 46 04 98* – *Mon-Sat 3pm-1am, Sun 5pm-1am*. For those who love Irish folk music. This pub is also owned by a real Irish person, who in fact barely speaks French. Music (jam sessions) Thursday and Sunday evenings.

Shopping

Markets – All day every day at the Halles St-Louis; every morning at the Halles St-Martin; mornings, Monday through Saturday, at the Halles du Pilier Rouge.

Kerjean – 79 rue de Siam. It is a store, but it seems more like Ali Baba's cave! Those who enjoy subtle and exotic aromas will be delighted (the Turkish Delight is out of this world).

Sports

Sailing: Station Voile Rade de Brest – *Centre nautique municipal, port du Moulin-Blanc, 29200 Brest*. ☎ *02 98 34 64 64*.

Windsurfing – *Les Crocodiles de l'Élorn, port du Moulin-Blanc* – ☎ *02 98 41 73 81*.

Scuba diving – *Groupe Manche-Atlantique de plongée, port de Commerce* – ☎ *02 98 43 15 11*.

Boat Trips

Sailing on the schooner – *La Recouvrance* – ☎ *02 98 44 66 77*. With its 430m²/1 411sq ft of sails, it offers cruises for 2 to 4 days. A replica of the original, but the pleasure is genuine.

Île d'Ouessant★★ – *See Île d'OUESSANT*.

Boat trip on the roadstead★ – Two companies offer boat trips of Brest's roadstead. *Guided tour of the military port and of the roadstead (1hr 30min); "restaurant cruises" (lunch or dinner) on request (3hr 15min); "crossing from Brest to the Presqu'île de Crozon" on board a fast motorboat. Compagnie maritime Azénor*. ☎ *02 98 41 46 23*.
Apr-Oct, tour of the military port (1hr 30min), 5 departures daily. Mid-Mar to mid-Oct, Presqu'île de Crozon (45min), 3 return trips daily. Depending on the tides, sailing up or down the Aulne and Elorn rivers. Compagnie des vedettes armoricaines, 1er bassin, Port de commerce. ☎ *02 98 44 44 04*.

Crossing the roadstead★ – *25min*. This trip links Brest (pleasure port) to the port of Fret on the Presqu'île de Crozon. *Apr-Sept departures from Brest at 7.30am, 12.30pm, 5.45pm (July and Aug additional departure at 10am); departure from Fret at 8.10am, 1.10pm, 6.10pm (July and Aug additional departure at 10.35am). Compagnie maritime Azénor*. ☎ *02 98 41 46 23*.

Sea and air links with the islands

BY SEA

With Ouessant – *Departure from Brest at 8.30am (and 8.15am in season); departure from Ouessant at 5pm (4.30pm out of season). 180F (children 108F). Compagnie Penn Ar Bed*. ☎ *02 98 80 24 68*.

With Molène – *Departure from Brest at 8.30am; departure from Molène at 5.30pm (5pm out of season). 160F (children 96F). Compagnie Penn Ar Bed*. ☎ *02 98 80 24 68*.

With Sein – *July to Aug: departure from Brest at 8.15am; departure from Seine at 5pm. 122F (children 72F). Compagnie Penn Ar Bed*. ☎ *02 98 80 24 68*.

BY AIR

From Brest to Ouessant, from Molène to Ouessant and to Ouessant-Sein, tour of Ouessant. For times, call Compagnie Finist'air, ☎ *02 98 84 64 87*.

Later the *Québec* blew up with the wounded Farmer. Du Couëdic also died from his wounds. The *Surveillante* was brought back to Brest in triumph, and Du Couëdic was laid to rest in the church of St Louis (destroyed in 1944).

Brest during the war – In June 1940, when the impending arrival of the German forces was announced, the French naval and commercial authorities hastily cleared the port, destroying the installations and putting several bridges and buildings and four submarines undergoing repair work out of operation. Nonetheless, the port was immediately put to use by the German navy, which built a concrete shelter for submarines at **Laninon**. The port thus occupied a highly advantageous strategic position and represented a considerable threat to Allied forces sailing between the USA and Great Britain. As a consequence, the town was heavily bombarded for four years. When the Americans finally managed to enter the town in September 1944, after a siege of 43 days, they were greeted by nothing but ruins.

SIGHTS

Naval Town *half a day*

Cours Dajot (EZ) – This fine promenade was laid out on the ramparts in 1769 by convicts from the naval prison.

★★**View of the roadstead** – From the viewing table at the east end of the promenade, you see the Brest roadstead from the mouth of the Élorn, and past the Ménez-Hom and the Pointe de Roscanvel right over to Pointe de Portzic. The anchorage is vast (150km²/258sq mi) and deep (12-20m/6-10 fathoms – over large areas), framed between heights and connected with many big estuaries. It communicates with the Atlantic through a channel with steep banks, 5km/3mi long and about 1800m/1mi wide. This configuration explains why Brest has had such great military importance for more than 2000 years.

To the left the Élorn estuary, spanned by Albert-Louppe Bridge (Pont Albert-Louppe), makes a safe anchorage for yachts. In the foreground is the commercial port. Beyond lies the Île de Plougastel, hiding the southeast of the roadstead. On the south side of the roadstead, at Lanvéoc, is the Naval School; nearby the nuclear submarine base is situated on the Île Longue. On the horizon to the right you see the Presqu'île de Crozon and the opening of the channel between Portzic Fort and the Pointe des Espagnols. In front of the castle, the inner harbour, protected by its breakwater, serves as anchorage for the fleet.

The building overlooking the roadstead between Brest and Ste-Anne-du-Portzic houses the naval base and school.

C. Chevalier

Brest – Training ships with the castle of Brest in the background

Château (**DZ**) – The castle is the sole reminder of Brest's history.
It was in the 11C that Brest's stronghold first put in an appearance at the mouth of the River Penfeld on a site which had already been fortified by the Romans. It was to fall victim to innumerable sieges over the centuries. Towers and fortifications were built from the 12C to the 17C. Richelieu, Colbert, Duquesne and Vauban, from 1683, were to strengthen the fortifications of the site.
The curtain wall was restored after the last war. The museum and the ramparts are all that is open to the public; the castle houses the offices of the Harbour Police (Préfecture Maritime).

★**Musée de la Marine** ⊘ (**DZ M²**) – This museum is an offshoot of the Maritime Museum in Paris and displays valuable **models** of ships, navigation instruments and charts illustrating the feats of the navy of sailing ships during the 18C.
The museum is entered through the Madeleine Tower (Tour Madeleine – 3C to 15C), from the top of which there is a good view of the port and the roadstead. At the foot of the terrace there is a display of the 5622 pocket submarine, 11.87m/39ft long by 1.68m/5.5ft wide, and the taking aboard of the boat-people rounded up in the South China Sea by the teaching ship *Jeanne d'Arc* in 1988. The tour continues along the watch-path of the Paradis Tower (Tour Paradis) (15C) in which there is an exhibition on the history of the castle. In the keep (14C to 17C) there are models of the *Cordelière*, a display of the various stages of ship-building in the 18C and interesting exhibits of ship decorations. There is a representation of Brest prison.
The 13C Azénor Tower (Tour Azénor) gives a view of the Penfeld with the Recouvrance Bridge (Pont de Recouvrance), Tanguy Tower (Tour Tanguy) and the dockyard.

Pont de Recouvrance (**DZ**) – Inaugurated in 1954, this drawbridge is the largest in Europe. The steel span, about 87m/285ft long and weighing some 530t, swings between four concrete pylons 64m/209ft high. The bridge crosses the River Penfeld just above the oldest section of the dockyard. Operated by a system of pulleys, the drawbridge can be fully raised within 150 seconds. Under the bridge you can see a 380mm cannon which came from the *Richelieu*, a 35 000t battle-ship. Further upstream, the **Pont de l'Harteloire** (634m/2 080ft long) spans the dockyard at a height of 40m/128ft; note the series of storerooms, workshops, lifting appliances, slipways and dry docks.

★**Brest Naval Base (Base Navale) and Dockyard (Arsenal)** – It was in 1631 that **Cardinal Richelieu** decided to turn the city of Brest into a harbour. In 1666, **Colbert** developed the infrastructure that already existed along the banks of the Penfeld: the meandering, enclosed estuary of this river was a perfect site, able to protect the boats from heavy storms. From 1740 to 1790, **Choquet de Lindu** undertook to build a huge dockyard and, as early as 1742, the first three dry docks of Pontaniou were built. In the late 19C a pier was erected, defining the boundaries of a vast roadstead; in 1970 two jetties able to accommodate large-tonnage vessels (aircraft-carriers, cruisers, frigates) were added onto the pier. Docks no 8 (for careening only) and no 9 (construction work) were built in 1918 and extended in 1953. Their huge size (300m/985ft long by 49m/160ft wide) enables them to receive the largest ships belonging to the French fleet, over 250m/820ft long and weighing more than 35 000t. At the same time, two other quays were built: Quai de l'Armement (555m/1 821ft long), designed to equip and repair ships, and Quai des Flotilles (752m/2 468ft long), which brings together most of the war vessels that make up the Atlantic fleet.

During the German Occupation in the Second World War, an underwater naval base was set up in Brest within 500 days. Its purpose was to protect the German submarines stationed in the Atlantic Ocean. As soon as the base became operational, it could accommodate up to 30 submarines. With a total area of 65 859m²/79 030sq yd covered by a 4m/13ft thick slab, it was practically invulnerable; during the bombing of 5 August 1944, the impacts made by ten 6t bombs caused only minor damage. This base is still in service today.

Visite de l'Arsenal (Tour of the Dockyard) ⊘ *(Access by Porte de la Grande Rivière west of the plan by Pont de Recouvrance – Open to French nationals only)* – A tour of the naval base will provide a good introduction to the French Atlantic fleet: the frigates and despatch boats *(avisos)* of the Groupe d'Action Sous-Marine, the mine sweepers, the helicopter-carrier *Jeanne d'Arc* and the aircraft-carrier *Charles-de-Gaulle*, with its huge steel hull moored along Quai de l'Armement (scheduled to be operational by July 1999). Visitors may also be shown round a warship, depending on the number of boats available.

Port de Commerce (EZ) – *As seen from the Cours Dajot.*
This was established in 1860, once the Penfeld became inadequate for accommodating both military and commercial shipping, for the use of the Brest Chamber of Commerce and Industry.
Traditional traffic is closely linked with the agricultural activities of west Brittany, and amounts to almost two million tonnes a year.
The commercial port imports oilseed and other products destined for livestock, as well as hydrocarbons and fertilisers; it exports mainly frozen poultry (for which it ranks as the world's number one port), potatoes and oils.
The port is also an important centre for naval repair work and encompasses three types of dry dock. The most recent of these, built in 1980, has the capacity to accommodate the largest commercial ships yet made (over 500 000t). These installations, which include wet repair docks and a gas extraction station, make Brest the foremost French naval repair complex.

TOWN CENTRE *2hr*

★**Musée des Beaux-Arts** ⊘ (EZ M¹) – The room on the first floor contains 17C and 18C paintings from the Italian (Crespi: *Martyrdom of St Sebastian*; Dolci: *St Philip Benizi*; Giordano; Canaletto), French (Bourdon; Van Loo; J-B Regnault) and Dutch Schools (Schlacken: *Mary Magdalene at Prayer*). Note the painting of Brest Port (1774) by L van Blarenberghe.
On the ground floor, to the left, there is a display of ships by local artists (Gilbert; Noël: *Sailing Ships in Brest Roadstead*), works by Orientalists such as Guillaumet, Fromentin and Leroy *(Portrait of a Young Guide)*, as well as *Two Parrots* by Manet. Perhaps the most interesting section for the visitor is the large collection of canvases by artists of the Symbolist movement (pastels by Lévy-Dhurmer, Henri le Sidaner and R Ménard) and more particularly the Pont-Aven School. Note *By the Sea in Brittany* by Emile Bernard, *Green Corn at Pouldu* and *The Water-Carriers* by Paul Sérusier and *Day in September* by Maurice Denis.
The visit ends in a small room containing sculptures and drawings by Anne Quinquaud, which reflect a strong African influence.

Église St-Louis (EY) – This large modern church (1957) is in keeping with the vast place St-Louis, which it overlooks. The impression of height is increased by the vertical lines of the adjoining bell-tower.
The interior, which is very plain, emphasises the vertical theme. There are stained-glass windows by Léon Zack and Paul Boni (St-Louis), a Crucifixion by Kaeppelin and a modern tapestry by Olin.

Tour Tanguy ⊘ (DZ) – The tower stands opposite the castle, on the far bank of the Penfeld, overlooking the dockyard. This 14C construction, once the Quilbignon stronghold, houses the **Musée du vieux Brest**. Dioramas by Brest painter Jim-E-Sévellec depict the most significant periods of history in Brest: pre-Revolution (first floor); from the Revolution to the present (second floor).

★★OCEANOPOLIS ⊘ *2hr*

The enormous crab-shaped complex of Océanopolis is located east of the commercial port *(port de commerce)* alongside the Moulin Blanc marina *(port de plaisance)*.
This scientific and technical centre on marine life provides a window on all the activities linked with oceanology. Océanopolis also aims to be a "living place" where researchers, professional people, industrialists and the general public can be

brought into contact with each other. In view of the tremendous variety of subject matter linked with the sea, Océanopolis is constantly improving and updating its exhibitions.

The visit begins on level 1.

Level 1 (Niveau 1) – This is mainly given over to temporary exhibitions on oceanographic research. Permanent features include a satellite image receiver enabling visitors to admire the view of earth seen from space. One room is entirely given over to a display on the "Brest roadstead". The bridge of a ship has been reconstructed and equipped with remote controls above an indoor pool with various model boats floating in it, giving visitors a chance to familiarise themselves with navigation and the problems associated with safety at sea.

Behind the ship's bridge, a door leads out to the outdoor section of the seals' pool. Inside once more, there is a model of a cliff with birds representing the main species to be found nesting on the Breton coast. A question-and-answer computer game in which visitors pretend to be a particular species of bird evaluates the reliability of their own nesting instincts!

Level 0 (Niveau 0) – Several giant aquariums illustrate the variety of submarine life along the Breton coastline. All the tanks are interesting and well-presented; some particularly memorable ones are described below:

Aquarium 16 – This simulates life on the continental shelf, the submerged, almost flat part of the continents, covered in sand and continental mud. This is the home of the pollack, the grey gurnard and the snub-nosed gurnard.

Aquarium 17 – The large mudflat that hugs the south coast of Brittany is between 50-100m/164-328ft deep and maintains a relatively constant temperature of 10-12°C/50-53.6°F. This is the ideal environment for large shellfish like the lobster.

Aquarium 22 – Here, the submerged section of a cliff is alive with the dainty wrass, small spotted dogfish, brill and dab.

Aquarium 19 – The Molène-Ouessant archipelago, a protected area which is part of the Parc naturel régional d'Armorique, houses colonies of grey seals. Sild and Ida, the seals which live in this aquarium, are sea calves which can be found in this area from time to time. They were born in captivity in Denmark in 1988.

Aquarium 21 – The Ocean Column, 3m/10ft high, enables tiny fish to form shoals, thanks to a system of constant rotation of the water in the column. The water level is controlled with a suction pump activated by an ultrasonic monitor.

Aquarium 24 – The bed of zostera, elongated plants which make up a sort of submarine meadowland, reconstitutes this fragile coastline environment, which is particularly susceptible to pollution. Closer examination reveals the presence of the seahorse, the only fish in the world which swims in an upright position.

A model of a whale (rorqual) with some dolphins forms an eye-catching centrepiece to level 0.

Océanopolis is also a scientific research centre focusing on the study of marine mammals which live off the coasts of France, and a rescue centre for seals stranded on the shore. A reference library enables visitors to either consult or borrow (under certain conditions) books, magazines and videotapes on the subject of the sea. The Auditorium screens films produced by Océanopolis.

A souvenir shop offers a large selection of books on the subject of the sea.

The marina can be reached via the restaurant (not connected with Océanopolis).

★**Conservatoire botanique national de Brest** ⊘ – *East of the town by rue Jean-Jaurès, then by the road to Quimper.* This site was always a popular place for picnics and weekend strolls among the residents of Brest. However, over the years, the setting deteriorated to such an extent that the idea of a botanical park aimed to preserve "endangered plant species" saw the light of day. Today, the Vallon du Stang-Alar houses one of the most prestigious botanical gardens in the world. As well as a beautiful public garden boasting a wide variety of both common and rare exotic ornamental plants, the greenhouses and other conservatories contain many species threatened with extinction. The role of this park is not only to preserve endangered varieties, but also to study them and to try to revive them in their natural environment. Thus attempts have been made to resuscitate the *Hibiscus fragilis*, the *Lobelia parva*, the *Narcissus triandrus ssp capax*, which almost disappeared from the Îles de Glénan a few years ago, or the *Limonium dendroides*, of which only four specimens remained in the wild. Playing areas for children and sports activities will delight nature lovers of all ages.

Brest – Conservatoire botanique – Hibiscus Boryanus

L. Ruellau/Conservatoire Botanique National. Brest

BOAT TRIPS ⊘

★★Île d'Ouessant – *See Île d'OUESSANT.*

★On the roadstead – The tour includes a visit of the naval port, the commercial port and the fortified channel (Goulet de Brest). *1hr 30min.*

★Across the roadstead – The crossing links Brest to Le Fret on the Crozon Peninsula. *45min.*

EXCURSIONS

★Presqu'île de Plougastel – *Round tour of 56km/35mi – about half a day. Leave Brest by ⑤ on the town plan.*
You pass on the left the road leading to **Kerhuon**, a resort nicely situated on the west bank of the Élorn.

Pont Albert-Louppe – Inaugurated by President Gaston Doumergue in 1930, this bridge crosses the Élorn estuary. It is 880m/2 887ft long and has three 186m/610ft spans. Four statues by the sculptor Quillivic stand at each end: a man and a woman from the Léon region on the Brest shore and a man and a woman from Plougastel on the opposite shore.
The bridge rises over 42m/137ft high above the river and offers a very fine **view★** over Élorn Valley and the Brest roadstead.

1km/0.5mi after the bridge bear right towards Plougastel-Daoulas.

Plougastel-Daoulas – *See PLOUGASTEL-DAOULAS.*

★Presqu'île de Plougastel – *See PLOUGASTEL-DAOULAS for details of the rest of the drive.*

Fort Montbarey – Mémorial du Finistère ⊘ – *Leave Brest to the west over the Pont de Recouvrance towards Le Conquet; the fort is on the right as soon as you join D 789.*
This fort was built in 1784 on the orders of Louis XVI. It bears the name of one of the king's ministers (1732-96). Several years ago it was converted into a major memorial site for Finistère. An organisation, AME, undertakes the maintenance of a list, by *commune*, of all the natives of Finistère who "died during and because of the war" between 3 September 1939 and 19 December 1946 (the date when the volunteers returned from fighting Japan). Visitors can see photographs, literature, objects and military equipment recalling the siege of Brest in 1944. Several vaulted rooms have been reconstructed as the various garrisons of the fort (butcher's, baker's, chemist's etc).

★Abers – *Round tour of 197km/122mi – allow 1 day. See ABERS.*

Coastal tour to Le Conquet – *Round tour of 61km/38mi – about 2hr 30min. Leave Brest west by Pont de Recouvrance (**DZ**) and turn left into rue St-Exupéry to reach route de la Corniche. This road overlooks the naval dockyard.*

At 4-Pompes drive straight on; turn left at the entrance to Cosquer.

Ste-Anne-du-Portzic – It is located along the beach in Ste-Anne Bay; walk a short distance along the coastal path to enjoy fine views.
An uphill road leads to the **Centre Océanographique de Bretagne** at the Pointe du Diable on the sound (Goulet de Brest). The centre is the headquarters, on terra firma, of IFREMER (French Institute of Research for the Exploitation of the Sea). Since 1968 a campus has been built to accommodate the centre, with a port, fish farm and marine research facilities.

Take D 789.

The road runs parallel to Trez-Hir beach, giving a good view of Bertheaume Bay, then goes through Plougonvelin.

Fort de Bertheaume ⊘ – A pleasant walk along a coastal foot path leads to one of Vauban's fortified creations, at the entrance to the Brest Channel.

Carry on along D 85.

Hostellerie de la Pointe St-Mathieu – ☎ 02 98 89 00 19 – *closed mid-Jan to mid-Feb – 21 rooms 270/590F – breakfast 39F – restaurant 98/400F.* Near the big lighthouses and the old abbey, the building was once a private home; the hotel rooms are in a modern extension. Meals are served in an attractive room with a vaulted ceiling and fireplace; for a quick lunch, you can also choose to eat in the brasserie.

Before you reach the Pointe de St-Mathieu, note on the right, near a house, two Gallic steles *(stèles)* topped by a cross, which are known as the Monk's Gallows.

★★ Pointe de St-Mathieu – St-Mathieu, which was an important town in the 14C, is now only a village known for the ruins of its abbey church, its site and its lighthouse.

Lighthouse (Phare) ⊘ – The lighthouse has a considerable system of lights; two auxiliary lights are reserved for air navigation. There is also a radio beam. The main light is served by a 600-watt halogenous lamp, giving it an intensity of about 5 000 000 candlepower, with a range of 60km/38mi.

From the top *(163 steps)* there is a superb **panorama★★**; from left to right – the mouth of the Brest Sound, Presqu'île de Crozon, Pointe du Raz, Île de Sein (in clear weather), Pierres Noires reef, and the Islands of Béniguet, Molène and Ouessant. Beyond Béniguet, 30km/18.5mi away, you can sometimes distinguish Jument Lighthouse.

★**Église abbatiale** – The abbey church ruins are the remains of a Benedictine monastery (6C) which, according to legend, had as a relic the head of St Matthew. The 13C chancel, which has pointed vaulting, is flanked by a square keep. The nave with rounded or octagonal pillars has a single aisle on the north side and two 16C aisles on the south side. The church has a 12C façade pierced by a round arched doorway and three narrow windows.

In front of the restored Chapelle Notre-Dame-des-Grâces, note the 14C porch, a relic of the former parish church.

Go round the lighthouse enclosure to reach the tip of the point.

At the tip of the point, a column, erected to the memory of the French sailors who died in the First World War, is the work of the sculptor Quillivic. There is a magnificent **view** from the edge of the cliff.

At a point 300m/300yd from St-Mathieu going towards Plougonvelin are two Gallic **steles** (on the left near a house) surmounted by a cross and known as the Monks' Gibbet (Gibet des Moines).

Return to Brest by the direct road, D 789.

BRIGNOGAN-PLAGES ⌂

Population 836

Michelin map 58 folds 4 and 5 or 20 folds 3 and 4 – Local map see ABERS

A seaside resort lying at the end of Pontusval Bay and possessing a magnificent sandy beach. On either side of Brignogan rock piles, sometimes curiously shaped, divide small beaches.

Pointe de Pontusval – This walk crosses a countryside dotted with blocks of granite. The Men Marz, at mid-distance, is a fine example of a menhir, 8m/25ft high, surmounted by a Cross.

Chapelle Pol – The 19C chapel, Calvary and small watchtower, built on two rocks, are worth seeing.

EXCURSION

Goulven – *7.5km/5mi southeast. Take the road to Lividic Beach, then the coast road along Goulven Bay. At Plounéour-Trez, turn left just after the church.*

This little village has a restored 15C-16C **church**. The **belfry★**, which dates from the Renaissance, is one of the finest in Brittany. To the right of the porch, which opens under the bell tower, is a fine Gothic doorway with twin doors and a carved stoup on the pier between them.

Inside the church are a monumental Renaissance stoup, a high altar in Kersanton granite and an altar decorated with six carved and painted panels illustrating St Goulven's miracles. The 16C organ loft has been built onto a former rood screen. Two fine 17C embroidered banners are displayed in the chancel in the summer months.

CAMARET-SUR-MER

Population 2 933

Michelin map 58 fold 3 or 20 folds 16 and 17 –
Local map see Presqu'île de CROZON

An important spiny lobster port, Camaret is also a quiet, simple seaside resort.

On the shore, to the left of the *Sillon*, a natural dike which protects the port, is Corréjou Beach.

The landing of 1694 – The Presqu'île de Crozon, which forms an advanced bastion for Brest, has been attacked many times by the British, Spanish and Dutch. Vauban, the military architect, fortified it in 1689. Five years later, during the reign of William III, an Anglo-Dutch fleet tried to make a landing, but the fort and hidden batteries covering the port were very effective; several ships were put out of action, and the landing troops were decimated. A charge by dragoons scattered the attackers, and the coastguard militiamen, with their pitchforks and scythes, completed the rout.

Submarine experiment – It was in Camaret Bay in 1801 that the American engineer **Fulton**, who had settled in France in 1797, carried out an underwater experiment. He had built a small vessel which, with a crew of five, could be propelled under water with jointed oars at a speed of two knots. It could stay under water for 6hr. This rudimentary submarine was intended to affix to the hull of an enemy ship a bomb or "torpedo" containing 100lb of powder, which was to be exploded by a time mechanism. A British frigate, at anchor in the bay, was to serve as the target. Fulton attacked but, unfortunately for him, the ship, though unaware of his approach, weighed anchor and sailed away. This failure spoilt the inventor's chances and he returned to America. It was not until the end of the 19C that this ingenious idea was realised.

Hotels

OUR SELECTION

Hôtel Thalassa – ☎ *02 98 27 86 44 – closed 1 Oct-3 Apr* – ◘ – *46 rooms 320/600F – breakfast 48F – restaurant 110/295F.* Some of these rooms, with cane furniture, open onto balconies that look out over the port; others, without balconies, look onto the swimming pool. The hotel's modern architecture boasts light open spaces, It is also a pleasant place to have a nice meal at good prices.

Boat Trips

To the Islands of Ouessant and Sein – *July-Aug – contact the tourist office.*

Schooner trips – *May-Oct – outings on the "Belle Étoile" (a lobster boat with sails)* – ☎ *02 98 27 86 91.*

SIGHTS

Chapelle Notre-Dame-de-Rocamadour – This chapel stands at the end of the dike. It was built between 1610 and 1683 and restored after a fire in 1910. It was originally a pilgrimage chapel on the pilgrims' route to Rocamadour in Quercy; from the 11C the pilgrims from the north, who came by sea, used to disembark at Camaret to continue the journey by land. A *pardon* is held on the first Sunday in September.

Château Vauban – A massive tower surrounded by walls was built by the military architect Vauban at the end of the 17C on Sillon Point. It now houses temporary exhibitions from time to time. There are fine views of the Brest Channel, Pointe des Espagnols and the port and town of Camaret.

EXCURSIONS

★★★**Pointe de Penhir** – *3.5km/2mi southwest by D 8. See Pointe de PENHIR.*

★★**Pointe des Espagnols** – *Round tour of 36km/23mi north – about 30min. Leave Camaret towards Crozon; turn left at the top of a hill after passing the last houses. The rest of the drive is described under Presqu'île de CROZON.*

BOAT TRIP ⊘

Les Tas de Pois – *See Pointe de PENHIR.*

CANCALE★

Population 4 910

Michelin map 59 fold 6 or 230 fold 12 – Local map see CÔTE D'ÉMERAUDE

The **setting★** of this fishing port and seaside resort is picturesque. To get a good view take the tourist road *(route touristique – one-way)* which branches off D 76 to the right 2.5km/1.5mi after the Portes Rouges crossroad. As you drive into Cancale the **views★** of the resort and Mont-St-Michel Bay are splendid.

The town has derived its gastronomic reputation for centuries from the **oysters** which flourish in the beds in the bay *(parc à huîtres)* and which oyster lovers come to eat in the hotels and bars around the port. Sales reached their highest level in the First Empire with 48 million oysters in one season.

Now only young oysters brought from Auray are cultivated in the bay, for a mysterious disease around 1920 decimated the native spat. Since then spat has begun to flourish in the immense beds in the open sea, and an oyster with a particular flavour is developing due to the richness of the plankton of Mont-St-Michel Bay.

CANCALE

D Monument aux Morts
E Maison de Jeanne Jugan
M¹ Musée des Bois sculptés
M² Musée des Arts
      et Traditions populaires
M³ La Ferme Marine
      Musée de l'Huître et du
      Coquillage

SIGHTS

★**Port de la Houle** (**Z**) – A bustling, animated area, the quays along the port teem with people unloading oysters, repairing nets, cleaning boats, or just waiting for the arrival of the fishing fleet at high tide.
Go to the Fenêtre jetty for a view of the bay and, at low tide, of the oyster beds.
The port is surrounded by a picturesque district where sailors and fishermen lived. A street, the Vaubaudet or Val du Baudet, was the only link with the town of Cancale, the upper district, where the landsmen and traders lived.

★**Pointe du Hock and Sentier des Douaniers** (**Z**) – Sentier des Douaniers (Customs Officers Path), a watch-path, runs into rue du Port (after some steps); it continues on 7km/4mi to the Pointe du Grouin. From the Pointe du Hock you get a **view**★ over Cancale Rock (Rocher de Cancale), Mont-St-Michel Bay and the mount itself; below on the right, at the foot of the cliff, are the oyster beds. On either side of Pointe du Hock you may take Sentier des Douaniers and enjoy a walk overlooking the shore. If you follow the coastline as far as Port-Mer, you will get a splendid view of Pointe de la Chaîne opposite Cancale Rock.

Église St-Méen ⊘ (**Z**) – From the church tower's upper platform (189 steps), where there is a viewing table, you can enjoy a wide **panorama**★ of Mont-St-Michel Bay, Granville and some 40 belfries. In clear weather you can see the îles Chausey.

Musée des Bois sculptés ⊘ (**Z M¹**) – An amazing collection of wood carvings by Abbot Quémerais (born in Cancale 1879, d 1955) are exhibited here. More than 300 figures are sculpted in high relief on oak panels with such minute detail that each scene (*Ode to the Apple, Apotheosis of Sport...*) appears to be animated.

Fines de Claire

89

La Ferme Marine Musée de l'Huître et du Coquillage ⊘ (**Z M³** – via ①) – This museum is located in St-Kerber, at the heart of an oyster-breeding farm, and has displays on the evolution of oyster-breeding techniques as well as the activities of oyster farmers across the centuries. A lovely collection of shellfish (more than 2 000 from all over the world), films and dioramas illustrate the way of life of this "gardener of the sea". There is a guided tour of the workshops, pools and shellfish tanks, as well as an explanation of tides, some of which here are the strongest in Europe.

Musée des Arts et Traditions populaires ⊘ (**Y M²**) – Housed in the old Église St-Méen (1714, now deconsecrated), the museum is devoted to the popular arts and traditions of the Cancale region (fishing, oyster-breeding, farming, costumes, furnishings...) and to the life of Jeanne Jugan. There is also a presentation relating to the sailing school (École de Navigation des Rimains), which has been located in the town for over 100 years.

Monument aux Morts (**Z D**) – This war memorial affords an extensive view of Mont-St-Michel Bay, Mont-Dol and the port and the oyster beds below.

Maison de Jeanne Jugan ⊘ (**Y E**) – The house is the birthplace of Jeanne Jugan (1792-1879), founder of the order known as the Little Sisters of the Poor.

EXCURSION

★★**Pointe du Grouin** – *4.5km/2.5mi north by the D 201 – about 30min – local map see CÔTE D'ÉMERAUDE. Leave Cancale by rue du Stade (**Y 27**), then turn right onto the road which leads straight to the Pointe du Grouin. At the end of the road, after the Hôtel de la Pointe du Grouin, leave your car in a vast parking area and take a path, to the right of the signal station, which leads directly to the point.* In a fine setting, this wild, rocky headland overlooks the sea from a height of 40m/131ft and affords a **panorama** which stretches from Cap Fréhel to Granville and Mont-St-Michel Bay with, in the distance, the Îles Chausey. At low tide one can take a path to a cave in the cliffside (height 10m/32ft, depth 30m/98ft).
The Île des Landes, opposite, is an island with a bird sanctuary and nature reserve. Housed in the blockhouse is an exhibition on sea birds.

Travellers' addresses

Hotels

OUR SELECTION

Hôtel Pointe du Grouin – *On the Pointe du Grouin* – ☎ *02 99 89 60 55* – *closed 2 Oct-31 Mar* – 🅿 – *21 rooms 400/520F – breakfast 48F – restaurant 118/315F.* In an exceptional location, this cozy little hotel opens its windows onto the islands and the Mont St-Michel. Very popular during the day, the Pointe rediscovers to its calm in the evening, and you can enjoy the deep nighttime tranquillity. Restaurant with view.

TREAT YOURSELF!

Les Maisons de Bricourt – *Rue Duguesclin* – ☎ *02 99 89 64 76* – 🅿 – *19 rooms from 750F – breakfast 90F – 2 restaurants 115/680F.* Give in to the temptation of the beautiful Hotel de Bricourt-Richeux and its restaurant Le Coquillage, la Maison des Rimains with rooms on the sea, or la Maison de Bricourt – the Olivier Rœllinger's starred restaurant... The charm of these four establishments will take your breath away!

Eating Out

BUDGET

Surcouf – *7 quai Gambetta* – ☎ *02 99 89 61 75 – closed 15 Nov-16 Dec, Tues evening Sept-June and Wed – 98/235F.* Here, food lovers can regale themselves without going broke! Served on the latticed terrace or in the chic dining room, the menu is created around regional specialities and fresh fish. Excellent quality for the price.

Crêperie du Port – *1 place du Calvaire, on the harbour* – ☎ *02 99 89 60 66 – closed Tues except during school holidays – 40/70F.* This crêperie *has a nautical atmosphere, from its walls covered with paintings and* posters to its ceiling fresco. Notice the beautiful sailboat model also on display. Everyone will enjoy its all-season terrace facing the port.

The Oyster Market – *At the end of quai Thomas – no credit cards – 16/60F.* "Direct from the producer to the consumer": here you can sit in the sea air on a low wall at the end of the quay, and savour fresh oysters direct from the oyster farmers. They will open the oysters for you to taste immediately from Easter to September, and take-out (unopened) is available all year.

CARHAIX-PLOUGUER

Population 8 198
Michelin map 58 fold 17 or 230 fold 20 – Local map see MONTAGNES NOIRES

In the Roman era Carhaix was an important town commanding seven main roads; even today it is still the hub of a roadway network. In the centre of a cattle-rearing district, the town is a milk production centre.

La Tour d'Auvergne (1743-1800) – Carhaix's famous son is **Théophile-Malo Corret**, known as La Tour d'Auvergne. When still very young, he became keenly interested in the Breton language but he was a soldier at heart. During the Revolution his exploits were such that he, a junior captain at 46, was offered the most exalted rank; but he refused – he wanted to remain with his troops.

When there was a pause in his campaigns, he would bring his faithful Celtic grammar out. He finally retired and spent all his time studying his favourite subject.

When the son of his Celtic master was called up for the army, La Tour, moved by the old teacher's grief, took the young man's place and enlisted, at 54 years of age, as a private soldier in the 46th half-brigade. New exploits followed. Bonaparte offered La Tour a seat on the Legislative Council, but failed to overcome his modesty. He was awarded a sword of honour and the title of "First Grenadier of the Republic". He was killed in 1800, during the Rhine campaign. All the army mourned him.

Every year, on the Saturday preceding 27 June, Carhaix celebrates the name-day of La Tour d'Auvergne.

Église St-Trémeur – Rebuilt in the 19C, the church's porch opens onto the bell-tower (16C); the tympanum over the doorway is adorned with the statue of St Trémeur, whose legend dates from the 6C.

Maison du Sénéchal – *No 6 rue Brizeux*. This building has a 16C façade. The ground floor is of granite decorated with carvings and the corbelled upper storeys are faced with slate and adorned with statuettes. The tourist office *(syndicat d'initiative)* has its premises here (temporary exhibitions), and a small **Musée d'Ethnographie locale** (Museum of Local Ethnography) ⊙ is open to the public on the first floor.

PLATEAU DU HUELGOAT

Round tour of 80km/50mi – 4hr. Leave Carhaix by rue Oberhausen and rue des Abattoirs in the direction of Plounevézel. Turn right at Croissant Marie-Joffré. 3km/1.2mi further on, past the Lesquern hamlet on the left, take a bend on the right onto an unsurfaced road.

Chapelle St-Gildas – The road leads through woodlands to the 16C chapel which has a square bell-tower crowned by a stone spire and grotesques at the east end. The beacon of St-Gildas (238m/781ft) stands to the right.

Return to the main road and turn right.

After the junction for Carnoët, there is a view of the Monts d'Arrée.

Bear left towards Plourac'h.

Plourac'h – The Renaissance church in the form of a T was built largely in the 15C and 16C. The south face is the most ornate. The porch, which is Gothic in character, contains statues of the Apostles surmounted by canopies. A beautiful Renaissance doorway with windows on either side is crowned by three gables adorned with coats of arms. Near the font is an 18C altarpiece depicting the mysteries of the rosary and statues of St Adrian and St Margaret. Among the many statues ornamenting the church should be noted those of St Guénolé and St Nicodemus, dressed as a doctor of law, and a Descent from the Cross in which the Virgin wears a Breton cloak of mourning.

Continue towards Callac.

Fine views of this undulating countryside.

Callac – This town is dominated by the ruins of Botmel Church. In front of the stud farm stands a bronze statue of the stallion Naous, by Guyot. The town is also the home of the Breton spaniel, a pointer.

Take the road towards Guingamp and after 4km/2.5 mi turn right.

Bulat-Pestivien – A former pilgrimage centre, a *pardon* takes place in town on the Sunday

Camping Municipal de la vallée de l'Hyères – *2.3km/1.3mi on the road to Morlaix, then the road in front of the gendarmerie, on the banks of the River Hyères* – ☎ *02 98 99 19 58 – open 15 June-Sept – no credit cards – 62 sites 34F*. This is the ideal campground for those who love to fish. In the heart of the natural landscape, it is located on the riverbank near a duck pond. The scenery is very relaxing. Nearby, you will find opportunities to ride horses, go canoeing, or stay overnight in a cottage.

M. Cambazard/EXPLORER

Plourac'h – Apostles on the south doorway

after 8 September. This fine **church★** was put up in the 15 and 16C. The Renaissance tower, had a spire added in the 19C. There are remarkable porches.

Inside is a monumental sacristy – adorned with a frieze of macabre design – with a loggia which projects into the church. There is a curious lectern representing a peasant in the local Vannes costume; and a massive table dating back to 1583. Bulat possesses three sacred fountains: the fountain to the Virgin (1718) in the cemetery and, on either side of the Callac road out of town, the fountain of the Seven Saints (1683) and the Cock fountain (16C). There is a fine Calvary (1550) with a striking Entombment at **Pestivien** *(1km/0.6mi north of Bulat).* Unfortunately it has been defaced.

You arrive at Burthulet by the Rostrenen road.

Burthulet – The simple 16C chapel, with wall belfry, stands in melancholy surroundings; one does not question the legend that says: "The devil died of cold here".
Make for Ty-Bourg and bear right.

St-Servais – The writer Anatole Le Braz was born here. 16C church.
Take the road opposite the church towards St-Nicodème. After 2km/0.6mi turn right.

★**Gorges du Corong** – *1hr on foot there and back. From the roundabout at the end of the road follow the path leading to the gorges.* The path runs along the river and into the Duault Forest. The river disappears beneath a mass of rocks to reappear as a series of cascades.
Turn round and bear right and right again in the direction of Locarn.

Locarn – Its **church** ⊘ contains 17C furnishings (altarpiece, pulpit, statues), a remarkable 16C stained-glass window, a carillon wheel and the panels of a Flemish altarpiece, also of that period. Displayed in the presbytery is the **treasury★**. Note the following objects made of silver-gilt: St Henrin's bust and reliquary (in the form of an arm) both 15C, a processional cross (late 16C) and a 17C chalice.
Return to Carhaix-Plouguer via Trebrivan.

CARNAC★

Population 4 243
Michelin map 63 fold 12 or 230 folds 35 and 49

Carnac was already known as a prehistoric capital. The name of Carnac is often associated with megalithic monuments.

SIGHTS

★★**Musée de Préhistoire J.-Miln-Z.-Le Rouzic** ⊘ (**M**) – This Museum of Prehistory was founded in 1881 by the Scotsman James Miln (1819-81), who had excavated in Carnac and Kermario, and enriched by Zacharie Le Rouzic, native of Carnac. In its new surroundings, these exceptional, beautifully displayed collections, cover prehistory from the Lower Paleolithic (450 000 BC) to the early Middle Ages.
The tour starts on the ground floor with an audio-visual presentation positioning the region's prehistory and archeology in world prehistory; the stratigraphic column presents, via the different strata, the different civilizations.

Proceeding chronologically, the visitor is presented: Lower Palaeolithic (chipped stone, scrapers, points); Middle and Upper Paleolithic (panels and documents); Mesolithic (primitive tools in wood or bone, shell ornaments, a reconstructed burial chamber); Neolithic Period, when man lived in settled communities and turned to crop growing and stock raising, marked by the realisation of megalithic tombs: dolmens or collective burial tombs (placed with the dead were pottery, polished axes, jewellery); menhirs and alignments. Also exhibited here are necklaces made of variscite (a green semi-

precious stone), fine polished axes in jadeite or fibrolite, beads and pendants, pottery, engraved stones, dolmens and objects related to daily life. The first floor covers the Bronze Age (socketed axes, gold jewellery), Iron Age (reconstructed burial tomb, salt oven, Celtic gold coins), to the Roman era (model of a villa, statuettes of Venus, coins, objects related to daily life).

*Church – Pardon: see Calendar of events. This 17C church is dedicated to **St Cornely**, the patron saint of horned cattle; his statue stands on the façade between two oxen. A massive bell-tower topped by an octagonal spire dominates the building. The porch on the north side is surmounted by a canopy in the form of a crown. Inside, the wooden vaults are covered with curious 18C **paintings** depicting the lives of the saint, Christ and St John the Baptist, and the Virgin. The communion table,

Hotels

OUR SELECTION

Hôtel Lann Roz – 36 avenue de la Poste – ☎ 02 97 52 10 48 – closed 2 Jan-Feb and Mon (except in summer) – 🅿 – 13 rooms 380/400F – breakfast 38F – restaurant 100/250F. This hotel stands in a garden and has a grandmotherly touch about it. The decor elegantly mixes old-fashioned details and more recent ones, such as the flowery fabrics and the cane furniture in the rooms. Terrace in the summer.

Eating Out

BUDGET

Crêperie Les Kerguelen – Route de la Trinité-sur-Mer via D 781, 2km/1.6mi – ☎ 02 97 52 28 21 – reservations required in summer – 55/120F. For crêpe-lovers, the short excursion to this inn outside of Carnac, is well worth it; you won't be disappointed... Others will enjoy the very reasonable prices. And for the curious, this restaurant has invented a delightful dish called the "quizza!"

OUR SELECTION

La Côte – At the Alignements de Kermario, 2km/1.6mi on route d'Auray – ☎ 02 97 52 02 80 – closed 17-28 Nov, 5 Jan-12 Feb and Mon except from 14 July to 15 Aug – 120/250F. An indispensable stopover after touring the megaliths. In this former farm, which opens its terrace in nice weather, you can taste the young chef's delicious and original cuisine. Good quality for the price.

pulpit and chancel screen are of the 18C and in wrought iron. In the chancel entrance, on the left, is a reliquary bust of St Cornely (18C gilt wood). The church's treasury is exhibited in the south aisle: chasuble, cross, chalices, monstrance etc. The organ was built in 1775.

⌂CARNAC-PLAGE

Carnac-Plage, with its gently shelving beach, has been developed in the shelter of the Presqu'île de Quiberon. View of the coast, Houat, Belle-Ile and the Presqu'île de Quiberon.

★★MEGALITHIC MONUMENTS (MÉGALITHES) *2hr 30min.*

A tour of the numerous megalithic monuments (alignments, dolmens, tumuli) to the north of Carnac makes a fascinating excursion.

Since the footsteps of innumerable visitors pose a serious threat to the soil (which is essential for the study of the mysterious origins of the megaliths) the public authorities have had to take action to protect the Ménec, Kermario and Kerlascan Alignments. If plant life is allowed to grow again, this will prevent any further erosion of the soil, which will in turn prevent the foundations of the menhirs from becoming exposed. At Kermario, if conditions are favourable, a temporary foot-bridge enables visitors to observe the alignment in its entirety, while reflecting that it is an example of Western Europe's first ever architecture.

★★**Alignements du Ménec** – The Ménec Alignments, over 1km/0.8mi long and 100m/330ft wide, include 1170 menhirs arranged in 11 rows. The tallest is 4m/12ft high.

They begin with a semicircle of 70 menhirs partly surrounding the hamlet of Ménec.

★**Alignements de Kerlescan** – In this field (880 x 139m/962 x 153yd), 540 menhirs are arranged in 13 rows and the whole is preceded by a semicircle of 39 menhirs.

★**Alignements de Kermario** ⊘ – 990 menhirs in 10 rows occupy an area similar to the Ménec Alignments.

Alignements de Kerlescan

S. Chirol

★**Tumulus St-Michel** – The tumulus is 120m/395ft long and 12m/38ft high (395 x 38ft), a mound of earth and stones covering two burial chambers and some 20 stone chests. Most of the artefacts found there are now in Carnac's Musée de Préhistoire and the Musée archéologique du Morbihan in Vannes. The galleries were first explored in the early 20C, but for safety reasons visitors are no longer allowed inside.

Dolmens de Mané-Kerioned – A group of three dolmens; the first has eight uprights with stylised engravings: axes, spirals, coats of arms etc.

Tumulus de Kercado ⊘ – *Leave the car at the entrance to Kercado Castle.*
This tumulus (3800 BC) is 30m/98ft across and 3.50m/11ft high and covers a fine example of a dolmen. A menhir stands on the summit. Note the carvings on the table and four uprights.

EXCURSIONS

★Other Megaliths – *8km/5mi northwest. Leave Carnac on the road to Lorient.*

Dolmens de Rondossec – *To the left on leaving Plouharnel.* Three underground chambers.

Menhirs du Vieux-Moulin – *After the level crossing.* These stand in a field to the right of the road.

Alignements de Ste-Barbe – *Near the road on the left in the direction of Kersily camp site.* Four menhirs on the edge of a field.

Dolmen de Crucuno – *Take a road to the right.* It rises against a farm in the centre of the hamlet of Crucuno. Only one chamber remains with the great table supported by 11 uprights.

Dolmen de Mané-Croch – *500m/0.7mi beyond Crucuno, on the left.* A typical dolmen with side chambers.

Alignements de Kerzerho – *To the right of the road at the entrance to Erdeven.* 10 rows include 1 129 menhirs.

Abbaye St-Michel-de-Kergonan – *4km/2.5mi by D 781 towards Plouharnel.*
This Benedictine abbey, founded in 1898, is part of the Abbaye St-Pierre in Solesmes *(see The Green Guide to Chateaux of the Loire)*. An imposing granite building includes a plain church with wooden vaulting held up by granite pillars. Beyond the abbey shop (books, produce and objects made by the nuns), a gallery houses an exhibit on the Benedictine Order: its origin, Cistercian Law, expansion, the height of its power with Cluny etc and Gregorian chants.

CHÂTEAUBRIANT

Population 12 782
Michelin map 63 folds 7 and 8 or 230 fold 41

On the border of Brittany and Anjou, surrounded by woods dotted with pools, stands this old fortified town with its imposing castle.
At the town gates, on the road to Pouancé, at Carrière des Fusillés, there is a memorial to the 27 hostages executed by the Nazis on 22 October 1941. The recesses at the base contain soil from the place of execution.

Françoise de Foix and François I (16C) – Among the ladies of Châteaubriant were two whose memory has survived the centuries. One, Sibylle, gave a rare example of conjugal love; when her husband returned from a Crusade in 1250, she died of joy embracing him.
The story of the second, Françoise de Foix, is less edifying. At the age of 11 she was married to Jean de Laval, Count of Châteaubriant. He was terribly jealous; he tried to keep his child-wife away from the dangers of the outside world and sulked in his castle. Nonetheless, Françoise grew in beauty, wit and culture and aroused great curiosity.
François I sent word to the Count that he would like to meet her. Laval took no notice. When the king insisted, Laval went to court, but unaccompanied; his wife, he said, liked to be alone, and moreover she was weak minded. The Count had arranged with his wife that she should join him only at a certain signal. A servant came upon the secret and sold it to the king. One fine day Laval saw Françoise alighting from her coach and being received with great honours. Mad with rage, he left the court, leaving his wife unprotected. Dazzled by this brilliant new life, she yielded and became the King's favourite.
However, royal loves are not eternal and she was superseded by the Duchess of Étampes. Laval returned, took his wife back to Châteaubriant and shut her up, with her daughter, aged seven, in a room hung with black. The child sickened and died. The mother held out for 10 years, whereupon, it has been said her husband hastened her end in 1537 with a thrust of his sword.

SIGHTS

★Château ⊘ – A part of the castle, which has been remodelled several times, is feudal while another part, dating from the Renaissance, was built by Jean de Laval.
You can stroll round it along the esplanade and the gardens which go right down to the Chère.
Enter through place Charles de Gaulle.
All that remains of the feudal castle is a large keep on a height,

Auberge Bretonne – *23 place Motte –* ☎ *02 40 81 03 05 – 78/285F.* A friendly local restaurant with a pleasant dining room, recently redecorated. A young chef oversees the kitchen, and the inn also has some rooms to let.

connected with the entrance fort and the chapel by walls against which the two wings of the main building stand. The three wings of the Seigneurial Palace (Palais Seigneurial), opposite, are connected by elegant Renaissance pavilions. The roof is ornamented with dormer windows, which are emblazoned with the coats of arms of Châteaubriant, Laval and Montmorency.

The tour takes you up the central staircase (**1**) to a balcony from where there is a lovely view onto the Main Courtyard, embellished with gardens and a huge chestnut tree, the keep, and the city's rooftops. Continue on to the room (**2**) of Françoise de Foix with its coffered ceiling and monumental early-17C carved wood chimney. Next to it is the oratory (**3**) with the tombstone of Françoise de Foix on which is carved an epitaph by Clément Marot (French Renaissance poet).

The Magistrate's Court (Tribunal d'Instance – **J**) occupies a part of the palace while the public library (**B**) is housed in the south wing.

There are only two sections left of the colonnade which surrounded the Main Courtyard: the covered gallery (**4**) which ends at a charming staircase-pavilion and the other section (**5**) enclosing the Main Courtyard.

Église de St-Jean-de-Béré – The church's oldest parts comprising the chancel and the transept crossing, which are built of fine red sandstone, date from the end of the 11C; the nave is 12C.

Outside, near the picturesque south porch (16C), is a rustic altar from which services were held at the time of the plague.

Inside you will see the ornately decorated altarpiece at the high altar (1665), in the north transept the altarpiece of the Virgin (1658) and left of the nave the altarpiece of St Blaise (1693).

A 17C panel representing the Eternal Father is placed in the nave across from the entrance; a Virgin and a statue of St Julian (15C) and other 17C statues including a St Elizabeth represented by Maria Theresa, Louis XIV's wife and St Augustine are also noteworthy. On the end wall are two low-relief sculptures representing the Annunciation (13C) and the Visitation (15C).

EXCURSION

Abbaye de Melleray – *21km/12mi south via D 178; turn left on D 18 at La Meilleraye-de-Bretagne (towards Riallé).*

Founded in 1142 near a lovely lake, this Cistercian abbey has buildings which date from the 18C. The **Église Notre-Dame-de-Melleray**, completed in 1183, has been restored to its Cistercian severity, including a series of grisaille windows. Note the pointed white-stone arches resting on square pink-granite pillars. In the flat chevet, admire the gracious 17C wood polychrome **statue of the Virgin**.

Opposite the entrance avenue there is a curious 15C granite Calvary.

COMBOURG★

Population 4 843

Michelin map 59 folds 16 and 17 or 20 fold 26

This picturesque old town stands at the edge of a great pool and is dominated by an imposing feudal castle. The tourist office is on place Albert-Parent, inside the restored 16C Maison de la Lanterne. Tourists who only want to take a quick look at the castle from the outside should walk along the local road which branches off the Rennes road and runs beside the pool, facing the castle and the village.

Chateaubriand at Combourg – The castle, which was built in the 11C, was enlarged in the 14Cand 15C and restored in the 19C. It belonged first to the Du Guesclin family, and then in the 18C to the Count of Chateaubriand, father of François-René, the great Romantic writer.

In his *Memoirs*, Chateaubriand recalled the two years he spent at Combourg in his youth, adding still more to their romantic nature. The Count, a sombre and moody man, lived very much in retirement; when the family met he would walk up and down for hours in the drawing room, in silence, while no one dared to speak. The Countess, who was unwell, kept only a distant eye on the children. Months passed without a visitor. Left to themselves, the young Chateaubriand and his sister Lucile grew close, sharing their boredom, their dreams and their fears.

The old castle, almost deserted, was gloomy; the pool, the woods and the surrounding heath exuded melancholy. The Cat Tower (Tour du Chat), in which François-René had his lonely room, was haunted; a former Lord of Combourg was said to return there at night in the form of a black cat, which the boy watched for anxiously. The owls fluttering against the window and the wind rattling the door and howling in the corridors made him shiver.

It was there that the dreamy and melancholy soul of one of the great Romantic writers, was formed, or perhaps confirmed.

★**Château** ⊘ – The exterior of the castle appears like a powerful fortress: its four massive towers, with pepper-pot roofs, its crenellated parapet walk, and its thick walls slit by narrow openings. The interior was rearranged in 1876. The tour takes you to the chapel, the drawing room (now divided in two), the Archives, where souvenirs of the author are displayed: autographs, awards, furniture etc and to François-René's austere bedroom in Cat Tower.

From the parapet walk there are views of the locality, the lake and the pretty, fragrant **park** ⊘.

Hôtel du Château – *Place Châteaubrand –* ☎ *02 99 73 00 38 – closed 15 Dec-15 Jan, Sun evening 15 Oct-15 May and Mon noon –* ▣ *– 35 rooms 310/520F – breakfast 47F – restaurant 95/290F. At the foot of the château, this old manor is very elegant. The rooms, modern in style, are pleasant, and have views of the château, the garden or the lake. This is a good place to set out for a trip around Haute-Bretagne.*

EXCURSIONS

Château de Lanrigan ⊘ – *5km/3mi east. Leave Combourg on the road to Rennes and after the lake bear left onto the road that runs along the lake's south bank to the château.*
The small Château de Lanrigan with its well-balanced proportions would recall the smaller châteaux of the Loire if it were not built of granite. The château has a charming Renaissance façade; in the angle formed by the main building and its flanking tower, a gracefully constructed gallery adds an original note.

Cobac Parc ⊘ – *10km/6mi northwest on D 73. At Lanhélin, follow the signs for the Parc de Loisirs.*
This country park, covering 10ha/25 acres, is one in which animals roam free (ponies, kids, donkeys) against a background of greenery. Amusements offered for young and old include a small train, merry-go-rounds, rope walk, boat rides... as well as a museum (200 of the region's animals, stuffed). There is a picnic area and a restaurant.

Antrain – *21km/10.5mi east on D 796 and D 313.*
High on a promontory, Antrain is a market town with steep little streets and 16C and 17C houses. **Église St-André** (for the most part from the 12C) hosts an imposing 17C bell-tower, topped by a dome with lantern turrets.

Château de Bonne-Fontaine ⊘ – *1.5km/1mi south. Leave Antrain by Rues Général-Lavigne and Bonne-Fontaine.*

Built in 1547 as a feudal manor-house and remodelled in the 19C, this castle rises in the centre of a beautifully maintained park. The elegant turrets adorning the massive main range, the tall windows and the carved dormer windows balance the severity of the squat, machicolated pepper-pot towers.

Château de la Balue – *5km/2.5mi southwest of Antrain on D 313 which intersects D 155, turn right towards Bazouges-la-Pérouse, then follow the signs.* In the eyes of some Romantic writers, this residence symbolised the royalist rebellion, and for this reason was visited by Musset, Balzac and Hugo. The English garden holds many surprises for the visitor.

CONCARNEAU★★

Population 18 630
Michelin map 58 fold 15 or 20 folds 32 and 33

Concarneau offers a fascinating picture of a bustling fishing port, the charm of a walled town, enclosed in granite ramparts, and the facilities of a popular resort. France's first fishing port, it is the leading market for tunny caught in African waters and in the Indian Ocean, and possesses three fish canneries and holds a colourful **fresh fish auction** *(criée)* ⊘.

There is an attractive **general view★** of Concarneau, its fishing port and the bay from Moros Bridge (Pont du Moros) on entering the town by ② on the town plan.

The **Fêtes des Filets Bleus★** (Blue Nets Festival; *see Calendar of events*) includes various folk events (dances and processions in local costumes). First held in 1905, it was originally organised to aid sardine fishermen and their families.

Annually on 14 July, in celebration of Bastille Day, about 100 old sailing ships gather in the bay.

★★WALLED TOWN (VILLE CLOSE) *2hr*

Narrow alleys cover the islet of irregular shape (350 x 100m/1 150 x 330ft) linked to the mainland by two small bridges between which stands a fortified building. Massive ramparts, built in the 14C and completed in the 17C, surround the town. Cross the two small bridges and pass under a gateway leading to a fortified inner courtyard. There is a fine well.

★Musée de la Pêche ⊘ **(M¹)** – This fishing museum is located in what used to be the arsenal which also served as barracks and a fishing school. In the courtyard *Commandant Garreau*, a lifeboat built in 1894, is exhibited. Accompanying notices, models, photographs, dioramas, and some 10 boats explain the history of Concarneau, its evolution as a port, traditional and modern fishing techniques (whale, cod, sardine, tuna, herring), boats, canning industry, shipbuilding, navigational equipment and rescue operations.

A large hall is devoted to exhibits relating to fishing in distant waters: an Azores whaleboat among other boats, a harpoon gun, a giant Japanese crab, a coelacanth (a fish whose origins date back 300 million years). The aquariums hold fish and other forms of marine life.

Outside (via Major's Tower – Tour du Major) a fishing boat is moored; climb aboard *Hémérica*, a trawler put out of commission in 1981, and relive the hard life of the fishermen.

Walk round the ramparts ⊘ – *Follow the signs. For the first part of the tour, go up a few steps on the left and follow the wall walk.*

Glimpses of the inner harbour and the fishing fleet can be caught through the loopholes. You also get an overall impression of the New Tower (Tour Neuve).

For the second part of the tour, return by the same path to the starting-point and descend the steps. After skirting Esplanade du Petit Château, giving onto the marina, you overlook the channel between the two harbours.

When you reach a big tower turn a sharp left and go down a ramp to a walkway beneath the ramparts. Return to the town by Porte du Passage. By the corner of the Hospice take rue St-Guénolé, which bears left towards place St-Guénolé.

From place St-Guénolé a short alley to the right leads to **Porte aux Vins** (Wine Gateway) through the ramparts. As you go through the gate *(porte)* you will get a typical view of the trawlers moored in the harbour. Rue Vauban brings you back out of the walled town.

ADDITIONAL SIGHTS

The harbours – By way of avenue Pierre-Guéguin and Quai Carnot, take a quick look at the fishing port *(port de pêche)*, where the main fishing fleet (trawlers and cargo boats) is moored; you may see the day's catch being unloaded. Then follow avenue du Dr-P.-Nicolas and walk round the pleasure boat harbour. The embarkation point for excursions is at the end of this quay, on the left.

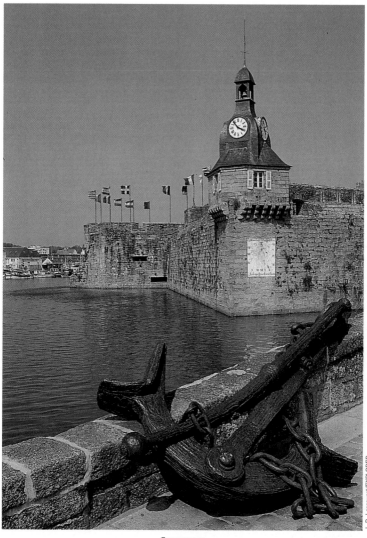

Concarneau

On the left of Quai de la Croix is the marine laboratory (Laboratoire Maritime) of the Collège de France. Inside visit the **Marinarium** ⊘ (**B M²**), an exhibition devoted to the sea world: aquariums, dioramas and audio-visual displays.

After passing the picturesque old fish market where fish used to be sold by auction, the 15C Chapelle Notre-Dame-de-Bon-Secours and a small lighthouse, you may skirt Port de la Croix (follow boulevard Bougainville), which is sheltered by a jetty. Looking back, there is a good view of the Pointe du Cabellou and, further on, of the Pointe de Beg-Meil. Out at sea are the Îles Glénan.

The beaches (**A**) – Go along boulevard Katherine-Wylie, which runs beside Mine Beach and affords good views of La Forêt Bay and the Pointe de Beg-Meil, then take boulevard Alfred-Guillou which leads to Cornouaille Beach.

ENVIRONS

Beuzec-Conq –This town is home to the **Kériolet Mansion**, built in the 15C and transformed in the 19C into a medieval-style fantasy dwelling by the wealthy Russian princess Zenaïde Narischkine-Youssopoff.

Rosporden – The church **bell-tower**★ is reflected in a pool formed by the River Aven. There are many canning factories in the town which is also famous for its mead (*chouchen* in Breton).The building dates from the 14C-15C and was remodelled in the 17C.

Hotels

OUR SELECTION

Hôtel de l'Océan – *Plage des Sables Blancs* – ☏ *02 98 50 53 50* – 🅿 – *56 rooms 490/600F – breakfast 52F – restaurant 99/260F.* Facing the beach, this modern hotel on the side of the road has improved its comfort over the years. Its rooms are relatively spacious, sound-proof, and functional. The restaurant, decorated like a cruise liner, has been entirely redone.

Ker Moor – *Plage des Sables Blancs* – ☏ *02 98 97 02 96* – 🅿 – *12 rooms 320/450F – breakfast 40F.* Right on the sea, this turn-of-the-century villa's discreet façade hides a resolutely maritime decor: white wainscotting, engravings, photos and ship models. All the rooms open onto the sea; three of them have terraces.

Eating Out

BUDGET

Chez Armande – *15 bis avenue du Dr-Nicolas* – ☏ *02 98 97 00 76* – *closed 20 Dec-4 Jan, Feb school holidays, Wed, Tues evenings except in summer* – *96/188F.* A very nice stop, facing the pleasure port. There's a small bar at the entrance, and its straw-bottomed chairs and pretty ceiling give it a warm and friendly atmosphere. Delightful cuisine at very good prices.

La Porte au Vin – *9 place St-Guénolé (Ville Close)* – ☏ *02 98 97 38 11* – *closed mid-Nov to mid-Dec, 3 Jan-8 Feb and 7-31 Mar* – *63/120F.* This building is located right beside one of the doors to the old walled city, which in days past allowed wine to be delivered. Its reasonably priced dishes are served in an authentic decor of stone, beams, grand fireplaces, old-time photos and paintings of the region.

OUR SELECTION

Coquille – *Quai Moros* – ☏ *02 98 97 08 52* – *closed 10 Jan-10 Feb, Mon, Sun evenings except in summer* – *150/390F.* This seafood restaurant is located on the fishing port, but first one must pass through a local bar to get there. In the three comfortable dining rooms, you can taste seafood and the chef's selection of local specialities.

Recreation

Beaches – The boulevard Katherine-Wylie follows the Miné beach and offers beautiful views over the bay, then le boulevard Alfred-Guillou leads to Cornouaille beach. Further on is the Sables Blancs beach.

Boat trips – Motorboat service is available to the Isles de Glénan, and on excursions on the River Odet. In season, a motorboat links Concarneau to Beg-Meil.

Festivals – The **Fête des Filets Bleus★**, begun in 1905 to aid sardine fisherman and their families, has taken on a folkloric look with lively groups in costume, dancing and parades.

EXCURSIONS

From Concarneau to Pont-Aven by the coast road – *45km/28mi – about 2hr. Leave Concarneau by ② on the town plan towards Quimperlé and after 2.5km/1.25mi bear right.*

★**Pointe du Cabellou** – *Go round the point starting from the right.* The car park affords a fine **view★** of the site of Concarneau and the walled town. The road skirts the rocky coastline amid the villas and pine trees and offers pretty views of Baie de la Forêt and the Îles de Glénan.

Return to the main road and make for Quimperlé. Turn right at Pont-Minaouët and right again at Kermao.

The road goes through **Pouldohan** (fine beach and large sailing school) and Pendruc.

Pointe de la Jument – *15min on foot there and back.* Fine rocky site and view of Cabellou, the bay and Beg-Meil, and the coast of Loctudy in the distance.

Make for the Pointe de Trévignon going via Lambell where you turn right, Lanénos and Ruat.

On the way, note the vertical granite panels forming the walls of the farm buildings.

Pointe de Trévignon – An old fort stands at the tip of the headland; fishing boats and the lifeboat are berthed in the tiny port to the west. Fine **view★** to the right of La Forêt Bay and Beg-Meil, Bénodet Bay, and on the left of the Îles de Glénan and near the coast of Verte and Raguenès Islands.

Follow the road along Kersidan Beach. Bear right onto the Glénan coast road, a good viewing platform; continue along rue de Beg-Foz and turn right.

Raguenès-Plage – Sheltered by Raguenès Island which can be reached at half tide.

Continue in the direction of Port-Manech. At Trémorvézen, turn right after the chapel.

Kerascoët – A quiet hamlet with typical thatched farms.

The road then descends to the **Anse de Rospico** (Rospico Bay), a small cove with a beach.

At Kerangall, turn right towards Port-Manech. The remainder of the excursion is described in the opposite direction under PONT-AVEN: Excursions.

From Concarneau to Bénodet by the coast road – *40km/25mi – about 3hr. The excursion is described in the opposite direction under BÉNODET: Excursions.*

CORNICHE BRETONNE★★

Michelin map 59 fold 1 or 20 folds 6 and 7

The scenic Breton coast road which joins Perros-Guirec and Trébeurden, following the Pink Granite coast which starts at the Pointe de l'Arcouest, is quite probably one of the most interesting runs in north Brittany.

The strange forms of the enormous rocks, which are the attraction of the Corniche Bretonne, are due to erosion. Granite is composed of quartz, mica and feldspar. The feldspar turns into kaolin (china clay), which is washed away by water, and the residue of quartz grains makes sand, which is carried away by rain and waves. Little by little, the stone changes shape and takes on surprising forms: almost perfect spheres, chiselled and fretted masses, boldly balanced piles and swaying stones. Erosion here has been very severe because the rocks are coarse grained and, therefore, easily broken up.

Local imagination has given names to some of the rocks: Napoleon's Hat, St Yves, the Gnome, the Witch, the Death's Head, the Elephant, the Whale, the Ram, the Rabbit, the Tortoise, the Horse, the Thimble, the Torpedo, the Armchair, the Umbrella, the Sentinel, the Corkscrew etc.

FROM PERROS-GUIREC TO TREBEURDEN
27km/17mi – 6hr – local map see below

Perros-Guirec – *See PERROS-GUIREC.*
After the town of Perros-Guirec, the road skirts the small hill on which the signal station stands and a **view★** opens up straight ahead onto the rocks of Ploumanach, seaward of Sept-Îles, looking back of the beaches of Perros-Guirec and, in the distance, of the Port-Blanc coast.

Chapelle Notre-Dame-de-la-Clarté – *See PERROS-GUIREC.*

★★ Ploumanach – *See PLOUMANACH.*

Trégastel-Plage – *See TRÉGASTEL-PLAGE.*
As you leave the village, on the right, at the end of a short rise, you get a view looking backwards, of Sept-Îles.
After 1.2km/0.8mi, turn left and then right.

Dolmen and Allée couverte de Kerguntuil – From the dolmen, by the roadside to the left, the passage grave can be seen at the end of a field; it is reached by walking in front of the farm buildings.
Then the road runs close to the sea, at high tide the shore can become wild and picturesque. It is a strange coast, dotted with islands and reefs.
Soon after a discotheque, right off the road, a dolmen looks down onto Kerivon shore.
Turn left towards Pleumeur-Bodou. At Penvern, bear left after the Café du Menhir.

★ Menhir de St-Uzec – A giant menhir is surmounted by a Crucifixion with instruments of the Passion surrounding the figure of a praying woman.
Take the road below the menhir to rejoin the Pleumeur-Bodou road, then turn left and 400m/437yd further on, left again.

Pleumeur-Bodou – This village, situated between Lannion and Penvern, has given its name to the radar dome, near which a telecommunications museum and planetarium have been set up.

★ Radôme and Musée des Télécommunications ⊘ – The Pleumeur-Bodou telecommunications centre, inaugurated in 1962 and situated 1km/0.6mi from the sea between Lannion and the pink granite coast, is the historic site of the first transatlantic communication via the satellite **Telstar** between France and the United States (Andover) on 11 July 1962. Besides the radar dome and the museum, the Pleumeur-Bodou site is occupied by a dozen or so giant antennae which communicate with the five continents.
The **Telecommunications Museum**, situated in a building shaped like an immense Delta wing, retraces one and a half centuries of inventions, progress and continuously updated technology.

★ Planétarium du Trégor ⊘ – Beneath a dome (20m/65.5ft in diameter), the spectator travels through the universe. In the entrance hall is an exhibit on astronomy and astrophysics.

Musée des Télécommunications and Radôme

Île Grande – *Cross the bridge*. The island offers a landscape of heaths bordered by blue granite shores. There are megalithic remains, in particular a passage grave *(allée couverte)* northeast of the village.

A sort of hospital for seabirds, this **Station ornithologique** ⊘ presents different bird species (guillemot, herring gull, black-headed gull, puffin, northern gannet and razorbill) on Sept-Îles. An audio-visual system provides a glimpse of the northern gannet in its natural habitat.

Return to the coast road and turn left towards Trébeurden.

⌂ **Trébeurden** – This seaside resort has several beaches; the two main ones are well situated and separated by the rocky peninsula of Le Castel: Pors-Termen Beach, which is a continuation of the Trozoul opposite the harbour and Tresmeur Beach which is much larger and more frequented.

★**Le Castel** – *30min on foot there and back. Follow a path along the isthmus (car park) between the two beaches of Trozoul and Tresmeur.*
Le Castel commands an extensive **view**★ of the coast and the Milliau *(access by boat or on foot during low tide)*, Molène, Grande and Losquet Islands.

★**Pointe de Bihit** – *Round tour of 4km/2.5mi. The Porz-Mabo road overlooks Tresmeur Beach and offers views of Grande, Molène and Milliau Islands. Take the road to the right.*
From the viewing table there is a fine **view**★ of the coast from the Île de Batz and Roscoff right over to the Île Grande and Triagoz Lighthouse out to sea with Trébeurden and its beaches down below.

The road, which has covered a quarter of a circle, goes on to Porz-Mabo, a nice sand beach. A road goes from the beach to Trébeurden.

CORNICHE DE L'ARMORIQUE★

Michelin map 58 folds 6 and 7 or 20 fold 6

This short section of the Channel coast, which is part of the Golden Belt and is also known as the heather coast, should be seen by all tourists who visit northern Brittany. The Lieue de Grève, a long, majestic stretch of sand, is followed by steep headlands skirted from a distance by the Armorican coast road proper.

FROM ST-MICHEL-EN-GRÈVE TO MORLAIX

59km/37mi – 5hr

St-Michel-en-Grève – A small seaside resort. The church is nicely situated near the sea.

★**Lieue de Grève** – This magnificent beach, 4km/2.5mi long, lies at the bottom of a bay which goes out 2km/1mi at low tide. Trout streams run into the sea through small green valleys. The road, which is very picturesque, follows the wooded coast and skirts the rocky mass of the Grand Rocher.

★**Climbing the Grand Rocher** – *45min on foot there and back.* A road to the left, just before the Grand Rocher, leads to a car park nearby from which a path runs to this 80m/261ft vantage point. There is a very fine **view**★ of the Lieue de Grève. At high tide and especially with a northwesterly blowing in winter, the sight of the endless foaming rollers breaking on the beach and dashing against the seawall that protects D 786 gives an excellent idea of the undertow.

St-Efflam – Next to the Chapelle St-Efflam, half hidden by lush vegetation, there is a fountain, which is surmounted by a massive dome. Efflam, a hermit who came from Ireland, landed with seven companions in AD 470 on the beach of the same name.
Bear left towards Plestin.

Plestin-les-Grèves – It was here that Efflam lived, founded a monastery and died in AD 512. The 16C **church**, which burned down in 1944, has been restored; it contains the tomb of St Efflam adorned with his recumbent figure (1576). In the south aisle, to the left of the altar, a statue shows him vanquishing a dragon, the symbol of paganism. Modern stained-glass windows.
Near the port of Toul-an-Hery, the Hogolo Roman baths have recently been unearthed and are gradually being restored.
Return to the coast road.

★**Corniche de l'Armorique** – Between St-Efflam and Locquirec the road picturesquely follows the heavily indented coast. After the Pointe de Plestin there is a fine view of the cove of Locquirec and its headland at high tide. Before reaching the village you will see, on the right and in the distance, the Corniche Bretonne as far as Trébeurden; and on crossing the bridge, to the left is the attractive Tour d'Argent Manor-House.

⌂ **Locquirec** – Built on a rocky peninsula, Locquirec is a small fishing port and marina as well as a seaside resort.
Once the property of the Knights of Malta, the charming **church**★ has a Renaissance turreted bell-tower. Inside, the panelled vaults of the chancel and transept are covered with 18C paintings. At the high altar is a 16C **altarpiece**★ illustrating scenes of the Passion in high relief in a simple style. On the left of the chancel is a niche containing the statue of Our Lady of Succour, flanked by a Tree of Jesse and six low-relief sculptures depicting the life of the Virgin. In the south transept there is a 15C Trinity. In the nave, spanned by a handsome rood beam, and to the left against the pillar nearest to the chancel, is a 16C alabaster Pietà.

★**Pointe de Locquirec** – *30min on foot there and back.* A walk starting near the church's east end round the Pointe de Locquirec offers fine views of Lannion Bay and coastline.
Beyond the mill, Moulin de la Rive, take the coast road overhanging the sea.

Marc'h Sammet Viewing Table – Built on a rocky headland, it commands splendid **views**★: to the east the beaches of Moulin de la Rive and the Sables Blancs and the rocky Point du Corbeau; to the north the Île de Losquet; to the west the Poul Rodou Beach (access 800m/2 265ft below).

Go to the village of Christ and turn right. Follow the signposts to the scenic road (route touristique).

From the coast road there is a good view of the coast from the Pointe de Trégastel to the Pointe de Primel.

At St-Jean-du-Doigt Beach, bear left.

★**St-Jean-du-Doigt** – This picturesque village owes its name to the relic kept in its church since the 15C. It celebrates its *pardon*, which is attended particularly by people suffering from ophthalmia, on the last Sunday in June.
The Parish close has a 16C triumphal gateway and, on the left, a pretty Renaissance **fountain**★ dominated by God the Father blessing the baptism of His Son performed by St John the Baptist. To the right of the church porch is a small chapel (1577) adorned inside with a frieze and sculpted beams.

★**Church** – St John the Baptist's finger, which was brought to the Chapelle St-Mériadoc c 1420, worked miracles. The construction of a great church was started in 1440, but building went slowly and was finished only in 1513 thanks to the generosity of Anne of Brittany.
The church, built in the Flamboyant style, has a flat east end. The bell-tower, which has lost its spire, abuts onto the first bay in the nave, which includes eight bays in all. At its base, abutting onto the buttresses, are two small ossuaries; that on the right is Gothic, the other, Renaissance in style.
The **treasury**★★ ⊘ contains several reliquaries, one of which holds the first joint of the index finger of St John the Baptist. There is also a **processional cross**★. The finest piece is a silver-gilt Renaissance **chalice**★★.

Plougasnou – At the centre of this small town, the church, which is mostly 16C, has a Renaissance porch opening onto the square. In the chancel are fine 17C altar-pieces. In the south aisle, the Chapelle de Kéricuff closed off by an elegant Gothic arcade in oak contains a 16C wooden Trinity. A road from the church's east end leads (300m/328yd from town) to the **Oratoire Notre-Dame-de-Lorette**, a granite oratory with a stone roof and two telamones framing the entrance.

Take the road past the tourist office and at the third junction turn right.

Go through Ste-Barbe. On the way down, the view extends over Primel, the beach, point and rocks.

★**Primel-Trégastel** – This beach of fine sand lies in a good setting near rocks comparable with those of Ploumanach and Trégastel.

★**Pointe de Primel** – *30min on foot there and back.* The point is a jumble of pink rocks. From the central spur, there is a fine **panorama** extending from the Baie de St-Pol-de-Léon to the Trébeurden coast. Out at sea are the Île de Batz Lighthouse and the Sept-Îles. The tip of the point is separated from the rest of the peninsula by a fissure (which can be crossed at low tide); a cave lies at the bottom of it.

After 1km/0.6mi turn right. The road passes near the fish ponds.

Pointe de Diben – At Le Diben, a picturesque fishing village, turn right in the direction of the fish farms (Viviers-le-Port) and port; 100m/110yd further on take the road opposite towards the port which leads to a dike. Just before this, bear left onto a path leading to the Pointe Diben: fine view over the bay and of the Pointe de Primel. Return to D 46^A2 and follow a road to the right towards Port-Blanc, which gives access to a car park from which a track *(15min on foot there and back)* leads to a rock jutting out over the sea: lovely view of Port-Blanc Islet.
The road passes the attractive Guerzit and St-Samson Beaches on the right.

Térénez – This small, very pleasant and typically Breton port is a sailing centre.
The coast road offers **glimpses**★ of Morlaix estuary, the Château du Taureau and the peninsula topped by the Cairn de Barnenez.

At the entrance to St-Gonven, turn right.

★**Cairn de Barnenez** – *See MORLAIX: Excursions.*

Continue in the direction of Morlaix.

Beyond Plouézoch, a fine tree-lined road descends into the picturesque valley of Le Dourduff where the fleet of spruce fishing boats belonging to the small oyster port of **Le Dourduff** is moored. After the bridge, the coast road runs along the River Morlaix and gives views of the sand dredging port, the yachting port with its lock, and the charming setting of the town, river and viaduct.

ENVIRONS

Château de Rosanbo – The **château** ⊘ stands on the foundations of an old 14C castle, overlooking the Bô Valley, hence its Breton name meaning "rock *(ros)* on the *(an)* Bô".
The different periods of construction can be seen as you enter the courtyard: the 15C manor-house to the west, which was enlarged in the 17C (with mansard roofs) and 18C, and finally restored in the 19C.

The rooms open to the public are furnished and decorated with good taste: seigneurial chapel, Breton room, kitchen, dining room and neo-Gothic drawing room. Archive documents have recently made it possible to reconstruct the most authentic rooms of the residence, the dining room and the 18C drawing room. The **library** contains over 8 000 volumes dating mainly from the 17C. The vast room overlooks a terrace with an enormous ornamental pond.

The château is bordered to the northeast by a magnificent **French style garden**, which is the work of Achille Duchêne, the famous 19C landscape architect. Note in particular the **hedges**, almost 2 500m/2 734yd long, and the green arbours (small clearings in shrubs) which once had specific functions, such as horse-riding ring, training area, tennis area etc.

Lanmeur – The small town of Lanmeur is situated in a market garden area on the Trégorrois Plateau. Only the crypt and the bell-tower of the original **church** have been retained in the edifice rebuilt in 1904. Note the curious statue of St Mélar. The pre-Romanesque **crypt**★ *(access to the left of the main altar, light switch at the foot of the stairway)* is ascribed to the 8C and is one of the oldest religious buildings in Brittany. The vaulting rests on eight massive pillars, two of which are decorated. A fountain stands to the right of the west door.

Excavations have brought to light two rare and very old (perhaps 6C) carved gold figurines.

In the cemetery close, the impressive **Chapelle de Kernitron** has a 12C nave and transept and 15C chancel. Look at the outside of the Romanesque doorway of the south transept: the tympanum depicts Christ in Majesty surrounded by the symbols of the Evangelists.

Inside, at the entrance to the south aisle, there is a fine carved wooden screen; in the nave, a rood beam carries Christ on the Cross between the Virgin and St John; to the right of the high altar stands a statue of Christ in Fetters and in the chapel facing the entrance a statue of Our Lady of Kernitron (*pardon* on 15 August) with, to the right in a small chapel, a charming statue of St Anne and the Virgin.

CORNOUAILLE★★

Michelin map 58 folds 13, 14 and 15 or 20 folds 16, 17, 18, 31 and 32

Historic Cornouaille, the kingdom and then the duchy of medieval Brittany, extended far to the north and east of its capital, Quimper, reaching Landerneau, the neighbourhood of Morlaix and Quimperlé.

The area included in our tour is much smaller and is limited to the coastal districts of Cornouaille, west of Quimper. This very extensive coastline is marked by two rocky peninsulas, Cap Sizun, "Le Cap", and the Presqu'île de Penmarch, which are its main tourist attractions. This is a maritime country in which fishing plays an important role; the ports of Guilvinec, Audierne and Douarnenez specialise in sardines and spiny lobster.

The interior is densely cultivated (potatoes and early vegetables), and the countryside with its tranquil horizons is covered with small hamlets of whitewashed houses.

CAP

★★CAP SIZUN

From Quimper to Plozévet

158km/98mi – one day

★★**Quimper** – *See QUIMPER.*

Leave Quimper northwest by rue de Locronan and rue de la Providence.

The road goes up the rural valley of the Steïr with its wooded slopes and then through undulating countryside.

Plogonnec – The 16C **church**, remodelled in the 18C, has a fine Renaissance bell-tower; it also has 16C stained-glass windows; in the chancel to the left of the high altar the windows recount the Transfiguration, above the altar the Passion and to the right the Last Judgement. At the entrance to the *placître* at the east end of the church, there is a Gothic triumphal arch.

★★**Locronan** – *See LOCRONAN.*

The Douarnenez road with Forest of Nevet on its left, leads to the sea.

Kerlaz – 16C and 17C church with a pierced bell-tower.
There is a good view of Douarnenez, which is reached after skirting the fine Ris Beach.

★**Douarnenez** – *See DOUARNENEZ.*

Leave Douarnenez, go through Tréboul and make for Poullan-sur-Mer where you turn left and then right and right again.

Chapelle Notre-Dame-de-Kérinec – The chapel, surrounded by trees, dates from the 13C and 15C; the elegant bell-tower was struck by lightning in 1958 but an exact replica, as it appeared in the 17C, has been rebuilt. Note the flat east end and to the left the rounded pulpit dominated by a Calvary. Inside, look at the massive pillars of the transept crossing which suggest that a central bell-tower was to be built but the project was most likely abandoned and in its place, a belfry-porch was erected.

Église Notre-Dame-de-Confort – The 16C church with its galleried bell-tower dating from 1736, has 16C **stained-glass windows** in the chancel, one of which is a Tree of Jesse. Over the last arch in the nave, on the north side, hangs a carillon wheel with 12 little bells. The chimes are rung to beg the Virgin for the gift of speech for children who have difficulties in speaking.
Alongside the chapel is a Calvary with a triangular base dating from the 16C; the 13 statues of the Apostles were redone in 1870.

Leave Confort in the direction of Pont-Croix and turn right, then left towards Beuzec-Cap-Sizun and again right after 2km/1mi.

★**Pointe du Millier** – A small lighthouse stands on this arid site. From the point *(15min on foot there and back)* there is a **view**★ of Douarnenez Bay and Cap de la Chèvre.

On leaving Beuzec-Cap-Sizun bear right.

SIZUN

A cormorant from the Réserve
du Cap Sizun

D'après photo J.-L. Lemorque/AZIMUT

Lapwing

★**Pointe de Beuzec** – From the car park there is a **view**★ of the approach to Douarnenez Bay, the Presqu'île de Crozon and in fine weather, of the Pointe de St-Mathieu.

★**Réserve du Cap Sizun** ⊙ – The most interesting time for a visit is at nesting time in the spring. Starting in March, most birds finish nesting by mid July. The adults and chicks then leave the sanctuary progressively through the month of August. In the magnificent and wild setting of the Castel-ar-Roc'h, more than 70m/230ft above sea level, such seabirds as guillemots, cormorants, common herring gulls, lesser black-backed gulls, great black-backed gulls, which are the rarest of all, and black-legged kittiwakes can be seen, sitting on their nests and feeding their young.

★**Pointe de Brézellec** – *Park the car by the lighthouse enclosure.* Go to the rock platforms nearby. There is a magnificent **view**★ along an exceptionally long stretch of coast of saw-tooth rocks and sheer cliffs: Presqu'île de Crozon, Pointe de St-Mathieu, Pointe du Van and Pointe de Tévennec can be seen. A narrow road (surfaced) descends steeply to a small fishing port.

Turn back and turn right towards Pointe du Van.

★★**Pointe du Van** – *1hr on foot there and back.* The 15C **Chapelle St-They** stands on the left of the path. On the point itself follow the half-hidden path, bearing always to the left, which goes right round the headland. The Pointe du Van, which is too big to be seen all in one glance, is, nevertheless, less spectacular than the Pointe du Raz, but it has the advantage of being off the tourists' beaten track. There is a **view**★★ of the Pointe de Castelmeur, the Pointe de Brézellec, the Cap de la Chèvre, the Pointe de Penhir, the Pointe de St-Mathieu and the Tas de Pois rocks on the right; the Île de Sein, the Vieille Lighthouse and the Pointe du Raz on the left. It is recommended that you do not climb down the cliffs.

The landscape becomes ever harsher: no trees grow; stone walls and barren moss cover the final headland.

Turn round and take, immediately on the right, a small road which hugs the coast leading to the Baie des Trépassés and affording fine views of the jagged coastline from the Pointe du Raz to the Île de Sein.

Baie des Trépassés – It was once thought that the drowned bodies of those who had been shipwrecked, and which the currents brought to the bay, gave the bay its name of Bay of the Dead. Another, less macabre explanation, based on the existence of a stream that flowed in the marshes, was that the original Breton name for the bay was "*boe an aon*" (bay of the stream), which became "*boe anaon*" (bay of the troubled souls). Now it is believed that the bay was the embarkation point from the mainland for Druids' remains which were taken over to Île de Sein for burial. According to local legend, the town of Is once stood in the little valley which is now covered in marshes.

The swell runs unimpeded into the bay, where it breaks with an impressive display of force.

★★★**Pointe du Raz** – *See Pointe du RAZ.*

Take the road in the direction of Audierne and after 10km/6mi, turn right towards St-Tugen.

★**St-Tugen** – The nave and the tower of the **chapel** are in the 16C Flamboyant Gothic style, the transept and the east end in the 17C Renaissance style. There is a fine south porch surmounted by an elegant pierced tympanum, containing six statues of Apostles in Kersanton granite and three 16C statues of Christ, the Virgin and St Anne.

Inside may be seen interesting 17C furnishings, including several altarpieces and a curious catafalque flanked at each end by statues of Adam and Eve. The baptismal chapel, surrounded with balustrades and painted panels, contains a chimney with granite firedogs. In the chancel the 17C statue of St Tugen stands. There is a 16C fountain below the chapel. A *pardon* is held *(see Calendar of events).*

★**Audierne** – This pleasure port and fishing village (mainly lobster and crabs) lies on the estuary of the Goyen, at the foot of a wooded hill in a **pretty setting**★.

Grands Viviers ⊙ – *Access by Quai Pelletan and the scenic coast road.* This fish farm boasts some 30 pools full of crustaceans (lobster and crab).

La Chaumière ⊙ – *Opposite the fish farm.* The thatched cottage's fine interior contains 17C and 18C Breton furniture as well as objects used in everyday life of that period.

★**Pont-Croix** – A small town built up in terraces on the south bank of the Goyen, also known as the River Audierne. Its narrow streets, hemmed in between old houses, slope picturesquely down to the bridge. A great procession take place there on 15 August. Take Petite and Grande-Rue-Chère; the latter is a charming stepped street. The church, **Notre-Dame-de-Roscudon**★, is interesting with its Romanesque nave dating from the early 13C. The chancel was enlarged in 1290 and the transept was built in 1450 and crowned by the very fine belfry with a steeple 67m/223ft high. There is an elegant south **porch** (late 14C) with three tall decorated gables. Inside, the church contains fine furnishings: in the apsidal chapel is a **Last Supper** carved in high relief in wood (17C); on the right of the chancel, the Chapel of the Rosary (Chapelle du Rosaire) has fine **stained glass** (c 1540); and in the adjacent

Hotels

OUR SELECTION

Hôtel Sterenn – *Route phare d'Eckmühl, 29760 Penmarch – ☎ 02 98 58 60 36 – closed 11 Oct-14 Apr and Mon except from 21 June to 20 Sept –* ▣ *– 16 rooms 350/450F – breakfast 40F – restaurant 80/300F.* Facing the sea, between Saint Guénolé and the Eckmühl lighthouse, this modern hotel is very welcoming. Almost all of its well-kept rooms have bay views. And its restaurant is well-known to food lovers from near and far!

Hôtel Roi Gradlon – *On the beach, 29700 Audierne – ☎ 02 98 70 04 51 – closed 5 Jan-20 Feb –* ▣ *– 19 rooms 330/380F – breakfast 45F – restaurant 130/250F.* All the rooms in this little hotel look onto the sea. It offers simple comforts, but is beautifully situated and provides a good starting point for dis-covering the Cournouaille. Its dining room serves seafood with a good view. Children's menu.

Hôtel La Baie des Trépassés – *29770 La Baie des Trépassés, 3km/1.8mi from the Pointe du Raz via D 784 – ☎ 02 98 70 61 34 – closed 5 Jan-12 Feb –* ▣ *– 27 rooms 280/376F – breakfast 42F – restaurant 102/295F.* The location of this hotel alone is worth making a detour. It stands on the beach, 3km/6mi from the Pointe du Raz, and offers a unique view over the bay, the Pointe and the Île de Sein. Its rooms resemble the rest of the establishment: functional and clean. There is a bar, an ice-cream salon, and a restaurant.

Eating Out

BUDGET

L'Étrave – *Route de la pointe du Van sur D 7, 2km/1mi, 29770 Cléden-Cap-Sizun – ☎ 02 98 70 66 87 – closed 2 Nov-27 Mar and Wed – 90/260F.* Opposite the Pointe de Brezellec, this restaurant looks like a private home. Inside, it is decorated with a touch of maritime decor, which is reinforced by the ceiling in the shape of an inverted boat's hull. The food is simple and fresh. Children's menu.

OUR SELECTION

La Pêcherie – *15 rue Pasteur, 29770 Audierne – ☎ 02 98 75 04 26 – 105/160F.* "No meat, no French fries, no frozen food": that's the motto of this nice little bistro located slightly back from the port. Its fresh fish, garden vegetables and its convivial atmosphere make it an essential stop. Whether you come for a full course meal, or just one dish, you will always receive a warm welcome.

Sports

Scuba diving at Cap-Sizun – Club des plongeurs du cap Sizun – *Open year round – ☎ 02 98 70 24 10.* This club organises diving outings for novices and for the more advanced. (A medical certificate certifying no physical counter-indications to scuba-diving is required).

Surfing at La Torche – École de surf de Bretagne "Beg An Torchen" – *La Torche – ☎ 02 98 58 53 80 – open Easter-Oct.*

Deep-sea fishing – On board the Yannick – *At Lechiagat (near Guilvinec) – ☎ 02 98 58 10 10.* The excursion lasts half a day.

BEACHES IN AUDIERNE

Beach Clubs – Les Dauphins (☎ 02 98 70 08 47) at the big Trescadec Beach, and Le Jardin des Mers at the Ste-Evette beach.

Sea kayaking – *Quai Ouest* – ☎ 02 98 70 12 20.

Wind-surfing – *At Esquibien* – ☎ 02 98 70 21 69. Le Club Nautique de la Baie d'Audierne is open all year.

Chapel of the Holy Family (Chapelle de la Sainte-Famille) and the Chapel of the Dead (Chapelle des Trépassés) in the north transept are stained-glass windows by Gruber (1977-78). The organ loft dates from the 16C.

Go to Plouhinec, the native town of the sculptor Quillivic, and after the church turn right towards **Pors-Poulhan**, a tiny port sheltered by a pier. Before Plozévet, there are fine views of Audierne Bay and the Phare d'Eckmühl.

Plozévet – There is a 15C porch to the Gothic church. Five arches in the wooden vaulted nave are Romanesque and date from the 12C. To the right of the building flows a sacred fountain. A menhir has been placed here as a 1914-18 war memorial.

Follow the route 1km/0.6mi further north.

Chapelle de la Trinité – The chapel is T-shaped; the nave was built in the 14C and the remainder added in the 16C. Outside note the charming Louis XII decoration (transitional style between Gothic and Renaissance with Italian influence) of two walls on the south transept side. Inside, the nave arches come down onto groups of columns with florally decorated capitals.

★PRESQU'ÎLE DE PENMARCH

From Plozévet to Quimper

100km/62mi – half a day

The journey is made through *bigouden* country, which has become known through the women's local costume, in particular their unique headdress in the shape of a little lace menhir.

From Plozévet to the tip of Penmarch Peninsula the sea breaks against a great sweep of shingle, continually rolling and knocking the stones of the some 20km/12mi arc. The even coastline is altogether inhospitable and desolate. The little villages with their white houses, which lie back from the coast, turn to the hinterland for their livelihood.

The **Presqu'île de Penmarch** was one of the richest regions in Brittany up to the end of the 16C: cod-fishing (the "lenten meat") brought wealth to the 15500 inhabitants. But then the cod deserted the coastal waters, and a tidal wave brought devastation. Final disaster came with the brigand **La Fontenelle** who took the locality by surprise in spite of its defences. He killed 5000 peasants, burned down their houses and loaded 300 boats with booty which he then took back to his stronghold on the Île Tristan.

Plozévet – *Description above.*

Leave Plozévet south towards Penhors; the road then follows the coastline.

Penhors – *For access to the chapel, make for the beach.* On the first Sunday in September the great *pardon* of Notre-Dame-de-Penhors, one of the largest of Cornouaille *(see Calendar of events)* takes place. The night before (Saturday) there

Ruined chapel at Languidou

Ch. Braud/DIAF

PRESQU'ÎLE DE PENMARCH

is a procession with torches. On Sunday afternoon the procession walks through the countryside until it comes to the shore line and back to the chapel where the benediction of the sea takes place.

Proceed to Plovan.

Plovan – A small 16C **church** adorned with beautifully coloured modern (1944) stained-glass windows and a fine turreted belfry. Nearby is a 16C Calvary.

Chapelle de Languidou – The ruined 13-15C chapel still has some interesting elements, particularly the fine rose window.

Make for Plonéour-Lanvern via Tréogat.

Chapelle de Languivoa ⊘ – *1.5km/1mi to the east of Plonéour-Lanvern.* This 14C and 17C chapel (restored) forms an imposing ensemble adorned by rose windows and Gothic arcading. The dismantled belfry porch still dominates the devastated nave and Classical style entrance with its engaged Doric columns. The chapel contains the Virgin of Notre-Dame-de-Languivoa suckling her child. A pardon is held on 15 August.

At Plonéour-Lanvern take the road to Plomeur and after 2km/1mi turn right.

★★**Calvaire and Chapelle Notre-Dame-de-Tronoën** – The Calvary and Chapelle of Notre-Dame-de-Tronoën stand beside Audierne Bay, in the bare and wild landscape of the dunes.

The **Calvary**★★ (1450-60) is the oldest in Brittany. The childhood and Passion of Christ are recounted on two friezes. The intensity and originality of the 100 figures are remarkable. Details of the sculpted figures, although worn by exposure, can be fully appreciated. The scenes are depicted in the round or in high relief in a coarse granite from Scaer, which is friable and tends to attract lichen (the Last Supper and the Last Judgment on the south face are greatly damaged). Three scenes on the north face are in Kersanton granite: the Visitation, an unusual Nativity with a sleeping Joseph and the Magi in 15C vestment. Christ and the thieves are also carved in hard granite.

The 15C **chapel** has a pierced belfry, flanked by turrets. Beneath the vaulted roof are old statues. The ornate south door opens on to the Calvary. A *pardon* takes place annually *(see Calendar of events)*.

Continue along the road bearing right and right again.

Pointe de la Torche – The name is a corruption of the Breton "Beg an Dorchenn": flat stone point. Fine **view**★ of the St-Guénolé rocks and Audierne Bay. There is a tumulus with a large dolmen.

Plage de Pors-Carn – This great sandy beach along La Torche Bay is the terminal point of the telephone cable linking France and the USA.

★Musée préhistorique finistérien ⊘ – *At the entrance to St-Guénolé.* A series of megaliths and Gallic steles or obelisks called lec'hs stand around the museum. Start the visit from the left to see the exhibits in chronological order, from the Stone Age to the Gallo-Roman period. On display are, in the first gallery, a reconstruction of an Iron Age necropolis, Gallic pottery with Celtic decorations and a Gallic stele with spiral carving; in the south gallery, polished axes of rare stone, flint arrowheads, bronze weapons and chests with grooves.

The museum contains all the prehistorical antiquities discovered in Finistère except for the rich collection displayed in the Musée des Antiquités Nationales at St-Germain-en-Laye *(see the Michelin Green Guide to Flanders, Picardy and the Paris Region).*

St-Guénolé – The modern church is charming although a little dark; it stands near the old square tower, all that remains of the 15C church. Behind the fishing port (coastal fishing) are the famous **rocks** against which the sea breaks furiously.

Chapelle Notre-Dame-de-la-Joie – This 15C chapel with its pierced bell-tower is flanked by turrets. The 16C Calvary is adorned with a Pietà. A *pardon* is held on 15 August.

★Phare d'Eckmühl ⊘ – Eckmühl Lighthouse stands at the very end of the Pointe de Penmarch. The lighthouse is 65m/213ft tall and its light of 2 million candlepower has a range of 54km/33.5mi. From the gallery at the top of the tower (307 steps) there is a **view★★** of Audierne Bay, the Pointe du Raz, the lighthouse on Île de Sein, the coast of Concarneau and Beg-Meil and the Îles de Glénan. Passing to the left of the lighthouse, you will reach the very tip of the point on which the old lighthouse – it now serves as a marker for ships at sea – a small fortified chapel and a signal station stand. The sea is studded with reefs covered in seaweed.

Further east, as at Penmarch, the coast is a succession of rocky points and dunes.

Kérity – Small fishing port leaning more and more towards pleasure boating. The Église Ste-Thumette (1675) has an elegant gabled front flanked by a turret.

★Penmarch – The parish includes several villages: St-Guénolé, Kérity, Tréoultré and St-Pierre. **St-Nonna★** ⊘ was built in the 16C in the Flamboyant Gothic style.

At the east end and on the buttresses on either side of the doorway, ships and caravels are carved into high or low-relief sculptures, recalling that the church was built with donations from shipowners. A gabled bell-tower crowns the roof. Inside there are several old statues: in the south chapel, St Michael and St Anne carrying the Virgin and Child; in the south aisle hangs the *Vow of Louis XIII.*

Proceed to Guilvinec by the coast road.

Guilvinec – This very active trawler and tunny fishing port has three fish canneries, which handle fish as it is unloaded. With **Lechiagat**, where numerous pleasure boats anchor, it forms a well-sheltered harbour. Beaches unfold behind the dunes as far as Lesconil.

Lesconil – Small but bustling trawler fishing port. A picturesque scene occurs when the boats come in around 5.30pm.

Make for Loctudy via Palue-du-Cosquer and Lodonnec.

Loctudy – *See PONT-L'ABBÉ.*

★Manoir de Kérazan – *See PONT-L'ABBÉ.*

Pont-l'Abbé – *See PONT-L'ABBÉ.*

Leave Pont-l'Abbé by ① on the town plan and return to Quimper.

★★Quimper – *See QUIMPER.*

CÔTE D'ÉMERAUDE★★★

EMERALD COAST – Michelin map 59 folds 4, 5 and 6 or 230 folds 9, 10 and 11

This name is given to the part of the coast between the Pointe du Grouin and Le Val-André, which includes some famous beaches: Dinard, St-Lunaire, Paramé etc and the city of the privateers: St-Malo. The Côte d'Émeraude, which means Emerald Coast, is rocky, heavily indented and very picturesque. A series of points, from which fine panoramas can be seen, project into the sea. The coast is bisected by the Rance estuary. An enjoyable boat excursion between Dinan and St-Malo can be made on the estuary.

The scenic road along the Emerald Coast is among the major tourist attractions of Brittany's north coast. Although it does not hug the coastline all the way, it offers many excursions to the points, enabling the visitor to enjoy spectacular sites with views and panoramas typical of this jagged coastline.

1 FROM CANCALE TO ST-MALO 23km/14mi – 5hr

★**Cancale** – *See CANCALE.*
Leave Cancale by ② on the town plan, turn right towards Pointe du Grouin 300m/about 0.5mi further on.

★★**Pointe du Grouin** – *See CANCALE: Excursion.*
The coast road follows the line of the cliffs as far as Le Verger, offering lovely views.

Chapelle Notre-Dame-du-Verger – *Bear right towards the beach.*
This small chapel, rebuilt in the 19C, is venerated by the sailors of Cancale (pilgrimage 15 August).
Inside there are models of different kinds of sailing vessels: sloops, three-masted ships, schooners etc.
After Le Verger, there is a good view of the Du Guesclin Cove and Island. A small fort stands on it.

La Guimorais – A quiet seaside resort. Chevrets Beach stretches between Pointe du Meinga and the Presqu'île Bénard which encloses the harbour of Rothéneuf on the east.
The road skirts the harbour of Rothéneuf. This stretch of water almost completely empties itself at low tide; the flow of the tides was once used to work a mill.
On the right, the elegant 17C **Château du Lupin**, a *malouinière* built by a wealthy St-Malo shipowner, is of interest.

Rothéneuf and Le Minihic – *See ST-MALO: Rothéneuf.*
The road offers fine glimpses of the Bay of St-Malo.

Paramé – *See ST-MALO: Paramé.*

★★★**St-Malo** – *See ST-MALO.*
St-Malo extends southwards to St-Servan-sur-Mer.

2 FROM ST-MALO TO DINARD

Here the tourist has a choice of two excursions *(see Vallée de la RANCE)*:
The **crossing of the Rance estuary**, which goes over the crown of the Rance tidal power scheme *(usine marémotrice)* and affords fine glimpses of the estuary.
A **round tour**★ of the **Vallée de la Rance**★★ *(allow one day)*, a picturesque excursion; the visit to Dinan is worth the detour.

3 FROM DINARD TO CAP FRÉHEL 67km/42mi – 4hr

The coastal road is dotted with pleasant resorts, offering fine sandy beaches.

Dinard – *See DINARD.*
Unfortunately, the road does not follow all the indentations of the coast between Dinard and Cap Fréhel. However, it has interesting overhanging sections and opens up fine panoramas and remarkable scenery. Many fashionable and family resorts lie along the coast.

St-Lunaire – *See DINARD.*

★**Pointe de la Garde Guérin** – *15min on foot* there and back. After crossing the point at its base, turn right onto a road as it descends to the foot of the hill, which is honeycombed with casemates *(car park)*. Climb on foot to the top of the promontory, from which a fine **panorama**★★ extends from Cap Fréhel to Pointe de la Varde.
The road traverses the Dinard golf course (60ha/148 acres).

St-Briac-sur-Mer – This pleasant resort with its picturesque and varied sites, has a fishing harbour and a marina, and many good beaches. There are good views of the coast from the Emerald Balcony (Balcon d'Émeraude) and the Sailors' Cross (Croix des Marins – *access: from the Emerald Balcony by a path on the left, just before a bridge)*.
As you come out of St-Briac cross River Frémur on a bridge 330m/984ft long.
Fine views on the right of the resort and an islet with its castle.

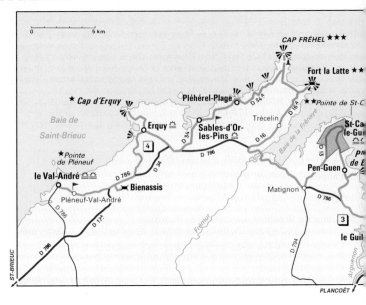

Lancieux – This village has a very extensive beach of fine sand, from which there is a lovely view of Ebihens Island and the advanced points of the coast, St-Jacut-de-la-Mer, St-Cast and Cap Fréhel. In the centre of the village stands the old bell-tower of the former church. The square tower is capped by a dome and its lantern turret.
In Ploubalay take the road towards Dinard and 800m/0.5mi further on turn left.

St-Jacut-de-la-Mer – The road follows a long peninsula and goes through St-Jacut-de-la-Mer, a small fishing port and seaside resort. After skirting the beach of Le Rougeret, you will reach the high and picturesque cliff of the **Pointe du Chevet**; there is a fine **view★** of the Île Ebihens, opposite, and its tower; also, to the left, of the Bay of Arguenon (note the upstanding poles – *bouchots* – where mussels mature) and St-Cast, and to the right of the Bay of Lancieux.

Le Guildo – This village lies in a picturesque setting on the shore of the Arguenon estuary. From the bridge across it you will see, on the east bank, the ruins of Le Guildo Castle. In the 15C this was the seat of Gilles de Bretagne, a carefree and gallant poet, who led a happy life at Le Guildo. However, Gilles was suspected of plotting by his brother, the reigning duke, and thrown into prison. As he did not die fast enough, he was smothered. Before Gilles died he summoned his brother to the judgement of God. A short time later the Duke, prostrate with remorse, expired.

Les Pierres Sonnantes – *3km/2mi west on D 786, the road to Erquy. After the bridge, bear right on the road which goes to the harbour, leave your car on the quay (car park) and take a lane along the Arguenon (15 min there and back).*
Opposite the ruins of the castle *(to the right, on the far bank)*, you will find a pile of rocks known as "the ringing stones" which emit a metallic note when you strike them with a stone of the same type. This resonance is due to the perfectly even grain of the rocks.
Go towards St-Cast by the coastal road.

Pointe de Bay – A good road on the right leads to a large car park. The **view★** includes the Arguenon estuary with its lines of mussel poles and the Presqu'île de St-Jacut and the Île Ebihens.

Pen-Guen – Fashionable fine sandy beach.

★★St-Cast-le-Guildo – *See ST-CAST-LE-GUILDO.*
Leaving St-Cast the road makes a big loop round the head of the bay of La Frênaye.
After Trécelin, take D 16ᴬ which leads to the fort (car park).

★★Fort la Latte – *See Cap FRÉHEL*

★★★Cap Fréhel – *See Cap FRÉHEL.*

④ FROM CAP FRÉHEL TO LE VAL-ANDRÉ
34km/21mi – about 2hr 30min

★★★Cap Fréhel – *See Cap FRÉHEL.*
The tourist road, which twists and turns in the moor, affords striking **views★★** of the sea, cliffs and golden beaches. It goes through pine forest.

Pléhérel-Plage – The beach is on the right after a forest of conifers. A scenic view of Cap Fréhel and, in the foreground, a succession of tiny coves carved into the dunes may be enjoyed.

☖ **Sables-d'Or-les-Pins** – The Channel can be seen through the pine forest. From the fine sandy beach a group of small islands can be distinguished, especially that of St-Michel and its chapel.
After the Plurien intersection, the St-Quay coastline comes into view across St-Brieuc Bay.

As you enter Erquy go towards the cape.

★**Cap d'Erquy** – *30min on foot there and back.* From the point where the road ends, there is an extensive view of grey-pink shingle beaches lapped by clear waters, opposite Caroual Beach, Vallées seashore, the Pointe de Pléneuf and Verdelet Islet and beyond St-Brieuc Bay, the Pointe de l'Arcouest and the Île de Bréhat.
Pleasant footpaths bordered by bracken cross the heath dotted with patches of yellow and mauve and afford glimpses of the reefs: guided tours of this area are organised in July and August.

Hotels

OUR SELECTION

Manoir de la Salle – *Rue du Lac, 22240 Sables-d'Or-les-Pins, 1km/0.6mi southwest via D 34 –* ☎ *02 96 72 38 29 – closed 1 Oct-31 Mar –* 🅿 *– 14 rooms 250/700F – breakfast 40F.* Despite being entirely renovated, this 16C Breton manor house has retained its character: its stone façades are superb. Inside, except for one large salon with a fireplace, all the rooms are modern and functional.

Manoir St-Michel – *At La Carquois, 22240 Sables-d'Or-les-Pins, 1.5km/1mi east via D 34 –* ☎ *02 96 41 48 87 – closed 3 Nov-31 Mar –* 🅿 *– 17 rooms 280/600F – breakfast 42F.* In this old manor house with rose-coloured sandstone walls, you can enjoy the large garden overlooking the sea and a duck-pond. The rooms are slightly out-of-date, but nonetheless are welcoming. Duplex for families; attractive prices off-season.

Hôtel Les Pins – *22240 Sables-d'Or-les-Pins –* ☎ *02 96 41 42 20 – closed 1 Oct-31 Mar – 22 rooms 290F – breakfast 36F – restaurant 68/140F.* A large establishment in a garden planted with pines, of course! This hotel is well-kept and has retained its familial atmosphere, which accounts for its simple and welcoming decor: the rooms are light and the dining room is warm and inviting.

Sport

Golf de St-Briac-sur-Mer – *54, boulevard Houle –* ☎ *02 99 88 32 07.* This 18-hole golf course is open all year, and is one of the oldest in France.

Erquy

⌂ **Erquy** – In the 19C, a number of historians believed that Erquy was located on the alleged site of Reginea, a former Gallo-Roman settlement. It now appears they may have been mistaken. However, due to this misunderstanding, the inhabitants of Erquy have retained the charming name of "*Réginéens*".

Set against a backdrop of rugged cliffs, this busy fishing port (2 000t of scallops in 1993) is gradually extending its influence. Its fishing fleet is made up of around 80 boats specialised in coastal fishing: fish (sole, turbot, gurnard, John Dory) and shellfish (scallops but also clams and queen scallops). Among the many beaches, that of Caroual stands out on account of its **view** of the bay and Cap d'Erquy, as well as its natural topography, which ensures safe bathing for children.

On the edge of the road leading to Cap d'Erquy stand two small guard-rooms – the vestiges of Vauban's fortifications – along with a curious-looking cannon-ball foundry; its purpose was to manufacture cannon-balls for the batteries of artillery to fire at the approaching English, sailing forth in their 17C wooden ships.

Château de Bienassis – *See Le VAL-ANDRÉ: Excursion.*

Via Pléneuf-Val-André return to Le Val-André.

⌂⌂ **Le Val-André** – *See Le VAL-ANDRÉ.*

LE CROISIC★

Population 4 428

Michelin map 6 fold 14 or 20 fold 51 – Local map see Presqu'île de GUÉRANDE

This pleasant fishing port is located on a peninsula and overlooks the Grand Traict lagoon which feeds the salt marshes of Guérande. It is only accessible by N 171. Originally one of the first seaside resorts, today Le Croisic still attracts many summer holiday visitors.

SIGHTS

Port – The port is well protected by the Tréhic jetty and is divided into several basins by three islets. It is a picturesque and busy scene in winter with the arrival of prawn boats, and in summer is enlivened by tourists.

Hôtel d'Aiguillon – The pretty 17C building houses the town hall. Dumas' "D'Artagnan" stopped here.

Église Notre-Dame-de-Pitié – This unusual 15C and 16C church, with its 17C 56m/84ft **lantern tower,** overlooks the port. Inside it has a short nave, with a flat east end illuminated by a window with Flamboyant tracery and three side aisles.

Old houses – To admire the beautiful corbelled and half-timbered houses, walk through the little streets near the church. Note nos 25, 20 and 28 in rue de l'Église, no 4 place du Pilori and nos 33 and 35 in rue St-Christophe.

Mont-Esprit – This artificial mound (30m/98ft high) was formed between 1814 and 1816 by the ballast of ships coming to load salt.

Mont-Lénigo – Ships at one time unloaded their ballast here and in 1761 trees were planted. The **view★** goes over the roadstead, the Tréhic jetty (850m/2 789ft long), and its lighthouse (1872) at the entrance to the port; the Pen Bron dike (1724) is across the way as is its marine centre. A shaded walk goes down to the esplanade where there is the memorial (1919) by René Paris, erected to Hervé Rielle, the coxswain, who saved 22 ships of the French fleet from disaster in 1692, by directing them to St-Malo.

★ **Océarium** ⊘ – The Océarium (Marine Information Centre) presents displays about commercial fish-breeding and houses a collection of wonders of the deep from both temperate and tropical waters. It contains 700 000l/150 000gal of seawater, and a marvellous 11m/36ft long tunnel through the pool. (containing 300 000l/66 000gal seawater) offers a unique view of the fish living there. At 4pm, a diver feeds the fish by hand.

Sea trips ⊘ – Two companies offer boat trips to Belle-Île. A ferry service crosses the roadstead to La Turballe.

★CÔTE SAUVAGE

Round tour of 26km/16mi – 2hr – local map see Presqu'île de GUÉRANDE. Leave Le Croisic by D 45, the coast road.

After St-Jean-de-Dieu, the road follows the coast passing St-Goustan and its salt-marsh where eels are raised. The Côte Sauvage (meaning wild coastline) with oddly shaped rocks (appropriately named the Bear, the Altar) ends at the **Pointe du Croisic**. Further on the view opens out over Pornichet, the Loire estuary and the coast as far as the Pointe St-Gildas.

⌂ **Batz-sur-Mer** – Against a background of the ocean and the salt-marshes, Batz's tall church bell-tower acts as a landmark for the town. The rocky coastline is broken by the sandy beaches of Valentin, La Govelle (fun-board) and St-Michel, a small strand where locals gather to watch the waves crashing on the dike.

★ **Église St-Guénolé** – The church was rebuilt in the 15C-16C. Its **bell-tower**, 60m/190ft high, surmounted by a pinnacled turret, dates from 1677. In the **interior**, you will notice at once that the chancel is off-centre, that massive pillars support Gothic arches and that the wooden roof is shaped like the keel of a boat. The top

Hotels

OUR SELECTION

Hôtel Les Nids – *15 rue Pasteur à Port-Lin* – ☎ *02 40 23 00 63 – closed Nov-Easter* – *23 rooms 380/466F – breakfast 38F – restaurant 100/250F.* You will be warmly welcomed in this modernised familial hotel situated in a flower garden. The medium-sized rooms are cozy and colourful. There is also an indoor swimming pool.

Hôtel Lichen – *At Manérick, 5km from Croisic by the coast road D 45, 44740 Batz-sur-Mer* – ☎ *02 40 23 91 92* – ▣ – *14 rooms 300/790F – breakfast 45F.* This large white slate-roofed villa overlooks the sea. Built in 1990 in the regional style, it has a devoted clientele of regulars who come to enjoy its light, airy rooms with ocean views, its garden and its proximity to the beach.

TREAT YOURSELF!

Hôtel Fort de l'Océan – *Pointe du Croisic* – ☎ *02 40 15 77 77 – 9 rooms from 800F – breakfast 80F – restaurant 265/420F.* If you want to break into your piggy-bank, this is the place to do it! In this 17C fort, located on the rocky Côte Sauvage, the tastefully decorated rooms combine beautiful fabrics and refined details for truly excessive comfort. The view, the swimming pool and the bicycles at your disposal add to the luxury of this stopover.

Eating Out

BUDGET

Lénigo – *11 quai Lénigo* – ☎ *02 40 23 00 31 – closed Mon and Tues except in summer, and evening Dec-Mar – 88/165F.* You can almost feel the ocean spray in this seafood restaurant with its wainscotted walls decorated with ship ropes and parts of boats. In nice weather, the terrace offers a pretty view of the port and the Presqu'ile of Penbron.

Beaches

The **Port-Lin Beach**, facing the open sea, is located 800m/875yd from the town centre; the **St-Goustan Beach** is 1km/0.6mi farther along the roadstead.

of the **bell-tower** (182 steps) offers an extensive **panorama★★** along the coast from the Pointe St-Gildas, south of the Loire, to the shores of the Presqu'île de Rhuys and, at sea, to Belle-Île and Noirmoutier.

★ **Chapelle Notre-Dame-du-Mûrier** – Legend has it that this fine Gothic chapel, now in ruins, was built in the 15C by Jean de Rieux de Ranrouët to keep a vow he made when in peril at sea. He was guided to safety by a burning mulberry bush (hence the name *mûrier*).

Musée des Marais salants ⊘ – This museum of popular arts and traditions contains a 19C Batz interior, salt workers' clothes, and other exhibits covering all aspects of working with salt. The tour ends with an audio-visual presentation on the salt-marsh and its fauna. **Guided toursa** of the salt-marshes are available.

Take D 45 back to Le Croisic.

Presqu'île de CROZON★★★

Michelin map 58 folds 3, 4, 13 and 14 or 20 folds 16 and 17

The Crozon Peninsula affords many excursions typical of the Breton coast. Nowhere else, except perhaps at Raz Point, do the sea and coast reach such heights of grim beauty, with the giddy steepness of the cliffs, the colouring of the rocks and the fury of the sea breaking on the reefs. Another attraction is the variety of views over the indentations and estuaries of the Brest roadstead, the Goulet, the broken coast of Toulinguet, Penhir, Dinan Castle, Cap de la Chèvre and Douarnenez Bay. From the summit of the Ménez-Hom all these features can be seen arrayed in an immense panorama.

★★★ ① FROM POINTE DE PENHIR TO POINTE DES ESPAGNOLS

Round tour starting from Crozon – 45 km/28mi – 2hr 30min

Crozon – The town stands in the middle of the peninsula of the same name. The **church** is modern. The altar to the right of the chancel is ornamented with a large 17C **altarpiece★** depicting the martyrdom of the Theban Legion. Below are two 17C panels: the Flagellation, on the left, and the Bearing of the Cross, on the right. Note the pulpit after which that at Locronan was modelled.

Leave Crozon by D 8, west of town and make for Camaret.

To the left, by Kerloch, there is a fine view of Dinan Bay and Point, the vast beaches of Kerloch and Goulien and, on a fine day, of the Pointe du Raz.

Camaret-sur-Mer – *See CAMARET-SUR-MER.*

Pointe du Toulinguet – An isthmus bounded by Pen-Hat Beach leads to the point on which a French Navy signal station stands. There is a view of Toulinguet rocks and of the Pointe de Penhir.

Return to the entrance to Camaret and bear right.

Alignements de Lagatjar – They include 143 menhirs discovered since the early 20C *(details on prehistoric monuments in the Introduction).*

★★★ **Pointe de Penhir** – Penhir Point is the finest of the four headlands of the Presqu'île de Crozon. A memorial (150m/164yd off the road) to the Bretons of the Free French Forces has been erected on the cliff.

Leave the car at the end of the surfaced road. Go onto the platform at the end of the promontory for a view of the sea 70m/229ft down below. Telescopes. 45min.

The setting is magnificent as is the **panorama**: below are the great isolated rocks called the **Tas de Pois** (literally, "pile of peas"!); on the left is the Pointe de Dinan; on the right, Pointe de St-Mathieu and Pointe du Toulinguet, the second with its little lighthouse, and at the back the Ménez-Hom. In the distance, the Pointe du Raz and the Île de Sein can be seen on clear days to the left, and Ouessant over to the right.

Tourists who enjoy scrambling over rocks should take a path going down to the left of the platform and monument. Halfway down the sheer drop of the cliff there is a view of a little cove. Here take the path on the left which climbs towards a cavity covered with a rock beyond which is the **Chambre Verte**, a grassy strip. From here there is an unusual view of the Tas de Pois Rocks and the Pointe de Penhir.

Return to the car and take the Camaret road again. Turn right after 1.5km/1mi towards Crozon, to avoid the town; then take the road to Roscanvel, once a strategic road.

The view opens out to show Camaret Bay on the left and, on the right, the Brest roadstead. The road enters the walls which enclose the Presqu'île de Roscanvel before Quélern. These fortifications date from the time of Vauban and the Second Empire.

This road running west is picturesque. The curious contrast between the slopes on either side of the peninsula is striking: the western slope, facing the west wind and the sea, is moorland and lacks vegetation; the eastern slope is covered with trees and meadows.

The road affords views of the Atlantic, Pointe du Toulinguet, Pointe du Grand Gouin, Camaret Bay, the Brest Sound and in the far distance, Pointe de St-Mathieu.

★★**Pointe des Espagnols** – From here one can see a remarkable **panorama** which includes the Brest Sound, overlooked by CNEXO (Centre National d'Exploitation des Océans), town and harbour of Brest, the Elorn estuary, the Pont Albert-Louppe, the Presqu'île de Plougastel, and the end of the roadstead.

Then the road skirts the eastern coast of the peninsula affording a good view on the left of the Brest roadstead, the Presqu'île de Plougastel and Longue, Morts and Trébéron Islands.

Roscanvel – The church was rebuilt after a fire in 1956 and now possesses fine dark stained-glass windows by Labouret, and a coloured terracotta Stations of the Cross by Claude Gruher.

Note the hedges of fuschia between the gardens.

The road, which to the south of Roscanvel goes round the end of the roadstead, affords fine views of Île Longue (nuclear submarine base – no entry), and in the foreground, of the two smaller islands, Trébéron and Morts. You leave the peninsular territory once more by the ruined fortifications.

About 500m/545yd beyond St-Fiacre, turn left.

Le Fret – A small port with regular boat service to and from Brest. View of the Presqu'île de Plougastel from the jetty.

The road runs along the jetty bordering Le Fret Bay.

When you come to a fork, leave the Lanvéoc road on your left and turn right to Crozon.

Enjoy a last look back at the roadstead.

Hotels

OUR SELECTION

Hostellerie de la Mer – In Fret 5.5km/30mi north of Crozon via D 155 and D 55 – ☎ 02 98 27 61 90 – closed 3 Jan-10 Feb – 25 rooms 297/385F – breakfast 46F – restaurant 105/270F. This little discreet hotel is ideally located in the charming port of Fret, in the heart of the Parc naturel régional d'Armorique. The comforts are modest, but you can enjoy the magnificent surroundings of the Ppresqu'île de Crozon.

Grand Hôtel de la Mer – 29160 Morgat – ☎ 02 98 27 02 09 – closed 1 Nov-2 April – ▣ – 78 rooms 485/595F – breakfast 58F – restaurant 110/198F. Near the beach, with its park planted with palm trees, this beautiful hotel was built in the early 1900's by the Peugeot family. It was entirely renovated in 1993. You will quickly overlook the rather functional decor once seated at a table in its restaurant: the view is magnificent!

★★ ② FROM CROZON TO POINTE DE DINAN

6km/4mi – 2hr

Crozon – See Presqu'île de CROZON.

Leave Crozon west by D 308.

Windswept heathland follows after the pine groves.

Pointe de Dinan – *1hr. Leave your car at the car park; continue on foot, by the path on the left for about 500m/545yd.* A fine **panorama** can be seen from the edge of the cliff; on the left are Cap de la Chèvre, the coast of Cornouaille and Pointe du Raz; on the right, Pointe du Penhir and the Tas de Pois. Skirting the cliff to the right you will see the enormous rocky mass of **Dinan Castle** ("Château" de Dinan), where the point ends; a natural arch joins this rock, which looks like a fortified castle in ruins, to the mainland *(30min on foot there and back, over rocky ground; wear non-slip soles)*. Take the path over the natural arch.

★ ③ FROM CROZON TO CAP DE LA CHÈVRE

11km/7mi – 2hr

Crozon – See section ① of tour described above.

Leave Crozon by D 887 southwest.

⌂ **Morgat** – Morgat is a well-sheltered seaside resort. The great sandy beach is enclosed to the south by a point covered with pine woods, Beg-ar-Gador. On the north side, a rocky spur separates Morgat Beach from that of Le Portzic. Fishing boats go out from the **harbour**, sheltering behind a jetty where 400 pleasure craft can also anchor. Morgat offers all types of fishing to the keen sportsman. From the new jetty, there is a good **view** over the cliff, the natural arch or Gador Gate, Douarnenez Bay and Ménez-Hom.

★**Les grandes grottes** ⊘ – The first group of big caves, situated beyond Beg-ar-Gador, includes Ste-Marine and the Devil's Chamber (Chambre du Diable). The second group is at the other end of the bay. The finest grotto is that of the Altar (l'Autel), 80m/262ft deep and 15m/49ft high. One of its attractions is the colouring of the roofs and walls.

Les petites grottes – Small caves at the foot of the spur between Morgat and Le Portzic beaches can be reached at low tide.

From Morgat to Cap de la Chèvre the road runs through an austere landscape of rocks and stunted heath, open to the ocean winds, with little hamlets of houses huddled together which seem to hide in the folds of the ground. To the left, the view gradually opens out over Douarnenez Bay, with the massive outline of the Ménez-Hom in the distance.

A short distance past Brégoulou, leave the car in the car park from which you can enjoy a good view of the Tas de Pois and Pointe du Raz.

★**Cap de la Chèvre** – *30min.* There is a French Navy signal station on the site. *Go round the signal station to the right to reach the point.* Telescope. From the former German observation point there is a fine **view** over the Atlantic and the advanced points of Finistère: (left to right) Pointe de Penhir and the Tas de Pois, the Île de Sein, Cap Sizun and its headlands, Pointe du Van and Pointe du Raz to the south of Douarnenez Bay.

A **monument**, representing the wing of an aircraft stuck into the ground, is dedicated to the aircrew personnel of Aéronautique Navale killed or missing in active service in the Atlantic and Scandinavian regions. The names of the people concerned are engraved on the sides of a circular trench.

DAOULAS★

Population 1 640
Michelin map 58 folds 4 and 5 or 20 fold 18

This small town is located on the banks of the river which shares its name. The river's estuary forms one of the many inlets in the Brest roadstead.

The town owes its development largely to the presence of the abbey built here; the fates of both have been closely linked over the centuries.

Daoulas has inherited many artistic features which bear witness to its past. There are still some 15C and 17C houses along rue de l'Église.

★**Parish Close (Enclos paroissial)** – The old abbey buildings are to the left. Opposite, and slightly to the right, a 16C **porch★** takes the place of a bell-tower and leads into the cemetery. The old **abbey church** still has the original 12C west door, nave and north side aisle. In the east end the ossuary has been converted into a sacristy.

Ancienne abbaye – The abbey was founded around the year 500 and, until the 10C, played a major part in the history of Daoulas. It was razed by the Vikings, then rebuilt in the 12C by Augustinian canons, under whose care it flourished until the Revolution.

The abbey now belongs to the Conseil Général of Finistère, which has converted it into a cultural centre, more particularly a venue for international archeological exhibitions.

★**Cloître and centre culturel** ⊘ – The garden in front of the cloisters contains several statues of saints (Augustine, Sebastian, Andrew).

The Romanesque cloisters, built in 1167 to 1173 (only three walls are still standing), is the only surviving example of this style of architecture in Brittany. The decoration consists of geometric designs and leaf motifs. A large basin decorated with 10 masks in between panels with geometric patterns occupies the centre of the cloisters' central open space. Important excavations currently being carried out have revealed the remains of a building dating back prior to the 12C on this site.

A path leads to a garden where herbs and medicinal plants are cultivated and a fountain as well as the **Oratoire Notre-Dame-des-Fontaines**, the fountain dating from 1550, with Catherine of Siena depicted in bas-relief work on it.

DINAN★★

Population 11 591
Michelin map 59 folds 15 and 16 or 20 fold 25 – Local map see Vallée de la RANCE

Dinan's old town is a small gem; its old houses and streets are girt by ramparts and guarded by an imposing castle. Enhanced by trees and gardens, it stands on a plateau overlooking the Rance and the pleasure port 75m/279ft below.

HISTORICAL NOTES

Du Guesclin against Canterbury – In 1357 the Duke of Lancaster besieged Dinan, which was defended by Bertrand Du Guesclin and his brother Olivier. After several encounters with the superior English forces, Bertrand asked for a 40-day truce, after which, he promised, the town would surrender if it were not relieved. In violation of the truce, Olivier, who had gone out of the town unarmed, was made prisoner by an English knight, Canterbury, who demanded a ransom of 1 000 florins. Bertrand challenged the Englishman to single combat. The encounter took place at a spot now called place du Champ; a stele marks the spot. Lancaster presided. Canterbury lost and had to pay Olivier the 1 000 florins he had demanded and surrender his arms to Bertrand. He was also discharged from the English army.

Du Guesclin's tombs – After more than 20 years of campaigning for the King of France, Bertrand du Guesclin died on 13 July 1380, at the gates of Châteauneuf-de-Randon, to which he had laid siege. He had asked to be buried at Dinan. The funeral convoy, therefore, set out for that town. At Le Puy the body was embalmed and the entrails buried in the Jacobins' church (now the Église St-Laurent). As the embalming was inadequate, the remains were boiled at Montferrand and the flesh was removed from the skeleton and buried in the Franciscans' church (destroyed in 1793). At Le Mans an officer of the King brought an order to bring the body to St-Denis; the skeleton was then handed over to him. Only the heart arrived at Dinan, where it was deposited in the Jacobins' church. It has since been transferred to the Église St-Sauveur. So it was that, while the kings of France had only three tombs (for the heart, entrails and body), Du Guesclin had four.

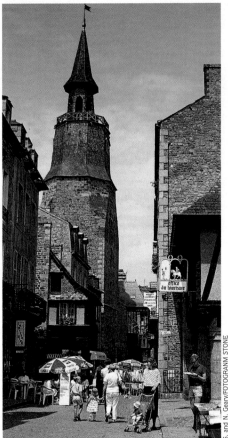

Dinan – Rue de l'Horloge

★★OLD TOWN
(VIEILLE VILLE)
1hr 30min

A medieval atmosphere can be felt as you walk through Dinan's old streets with their beautifully restored, picturesque half-timbered houses.

Place Du-Guesclin (BZ) – In this square, bordered with 18C and 19C town houses, stands the equestrian statue of Du Guesclin; the square, with place du Champ, served as a fairground during the Middle Ages.

Bear right on rue Ste-Claire, then left on rue de l'Horloge.

Hôtel Kératry (BZ B) – This attractive 16C mansion with three granite pillars, houses the tourist office.

Maison du Gisant (BZ D) – During the restoration of this 17C house, the 14C recumbent figure (exhibited outside) was found.

Tour de l'Horloge (BZ E) – Exhibited in the belfry are the clock, bought by the town in 1498. From the top of the Clock Tower (158 steps), there is a vast **panorama★★** of the town and its principle monuments and the surrounding countryside. Exhibition on Anne of Brittany.

★**Place des Merciers (BYZ 33)** – The old well and lovely old triangular-gabled houses with wooden porches paint a pleasant scene. Glance into nearby rue de la Cordonnerie and rue du Petit-Pain lined with corbelled houses. At no 10 rue de la Mittrie, Théodore Botrel (1868-1925), the songwriter, was born.

Take the pretty rue de l'Apport.

Different types of half-timbered houses, characteristic of 15C to 17C Dinan architecture, can seen in rue de l'Apport: houses with the upper floor resting on thick wooden pillars, under which the merchants and tradesmen exposed their wares, houses with overhanging upper storeys and houses with large projecting display windows.

Cross place des Cordeliers and take the Grande-Rue on the left to reach St-Malo Church.

Église St-Malo (AY) – This Flamboyant Gothic church was begun in 1490 and finished in the 19C. The late-15C transept, chancel and chevet make a striking impression. The **stained-glass windows** date from the 20C and depict life in the various districts of Dinan during major religious festivals.

Before reaching the Basilique St-Sauveur, go down rue de la Lainerie, in which there is a **well**, and at **Porte St-Malo** (St-Malo Gate), take the pretty walk along the watch-path of the ramparts. The walk leads past Tour du Gouverneur **(view)★★**.

★**Rue du Jerzual (BY)** – This lovely cobbled street slopes steeply downhill. The 15C and 16C **shops** lining the street are now occupied by artists: glass-blowers, sculptors, weavers etc. This was once the main street leading down to the port; imagine the constant comings and goings of the bourgeois, the hawkers with their overflowing carts and the tradesmen and apprentices running about.

Ancien hôtel Beaumanoir (BY N) – A beautiful Renaissance porch, called the Pelican, adorns the entrance of this old mansion. In the courtyard, note the decoration of the windows and a 16C turret, which houses a lovely staircase.

Basilique St-Sauveur (BZ) – This basilica features a Romanesque porch surmounted by a Flamboyant Gothic gable opening off the façade. Construction stretched from the 12C (the wall to the right) to the 16C. The original dome of

B	Hôtel Kératry	**F**	Maison du Gouverneur
D	Maison du Gisant	**L**	Ancien couvent des Cordeliers
E	Tour de l'Horloge	**N**	Ancien hôtel Beaumanoir

the tower, which was destroyed by lightning, was replaced in the 18C by a timber steeple covered with slate.

Inside, the building's lack of symmetry is striking; the south side is Romanesque, while the north side, the transept and the chancel are Flamboyant Gothic. In the north transept, the heart of Du Guesclin is preserved behind a 14C tomb stone incorporated in a 19C tomb. The modern stained-glass windows were made in the Barillet workshop.

As you leave the basilica, on place St-Sauveur, there is a house with pillars on the left, in which Auguste Pavie, diplomat and explorer of Indochina, was born in 1847.

Jardin Anglais (BYZ) – The terraced garden offers a good overall **view★★**, especially from Tour Ste-Catherine, of the River Rance, the port, the enormous viaduct, 250m/820ft long and 40m/128ft high, and the ramparts.

Maison du Gouverneur (BY F) – No 24. This is a fine 15C mansion in which a weaving and high-warp tapestry workshop has been installed.

ADDITIONAL SIGHTS

Promenade de la Duchesse-Anne (BZ) – From this promenade along the ramparts, there is a lovely **view★** of the Rance, the viaduct and the port.

Promenade des Petits-Fossés (AZ) – This promenade skirts the outside of the 13C-15C ramparts. Looming above are the castle, and the Connétable and Beaufort Towers.

Promenade des Grands-Fossés (ABY) – This magnificent avenue is embellished by the St-Julien, Vaucouleurs and Beaumanoir Towers and the Porte St-Malo.

⊠ Banks of the Rance – *1hr on foot. Go down to the Rance and cross the Gothic bridge (Pont Gothique).*
On the right, take the old towpath which passes under the viaduct and follows the river in a green and sheltered **setting**, where it is pleasant to stroll.

★Castle (Château) ⊘ **(AZ)** –The 13C Porte du Guichet is framed by towers pierced with arrow slits. The 14C dungeon, with its bold machicolations, houses a **museum** of the history of Dinan from prehistoric times to the early 20C. It also contains exhibits of local crafts. The top room displays works by painters who have drawn inspiration from the town and surrounding area, and by late-19C sculptors who worked in Dinan. From the terrace overlooking the watch-path there is a lovely **panorama★** of the region. The Tour de Coëtquen, the old artillery tower, exhibits tombstones in a ground floor room.

Ancien Couvent des Cordeliers ⊘ (AY L) – The 15C Gothic cloisters and the 13C turreted (pepper-pot roofs) main courtyard are all that remain of the monastery.

Maison d'Artiste de la Grande Vigne ⊘ – The former house of **Yvonne Jean-Haffen** (1895-1993), a friend and student of the painter Mathurin Méheut, displays several hundred paintings and drawings depicting the Brittany of bygone days.

EXCURSIONS

Léhon – *2km/1mi south.* In this village, nestled in the Rance Valley, stands the **Prieuré St-Magloire**, a priory built in the 12C. *45min.*

Church – The church, rebuilt in the 13C and restored in the late 19C, has a rounded doorway adorned with small columns and surmounted by a horizontal string-course decorated with heads. The Angevin-style pointed vaulted nave contains the tombs of the Beaumanoir family and a 13C stoup, where harvesters came to sharpen their sickles.

Conventual Buildings – A small **museum** ⊘ exhibits capitals of the old Romanesque cloisters. The 13C **refectory**, the oldest room in the Abbey, has been beautifully restored. Note the reader's chair with its staircase and rostrum. The dormitory houses several treasures including the reliquary of St-Magloire.

Hotels

BUDGET

Camping Municipal de la Hallerais – *In Taden, 22100, 3.5km/2mi from Dinan, road to Dol-de-Bretagne and D 2 – ☎ 02 96 39 15 93 – 15 Mar-Oct – 228 sites, 116F.* This campground overlooks the Rance, on the Taden plain, not far from the medieval city of Dinan. Put up your tent on one of the spots with a shaded terrace, or rent a mobile home. Swimming pool, tennis court, and mini-golf.

OUR SELECTION

Hôtel Challonge – *29 place Du-Guesclin – ☎ 02 96 87 16 30 – 18 rooms 280/370F – breakfast 38F – restaurant 98/170F.* Located near the city ramparts, this chic-looking hotel has been entirely renovated in a nostalgic style. In addition to its modern rooms, it has a brasserie decorated like an English pub, with dark woodwork and a grand bar: Le Longueville. Children's menu.

TREAT YOURSELF!

Hôtel Avaugour – *1 place du Champ – ☎ 02 96 39 07 49 – 24 rooms from 580F – breakfast 50F – restaurant 135F.* Situated on the ramparts, this hotel provides a pleasant stopover in an historic city. The hotel occupies an old building of traditional regional architecture, but the restaurant is located at the end of the garden in a fortified tower from the 15C. The renovated rooms are relatively refined.

Eating Out

BUDGET

Crêperie des Artisans – *6 rue du Petit-Fort – ☎ 02 96 39 44 10 – closed mid-Oct to Palm Sun and Mon except in summer – no credit cards – 52/69F.* Go up this little street between the port and the old part of the town, and stop in at this *crêperie* to gather your forces beside the fire. While enjoying traditional crêpes and farm products, you can also admire their collection of percolators and coffee-makers.

OUR SELECTION

Mère Pourcel – *3 place des Merciers – ☎ 02 96 39 03 80 – closed Feb, school holidays, Sun evening and Mon except in summer – 162/370F.* With its slightly askew half-timbered façade, this 15C Breton house is worth visiting for its decor: notably for its staircase and its enormous ceiling beams in dark wood, very typical of Dinan architecture. Traditional cuisine.

Le Bistrot du Viaduc – *On the road to Dol-de-Bretagne – ☎ 02 96 85 95 00 – closed 20 Dec-15 Jan, Sun evening off-season, Sat lunch and Mon – 160/185F.* At the end of the viaduct, this bistro overlooks Dinan's port and offers a beautiful view of the ramparts and the town. You'll pass in front of the kitchen before discovering the generous traditional cuisine served in a tasteful old-style decor.

Gardens ⓣ – Excavations have uncovered an underground passage which was, in fact, a covered canal linking the abbey to the Rance running down below.

Corseul – *11km/7mi. Leave Dinan by T on the town plan, bear right onto the road to Plancoët.*
Already known to the Celts, Corseul was conquered and extensively modified by the Romans, as was most of the Armor area. Many artefacts from those periods are gathered here, notably in the Garden of Antiquities (Jardin des Antiques), (columns and capitals) and in the **Musée de la Société archéologique de Corseul** ⓣ on the second floor of the town hall (fossils from the Falun Sea, polished and dressed stones, funerary urns, coins, Roman murals, everyday implements from Gallo–Roman times). The most remarkable vestige is the **Temple du Haut-Bécherel**, said to be the Temple of Mars *(1.5km/1mi on the road to Dinan and right on an uphill road)*. It is a polygonal tower with masonry in small courses, dating from Emperor Augustus's reign.

★ **Château de la Bourbansais** – *14km/8.5mi southeast.* Standing in an immense park, this impressive late-16C building was embellished by three generations of the Huart family, counsellors to the Breton Parliament.

Parc zoologique et jardin ⓣ – The zoo protects more than 500 animal species from the five continents. *After the zoo go to the château.* The main building is flanked by pinnacled turrets and saddleback-roofed pavilions characteristic of the 18C.

Château interior ⓣ – On the ground floor the rooms are decorated and furnished in the 18C style and contain 17C Aubusson tapestries and a fine collection of porcelain from the Dutch India Company. In the peristyle, there is a display of documents, archives and personal objects belonging to the past owners, evoking the château's history.

Going Out

Le Bistrot d'en bas – *20 rue Haute-Voie* – ☎ 02 96 85 44 00 – *Oct-May, Tues-Sun 11am-1am; June-Sept, daily 11am-1pm.* This wine bar has an extensive list of Anjou wines. Against a backdrop of jazz or French songs, you can enjoy tartines of special bread with charcuterie or cheese. Terrace in the pedestrian street.

À la Truye qui file – *14 rue de la Cordonnerie* – ☎ 02 96 39 72 29 – *Tues-Sat noon-1am, Tues-Sat noon-1am, Sun 5.30pm-1am.* In the 15C, a sow spun wool with its tail on place de Grève, an act which, at that time, was considered to be sorcery. So, the sow and its trainer were burned alive. In homage to *"la truye qui file"* ("the sow that spun wool"), a dozen or so bars in France have this name, and one of them is located in Dinan. The owner, called "Nounours" ("Teddy Bear") is a former professional musician, and has been known to spin some tender music in remembrance of this talented sow.

La Licorne – *6 rue de la Poissonnerie* – ☎ 02 96 39 08 13 – *Mon-Sat 10am-1am.* Dating from 1495, this is one of oldest establishments in Dinan. Today, it is one of the most popular bars, especially with a very young clientele. A drink in hand, they crowd around the fireplace that is classed as a "monument historique".

Le Myrian – *3 rue du Port* – ☎ 02 96 87 93 36 – *May-Sept, daily 10am-1am; Oct-Apr, closed Thur.* Away from the usual crowds, this bar enjoys the considerable advantages of being located on the banks of the River Rance and of looking out onto both the viaduct and the old bridge. One of the best places to stop between two walks. The pizzeria next door belongs to the same owner.

Le Poche Café – *1 rue Haute-Voie* – ☎ 02 96 39 98 60 – *Mon 2pm-7pm, Tues-Sat 10am-7pm.* It is first of all "a bookstore of 6 000 paperback titles", explains the owner, but it is also a bar where one can drink a cup of coffee and authors' prose. It hosts monthly exhibitions of paintings and photographs, and a literary evening two Saturdays a month.

Rue de la Cordonnerie – La rue de la Cordonnerie is the ideal place to quench your thirst. On this small street are no less than eight bars, all with different styles.

Boat trips

In season, you can go down the River Rance by boat, however the return trip, the same day, must be made by bus or by train.

Shopping

Flea market – Held every Wednesday in July and August, and on the first Wednesday of the month the rest of the year.

Boutique Locmaria – *9 rue du Château* – *July-Aug, daily.* Three Dinan culinary specialities: *gavottes* (with butter), *corbelets* (with almond paste), and *clopinettes* (with pralines).

DINARD ✿✿✿

Population 9 918

Michelin map 59 fold 5 or 20 fold 11 – Local maps see CÔTE D'ÉMERAUDE
and Vallée de la RANCE

This smart resort, which lies in a magnificent setting on the estuary of the Rance, opposite St-Malo, is frequented by the international set and in particular by the British and Americans. The place was "launched" about 1850 by an American named Coppinger and developed by the British. Before that it was a small fishing village and an offshoot of St-Énogat.

The tourist will be interested by the extraordinary contrast between Dinard and St-Malo: the former, a luxurious resort with modern installations, intense social activity, princely villas and splendid gardens and parks; the latter, an old city surrounded by ramparts, possessing a family beach and a commercial port.

SIGHTS

★★Pointe du Moulinet (BY) – *Start from Grande Plage.*

A walk round this point offers a series of magnificent **views** of the coast from Cap Fréhel, on the left, to St-Malo on the right and, a little further on, of the Rance estuary.

DINARD

Féart (Bd)	**BYZ**	Boutin (Pl. J.)	**BY** 9	Levavasseur (R.)	**BY** 29
Leclerc (R. Mar.)	**BYZ** 28	Clemenceau (R. G.)	**BY** 10	Lhotellier (Bd)	**AY** 31
		Coppinger (R.)	**BY** 12	Libération (Bd de la)	**AZ** 32
		Corbinais (R. de la)	**AZ** 13	Malouine (R. de la)	**BY** 34
Abbé Langevin (R.)	**AY** 2	Croix-Guillaume		Mettrie (R. de la)	**BZ** 35
Albert-1er (Bd)	**AB** 3	(R. de la)	**AZ** 15	Pionnière (R. de la)	**ABY** 38
Anciens Combattants		Douet-Fourchet		Prés.-Wilson (Bd)	**BY** 40
(Rue des)	**AZ** 5	(R. du)	**AZ** 17	Renan (R. E.)	**AY** 43
Barbine (R. des)	**AZ** 7	Dunant (R. H.)	**AY** 19	République (Pl. de la)	**BY** 44
		Français-Libres (R.)	**BZ** 22	St-Lunaire (R. de)	**AY** 48
		Gaulle (Pl. du Gén.-de)	**BZ** 25	Vallée (R. de la)	**BYZ** 50
		Giraud (Av. du Gén.)	**BZ** 26	Verney (R. Y.)	**BY** 52

M¹ Musée du Site Balnéaire   M² Aquarium et Musée de la Mer

126

Where to Stay

OUR SELECTION

Hôtel Printania – *5 avenue George-V* – ☎ *02 99 46 13 07* – *closed 21 Nov-19 Mar* – *59 rooms 270/450F* – *breakfast 40F* – *restaurant 95/135F*. If it's Breton folklore you're after, you'll find it here! The dining room and lounge of this seafront hotel are steeped in local style: rustic wood furnishings and old paintings abound. The waitresses wear traditional local costumes.

Résidence Crystal Appartements – *15 rue Malouine* – ☎ *02 99 46 66 71* – *18 apartments 2/4 people, week 2500/5900F*. This modern building is very well located, providing direct access to the beach and a nice view of the water and St-Malo. The apartments are functionally equipped and many have terraces. For a short stay, you may prefer the hotel.

Hôtel du Golf – *6km/3.6mi west of Dinard via D 786, boulevard Houle, 35800 St-Briac-sur-Mer* – ☎ *02 99 88 30 30* – 🅿 – *40 rooms 400/520F* – *breakfast 45F* – *restaurant 90/149F*. A modern building, in a quiet place, well suited as a base for excursions. The rooms are spacious and well-equipped, the bar and lounge are bright and friendly. Nearby, the oldest golf course on the continent is an added plus for lovers of the game.

TREAT YOURSELF!

Hôtel Reine Hortense et Castel Eugénie – *19 rue Malouine* – ☎ *02 99 46 54 31* – *closed 16 Nov-25 Dec and 4 Jan-24 Mar* – 🅿 – *13 rooms 780/980F* – *breakfast 60F*. Two villas, dating from 1900, face the sea. The rooms may make you feel as if you've wandered into an old engraving: antique furniture and a refined decor recall the days of Queen Hortense, who also must have enjoyed the superb view over St-Malo. Private access to the beach.

Eating out

BUDGET

Présidence – *29 boulevard du Prés.-Wilson* – ☎ *02 99 46 44 27* – *closed school holidays at Christmas and in Feb, Sun evening off-season and Mon* – *92/135F*. Across from the casino, this family restaurant is unpretentious and colourfully decorated; fresh fish and fresh local products are served in the long, narrow dining room. Fixed price menus and children's menu available.

Restaurant du Yacht Club de Dinard – *9 promenade du Clair-de-Lune, 1st floor* – ☎ *02 99 16 48 74* – *closed 3 weeks in Jan, Tues evening and Wed off-season - 85/169F*. You needn't be a member of this venerable institution to benefit from the remarkable view on the Rance estuary and the superb roof garden. "Clubby" ambience in the midst of souvenir photos and trophies.

OUR SELECTION

La Brasserie du Casino – *4 boulevard Wilson* – ☎ *02 99 16 30 30* – *120/220F*. If you have any money left after crossing the line of one-armed-bandits, you can enjoy a meal in this brasserie designed to look like a cruise ship inside. Located just above the main beach, the restaurant offer a wide choice of items to satisfy your appetite.

A welcome break

L'Amirauté – *1 pointe du Décollé, 35800 St-Lunaire* – ☎ *02 99 46 33 38* – *off-season, Mon-Tues, Thur-Sat noon-3pm, 7pm-10pm, Sun noon-10pm; July-Aug, daily 10am-11pm*. On the Pointe du Décollé, this bar and crêpe restaurant has a panoramic view of the bay at Saint-Malo, the sea and the rocks white with foam. The ice cream is made by a specialist, and is truly delicious – enjoy some on the large terrace away from the bustling crowds.

Going out

Rue Yves-Verney – *Rue Yves-Verney*. If you are looking for a place to have a fun night out, head for this street, with a half a dozen bars, each with its own ambience: American-style at Davy's, the yachting crowd at Newport, the Croisette is classy, and la Fonda is hip.

La Chaumière – *Pointe du Décollé, 35800 St-Lunaire* – ☎ *02 99 46 01 76* – *off-season, Fri-Sat; July-Aug, Thur-Sun*. On the Pointe du Décollé, with a great view over the ocean, this disco is the best known in the region. In the wee hours, the cool sea breeze will calm your Saturday Night Fever.

Shows – La promenade du Clair de Lune is the scene of a sound and light show, daily from June through Sept.

Shopping

Marché de Dinard – *Place Crolard – Mar, Thur, Sat morning.* This market is known throughout the region and has many faithful customers, some of whom come from quite a distance to do their shopping, especially on Saturday.

Sports

Wishbone Club Dinard – *Plage de l'Écluse – ☎ 02 99 88 15 20 – Mar-June, Sept-Dec, daily 10am-noon, 2pm-6pm; July-Aug, daily 9am-10pm.* This nautical club organises sessions for sailing instruction, rents windsurfers, catamarans, day-sailers and kayaks.

Dinard Équitation – *20 rue du Val-Porée – ☎ 02 99 46 23 57 – daily 9am-noon, 2pm-6pm.* This riding centre gives lessons, organises workshops and day trips. In August, there is an international jumping competition.

Boat trips

St-Malo★★★ – *Crossing 10min – see SAINT-MALO.*

Dinan, via la Rance★★ – *See Vallée de la RANCE.*

Cruises to cap Fréhel★★★ – *See Cap FRÉHEL.*

Cruises on la Rance and to Cézembre Island – On these cruises, you can discover hidden inlets and secret landscapes, or sail to Cézembre Island, where the vast white sand beach faces south. *Information from the tourist office or at the dock.*

From the air

There is regular service to the Channel Islands of Jersey and Guernsey, as well as to Southampton and London. Information from the Dinard/Pleurtuit airport (☎ 02 99 46 18 46); from the Aéro-club de la Côte d'Émeraude (☎ 02 99 88 23 42); from Aurigny-Air-Services or British Airways (☎ 02 99 46 70 28); from Assistance et Loisirs (☎ 02 99 46 96 86) or the tourist office.

★**Grande Plage or Plage de l'Écluse** (BY) – This beach of fine sand, bordered by luxurious hotels, the casino and convention centre (Palais des Congrès), extends to the end of the cove formed by Moulinet and Malouine Points.
Following the promenade along the beach to the left you will reach a terrace from which you can see St-Malo.

★**Promenade du Clair de Lune** ☺ **and Plage du Prieuré** (BYZ) – This walk *(pedestrians only)* lies along a sea wall which follows the water's edge and offers pretty views over the Rance estuary. Lovely multicoloured flower beds and remarkable Mediterranean vegetation embellish the Promenade.
The **Plage du Prieuré** is at the end of the Promenade. It owes its name to a priory founded here in 1324.

Musée du Site Balnéaire ☺ (BZ M¹) – The regional museum is housed in Villa Eugénie, built in honour of Napoleon III's wife, who was to have inaugurated the season in 1868. An exhibit traces the history of the six *communes* – Dinard, Pleurtuit, La Richardais, St-Briac, St-Lunaire, Le Minihic – which form the *canton*. A large section displays late-19C and early-20C resort life, an era of opulence, when magnificent villas and great hotels (Grand Hôtel, Grand Hôtel des Terrasses, Crystal Hôtel, to name a few) were built and excellent food was served.

Aquarium et Musée de la Mer ☺ (BY M²) – The **Muséum d'Histoire naturelle** (Natural History Museum) comprises an **aquarium** with 24 pools filled with fish and crustaceans from Breton waters.
Next is the **Musée de la Mer** (Marine Museum), which presents mementoes of Commandant Charcot's polar expeditions.

Pointe des Étêtés (AY) – View of the islands and the coast beyond St-Malo.

Jardin du Port-Riou (AY) – This terraced garden, below Pointe des Étêtés, offers a fine **view** as far as Cap Fréhel.

Plage de St-Énogat (AY) – The beach lies in a picturesque setting under steep cliffs.

★★**Pointe de la Vicomté (BZ)** – *2km/1mi – 1hr on foot there and back*. The Vicomté, a fine estate divided into lots, is becoming one of Dinard's most fashionable quarters. Walk along the circular road *(chemin de ronde)*, which starts at Avenue Bruzzo and offers splendid **vistas** towards the roadstead, the Rance estuary and the Usine marémotrice de la Rance.

Excursions

≙≙**St-Lunaire** – This smart resort, not far from Dinard, has two fine beaches: to the east that of St-Lunaire, which is the more frequented facing St-Malo, and to the west that of Longchamp, which is the larger of the two opposite Cap Fréhel.

Vieille église St-Lunaire ⊘ – The church stands among the trees in a former cemetery. The nave is 11C; the side aisles and canted chancel were rebuilt in the 17C. In the middle of the nave lies the tomb of St Lunaire with the recumbent figure of the saint (14C) resting on a Gallo-Roman sarcophagus. The transept contains seven tombs; in the Chapelle des Pontbriand in the north arm, note the tombs of a squire and a lady (15C), and in the Chapelle des Pontual in the south arm, the tomb of a lady of the Pontual family (13-14C), richly carved in high relief.

★★**Pointe du Décollé** – The point is joined to the mainland by a natural bridge crossing a deep fissure and known as the Cat's Leap (Saut du Chat); the Décollé promenades are laid out beyond the bridge.

To the left of the entrance to the Décollé Pavilion, take the road leading to the point, on which stands a granite cross.

From here the vantage point affords a very fine **view**★★ of the Côte d'Émeraude, from Cap Fréhel to Pointe de la Varde.

★**Grotte des Sirènes** – From the bridge crossing the cleft through which it opens to the sea, you can see the bottom of the grotto. The wash of the sea at high tide is spectacular.

DOL-DE-BRETAGNE★

Population 4 629
Michelin map 59 fold 6 or 20 fold 12

Dol, a former bishopric and proud of its fine cathedral, is now the small capital of the "Marais" (marsh) district. It stands on the edge of a cliff, about 20m/64ft high, which was washed by the sea until the 10C, when marine deposits began forming; the deposit enabled the construction of the sea dike, now a section of the Pontorson-St-Malo tourist road.

SIGHTS

★★**Cathédrale St-Samson** – *30 min*.
The cathedral is a vast structure, built of granite in the 12C and 13C and completed during the next three centuries. It gives an idea of the importance that the bishopric of Dol then enjoyed.
On the outside, the most interesting part is the south wall, which includes two porches: the splendid **great porch**★ (14C) and the little porch (13C) with its fine pointed arcade. Seen from the north, the cathedral looks like a fortress; its crenellated parapet was linked to the old fortifications of the town.
The interior, 100m/328ft long, is impressive. Notice in the chancel: the medallion-glass **window**★★ (13C restored), the eighty stalls (14C), the carved wood Bishop's throne (16C) and, above the high altar, the 14C wooden Statue of the Virgin, coloured in 1859. In the north arm of the transept, is the tomb of Thomas James, Bishop of Dol (16C); it is the work of two Florentine sculptors, Antoine and Jean Juste. In the north aisle note the Christ Reviled; in the axial chapel there are two 18C reliquary figures of St Samson and St Magloire.

★**Cathédraloscope** ⊘ – This exhibit, installed in the former residence of the bishops of Dol, is devoted to the subject of cathedrals, and is especially attractive to children. In a modern and uncluttered setting, which lends itself to contemplation, various models of cathedrals and the machines used to build them are on display, as well as items relating to the craftsmanship of stained-glass windows and sculpture.

★**Promenade des Douves** – This public garden (also known as Promenade Jules Revert) has been traced along the north part of the old ramparts. One of the 12 defence towers, the large Tour des Carmes, can still be seen. Its offers a fine **view**★ of the Mont Dol and the Marais de Dol.

DOL-DE-BRETAGNE

Museum (Musée historique de Dol) ⓥ – The museum is installed in the 16C treasury and is devoted, for the most part, to the history of Dol: dioramas, wax figures, models and arms; there is also a section on the Revolution (dioramas). The treasury contains a fine collection of polychrome wooden statues (13C-19C) of saints as well as 17C-18C glazed earthenware from different Breton Schools (in particular rare statues of Virgins).

Old houses – The streets near the cathedral precincts have interesting old half-timbered houses, town houses, and shops.

Grande-Rue des Stuarts (10) – No 17 (florist) dates from the 11C and 12C and has Romanesque arcading; no 27 (antique-dealer) is 13C; no 33 is a 1617 dwelling with fine dormer windows; no 18, a former Templars' inn with a 12C vaulted cellar, is now transformed into a bar-*crêperie*; a charming 16C courtyard is at no 32.

Rue Le-Jamptel (12) – No 31 (hardware store) dates from the 12C or 13C; no 27 is a 15C house decorated with pillars.

Rue Ceinte (6) – This street where the chapter-house used to be located. No 1, an old shop with a granite counter, and no 4, now a *crêperie*, are both 15C; no 16 dates from 1668.

EXCURSIONS

★Mont Dol

This granite mound, though only 65m/208ft high, overlooks a great plain and resembles a small mountain. The remains of many prehistoric animals – mammoth, elephant, rhinoceros, reindeer etc – and flint implements have been unearthed on its slopes.

It is possible to go round the mound by car by way of the surface road.

★**Panorama** – To the north, from the top of the tower, there is a view of the Îles Chausey and Cancale and Grouin Points; to the northeast, Mont-St-Michel, Avranches and Granville. From the Calvary, to the south, on the edge of the Dol Marsh, Dol and its fine cathedral can be seen with the Hédé heights in the background; and below, the Dol Marsh.

Marais de Dol – This is the name given to land reclaimed from the marshes and the sea in Mont-St-Michel Bay. Seen from the mound the countryside looks strange and monotonous; it extends for about 15 000ha/40 000 acres from the mouth of the River Couesnon to near Cancale. The old shoreline ran through Cancale, Châteauneuf, Dol and St-Broladre and along the stretch of road between Pontorson and St-Malo.

This former marshy area consists of two land-types: white marsh, made up of silt from a marine deposit and black marsh, made up of peat bogs.

Some 12 000 years ago, the sea covered the Marais de Dol, it then receded uncovering a large part of the bay. Bit by bit, forest and vegetation took possession of the land abandoned by the sea.

The establishment of large-scale mussel-beds in the area around Le Vivier-sur-Mer, in full expansion, has somewhat modified its appearance.

Tour of the countryside – *30km/18.5mi – 1hr 45min.*

Leave Dol southeast of the town plan on D 795. Leave the road to Épiniac on your left, 600m0.3mi further turn left then turn right onto a tarmac road.

Menhir de Champ-Dolent – The dolmen, one of the finest in Brittany, stands 9.50m/30ft high (width: 8,70m/31ft). The granite comes from Bonnemain located 5km/3mi south. The name *Champ-Dolent* ("Field of Pain") refers to a legendary struggle which is supposed to have taken place here.

Return to the road to Combourg.

Musée de la Paysannerie ⊘ – At **Baguer-Morvan**. Made up of three large buildings, this museum retraces the past 100 years in the life of the peasant farmer: reconstructed furnished interiors, photographs and postcards, farming equipment (tractors, threshers, harvesters...) and tools (rakes, knives, hammers...). Cider tasting is offered at the end of the tour.

Continue on D 795 and then left towards Épiniac.

Épiniac – In the north aisle of the **church**, on the altar, is a 16C polychrome high relief representing the Dormition of the Virgin; in the chancel is a finely carved 17C wood canopy.

Follow D 85 then bear left.

Broualan – In the centre of the village near a small yet remarkable Calvary stands a 15C church, enlarged in the 16C. The east end is decorated with pinnacled buttresses and lovely Flamboyant windows. The small columned bell tower rests on the large arch which separates the nave from the chancel. Inside, several small granite altars and finely worked credences (side tables) can be seen. The tabernacle of the high altar is supported by angels. Note the 16C polychrome stone Pietà.

Via La Boussac return to Dol-de-Bretagne.

Abbaye Notre-Dame-du-Tronchet – *10km/6mi. Leave Dol southwest of the town plan on N 176 and bear left towards Le Tronchet.* This former Benedictine abbey was built in the 17C. Large cloisters and a hostel (which houses the presbytery) stand amid the ruins. The church contains beautiful 17C woodwork.

DOUARNENEZ ★

Population 16 457

Michelin map 58 fold 14 or 20 fold 17 – Local map see CORNOUAILLE

The four localities of Douarnenez, Ploaré, Pouldavid and Tréboul have merged to form the *commune* of Douarnenez, which today is known as a city boasting three ports (museum-port, fishing port and sailing harbour), a European centre for fish canning, a seaside resort and a thalassotherapy spa. The town itself, nestling in a prettily curved bay, presents colourful, picturesque façades that have seduced many an artist, namely Auguste Renoir, Eugène Boudin, Emmanuel Lansyer etc. Although "the era of the sardine" now belongs to the past, visitors will appreciate the old-fashioned atmosphere which permeates the maze of narrow streets encircling the port.

According to local tradition, Douarnenez was the original site of the palace belonging to King Marc'h; the island located at the entrance to the estuary of Pouldavid bears the name of his nephew Tristan. Before being called Douarnenez in 1541 (*douar an enez* means the land of the island), the harbour was known as Hameau de St-Michel (St-Michael's Hamlet) and then, in 1520, Bourg de l'Île Tristan (Village of Tristan's Island).

La Fontenelle (16C) – According to local tradition, the palace of King Marc'h was at Douarnenez and the island at the mouth of the Pouldavid estuary was, therefore, given the name of his nephew, Tristan.

In the 16C this island was the lair of Sire Guy Eder La Fontenelle, the most dangerous of the robber barons who devastated the country during the conflicts of the League. La Fontenelle seized the Île Tristan. To obtain materials for fortifications he demolished those of Douarnenez. His cruelty was legendary. In 1598 he agreed to lay down his arms on condition that he be allowed to keep the island; this was granted by Henri IV. But in 1602 the King took his revenge: involved in a plot, La Fontenelle was sentenced to be broken on the wheel in Paris.

SIGHTS *3hr*

Start from place de l'Enfer.

★★ **Port-Musée** ⊘ – This Port Museum is both a centre of conservation of boats and a permanent workshop where expertise in this field is passed on. It offers a good opportunity to rediscover the recent maritime past. The various elements of the Port Museum, established on the wonderful site of Port-Rhu, once the commercial harbour of Douarnenez, contain displays on all aspects of maritime and harbour life, from ships afloat, to construction sites and an onshore museum containing 230 boats.

DOUARNENEZ

E Chapelle St-Michel
M Musée du Bateau

Musée du Bateau (YZ M) – This Boat Museum is located in an old canning factory and contains an **outstanding collection★** of fishing, transport and pleasure boats from France and abroad. The Irish curragh can be found beside the Welsh coracle or the Norwegian *oselvar*; clinker-built ships are next to carvel-built ships. Most of the exhibits are of wood; however, there are some boats made from the skins of horses, deer, seals or even whales. Many of the craft are displayed in full sailing rig.

Musée à flot – This comprises about 40 boats, 26 of which are open to visitors, moored in three harbour docks. In the first basin, **fishing boats** include: trawlers, lobster boats, shellfish boats, sardine boats and tuna boats. Visitors can go aboard one of the lobster boats, the *Notre-Dame-de-Rocamadour*. In another basin are larger **coastal vessels** such as the *Saint-Denys*, the *Anna Rosa* or the *Northdown*. The variety of boats displayed encompasses a British steam tug, a Norwegian coaster and a Breton *sablier* (used for transporting sand). **Pleasure craft** include the *Ariane*, built in 1927, the *Viviane*, dating from 1859, as well as cruising vessels and modern racing boats moored on the premises.

Chantier naval – A 53m/174ft 19C three-master clipper on which construction work is expected to last several years is currently on place de l'Enfer, at the centre of the shipyard. Along the quays, a wooden breakwater has been reconstructed in the old-fashioned style with repair workshops and presentations which enlighten visitors on the trades of marine rope-makers, sail-makers and carpenters.

The Port-Rhu floating musem

At the centre of the wet dock, the *Scarweather*, a British lightship can be visited from the bridge down in the hold, going through the radio room.

Trips out to sea, by the hour or half-day, organised by the associations in charge of conventional boats, round the visit off nicely.

Take boulevard Camille-Réaud.

This route brings the visitor to the viewpoint of the "Guet", where the Port-Rhu River runs into the bay.

Port-Rhu River and Plage des Dames (Y) – A *corniche* road runs along the shore and affords picturesque views of Tristan Island, a superb view of the bay, the Tréboul district, the narrow streets clustering round the port, and the estuary, which is spanned by a viaduct 24m/78ft high. There lies Port-Rhu, the former commercial port of Douarnenez. The path skirts Plage Porscad, then Plage des Dames.

★ **Boulevard Jean-Richepin and Nouveau Port** (Y) – Follow this boulevard, which offers superb **views**★ of Douarnenez Bay. You will see the new fishing port, which is developing in the shelter of a jetty some 741m/800yd long. The view from the new jetty is worth admiring as you get a wider view of the bay.

★ **Port du Rosmeur** (Y) – This fishing port, the pulse of the local economy, is ranked 6th in France in terms of tonnage. Here you may witness typical scenes of a coastal fishing town: the return of the boats loaded with the day's catch at 11pm, the open-air fish market at 6.30am *(for guided tours, apply to the tourist office)*. The most common types of fish caught off Douarnenez include mackerel, cod, whiting, monkfish, coalfish, tunny fish, sardine and crayfish. A walk along Rosmeur pier also offers a good view of the harbour district.

Take rue A.-France uphill to the left.

Chapelle Ste-Hélène (Y) – This chapel, in the Flamboyant Gothic style, was remodelled in the 17C and 18C. Over the side altars are 18C pictures and at the end of the nave, two 16C stained-glass windows.

Return to place Gabriel-Péri by way of the covered market. Every morning there is a charming, bustling open-air market.

Continue along rue Jean-Bart and turn left onto rue de Port-Rhu.

Chapelle St-Michel ⊘ (Y E) – This was built in 1663 and has a semicircular chancel and transept, and a small domed belfry. 17C paintings on the vaulting.

Return to place de l'Enfer.

Tréboul – Tréboul is linked to Douarnenez by a pedestrian passageway running along the estuary of Port-Rhu and the outer walls of the Port-Musée (offering visitors a charming stroll in a pleasant setting) as well as by Grand Pont, a large metal bridge for cars spanning the Port-Rhu estuary and affording a splendid **view** of the Port-Musée site.

Port de Plaisance (Yachting Harbour) – Set up in the bay of Tréboul, it can accommodate up to 700 boats. The bay serves as a fantastic natural venue for nautical events and a great many competitions are staged here every year.

PLOARÉ

Church ⊘ – Rue Laënnec. Access by ② on the town plan, D 57. The church dates from the 16C and 17C. It is crowned by a fine Flamboyant and Renaissance **tower**★, 55m/180ft high, with a crocketed steeple with four pinnacles at the corners (two Gothic, two Renaissance).

The façade is flanked with Gothic buttresses surmounted by pinnacles, while the buttresses of the apse and transept are crowned with small Renaissance lanterns. Inside note the high altar's carved altarpiece and a 17C painted wooden group representing the Holy Trinity.

Laënnec (1781-1826), the inventor of the stethoscope, is buried in the cemetery. Kerlouarnec, the country house where this eminent physician died, can be seen at the end of a fine avenue leading to the Chapelle de Ste-Croix (1701).

POULDAVID

By ② of the town plan, D 765 towards Audierne, and take the first road on the left.

Church ⊘ – 32 steps. Built on the hillside, the church has a 15C porch, a 14C arcaded nave and a 16C chancel. The chancel vaulting is adorned with sixteen 16C painted panels illustrating scenes from the Passion. Housed inside are several old statues; note the late-16C Pietà on the stone altar.

EXCURSIONS

★**Sentier des Plomarc'h and Plage du Ris** (**Z**) – *2hr 30min on foot there and back. Access via rue des Plomarc'h east of the town plan.*
The path begins at Port du Rosmeur and runs along the side of a slope affording some very picturesque **views**★ of Douarnenez. It leads to Plage du Ris. Return by the Locronan road.

★**Pointe de Leydé** – *Round tour of 6km/4mi to the west. At Sables-Blancs Beach (Tréboul district), turn left onto the road to Roches Blanches and leave the car on the parking area just after the Village de Vacances. Follow the Roches Blanches coastal path (signposted in orange) which runs along the sea and leads to the Pointe de Leydé.* The point affords a lovely **view**★ of the bay of Douarnenez.
From there, you can either return by the road leading back to Tréboul, or continue by the path leading to the localities of Poullan-sur-Mer and Beuzec.

Le Juch – *8km/5mi. Leave Douarnenez by* ② *on the town plan, D 765. 6km/4mi further on, turn left for Le Juch.*
Fine **view** of Douarnenez Bay, the Presqu'île de Crozon and Ménez-Hom. Inside the 16C-17C **church** ⊙, the old 16C stained-glass window at the east end shows scenes from the Passion; to the left and right of the chancel are statues depicting the Annunciation, placed in niches with 16C painted shutters. To the right of the sacristy door, in the north aisle is St Michael overcoming a dragon known as the Devil of Le Juch. *Pardon* on 15 August.

Guengat – *14km/9mi by* ② *on the town plan, D 765. 11km/7mi further on, turn left, for Guengat.*
In the Gothic church at the entrance to the choir is, on the left column, a Flemish statue of St Barbara and, on the right column, a 16C Virgin and Child. In the choir itself are 16C **stained-glass windows**★ depicting the Passion (centre), the Last Judgment (right) and the Virgin between St John the Baptist and St Michael (right), and a carved frieze with animals (hare, fox, wild boar), people and floral decoration. It is worth going into the cemetery to see the fine Calvary.

Hotels

OUR SELECTION

Hôtel Ty Mad – *Near Chapelle St-Jean, 29100 Tréboul – 3km/1.8mi northwest of Douarnenez – ☎ 02 98 74 00 53 – closed 1 Oct-31 Mar – ▯ – 23 rooms 250/340F – breakfast 40F – restaurant 70/190F.* This villa where Max Jacob lived is simple and unpretentious, but is surrounded by a pretty garden where you can have your breakfast in the sun, or enjoy one of the barbecues organized on summer evenings. The rooms are modern, and the charming restaurant has a veranda.

Chambre d'hôte Manoir de Kervent – *4km/2.4mi from Douarnenez on the road to Audierne (D 765), then turn right and follow signs – ☎ 02 98 92 04 90 – no credit cards – 3 rooms 200/280F.* Located out in the country, this family residence hosts three standard rooms. The lady of the house will serve you a copious breakfast, full of Breton flavours, before offering you a tour of the barrel-making workshop next door.

Eating Out

BUDGET

Crêperie Tudal – *Au Goûter Breton – 36 rue Jean-Jaurès – ☎ 02 98 92 02 74 – closed 8-23 June, 15 Nov-8 Dec, Sun and Mon except during school holidays – 46/87F.* This restaurant is the talk of the town. It has a youthful and noisy ambience, and serves original crêpes, such as with marinated sardines or with chouchen jelly, in a warm atmosphere between a fireplace and wall fresco.

Recreation

Sea excursions – You can go on excursions to discover sea caves, to fish, or to enjoy a cruise to Morgat. *Apr to mid-July, departing from the fishing port, excursions to the bird sanctuary of cap Sizun; Apr to mid-Sept, sea-fishing expeditions, and guided tours of the bay of Douarnenez – ☎ 02 98 92 83 83.*

For children – In July and August, they can navigate miniature electric boats: Treiz wharf, Port Rhu. ☎ 06 81 12 32 53.

Sailing and wind-surfing – *Fun Evasion, Sables-Blancs beach at Tréboul – ☎ 02 98 74 33 33 – fun-evasion@kerys.com – open all year.*

Les ENCLOS PAROISSIAUX ★★

Michelin map 58 folds 5 and 6 or 230 folds 4, 5, 18 and 19

Parish closes, which are a special feature of Breton art, are to be found mostly in Lower Brittany. The route runs through the picturesque Élorn Valley and the foothills of the Monts d'Arrée and includes only a few of the more interesting ones. There are many others, especially that of Pleyben, further to the south.

ROUND TOUR STARTING FROM MORLAIX

130km/81mi – one day

★**Morlaix** – *See MORLAIX. Leave Morlaix by ③ on the town plan.*

★★**St-Thégonnec** – *See ST-THÉGONNEC.*
Go round the east end of the church and bear left.

★★**Guimiliau** – *See GUIMILIAU.*
On the outskirts of Guimiliau, before the bridge under the railway, note lower down on your left a fountain decorated with three figures.

★**Lampaul-Guimiliau** – *See LAMPAUL-GUIMILIAU.*

Landivisiau – Landivisiau is a busy town. Its cattle fairs are among the largest in France. The **Église St-Thivisiau** is a modern church in the Gothic style, which still has the bell-tower and the fine granite **porch★** of a former 16C church. Note the elegant canopies above the statues of the Apostles and the delicate ornamentation round the doors.
Take the narrow rue St-Thivisiau to reach the **Fontaine de St-Thivisiau**, a 15C fountain decorated with eight granite low-relief sculptures. The chapel in middle of the churchyard, dedicated to St Anne, was an ossuary in the 17C. The façade is adorned with six caryatids. Death is represented to the left of the west doorway. In the village of **Lambader**, 8km/5mi north, the Chapelle Notre-Dame has a lovely rood screen in the Flamboyant Gothic style (1481).
Head towards Landerneau, then turn right via the intersection at La-Croix-des-Maltotiers.

Bodilis – *15min.* The **church★** (16C) is preceded by a Flamboyant bell-tower pierced with three openings at the base. The large 17C sacristy, jutting out from the north aisle, is very handsome, with a roof in the shape of an inverted hull, a richly decorated cornice and buttresses ornamented with niches. A porch opens on the south side. The interior has remarkable **decorations★**: purlins, tie-beams, hammerbeams, statues and gilded altarpieces. The font canopy is carved from Kersanton granite. There is also a colourful Entombment in high relief on the porch wall.
Rejoin D 712 Landerneau and bear right.

Moulin de Brézal – The mill, which has an interesting façade with a Flamboyant doorway, stands in a pleasant setting below a pool. On the opposite side of the road is the ruined Chapelle de Pont-Christ (1533).

★**La Roche-Maurice** – The village, situated on a hillside and dominated by the ruins of a castle, has a fine parish close, featuring three crosses with Christ and the thieves.

Church – An elegant, twin-galleried belfry crowns the 16C building. The **south porch★** is delicately carved with bunches of grapes and statuettes of saints. Inside, note the Renaissance **rood screen★** decorated on the side facing the nave with 12 statues carved in the round, including nine Apostles and three Popes, and on the chancel side with low-relief sculptures of saints. Behind the high altar, a large **stained-glass window★** (1539) illustrates the Passion and the Resurrection of Christ. Also of interest is the panelled ceiling adorned with angels and coats of arms, carved purlins and beams.

★**Ossuary** – This ossuary dates from 1640 and is one of the largest in Brittany. Above the outside font, Death is shown armed with an arrow, threatening small figures framed in medallions representing all social classes: a peasant, a woman, a lawyer, a bishop, St-Yves, a pauper and a rich man; an inscription reads "*Je vous tue tous*" (Death comes to all).

Landerneau – *See LANDERNEAU.*
Leave Landerneau by ② on the town plan, towards Sizun.
The road follows a pleasant wooded valley studded with fine rocks.

★La Martyre – *Left after 7km/4mi – 15min*. This **parish close★**, the oldest in the Léon region, opens onto a triumphal arch with a Flamboyant balustrade and a small Calvary. The ossuary (1619) is adorned with a curious caryatid and macabre motifs. The 14-16C church has a fine historiated **porch★** (c 1450) on its south side. Inside, note the carved purlins, tie-beams, altarpieces and 15C chancel screen. The chancel is lit by 16C **stained-glass windows★**. A *pardon* is held on the second Sunday in May and the second Sunday in July.

Ploudiry – The village, formerly the largest parish of the Léon region, has an interesting close. On the façade of the ossuary (1635), Death is depicted striking down men of all social classes. The church, rebuilt in the 19C, retains a fine south **porch★** dating from 1665. The high altar, adorned with polychrome high-relief carvings and the side altars are good specimens of 17C Breton art. In the chancel is a 17C window depicting the Passion.

Pass through Le Traon and turn left towards Sizun.

★Sizun – *See SIZUN.*

Proceed to Carhaix.

Moulins de Kerouat ⊙ – Under the auspices of the Parc naturel régional d'Armorique, the 19C village of Kerouat has been revived. You will see its mills, dwelling house, outbuildings (stable, barn) and bread oven; learn how a water mill functioned with its scoop wheel and mechanism (gears on the ground floor, millstone on the upper floor), and how the miller lived.

The overseer's house is characteristic of the region with its projecting wing perpendicular to the main part of the building; it is where meals were served.

Continue onto Carhaix and at Ty Douar bear left.

Commana – The village stands on an isolated foothill of the Monts d'Arrée. Within the close is a 16C-17C **church★** with a fine south porch. Inside, there are three interesting altarpieces. Note the **altar★** to St Anne (1682) in the north aisle and an Ecce Homo in wood on a pillar in the transept, to the right. The canopied font is ornamented with five statues: Faith, Hope, Charity, Justice and Temperance.

In the summer there is an exhibit of sacred art in the charnel-house.

Mougau-Bian – Beyond the hamlet, to the right, is a **covered alleyway★**, 14m/46ft long; some of the uprights are carved on the inside with lances and daggers.

Return to the road to Carhaix and bear right; 1km/0.5mi further on, take an uphill road to the right to join the Morlaix road, and turn left.

★★Roc Trévezel – *see Monts d'ARRÉE*

Near Plounéour-Ménez, turn right.

Le Releg – Nestling in the valley, a 12C-13C church and the ruins of the monastery buildings, are all that remain of the former Cistercian abbey. It is a simple, austere building, although the façade was restored in the 18C; note the staircase leading up to the monk's dormitory. Around the chancel are statues of St Benedict and St Bernard. Two *pardons* are held every year: Ste-Anne's with a Celtic music concert and that of Notre-Dame-du-Releg.

Turn back and bear right towards Morlaix.

Pleyber-Christ – It has a small parish close. The Gothic-Renaissance **church** is preceded by a triumphal arch (1921) dedicated to the dead of the First World War. Inside the building, which has fine carved purlins and remarkable beams, are some old pews and three lovely altarpieces. There is a small ossuary to the left of the church.

Continue towards Ste-Sève; after 3.5km/2mi, take the road on the right to return to Morlaix.

Rivière d'ÉTEL

Michelin map 230 fold 35

This very short river, which forms a bay west of the Quiberon Peninsula, follows a course which covers 15km/9mi from its source to the sea, and yet the banks are so winding that the length of them stretched out would measure 100km/60mi! This makes it a lovely place to walk and enjoy nature.

Barre d'Étel – The River Étel is known for its treacherous bank of quicksand *(barre)*, which offers a spectacular scene in bad weather. Navigation is difficult and requires constant surveillance. The view extends over Groix Island, Belle-Île and the Quiberon peninsula. The small fishing port of **Étel** lies on the river's south bank. It is home to a fleet of about 10 fishing boats, which sail to the Azores, and a small fleet of trawlers, which fish along the coast.

The river, which abounds in fish and oysters, flows inland to the commune of Nostang.

Pont-Lorois – This short and pretty run gives a glimpse of the wide estuary, which on the left opens out into a bay and on the right narrows into a deep channel which winds down to the sea.

Left Bank

Chapelle St-Cado – *15min on foot there and back*. This chapel, like the church at Merlevenez, is one of the few Romanesque buildings in the Morbihan. Its general simplicity, with unornamented rounded arches, capitals with very plain decoration and dim lighting, contrasts with the fine Flamboyant style gallery running on the inside of the 16C façade. It is in this chapel that the deaf sought help from St Cado whose stone bed and pillow can still be seen. The chapel, the Calvary and the little fishermen's houses make a charming Breton **scene**★ especially at high tide. The St-Cado fountain stands below the east end.

Pointe du Verdon – As with all the points of the bay, the far end of the Pointe du Verdon is devoted to oyster farming; after crossing the isthmus and before taking the uphill road through the pines, bear right to reach a platform from which there is a fine view over the oyster beds. At low tide it is possible to walk round the point.

Right Bank

Presqu'île de Nestadio – This village has some 16C houses. At the end of the peninsula, stands a small chapel dedicated to St-Guillaume.

Pointe de Mané-Hellec – *By a small transformer station, turn left onto a surfaced road*. Lovely view of St-Cado and its chapel, Pont-Lorois, the River Étel and the Forêt de Locoal-Mendon.

★**Merlevenez** – This little town's **church**★ is one of the few Romanesque churches in Brittany which has kept intact its elegant doorways with chevron and saw-tooth archivolts, its depressed arches in the nave, its historiated capitals and dome on squinches rising above the transept crossing. Modern stained-glass windows by Grüber illustrate scenes from the Life of the Virgin.

The length of time given in this guide
 – for touring allows time to enjoy the views and the scenery;
 – for sightseeing is the average time required for a visit.

LE FAOUËT

Population 2 869
Michelin map 58 fold 17 or 230 fold 20

This village is the centre of a very picturesque district extending between the Stêr Laër and the Ellé, two rivers flowing from the Montagnes Noires.

Halles – The covered market with its great slate roof supported at the sides on short granite columns and at the ends by massive porches, was built in 16C. Inside, three aisles lie under the fine timber work. A domed pinnacle crowns the building.

Grand-Place – In this shady square in front of the market, stands a monument to **Corentin Carré**, the youngest soldier of France. In 1915 he enlisted at the age of 15, and died in aerial combat in 1918. He was then a sergeant-major.

EXCURSIONS

★**Chapelle St-Fiacre** – ⏱ *2.5km/1.5mi southeast on D 790*. The chapel is a fine 15C building. The façade has one of the best gable-belfries in Brittany *(see photograph p 44)*.
Inside, the **rood screen★★** of lace-like woodcarving is a Flamboyant work of 1480 *(see photograph p 46)*. On the nave side, scenes of the Temptation of Adam and Eve, the Annunciation and the Calvary are related. The most curious figures are on the chancel side; they picture theft (a man picking fruit from a tree), drunkenness (a man vomiting a fox), lust (a man and a woman) and laziness (a Breton peasant playing bagpipes and a bombard). The decoration of the panels of the gallery and the corbels is quite varied. The stone altarpiece against the left pillar shows the martyrdom of St Sebastian. There are fine 16C **stained-glass windows** in the chancel and transept: the Passion (chancel), the Life of St John the Baptist (south transept), the Tree of Jesse and the Life of St Fiacre (north transept). The statues of St Apollinia, St Fiacre (in a painted wooden niche) and a Breton duke in court dress date from the 15C and 16C.

Chapelle Ste-Barbe ⏱ – *3km/1.8mi northeast of Le Faouët via D 790*. This Flamboyant-style chapel is built in a rocky cleft on the side of a hill. The **site★** is very pretty; from a height of some 100m/300ft, it overlooks the small Ellé Valley. The great stairway *(78 steps)*, built in 1700, leading up to the chapel, is linked by an arch to the St Michael Oratory (Oratoire St-Michel) crowning a rock spur. Nearby, in a small building, is the bell tolled by pilgrims to call down blessings from heaven.
Owing to its position and orientation, the chapel has only a single aisle and a small apse. Inside are Renaissance stained-glass windows and the lords' gallery with finely carved panels. Two *pardons* are held every year.
Paths lead down to the sacred fountain, below the chapel.
From a rocky platform reached by a path starting on the right half-way along the car park, there is a good view of the sunken, wooded Ellé Valley.

LE FOLGOËT★★

Population 3 094
Michelin map 58 fold 4 or 230 folds 3 and 4 – Local map see ABERS

You should see this little village and its magnificent Basilica of Our Lady (Notre-Dame) during the great pardon *(See the Calendar of events at the end of the guide)*. It is the best known in the Léon region and one of the largest in Brittany. The ceremonies begin at 6pm the day before and continue the next day. The *pardon* of St Christopher with the blessing of cars is on the fourth Sunday in July.

Legend – The name Folgoët (Fool's Wood) recalls the legend attached to the foundation of the shrine. In the mid 14C, a poor half-wit named Salaün lived in a hollow oak in a wood, near a spring not far from Lesneven. He knew only a few words, and he constantly repeated them: "Itron Gwerc'hez Vari" (Lady Virgin Mary). After his death a lily grew on his grave; the pistil made the words "Ave Maria" in gold letters. Men dug up the earth and found that the lily sprang from Salaün's mouth. News of the miracle spread in Brittany. The War of Succession was raging at the time. The Pretender Montfort vowed that if he won he would build a sumptuous chapel to the Virgin. After his victory at Auray, he gave orders for the building to begin. The altar was to stand over the spring where the simpleton used to drink. The work was completed by Montfort's son in 1423.
The chapel was pillaged during the Revolution. To save it from being demolished, 12 farmers joined together to buy it. It was returned to the parish at the Restoration, and has been gradually repaired since.

★★Basilique – *30min*. A great esplanade with inns on each side leads up to the basilica, but is not even wide enough to hold the crowd on *pardon* days. The **north tower★** of the façade supports one of the finest bell-towers in Brittany.

The basilica is square in shape, which is unusual; the Chapel of the Cross, whose east wall is an extension of the flat east end, branches off the chancel. This chapel has a fine **porch★**. Salaün's fountain, where pilgrims come to drink, stands outside, against the east wall. The water comes from the spring under the altar.

Inside is a masterpiece of Breton art of the 15C, the admirably carved granite **rood screen★★**. Five 15C Kersanton granite altars stand in the east end. The Chapel of the Cross and the apse are adorned by fine rose windows. There is a 15C statue of Our Lady of Folgoët.

Left of the basilica the little 15C manor house of **Le Doyenné**, though much restored, forms an attractive group with the pilgrim's inn and the church.

In the inn, a small **museum** ⊙ contains a collection of 15C, 16C and 17C stone statues, archives and 15C furnishings.

EXCURSION

Lesneven – *Northeast of Folgoët*. Lesneven was founded in the 5C by the Breton chief Even. There are several 17C and 18C granite houses.

Musée de Léon ⊙ – Located in the Ursuline convent's chapel, this museum is devoted to the history of the Léon region.

Note the authentic decree signed by Louis XIV authorising the creation of an Ursuline convent in Lesneven; a section pertains to General Le Flô. Displayed in the popular arts and traditions section are fine furnishings and 19C costumes.

FOUESNANT★

Population 6 524

Michelin map 58 fold 15 or 230 fold 32

This town is in the middle of one of the most fertile areas in Brittany; the villages stand among cherry and apple orchards. This is also where the best Breton cider is produced. The costumes and headdresses of Fouesnant are a very pretty sight at the feast of the apple trees and at the *pardon* of St Anne *(see Calendar of events)*.

Its beaches and small ports make it a popular seaside resort.

Church – Built in the 12C, the church, remodelled in the 18C, was restored. On the square stands a small 17C Calvary; the monument to the dead, left of the porch, the work of the Breton sculptor Quillivic, is remarkable for the stately yet serious expression of the peasant woman wearing a local headdress.

Hotels

OUR SELECTION

Manoir du Stang – *29940 La Forêt-Fouesnant, 1.5km/1mi north of la Forêt-Fouesnant on V 7* – ☎ *02 98 56 97 37* – *closed 26 Sept-4 May* – 🅿 – *24 rooms 490/950F* – *breakfast 45F* – *restaurant 180/190F*. Generations of this family of "gentleman farmers" have been living in this magnificent 16C residence for over 200 years. Even England's Queen Mother graced them with a visit in 1990! Its large flower park and its elegant rooms will seduce you as well. The restaurant is open only in the summer for dinner.

Pointe Moussterlin – *6km/4mi southwest of Fouesnant on D 145 and D 134* – ☎ *02 98 56 04 12* – *closed 16 Oct-1 Apr* – 🅿 – *47 rooms 465F* – *breakfast 43F* – *restaurant 95/200F*. The three buildings of this hotel offer the guest a variety of choices: traditional or modern rooms with sea and beach or garden views. It is a very pleasant establishment, well-run by a mother and daughter team.

Festivals

Les "Festimusicales" – In the summer, 120 free open-air concerts are given facing the ocean.

Nature outings

The tourist office organises "nature outings" from February to November, with excursions to the Îles de Glénan in April to admire the special narcissus flowers there (☎ 02 98 56 00 93, bring a picnic).

Getting to the Îles de Glénan

From Fouesnant – *In season, 2 departures per day: morning and afternoon. Information from the tourist office at* ☎ *02 98 56 00 93.*

From Bénodet – *In season, 2 departures per day: morning and afternoon. Information from the tourist office at* ☎ *02 98 57 00 14.*

From Concarneau – *In season, 2 departures per day: morning and afternoon. Information from the tourist office at* ☎ *02 98 97 01 44.*

From Loctudy – *In season, 2 departures per day: morning and afternoon. Information from the tourist office at* ☎ *02 98 87 53 78.*

Inside the church, the tall granite pillars are adorned with fine Romanesque capitals. An unusual stoup is built into an engaged pillar. A triumphal arch, with pointed arch and four recessed orders, separates the nave from the transept where the altar stands. Naive statues are located in the chancel and entrance.

EXCURSION

Commemorative monument, La Forêt-Fouesnant

La Forêt-Fouesnant – *3.5km/2.2mi east.* This village possesses a **parish close** and a 16C Calvary with four corner pilasters. The church porch, dating from 1538, is adorned with two old, rough-hewn statues of St Roch and St Mélar. Inside, at the high altar are an altarpiece and, on either side, two 17C statues. The chapels at the far end of the church contain, to the right, a wooden statue of St Alan and to the left, a font (1628) with a piscina and a basin hewn from the same block. In the chapel on the south side of the chancel stands a Pietà. Breton and Celtic music is played in the background all day.

Port-la-Forêt – This port for pleasure craft has been built near La Forêt-Fouesnant; it can hold 800 boats. There are boat services to the Îles de Glénan and up the Odet.

Cap-Coz – This small resort is built on a sandy spit, between the cliffs of Beg-Meil and the channel to Port-la-Forêt. The view extends on one side over La Forêt Bay, Beg-Meil and Concarneau and on the other side over Port-la-Forêt and La Forêt-Fouesnant.

A pleasant excursion can be enjoyed by taking the **coastal path** *(1hr on foot there and back – access through a door after the pine grove at the far end of the great wall along the road leading to the beach).* This path runs along La Forêt Bay as far as La Roche-Percée, overlooking or crossing small coves and affording fine views of the coastline from Kerleven to the Pointe de Trévignon.

Beg-Meil – Beg-Meil (meaning the Point of the Mill) is located at the mouth of Baie de La Forêt and opposite Concarneau. This resort has beaches both on its bay and ocean front. On the bay side there are small rocky wooded coves: Oiseaux Beach and La Cale Beach. On the ocean side there are dunes: the well-equipped Sémaphore Beach, while from the vast Dunes Beach (or Grande Plage), the Glénan archipelago is visible in the distance. From **Pointe de Beg-Meil** (Beg-Meil Point), there is a fine view of Concarneau and Baie de La Forêt.

Pointe de Mousterlin – From the end of the point, there is an extensive view of the coast from the Pointe de Lesconil to the Pointe de Trévignon, with in the distance the Île aux Moutons and the Îles de Glénan. The Eckmühl Lighthouse can be seen on the right after dark.

★**Île de Glénan** – The archipelago consists of nine islets surrounded by reefs and lies off Concarneau.

Tour – Boats go to the **Îles St-Nicolas** which has a few houses, a skin diving school (Centre International de Plongée) and a breeding pool for crustaceans. A footpath goes round the island affording good views of the coast from Penmarch to Le Pouldu.

To the north lies the **Île Brunec** and to the south the **Île du Loch**, which can easily be distinguished by the chimney from a former seaweed factory. Both are privately owned.

Penfret with its lighthouse, **Cigogne** (The Stork) identified by its 18C fort and the annexe of the marine laboratory of Concarneau, **Bananec**, which is linked to St-Nicolas at low tide, and **Drénec** are islands from which the internationally famous sailing school, the Centre Nautique de Glénan, operates.

The **Île Giautec** and other uninhabited islands are kept as bird sanctuaries: gulls, terns, oyster catchers and cormorants nest there.

FOUGÈRES★★

Population 22 239
Michelin map 59 fold 18 or 230 fold 28.

This former stronghold is built in a picturesque setting on a promontory overlooking the winding valley of the Nançon. Below it, on a rocky height almost entirely encircled by the river, stands a magnificent feudal castle whose walls, with their 13 big towers, are among the most massive in Europe.

The town centre (place Aristide-Briand, place du Théâtre, rue Nationale and the neighbouring streets) has been transformed into a pedestrian precinct. The Classical buildings in this area are the works of Gabriel.

HISTORICAL NOTES

A frontier post – Standing on the border of Brittany and France, Fougères acquired great military importance in the early Middle Ages, when its barons were very powerful. The most famous was Raoul II. He lived in the mid 12C under Conan IV, known as "the Little", Duke of Brittany. This weak duke submitted to Henry II Plantagenet, King of England and Duke of Normandy, but the proud Raoul revolted against the English yoke. He formed a league with some of the Breton nobles and rebelled against Henry II. In 1166 Henry II surrounded Fougères, which capitulated after three months' siege. The castle was completely demolished, but Raoul immediately began to rebuild it, and part of his work still stands.

In the 13C the fief passed to some Poitou noblemen, the Lusignans. They claimed to be descendants of the fairy Mélusine and gave her name to the finest of the towers that they added to the walls.

Fougères is an example of a formidable fortress which was often taken. Among those who fought their way into it were St Louis, Du Guesclin, Surienne, a leader from Aragon in the service of the English (at night without striking a blow), La Trémoille, the Duke of Mercœur and the men of the Vendée.

After the union of Brittany and France, there were a succession of governors at Fougères; 10 of its towers bear their names. The castle was then mainly used as a prison. In the 18C it became private property. The town bought it in 1892.

Chouan country – Victor Hugo, in *Quatre-vingt-treize* (Ninety-three), and Balzac, in *Les Chouans*, introduced Fougères and its region into their stories of the royalist rebellion. They gleaned their information on the spot. In 1836 Hugo, accompanied by Juliette Drouet (who was born at Fougères), gave a glowing account of the town and castle. "I should like to ask everyone," he wrote, "have you seen Fougères?" Balzac stayed with friends at Fougères, explored the neighbourhood with survivors of the rebellion and wrote his novel there in 1828.

The Breton and Vendéen revolt continued, with a few pauses, from 1793 to 1804. Its supporters were named after their call imitating the hoot of an owl *(chat-huant)*. The instigator of the movement was the Marquis of La Rouërie (1756-93), who was born at Fougères. His life was a real adventure story. A turbulent youth resulted in a warrant for his arrest; to avoid the Bastille prison, he fled to Switzerland. Thinking he had a religious vocation, La Rouërie shut himself in a Trappist monastery. But he then felt the call to arms. Discarding the habit, he went to America, where the War of Independence was being fought, and became a general in the American Army. He returned to France on the eve of the Revolution. When it broke out the Marquis refused to emigrate and prepared for resistance by ambuscade, well suited to the Breton countryside.

He organised stores of hidden arms and provisions and recruited a secret army which would rise at a sign. But the plotter was betrayed and obliged to flee. He went into hiding and died, worn out, in January 1793. The following month the Convention decreed the mass levy: Brittany rebelled, and the war foreseen by La Rouërie broke out.

Fougères

★★ THE CASTLE ⏱ 1hr 30min

The castle is a fine example of military architecture of the Middle Ages. There is an interesting general view from the public garden.

The site is curious. A loop in the river, washing a rocky eminence, shaped like a very narrow peninsula, formed an excellent defensive position. Military architects took advantage of this site to build ramparts and towers and turn the peninsula into an island by a short diversion of the Nançon at the base of the loop. As the castle was connected with the upper town by the city ramparts, the garrison could take part in its defence; they also had the advantage of being able to retire into the fortress and hold it as a frontier post for the Duchy of Brittany should the town fall. The fortress, as we see it, has suffered greatly over the centuries. The wall is complete, with its curtains closely following the lie of the land and its 13 towers. Unfortunately, we can no longer see the high keep that commanded all the defences; it was razed in 1166 by King Henry II of England and there are now only traces which can be seen when visiting the castle's interior. The main buildings which occupied part of the inner court were also demolished down to their foundations, in the beginning of the 19C. History tells us that the defenders often succumbed and that attackers were able to seize these high walls, either by surprise attack or after long sieges. An outer tour of the castle shows the attackers' point of view; an inner tour, that of the defenders.

★ Around the fortifications – *Park your car in place Raoul-II, skirt the fortifications and then, left, along rue Le Bouteiller.*

As you circle the walls you will see the splendid towers in all their variety of appearance and structure. At the start you will also see, in the middle of the north rampart, the 14C Guibé Turret, a corbelled sentry-post built onto the wall.

Going round the spur formed by the ramparts towards the west, you will see how massively the defences are concentrated at this point. The whole forms a triangle with two towers at the base and a postern at the apex. The 15C postern today looks out on empty space, but it was once connected with a double arcade that crossed the moat to communicate with an outwork. The 13C and 14C Gobelin Tower, to the left of the postern, and the 14C Mélusine Tower, to the right, are round and overlook the walls from a height. Stripped of their machicolations and with their upper parts probably rebuilt, they have lost much of their proud aspect. The Mélusine Tower is regarded as a masterpiece of military architecture of the period; it is over 13m/41.5ft in diameter, with walls 3.50m/11ft thick and rising 31m/99ft above the rock.

Further on are two squat, horseshoe-shaped towers, the Surienne and the Raoul, which mark the last stage in the building of the castle (15C). Built to serve as platforms for artillery, they contain several storeys of very strong and well-preserved gun platforms. To resist enemy artillery fire, their walls are 7m/22ft thick. At the end of the 15C, artillery had been in use for nearly a century and a half, and siege warfare often took the form of an artillery duel at short range.

Opposite the two towers stands the Église St-Sulpice. On the right is the Marchix District (see Additional Sights below).

Still following the walls, you will see the 13C Cadran Tower, two centuries older than the others. It is small, square and badly damaged, not nearly as strong as its neighbours and recalling the time when firearms had not yet taken the place of bows and arrows. Further on, Our Lady's Gate is the only one left of the four rampart gateways preceding the four gates in the walls which encircled the town. The left-hand tower, which is higher and is pierced with narrow loopholes, dates from the 14C; that on the right, with very ornamental machicolations, dates from the 15C, as do the Surienne and Raoul Towers.

Go under the gate and follow rue de la Fourchette, then turn a sharp right on rue de la Pinterie. To leave the garden, go under the ruins of a beautiful chapel doorway and go once more into rue de la Pinterie on the left. This leads to the castle entrance.

★★ **Inside the castle** – The entrance, preceded by a moat filled from a diversion of the Nançon, is through the square tower of La Haye-St-Hilaire. To reach it, you first had to go through a town gate and the wall before it. The castle has three successive walls. The *Avancée* (advanced wall) was guarded by three 13C towers pierced with loopholes. When this line of resistance had been crossed, attackers would enter a small courtyard on the island formed by a second diversion of the river, and would come under the converging fire of defenders posted on the four sides. Thus exposed, the attackers had to cross a second moat before reaching the

H Hôtel de ville
J Hôtel de la Belinaye
  (Tribunal d'instance)

M Musée Emmanuel-de-la-Villéon

main ring of fortifications, guarded by four towers dating from the 12C and 15C. When both lines had been stormed, they would burst into the main inside courtyard; but the defenders still had a chance to rally. A third position, the redoubt, girt with a wall and two towers, and the keep (demolished after the 12C), made a long resistance possible, and from these positions the garrison could still seek safety in flight through the postern.

Entering the main inside courtyard, go round the walls on the wall walk. This enables one to appreciate the might of such a fortress and also to enjoy some good views of Fougères.

At the end of the highest wall of the castle is Mélusine Tower, which from the top *(75 steps)* commands a fine view of the castle and the town. Further on are the remains of the keep and north wall, and beyond, the Guibé Turret and the Coigny Tower (13C and 14C), whose second and third storeys were turned into a chapel in the 17C. The summit was disfigured by the addition of a loggia during its first restoration in the 19C.

Hotels

BUDGET

Chambre d'hôte Ferme de Mésauboin – *10km/6mi down the road to Vitré via Billé (D 179) then follow road to St-Georges-de-Chesne – ☎ 02 99 97 61 57 – reservations required – 5 rooms 180/232F – meal 92F.* The calm and simplicity of this 17C farm-manor will seduce visitors who love being in the country. You can enjoy home-made regional specialities, sleep in the small, cozy bedrooms, or perhaps in the summer choose to stay in one of the two gîtes.

Eating Out

BUDGET

Crêperie des Remparts – *102 rue de la Pinterie – ☎ 02 99 94 53 53 – closed Jan, Wed and Thur off-season (except school holidays) – 40/80F.* Near the château, one of the oldest buildings in Fougères houses this *crêperie* with its massive ceiling beams and its walls decorated with old photographs. In nice weather, it opens its terrace along the public park which borders the ramparts.

OUR SELECTION

Haute Sève – *37 boulevard J.-Jaurès – ☎ 02 99 94 23 39 – closed 20 July-16 Aug, 1 Jan-15 Jan, Sun evening and Mon – 120/280F.* A young couple has been running this small restaurant in Fougères for several years. In its long and narrow dining room, you can enjoy fresh cuisine created around regional specialties. The service is amiable and attentive.

Night-life

Les Oubliettes – *71 rue de la Pinterie – ☎ 02 99 94 15 62 – Tues-Sun 3pm-1am.* This little cocktail bar is run by a young Parisian couple. whose motto is "a good cocktail is worth several beers."

Le Coquelicot – *18 rue de Vitré – ☎ 02 99 99 82 11 – Tues 4pm-1am, Wed-Sat 4pm-3am.* Every Thursday for 20 years now, this seemingly ordinary little music-bar, has been hosting well-known rock , jazz and blues artists. More than 800 concerts have been held here, since its tumultuous beginnings which landed its owner in jail for two weeks for disturbing the peace.

Guided Tour

Tourist train – *Departure place Pierre-Symon – ☎ 02 99 99 71 72.* Guided tour of the town (30min).

Market

The Aumaillerie market is the most important livestock market in western France: it is held every Friday morning starting at 5.30am.

Recreation

Ferme de Chênedet – *Route forestière to Villeboeuf, in Landéan, 8 km/4.8mi northwest of Fougères – ☎ 02 99 97 35 46 – Mon-Sat 9am-6pm.* In the heart of the Fougères forest, this recreation centre offers both equestrian activities (equitation classes, and horseback riding outings), and water sports (kayak and row-boat rentals in the summer). Off road-vehicle rentals all year.

ADDITIONAL SIGHTS

★Église St-Sulpice (AY) – A Gothic building in the Flamboyant style; although erected between the 15C and the 18C, it has great homogeneity. It has a slim 15C slate-covered steeple. The inside is enriched with 18C woodwork; nonetheless the 15C granite **altarpieces★** in the chapels are the most noteworthy. The Lady Chapel (on the left) contains the altarpiece dedicated to Anne of Brittany, the church's donor. In the niche, underneath Brittany's coat of arms, is the miraculous 12C statue of the Nursing Virgin (Notre-Dame des Marais). Off the south aisle, in the Chapelle des Tanneurs, there is an imposing altarpiece adorned with vine leaves, crockets, small animals and the instruments of the Passion.

★Jardin Public (AY) – This lovely garden, at the foot of St-Léonard and the town hall, is laid out partly in terraces on the site of the former town walls and partly on the slopes down into the Nançon river valley. Follow the low wall prolonging the balustrade to the entrance for an extensive view of the woodlands typical of the Fougères region. From the terrace closed off by the balustrade, there is an interesting general **view★** of the castle.

Quartier du Marchix – This area around place du Marchix (the site of the former market at the heart of the old town) (AY), with its picturesque old houses, has always been of interest to painters.

Take rue Foskeraly.

From rue Foskeraly, which skirts the Nançon, there are good views of the old ramparts now converted into a public garden. Take a walk along rue du Nançon with its 16C houses. There are other interesting houses at the corner of rue de la Providence and rue de Lusignan as well as in rue de Lusignan.

On place du Marchix are two fine 16C houses, nos 13 and 15. Take rue des Tanneurs to cross the bridge over the Nançon; looking back, you will see a picturesque group formed by the backs of the houses of place du Marchix.

Église St-Léonard (AY) – The 15C-16C church has a richly decorated 16C north façade and a 17C tower. It is lit through modern stained-glass windows by Lorin; however, in the Chapel of the Cross, on the left as you go in, are two 12C scenes of St Benedict's life, and in the baptismal chapel pieces of 16C **stained-glass windows★**.

Town Hall (Hôtel de Ville) (AY H) – A 16C building with a Renaissance doorway (partly walled up).

Musée Emmanuel de la Villéon ⊘ (ABY M) – The museum is located in a 16C house (restored) with a porch with wood and granite pillars.

It displays the works (drawings and watercolours) by **Emmanuel de la Villéon** (1858-1944), an Impressionist painter, born in Fougères. His works were inspired by the landscape and people of his native Brittany.

Beffroi – Rising proudly above the ramparts, this octagonal belfry was built in the 14C and 15C. It is decorated with gargoyles and topped by a slate-covered steeple.

Place Aristide-Briand (BY 5) – The **Hôtel de la Belinaye** (J), which presently houses the Magistrates' Court, was the birthplace of **Charles Armand Turpin de la Rouërie**. A statue was erected in 1993 to commemorate the bicentenary of his death.

Cattle Fair (Marché aux Bovins de l'Aumaillerie) – *2km/1mi to the southeast. Leave Fougères by ②.*

Forêt domaniale de Fougères – *3km/1.8mi northeast. Leave Fougères on ① on the town plan, the road to Flers.*

Those who like walking in a forest will spend hours strolling in the fine beech woods, along the forest roads. They can see two dolmens in ruins and a line of megalithic stones called the Druids' Cord (Cordon des Druides) near the Chennedet crossroads (Carrefour de Chennedet).

At Landéan, on the edge of the forest, near the Recouvrance crossroads (Carrefour de la Recouvrance) are the 12C cellars (now closed) once used as a secret hideout by the lords of Fougères.

Cap FRÉHEL★★★

Michelin map 59 fold 5 or 230 fold 10 – Local map see CÔTE D'ÉMERAUDE

The **site** ⊙ of this cape is one of the grandest on the Breton coast. Its red, grey and black cliffs rise vertically to a height of 70m/229ft and are fringed with reefs on which the swell breaks heavily. The coastal **panorama★★★** is vast in clear weather: from the Pointe du Grouin, on the right, with the Cotentin in the background, to the Île de Bréhat, on the left. The famous outline of Fort la Latte is visible on the right.

The **lighthouse** ⊙ *(145 steps)*, built between 1946 and 1950, is lit by a xenon flash lamp; the light carries only 200m/656ft in foggy weather but it can be seen 120km/74.5mi away when it is clear. From the gallery at the top of the tower, there is an immense view of the horizon: you may see Bréhat to the west, Jersey to the north, Granville, a part of the Cotentin Peninsula and the Îles Chausey to the northeast. At a point 400m/437yd from the lighthouse a siren mounted in a shelter gives two blasts every minute in foggy weather.

Walk round the cape *(30min)*, beginning left of the lighthouse. After passing the extreme point where the siren stands, you can look down on the Fauconnière rocks, crowded with seagulls and cormorants; the contrast between the mauvish-red of the rocks and the blue or green of the sea is striking. Near the Restaurant de la Fauconnière take a steep path on the right; halfway down, it reaches a platform from where there is another fine view of the Fauconnière rocks and the deep blue sea.

Boat trips ⊙, to view Cap Fréhel from the sea, leave from St-Malo and call in at Dinard.

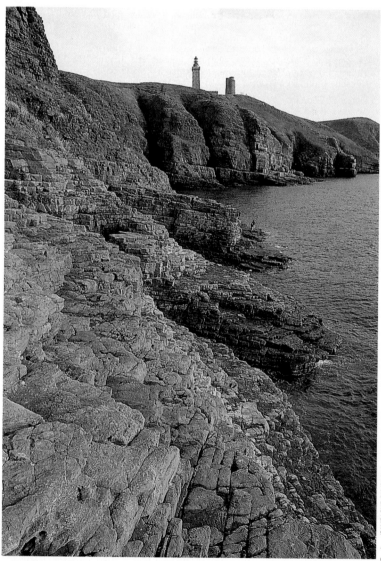

Cap Fréhel

Hotels

BUDGET

Hôtel du Fanal – *22240 Fréhel, 2. 5km/1.5mi south of Cap Fréhel via D 16* – ☎ *02 96 41 43 19* – *closed 26 Sept-6 Apr* – ▣ – *9 rooms 240/340F* – *breakfast 35F*. On the road leading to the cape, this wood-panelled hotel is simple and well-kept. Its few standard rooms are furnished in pine or rustic wood. The amiable welcome adds to the pleasure of this peaceful little stopover.

OUR SELECTION

See the addresses for La Côte d'Émeraude.

Eating Out

OUR SELECTION

Fauconnière – *At the end of the cape, 22240 Fréhel* – ☎ *02 96 41 54 20* – *closed 1 Oct-19 Mar and evening off-season* – *105/175F*. This restaurant must be reached on foot. Built beside the cliffs in an exceptionally wild site, it features a magnificent view onto the sea and the coasts. It is very popular with tourists, and offers several menus at reasonable prices.

EXCURSION

★★**Fort de la Latte** – A gate marks the entrance to the park. Follow the lane to the fort; you will pass a menhir known as Gargantua's Finger.

This stronghold, built by the Goyon-Matignons in the 14C, remodelled in the 17C and restored in the early 20C, has kept its feudal appearance. It stands on a picturesque **site**★★, separated from the mainland by two gullies, which are crossed by drawbridges. You will visit in succession: the two fortified enclosures, the inner courtyard, around which are located the guard-room, the Governor's living quarters, the cistern and the chapel. Cross the thick walls made to shield the defender from cannon-balls and go to the Échauguette Tower (Tour de l'Échaugette) and the cannon-ball foundry. A look-out post takes you to the keep. From the parapet walk, there is a **panorama**★★ of Sévignés Cove, Cap Fréhel, the bay of La Frênaye, Pointe de St-Cast, the Hébihens archipelago, the resorts of St-Briac and St-Lunaire, Pointe du Décollé, St-Malo, Paramé and Rothéneuf, the Île de Cézembre, the Pointe du Meinga and the walls of the fort. It is possible to walk up to the top of the tower *(difficult steps)*.

La GRANDE BRIÈRE★★

Michelin map 63 folds 14 and 15 or 230 fold 52

Also known by the name of **Grande Brière Mottière**, this region covers 7 000ha/17 297 acres of the total 40 000ha/98 840 acres belonging to the **Parc naturel régional de Brière**. Lying to the north of St-Nazaire, the area is renowned for its wildfowling and fishing. The world at large was to discover this region in 1923, through the pages of Alphonse de Chateaubriant's novel, *La Brière*.

Brière in the past – In early geological times the area was a forested, undulating basin which reached the hills of Sillon de Bretagne. Neolithic man (7500 BC) was expelled from the area, when there was a momentary maritime incursion. Marshes formed behind the alluvial banks deposited by the Loire. The trees died and were submerged and vegetable matter decomposed to form **peat bogs**, often entrapping fossilized tree trunks, known as "**mortas**", over 5 000 years old.

Brière from the 15C to the 20C – This swampy area was subdivided, water pumped and the drainage improved. In 1461, the Duke of Brittany, François II, decreed the area the common property of all Briérons, an act which was to be confirmed by several royal edicts. For centuries the Briérons (17 parishes divided into 21 *communes*) have cut the peat, gathered the reeds and rushes for thatching, woven baskets with the buckthorn, tended their gardens and kept poultry. They have trapped leeches, harpooned eels, placed eel-pots in the open stretches of water and wickerwork traps to catch pike, tench and roach; and hunted with their dogs in a boat hidden by a clump of willow trees. For ages the Briéron has propelled with a pole his **blin**, a flat-bottomed boat, loaded with cows or sheep going to pasture. In spite of these activities, the Briéron women also had to work to make ends meet. In the 19C and early 20C, two workshops in St-Joachim employed approximately 140 women to make wax orange blossoms. These flowers were used to make splendid brides' headdresses exported throughout Europe *(see Bride's House below)*.

Hotels

BUDGET

Chambre d'hôte Ty Gwen – *25 Île d'Errand, 44550 St-Malo-de-Guersac, 3km/2.4mi from St-Malo, after the church go straight on* – ☎ *02 40 91 15 04 – closed Oct-Mar – no credit cards – 4 rooms 220/300F – meal 120F.* Incredibly romantic, this pretty thatched cottage welcomes its guests with cozy comfort. Ceiling beams, fireplace and well-chosen fabrics create a refined atmosphere. Its charming garden and swimming pool add to the pleasure of stopping here. Rooms reserved for non-smokers only.

Eating Out

OUR SELECTION

Auberge de Kerbourg – *In Kerbourg, 44410 St-Lyphard, 6km/3.6mi south-west of St-Lyphard via D 51 (road to Guérande)* – ☎ *02 40 61 95 15 – closed 15 Dec-15 Feb, Sun evening off-season, Mon (but open evening in season), Tues lunch – 200/350F.* The authentic details of this old thatched cottage have been scrupulously preserved. The owners welcome their clients as if they were personal friends in the two meticulously decorated dining rooms, where the meal is also congenial and tasty.

Auberge du Parc – *44720 St-Joachim, Île de Fedrun* – ☎ *02 40 88 53 01 – closed Mar, Sun evening and Mon off-season – 150/380F.* You will be well-received in this attractive inn, with its blue shutters and thatched roof. In the muted dining room, you can enjoy a refined meal, or simply spend a peaceful night in one of its lovely rooms. A very charming stop!

Auberge de Breca – *Road to Breca (follow the signs to the restaurant) – July-Aug, daily 10am-6pm; Sept-June Fri-Wed.* This restaurant and ice-cream salon, located in an old hunting lodge, offers a quick bite or a little refreshment to those enjoying long row-boat outings.

Barge outings

Barge outings★★ are available all year; refer to the map of the park to find embarking points. The Brière is delightful in every season: abloom in the spring, lush green in the summer, orange and red in the autumn, and silver in the winter.

The Briéron of the 20C has remained closely attached to the land but, by force of circumstance, he is turning more to local industries: metallurgy in Trignac and dockyards and aeronautics at St-Nazaire. Nevertheless, he continues to fish, shoot, graze animals or cut reeds and pay his annual fee. Change is inevitable, roads now link the islets, locks have been built, marsh has become pastureland but despite it all, La Grande Brière has retained its charm and when the Briéron returns home he fishes and shoots for his own pleasure. Many of those who have boats will take visitors on trips along the canals and smaller channels beautiful with yellow irises (mid-May to mid-June) and pearl-white water lilies (mid-June to late July)

PARC NATUREL RÉGIONAL DE BRIÈRE

Created in 1970, the Brière Regional Nature Park covers 21 *communes* spread over 40 000ha/98 840 acres of which 15 000ha/37 000 acres are marshland. Its duties include the creation of traditional types of housing (the Lock Keeper's House, Brière thatched cottage...), the restoration of a typical Brière village (Kerhinet), exhibits, and cultural (folklore events) and recreational (rambling, cycling, canoe, kayak) activities.
The park also offers excellent opportunities for the study and observation of the local bird population.

Maison du Parc – 177 Île de Fédrun – 44720 Saint-Joachim – ☎ 02 40 91 68 60.

Round tour starting from St-Nazaire

83km/52mi – half a day

St-Nazaire – *3hr. See ST-NAZAIRE.*
Leave St-Nazaire by N 171, the road to Nantes.

Trignac – This rural community has seen the implantation of new industries. A road to the left leads to the **Pont de Paille** which affords a **view** of Trignac Canal. At **Montoir-de-Bretagne** turn left onto D 50.

St-Malo-de-Guersac – This, the largest of the islets (13m/43ft high), offers a **view** from Guérande in the west to the hilly region, Sillon de Bretagne, to the east. The road passes near new slate-roofed houses.

Rosé – A boat-building centre, this small port, was the former departure point for the boats plying upstream to Nantes and Vannes.

Maison de l'Éclusier ⊙ – The house is located on Rosé Canal. The lock keeper operated the two locks which regulated the water level of the marsh. There is an exhibit devoted to the fauna (stuffed animals) and flora to be found in the marshland. An aquarium contains the main species of Brière fish. Slides and various documents illustrate the formation and evolution of the marsh. Docked alongside the canal is a reconstruction of the *Théotiste*, which was used to transport peat.

Parc animalier ⊙ – *Field-glasses can be hired. Cross the bridge over the canal and take the path to the right to the reception building* (pavillon d'accueil) *800m/875yd further on. It can also be reached by boat (landing-stage to the right of the bridge). A path (about 1.8km/1mi) cuts through this nature reserve (26ha/64 acres), with observation posts where silence and patience will be rewarded. There are descriptive panels to help you identify the flora and fauna. In a wood and reed building Brière activities are displayed.*

Bear left before St-Joachim.

★**Île de Fédrun** – Linked to the St-Joachim road by two bridges, this, the most attractive of the islets, is entirely surrounded by marshland. The islet has two roads: one which divides it in two and the other which runs around it. At no 130 of the circular road is the **Maison de la Mariée** (Bride's House) ⊙. The interior of the house, arranged in typical Brière style, displays a collection of bridal headdresses decorated with wax orange blossoms and an explanation of how they are made. At no 180 are the administrative services of the Regional Nature Park (Maison du Parc).

No 308, the **Chaumière Briéronne** (Brière Thatched Cottage), shows a typical Brière cottage interior with costume exhibits, farming tools and equipment, an 1862 cadastral plan (has not been revised since), and a display of ducks' webbed feet: each webbed foot has been marked to identify its owner.

An audio-visual presentation illustrates marsh life, peat harvesting and a Brière wedding. The low, flower-bedecked houses retain the traditional thatched roof. The cottages on the islet's outer shores are backed by a **dike**, often planted with vegetables and fruit trees, which, itself borders the **canal** *(curée)* where the residents tie up their boats.

St-Joachim – The village, once a wax orange blossom manufacturing centre, extends along the two islets of **Brécun** (alt 8m/26ft) and **Pendille**, dominated by the tall white spire of its 19C **church** with very low aisles. The altar is adorned by a stone Calvary and the ambulatory has fine Romanesque arcading.

The road crosses the sparsely populated islets of **Camerun** and **Camer**.

La Chapelle-des-Marais – At the entrance to the village, on the right, is the **Maison du Sabotier** (Sabot-Maker's House), where the last Briéron craftsman lived. In the **church**, the granite pillars stand out against the white stone; in the chapel to the right of the chancel, there is a polychrome statue of St Corneille, protector of the flocks.

Take the road in the direction of Herbignac and after 4km/2.5mi turn left.

Château de Ranrouët ⊘ – *Leave the car in the car park (grassy) and go behind the old farm buildings.* This 12C-13C fortress, dismantled in 1618 by Louis XIII and burnt during the Revolution, is spectacular with its six round towers and moat (dried-up). Note in particular the 16C modifications designed to counter improved artillery (barbican, fortified curtain wall). Cannon-balls embedded in the right tower wall recall that the castle once belonged to the Rieux family, whose coat of arms included 10 gold cannon-balls.

Turn around and bear right towards Pontchâteau; at Mayun, turn right.

Les Fossés-Blancs – From a landing-stage on the canal to the north, there is a fine view of the Brière. A tour of the marsh provides an opportunity to study the flora and, occasionally, the fauna.

St-Lyphard – In the **church's belfry** ⊘ *(135 steps)* a lookout point has been set up. A **panorama**★★ extends onto the Brière and from the Loire estuary to the mouth of the Vilaine encompassing Guérande and its salt marshes.

Follow the road towards Guérande and turn left.

★**Dolmen de Kerbourg** – This covered alleyway stands on a mound near a windmill.

Continue in the direction of Le Brunet.

Kerhinet – A group of thatched cottages (restored) make up the **Musée du Chaume** ⊘, a charming hamlet *(visited on foot only)*. One of the cottages presents a modest **Brière interior** (dirt floor, meagre furnishings and kitchen utensils). In the shed are tools used for peat harvesting, farming and fishing.

In season, the arts and crafts centre *(maison des artisans)* displays works by artists from Guérande Peninsula.

Go onto Le Brunet and from there the road continues to Bréca.

Bréca – Good view over the Brière and Bréca Canal.

Return to Le Brunet; continue to La Chaussée-Neuve via St-André-des-Eaux.

La Chaussée-Neuve – It was from this former port that the boats loaded with peat used to leave. From here there is a wide **view**★ over the Brière.

Return to St-André-des-Eaux, and bear left to return to St-Nazaire.

EXCURSIONS

Pontchâteau – The church of Pontchâteau, which is perched on a hill in a region of windmills, now no longer in use, overlooks the little town with its houses built in terraces on the banks of the River Brivet.

Calvaire de la Madeleine – *4km/2.5mi west. Leave Pontchâteau on D 33 towards Herbignac. Leave the car in the car park on the left side of the road.*

St Louis-Marie Grignion de Montfort (1673-1716), a famous preacher, had the Calvary built in 1709 on the heath of the same name. Destroyed under Louis XIV, it was rebuilt in 1821.

From the Temple of Jerusalem, a fortress-type oriental palace, an alley crosses the park and leads to Pilate's Court or Scala Sancta, the five high-relief sculptures of which represent the Passion. It is the first station in the Stations of the Cross which,

Thatched roof in the Grande Brière region

further on (on the left) are continued by large white statues derived from the local folklore. From above the Calvary the view extends to the Brière, St-Nazaire and Donges. The small chapel at the foot of the Calvary houses the original Christ (1707) in wood as well as frescoes recounting the life of the preacher, Montfort. *(Pilgrimages on Sundays in summer).*

Fuseau de la Madeleine – *800m/875yd from the Calvary. Take the road to the left of the statue of the Sacred Heart, cross the park and bear left at the first crossroads.*
This menhir, 7m/23ft tall and 5m/16ft in circumference, stands in the middle of a field.

Île de GROIX★

Michelin map 58 fold 12 or 230 fold 34

Groix Island is smaller than its neighbour, Belle-Ile, but has the same geological form – a mass of schist rock. The coast to the north and west is wild and deeply indented: there you will see cliffs and giant rocks, valleys and creeks; while the east and south sides are flatter and along the coast there are many sheltered sandy creeks. Small villages dot some of the still cultivated fields and the vast expanses on which gorse and heather grow.

TOUR ⏱ *1 day*

Groix – This is the island's capital with its low slate-roofed houses grouped round the church. The bell-tower is crowned by a tunny fish weather vane, recalling the island's great tunny fishing days of the early 1900s.

Locmaria – Facing the open sea, this village, with its winding streets, has a small harbour, where fishing and pleasure boats seek shelter behind a jetty.

Pen-Men – The western tip of the island, to the right of Pen-Men Lighthouse, is a rocky headland, offering splendid views of the Morbihan coast extending from Talut Point to Port-Manech. This, the **Réserve naturelle François Le Bail**, is home to thousands of birds.

Plages des Grands Sables – This is the island's largest beach; garnets can sometimes be found in the sand.

Pointe de Bileric – Near the Beg-Melen signal station *(not open to the public)*, many black-legged kittiwakes can be seen nesting in this bird sanctuary.

Pointe des Chats – On this point, the lowest part of the island, stands a small lighthouse; fine view of the south coast. There is a mineralogy reserve where visitors can see garnets, needles of blue glaucophane and green lepidolite, but of course the taking of samples is strictly forbidden.

Port-Lay – This safe anchorage, where trawlers used to shelter, lies in a beautiful **setting★**.

Getting there

Daily departures from Lorient (45mi, 4 to 8 round trips per day, depending on the season) – 105F there and back off-season, 110F there and back high season – Société morbihannaise et nantaise de navigation (Lorient) – ☎ 02 97 64 77 64.

Hotels

BUDGET

Hôtel de la Marine – *In town* – ☎ *02 97 86 80 05* – *closed 3 Jan-3 Feb, Sun evening and Mon off-season, except during school holidays* – *22 rooms 248/450F* – *breakfast 46F* – *restaurant 80/140F*. What a jewel! This little hotel harbours delights: its pretty sunlit terrace, its charming garden and its simple and well-kept rooms. And in addition, its carefully prepared meals attract food lovers from miles around! Don't miss it!

OUR SELECTION

Hôtel Ty Mad – *On the harbour* – ☎ *02 97 86 80 19* – *closed Jan* – ▣ – *32 rooms 300/400F* – *breakfast 40F* – *restaurant 80/180F*. Located on the harbour, this hotel offers modern rooms in its recent wing. The view is certainly not spectacular, but the rooms are spacious and lighter than those in the older building. Heated swimming pool.

Night-life

Ty Beudeff – *Rue du Général-de-Gaulle* – ☎ *02 97 86 80 73* – *open daily 6pm-2am*. This incredible café has a world-wide reputation; its legendary owner, Alain, explains, "it's really more of a boat than a bar, in the sense that there are just a bunch of benches ...". And indeed, these benches are occupied by sailors or pretty mermaids who enjoy singing sea ballads in unison in this festive and slightly licentious atmosphere.

Port-Melin – The little creek can only be reached on foot down a steep slope. From the platform, there is a good **view** of the approach to Port-Tudy and of the Lorient coast in the distance.
The statue is of the Breton poet, J.-P. Calloc'h, native of the island (1888-1917), who wrote in Celtic, under the pseudonym of Bleimor.

Port-Mélite – A rocky cove with a beach. The view extends from the Étel Bar to the Pointe du Talut.

Port-St-Nicolas – A large bay with deep, clear waters hemmed in by cliffs.

Port-Tudy – Sheltered by two piers, this port offers a direct link with Lorient, on the mainland. Former tunny fishing port, it is now a safe harbour for trawlers and pleasure boats.
Housed in an early-20C canning factory, the **Ecomusée de l'Île de Groix** ⊘ presents interesting exhibits (explanatory panels, photographs...) on the island's geography, history and ethnography. The displays include the island's soil, its people and their different occupations: farming (the women worked the land, while the men were at sea), fishing (from 1870-1940 the Île de Groix possessed France's most

important tunny fishing fleet; note the ship model of a two-masted tunny fishing boat) and family life. Utensils, costumes and household items complete the exhibit. The *Kenavo*, the last coastal fishing cutter built on the Île de Groix, can be hired for a boat trip round the island; contact the tourist office *(syndicat d'intiative)*, for details.

★**Trou de l'Enfer** – This deep opening ("the Devil's Hole") in the cliff face into which the sea surges with great force, is a wild barren site with a beautiful **view** of the Pointe St-Nicolas and the rocky coast.

Presqu'île de GUÉRANDE★

Michelin map 63 folds 13 and 14 or 230 folds 51 and 52

This is a very interesting district in which you may see, besides the curious landscape of salt-marshes, several beaches, of which La Baule is the finest, the picturesque Côte Sauvage, busy fishing ports, Guérande and its ramparts, and Batz and its church.

The former gulf – In the Roman era, a great sea gulf stretched between the rocky Île de Batz and the Guérande ridge. A change of level of approximately 15m/50ft turned the gulf into marshland.

Sand brought down by the currents linked the Île de Batz with the mainland through the strip on which La Baule and Le Pouliguen stand. To the west the sandy Pen Bron Point has not quite reached the island; a channel remains open opposite Le Croisic through which the sea flows at high tide into the Grand and Petit Trait, vestiges of the former gulf. At low tide it retreats, exposing mud flats on which the coast dwellers raise oysters and mussels, clams and periwinkles. The rest of the marsh is used for salt pans.

Salt-marshes – The salt-marshes cover 1 800ha/4 448 acres divided into two basins: Mesquer and Guérande, forming a huge quadrilateral delimited by clay embankments. The sea, brought in by the tides through canals *(étier)*, irrigates the salt-marsh. Every 15 days, during the salt harvest, the salt pan worker allows the seawater to flow through a gate into a type of settling pond *(vasière)* used for removing the impurities (sand, clay etc). Then with the drop in water level the water flows through a series of evaporating ponds where the wind and sun cause the water to evaporate, producing brine. In the 70m²/853sq ft pools called *œillets* the brine finally rests and crystallises.

From June to September the salt-pan worker harvests two kinds of salt: table or white salt collected (3-5kg/7-11lb per day per *œillet*) with a flat spade *(lousse)* and coarse or grey salt collected (40-70kg/88-154lb per day per *œillet*) at the bottom of the pond with a large flat rake *(lasse)* onto a tray. The salt is put to dry on little platforms *(trenet)* built on the banks, then piled in large heaps *(mulons)* at the edge of the salt-pans before being stored in sheds in September.

When not harvesting salt, the salt-pan worker looks after the salt-marsh: repairing the dikes, raking the settling pond (October-March), cleaning and preparing the salt pans (April-May) and removing the salt before the next harvest.

A hard struggle – The salt pans of Guérande were very prosperous until the Revolution, for, thanks to a relic of the former rights of the province, the salt could be sent all over Brittany without paying the gabelle or salt tax. Dealers or salt makers could exchange it in neighbouring provinces for cereals. Trafficking by "false salt makers" or smugglers often occurred.

Today about 8 000 *œillets* are harvested, they produce an average of 10 000t of coarse salt a year. Guérande salt is rich in sodium chloride and weak in magnesium, potassium and other trace elements.

Cliffs and dunes – The cliffs and rocks of the Côte Sauvage, between the Pointe de Penchâteau and Le Croisic, offer a striking contrast to the immense sandy beach at La Baule.

In 1527 a violent wind spread the sand accumulated in the Loire estuary over the village of **Escoublac**. After this gale, which lasted for several days, sand continued to accumulate, and in the 18C the last inhabitants finally left. The village was rebuilt several miles further back. The pines planted to fix the dunes form the Bois d'Amour of La Baule. The coast, which became very popular in the 19C, took the name of **Côte d'Amour**.

A salt marsh worker

Hotels

BUDGET

There is a site for **camping-cars** on rue Jean-Baptiste-Legeay.

Chambre d'hôte Ker Kayenne – *744 boulevard Lauvergnac – 44420 La Turballe, 1km/0.6mi from La Turballe, on D 333 between Guérande and Piriac – ☎ 02 40 62 84 30 – closed 15 Nov-15 Mar – no credit cards – 8 rooms 210/300F.* In its flower garden, this Breton residence is very attractive with its old stone walls and slate roof. Inside, the small rooms have white walls and pretty woodwork. The outbuilding, however, has less charm. Swimming pool.

OUR SELECTION

Chambre d'hôte Les Rochasses – *58 rue Bellevue, 44420 La Turballe – ☎ 02 40 23 31 29 – no credit cards – 5 rooms 300F.* You will enjoy the park, the indoor swimming pool, the undeniable comforts of the rooms and the owner's warm welcome in this grand modern villa. Breakfast, served on the pretty veranda on the garden, is delightful.

Eating Out

BUDGET

Chaudron – *Route de Guérande 1.5 km/1mi, 44420 La Turballe – ☎ 02 40 23 32 52 – closed 12 Nov-10 Dec, Tues evening and Wed except in summer – 85/170F.* On the road to Guérande, this small old house welcomes its clients on its pretty terrace, as soon as the weather is pleasant. In the warm and attractively arranged dining room, you can taste fresh cuisine, presented with flair.

Crêperie la Flambée – *12 rue Saillé (in town) – ☎ 02 40 24 73 82 – open school holidays, Easter-Oct and weekends except Jan, closed evening in Nov, Dec and Mar – 40/80F.* This *crêperie* faces two wall frescoes depicting the neighbouring salt-marshes and salt works. Inside, the fire crackles gaily as the crêpes are prepared with organic flour.

Ar Blaz Mad – *40 rue St-Michel, in Guérande – ☎ 02 40 15 63 70 – closed Mon off-season and evening in winter, except during school holidays – 50/80F.* "Au bon goût": this boutique selling regional products hides a small, cute dining room where it is a pleasure to linger and nibble on a variety of tartines and to savour the home-made pastries. Pretty garden in the summer.

OUR SELECTION

Remparts – *Boulevard Nord in Guérande – ☎ 02 40 24 90 69 – closed 1 Dec-15 Jan, Sun evening and Mon except in summer – 105/250F.* Facing the Guérande ramparts, this family run establishment looks simple and typical, but you can enjoy a very pleasant meal in its small modern dining room. Several menus are available, including one for children. Also has a few rooms.

TOUR

Round tour of 62km/39mi – half a day

La Baule – *See La BAULE.*
Leave La Baule to the south. On reaching Le Pouliguen turn left immediately after the bridge.

★Le Pouliguen – *See La BAULE.*
The road hugs the coast and there is soon a fine view of the shore south of the Loire as far as the Pointe de St Gildas and Banche Lighthouse.

★Côte Sauvage – *See Le CROISIC: Excursion (opposite direction).*

Le Croisic – *See Le CROISIC.*

Batz-sur-Mer – *See Le CROISIC.*

Kervalet – A small village of salt-marsh workers with a chapel dedicated to St Mark.

Saillé – Built on an island amidst the salt-marshes, this town is the salt capital. A former chapel contains the **Maison des Paludiers** ⊙. Engravings, tools, furnishings and costumes illustrate the life of the salt-marsh worker.
Turn left onto the road to Turballe through the salt flats.

La Turballe – The town stretches along the seafront. The fish auction (La Criée) stands in the middle of the busy artificial port which receives both pleasure craft and sardine boats. The modern granite Église St-Anne has a low bell-tower adjoining the apse. The chancel is lit by small stained-glass windows (1937). The **view** is beautiful along the coast after Lerat.
After Penhareng, turn left twice.

★Pointe du Castelli –
*From the car park a
path along the cliff ridge
takes you to the point.*
There is a nice view of
the rocky creeks. On the
right Île Dumet and the
low shore of Presqu'île
de Rhuys are visible. On
the left are the road-
stead and peninsula of
Le Croisic with the
church towers of Batz
and Le Croisic.

Piriac-sur-Mer – A
small resort and fishing
village. In the square, in
front of the church,
there is a fine group of
17C houses.

*To leave Piriac take the
road that runs beside
the harbour towards
Mesquer, turn right to-
wards Guérande. Go
through St-Sébastien.*

Trescalan – The main square is dominated by a small Calvary topped with a pediment. The church with buttresses has fine columns with capitals and inside, in the
south aisle, is a statue of St Bridget.
From D 99, as it runs along the Guérande ridge, there is a fine view of the salt-
marshes and the harbour of Le Croisic. In the evening the light effects on the
marshes are remarkable.

★Guérande – The town surrounded by ramparts, standing on a plateau overlooking
the salt-marshes, has kept the appearance of the Middle Ages.
Every year in August there is a three day Interceltic Festival at the foot of the fortifications.

Guérande salt-marshes

★Walk round the ramparts – The ramparts, in which there is still no breach, were built in the 14C and 15C. They are flanked by six towers and pierced by four fortified gateways. In the 18C the Duke of Aiguillon, Governor of Brittany, had the moats filled in (although the north and west sections still contain water) and arranged the present circular promenade, which the tourist can follow by car or on foot *(the watch-path is not open to the public)*.

★Collégiale St-Aubin – This collegiate church, built from the 12C to the 16C on the site of a baptistery, features a granite west façade decorated with bell turrets and crocketed pinnacles. To the right a 15C outside pulpit is embedded into a buttress. The **interior** is imposing with large 15C pillars in the transept. The Romanesque columns of the nave support Gothic arches with **capitals** portraying grotesque and floral decoration. The 15C chancel, with aisles opening onto four 16C chapels, is lit by a magnificent 18C **stained-glass window** showing the Coronation of the Virgin and the Assumption. The chapel to the right, oddly enough called the **crypt**, contains a Merovingian sarcophagus (6C), a recumbent figure and a tombstone, both 16C. In the nave is a 16C carved wooden Christ.

Porte St-Michel (**Château-Musée**) ⊙ – The gatehouse was once the governor's house (15C) and is now a local museum; a spiral staircase goes up to the different floors. On the first floor, once the soldiers' living quarters, two interiors have been reconstructed: that of the Briéron inhabitant with its waxed furniture and that of the salt-marsh worker with its furniture painted a deep plum-red colour. The second floor, where the governor resided, is embellished with paintings, porcelain from Le Croisic, pottery and other everyday objects typical of the area, as well as part of the collegiate church's rood screen. On the third floor (note the beautiful timber work) a weaving loom (1832), and old bourgeois, salt-marsh worker and farm tenant costumes, on life-size figures, are exhibited.

Château de Careil ⊙ – The first fortified castle was built in the 14C; renovated in the 15-16C, it is still inhabited today.

GUÉRANDE

M Porte St-Michel
(Château-Musée)

La GUERCHE-DE-BRETAGNE

Population 4 123
Michelin map 63 fold 8 or 230 folds 41 and 42

This small town, once a manorial estate with Du Guesclin as its overlord, still retains some old houses and an interesting church.
Every Tuesday, since 1121, an important fair and market is held around the town hall and the squares in the town centre.

Church (**Église**) – Only the chancel, with its triple-sided apse, and the Romanesque tower, with its massive buttresses, remain from the original building erected in 1206. The nave and south aisle were rebuilt in the 16C; the north aisle and the bell-tower, with openings at the top, date from the end of the 19C. The splendour of this church lies in its 16C stalls with their amusing Gothic misericords – the carved decoration of the woodwork is clearly of the time of Henri II (1547-59) a more advanced period – and the remains of the 15C and 16C stained-glass windows in the south aisle. Note the purlins embellishing the nave's wooden vaulting and at the rear of the apse a stained-glass window depicting the Assumption.

Old houses – About 15 porched and half-timbered houses dating from the 16 and 17C can be found on place du Général-de-Gaulle, near the church, and in the neighbouring streets of rue du Cheval-Blanc and rue de Nantes.

La Roche-aux-Fées

EXCURSIONS

★**La Roche-aux-Fées** – *Round tour of 43km/27mi – about 2hr 30min. Leave La Guerche west on the Rennes road, D 463. At Visseiche turn left.*
You soon reach an arm of Marcillé Lake (Étang de Marcillé) formed by the junction of the Seiche and Ardenne Valleys; hence its curved shape.

On leaving Marcillé-Robert, cross the Seiche and bear left towards Retiers which follows the bank of the other arm of the lake. Turn right after 800m/0.5mi to Theil and then right again 3km/2mi further on. On the right, a short distance from the road, stands La Roche-aux-Fées (Fairies' Rock).

★**La Roche-aux-Fées** – This is one of the finest megalithic monuments in Brittany. Built in purple schist, it consists of 42 stones, of which half a dozen weigh between 40 and 45t each. There is a massive portico entrance and then a low ceilinged corridor leading to a large, very high compartmented room.
Turn round and go to Le Theil then turn left towards Ste-Colombe.

Lac des Mottes ⊘ – Charming artificial lake amid magnificent trees.
When within sight of Ste-Colombe, turn left.

Retiers – Pretty small town where the church contains five paintings and three 17C and 18C altarpieces in carved wood.
Cross Arbrissel, the birthplace of Robert d'Arbrissel who founded the famous abbey of Fontevraud where he is buried.

From Rannée (The Green Guide Châteaux of the Loire) return to La Guerche.

Lac de GUERLÉDAN★★

Michelin map 59 fold 12 or 230 folds 21 and 22

At the heart of the Argoat, the waters of the River Blavet form a winding reservoir known as Guerlédan Lake, a magnificent stretch of water surrounded by trees. It is one of the finest sights of inland Brittany and a lovely place for water sports.

★★**Boat trips** ⊘ – Boats, leaving from Beau Rivage and Sordan Bay, offer tours of this beautiful lake.

TOUR OF THE LAKE

Round tour of 44km/27mi starting from Mur-de-Bretagne – 3hr 30min.

Mur-de-Bretagne – This is one of the liveliest towns in the interior of Brittany. The **Chapelle Ste-Suzanne** stands to the north of the town in a very pretty wooded setting. The splendid oak trees which surround it are several centuries old and inspired the painter Corot (1796-1875) on several occasions. The chapel's elegant **belfry-porch** dates from 1760. Inside, the remarkable 18C **painted ceiling★**, recently restored, is dedicated to St Suzanne.
In the village, a road to the right leads to a roundabout, which affords a lovely **view★** of Guerlédan Lake and dam.

Take D 35 southwest and after crossing two bridges over the canal and the Blavet, turn right.

St-Aignan – In the charming 12C **church** note in particular a beautiful carved wooden image of the Tree of Jesse to the north of the chancel and a depiction of the Trinity surrounded by Evangelists, in the same medium, to the south. There is also a statue of St Mark and a Pietà.

On leaving the village, to the left, an **Électrothèque** ⊘ has been set up in the Regional Centre (Maison du pays) and contains a display on the construction of the Barrage de Guerlédan, as well as collections of exhibits evoking the history of electricity: measuring instruments, electric household appliances or electrical equipment used by the railway services. Visitors can operate some of these exhibits themselves.

Barrage de Guerlédan – A viewpoint overlooks this dead-weight dam (45m/147ft high, 206m/240yd long along the top and 33.50m/109ft thick at the base) and extending over 12km/7mi in the Blavet Gorges.

Come back by the same road and bear right.

The road runs through a countryside of fields and pastureland.

Before entering the Forêt de Quénécan bear right.

Anse de Sordan – Pleasant site on the edge of the Lac de Guerlédan.

Eating Out

BUDGET

Beau Rivage – *On the lake, 2km/1mi via D 111, 22530 Caurel –* ☎ *02 96 28 52 15 – closed 15-30 Oct, Feb school holidays, Mon evening and Tues – 90/350F.* In this little hotel, the dining room's bay windows look out over the lake. In addition to the very pretty view, you can also enjoy its simple and fresh family-style cuisine. Its few rooms are neat, tidy and no-frills.

Recreation

Boat trips★★ – *July-Aug, cruises (1hr 30min) departure at 2.30pm, 3pm, 4pm; Apr-June and Sept-Oct, inquire – 40F (children 22F) – luncheon cruise (3hr), reservations required – cruise on the canal from Nantes to Brest –* ☎ *02 96 28 52 64.* From Beau-Rivage or the cove of Sordan, motorboats will take you out on the lake so you can better appreciate the beauty of this site.

Water-skiing – *Ski club de Guerlédan –* ☎ *02 96 26 02 18.* In season, at Beau-Rivage.

Paddle-boats – Can be rented at Beau-Rivage, at the cove of Sordan, and at the roundabout du Lac at Mur-de-Bretagne.

Swimming – Whether at Beau-Rivage or at the cove of Sordan, swimming is unsupervised. In Gouarec, the swimming pool with solarium is open all year. (L'Aquadélis, ☎ 02 96 24 86 15).

Forêt de Quénécan – The forest of 2 500ha/6 175 acres stands on an uneven plateau overlooking the Blavet Valley. Apart from beech and spruce around Lake Fourneau (Étang du Fourneau) and Les Forges des Salles, the forest, abounding in game (deer, wild boar), consists of pine, scrubland and heath.

Les Forges-des-Salles – Les Forges **Hamlet** ○, tucked at the bottom of a wooded valley, was the site of an iron and steel industry in the 18C and 19C. Quite apart from the site's remarkable testimony to a complete period of industrial history, the setting itself is charming. Since the mining and processing of iron ore was stopped, in 1880, this collection of well-designed buildings has not been altered. The buildings of schist, which are arranged around the ironmaster's house, include some which are open to visitors; these are the former homes of blacksmiths (arranged as exhibition rooms). Some have been furnished according to their original style and function: the school, the accounts office, the canteen, the chapel, the joiner's workshop and a small smithy.

East of the castle, at the top of the terraced pleasure garden (the **Thabor**), there is a lovely view over the valley and the various stretches of water in it.

Continue in the direction of Ste-Brigitte.

There are fine views on the right of Lake Fourneau.

Via Les Forges des Salles return to the main crossroads, then bear left.

The road runs down the valley of the Forges stream, then enters the Blavet Valley.

Leave the car in the car park before the bridge to the left.

Écluse de Bon-Repos – The lock on the River Blavet, the old corbelled bridge, the former lock keeper's house and the overflow form a pretty picture.

Go over the bridge and take the towpath to the right.

Abbaye de Bon-Repos ○ – This 12C Cistercian abbey, a dependent of the Abbaye de Boquen, rebuilt in the 14C and embellished in the early 18C, was sacked and destroyed during the Revolution. The fine façade of the abbot's lodging, the sober architecture of the conventual buildings and the vast size of the church may still be admired.

Make for N 164 and turn left towards Gouarec; immediately after the bridge bear right to Daoulas Gorges.

★**Gorges du Daoulas** – Go up the gorges. The fast-flowing waters of the Daoulas run in a narrow, winding valley with steep sides covered with gorse, broom and heather. To join the Blavet, which has become the canal between Nantes and Brest, the river has made a deep cut through a belt of schist and quartzite. The slabs of rock rise almost vertically; some end in curious needles, with sharp edges.

2km/1mi further on reverse into a lane before two houses at the place known as Toulrodez and turn back.

The road towards Loudéac, which you take to the left, crosses undulating country and provides views of the lake. After 5km/3mi turn right into the road towards the water, after dropping down into a small pine wood it provides a beautiful **view**★ of the Lac de Guerlédan.

Beau-Rivage – Leisure and sailing centre.

Proceed to Caurel and turn right towards Loudéac. After 3.5km/2mi turn right to return to Mur-de-Bretagne.

GUIMILIAU★★

Population 791
Michelin map 58 folds 5 and 6 or 230 folds 4 and 5
Local map see Les ENCLOS PAROISSIAUX

The fame of the small village of Guimiliau is due to its remarkable parish close and to the magnificently ornamented furniture of its church.

★★PARISH CLOSE *45min*

★★**Calvaire** – The Calvary, the most curious and one of the largest in the region, dates from 1581-8 and includes over 200 figures. On the upper part stands a large cross with a thorny shaft bearing four statues: the Virgin and St John, St Peter and St Yves. On the platform are 17 scenes from the Passion and a composition representing the story of Catell-Gollet above the Last Supper. The figures on the frieze are numerous and depict, in no chronological order, 15 scenes from the life of Jesus. The four Evangelists stand at the corners of the buttresses.

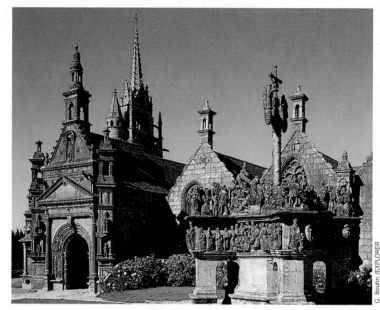

Guimiliau parish close

★**Church** – This 16C building was rebuilt in the Flamboyant Renaissance style at the beginning of the 17C.

Go round the south side of the church to see the charming triple-panelled apse. Continue round the building, to the façade where the bell tower (1530) stands, all that remains of the original church.

The **south porch**★★ is remarkable. The recessed arches adorned with statuettes give an interesting picture of the Bible and the Gospels. Above the triangular pediment over the porch is the statue of St Miliau, King of Cornouaille and patron saint of the area. To the left of the porch is a small ossuary with low-relief sculptures depicting scenes from the life of Christ. The inside of the porch is a fine example of a form of decoration frequent in Brittany. Under the usual statues of the Apostles is a frieze ornamented with rose medallions, strapwork and scenes from the Old Testament. Note on the left side, near the date 1606, the Creation of Woman. In the end wall two round arched doorways, surmounted by a statue of Christ, frame a Kersanton granite stoup.

Inside, the nave and side aisles are roofed with panelled vaulting. At the end of the north aisle is a fine carved oak **baptistery**★★ dating from 1675. Eight spiral columns support an elaborately carved canopy, crowned by a dome which shelters a group representing the baptism of Our Lord. To the right of the organ are two beautiful embroidered banners (1658).

In the **organ loft** are three 17C **low-relief sculptures**★; on the nave side, David playing the harp, and St Cecilia at the organ; opposite the baptistery, the Triumph of Alexander.

The **pulpit**★, dating from 1677, is ornamented at the corners with statues of the four Sibyls. The panels carry medallions representing the Four Evangelists surrounded by the Cardinal Virtues.

The chancel with its central stained-glass window (1599) is closed by a 17C altar rail. Note from right to left: the colourful **altarpiece of St Joseph**, on which can be seen St Yves, the patron saint of barristers between a rich man and a poor one, and the blind St Hervé with his wolf; the **altarpiece of St Miliau**, representing scenes from the saint's life; the **altarpiece of the Rosary**, with 15 mysteries in medallions, is surmounted by a Trinity.

Chapelle funéraire – The funerary chapel in the Renaissance style, dating from 1648, has an outdoor pulpit set in one of the windows.

*The **Michelin Maps scale 1:200,000** for this region are shown in the diagram on page 6*
The text refers to the maps which, owing to their scale or coverage, are the clearest and most appropriate in each case

GUINGAMP

Population 7 905
Michelin map 59 fold 2 or 230 folds 7 and 8

Located on the edge of Armor and Argoat, Guingamp is a commercial and industrial (electronic construction, food processing) town, which has greatly developed in the past 20 years.

SIGHTS

★**Basilique Notre-Dame-de-Bon-Secours** (**B**) – This church was built in the Gothic style in the 14C (a Romanesque part remains at the transept crossing); but two centuries later the south tower collapsed, demolishing the nave's south side. The town asked several architects to plan its reconstruction. One old master presented a purely traditional Gothic design; but a young man named Le Moal submitted plans in which the Renaissance style, almost unknown in Brittany at that time, appeared. Quite unexpectedly the people of Guingamp awarded the prize to the innovator. Since then the church has had the unusual feature of being Gothic on the left and Renaissance on the right.

At the west end, two tall towers, the 13C Clock Tower to the left and the Renaissance Tower to the right, frame a very fine round arched doorway with delicate decorations, half sacred and half profane.

Enter by the Notre-Dame-de-Bon-Secours doorway which opens into rue Notre-Dame.

Transformed into an oratory, the chapel houses a Black Virgin, the church's patroness. A great *pardon* draws thousands of pilgrims. After the torch-lit procession, three bonfires are lit on place du Centre in the company of the bishop, who also presides over the ceremony.

Inside, the church is unusual with its numerous pillars and graceful flying buttresses in the chancel. The triforium is adorned with trilobed arches with a quadrilobed balustrade while lower down the nave has striking Renaissance decoration.

Place du Centre (**AB**) – On the square are a few old houses (nos 31, 33, 35, 39, 48) and at the corner of rue St-Yves and rue du Cosquet. The fountain called **"la Plomée"**, with three lead and stone basins dating from the Renaissance is popular.

Hôtel de Ville ⊘ (**B H**) – The town hall (1699) housed in the old hospital (Hôtel-Dieu), was formerly an Augustinian monastery. The cloisters, great staircase and fine Italian-style chapel (1709) may be visited. In the chapel, in season, temporary exhibitions are held.

Among the permanent collection are paintings by Sérusier (in the great hall) and the Pont-Aven School.

Ramparts – Standing on place du Vally (**B 13**) are all that remains of the castle (1438-42) – the ramparts.
Ruins of the fortifications which once surrounded the town can be seen not far from rue du Maréchal-Joffre (**AB**) and place St-Sauveur (**A**).

EXCURSIONS

★**Menez-Bré** – *13km/8mi west – 1hr 15min. Leave Guingamp on ⑦, the road to Brest. 11.5km/7mi from Guingamp, after a house on the right, turn right (signposted) onto a steep uphill road which leads to the summit of the Menez-Bré. See BELLE-ISLE-EN-TERRE: Excursions.*

Grâces – *3.5km/2mi. Leave Guingamp on D 54, west on the town plan. Turn right after 2km/1mi; in the village centre stands the large church.*
Originally the **Église Notre-Dame** (Church of Our Lady) would appear to have been a pilgrims' chapel, probably founded by Queen Anne. Built in the 16C, it was slightly altered in the 17C and restored in the 19C. The four gables of the single aisle give it a saw-tooth silhouette from the south.
Inside, note the nave's tie-beams and the superb carved purlins. A satirical picture of drunkenness is the main theme; but there are also hunting scenes, monsters, and a poignant Holy Face surrounded by little angels. A wooden shrine contains the relics of Charles of Blois, killed at the Battle of Auray.

Châtelaudren – This little town stands on a bend of the Aulne, in the green and deep valley through which the canalised river flows. Two lines of shady quays are its most decorative feature. The tide does not reach Châteaulin but dies out a little way downstream, at Port-Launay, where small seagoing ships are tied up to the quay.

VALLÉE DU TRIEUX

Round tour of 39km/24mi – 2hr. Leave Guingamp on ⑤ on the town plan.

The road follows the Trieux Valley and then, for a short while, goes into Kerauffret Wood which lies over on the left. The almost flat countryside is pleasant.

Château de Brélidy – *22140 Brélidy, 15km/9mi north of Guingamp – ☎ 02 96 95 69 38 – closed 3 Nov-1 Apr – ▣ – 10 rooms from 500F – breakfast 55F – restaurant 145/185F. This well-kept little 16C château is very restful; the rooms are spacious and quiet, with stylish furnishings. The vast park offers a private fishing area and a swimming pool.*

Bourbriac – Rising in the centre of the town and surrounded by gardens, is the church with its soaring belltower 64m/210ft high. There have been several buildings erected on the site: of the first there remains a crypt probably of the 10C or 11C; of the Romanesque church which followed, there is the very high transept crossing – the tower above it was burnt down in the fire of 1765 and has been replaced by a pinnacle. In 1535 building on the west tower began; it is a remarkable example of the style that was to come: while the big pointed arched porch and all the lower floor are in the Flamboyant style, the remainder of the tower is definitely Renaissance. The spire was added in 1869. Inside, the sarcophagus of St Briac, dating from Merovingian times, is invoked as a cure for epilepsy.

Go towards Plésidy and then in the direction of St-Péver.

After 2km/1mi, note on the left below the road the small **Manoir de Toul-an-Gollet**, a pleasant 15C granite with a pepper-pot turret and mullioned windows.
Turn left at the crossroads and before the bridge over the Trieux, take a small road to the right.

Chapelle Notre-Dame-de-Restudo ⊘ – This 14C-15C chapel retains traces of 14C frescoes depicting the Last Supper and chivalric scenes in the nave and chancel which are separated by a great pointed arch. *Pardon on 30 June in honour of St Eligius.*

Turn back and take the road back to Guingamp.
The Trieux Valley offers varied scenery.
After 2km/1mi bear right to Avaugour.

Chapelle d'Avaugour ⊘ – The chapel stands in an attractive setting and contains a finely carved wood sacrarium (shrine) of the 16C and interesting statues of the Apostles.

Make your way up the Trieux Valley back to Guingamp on ④ of the town plan.

Île de HŒDIC and Île d'HOUAT

Population 140 and 390
Michelin map 63 fold 12 or 230 fold 50
Access: boat service from Quiberon and Vannes ⓥ

These islands in the Ponant archipelago are about 15km/8mi from the coast. Tourism and fishing are the main activities. Peace and quiet guaranteed.

HŒDIC

Separated from the Île d'Houat by the Sœurs Channel, Hoedic is the smaller of the two (2.5 x 1km/1.5 x 0.5mi); it has the same granite formation with beaches and rocky headlands. Two lagoons extend east of the town while the island is covered in sparse heathland where wild carnations, a few cypresses, fine fig trees and tamarisks grow. Fresh water is supplied by an underground water bearing bed. The boats dock at Argol Harbour. There are two other harbours – Port de la Croix and Port Neuf – which attract pleasure craft to the island. A gently sloping road leads to the town with a small chapel on the right and a menhir on the left.

Town – The south-facing houses stand in groups of three or four. Near the former beacon is the **Église St-Goustan** named after a Cornish hermit, who came to the island for a few years. It has fine 19C **furnishings**; note the two angels in white marble by the high altar.

Ancien fort – The old fort, built in 1859 and partly hidden by the dunes, can be seen on the road to Port de la Croix. There is also a ruined 17C English fort at Beg-Lagatte.

Footpaths by the sea take you round the island to discover the beaches and admire the lovely **view** of the mainland, Houat Island, Belle-Ile and of the reefs.

HOUAT

This island (5km/3mi long and 1.3km/1mi wide) is a granite ridge fringed by cliffs. Because of its location commanding the access to Quiberon Bay, it was occupied three times by the English in the 17C and 18C. The boats dock in the new harbour on the north coast. A road leads uphill to the town.

Town – Pretty houses, whitewashed and flower-bedecked, line the winding streets and alleyways leading to a square in the centre of the town in which stands the communal well, and to another square next to the church.

The church, built in the 19C, commemorates St Gildas, an English monk and patron of the island, who visited Houat prior to founding the monastery of St-Gildas-de-Rhuys.

Go round the church and follow the path skirting the cemetery.

From the look-out point, there is a fine **view★** of the harbour and of the Presqu'île de Rhuys.

Beaches – There are numerous beaches nestling in small creeks but the loveliest extends to the west, facing the Île de Hœdic, near the old harbour which was damaged in a violent storm in 1951.

HUELGOAT★★

Population 1 742
Michelin map 58 fold 6 or 230 fold 19 – Local map see Monts d'ARRÉE

The forest, lake, running water and rocks make Huelgoat one of the finest **sites★★** in inner Brittany which come under the aegis of the Parc natural régional d'Armorique. Huelgoat is not only a good excursion centre but a favourite place for anglers (especially for carp and perch in the lake and trout in the river).

★★THE ROCKS *1hr 30min on foot*

🔁 **Access** – *In rue de Berrien past the lake and follow the signposted path.*

Chaos du Moulin – The path cuts through the rocks dominating the course of the River Argent. This pile of rounded granite rocks, surrounded by greenery, is very picturesque.

Grotte du Diable – *To reach this, climb down an iron ladder.* A brook babbles under the rocks.

Théâtre de Verdure – Beautiful setting.

Roche Tremblante – *Left bank.* By leaning against this 100t block at a precise point, you can make it rock on its base.

Ménage de la Vierge – An enormous pile of rocks shaped rather like kitchen utensils.

An uphill path, known as Lovers' Walk (Sentier des Amoureux), leads directly through the woods to Artus's Cave and to Boars' Pool (see The Forest below).

Allée Violette – A pleasant path in the woods along the left bank of the River Argent.

To return to the centre of Huelgoat, at Pont-Rouge, turn right oto the road from Carhaix and then take rue du Docteur-Jacq.

★THE FOREST

Extending over 1 000ha/2 471 acres, the Forest of Huelgoat lies at the foot of the southern slope of the Monts d'Arrée mountain range. Its tortured topography consists of a series of hills divided by deep valleys. The forest features a great many different landscapes and colours; it also contains strange, picturesque sites which have inspired many traditional tales and legends. *(Visitors can discover these sites with the help of signposts and car parks; see below).*

🔳 **Promenade du Fer à Cheval and Le Gouffre** – *30min on foot. After Pont-Rouge, take the Horseshoe Walk on the right.*
A pleasant walk through the woods along the River Argent. *Then return to the Carhaix road for 300m/328yd.* A stairway *(39 steps)* leads down to the chasm. The River Argent flowing from the Lac d'Huelgoat, falls into a deep cavity to reappear 150m/164yd further on. A path leads to a lookout point *(15min there and back – difficult and no security ramp)* commanding a view of the chasm. You can continue this walk through the woods by the river passing near the Mare aux Fées (Fairies Pool) and combining it with the Promenade du Canal.

Follow the signposts to the mine (La Mine), turn right at the bridge into an unsurfaced road and at the former mine, continue along an uphill path to the right to the power station (usine électrique). *A footbridge spans the canal and leads to the opposite bank.*

🔳 **Promenade du Canal** – *2hr on foot there and back on rue du Docteur-Jacq.* This walk follows the bank of the upper canal. A reservoir and two canals were dug in the 19C to work the silver-bearing lead mines, already known to the Romans. The waters were used to wash the ore and drive a crusher. From the far end of the canal walk you may continue on to the chasm; *this walk is described in the opposite direction see below.*

🔳 **Walk** – *1hr 30min on foot there and back. From the car park after Pont-Rouge, take Allée du Clair-Ruisseau.*
This path half-way up the slope affords fine views of the rock-strewn stream bed. A stairway *(25 steps)* on the left leads down to the **Mare aux Sangliers** (Boars' Pool) in a pretty setting of rocks shaped rather like boars' heads, hence the name. Cross over the rustic bridge to Allée de la Mare on the left.

Rocks at Huelgoat

After the great stairway *(218 steps)*, which provides the quickest access to **Camp d'Artus** (Artus's Camp), you can see up above, on the right, the entrance to **Grotte d'Artus** (Artus's Cave).

Continue up the path which after 800m/0.5mi takes you to the camp. Boulders mark the entrance which was dominated by an artificial mound.

It is an important example of a Gallic fortified site, bordered by two enclosures. In spite of the encroaching vegetation, it is possible to go round the camp by a path *(1km/0.6mi)* following the remaining second elliptical enclosure which is fairly well preserved.

Hôtel du Lac – ☎ *02 98 99 71 14 – closed 11Nov-11 Jan – ◻ – 15 rooms 260/320F – breakfast 36F – restaurant 100/160F.* Although it doesn't have a particularly engaging façade, this recently renovated hotel is a good bargain. The rooms are well-lit, clean and comfortably furnished, and the restaurant has a nice view over the lake. Grilled steak and pizza are featured on the menu.

ADDITIONAL SIGHTS

Church – A 16C church with a modern belfry stands near the main square in the town centre. Inside there are sculpted purlins and to the left of the chancel is a statue of St Yves, the patron saint of the parish, between a rich man and a pauper.

Chapelle Notre-Dame-des-Cieux – Overlooking Huelgoat, this Renaissance chapel with its 18C bell tower, has curious painted low-relief sculptures depicting scenes from the life of the Virgin and the Passion around the chancel and the side altars. A *pardon* takes place on the first Sunday in August.

La Roche Cintrée – *Take the road to Carhaix and follow the signposts. After 100m/110yd take the uphill road on the left.*
From the top of the rock *(15min on foot there and back)*, there is a view of Huelgoat (somewhat limited), north onto the Monts d'Arrée and south onto the Montagnes Noires.

A new concept in travel planning.
When you want to calculate a trip distance or visualise a detailed itinerary; when you need information on hotels,
restaurants or campsites, consult Michelin on the Internet.
Visit our Web site to discover our full range of services for travellers:
www.michelin-travel.com.

This small town stands in a picturesque setting. Its river, the Oust, reflects the famous castle of the Rohan family. Behind the fortress-castle, on the sides and the summit of a steep ridge, old houses with slate roofs are scattered around the basilica of Our Lady of the Brambles (Basilique Notre-Dame-du-Roncier).

The prosperity of the region depends on tourism and local industries such as meat canning and cardboard manufacturing.

HISTORICAL NOTES

The Battle of the Thirty (14C) – By the middle of the 14C Josselin Castle had already been razed and rebuilt. It belonged to the Royal House of France; Beaumanoir was its Captain; the War of Succession was raging. Josselin supported the cause of Blois; the Montfort party held Ploërmel, where an Englishman, Bemborough, was in command. At first the two garrisons had frequent encounters as they ravaged the countryside; then the two leaders arranged a fight between 30 knights from each camp: they would fight on foot, using sword, dagger, battle-axe and pike.

After taking Communion and praying all night at Our Lady of the Brambles, Beaumanoir's men repaired, on 27 March 1351, to the rendez-vous on the heath at Mi-Voie, between Josselin and Ploërmel (5km/3mi from Josselin at a place called Pyramide; a stone column marks the spot today). In the opposite camp were 20 Englishmen, six Germans and four Bretons. The day was spent in fierce hand-to-hand fighting until the combatants were completely exhausted. Josselin won; the English captain was killed with eight of his men, and the rest were taken prisoner. During the struggle, which has remained famous as the Battle of the Thirty, the Breton leader, wounded, asked for a drink. "Drink your blood, Beaumanoir, your thirst will pass!" replied one of his rough companions.

Constable de Clisson (14C) – Among the owners of Josselin the greatest figure was Olivier de Clisson, who married Marguerite de Rohan, Beaumanoir's widow. He acquired the castle in 1370. He had a tragic childhood; for when he was only seven his father was accused of betraying the French party in the War of Succession and beheaded in Paris. His widow, Jeanne de Belleville, who had been quiet and inconspicuous hitherto, became a fury. She hurried to Nantes with her children and, on the bloody head of their father nailed to the ramparts, made them swear to avenge him. Then she took the field with 400 men and put to the sword the garrisons of six castles which favoured the French cause. When the royal troops forced her to flee, she put to sea and sank every enemy ship that she met.

The Rohans at Josselin (15 and 17C) – In 1488, to punish Jean II de Rohan for having sided with the King of France, the Duke of Brittany, François II, seized Josselin and had it dismantled. When his daughter Anne became Queen of France she compensated Jean II, who was able in the rebuilding of the castle to create a masterpiece worthy of the proud motto of his family: *"Roi ne puis, Prince ne daigne, Rohan suis"* (I cannot be king, I scorn to be a prince, I am a Rohan). The owner of Josselin showed his gratitude to the Queen in the decoration of the palace; in many places, the letter A is carved in the stone, crowned and surmounted by the girdle which was Anne's emblem, and accompanied by the royal fleur-de-lis. In 1629, Henri de Rohan, the leader of the Huguenots, Richelieu's sworn enemies, met the Cardinal in the King's antechamber where the cleric, who had just had the keep and five of the nine towers of Josselin razed, announced with cruel irony: "I have just thrown a fine ball among your skittles, Monsieur."

★★CHÂTEAU ⊘ 45min

To get a good **view★** of the castle stand on Ste-Croix Bridge, which spans the River Oust. From this point the building has the appearance of a fortress, with high towers, curtain walls and battlements. The windows and dormer windows appearing above the walls belong to the palace built by Jean II in the 16C.

The castle is built on a terrace of irregular shape, surrounded by walls of which only the bases remain, except on the side which is seen from the bridge. The isolated "prison tower" marked the northeast corner of the enclosure.

The delightful **façade★★** of the main building which looks out onto the old courtyard, now the park, makes a striking contrast with the fortifications of the outer façade. Nowhere else in Brittany has the art of the sculptor in that hard material, granite, been pushed to such limits: brackets, florets, pinnacles, gables, crowns and curled leaves adorn the dormer windows and balustrades.

Only the ground floor, restored in the 19C, is open to the public. In the panelled dining room stands an equestrian statue of Olivier de Clisson by Frémiet. After the antechamber, in which are hung portraits of the Rohan family, is the richly furnished drawing room with its delicately carved chimney which bears the current Rohan motto, "A plus" (To more). There are over 3 000 books and some portraits in the library.

Morcime/CAMPAGNE CAMPAGNE

Josselin

Musée des Poupées ⊘ (**B M**) – In the castle's old stables, 500 dolls from the Rohan collection are exhibited. These come from many different countries (France, Netherlands, Austria, North America etc) and date from the 17C to the 20C. The dolls (in wood, wax, celluloid, porcelain...) are dressed in religious or traditional costumes. Miscellaneous doll accessories are also exhibited. There are temporary exhibitions here in summer.

ADDITIONAL SIGHTS

★**Basilique Notre-Dame-du-Roncier** (**B**) – Founded in the 12C and several times remodelled (east end's spire built in 1949), the basilica is, generally speaking, Flamboyant in style; note the wonderful gargoyles which adorn its three sides and the stone statue of the Virgin at the entrance door. It is famous for its great *pardon (see Calendar of events)*. This has been called the "barkers' pardon" since 1728, when three children were cured of epilepsy at the festival.

The name, Our Lady of the Brambles, is based on a very old legend. Around the year 800 a peasant, cutting brambles in his field, discovered a statue of the Virgin, hence its name. An oratory made of branches, followed by a chapel in wood, then, in c 1000, by a Romanesque chapel (rebuilt in the late 12C) were built on this spot.

Inside, in the south chapel, is the **mausoleum**★ of Olivier de Clisson and his wife Marguerite de Rohan (15C). The chapel of the Virgin of the Brambles is left of the chancel (modern statue; the former statue was burned in 1793). In the nave is a fine wrought-iron pulpit of the 18C. The organ case is 16C. The modern stained-glass window in the north transept was designed by Grüber.

JOSSELIN

M Musée de Poupées

Hotels

BUDGET

Hôtel France – *Place Notre-Dame* – ☎ *02 97 22 23 06* – *closed Jan, Sun evening and Mon off-season* – 🅿 – *20 rooms 200/280F* – *breakfast 36F* – *restaurant 81/205F.* Opposite the basilica, this hotel's old façade hides a renovated interior. Its modern rooms are well-equipped, if slightly narrow. The attic rooms only have a shower. Small terrace.

OUR SELECTION

Hôtel du Roi Arthur – *56800 Ploërmel, 14km/8mi east of Josselin via N 24 and D 8, at the Lac au Duc* – ☎ *02 97 73 64 64* – *closed 6-20 Feb* – 🅿 – *46 rooms 400/560F* – *breakfast 55F* – *restaurant 135/240F.* This modern hotel is located between a lake and a golf course, in a lush, green setting, and also features an indoor swimming pool and a fitness centre. Its large rooms are well-equipped. Duplexes are available for families and long stays.

Sports

The tourist office in Josselin offers three **bike trails** (from 11km/7mi to 18km/12mi).

Lac au Duc – ☎ *02 97 74 14 51.* You can fish, swim, water-ski and sail in this lake of 250ha.

Ascent to the tower ⊘ – *Access from place A.-de-Rohan.* The tower commands a view of the northeast façade, the castle's inner courtyard and the countryside beyond.

Chapelle Ste-Croix ⊘ (**A**) – Built on the side of the hill is this chapel with its 11C nave. From the surrounding cemetery, which is ornamented with a Calvary (16C), there is a pretty view of the Oust and the castle.
After a visit to the chapel, stroll in the picturesque Ste-Croix district with its narrow streets and old houses some of which are corbelled.

Fontaine N.-D.-du-Roncier (**B**) – Built in 1675, the fountain is still a place of pilgrimage.

Old houses – The old houses are found in the basilica's precinct especially on rue des Vierges and place Notre-Dame. Nevertheless, the most picturesque are in rue des Trente; there is the picturesque house at no 7, dating from 1624 and beside it a house built in 1663.

EXCURSIONS

Guéhenno – The **Calvary**★ stands in the cemetery near the church. It dates from 1550, was destroyed in 1794 and restored in the last century. All its beauty lies in its perfect composition. Carved in the shaft of the central cross is Jesse, father of David. In front of it stands a column, with the instruments of the Passion, on which a cock is perched, in allusion to the denial of St Peter. Behind this monument is a small ossuary, whose entrance is protected by the figures of two guards on duty. A low relief framed in the left gable depicts the Passion.

Ploërmel – This little town, in the centre of an agricultural area at the limit of Upper Brittany, was once the seat of the dukes of Brittany and it was from Ploërmel that the Englishman, Bemborough, set out for the Battle of the Thirty (1351). The **church**★ is dedicated to St Arthmael, who founded the town in the 6C; he is shown taming a dragon which he leads away with his stole.
The church dates from the 16C. The Flamboyant Gothic and Renaissance north **portal**★ presents two finely carved doors. The scenes depicted take both religious (Christ's Childhood, Virtue Trampling on Vice) and comic themes. The Apostles have been sculpted on the door panels.
The magnificent 16C and 17C **stained-glass windows**★ have been restored: Tree of Jesse (in the side aisle), life of St Arthmael (in the north transept); there are also modern windows by Jacques Bony.
In the chapel to the north of the chancel are white marble statues of Duke Jean II and Duke Jean III of Brittany (14C). In the south transept, behind the Kersanton granite tomb of Philippe of Montauban and his wife, is a fine 14C recumbent figure in white marble. Below the wood vaulting the purlins are worth noticing (*light switch*).

Old houses – Rue Beaumanoir, so-called in memory of the hero of the Battle of the Thirty, contains (at no 7) the 16C **Maison des Marmousets★** (**Y D**) adorned with woodcarvings, and opposite the 16C former house of the dukes of Brittany. Other old houses may be seen in rue des Francs-Bourgeois.

Maison-Mère des Frères de Ploërmel (**YZ E**) – The order was founded in 1819 by the abbot Jean-Marie de La Mennais (1780-1860), brother of the famous author Lamennais.

Astronomical Clock (Horloge astronomique) – *Enter the abbey's courtyard via place J.-M.-de-La-Mennais.*
The clock was created between 1850 and 1855 and was intended for the instruction of the future teachers of the coastal schools.

Musée du Père Jean-Marie de la Mennais ⊙ – It is housed in one of the community buildings, near the Astronomical Clock. There is an exhibition on the Ploërmel Order in front of it. The tomb of Father La Mennais is in the chapel.

Étang au Duc – *2.5km/1.5mi north. Leave Ploërmel by boulevard du Maréchal-Foch west of the plan.*
🏃 Locally known as "the lake" it is a popular excursion (with an area of 250ha/718 acres). There is an artificial beach and a water sports centre.

Château du Crévy ⊙ – *8km/5mi south or N 166 to La Chapelle-Caro.* This castle dates back originally to the 3C, was rebuilt in the 14C, and has since been frequently remodelled.
The castle houses a **Musée du Costume★** (Costume Museum) with a remarkable collection of men's, women's, and children's fashion and dress from the 18C to the present. Tableaux with dressed models and furnishings of the period (Ancien Régime, Napoleonic period, Belle Époque...) illustrate the fashions and tastes of the time.

Malestroit – Near the Lanvaux Moors, this picturesque town, built along the Oust Canal, contains interesting Gothic and Renaissance houses. Malestroit was, during the Middle Ages, one of Brittany's nine baronies.

Old houses – Half-timbered or in stone, these houses are located mostly in the St Gilles precincts. On place du Bouffay one of the residences has humorous carvings on its façade, another has a pelican in wood. Stroll along rue au Froment, rue aux Anglais, rue des Ponts and the rue du Général-de-Gaulle.

Église St-Gilles – This 12C and 16C church is curious for the juxtaposition of styles and the double nave. Notice the south doorway, with its two doors with 17C carved panels, flanked by massive buttresses adorned with the symbolic attributes of the four Evangelists. The lion of St Mark is mounted by a youth symbolising St Matthew, and St Luke's ox rests on a pedestal adorned with the eagle of St John. About 3pm the shadows of the ox and the eagle between them suggest the well-known profile of Voltaire. Left of the high altar is a 16C stained-glass window dedicated to St Gilles and in the south chapel a 16C Pietà.

Musée de la Résistance bretonne ⊙ – *3km/2mi west on D 321 to St-Marcel.*
Spread over a forested park is the **Museum of Breton Resistance**, which vividly retraces this very important part of local Breton history.

The visit starts with a film which summarises the important events in the Second World War: German war effort, invasion of Europe, Allied preparation of the landing and the landing itself, and the Liberation.
Then follow exhibits, organised chronologically, with explanatory panels, slides and films, models, arms, uniforms etc evoking the war and its effect on Brittany. To illustrate wartime rationing, a street has been reconstituted, with its local grocery, petrol pump and restaurant; the black market and the collaboration are also explained. In the park part of the Atlantic Wall has been rebuilt; further on there is a garage, during the Occupation, with its gas-run cars, an American Army camp and finally a collection of military vehicles and weapons belonging to both the German and Allied armies.
Bear left 1km/0.5mi on leaving, to find a monument commemorating the battle which occurred between members of the Maquis (French Resistance Movement) and the Germans on 18 June, 1944.

Morcime/CAMPAGNE CAMPAGNE

Carved figure on a house in Malestroit

Domaine de KERGUÉHENNEC

Michelin map 69 fold 3 or 230 folds 36 and 37

The Kerguéhennec **estate**, in a pleasant, verdant setting, includes a Classical-style château, wooded park and lake. It was acquired by the Morbihan *département* in the 1970s and transformed into a **Contemporary Art Centre** ⓒ.

Park and Sculptures – An arboretum with fine trees is located in the 170ha – 442 acre park. Dotted throughout the park are modern sculptures including Giuseppe Penone's bronze *Charm's Way* (1986), Étienne Hajdu's *7 Columns to Stéphane Mallarmé* (1969-71), and Ulrich Ruckrien's blue granite *Bild Stock* (1985). On the lake float red polyester sculptures (1986) by Marta Pan.

Château – The château, built in the early 18C by local architect Olivier Delourme, consists of a main building, with two projecting wings and symmetrically opposed outbuildings, the whole enclosing a vast court of honour, closed by a fine grille. The inside, restored in the late 19C, can be visited: dining room, drawing room with its fine chandeliers and candelabra, billiard room, and library.

Temporary exhibitions and seminars are held in the old stables.

The greenhouse contains bright red flowerpots, the work of Jean-Pierre Raynaud, called *1 000 Cement Pots Painted for an Old Greenhouse* (1986).

EXCURSION

Locminé – The name of this town (*lieu des moines* meaning a place where the monks are), derives from the abbey founded here in the 6C, which had two churches identical in plan: Église St-Sauveur (16C) and Chapelle of St-Colomban. Only their façades remain; behind is a modern church (1975) built on the site of the nave and aisles. In the square are two corbelled houses; one is adorned with two wooden statues.

Chapelle Notre-Dame-du-Plasker – *To the left of the east end of the modern church.* This 16C rectangular chapel is decorated in the Flamboyant style.

KERNASCLÉDEN★★

Population 382
Michelin map 58 fold 18 or 230 folds 21 and 35

This small village possesses a beautiful church built by the Rohan family.

★★**Church** – Though the church at Kernascléden was consecrated in 1453, 30 years before the Chapelle de St-Fiacre *(see Le FAOUËT)*, there is a legend that they were built at the same time and by the same workmen. Every day, angels carried the men and their tools from one site to the other.

A characteristic feature of this church is the striving for perfection that appears in every detail. The very slender tower, the foliated pinnacles, rose carvings and delicate tracery help to adorn the church without overloading it. Two porches open on the south side. The left **porch★**, which is the larger, is ornamented with statues (restored) of the twelve Apostles.

Inside, the church has pointed stone vaulting. The vaults and walls surmounting the main arches are decorated with 15C **frescoes★★** representing episodes in the lives of the Virgin and Christ. The finest are the Virgin's Marriage, Annunciation (left of chancel) and Burial (right of chancel). In the north transept are eight angel-musicians; over the triumphal arch (on the chancel side), the Resurrection of Christ. On the walls of the south arm are fragments of a dance of death and a picture of Hell (facing the altar), which is remarkable for the variety of tortures it depicts. There are many 15C statues in wood and stone: Our Lady of Kernascléden to the left of the high altar, St Sebastian and a Pietà in the nave.

EXCURSIONS

Château et Forêt de Pont-Calleck ⓒ – *4km/2mi south. Take D 782 in the direction of Le Faouët and at Kerchopine, turn left.*

The road skirts the site of Notre-Dame-de-Joie, a children's home housed in **Château de Pont-Calleck** (Pont-Calleck Castle) which was rebuilt in 1880 *(only the park is open to visitors)*. The tiny Chapelle Notre-Dame-des-Bois stands at the entrance to the park.

Continue towards Plouay.

The road runs through the **Forêt de Pont-Calleck** (Forest of Pont-Calleck). A small road to the left runs down steeply and leads to a lake which affords a lovely view of the castle's site. Return to the Plouay road for a pleasant drive through the narrow valley of the Scorff.

Ploërdut – The **church** (13C-17C) has a fine Romanesque nave and side aisles. The rounded arches rest on solid square **capitals★** adorned with geometrical designs. Note the charnel-house abutting the south side of the church, which has a granite enclosure.

LAMBALLE

Population 9 874
Michelin map 59 folds 4 and 14 or 230 folds 23 and 24

Lamballe is a picturesque commercial town built on the slope of a hill crowned by the church of Notre-Dame-de-Grande-Puissance. It is an important market centre.

Bras-de-Fer before Lamballe (1591) – The town, which was the capital of the County of Penthièvre from 1134 to 1420, suffered a great deal in the War of Succession. During the League it was one of the strongholds of Mercœur, Duke of Penthièvre (Charles IX made the county a duchy). In 1591 Lamballe was besieged by the famous Calvinist captain La Noüe, nicknamed Bras-de-Fer (Iron-Arm), because he wore a metal hook in place of the arm he had lost; he was seriously wounded during the siege and transported to Moncontour where he died. Henri IV felt his loss keenly. "How terrible", he exclaimed, "that such a little fortress destroyed so great a man; he alone was worth an army!" In 1626 César de Vendôme, Lord of Penthièvre, the son of Henri IV and Gabrielle d'Estrées, conspired against Richelieu and the castle was razed by order of the Cardinal. Only the chapel remains.

The Princess of Lamballe (Revolution) – In 1767, at the age of 20, the Prince of Lamballe (the heir to the Duchy of Penthièvre) led such a dissolute life that his father, the duke, in an effort to reform him, married him to a Piedmontese princess; but the heir did not mend his ways, and he died, worn out with debauchery, three months later.

In 1770, when Marie-Antoinette married the future Louis XVI, she made friends with the young widow, who remained faithfully attached to her for 20 years. When the tragedy of the Revolution took place, the Princess of Lamballe bravely stood by the Queen. She died a year before her: in the massacres of September 1792, the rioters cut off her head and paraded it on a pike.

SIGHTS

★**Haras national (Stud Farm)** ⊙ – Founded in 1825, the stud contains 70 stallions (draught horses). From the beginning of March to mid-July, all the stallions are sent out to breeding stands in the Côtes d'Armor and the north of Finistère. The stud houses a school of dressage (40 horses) and a riding centre (20 horses). The visit includes the stables, blacksmith's shop, carriage house, harness room, riding school and main court.

J.D. Sudres-DIAF

The "Executioner's house" is now the tourist office

Place du Martray – Old half-timbered houses. The most remarkable is the 15C **Maison du Bourreau** (Executioner's House) (**M**) which now contains the tourist office and two museums.

Musée du Pays de Lamballe ⊘ – *Ground floor*. Devoted to popular arts and traditions, displays of pottery from Lamballe, etchings of the old town, headdresses and costumes of the region are shown.

Musée Mathurin-Méheut ⊘ – *First floor*. Works by the local painter M Méheut (1882-1958) as well as Breton costumes, *pardons* and traditional trades.

Collégiale Notre-Dame ⊘ – The Gothic collegiate church has Romanesque features, in particular the remarkable north doorway with slender columns and carved capitals supporting the recessed arches, a bay in the nave and the north transept. At the entrance to the south aisle in the chancel is a fine carved wood rood screen in the Flamboyant style. On the south side of the church with its buttressed gables, there is a terrace, built in the 19C, which affords a fine view of the town and the Gouessant Valley.

A shady esplanade is located left of the church.

Tour d'Argent – *2 rue du Dr-Lavergne – ☎ 02 96 31 01 37 – 31 rooms 290/380F – breakfast 40F – restaurant 88/210F*. Not to be confused with the famous Parisian restaurant of the same name, this hotel has an old half-timbered façade. The rooms are located in three different buildings and are quite modern, as is the rest of the establishment.

Église St-Martin – The old priory of Marmoutier Abbey was remodelled many times in the 15C to the 18C. In front of the church is a small, shady square. On the right is an unusual little porch (11C-12C) with a wooden canopy (1519). The handsome belltower has an 18C steeple.

ENVIRONS

★**Château de la Hunaudaye** – The **castle ruins** ⊘ of La Hunaudaye Castle rise in a lonely, wooded spot. Still impressive and severe, they reflect the power of the great barons, equals of the Rohans, who built the castle.

The castle, built in 1220 by Olivier de Tournemine, was partly destroyed during the War of Succession. Rebuilt and enlarged by Pierre de Tournemine in the 14C, enriched in the early 17C by Sébastien de Rosmadec, husband of one of the Tournemine heiresses, it was dismantled and then burnt by the Republicans at the time of the Revolution. The pillage of the castle stones was only stopped when the property was bought by the French government in 1930.

The shape is that of an irregular pentagon with a tower at each corner. The two smallest derive from the first building, the other three were built in the 14C-15C. The moat was once fed by two lakes. A bridge, replacing the original drawbridge, gives access to a large rounded doorway surmounted by a coat of arms. This leads to the courtyard.

Tour de la Glacière – This 15C tower is north facing, hence its name (*glacière* meaning ice-house). Go up the spiral staircase to admire the elegant structure and chimneys, and the view of the moat.

Logis seigneurial – 15C-16C. The walls and the splendid Renaissance stairway give some idea of the lay-out of this great manor house.

Donjon seigneurial – This 15C tower of this manorial keep with its spiral staircase (73 steps) is the best preserved. The monumental chimney-pieces and loopholes in the walls are note worthy. View of the courtyard and moat.

The fifth tower closing off the pentagon is the 13C-14C Chapel Tower.
This site is the setting for a performance, in period costume, of various aspects of life in a medieval castellany. The actors belong to the Compagnie Médiévale "Mac'htiern".

Ferme d'antan de St-Esprit-de-Bois-en-Plédeliac – Go into the courtyard surrounded by the traditional buildings on a small holding with their usual implements: outbuildings, cart and wood sheds, stables, cellar, bread oven, 1873 forge, recently restored and enhanced by the addition of a collection of tools of days gone by. The communal living room, with its great chimney-piece, is furnished in typical Breton style.
The tour ends with a film projection illustrating the everyday life of a peasant family in this very farm at the beginning of the century.

Château de la Touche-Trébry ⊘ – Although built at the end of the 16C, La Touche-Trébry looks like a medieval castle. It stands, facing a pond, protected by its defensive walls forming a homogeneous whole, unaltered in character by the restorations that have taken place. Two pavilions, resting against two huge towers (the one on the right has crumbled), watch over the entrance which consists of two gates, one of which is smaller than the other, and is topped by a wall walk. The courtyard is regular in shape with the main building, with its symmetrical façade, at the far end. On either side, at right angles, are the two wings with pointed roofs; next to them are the outbuildings, not as tall, extending all the way to the two entrance pavilions. In the corners between the main building and the side wings stand four turrets. The towers and turrets all have domed roofs. Inside the castle there are some fine chimney-pieces.

LAMPAUL-GUIMILIAU★

Population 2 037
Michelin map 58 fold 5 or 230 fold 4 – 4km/2mi southeast of Landivisiau –
Local map see Les ENCLOS PAROISSIAUX

This village has a complete parish close. The church is especially noteworthy for its rich decoration and furnishings.

★PARISH CLOSE

Triumphal arch (Porte triomphale) – The round arched gateway to the cemetery is surmounted by three crosses (1669).

Funerary chapel (Chapelle funéraire) – The former ossuary (1667) abuts on the arch and has buttresses crowned with small lantern turrets. Inside is the altar of the Trinity, with statues of St Rock, St Sebastian and St Pol and his dragon.

Calvary (Calvaire) – Very plain (early 16C) and, sadly, damaged.

★**Church (Église)** – The church is dominated by a 16C bell-tower, whose steeple was struck by lightning in the early 1800s. The apse, with a sacristy added in 1679, forms a harmonious whole in which the Gothic and Classical styles are blended. The porch on the south side dates from 1533. Under it are statues of the twelve Apostles and, between the two doors, a statue of the Virgin and Child and a graceful Kersanton stoup.

★★**Interior** – A 16C **rood beam** spans the nave, bearing a Crucifix between statues of the Virgin and St John. Both its faces are adorned with sculptures representing, on the nave side, scenes from the Passion and, on the chancel side, the twelve Sibyls separated by a group of the Annunciation. The pulpit dates from 1759. At the end of the south aisle is a **font** surmounted by a fine canopy dating from 1651. Higher up, on the right of the St Lawrence altarpiece, is a curious stoup (17C) representing two devils writhing in holy water; above, the Baptism of Christ.

In the chancel are 17C stalls, and on each side of the high altar, carved woodwork: on the left, St Paul on the road to Damascus and his escape; on the right, St Peter's martyrdom and the divine virtues. The side altars have 17C altarpieces.

The Last Supper (detail)

G. Biollay/DIAF

The altar of St John the Baptist, on the right of the chancel, is adorned with low-relief sculptures of which the most interesting (left) represents the Fall of the Angels after Rubens. The altar of the Passion, on the left of the chancel, has an **altarpiece** in eight sections in high relief with lifelike figures and, on the top, the Resurrection. On either side are two panels showing the Birth of the Virgin (left), a rare theme in Brittany, and the Martyrdom of St Miliau (right), King of Cornouaille beheaded by his jealous brother. In the north side aisle is a 16C Pietà with six figures carved out of a single piece of wood and also a 17C banner, embroidered in silver on a velvet ground (in an open cupboard). The impressive 1676 **Entombment** in polychrome tufa was carved by the naval sculptor Anthoine. Note the expression of the Christ figure in particular. The organ case is 17C. The sacristy contains a 17C chest.

LANDERNEAU

Population 14 269

Michelin map 58 fold 5 or 230 fold 4 – Local map see Les ENCLOS PAROISSIAUX

Located between Léon and Cornouaille, Landerneau, once the capital of Léon, is a small port and active market town, on the Élorn estuary.

SIGHTS

Pont de Rohan – Built in the 16C, this picturesque bridge, lined with houses with overhanging upper storeys, is one of the last inhabited European bridges.
Walk to the front of the town hall and enjoy the scene of the bridge, with its slate-covered houses and overfall.

Église St-Houardon – The Renaissance domed tower and the porch (1604) on the south side of this church remain.

Église St-Thomas-de-Cantorbéry ⊘ – This 16C church has a belfry-porch (1607) with three superimposed balconies. Inside, note the amusing decoration of the purlins in the north aisle and the great 18C altarpiece at the high altar.

Ancien Ossuaire – This former ossuary was erected as an annexe to the church of St Thomas in 1635.

Old houses – These are to be found mainly on the right bank of the River Élorn: no 9 place du Général-de-Gaulle, the turretted house (1664) known as the house of Duchess Anne; the façade at no 4 rue de la Fontaine-Blanche; at no 5 rue du Commerce, house with decorated turret and dormer windows (1667) and at the corner of the Pont de Rohan and Quai du Cornouaille is the so-called Maison des Rohan (Rohan House) (1639) with its sundial.

LANDÉVENNEC ★

Population 374

Michelin map 58 folds 4 and 5 or 230 fold 18

Situated on the Presqu'île de Landévennec, which is part of the Parc naturel régional de l'Armorique, the village of Landévennec stands in a pretty **site**★ at the mouth of the River Aulne, which is best seen by taking the steep downhill road to the right from Gorréquer. A lookout point to the right offers a fine **view**★ of Landévennec. Below is the course of the River Aulne, with the Île de Térénez; beyond, the Presqu'île de Landévennec and the River Faou.
A steep descent leads to the settlement, a little summer resort surrounded by woods and water and, due to the mild climate, Mediterranean vegetation.

Nouvelle abbaye bénédictine St-Guénolé – *Halfway bear right onto a tree-lined alley and follow the signposts.*
An audio-visual show offers a glimpse of the abbey's life past and present. The very plain church contains a polychrome wood statue of St Guénolé (15C), in sacerdotal vestments and a monolithic pink granite altar. Services are held and there is a shop.

Ruines de l'ancienne abbaye ⊘ – The monastery founded by the Welsh St Guénolé (Winwaloe) in the 5C and remodelled several times ceased to exist in the 18C and only the ruins of the Romanesque church remain. The plan can be deduced from the column bases, wall remains and doorway: a nave and aisles with six bays, transept, chancel and ambulatory with three radiating chapels. At the entrance to the south transept, there is a monument thought to be the tomb of King Gradlon. Near the church lie the ruins of a 17C conventual building.
In 1990, an **abbey museum** ⊘ of a very modern design was inaugurated on this site. It houses objects unearthed during excavations, including a wooden sarcophagus predating the 10C, discovered in 1985, and models illustrating the different stages

of construction of the abbey (a number of panels on the history of the monastic movement in Brittany during the Middle Ages). An audio-visual display retraces the history of the abbey and its occupants to the present.

The tour of the site is completed with a visit to a room given over to archeological exhibits.

EXCURSIONS

Pont de Térénez – Spanning the River Aulne, this graceful bridge, whose central span 272m/893ft, offers a fine view of the valley

Le Faou – The town, at the head of the Faou estuary, occupies a **site**★ which is full of character at high tide.

Rue Principale – The main street is flanked, on one side, by old houses with overhanging upper storeys and slate-covered façades. The 16C **church** stands on the river bank. It has an elegant 17C domed bell-tower, a double transept, a canted east end and an ornately sculpted south porch.

LANNION ★

Population 16 958

Michelin map 59 fold 1 or 230 fold 6

Lannion, a port spread out on both banks of the River Léguer, will attract the tourist with its typical "Old Brittany" character and with its proximity to the main beach resorts of the Côte de Granit rose (Pink Granite Coast).

The Centre de Recherches de Lannion and the Centre National d'Études des Télécommunications, where research is undertaken in telecommunications and electronics, have been built 3km/2mi north of Lannion at the crossroads of the road to Perros-Guirec and that of Trégastel-Plage.

LANNION

Augustins (R. des) .... **Z** 3
Leclerc (Pl. Gén.) .... **Y** 17
Pont-Blanc
(R. Geoffroy-de) .... **Z** 25

Aiguillon (R. d') .... **Z** 2

Buzulzo (R. de) .... **Z** 4
Chapeliers (R. des) .... **Y** 6
Cie-Roger-de-Barbé (R.)... **Y** 7
Coudraie (R. de la) .... **Y** 8
Du Guesclin (R.) .... **Z** 9
Frères-Lagadec (R. des) .. **Z** 12
Keriavily (R. de) .... **Z** 14
Kermaria (R. et Pont)...... **Z** 16
Le-Dantec (R. F.) .... **Y** 18

Letaillandier (R. E.) .... **Z** 20
Mairie (R. de la) .... **Y** 21
Palais-de-Justice
(Allée du) .... **Z** 24
Pors-an-Prat (R. de) .... **Y** 26
Roud-Ar-Roc'h (R. de)..... **Z** 28
St-Malo (R. de) .... **Z** 29
St-Nicolas (R.) .... **Z** 30
Trinité (R. de la) .... **Y** 32

175

SIGHTS

★**Old houses** – The beautiful façades of the 15C and 16C houses, half-timbered, corbelled and with slate roofs, may be admired especially at place du Général Leclerc (nos 23, 29, 31, 33), rue des Chapeliers (nos 1-9), rue Geoffroy-de-Pont-Blanc (nos 1 and 3) and rue Cie-Roger-de-Barbé (nos 1 and 7). At the corner of the latter, on the left, a granite cross has been sealed in the wall at the spot where the Chevalier de Pont-Blanc distinguished himself in the heroic defence of the town during the War of Succession.

★**Église de Brélévenez** (Y) – The church was built on a hill by the Templars in the 12C and remodelled in the Gothic period. The bell-tower is crowned by a granite spire and dates from the 15C.

Access – *The church is reached on foot up a staircase (142 steps) which tends to be a meeting point for artists; by car, via rue Le-Dantec, rue du Faubourg-de-Kervenno and rue des Templiers to the right.*
When you reach the terrace, there is an attractive view of Lannion and Léguer Valley. Before entering look at the curious Romanesque apse which is decorated with engaged round pillars, carved capitals and modillions.
Inside, on the left, is a stoup, which was used to measure tithe wheat. In the chapels to the right and left of the chancel are 17C altarpieces. Under the chancel and ambulatory, the Romanesque crypt, which was remodelled in the 18C, contains a marvellous 18C **Entombment**★, in which the subjects, carved in polychrome stone, are depicted life-size.

Église de St-Jean-du-Baly ⊘ (Y) – 16C-17C. Over the door of the sacristy to the left of the high altar is a fine 18C portrait of St John the Evangelist.

Bridge (Pont) (Z) – From the bridge, there is a good view of the port and of the vast Monastère Ste-Anne.

EXCURSIONS

① Castles and chapels
Round tour of 50km/31mi – 3hr.

Leave Lannion on ④ on the town plan, the road to Plouaret. 1.5km/1mi after Ploubezre, bear left at a fork where five granite crosses stand and 1.2km/1mi further on, turn left.

★**Chapelle de Kerfons** ⊘ – In a lovely setting, the chapel in front of which is an old Calvary, is surrounded by chestnut trees. Built in the 15C and 16C, it has a flat east end, a modillioned cornice along the south wall and a pinnacle turret deco-

Eating Out

BUDGET
Crêperie La Sarrazine – *13 rue Jeanne-d'Arc* – ☎ *02 96 37 06 48* – *closed 15-30 Nov, Sun except evening in season and Mon off-season* – *40/70F*. This little restaurant serves traditional crêpes in its dining room with stone walls, or in its back garden when the weather is nice. The regulars especially enjoy its family atmosphere.

OUR SELECTION
Ville Blanche – *5km/3mi from Lannion via the road to Paimpol and D 786* – ☎ *02 96 37 04 28* – *closed 13-20 Oct, 3 Jan-11 Feb, Sun evening except in summer, and Mon* – *120/360F*. What a delightful stop this starred restaurant is! With its yellow walls, pretty tables and charming vegetable garden, where the two cooks, brothers, pick the herbs to subtly enhance their dishes. Reservations advised.

Guided Tours

From 1 July to 31 August, the tourist office organises guided tours, notably with *terroir et patrimoine* ("local patrimony") days.

Sports

Kayak – ☎ *02 96 37 43 90*. Instruction in either sea (in the bay of Lannion) or river (in the Léguer River) kayaking is available in July and August (every morning from Tuesday to Friday).

Golf at St-Samson – *Route de Kérénoc in Pleumeur-Bodou* – ☎ *02 96 23 87 34*. This 18-hole golf course is located 9km/6mi outside of Lannion.

rated with telamones crowning the gabled south transept. It contains a late-15C carved **rood screen★** and fragments of old stained glass remain in the windows of the chancel and north transept.

Turn back and take the road on the left.

Soon the road starts to wind downhill providing good views over the ruins of Tonquédec in the Léguer Valley. After crossing the swiftly flowing river you will see the castle on the left *(car park)*.

★Château de Tonquédec ⊘ – The ruins of the castle stand in very fine surroundings on a height overlooking the Léguer Valley. The castle, which was built in the early 13C, was dismantled by order of Jean IV in 1395; rebuilt at the beginning of the 15 C, it was again razed by order of Richelieu in 1622.

The entrance gate is opposite a pool now run dry. Enter a fortified outer courtyard. On the right, two towers connected by a curtain wall frame the main entrance to the second enclosure. Pass through a postern into the second courtyard. Opposite, standing alone, is the keep with walls over 4m/13ft thick. Go up a stairway *(70 steps)* to a platform to admire the plan of the castle and the local countryside: a wide, fertile and populous plateau intersected by deep, wooded valleys running north and south.

Turn back and at the first crossroads bear left to join the road to Plouaret, then turn left again; and after 1km/0.5mi turn left.

Château de Kergrist ⊘ – One of the principal attractions of the château lies in the variety of its façades. The north façade is Gothic with dormer windows set in tall Flamboyant gables; the main building, which belongs to the 14C and 15C, nevertheless features an 18C façade on the opposite side, while the wings running at right angles, which were built at an earlier date, have Classical fronts overlooking the gardens. The formal French gardens extend as far as the terrace which overlooks a landscaped English garden and the woods.

Return to the Plouaret road and bear left; after 2.2km/1.5mi, turn left.

Chapelle des Sept-Saints ⊘ – This 18C chapel, surrounded by greenery, is unusual in that it is built in part on top of an imposing dolmen. From the outside, a small door in the south arm of the transept leads under the dolmen which has been turned into a crypt for the cult of the Seven Sleepers of Ephesus. According to legend, seven young Christians walled up in a cave in the 3C woke up 200 years later. Every year, an Islamic-Christian pilgrimage *(see Calendar of events)* is held in this Breton chapel.

Via Pluzunet and Bardérou you will reach the road to Lannion, then bear left.

Caouënnec-Lanvézéac – The **church** ⊘ contains a lovely, ornate altarpiece.

Proceed towards Lannion and at Buhulien bear left in the direction of Ploubezre and 100m/110yd after a farm at Pont-Keriel, turn left onto an unsurfaced path through the woods.

Château de Coatfrec – There are fine ruins of this large 16C mansion.

Make for Ploubezre and turn right to Lannion.

② Tour of towns in the Léguer Estuary

Round tour of 32km/20mi – 2hr.

Leave Lannion by Quai du Maréchal-Foch.

The south bank of the River Léguer is very picturesque, especially at high tide.

Loguivy-lès-Lannion – This town on the outskirts of Lannion clings to the hillside in a pleasant setting. The **church**, nestled on the banks of the Léguer, is 15C. A curious outdoor stairway leads to the wall-belfry (1570). Inside the church, in the chapel to the right of the chancel, there is a 17C wooden **altarpiece** depicting the Adoration of the Three Wise Men with shepherds in Breton costume playing the bagpipes and the bombardon. The fine wooden balustrade in the chancel dates from the same period.

At the back of the chancel there is a beautiful polychrome statue of St Ivy, patron saint of the parish.

Against the wall of the parish close, to the right of the triumphal doorway, stands a 15C **fountain** which contains a statue of St Ivy in bishop's robes. In the cemetery, a second fountain, made in granite and dating from 1577, plays beneath yew trees which are several centuries old.

Le Yaudet – This hamlet, in its beautiful setting, was the episcopal seat in the early centuries of our era and was destroyed by the Danes (c 848); it has remains of Roman walls and an interesting **chapel** overlooking the bay. Inside, above the altar, is a curious sculpted panel depicting the Trinity: a recumbent figure of the Virgin with the Infant Jesus at her side; God the Father is sitting in an alcove at the foot of the bed over which hovers a dove symbolising the Holy Spirit. A *pardon* is held on the third Sunday in May and on 15 August.

From the car park, the Corps de Garde footpath leads to a viewpoint, which affords a lovely **view** of the Léguer.

Return to the centre of Le Yaudet and turn right.

The road descends to Pont-Roux and climbs up again to reveal a fine **view** of the Léguer estuary and of the coast as far as Trébeurden.

At Christ, bear right towards Locquémeau.

Locquémeau – The town overlooks the beach and the fishing harbour which are reached by a corniche road to the left at the entrance to the town. The 15C **church** ⊘, which has a wall-belfry flanked by a turret, contains interesting 18C altarpieces and fine sculpted tie beams, purlins and hammerbeams.

★**Pointe de Séhar** – Leave your car near the port of Locquémeau and make for the point, from which the **view**★ extends westwards as far as the Pointe de Primel and eastwards to the resort of Trébeurden.

Trédrez – St Yves was Rector of Trédrez from 1284-92. The **church** was completed in 1500 by Philippe Beaumanoir to whom we owe many of the region's churches, with their characteristic wall belfries. Note inside the 14C granite font crowned with a beautifully carved wood canopy (1540). In the south side aisle, there is an altar decorated with four 17C panels depicting episodes from the Life of Christ; further along, a small stone altar features a polychrome altarpiece covered in gold leaf, depicting a beautiful Virgin and Child in a Tree of Jesse (1520). At the end of every hammerbeam angels have been carved *(see illustration p 39)*. Note also the sculpted decoration of the purlins and the animals swallowing the end of the tie beams. Facing the pulpit is a fine 16C Christ.

Leave Trédrez by the road going towards Kerbiriou and follow the road that leads to the Beg-ar-Forn headland.

Shortly before the car park there is a good view of the bay and the Lieue de Grève.

Turn round and at the second junction turn right towards St-Michel-en-Grève.

The road runs beside the sea to the town and affords a good view.

St-Michel-en-Grève – *See CORNICHE DE L'ARMORIQUE.*

Take the road to Lannion on leaving St-Michel-en-Grève, then bear right.

Ploumilliau – The 17C **church** ⊘ contains, in the south transept, 13 wooden **panels**, carved and polychrome, which illustrate scenes from the Life of Christ (Last Supper, the Passion, the Resurrection). There is also, on the wall opposite the sacristy, a curious portrayal of Ankou (Death), so often mentioned in Breton legend.

Return to the Morlaix-Lannion road to the north; turn right towards Lannion.

Admission times and charges for the sights described are listed at the end of the guide. Every sight for which there are times and charges is identified by the symbol ⊘ in the Sights section of the guide.

LOCMARIAQUER★★

Population 1 309

Michelin map 63 fold 12 or 230 fold 50 – Local map see Golfe du MORBIHAN

The village commands the channel into Morbihan Bay.

SIGHTS

Up by the cemetery, take the signposted path to the car park.

★★**Ensemble mégalithique de Locmariaquer** ⊙ – This group of three megaliths is an important part of a programme of conservation and restoration of megalithic sites.

Grand Menhir brisé – This menhir was probably broken on purpose as long ago as the Neolithic period, when it measured 20m/64ft and weighed almost 350t. It is set on the axis of the Er-Grah tumulus, but its relation with this monument has not yet been clearly explained. It is the largest menhir known to us.

Table des Marchands – The origin of the name of this dolmen has provoked considerable dispute, and experts are not sure whether the dolmen in fact bears the name of the family to which it belonged. It has been restored recently, and its tumulus has been rediscovered. A 7m/23ft corridor leads to a funerary chamber in which the base stele is decorated with crooks arranged symmetrically. The slab which forms the ceiling is in fact part of a large menhir, the two other parts of which can be found at the Tumulus d'Er-Grah, not far from here, and in the Cavin de Gavrinis, 4km/2.5mi from here. This slab features axe and crook motifs and part of a bovine figure.

Tumulus d'Er-Grah – This very elongated monument is situated north of the other megaliths. It is thought that its original length was more than 170m/558ft. The tumulus is currently the object of examination.

The excavations carried out in the area immediately surrounding the dolmen have revealed not only traces of dwellings – fireplaces, fragments of earthenware, mills for grinding grain – but also an alignment of 16 ditches, suggesting that this was once the site of ancient dressed stones.

★**Dolmen de Mané-Lud** – It stands surrounded by houses on the right at the entrance to the village. The stones which remain standing inside the chamber are carved.

★**Dolmen de Mané-Rethual** – *In the centre of the village and to the right of the former town hall, take a path which passes by a group of houses and gardens.* A long covered alleyway leads to a vast chamber, the supports of which are carved.

Church (Église) – It retains its 11C oven vaulted chancel and transept. The nave and aisles were rebuilt in the 18C. There are remarkable **capitals** adorned with geometrical designs or foliage at the transept crossing and in the chancel, and a fine stoup.

Hôtel Les Trois Fontaines – *Route d'Auray* – ☎ *02 97 57 42 70* – *closed 16 Nov-22 Dec and 3 Jan-24 Mar* – ▣ – *18 rooms 400/600F* – *breakfast 53F.* There is a pretty garden in front of this attractive modern building, which is one of the better places to stop in the region. The rooms are spacious and the nautical motif of the wooden furnishings is repeated in the lounge.

BOAT TRIP

★★★**Golf du Morbihan** – *See Golfe du MORBIHAN.*

TOUR OF MEGALITHIC MONUMENTS – *5km/3mi*

On leaving the village take the road on the right leading to **Kerlud** village, a remarkable group of small farms built in granite. Opposite the last house is the partly hidden **Dolmen de Kerlud.**
Return to the main road and bear right; beside the beach turn right again.

★**Dolmen des Pierres-Plates** – A menhir indicates the entrance to this dolmen. Two chambers are linked by a long alleyway. Remarkable engravings decorate the supports. A terrace affords a fine view of the Pointe de Port-Navalo and the Pointe du Grand-Mont, the Île d'Houat with Belle-Île in the distance, and the Presqu'île de Crozon.
Turn round and follow the shoreline as far as the Pointe de Kerpenhir.

★**Pointe de Kerpenhir** – Continue past the blockhouse. The point where a granite statue of Our Lady of Kerdro stands protecting sailors (*kerdro* is Breton for safe return), affords a **view**★ onto the Morbihan channel.
The road to the left offers a fine glimpse of the bay.

★**Tumulus de Mané-er-Hroech** – *At Kerpenhir take a path to the left of the road which climbs up to the tumulus.* A stairway *(23 steps)* gives access to the funerary chamber and to the dry-stone structure forming the tumulus.
Return to Locmariaquer.

LOCRONAN★★

Population 796

Michelin map 58 folds 14 and 15 or 230 fold 18 – Local map see CORNOUAILLE

The little town once prospered from the manufacturing of sailcloth. Traces of its golden age are to be found in its fine **square**★★, with its granite houses built during the Renaissance, old well, large church and pretty chapel. There are fine houses in the side streets (Rues Lann, Moal, St-Maurice).

The Troménies – The hill or mountain of Locronan, which overlooks the town, presents a very original spectacle on days devoted to *pardons*, which are known here as *Troménies*. There are the **Petites Troménies** *(see Calendar of events)*, when the procession makes its way to the top of the hill, repeating the walk that St Ronan, a 5C Irish saint, according to tradition, took every day, fasting and barefooted.

The **Grande Troménie**★★ takes place every sixth year on the second and third Sundays in July *(2001 is on the schedule)*. Carrying banners, the pilgrims go round the hill (12km/7.5mi), stopping at 12 stations. At the different stations each parish exhibits its saints and reliquaries. The circuit follows the boundary of the former Benedictine priory – built on the site of the sacred forest, the "Nemeton", which served as a natural shrine – founded in the 11C, which was a place of retreat. Hence the name of the *pardon* Tro Minihy or Tour of the Retreat, gallicised as Troménie.

SIGHTS

★★**Église St-Ronan and Chapelle du Penity** ⏱ – The accoladed and inter-communicating church and chapel form a harmonious ensemble. The 15C church is remarkable for its unity of style and stone vaulting. The decoration of the **pulpit**★ (1707) relates the life of St Ronan, and the 15C **stained-glass window**★ in the apse depicts scenes of the Passion. Among the old statues note that of St Roch (1509). The 16C chapel houses the tomb of St Ronan (the recumbent figure dates from the early 16C and is one of the earliest works in Kersanton granite). Note too a 16C Descent from the Cross in polychrome stone with six figures. The base is decorated with two beautiful **bas-relief sculptures**★, depicting the apparition of the resurrected Jesus to Mary Magdalene and the disciples of Emmaus, and two 15C statues (Christ in Fetters and St Michael weighing souls).

From the cemetery behind the church there is a good view of the church's flat east end.

Chapelle Notre-Dame-de-Bonne-Nouvelle ⏱ – *Walk down rue Moal, which starts from the square and leads down the slope of the ridge.*

With the Calvary and the fountain (1698), this 14C chapel forms a typically Breton scene. Inside is an Entombment; note also the diaphragm arch between the nave and chancel and the stained-glass windows by Alfred Manessier.

Museum ⏱ – *On the Châteaulin road.*

The ground floor is devoted to the 19C: Quimper faience, sandstone objects, local costumes and recreation of a typical interior. On the first floor the exhibits relate to the *Troménies (see above)* and to ancient crafts. There are also pictures and engravings by contemporary artists of Locronan and the surrounding area.

Skritelleoueg Breizh, Conservatoire de l'Affiche en Bretagne ⏱ – This museum, located in the old manor house of the Daniélou family, is devoted to collecting, conserving and restoring posters of all types (political, cultural, advertising etc). Temporary exhibitions focus on various selections from this collection in more detail.

Hotels

OUR SELECTION

Manoir de Moëllien – *29550 Plonévez-Porzay, 3km/5mi northwest of Locronan via C 10* – ☎ *02 98 92 50 40 – closed 13 Nov-14 Dec and 3 Jan-24 Mar* – 🅿 – *18 rooms 370/740F – breakfast 50F – restaurant 128/300F.* This 17C manor house in the country welcomes its guests in its outbuildings. The attractive rooms open their French doors onto the bucolic and remarkably calm surroundings, only the restaurant with fireplace is located in the manor house.

Eating Out

BUDGET

Crêperie Breiz Izel – *Place de l'Église* – ☎ *02 98 91 82 23 – closed Oct-Easter and Sun off-season – no credit cards – 35/60F.* While you are visiting the town, don't hesitate to stop in at this former residence of the Comptoir de la Compagnie des Indes to enjoy the old fireplace, the beautiful dining room and the reasonably priced crêpes.

EXCURSIONS

★**Montagne de Locronan** – *2km/1mi east. Leave Locronan on the Châteaulin road.* Go straight along the steep road on the hillside and take in the views of the bay, Ménez-Hom and the Porzay hollow below.

From the top (289m/948ft), crowned by a **chapel** ⊘ (note the stained-glass windows by Bazaine), you will see a fine **panorama★** of Douarnenez Bay. On the left are Douarnenez and the Pointe du Leydé; on the right Cap de la Chèvre, the Presqu'île de Crozon, Ménez-Hom and the Monts d'Arrée. To the right of the entrance is a granite pulpit.

Chapelle de Kergoat – *3.5km/2mi on the Châteaulin road.* The Gothic chapel is dominated by its domed belfry; it has a fine 17C east end. The **stained-glass windows★** are old and one shows the Last Judgement (1555). Pilgrimage Sunday following 15 August.

Ste-Anne-la-Palud ⊘ – *8km/4mi northwest. Leave Locronan by D 63 to Crozon. After Plonévez-Porzay, turn left.*

The 19C chapel contains a much-venerated painted granite statue of St Anne dating from 1548. The *pardon* on the last Sunday in August, one of the finest and most picturesque in Brittany, attracts thousands.

On the Saturday at 9pm the torchlit procession progresses along the dune above the chapel. Afterwards, high Mass is celebrated outside. The following Sunday and Tuesday a high Mass and vespers are pronounced followed by a procession with people dressed in Breton costumes bearing crosses, statues and banners.

Manoir de l'Automobile à LOHÉAC★★

Michelin map 63 fold 6 or 230 fold 39

This **Motor Museum** ⊘, set up in La Courneuve manor house *(from Lohéac, take D 50 towards Lieuron)*, contains a collection of over 160 cars of all types, ages and nationalities, specialising particularly in private and sports cars.

The tour begins in the old manor house, taking in a collection of "golden oldies" from the turn of the century, before moving on to an impressive line-up of Alpines (A 210 Le Mans, Coach A 106, Berlinette Tour de France A 108, A 110 GT⁴, A 310 1600 VE). Further on, there are examples of essentially the whole Lamborghini production (from the 350 GT to the Diablo). Dozens of Maseratis, Ferraris, Porsches and Rolls-Royces rub fenders with Dauphine Renaults, R8s or R12s, Citroëns, Peugeots (convertibles 301-403, from the 1960s and 70s) and Volkswagens.

The next stop on the tour is the **Chapelle des Moteurs** (Engine Chapel), an original display of several vintage engines in an old chapel. Other features of the museum include the reconstructions of a forge, a garage and an old-fashioned filling station fully equipped with tools, materials and authentic equipment connected with vehicle repair and maintenance.

The spacious first floor houses an exhibition of lavish foreign cars known as the "*belles étrangères*" and at the end of it is a wall of illuminated signs bearing the names of leading manufacturers associated with the motor industry.

The area devoted to miniature models relates the glorious history of the steam engine, illustrated by over 3 000 exhibits. Finally, the museum has a projection room, in which good films of cars are shown.

LORIENT

Conurbation 107 088
Michelin map 63 fold 1 or 230 folds 34 and 35

The modern city of Lorient boasts proudly of being the site of 5 ports: the fishing port of Keroman, a military port, with dockyard and submarine base (capacity: 30 submarines), a passenger port, with ships crossing the roadstead and sailing to the Île de Groix, the Kergroise commercial port, which specialises in the importing of animal foodstuffs, and the Kernevel pleasure boat harbour, with a wet dock located in the centre of the city; it is the starting point for transatlantic competition.

An annual Interceltic Festival (Festival Interceltique, *see Calendar of events*) is held in Lorient.

Parc à bois – On your way into Lorient, coming from Lanester, after taking the Pont St-Christophe, skirt the River Scorff and you will see black posts sticking out, particularly striking at low tide. They are probably the remains of the mast pond started in 1826.

The wood, used for naval construction, was plunged into the muddy sand to protect it from rotting and from ship worms.

Hotels

BUDGET

Léopol – *11 rue W-Rousseau* – ☎ *02 97 21 23 16* – *closed 24 Dec-5 Jan* – *26 rooms 190/270F* – *breakfast 32F.* The owners have put a lot of effort into rejuvenating this hotel: its renovated rooms and its salon with wicker furniture remain simple, but on the whole it is clean and welcoming. A good address for tight budgets.

OUR SELECTION

Hôtel Les Mouettes – *56260 Larmor-Plage, 7km/4mi south of Lorient via D 29 and D 152, Anse de Kerguélen* – ☎ *02 97 65 50 30* – 🅿 – *21 rooms 350/420F* – *breakfast 42F* – *restaurant 100/250F.* You'll feel pleasantly at the end of the world on the beach of this hotel, built on a nature preserve. The architecture is somewhat austere and the interior decoration is in the very spare Modernist style, however, you can still enjoy being so secluded.

Eating Out

BUDGET

Tea For Two – *23 rue Paul-Bert* – ☎ *02 97 64 27 70* – *closed Sun and evening* – *60/80F.* Alone or in a group, you will surely like the serene atmosphere and warm colours in this lovely tearoom. Their home-made pastries, light meals, brunches and teas already enjoy a solid reputation.

Crêperie du Gaillec – *Hameau de Gaillec – from Lorient, 9km/5.4mi via the expressway, exit at Plœmeur – Lann-Bihoué, turn left and follow signs to Gaillec* – ☎ *02 97 83 00 26* – *closed last three weeks in Sept, Sun evening and Mon* – *30/80F.* Some things are worth the effort! Getting to this former farm is not particularly easy, however, once seated in the restaurant, you will enjoy their crêpes made with organic flour and their selection of local products.

OUR SELECTION

Jardin Gourmand – *46 rue Jules-Simon* – ☎ *02 97 64 17 24* – *closed 1-12 Aug, Feb school holidays, Sun and Mon* – *105/160F.* In a small stone house, this restaurant serves fresh and delicious cuisine. In the summer, you can eat in the small garden, and in the winter in the beige and lavender dining room. Lunch and dinner.

Night-life

Jame'son – *48 rue Jules-Simon* – ☎ *02 97 64 49 99* – *Mon-Sat 6pm-2am.* Renowned for its delicious punches, this cocktail bar is enlivened by the songs of Brassens, Brel and Piaf. After 30 years, it is still known for its courteous welcome.

HISTORICAL NOTES

The India Company – After the first India Company, founded by Richelieu at Port-Louis, failed, Colbert revived the project in 1664 at Le Havre. But as the Company's ships were too easily captured in the Channel by the British, it was decided to move its headquarters to the Atlantic coast. The choice fell on "vague and vain" plots of land located on the right bank of the Scorff. Soon afterwards, what was to be known as the "Compound of the India Company" was born. Since all maritime activities were focused on India and China, the installations built on that site bore the name "*l'Orient*" (French for the East). In those days, the arrogant motto of the India Company – *Florebo quocumque ferar* (I shall prosper wherever I go) – was fully justified by the flourishing trade which it exercised. But a new naval war loomed ahead. So Seignelay turned the "Compound" into a royal dockyard patronized by the most famous privateers (Beauchêne, Duguay-Trouin etc).

In the 18C, under the stimulus of the well-known Scots financier Law, business grew rapidly; 60 years after its foundation, the town already had 18 000 inhabitants. The loss of India brought the Company to ruin, and in 1770 the State took over the port and its equipment. Under the Empire it became a naval base.

Despite the loss of monopoly, the company resumed trading in 1785 as the New India Company but ceased its activities in 1794.

The war years – Lorient was occupied by the Germans on 25 June 1940. From 27 September 1940 the city was subject to bombardments, which intensified as the war raged on, and was destroyed in August 1944. The fighting between the entrenched German garrison and the Americans and locally based Free French Forces which encircled the Lorient "pocket" devastated the surrounding area so that when the townspeople returned on 8 May 1945, all that greeted them was a scene of desolation.

Villa Vanny – *10 place Jules-Ferry* – ☎ *02 97 64 57 81* – *Mon-Sat noon-2pm, Sun 6pm-2am.* The Villa Vanny is the current fashionable bar in Lorient. Its rum drinks and up-to-date music attract all the gilded youth in the city.

The Galway Inn – *18 rue de Belgique* – ☎ *02 97 64 50 77* – *daily 11am-1am.* This very convivial pub has been run by an Irishman since 1988. It hosts numerous concerts of Celtic music. Packed on the weekends.

Place Jules-Ferry – *Place Jules-Ferry.* This is the centre of Lorient's night-life. Everyone converges here – from chic young people (at Villa Vanny) to those slightly older (at Admiral Benbow). Around the place, you will also find a café-theatre, a pub, an Australian bar, and a couple of discotheques.

Villa Margaret – *Port de plaisance de Kernevel, 56260 Larmor-Plage* – ☎ *02 97 33 67 19* – *off-season, daily 9am-midnight; July-Aug, 7.30am-1am.* Young and old mingle in his peaceful bistro, located in a splendid residence which dates from 18C. In the summer, jazz rhythms pervade the shaded garden terrace which looks out onto the port of Kernevel.

Cultural Activities

Architectural tour of Lorient in the 1930's and 1950's – The tourist office distributes a small guide to the city's architecture.

Théâtre de l'Océan – *Larmor-Plage* – *information at the tourist office* – ☎ *02 97 33 70 02.* Plays and concerts facing the sea.

Recreation

Centre nautique de Kerguelen – *Road to Kerguélen, 56260 Larmor-Plage* – ☎ *02 97 33 77 78* – *Mon-Fri 8.45am-12.15pm, 1.45pm-6pm, weekends and public holidays 9am-noon, 2pm-5pm.* This enormous nautical complex offers a wide range of activities: scuba-diving, windsurfing, kayaking, regular and parachute water-skiing, and surfing.

Boat trips – Trips are available to the following destinations; see individual names: **Belle-Île★★**, **Port-Louis★**, and **Île de Groix★**.

Moulin Lorient Marée – *Fishing port* – ☎ *02 97 37 30 00* – *Mon-Sat 8am-noon.* Located on the fishing port of Keroman, this is the only store which sells fresh sea products retail. Fish auctions are also held there.

Guided tour of the fishing port – Organised by the tourist office (with break-fast at the port), from Monday to Wednesday, starting at 4.30am (19F + 21F for breakfast).

Sea-fishing – ☎ *02 97 21 00 52.* Departure from Larmor-Plage's marina for half-day or full-day fishing expeditions.

SIGHTS

Enclos du Port ⊘ – A tour of the dockyards recalls the heyday of the India Company: the Gabriel pavilion has been entirely restored in the original style. There are four dry docks designed for battleship repair. The *Tour de la Découverte* was built in 1786 and once served as a watchtower.

Port de pêche de Keroman (**Z**) – *Best seen in the morning when the fishermen return with the day's catch (depending on the tide).* Partly reclaimed from the sea, the port of Keroman is the only French harbour designed and equipped for commercial fishing; it is the leading port in France for the value and variety of fish unloaded. It has two basins set at right angles: the Grand Bassin and the Bassin Long (totalling 1 850m/6 070ft of docks). The Grand Bassin is sheltered by a jetty 250m/265yd long which is used as a loading and unloading quay for cargo steamers and trawlers. The basin has two other quays, one with a refrigerating and cold-storage plant for the trawlers and fish dealers; and the other, as well as the quay at the east end of the Bassin Long, where the trawlers unload their catch. In front of the quays is the 600m/650yd long market hall *(criée)* where auctions are held, and, close behind it, the fish dealers' warehouses which open onto the car park, where lorries destined for the rest of France are loaded.

In six bays of the slipway, trawlers can be dry-docked or repaired. A large area round the basins, available for the industries and commerce connected with fishing, completes the zone.

The port of Keroman sends out ships for all kinds of fishing all the year round. The largest vessels go to sea for a fortnight, especially to the Irish Sea for coal-fish and carry their own ice-making equipment (which can make up to 400t a day) to the fishing grounds.

LORIENT

0 300 m

HENNEBONT
PORT-LOUIS
LANESTER

QUIMPERLÉ / D 765

N 24 RENNES
N 165-E 60 VANNES

QUIMPER

KERENTRECH

Bd de Normandie
R. P.
Guiyesse
Laënnec
R. Prof. Perrin
Bd de Verdun
R. du Scorff
Cra

Dumanoir
Cosmao
Bd E. Svob
Mal Joffre
HÔPITAL DES ARMÉES

LE MOUSTOIR
Blum
LE MOUSTOIR
Léon R. J. Le Courailer
PALAIS DES CONGRÈS
des Indes
ARSENAL MARITIME

Av. Jean Jaurès
Av. du Gal de Gaulle
R. Du Guesclin
MERVILLE
NOUVELLE VILLE
R. Duguay-Trouin
Lazare
V. Hugo
R. de Carnel
Bd de la République
R. Carnot

PORTE GABRIEL
PORT-LOUIS
BELLE ÎLE
ÎLE DE GROIX

LARMOR-PLAGE
D 162, PLOEMEUR

PORTE DE LA BASE
N 465
Av. de la Perrière
PORT DE PÊCHE DE KEROMAN
HALLE DE CRIÉE
BASSIN LONG
GRAND BASSIN
BASE DES SOUS-MARINS

Y

Z

Assemblée-Nat. (R.) ...... **Z** 3
Foch (R. Mar.) .... **Z** 9
Liège (R. de) .... **Z** 15
Patrie (R. de la) .... **Z** 19
Port (R. du) .... **Z** 21

Anatole-France (Av.) ..... **Z** 2
Bart (Q. J.) .... **Z** 4
Du-Couédic (R.) .... **Y** 5
Du-Faouédic (Av.) .... **Z** 7
Ferry (Pl. Jules) .... **Z** 8
Leclerc (Bd Gén.) ..... **Y** 12
Le-Grand (R. J.) .... **Y** 13
Oradour-sur-
   Glane (Bd d') .... **Y** 17
Pierre (Bd A.) .... **Z** 22
Rohan (Q. de) .... **Z** 25
St-Christophe (Pont) . **Y** 28

B Église N.-D.-de-Victoire

★ **Base des sous-marins Ingénieur-Général-Stosskopf** ⊘ – The submarine base is named in honour of the Second World War maritime engineer who, by appearing to collaborate with the Germans, was able to keep abreast of activities on the base and inform Allies. When he was discovered, he was executed.

The three blocks were built in record time. The first two (1941) have slots for 13 submarines. The third (1943) has a protected reinforced concrete roof 7.5m/25ft thick.

At the end of the war, the French Navy took over the base for their Atlantic submarine operations, but have since abandoned it for this purpose. The last dry-dock operation took place in December 1996, and the *Sirène*, the last active submarine, left the base for the Toulon port in February 1997. The *Flore* is the only ship remaining; it has no military purpose but is kept up for display between blocks one and two. The Navy has progressively turned over the dockyards to the city of Lorient and various projects for the use of the area are underway or being considered.

Le Victor Pleven ⊘ – This ship was launched in Gdansk in 1971, and at the time was one of the largest fishing and packing ships to work the waters off Canada and New-foundland (90m/295ft long). This giant floating factory could bring 1000 tonnes of frozen fish into port.

Église Notre-Dame-de-Victoire (**YZ B**) – Better known to the locals as the church of St-Louis, it stands in place Alsace-Lorraine which is, itself, a successful example of modern town planning. The church is built in reinforced concrete and has very plain lines. It is square with a flattened cupola roof and a square tower flanking the façade. The beauty of the church lies in its **interior★**. Little panes of glass, yellow and clear, reflect the outside light into the building from the top of the rotunda and the bays in the lower section consist of brightly coloured splintered glass. Covering the wall at the back of the high altar is a mural in pastel tones, while in the nave a striking monochrome Entombment faces an Annunciation. The Stations of the Cross drawn in outline only, show each at its most dramatic moment.

THE COAST BETWEEN SCORFF AND LAÏTA

Round tour of 47km/29mi – 2hr 30min. Leave Lorient by ② on the town plan passing the Kernével road on the left.

⌂ **Larmor-Plage** – Looking out over the ocean, across from Port-Louis, Larmor-Plage has lovely, fine, sandy beaches much appreciated by the people of Lorient.
The parish **church**, built in the 12C, was remodelled until the 17C. The 15C porch, uncommonly situated on the north façade because of the prevailing winds, contains statues of the Apostles and above the door a 16C painted wood Christ in Fetters. The inside contains interesting furnishings: a 17C altarpiece at the high altar and in the north aisle, at the Jews' altar, a Flemish-style 16C altarpiece, which por-

trays 40 small figures on the slopes of the Calvary; to the right is a 16C poly-chrome statue of Our Lady of the Angels and in the south aisle a 16C Pietà in stone; from the same period are statues of St Efflam and St Barbara, in the chancel. Every year, on the Sunday before or after 24 June, there is a blessing of the Coureaux (the channel between the Île de Groix and the coast). By tradition, war-ships leaving Lorient salute the Church of Our Lady of Larmor with three guns, while the priest blesses the ship, has the church bells rung and hoists the flag. The old road from Larmor follows the coast fairly closely, passing many small seaside resorts. Note the kaolin quarries on the right. After Kerpape the drive affords extensive views of the coast of Finistère, beyond the cove of Le Pouldu and over to the Île de Groix.

In the foreground are the coastal inlets in which lie the little ports of Lomener, Perello Kerroch and Le Courégant and the large beach of **Fort-Bloqué** dominated by a fort. Go through Guidel-Plages on the Laïta estuary. From Guidel make for the Pont de St-Maurice *(6km/4mi there and back)* over the Laïta. The **view**★ up the enclosed valley is magnificent.

From Guidel continue on via Coatermalo and Gostel to Pont-Scorff. At Pont-Scorff take the road towards Quéven.

Zoo de Pont-Scorff ⊘ – In a woodland setting on the steep banks of the Scarve, the zoo, which specialises in breeding big cats, contains 13 species from the cat family: lions, tigers, leopards, ocelots, snow leopards, lynxes, pumas etc as well as many other types of animal from all over the world: bears, wolves, llamas, bison, hippopotamuses, web-footed animals, birds and monkeys.

Return to Lorient passing through Quéven.

LOUDÉAC

Population 9 820
Michelin map 59 fold 13 or 230 folds 22 and 23

This little town, at the heart of Brittany, still holds some large fairs and markets. The region specialises in intensive farming, mainly chicken and pigs, and the countryside is dotted with large hangars flanked by tall silos. Loudéac is also well known for its **race meetings** ⊘.
With the second-largest race track in Western France, Loudéac remains faithful to a history of horse breeding which began in the Middle Ages. The Rohan family kept a stud farm of about 100 fine horses here. Today, tourists have the opportunity of dis-covering the unspoiled landscapes astride a traditional mount.

EXCURSIONS

La Chèze – *10km/6mi southeast on the D 776.*
In this village, which has preserved the vestiges of a 13C castle, is the **Musée régional des Métiers de Bretagne** (Breton Crafts Regional Museum) ⊘. The centre evokes the crafts and trades of yesteryear with reconstituted workshops of the slate roofer, harness-saddle maker, cartwright, wooden shoemaker and blacksmith.

Querrien – *11km/7mi east.*
The little village of Querrien was the site of the miraculous apparition of the Virgin to a young shepherdess in the 17C. There is an annual pilgrimage in the sanctuary in honour of Our Lady of Infinite Succour (Notre-Dame-de-Toute-Aide).

La Ferrière – *16km/10mi southeast. Leave Loudéac on the road to Rennes and after 12km/7mi bear right towards La Trinité-Porhoët and right again 2km/1mi further on.*
In the village stands a vast 14C **church** with a belfry-porch. Inside, in the chancel is a stained-glass window depicting the Virgin (1551); in the north transept a window of the Tree of Jesse of the same date, a Romanesque Virgin in lime wood, the so-called Our Lady of La Ferrière and a granite late-15C Annunciation; in the nave a 16C Crucifixion (on the right).
The square opposite the church is adorned with a 15C Calvary cross.

MÉNEZ-HOM★★★

Michelin map 58 fold 15 or 230 fold 18

Ménez-Hom (alt 330m/1 082ft), a detached peak at the west end of the Montagnes Noires, is one of the great Breton viewpoints and a key position commanding the approach to the Presqu'île de Crozon. On 15 August a folklore festival is held at the summit.

Travelling from Châtealin towards Crozon along D 887 and D 83, you can see the mount above you. The final 2km/1mi climb is along a road which branches off, 1.5km/1mi after the Chapelle Ste-Marie-du-Ménez-Hom.

★★★ **Panorama** – *Viewing table.* In clear weather there is a vast panorama. You will see Douarnenez Bay, bounded on the left by the Cornouaille coast as far as the Pointe du Van, and on the right by the coast of the Presqu'île de Crozon as far as Cap de la Chèvre. To the right the view extends to the Pointe de St-Mathieu,

Hotels

BUDGET

Relais de Cornouaille – *Road to Carhai, 29119 Châteauneuf-du-Faou –* ☎ *02 98 81 75 36 – closed Oct, Sun evening and Sat –* 🅿 *– 20 rooms 210/280F – breakfast 35F – restaurant 70/200F.* This hotel is located in two adjoining houses – one recent, one old. Little by the little, the rooms, salon and reception area have been modernised. The restaurant's generous servings attract a large local clientele. Children's menu.

Eating Out

BUDGET

Bienvenue – *56110 Roudouallec, 9km/5.4mi west of Gourin on the Quimper road via D 1 –* ☎ *02 97 34 50 01 – closed Sun evening and Mon Oct-May – 72/235F.* Behind its quite ordinary façade, this restaurant serves delightful food... perfect for food-lovers passing through. In its unpretentious, but light and well-groomed, dining room, you can enjoy dishes which highlight regional specialities.

the Tas de Pois Rocks, the Pointe de Penhir, Brest and its roadstead, in front of which you will see the Île Longue on the left, the Île Ronde and the Pointe de l'Armorique on the right, with the estuary common to the River Faou and River Aulne, which nonetheless separate as they flow inland. The nearer valley – that of the Aulne – follows a fine, winding course, spanned by the suspension bridge at Térénez. In the distance are the Monts d'Arrée, the Montagne St-Michel crowned by its little chapel, the Châteaulin Basin, the Montagne de Noires Montagnes, Locronan, Douarnenez and Tréboul.

Go as far as the mark of the Geographical Institute (Institut géographique) to get a view of the horizon from all sides. You will then see, in the Doufine Valley, the village of Pont-de-Buis.

Chapelle Ste-Marie-du-Ménez-Hom – The chapel stands in a small parish close at the entrance to Presqu'île de Crozon. The close has a very plain rounded doorway, dated 1739, and a Calvary with three crosses rising from separate bases. The chapel, which has a twin-gabled façade, is entered through a doorway beneath the elegant galleried belfry, topped by a cupola which gives an upward sweep to the massive building. Inside, the ornate **altarpieces★** take up the whole of the east wall, without covering over the window apertures. While both the central altarpiece, with the family and life of the Virgin as its theme, and the north altarpiece, depicting the saints, have figures which are rather heavy and expressionless, the figures of the Apostles on the south altarpiece show life and elegance. The skill with which they were carved marks a step forward in Breton sculpture. The lovely purlins in the north transept, adorned with animals and various scenes, a remarkable St Lawrence and a graceful St Barbara in wood, are also noteworthy.

MONTAGNES NOIRES★★

Michelin map 58 folds 16 and 17 or 230 folds 19 and 20

With the Monts d'Arrée, the Montagnes Noires form what Bretons call the spine of the peninsula. These two little mountain chains, mainly of hard sandstone and quartzite, are not quite alike. The Montagnes Noires are lower (326m/1 043ft as against 384m/1 229ft); their crest is narrower; their slopes are less steep and their heaths are less extensive.

The chain's name (*noire* means black) suggests that it was once covered with forest. As in all inland Brittany, the ground became bare with time. Since the end of the last century reafforestation has been going on, and the fir woods, now numerous, once more justify the name of Black Mountains.

Quarrying of Breton slate carried out on a large scale in the past, is now concentrated on the eastern end of the chain, in the district of Motreff and Maël-Carhaix.

ROUND TOUR STARTING FROM CARHAIX-PLOUGUER

585km/53mi – half a day

Carhaix-Plouguer – *See CARHAIX-PLOUGUER.*

Leave Carhaix-Plouguer west towards Pleyben and after 2.5km/1.5mi turn left.

The road then enters the picturesque valley of the Hyère.

At Port-de-Carhaix, after crossing the Nantes-Brest Canal, bear right.

Some 1.5km/1mi further on, note the **Calvaire de Kerbreudeur** on the left, parts of which are thought to date from the 15C.

St-Hernin – In this place, where the Irish St Hernin is said to have settled, is a 16C parish close. The church and charnel house were remodelled in the 17C. On the beautiful slender Calvary note St Michael slaying the Dragon.

Take the road to Moulin-Neuf and bear right on the road Carhaix-Plouguer to Gourin.

Old slate quarries can be seen to the right and left.

Chapelle St-Hervé – *Access is via a road to the left.* This small 16C building with a pierced pinnacle is decorated in the Flamboyant Gothic style. A *pardon* is held on the last Sunday in September.

After crossing the crest of the Montagnes Noires, the road runs down to Gourin.

Gourin – Once a centre of slate production, Gourin also has white stone quarries and raises horses, cattle and poultry. The 16C church, topped by a domed bell-tower with lantern turrets, contains in the south aisle, to the left of the entrance, a 16C Pietà in polychrome wood.

At Gourin, take the Quimper road, and at the bottom bear right towards Châteauneuf-du-Faou.

La Trinité-Langonnet

This village possesses a fine Flamboyant-style church. The **timbering★** inside, dated 1568 and decorated with Renaissance designs, shows great craftsmanship and enhances the lofty, well-lit nave. In the richly ornamented chancel, note the carved recesses, corbels and purlins; and on the left of the chancel, a sacrarium, a fine stone cupboard.

The road climbs towards the crest of the Montagnes Noires.

★◪ Roc de Toullaëron – *30min on foot there and back; 5km/3mi from Gourin, leave your car and take a stony lane bordered with oak trees (private property, no picnicking) to the right. At the end of the lane, climb up the rocks.*
From the top, which is the highest point in the Montagnes Noires (326m/1043ft), a wide **panorama★** may be enjoyed in clear weather: to the west is the densely wooded valley of Châteaulin; to the north, the Monts d'Arrée; to the south, in the distance, the Breton plateau slopes gently down to the Atlantic.

Make for Spézet; on leaving Spézet take the Châteauneuf-du-Faou road, bear left.

★Chapelle Notre-Dame-du-Crann ⊘ – The chapel, built in 1532, stands on the side of the road in a verdant setting. It contains some remarkable 16C **stained-glass windows★★** and has a flat east end.
In the south aisle you will see the window illustrating the legend of St Eligius, who is the patron of farriers. In the south transept are the Death and Coronation of the Virgin. Above the south aisle, is the stained-glass window of St James the Greater, in three bays. The window in the chancel depicts scenes of the Passion in 12 bays.

Return to Spézet and before entering bear left and after 2km/1mi, left again. At the entrance to St-Goazec, turn right.

Écluse de Gwaker – This is one of the many locks on the Nantes-Brest Canal. There is a pretty waterfall at the end of the large pool, forming a pleasant setting.

After St-Goazec, bear right towards Laz.

The road climbs into the lovely forest of Laz, which is mostly coniferous.

★**Park and Château de Trévarez** ⊘ – This 85ha/210 acre forest park is laid out around an imposing neo-Gothic château built in the "Belle Epoque" style. The signposted paths wind their way through the woods, making for a pleasant stroll whatever the season: admire the camellias (April), the azaleas and hydrangeas (July), fuchsias and rhododendrons. A pond, a water garden and several fountains add a refreshing touch. The château terrace offers a **splendid view** of the Châteauneuf-du-Faou region. The former stables, whose original design was extremely modern for their time, have kept their stalls and loose-boxes; these have been converted into a small museum and are used for exhibitions and other educational activities organised throughout the year. This charming outing can be complemented by a train ride and a "Breton tea" (with traditional Breton cakes).

At Laz, turn right towards Kerohan.

The picturesque downhill road, hemmed in by rocky ridges, affords a fine view over the Aulne Valley.

After Ty-Glas, bear right towards Châteauneuf-du-Faou.

The road crosses and then follows the Aulne.

Châteauneuf-du-Faou – This village is built in very pretty surroundings on the slope of a hill overlooking the Aulne. It is an angler's delight with salmon swimming up the Aulne from the sea and also pike. In the church, the baptismal chapel decorated in 1919 with scenes from the life of Christ by **Paul Sérusier** (1865-1927), a painter of the Nabis group, is of interest. A *pardon* is held on the third Sunday in August at the Chapelle Notre-Dame-des-Portes.

The road from Châteauneuf to Carhaix-Plouguer is charming for the short distance that it follows the Aulne.

After 1.5km/1mi beyond the confluence with the Nantes-Brest Canal, bear left towards La Roche and then right after some 500m/547yd.

The road runs past farmyards to a hillock. From the top of the tumulus, there is a fine **view** of a loop of the Aulne.

Return to the road to Carhaix-Plouguer.

Cléden-Poher – The village has a fine **parish close**★ dating mainly from the 16C. The 15C-16C church contains interesting altarpieces: three Flemish-style 16C panels at the high altar; the altarpiece of the Rosary (1694) in the south aisle; the altarpiece of the Pentecost (17C) in the north aisle. Much of the vaulting has preserved its panelling painted in 1750. In the cemetery are an ossuary turned into a chapel with a fine timber roof, a Calvary (1575) and two curious sacristies with keel vaulting.

Return to Carhaix-Plouguer.

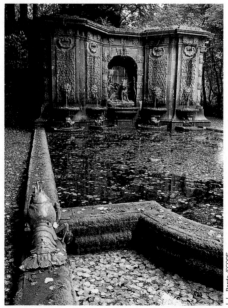

Fountain in Trévarez park

MONT-ST-MICHEL★★★

Population 72
Michelin map 59 fold 7 or 231 fold 38

The Mont-St-Michel has been called "the Marvel of the Western World" owing to its island setting, its rich history and the beauty of its architecture; at any season of the year it leaves an indelible impression. The rock and the immensity of nature around it, the Bay with both sand and grassy flats are all parts of a magical whole, which made it among the fist sites to be included on UNESCO's World Heritage List (1979). As the bay is already partially silted up *(see DOL-DE-BRETAGNE: Marais de Dol)*, the mount is usually to be seen surrounded by huge sand banks which shift with the tides and often reshape the mouths of the neighbouring rivers.

The course of the Cousenon, which used to threaten the dikes and polders with its wandering, has been canalised and the river now flows straight out to sea to the west of the mount. Its former course, northwest from Pontorson, used to mark the frontier between the duchies of Normandy and Brittany.

The movement of the tides in the bay is very great and the difference in sea level between high and low water can be over 12m/40ft, the highest in France. As the sea bed is flat, the sea retreats a long way exposing 15km/9mi of sand. The tide comes in very rapidly, not quite at the speed of a galloping horse, as has been said, but of a person walking at a brisk pace. This phenomenon, which is aggravated by numerous currents, can spell danger to the unwary.

The Mont-St-Michel has been silting up for several decades. Indeed, every year the sea deposits around 1 000 000m³/35 315 000cu ft of sediment in the bay. In part, this can be blamed on mankind since between the mid 19C and 1969 a number of regional initiatives were taken, resulting in constructions that accelerated the formation of polders (canalization of the River Couesnan, building of a dike then a dam). In 1995 a joint project was commissioned by the State and by local municipalities, intended to return the Mont to the sea. Ideally, this would make it possible to replace the dike by a footbridge under which cross-currents would once again flow between the mainland and the island. It would also help restore the scouring action of the Couesnan and the two other coastal streams. The implementation of this project is hoped to be completed in the year 2000.

St Michael's Mount, Cornwall

In the 4C BC ships came from the Mediterranean to the **Island of Ictis**, as they named it, to trade in tin, copper and gold; in AD 495, according to Cornish legend, fishermen saw St Michael standing on a westerly ledge of the granite rock which rises high out of the sea, whereupon the island became a place of pilgrimage. By the 8C, it is said, a Celtic monastery had been founded upon it which endured until the 11C.

At the same time, in AD 708 in France, St Michael appeared three times in a vision to Bishop Aubert of Avranches, who then built an oratory to the saint on the island from then known as Mont-St-Michel. By the time of the Battle of Hastings, the oratory in France had developed into an important Benedictine community to which St Michael's Mount passed as a dependency. The English house, always modest by comparison with the French monastery, was ultimately appropriated during the course of the Hundred Years War by Henry V as alien property and was finally suppressed in 1535.

HISTORICAL NOTES

An amazing achievement – The abbey's origin goes back to the early 8C, when the Archangel Michael appeared to Aubert, Bishop of Avranches, who founded an oratory on the island, then known as Mont Tombe. In the Carolingian era, the oratory was replaced by an abbey and from then until the 16C a series of increasingly splendid buildings, in the Romanesque and then the Gothic styles, succeeded one another on the mount which was subsequently dedicated to the Archangel.

The well fortified abbey was never captured.

The construction is an amazing achievement. The blocks of granite were transported from the Îles Chausey or from Brittany and hoisted up to the foot of the building. As the crest of the hill was very narrow, the foundations had to be built up from the lower slopes.

Pilgrimages – Even during the Hundred Years War pilgrims came flocking to the mount; the English, who had possession of the area, granted safe conduct to the faithful in return for payment. People of all sorts made the journey: nobles, rich citizens and beggars, who lived on alms and were given free lodging by the monks. In times of great calamity, the pilgrimage to Mont-St-Michel prompted such excessive

displays of religious fervour that the ecclesiastical authorities were obliged to inter-
vene. Hotels and souvenir shops flourished. The pilgrims bought medals bearing the
effigy of St Michael and lead amulets which they filled with sand from the beach.
Of the many thousands of people crossing the bay some were drowned, others were
lost in the quicksands; this gave rise to the longer dedication of St Michael in Peril
from the Sea.

Decline – The abbey came to be held *in commendam* (by lay abbots who received
the revenue without exercising the duties), and discipline among the monks grew lax.
In the 17C the Maurists, monks from St Maur, were made responsible for reforming
the monastery but they only made some deceptive architectural changes, tinkering
with the stonework. More dilapidation ensued when the abbey became a prison. From
being the local Bastille, before the Revolution, it was converted in 1811 into a national
prison where political prisoners such as Barbès and Blanqui were detained. In 1874,
the abbey and the ramparts passed into the care of the Historic Monuments
Department (Service des Monuments Historiques). Since 1969 a few monks have again
been in residence, conducting services in the abbey church.

Stages in the Abbey's Construction – The buildings date from the 11C to 16C.

Romanesque Abbey – 11C-12C. Between 1017 and 1144 a church was built on the top
of the mount. The previous Carolingian building was incorporated as a crypt – Our
Lady Underground (Notre-Dame-sous-Terre) – to support the platform on which the
last three bays of the Romanesque nave were built. Other crypts were constructed to
support the transepts and the chancel which projected beyond the natural rock.
The conventual buildings were constructed on the west face and on either side of the
nave. The entrance to the abbey faced west.

Mont-St-Michel

West   Abbey | Church   East

about 150m/492ft

West Platform

La Merveille

Refectory

Belle Chaise

Fort

Dungeons

N.D. sous Terre
(Carolingian Church)

Crypte des
Gros Piliers

Barbican

Chapelle
St-Aubert

Entrance level

258ft
165ft

Average sea level

North   Abbey | Church   South

about 150m/492ft

La Merveille

Abbatial Buildings

Cloisters

Salle des Chevaliers

Cellar

N.D. des
Trente Cierges

Ch.lle
St-Martin

Tour Claudine

Échauguette
du Nord

Entrance level

Porte du Roi

Tour
du Roi

165ft
258ft

Average sea level

Gothic Abbey – 13C-16C. This period saw the construction of:
– the magnificent Merveille buildings (1211-28) on the north side of the church, used by the monks and pilgrims and for the reception of important guests;
– the abbatial buildings (13C-15C) on the south side comprising the administrative offices, the abbot's lodging and the garrison's quarters;
– the fort and the outer defences (14C) on the east side, which protected the entrance, moved to this side of the mount.
The chancel of the Romanesque church had collapsed and was rebuilt more magnificently in the Flamboyant Gothic style (1446-1521) above a new crypt.

Alterations – 18C-19C. In 1780 the last three bays of the nave and the Romanesque façade were demolished.
The present bell-tower (1897) is surmounted by a beautiful spire which rises to 157m/515ft and culminates in a statue of St Michael (1879) by Emmanuel Frémiet.

★★★ THE ABBEY *Leave the car in the car park* ⊘

The **tour of the abbey** ⊘ does not go from building to building nor from period to period but from floor to floor through a maze of corridors and stairs.

Outer Defences of the Abbey – A flight of steps, the Grand Degré, once cut off by a swing door, leads up to the abbey. At the top on the right is the entrance to the gardens; more steps lead up to the ramparts.
Through the arch of an old door is a fortified courtyard overlooked by the fort, which consists of two tall towers shaped like mortars standing on their breeches and linked by machicolations. Even this military structure shows the builder's artistic sense: the wall is attractively constructed of alternate courses of pink and grey granite. Beneath a pointed barrel vault, a steep and ill-lit staircase, known as the Pit Steps (Escalier du Gouffre), leads down to the beautiful door which opens into the Guard-room, also called the Gatehouse (Porterie).

Guard-room or Gatehouse (**B**) – This hall was the focal point of the abbey. Poor pilgrims passed through on their way from the Merveille Court to the Almonry. The abbot's visitors and the faithful making for the church used the Abbey Steps.

Abbey Steps – An impressive flight of 90 steps rises between the abbatial buildings (left) and the abbey church (right); it is spanned by a fortified bridge (15C). The stairs stop outside the south door of the church on a terrace called the Gautier Leap (Saut Gautier – **E**) after a prisoner who is supposed to have hurled himself over the edge. The tour starts here.

West Platform – This spacious terrace, which was created by the demolition of the last three bays of the church, provides an extensive **view★** of the bay of Mont-St-Michel.

★★ Church – The exterior of the church, particularly the east end with its buttresses, flying buttresses, bell turrets and balustrades, is a masterpiece of light and graceful architecture. The interior reveals the marked contrast between the severe and sombre Romanesque nave and the elegant and luminous Gothic chancel.
The church is built on three crypts which are visited during the tour.

★★★ La Merveille – The name, which means the Marvel, applies to the superb Gothic buildings on the north face of the mount. The eastern block, the first to be built between 1211 and 1218, comprises from top to bottom, the Refectory, the Guests' Hall and the Almonry; the western block, built between 1218 and 1228, consists of the cloisters, the Knights' Hall and the cellar.
From the outside the buildings look like a fortress although their religious vocation is suggested by the dignity and purity of their line. The interior is a perfect example of the evolution of the Gothic style, from a simplicity which is almost Romanesque, in the lower halls, through the elegance of the Guests' Hall, the majesty of the Knights' Hall and the mysterious luminosity of the Refectory, to the cloisters which are a masterpiece of delicacy and refinement. The top floor comprises the cloisters and the Refectory.

★★★ Cloisters – The cloisters seem to be suspended between the sea and the sky. The gallery arcades display heavily undercut sculpture of foliage ornamented with the occasional animal or human figure (particularly human heads); there are also a few religious symbols. The double row of arches rests on delightful slim single columns arranged in quincunx to enhance the impression of lightness. The different colours of the various materials add to the overall charm. The *lavatorium* (lavabo), on the right of the entrance, recalls the ceremonial "washing of the feet" which took place every Thursday.

★★ Refectory – The effect is mysterious; the chamber is full of light although it appears to have only two windows in the end wall. To admit so much light without weakening the solid side walls which support the wooden roof and are lined with a row of slim niches, the architect introduced a very narrow aperture high up in each recess. The vaulted ceiling is panelled with wood and the acoustics are excellent.

Old Romanesque Abbey – The ribbed vaulting of this former abbey marks the transition between Romanesque and Gothic. The tour includes the Monk's Walk (Promenoir des Moines) and part of the old dormitory.

"Grande Roue" – This huge wheel brings back the days in which the abbey served as a prison. Operated by five to six prisoners who would tread inside it, the wheel was used for hoisting provisions and pieces of equipment.

Crypts – The chancel and transepts of the church are supported by three undercrofts or crypts; the most impressive is the **Crypte des Gros Piliers★** (Great Pillared Crypt) with its 10 pillars 5m/16ft round, sculpted in granite coming from the Îles Chausey.
The second floor consists of the Guest's Hall (Salle des Hôtes) and the Knights' Hall (Salle des Chevaliers).

★Guests' Hall – Here the Abbot received royalty (Louis IX, Louis XI, François I) and other important visitors. The hall, which is 35m/115ft long, has a Gothic ceiling supported on a central row of slim columns; the effect is graceful and elegant. At one time it was divided down the middle by a huge curtain of tapestries; on one side were the kitchen quarters (two chimneys) and on the other the great dining hall (one chimney). One can easily imagine the opulence of the banquets held in the Guests' Hall.

★Knights' Hall – The name of this hall may refer to the military order of St Michael which was founded in 1469 by Louis XI with the abbey as its seat.
The hall is vast and majestic (26 x 18m/85 x 58ft) and divided into four sections by three rows of stout columns.
It was the monks' workroom, where they illuminated manuscripts, and was heated by two great chimneys. The rooms on the lower floor are the Almonry and the Cellar.

Cellar – This was the storeroom; it was divided in three by two rows of square pillars supporting the groined vaulting.

Almonry – This is a Gothic room with a Romanesque vault supported on a row of columns.

Abbatial buildings – Only the Guard-room is open.

Hotels

BUDGET

Hôtel le Bretagne – *59 rue Couesnon, 50170 Pontorson, 9km/5.4mi south of Mt-St-Michel via D 976 – ☎ 02 33 60 10 55 – closed 10 Jan-15 Feb and Mon off-season - no credit cards - 12 rooms 200/380F – breakfast 39F – restaurant 85/260F*. This hotel reflects the regional style. In the small dining room, notice the pretty 18C woodwork, the grey marble fireplace and the radiator which doubles as a heating plate (quite unusual!). The muted bar is very British and the spacious rooms are pleasantly furnished.

OUR SELECTION

Beauvoir – *50170 Pontorson, 4km/2.4 from Mont-St-Michel via D 976 towards Pontorson – ☎ 02 33 60 09 39 – closed 12-Nov to Feb school holidays – no credit cards – 18 rooms 270/340F – breakfast 42F – restaurant 90/250F*. This large residence covered in Virginia Creeper is in the last village before Mont-St-Michel. It offers rooms of various sizes which are well-kept and subtly furnished. Half-board required. Children's menu.

Hôtel Manoir de la Roche Torin – *In lower Courtils, 50220 Courtils, 8,5km/5mi from Mont-St-Michel on the road to Avranches – ☎ 02 33 70 96 55 – closed 15 Nov-15 Dec and Jan to mid-Feb – ▣ – 13 rooms 460/810F – breakfast 62F – restaurant 120/320F*. The perfect spot from which to admire the bay view – in the foreground, sheep in the fields, against the backdrop of Mont-St-Michel. As for the manor house, you'll love its refined decor, its muted rooms and its splendid tranquillity.

Eating Out

BUDGET

La Sirène – *50116 Le Mont-St-Michel – ☎ 02 33 60 08 60 – 60/80F*. This 14C building has always served as an inn. Today, it also has a *crêperie*, reached by way of a spiral staircase. The wooden windows with pewter-lined panes testify to its authenticity.

Omelette de la Mère Poulard

Annette Boutiaut was born in Nevers in 1851. She was employed as a lady's maid by the architect Édouard Corroyer, a disciple of Viollet-le-Duc, who was commissioned by the Monuments Historiques (a State-run organisation) to restore Mont-St-Michel Abbey. Annette followed her employers there and met the son of a local baker. They married and took over the running of the St-Michel Tête d'Or Hotel. At that time (around 1875), the causeway had not been built yet so that tourists and pilgrims reached Mont-St-Michel on foot, on horseback or aboard a *maringotte* (a small two-wheeled horse-drawn cart), tide permitting. They were usually very hungry and could not bear to wait for food to be prepared. Annette knew that a good innkeeper should not be taken unawares. She therefore always had eggs in store and quickly beat up an omelette for her guests while they waited for more substantial dishes. Her welcome and the quality of the food she served gradually brought her fame. When Annette Poulard died in 1931, food critics speculated on the secret recipe of the omelette... Some talked about fresh cream, specially selected eggs and butter, others argued it was all due to fast cooking; Annette herself explained in a letter dated 1922: "I break the eggs in a bowl, I beat them up well, I put a nice knob of butter in the frying pan, I throw the eggs in and stir continuously."
Curnonsky (1872-1956), the "Prince of gourmets", said that the secret lay in the recipe of Dr Rouget, the hero of Balzac's *La Rabouilleuse*, who beat up the yolks and whites separately before mixing them in the frying pan!

★★THE TOWN

Outer Defences – The Outer Gate is the only breach in the ramparts and opens into the first fortified courtyard. On the left stands the Citizens' Guard-room (16C) which presently houses the tourist office; on the right are the "Michelettes", English mortars captured in a sortie during the Hundred Years War.
A second gate leads into a second courtyard. The third gate (15C), complete with machicolations and portcullis, is called the King's Gate because it was the lodging of the token contingent maintained on the mount by the king in assertion of his rights; it opens into the Grande-Rue where the abbot's soldiers lodged in the fine arcaded house (right).

LE MONT-ST-MICHEL

| B | Salle des Gardes ou Porterie | E | Terrasse "le Saut Gautier" |
| D | Maison ancienne "la Truie-qui-file" | | |

★**Grande-Rue** – This picturesque narrow street climbs steeply between old (15C-16C) houses, several of which have retained their original name – **Logis Saint-Etienne**, **Vieux logis**, **Sirène**, **Truie qui file** (**D**) – and ends in a flight of steps. In summer it is lively and crowded with restaurants and the stalls of souvenir merchants, as it was in the Middle Ages at the height of the most fervent pilgrimages.

★★**Ramparts** – These are 13C-15C. The sentry walk offers fine views of the bay; from the North Tower the Tombelaine Rock, which Philippe Auguste had fortified, is clearly visible.

★**Abbey Gardens** ⊘ – A pleasant place for a stroll with a view of the west side of the mount and the Chapelle St Aubert.

Archéoscope ⊘ – This magical mystery tour takes you back in time to the mount's origins. The seismic phenomenon of Scissy Forest, the Archangel Michael's appearance before Bishop Aubert, the different stages of the mount's construction and its architectural splendour, are all explained by sophisticated special effects coordinated by a computer: models emerge out of water, slides flash on screens, the whole show is accompanied by light and sound effects.

Église paroissiale St-Pierre – The building which dates from the 11C has been much altered. The apse spans a narrow street. The parish church contains a Crucifix and other furnishings from the abbey; the chapel in the south aisle contains a statue of St Michael covered in silver; in the chapel to the right of the altar there is a 15C statue of the Virgin and from the gallery hang numerous pilgrim banners.

Logis Tiphaine ⊘ – When Du Guesclin was captain of the mount, he had this house built (1365) for his wife, Tiphaine Raguenel, an attractive and educated woman from Dinan, while he went off to the wars in Spain: the Constable's room (tester bed, chest), dining room (six-door sideboard, chimney bearing the arms of Du Guesclin, 17C copperware) and Tiphaine's room (cupboard, tester bed, wax figure).

BOAT TRIPS

Baie du Mont-St-Michel – Starting at Vivier-sur-Mer, the *Sirène de la Baie*, an amphibious vehicle, takes you to Cancale; views of its oyster beds and mussel breeding poles.

Michelin Maps are updated constantly.
Always travel with the latest edition.

Golfe du MORBIHAN★★

Michelin map 63 folds 2, 3, 12 and 13 or 230 folds 36, 37, 50 and 51

The Morhiban Gulf, an inland sea dotted with islands, offers some of the most unusual scenery in Brittany. It has the most delicate light effects, and its sunsets are unforgettable. A visit, especially by boat, is essential.

HISTORICAL NOTES

In 1C BC the Veneti – after whom Vannes is named – lived around the Golfe du Morbihan. They were the most powerful tribe in Armor and when Caesar decided to conquer the peninsula he aimed his main effort at them. It was a stiff task, for the Veneti were fine sailors and had a fleet which made it useless to attack them by land. The decisive struggle, therefore, had to be waged afloat. The Roman leader had a large number of galleys, built and assembled at the mouth of the Loire which were under the command of his lieutenant, Brutus.

The encounter, which took place before Port-Navalo, is said to have been watched by Caesar from the top of the Tumulus de Tumiac. On the other hand, geologists declare that the gulf did not exist at the time of the Gallic War. In all events, it is certain that the battle took place off the southeast coast of Brittany.

The Gauls put to sea with 220 large sailing ships, with high, strong hulls. The Romans opposed them with their large flat barges, propelled by oarsmen. The total and unexpected victory of Brutus was due to several causes: the sea was smooth and this favoured the galleys, which could not face bad weather; moreover, the wind dropped completely during the battle, becalming the Veneti in their sailing ships. Finally the Romans had sickles tied to long poles. When a galley drew alongside an enemy sailing ship, an agile sailor heaved the sickle into its rigging. The galley rowed on at full speed, the rope drew taut and the blade cut the rigging; mast and sails came tumbling down. Two or three galleys then attacked the ship and boarded it.

After this victory Caesar occupied the country of the Veneti and made them pay dearly for their resistance. All the members of their Senate were put to death, and the people were sold into slavery.

GEOGRAPHICAL NOTES

Mor-bihan means "little sea", while *Mor-braz* means "great sea" or ocean. This gulf, which is about 20km/12mi wide and 15km/9mi deep from the sea to the inner shore, was made by a comparatively recent settling of the land. The sea spread widely over land already despoiled by river erosion leaving inlets and estuaries which run far into the interior, and innumerable islands which give the Morbihan its special character. The River Vannes and River Auray form the two largest estuaries. About 40 islands are privately owned and inhabited; the largest are the Île d'Arz and the Île aux Moines, both *communes*. The gulf is tidal; at high tide the sea sparkles everywhere around the low, flat and often wooded islands; at low tide, great mud-banks lie between the remaining channels. A narrow channel, before Port-Navalo permits passage both at high and low tide.

Morbihan is thronged with boats fishing between the islands, as well as with pleasure boats and oyster barges using Auray and the port of Vannes. There are many oyster beds in the rivers and along the islands.

★★★THE GULF BY BOAT

The best way to see the gulf is by boat. There are excursions starting from Vannes, Locmariaquer, Port-Navalo or Auray.

Île d'Arz – The island, 3.5km/2mi long, has several megalithic monuments.

★**Île aux Moines** ⊘ – This former monastic fief is the largest of the Morbihan Islands (7km/4mi long) and the most populous. It is a particularly quiet and restful seaside resort where mimosas and camellias grow among palm trees, lemon and orange trees. Its woods have poetic names: Bois des Soupirs (Wood of Sighs), Bois d'Amour (Wood of Love), Bois des Regrets (Wood of Regrets). The beauty of the island women, often sung by Breton poets, is no doubt responsible for these gallantries.

There are several sights worth visiting: the town with its picturesque alleyways; from Pointe du Trech, north of the island, there is a good view of Pointe d'Arradon and the gulf – note the odd-looking Calvary, its base composed of different levels and with stairs on its right side; southwards are the Boglieux and Penhap dolmens; and Pointe de Brouël, east of the island, affords a view of the Île d'Arz.

★THE SHORES OF THE GULF

☐ From Vannes to Locmariaquer
49km/30mi – 3hr 30min

★★**Vannes** – *2hr 30min. See VANNES.*

Leave Vannes on D 101. After 5km/3mi bear left towards Pointe d'Arradon. The road skirts Arradon.

★Pointe d'Arradon – *Turn left towards Cale de la Carrière.* From here there is a very typical **view★** of the Golfe du Morbihan in which you can distinguish, from left to right: the Îles de Logoden; in the distance, the Île d'Arz; then the Île d'Holavre, which is rocky and the Île aux Moines. To reach the point take the path bordering the rocks, behind the hotel.

Turn round and go to Le Moustoir and bear left.

At the place called Moulin de Pomper note on the left the old tidal power mill *(see Vallée de la RANCE).*

Turn left towards Port-Blanc where you will embark for the Île aux Moines.

★Île aux Moines – *2.5km/1.5mi – plus 15min by boat there and back. Bicycle rental. Description above.*

The road next skirts Kerdelan Creek (on the left there is a good view of the gulf and, in the distance, of the Île aux Moines), then passes by Pen-en-Toul marshes *(marais)* on its right.

Larmor-Baden – A little fishing port and large oyster-farming centre. From the port there is a fine view of the other islands and the entrance to the gulf.

★★Cairn de Gavrinis – *During the visit, you will be able to glimpse lovely views of the River Auray.* The Gavrinis Tumulus is the most interesting megalithic monument in Brittany. It is situated on the island of Gavrinis, at the mouth of the Golfe du Morbihan, south of Larmor-Baden, from which it can be reached. The tumulus, 6m/20ft high and 50m/164ft around, is made of stones piled on a hillock. It was discovered in 1832 and comprises a covered gallery 14m/46ft long with nine tables held up by 23 carved supports; the funeral chamber, probably a royal tomb (2.50m/8ft on one side), with a ceiling made of a single granite slab, resting on supports is also covered with carvings.

Cairn de Gavrinis (detail)

Piquer/CAMPAGNE CAMPAGNE

J. Kaken/CAMPAGNE CAMPAGNE

From the top of the tumulus there is a wide view of the Golfe du Morbihan.

On the tiny island of **Er Lanic**, a little south of Gavrinis, are two tangent circles of menhirs *(cromlechs)* in the form of a figure eight, half of which is submerged. This gives evidence of the subsidence of the soil which created the gulf in prehistoric times. At low tide the menhirs reappear.

Bono – From the new bridge is a picturesque **view**★ of Bono, its river and harbour and the old suspension bridge. You will notice piles of whitewashed tiles used to collect oyster spat *(see CANCALE)*. The **church** contains modern **stained-glass windows**★.

Before taking the new bridge towards Auray, bear left onto a downhill road.

As you leave Kernours, on the right in a small pine forest is a right-angled dolmen. On this same road continue to **Mané-Verh** which offers glimpses of the River Auray.

★**Auray** – *See AURAY.*

Leave Auray by ② on the town plan, then after 8km/5mi bear left.

The road skirts megalithic monuments.

★★**Locmariaquer** – *See LOCMARIAQUER.*

② From Vannes to Port-Navalo and Back

79km/49mi – about 4hr – local map right

★★**Vannes** – *2hr 30min. See VANNES.*

Leave Vannes on the Nantes road on the town plan. After St-Léonard, turn right.

The road runs along the east bank of the bay; there are several viewpoints.

★**Presqu'île de Rhuys** – At St-Colombier you enter the peninsula, which encloses the Golfe du Morbihan to the south. Its flora is reminiscent of that of the south of France.

Sarzeau – Birthplace of **Lesage** (1668-1747), satirical dramatist and author of *Turcaret* and *Gil Blas*. On the small square, to the right of the church, stand two lovely Renaissance houses.

From Sarzeau go towards Brillac, the road follows the coast for some distance.

Le Logeo – A pretty little port sheltered by the Gouihan and Stibiden Islands.

Go as far as Le Net and bear right.

★**Tumulus de Tumiac or Butte de Cézar** – *15min on foot. Leave your car in the car park and take a dirt track to the right.* From the top of the tumulus there is an extensive **view**★ of the gulf, Quiberon Bay and the islands. This was the observatory from which Caesar is supposed to have watched the naval battle agains the Veneti.

Hotels

BUDGET

Vacation village Île de Berder – *56870 Île de Berder* – ☎ *02 97 57 03 74* – *closed Nov-Feb* – *no credit cards* – *90 rooms full board 220/295F*. This former convent is admirably situated on a 57-acre island; however, its comforts are very modest (you must share sanitary facilities). Nevertheless, the family atmosphere, the conviviality and calm, and the events organised in the summer will make you quickly forget the spartan accommodation. Boarding only.

OUR SELECTION

Kerdelan – *56870 Larmor-Baden, Locqueltas, 2km/1mi along the road to Vannes* – ☎ *02 97 57 05 85* – *closed 15 July-30 Aug* – *no credit cards* – *4 rooms 310/360F*. In a beautiful park facing a golf course and the Île aux Moines, this white villa is especially for those who delight in luxurious idleness! All the rooms open onto a terrace, and the library, billiard room, and salon create a true holiday ambience.

Glann Ar Mor – *27 rue des Fontaines, 56640 Port-Navalo* – ☎ *02 97 53 88 30* – *8 rooms 295F* – *breakfast 38F* – *restaurant 98/120F*. A nice establishment near the golf course. The restaurant has marine accents, and the white rooms have been simply renovated. Full or half-board in-season.

TREAT YOURSELF!

Hôtel Miramar – *56640 Port du Crouesty* – ☎ *02 97 67 68 00* – *closed 29 Nov-26 Dec* – ▣ – *120 rooms from 1 155F* – *breakfast 105F* – *restaurant 255/275F*. The imposing white façade of this beautiful hotel looks like a cruise liner. Gangways and rails on the outside, inside, nice wood furniture and bay windows invite you into a dream-world ... whether you are there for the thalassotherapy, or simply for pleasure, let yourself be seduced by its comfort and luxury!

Résidence Pierre et Vacances – *56640 Port du Crouesty* – ☎ *02 97 53 85 35* – *closed 15 Nov-19 Dec and 6 Jan-6 Feb* – *350 apartments 4/5 pers, weekly rate from 6 000F*. Well situated between the pleasure port and the ocean, this modern village inspired by local architecture rents apartments that are functional, if slightly lacking in charm. Events and services specially adapted for families. Private swimming pools and thalassotherapy close by.

Eating Out

OUR SELECTION

Grand Largue – *At the landing-stage, 56640 Port-Navalo* – ☎ *02 97 53 71 58* – *closed 13 Nov-20-Dec, 3 Jan-7 Feb, Mon lunch in summer, Mon evening and Tues Sept-June* – *150/330F*. Located at the end of the wharf, this restaurant looks out over the sea. Whether you are seated on its terrace surrounded by beautiful hortensias or inside amid its dainty, flowered decor, you will be greeted by the restaurant's enthusiastic staff, who will be delighted to help you discover the chef's original cuisine.

San Francisco – *At the port, 56780 Île aux Moines* – ☎ *02 97 26 31 52* – *closed 15 Nov-24 Mar* – *120/240F*. This hotel-restaurant is worth a visit simply to admire its beautiful location. From the stone-walled dining room and the covered terrace, you can enjoy a beautiful view of the port. Two of its rooms also offer beautiful views.

Sports

Discover the gulf in a kayak – *Base nautique Varec'h, in Baden,* ☎ *02 97 57 16 16*. For beginners or experienced practitioners. Outings with a monitor are available in July and August.

Swimming – There are numerous small beaches on the gulf, notably on the Île aux Moines. However, the pretty beach at Suscinio (near its château) has two advantages: it is 3km/2mi long, and although the water may be cooler than in the gulf, it is also much clearer.

A Paradise for Children

Arzon – *Office de tourisme* – ☎ *02 97 53 69 69*. This town received the "label Kid" from the Tourist Ministry, offers workshops in kite-flying, science and music, as well as hiking outings – all this in addition to the traditional beach club activities.

Markets

At Port du Crouesty, every Monday morning in the summer. At Port-Navalo, Tuesday and Friday mornings. At Sarzeau, Thursday mornings, as well as a market-fair on the third Wednesday of each month.

Golfe du MORBIHAN

Arzon – In obedience to a vow made to St Anne in 1673, during the war with Holland, the sailors of Arzon march in the procession of Ste-Anne-d'Auray every year on Whit Monday. Two stained-glass windows (1884) in the chancel of the church recount the story of this vow.

Port-Navalo – A small port and seaside resort. The roadstead is enclosed to the south by a promontory on which stands a lighthouse (benches and telescope), and to the north by Bilgroix Point which offers a good **view★** of the Golfe du Morbihan. The beach faces the open sea.

Port du Crouesty – Located on the bay of the same name and southeast of Port-Navalois lies this pleasure boat harbour. Alongside it is a large residential complex. The four docks are well sheltered and can hold over 1 100 boats. From the tourist car park there is a good view of the site. Fine walk along the quayside.

St-Gildas-de-Rhuys – This village owes its origin to a monastery founded by St Gildas in the 6C. The most famous of the abbots who governed it was Abélard in the 12C.

★ Church ⊙ – This is the former abbey church built at the beginning of the 11C and largely rebuilt in the 16 and 17C.

The Romanesque chevet has pure, harmonious lines; it is ornamented with modillions; note a small carving depicting a tournament. Inside, the Romanesque **chancel★** is remarkable. Behind the Baroque high altar is the tomb of St Gildas (11C). In the north transept lies the 11C gravestone of St Goustan and in the ambulatory,

---

Abélard

A love story with his brilliant student, Héloïse, ended tragically when her outraged family had Abélard emasculated. The learned philosopher tried to find peace in this Breton solitude. His disillusion was quick and cruel: "I live", he wrote to Héloïse, "in a wild country whose language I find strange and horrible; I see only savages; I take my walks on the inaccessible shores of a rough sea; my monks have only one rule, which is to have none at all. I should like you to see my house; you would never take it for an abbey; the only decorations on the doors are the footmarks of various animals – hinds, wolves, bears, wild boars – or the hideous remains of owls. Every day brings new dangers; I always seem to see a sword hanging over my head."

However, the monks used poison, not a sword, to get rid of their abbot. It was a wonder he survived and managed to escape through a secret passage in 1132.

lit by modern stained-glass windows, 13C and 14C gravestones of Breton children and gravestones of abbots and knights. At the end of the nave is a stoup made up from two carved capitals. Another capital is found in the south aisle.

The **treasury★** ⊙ contains valuable antique objects, well displayed: 14C and 18C shrines, reliquaries (15C) containing the arms and legs of St Gildas, and his embroidered mitre, a 17C silver-gilt cross bejewelled with emeralds etc.

★**Château de Suscinio** ⊙ – The impressive ruins stand in a wild setting by the seashore, where they are buffeted by sea winds. It was the sea which used to fill the moat. The castle was built in the 13C and modified by the dukes of Brittany in the 15C, prior to becoming one of their favourite residences. It was confiscated by François I and fell into the hands of the French Crown which used it to house faithful servants and the current Royal favourite. In ruins at the end of the Ancien Régime, the castle was sold to a private individual during the Revolution and was used as a stone quarry. Six of the towers have survived. In 1955, the roofing of the New Tower (Tour Neuve) and the West Pavillion (Logis Ouest) were restored to its former glory. The rooms in the entrance pavilion, also restored, house a small **museum** devoted to the history of Brittany.

Having crossed the moat, enter the guard-room and the adjoining tower in which the history of the castle and its restoration are explained.

On the upper floors, the history of Brittany is described with the aid of literature, portraits, paintings and locally produced artefacts (*Scène de pardon* by Camille Chazal and a relief depicting Olivier de Clisson on horseback by Fremiet). Several rooms are devoted to splendid 13C and 14C **floor coverings** in varnished ceramic, which came from a chapel outside the castle's curtain wall, on the banks of the moat, which has since disappeared. The variety and quality of the decoration, which has been excellently preserved, make these an eloquent witness to medieval decorative art.

The Ceremonial Hall (Salle des Cérémonies), which opens onto a small chapel, provides access to the north façade and to the terraces, offering a lovely **panorama** of the peninsula and nearby ocean.

From St-Colombier return to Vannes on the road on which you came.

MORLAIX★

Population 16 701

Michelin map 58 fold 6 or 230 fold 5 – Local map see Les ENCLOS PAROISSIAUX

The first thing the tourist will notice at Morlaix is its colossal viaduct. This structure bestrides the deep valley in which lies the estuary of the Dossen, commonly called the River Morlaix. The town is busy but the port, though it is used mostly by yachts, has only limited commercial activity (sand, wood, fertilisers).

HISTORICAL NOTES

Queen Anne's Visit – In 1505, on King Louis XII's recovery from a serious illness, Queen Anne of Brittany decided to make a pilgrimage to the saints of her duchy. She stayed at Morlaix; a wealthy city, which received the Queen sumptuously. She was presented with a little golden ship studded with jewels and a tame ermine wearing a diamond-studded collar (the ermine is Anne of Brittany's emblem). The showpiece of the festival was a live Tree of Jesse representing all the sovereign's ancestors.

Cornic, the "blue" officer – Charles Cornic, known as Duchesne, was the great Morlaix seaman of the 18C. He was born in 1731, and at the age of eight he was sent against his will to work as a ship's boy on a privateer. His exploits were nonetheless such that the king made him lieutenant of a vessel in his Grand Corps. But Cornic was never to be more than an "upstart", a "blue" officer (those officers who had risen through the ranks wore a completely blue uniform), forever subjected to the taunts of the "red" officers (those who had been through the Marine Guard School, almost all of whom were of aristocratic birth, wore a red and blue uniform). He served for a while with the Merchant Navy, but finally left active service in 1778, retiring never having risen above the rank of captain.

After the Revolution, he was promoted to the rank of Colonel General of the Artillery of Bordeaux in 1790, then deputy minister of the Dalbarade Navy. He later returned to Morlaix, where he studied the setting of buoys in the bay and the defence of the coast. He died in Morlaix in 1809.

OLD MORLAIX *2hr*

Leave your car in place Cornic.

★**Viaduc** (**ABY**) – From place des Otages there is a good view of the viaduct, an imposing two-storeyed structure, 58m/190ft high and 285m/935ft long.

Go up the stairs to the right of the viaduct.

On the left is the 16C Hôtel du Parc, an impressive horseshoe-shaped building.

Aiguillon (R. d') ..... **BZ** 2
Brest (R. de)............ **AZ**
Carnot (R.)............. **BZ** 7
Grand'Rue .... **BZ**
Mur (R. du)........... **BZ** 13
Otages (Pl. des)...... **AY**
Paris (R. de) .... **BZ**

Allende (Pl. S.) .... **BZ** 3
Ange-de-Guernisac
  (R.)..................... **BY** 5
Bouchers (R. des).. **BZ** 6
Dossen (Pl. du) ..... **BZ** 8
Jacobins (Pl. des) .. **BZ** 12
Paris (Rte de) .... **BZ** 14
Poan-Ben
  (Allée du) .... **BZ** 16
Son (Venelle au)..... **BZ** 18
Traoulen (Pl.).......... **BZ** 20

B Maison "de la Reine Anne"   **M** Musée des Jacobins

Église St-Mélaine ⊘ (**BY**) – The present church, which dates from 1489, is in the Flamboyant Gothic style with an interesting porch on the south side.
Inside, note the modern stained-glass windows designed by Labouret and the vaulting adorned with purlins and tie-beams. A coloured wood panel in the south aisle depicts the Annunciation, the Nativity and the Flight into Egypt; in the north aisle are a font crowned with a carved wood canopy and a Descent from the Cross.

Rue Ange-de-Guernisac (**BY 5**) – This street is lined with fine corbelled and half-timbered houses: the Hôtel du Relais de France at no 13, and the houses at nos 9, 6 and 5 are of interest. Take a look in the picturesque alleyways, Venelle du Créou (**BY**) and Venelle au Son (**BZ 18**).
*Bear right into rue Carnot (**BZ 7**).*

★**Grand'Rue** (**BZ**) – *Pedestrian precinct.* Here you will see picturesque 15C houses adorned with statues of saints and grotesques, and low-fronted shops with wide windows, especially at nos 8 and 10. Originally these old houses, called **skylight houses**, comprised a large central area with skylights onto which opened the other rooms, linked by a spiral staircase supported by a lovely carved newel post. Queen Anne's House *(see below)* has a fine collection and many illustrations of newel posts.
Walk round place S.-Allende and up a ramp leading to rue du Mur.

Maison de la Reine Anne ⊘ (**BZ B**) – This 16C corbelled mansion, three storeys high, has a façade adorned with statues of saints and grotesques. With its court-yard lit by a skylight, the **interior**★ is a perfect example of the skylight house. In one of the courtyard's corners, there is a magnificent spiral staircase, 11m/36ft high, carved from one piece of wood. The newel post is adorned with saints carved in the round: St Roch, St Nicholas, St Christopher and St Michael. Between the first and second floors, note the fine sculpture of an acrobat with his barrel. There is a monumental stone chimney-piece opposite the staircase.

★**Musée des Jacobins** ⊘ (**BZ M**) – The museum is housed in the former church of the Jacobins, which has a fine early-15C **rose window**★ at the east end. The exhibits include the finds from archeological digs in the region, mementoes of Morlaix's famous citizens and of Old Morlaix with its skylight houses: 16C carved newel posts. Also on display are a large collection of 13C-17C religious statues, typical 17C furniture of the Léon region (chests, tester beds), household objects, farming and craft implements, and a collection of **modern paintings**★. On display is an old cannon from the privateer's ship *Alcida*, which sank at the mouth of the River Morlaix in 1747 (found in 1879).

Hotels

BUDGET

Hôtel de l' Europe – *1 rue Aiguillon, 29600 Morlaix –* ☎ *02 98 62 11 99 – 60 rooms 195/440F – breakfast 40F – restaurant 85/180F.* This hotel is well-situated and has lots of character. The rooms are pleasant enough, despite being less charming than the entrance or the restaurant with its pretty mouldings and nostalgic decor.

Eating out

BUDGET

Marée Bleue – *3 rampe St-Mélaine, 29600 Morlaix –* ☎ *02 98 63 24 21 – closed Oct, Sun evening and Mon except in summer – 78/230F.* Near the viaduct, this little restaurant serves pleasant cuisine in its three dining rooms. A young couple has been running it for several years now, and they renew its culinary offerings regularly. Good quality for the price.

OUR SELECTION

Cabestan – *In Carantec, on the port –* ☎ *02 98 67 01 87 – closed Nov, Jan, Mar, Mon Sept-June – 120/260F.* Located on the port, the restaurant and the brasserie are run by the same family. Opt for restaurant if possible; it may not have a terrace like the brasserie, but you'll never be disappointed by the cuisine.

Going out

Le Grand Café de la Terrasse – *31 place des Otages –* ☎ *02 98 88 20 25 – daily 7.30am-1am.* Founded in 1885, this pretty brasserie was frequented by nobles, who found pleasant diversion in its singers and magicians. Between 1907 and 1914, the Tour de France bicycle race began there. Then, during the war, the Germans razed absolutely everything, except the billard hall. It remained dormant until 1996, when the brassserie was bought and revived by the Quenech'du family who wanted to restore it to its former glory. Definitely a success!

Tempo – *Quai de Tréguier –* ☎ *02 98 63 29 11 – Mon-Thur 11am-midnight, Fri 11am-1am, Sat 5pm-1am.* On Morlaix's marina, this modern bar with metallic decor is a choice place to have a drink on the sunny terrace. Monthly exhibitions. A dozen wines sold by the glass.

Recreation

Sheltered beaches – The best beaches are at the Grève Blanche and at the longer Grève du Kélenn. They are pleasantly sheltered from the wind.

Shopping

Rue Ange-de-Guernisac – *Rue des Arts.* This is the street of arts, artists, and craftsmen where you will find painters, potters, sculptors, dressmakers, woodworkers …

Maison des vins – *Place des Viarmes –* ☎ *02 98 88 72 43 – Tues-Sat 9.30am-noon, 2pm-7pm.* This wine cellar occupies a magnificent 17C house. Among many other remarkable features, the lighting is worth noticing. As for wines, this establishment boasts over 1 000!

Martin – *29 place des Otages –* ☎ *02 98 88 01 65 – Tues-Sat 9am-12.30pm, 2pm-7.30pm, Sun 9am-1pm, 2.30pm-7pm.* Pastry and tea salon easily recognized by its unusual façade dating from 1830. The Martin family has been running it with brio for four generations. The house speciality is the Breton galette.

Festivals

Outdoor arts festivals – Each Wednesday from mid-July to mid-August, a large pedestrian area is given over to actors and to the public and makes for a vast, convivial theatre experience.

Église St-Mathieu ⊘ (**BZ**) – The church was rebuilt in 1824 but the tower is 16C. Inside, it has a basilical plan and Doric columns supporting a pointed barrel vault. To the left of the high altar is an unusual wood statue of the **Virgin**★ (c 14C) which opens. When closed it represents the Virgin suckling the Infant Jesus; open, it contains a group of the Holy Trinity. On the shutters are illustrated six scenes from the life of Christ: the Annunciation, the Nativity, the Presentation at the Temple, the Flagellation, the Resurrection and the Descent into Hell. In the north aisle stands a fine 16C wooden statue of Christ with the Virgin Mary and St John the Evangelist.

Via rue de l'Aiguillon and place des Otages, return to place Cornic.

Morlaix

D. Thaulin-Hommell

EXCURSIONS

★**Plougonven** – *12km/7mi southeast on D 9 towards Callac.*
This village, nestling at the foot of the Arrée Mountains, has an interesting parish close. The **Calvary★★** was built in 1554; the cross in two tiers, carries, above, the statues of the Virgin and St John, and, below, two guards; the thieves' crosses stand on either side. At the foot of the main cross there is a Descent from the Cross. On the platform and around the base are scenes depicting various episodes in the life of Christ: the Temptation in the Desert, His Arrest etc. The charnel house presents a trefoil arcade and a basket-handle arched doorway.
The **church**, built in 1523 and badly damaged by fire in the early 20C, is dominated by a graceful belfry with a balcony, a turreted staircase and striking gargoyles.

Carantec, which lies on a peninsula between the estuary of the Penzé and the River Morlaix, is a family seaside resort. There are several beaches suitable for bathing; the most important are Grève Blanche and Grève du Kélenn, the larger of the two.
A number of *pardons* are held at Carantec *(see Calendar of events)*. The apse of the modern **church** contains a fine silver **processional cross★** (1652) and a less ornate one in front of the altar.

Musée maritime ⊘ – The exhibits in this small maritime museum show the region's link with the sea (oyster breeding, privateering, Morlaix Bay's flora and fauna and seaweed collecting).

La Chaise du Curé – From this rocky platform, the **view★** extends from left to right over the Porspol and Blanche Beaches with St-Pol-de-Léon and Roscoff in the background, as far as the Pointe de Pen-al-Lann.

Pointe de Pen-al-Lann – *1.5km/1mi east, plus 15min on foot there and back. Take rue de Pen-al-Lann and leave your car at a roundabout. Take the downhill path through pine trees to a rocky height.*
The **view★** extends along the coast from the Pointe de Bloscon crowned by the Chapelle Ste-Barbe, near Roscoff, to the Pointe de Primel; opposite you can see the castle on Taureau Island, which guarded the mouth of River Morlaix.

Île Callot – From Grève Blanche port you can reach the island by car (car park) at mid-tide.
The **Chapelle Notre-Dame** ⊘ on the island was founded in the 16C and rebuilt in the 17C and 19C. Inside is a 16C statue of the Virgin. *Pardon* on the Sunday after 15 August. The island is excellent for fishing.

*If you are looking for a pleasant, quiet, well-located hotel anywhere in France, consult **The Red Guide**, published yearly.*

Conurbation 492 255
Michelin map 67 fold 3 or 230 folds 54 and 55 or 232 fold 28

Nantes is many cities combined: a city of the arts, a great industrial city, and the seat of a big university.

Located at the confluence of the rivers Loire, Sèvre and Erdre, Nantes is the historic capital of the dukes of Brittany and has now become the capital of the region called Pays de la Loire. The three ports of Donges, Nantes and St-Nazaire have merged and follow the estuary from Nantes up to the Atlantic Ocean.

At the heart of the city, opposite the southern station, the new **Cité des Congrès (HZ)** is equipped with high technology facilities which place it at the forefront of the conference centres on the Atlantic coast.

HISTORICAL NOTES

Nantes, capital of Brittany – Nantes, first Gallic and then Roman, was involved in the bloody struggle between the Frankish kings and the Breton noblemen. But it was the Vikings who did the most damage. In 843 the pirates landed, rushed into the cathedral, where the Bishop was saying Mass, and put the prelate, the clergy and the congregation to death. In 939, young Alain Barbe-Torte (Crookbeard), a descendant of the great Breton chiefs, who had taken refuge in England, returned to the country and drove the invaders out of Brittany. Having become duke, he chose Nantes as his capital and rebuilt it. Nantes was the capital of the Duchy of Brittany several times during the Middle Ages, in rivalry with Rennes. The dukes of the House of Montfort, especially **François II**, governed as undisputed sovereigns and restored the prestige of the town and its title of capital.

Edict of Nantes (13 August 1598) – In 1597, Brittany, tired of disorder and suffering caused by the League and also of the separatist ambitions of its Governor, Philip of Lorraine, sent a pressing appeal to Henri IV, asking him to come and restore order. Before the castle he whistled with admiration. "God's teeth", he exclaimed, "the dukes of Brittany were no small beer!" The royal visit was marked by a great historic event: on 13 August 1598, Henri IV signed the Edict of Nantes, which, in 92 articles, settled the religious question – or so he thought.

Sugar and "ebony" – From the 16C to the 18C, Nantes had two main sources of revenue: sugar and the slave trade, known discreetly as the "ebony trade". In the Antilles, the slaver would sell the slaves bought on the Guinea coast and buy cane sugar, to be refined at Nantes and sent up the Loire. The "ebony" made an average profit of 200%.

Philosophers inveighed against this inhuman traffic, but Voltaire, whose business acumen is well known, had a 5 000 *livres* share in a slave ship from Nantes. At the end of the 18C the prosperity of Nantes was at its height: it had become the first port of France; its fleet included 2 500 ships and barques. The big shipowners and traders founded dynasties and built the fine mansions on Quai de la Fosse and the former Feydeau Islet.

All drowned – In June 1793, Nantes numbered many royalists. The Convention sent **Carrier**, the Deputy of the Cantal, there as its representative in early October. Carrier had already spent some time at Rennes. His mission was "to purge the body politic of all the rotten matter it contained".

The revolutionary tribunal had filled the prisons with Vendéens, priests and suspects, and a problem arose: how to make room for new arrivals. Carrier chose drowning. Condemned people were put into barges which were scuttled in the Loire, opposite Chantenay. When informed, the Convention immediately recalled its delegate. He was put on trial and was sent before the Nantes Revolutionary court, sentenced to death and guillotined in December.

In 1832 tragedy gave way to farce. The **Duchess of Berry**, a mortal enemy of Louis-Philippe, was convinced that Brittany was still legitimist and scoured the Nantes countryside. Her failure was complete. She took refuge at Nantes but was betrayed. The police invaded the house (**HY B**) and found it empty, but kept it under surveillance. Feeling cold, they lit a fire in one room. Their surprise was great when the chimney-shutter fell open and out on all fours came the duchess and three of her followers, black as sweeps and half suffocated. They had spent 16hr in the thickness of the wall.

★★CHÂTEAU DES DUCS DE BRETAGNE ⊘ (HY) 2hr

The golden age of the castle was the age of Duke François II, when court life was truly regal: five ministers, 17 chamberlains and a host of retainers attended the Duke. Life was sumptuous and morals liberal.

The present building was begun by Duke François II in 1466 and continued by his daughter, Anne of Brittany. Defence works were added during the League by the Duke of Mercœur. From the 18C onwards the military took possession, destroyed

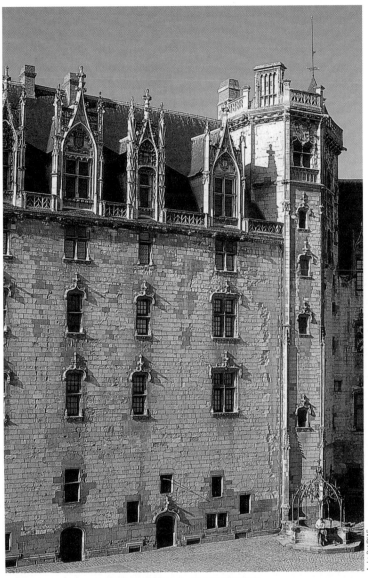

Nantes – Château des Ducs de Bretagne

some buildings and erected others lacking in style. The Spaniards' Tower (**1**), which had been used as a magazine, blew up in 1800 *(the north part of the castle was destroyed – the sites of the destroyed buildings are indicated by a broken line on the plan)*. From Charles VII to Louis XIV, nearly all the kings of France spent some time at the castle: Louis XII married Anne of Brittany in its chapel (1499); it was here that Henri IV signed the Edict of Nantes in 1598. Chalais, Cardinal de Retz, Gilles de Rais (Bluebeard) and the Duchess of Berry were imprisoned in its towers. An arm of the Loire washed the south, east and northeast walls until the building of a quay in the 19C and the filling up in the 20C of a branch of the Loire.

The fortress – The moat has now been re-established; the ditches which guarded the north and west sides have been turned into gardens and the old ditches have been restored on the other sides. An 18C bridge leads to the former drawbridge which is flanked by two massive round towers dating from the time of Duke François.

The palace – Behind the massive defensive walls, the court was used for jousting and tournaments, also for the performance of mystery plays and farces.
The 15C **Bakery Tower** *(not open to the public)*, also called Tower of Hell, was used as a prison, a theory confirmed by the graffiti one could see on the walls.

205

The elegant **Golden Crown Tower**★ (Tour de la Couronne d'Or), whose name may be explained by the presence of a nearby well, presents fine Italian-style loggias and connects two pavilions pierced by rows of windows The 15C **Jacobins Tower** was also used as a prison (carved graffiti).

The **main building**, built by François II and extended two storeys by Anne of Brittany, was the ducal palace. It is decorated by five tall Gothic dormer windows with ornate pinnacles.

This part of the castle took the name **Gover**nor's Major Palace after the 1670 fire, which destroyed a whole wing of the castle. It then became the home of the governor of Brittany. During the reign of the dukes, it had been their palace and had been used for meetings concerning the duchy.

Over the **well**★★, which probably dates back to the days of François II, there is a wrought-iron framework, which represents the ducal crown. The seven-sided curb of the well has seven pulleys and seven gargoyles for the overflow.

The Renaissance **Governor's Lesser Palace** was built under François I; the military **Saddlery**, dating back to 1784 was the armoury.

The old keep (**2**) is, in fact, one of the four polygonal towers, which enclosed the original castle built in the 13C and enlarged in the 14C; it is part of an 18C mansion, which houses the porter's lodge (**3**).

The **Horseshoe Tower** is 16C. In the restored rooms, special lighting enhances the vaulting with armorial-decorated keystones. Temporary exhibitions are held alternately, presenting the works formerly displayed in the Musée des Salorges.

Nantes derives its name from the *Namnètes*, a Gallic tribe who made the town their capital. The Romans developed it as a trading centre; the Vikings pillaged then occupied Nantes. In the early 20C, a plan for urban renewal greatly altered the face of the town, as did the massive destruction of the Second World War. The cathedral, striking for its Gothic unity despite the long building period, was bombed during the war, and had been nearly completely restored in 1972 when fire largely destroyed the roof. The medieval castle is remarkable for its contrasts: outside, a fortress with its crenellated towers; inside, a typical Renaissance palace. These rare historic buildings are the architectural pride of Nantes.

CATHÉDRALE ST-PIERRE-ET-ST-PAUL (HY) *30min*

This imposing building, begun in 1434, completed in 1893 and restored after serious fire damage in 1972, is remarkable for its austere façade restored in 1930: two plain towers frame a Flamboyant window; note the 15C canopied niches which decorate the pillars supporting the towers. The three portals reveal finely sculpted recessed arches and on the central portal stands a statue of St Peter. From the north side one can see the chevet with its ring of fine apsidal chapels crowned by graceful pinnacles.

★★**Interior** – Here, at Nantes, white stone replaces the granite used in purely Breton cathedrals. Being less heavy, this stone made it possible to build vaults 37.50m/123ft high (the vaulting of Westminster Abbey is 30.50m/100ft high). As you enter you will be struck by the nave's pure, soaring lines, a fine example of Flamboyant work. Stand under the organ loft to appreciate the effect; you will see a double row of vertical lines springing from the ground and shooting without a break up to the delicately carved keystones of the vaults, where they cross.

Nantes for tourists

Thematic guided tours – In the summer, the tourist office organises a variety of thematic tours, which last 2hr-2hr 30min. For information or reservations, call ☎ 02 40 20 60 00, or stop by the tourist office.

Horse-drawn carriage tours – *Facing the château entrance – ☎ 02 40 38 34 16 – 1 Apr-30 Sept, carriages depart every hour (11am-5pm); the rest of the year, by reservation only.*

Transports urbains – By tramway – Getting around by tramway is quick and convenient (operational all year, except on 1 May). There are two existing tramway routes (27 km/18mi, the longest tramway network in France) and another under construction. An individual ticket (8F) is valid for 1hr on both buses and tramways, and can be bought from automatic vending machines at tramway stops, from TAN establishments and TAN kiosks (the main one is at the stop known as Commerce). The best way to visit the town is to buy a daily pass, called a "ticket 24hr" (21F), which permits unlimited travel for one entire day. Info Allô TAN ☎ 0 801 444 444.

By bus – You may buy bus tickets from the bus driver, from automatic vending machines, or in TAN kiosks.

Regional information in the media – For information about events, cultural activities and movies, consult the newspaper *Ouest-France* (Nantes edition), the magazine *Nantes-Poche*, and the tourist office's monthly program, "*Des Jours et des Nuits*". You may also consult 3615 Nantes (booth at the tourist office) for other information about cultural activities and sports.

Radio stations Radio Sud-Loire 88.8 mhz ; Radio Nantes 100.9 mhz, Radio-France Bretagne Ouest 101.4mhz.

Hotels

BUDGET

Hôtel Graslin – *1 rue Piron – ☎ 02 40 69 72 91 – 47 rooms 250/400F – breakfast 40F.* Well situated in town, this hotel provides a good opportunity to combine business with tourism. The building is old, but the interior is modern. If your budget permits, choose one of the eight larger rooms.

OUR SELECTION

Hôtel La Pérouse – *3 allée Duquesne – ☎ 02 40 89 75 00 – 47 rooms 430/560F – breakfast 50F.* Resolutely contemporary, this hotel combines purity of form with comfort of materials. Lovers of design will especially appreciate its white walls treated with linseed oil, its blond parquets, its "zen" furnishings, and its transparent basins.

Eating out

BUDGET

Crêperie Heb-Ken – *5 rue de Guérande – ☎ 02 40 48 79 03 – closed 15 July-20 Aug and Sun – 40/80F.* Very reasonable prices for quality crêpes, served in two simple dining rooms, decorated with local photos. A pleasant place to stop while wandering around Nantes, located between place Royale and rue Crébillon.

Au Coup d'Canon – *12 rue Jean-Jacques-Rousseau – ☎ 02 40 71 88 04 – 80/110F.* Quite a cannon blast it is! Here, the wines flow freely, the food is very substantial, and the atmosphere joyous and noisy.

Chez l'Huître – *5 rue des Petites-Écuries – ☎ 02 51 82 02 02 – closed 24 Dec-2 Jan and Sun – 85/130F.* Oysters or smoked fish? If you love shellfish, this tiny bistro is the place for you! You'll get a grand gulp of sea air while tasting the shellfish platters ... and without breaking your piggybank. Summer terrace on the pedestrian street.

OUR SELECTION

Cigale – *4 place Graslin – ☎ 02 51 84 94 94 – 150F.* With its decor of turn-of-the-century ceramics which ranks it as an historic monument, this brasserie is one of the locals' favourite meeting places. Seated elbow to elbow, they enjoy the hearty cuisine and the lively atmosphere. Brunches on the weekend.

L'Atlantide – *quai Renaud, 4th floor – ☎ 02 40 73 23 23 – closed 1-23 Aug, Sat lunch and Sun – 200/330F.* This starred restaurant, with very understated decor, is located on the 4th floor of a modern building. Its gourmet cuisine is also contemporary and original, and you'll enjoy the lovely view of the Loire.

Le Bouche à Oreille – *14 rue Jean-Jacques-Rousseau* – ☎ *02 40 73 00 25* – *closed 1-21 Aug, Sun and public holidays* – *125/180F*. This bistro is so popular that you will need to reserve. It serves copious portions of regional dishes in a stunning decor that mixes old enamelled plaques, amusing curios and a very unusual collection of pigs … Also known for some culinary specialities of Lyon.

La Maison du Change – *2 place du Change* – ☎ *02 40 47 18 49* – *closed Sun* – *110/180F*. Travel back in time by admiring this house's 15C façade, and venturing into the medieval interior. The building is classed as an historic monument, and even the dishes have been inspired by history. The bar remains open when the restaurant is closed.

Night-life

La Civelle – *21 quai Marcel-Boissard, in Trentemout* – ☎ *02 40 75 46 60* – *Mon-Fri 11am-midnight, Sat 7pm-midnight*. If you are travelling by car, this bar-restaurant on the south bank of the Loire will enable you to discover the charming little pleasure port of Trentmout. Watching the sun set over the Loire from the terrace is marvellous.

Le Flesselles – *3 allée Flesselles* – ☎ *02 40 47 66 14*. Already legendary in Nantes, this café caters to the "hip" artistic crowd; the regulars seem to arrive in waves. If it seems too packed, there is another room on the 1st floor with amusing decorations which are renewed regularly.

Le Graslin – *1 rue Racine* – ☎ *02 40 69 81 79* – *Mon-Sat 11am-2am*. Beer-lovers of Nantes are particularly attached to this bar which serves around 400 different brands of beer a year, and usually has 200 different brands at any given time. Needless to say, the owners are experts on the subject, and have even created a game which you can play in this most convivial of bars.

Le Remorqueur – *Quai Malakoff* – ☎ *02 40 20 49 99* – *Tues-Sat 9pm-5am*. Tucked away in a turn-of-the-century barge, this inimitable all-night bar is run by an unusual character who has spent years fixing it up. Despite appearances, it does meet security regulations. World music.

Going out

Pannonica – *9 rue Basse-Porte* – ☎ *02 51 72 10 10* – *www.pannonica.com* – *Tues-Fri 10am-13pm, 15pm-6.30pm, Sat 10am-1pm*. Jazz, blues, and rock concerts … Holds an important place in the Nantes music scene due to its extremely high quality programming.

Théâtre Graslin – *Place Graslin* – ☎ *02 40 69 77 18* – *Mon-Fri 1pm-6pm, Sat 10am-5pm*. This 18C building in the classic Corinthian style houses one of Nante's cultural highlights. Operas, great classics of the theatre …

Everything is based on elevation and the dimension of 37.50m/123ft loses significance. Seen from this angle, the slender ribs of the pillars mask not only the flat wall surfaces that separate them but all the lines, curved or horizontal, of the arcades, the triforium or the upper windows which could break the harmony of this vista, composed entirely of parallel vertical elements.

Go round the building to the right.

In the south transept is the decorative masterpiece of the cathedral and a very great Renaissance work: the **tomb of François II★★**. It was carved between 1502 and 1507 by Michel Colombe, a sculptor who was born in Brittany but settled in the Touraine. It was commissioned by Anne of Brittany to receive the remains of her father, François II, and her mother, Marguerite of Foix, and it was placed in the Church of the Carmelites. The Revolutionary Tribunal ordered it to be demolished, but the courageous town architect of the time, instead of obeying the order, hid various pieces of the tomb in his friends' homes. It was reconstructed after the Revolution and transferred to the cathedral in 1817.

The Duke and Duchess recline on a black marble slab placed on a rectangular one in white marble. The statues grouped round them are symbolic: the angels supporting their heads represent their welcome to Heaven; the lion crouching at the feet of François stands for power, and Marguerite's greyhound for fidelity. The four large corner statues personify the four Cardinal Virtues: for the Duke, Justice (crowned and holding a sword) and Strength (helmeted and armed and expelling a dragon from a tower); Prudence and Temperance guard the Duchess. Prudence has two faces: in front, a young girl with a looking glass, symbolising the future, and behind, an old man representing the past. Temperance holds a bridle to signify control over passions, and a clock representing steadiness.

Below the recumbent figures are 16 niches containing the statues of saints interceding for the deceased, notably St Francis of Assisi and St Margaret, their patrons. Below the saints, 16 mourners, partly damaged, represent their people's sorrow. This magnificent group is lit by a superb modern **stained-glass window**, 25m/80ft high

Théâtre de Poche – *5 rue Lekain* – ☎ *02 40 47 34 44* – *open on the evenings of performances*. This is Nante's only café-théâtre, and presents essentially humorous entertainment.

Orchestre national des Pays de la Loire – *Cité des Congrès* – ☎ *02 51 25 29 29*. This national orchestra gives concerts twice a month.

Shopping

Markets – The Talensac market (rue de Talensac) is held daily except Monday; the Bouffay market (place du Bouffay), also daily except Monday; the Petite Hollande market(place de la Petite-Hollande), on Saturdays.

Flea market – Is held place Viarme, Saturday all day and Sunday morning.

George Gautier – *Rue de la Fosse* – *Tues-Sat 9am-7pm*. This magnificent chocolate shop dates from 1850 and is classed as an historic monument. Chocolate lovers will drool before the macaroons, the *"berlingots nantais"* or the *"vieux pavés"*… The establishment next door belongs to the same owner.

Festivals

Les Folles Journées – ☎ *02 51 88 20 00* – *follejournée@congres-nantes.fr*. Every year, this classical music festival attracts more and more different kinds of music lovers. La Folle Journée, devoted to a different composer each year, takes place on the last weekend of January.

Other events – Nantes is not lacking in events, whether cultural or simply festive: Carnaval (March-April), Printemps des Arts (May-June), Festival d'été (July), Rendez-vous de l'Erdre (end of Aug-early Sept), festival des 3 Continents (end of Nov-early Dec) etc. Information is available from the tourist office.

Boat trips on the River Erdre

Bateaux Nantais – *See Excursion: Boat trips*. This company organises daily cruises (lunches, dinners with dancing) on the lovely River Erdre. After nightfall, these cruises take on an enchanted quality. During school holidays, treasure hunts are organised for children.

Electric boats – ☎ *02 51 81 04 24*. Enjoy an outing in an electric boat; no licence is required. Departure from l'Île de Versailles.

Canoë-kayak – *Canoë-kayak nantais, route de la Jonelière* – ☎ *02 40 29 25 71*. This club organises canoe and kayak outings on the river.

and 5.30m/14ft wide devoted to Breton and Nantes saints, the work of Chapuis. You should pause at the transept crossing, where the impression of height is astonishing. In the north arm of the transept is the **Cenotaph of Lamoricière★**, the work of the sculptor Paul Dubois (1879). The General is shown reclining under a shroud. Four bronze statues represent Meditation and Charity (at his head) and Military Courage and Faith (at his feet). Lamoricière (1806-65), a great African campaigner who came from Nantes, captured the Arabian Emir Abd-el-Kaderin 1847 during the wars in Algeria. He later fell into disgrace and when exiled by Napoleon III commanded Papal troops against the Italians. It is the Catholic paladin who is honoured here. The apsidal chapel contains lovely abstract stained-glass windows by Jean Le Moal.

TOWN CENTRE

★★ Musée des Beaux Arts ⊙ (HY M¹) – The museum is housed in an imposing late-19C building, the main part of which is flanked by projecting wings. The collections, enriched by exhibits from the depository, cover the 13C to the present. A central patio is surrounded by large galleries with works exhibited in chronological order. Among the Italian Primitives note Perugino's *Saint Sebastian* portrayed as an elegant page holding an arrow; the 17C is represented by such masters as Rubens (*The Triumph of Judas the Maccabee*) and Georges de La Tour *(Saint Peter's Denial, The Angel Appearing to Joseph in His Dream, The Hurdy-Gurdy Player)*. Representing the 18C French School are Greuze *(The Guitarist)* and Watteau *(Harlequin, Emperor of the Moon)*. Classicism and Romanticism are represented by Ingres' fine portrait *Madame Senonnes*, Delacroix's *The Moroccan Chief* and Courbet's *The Winnowers*.

The 20C collections are displayed in seven large galleries. In the first, works illustrating the period from Impressionism to the Fauves include Monet's *Nymphéas*, Émile Bernard's *Apple Tree Beating*, representing the Pont-Aven School, Sonia Delaunay's *Yellow Nude*, a Fauve work, and *Château de Clisson* by Nantes artist Metzinger.

B   Maison « de la duchesse de Berry »
D   La Psalette
F   Église St-Nicolas
L   Manoir de la Touche
M¹ Musée des Beaux-Arts
M² Muséum d'Histoire naturelle
M³ Musée archéologique
M⁴ Musée de l'Imprimerie
M⁶ Musée de la Poupée et des Jouets anciens
M⁷ Maison de l'Erdre

NANTES

The second gallery contains a collection, which must be unique in a provincial museum, of paintings by Vasili Kandinsky executed during the years he taught at the Bauhaus (1922-33). The homogeneity of this collection, which features in particular *Black Frame* and the bright *Évènement doux*, revolves around the idea of a "microcosm". The third gallery exhibits different artistic movements from the period 1913-45, notably two works by the Constructivist Gorin, *Two Women Standing* by a Magnelli at the intersection of Futurism and Cubism, as well as two paintings by Chagall executed at a particularly testing time in his life, *Red Horse* and *Obsession*.

The fourth gallery plunges the viewer into the cultural context of the period 1940-60, with figurative works by Lapicque *(Sunset on the Salute)*, Hélion *(Still Life with Pumpkin)* and abstract works by Poliakoff, Hartung, Bissière and the Nantes artist Camille Bryen.

The fifth gallery covers the period 1960-75. It focuses principally on the Nantes artist Martin Barré, but also exhibits the interesting work of François Morellet, representing Kinetic art.

The sixth gallery is largely given over to the 1970s and 80s. Note in particular *Promenade of the Blue Cavalier*, a charming abstract work by Thiéval, large "canvases" by Viallat and above all two Picassos, among the master's last works, **Couple**★ and **Man Seated with Walking Stick**. Finally, there are three works by Dubuffet, including *Setting with two Figures F 106*.

The final gallery devotes a large area to contemporary European artistic expression. Rebecca Horn's *Hydrapiano*, with the bizarre behaviour of its long column of mercury, is particularly eye-catching.

Place Maréchal-Foch (HY) – Two fine 18C hotels, built from the plans by Ceineray, flank the Louis XVI Column which was erected in 1790. From the square, commonly called place Louis-XVI, which is prolonged by Cours St-André and St-Pierre, you can readily appreciate the dimensions of the cathedral, in particular its soaring height.

Porte St-Pierre (HY) – This 15C gateway stands on the remains of a 3C Gallo-Roman wall. The gateway is built into an elegant turreted building, which was once part of the episcopal residence.

Skirt the cathedral façade; go through the portal on the left.

La Psalette (HY D) – This 15C building with a polygonal turret formerly contained the chapter-house but is now part of the sacristy.

Take the vaulted passageway on the right.

From the small square you can see the other side of La Psalette.

Bear right on Impasse St-Laurent then left into rue Mathelin-Rodier (the name of the architect of the cathedral and part of the castle).

It was in the house at no 3 (**HY B**) that the Duchess of Berry was arrested.

Pass the Château des Ducs de Bretagne on the left.

Plateau Ste-Croix – It is an area where 15C and 16C half-timbered houses still stand: no 7 rue de la Juiverie, no 7 rue Ste-Croix, nos 8 and 10 rue de la Boucherie, no 5 rue Bossuet and place du Change.

Église Ste-Croix (GY) – This 17C church is surmounted by the former town belfry crowned with trumpeting angels. The palm tree decoration of the chancel vaulting contrasts with the round vaulting of the nave. Large Flamboyant windows open onto the aisles. The furnishings are 18C.

★**The 19C town** – It was the financier **Graslin**, Receiver General for Farmlands at Nantes, who was responsible for the creation of this area. By way of place du Pilori, surrounded by 18C houses, make for **place Royale** (GZ), which was built by Crucy, the architect of the Stock Exchange (Bourse). This is adorned by a fountain representing Nantes (1865).

Rue Crébillon (GZ 60) is narrow, commercial and very busy.

Opening onto rue Santeuil on the left, is a curious stepped shopping arcade, the **passage Pommeraye**★ (GZ 150), built in 1843, which goes down to the Stock Exchange. Great fluted columns support galleries lined with elegant shops, and statue-adorned pedestals serve as bases for lamps.

Return to rue Crébillon, the fine **place Graslin** (FZ) dominated by the Corinthian-style Grand Théâtre (1783). The café on the corner, La Cigale, still has a turn-of-the-century air and fine mosaics. Leading off from the same corner is **Cours Cambronne**★ (FZ) lined with late-18C and early-19C pilastered houses.

★★**Muséum d'Histoire naturelle** ⊘ (FZ M²) – Originally set up in the Cabinet Dubuisson in 1799, this Natural History Museum was later moved to the former Mint (Hôtel de la Monnaie) and inaugurated in 1875. It houses several important collections in such varied areas as zoology, regional fauna, osteology, paleontology, prehistory, sciences of the earth, mineralogy and ethnography. The section devoted to shells is remarkable on account of the sheer beauty and variety of the exhibits. A vivarium presents reptiles and batrachians from all over the world.

The museum features an auditorium (conferences and educational activities), a public library with scientific books, as well as a "Science and Nature" area specially designed for groups of pupils.

★**Palais Dobrée** (**FZ**) ⊘ – This Romanesque-style mansion was built in the 19C by the Nantes shipowner and collector **Thomas Dobrée** (1810-95).

On the ground floor Romanesque and Gothic sculptures from Nantes and the Val de Loire are presented in a modern setting: 4 large statues from the cathedral's bell-tower, decorated purlins and corner posts; the armoury exhibits items from the Bronze Age to the 19C. Displayed around the reliquary containing the heart of Anne of Brittany (1516) are medieval ivories and alabasters, champlevé enamels (12C-14C) from the Limousin, Rhine and Moselle regions, paintings and jewellery. On the first floor are 16C-19C furnishings, paintings, tapestries, painted enamels, gold and silversmith work, ceramics, portraits, jewellery and Dobrée family memorabilia.

Manoir de la Touche ⊘ (**FZ L**) – This house is known as Jean V's Manor-House, because Jean V, a duke and member of the Montfort family, died here in 1442. Exhibited inside are collections (arms, documents, paintings, costumes etc) evoking the French Revolution and the Wars of the Vendée (1793-5).

★**Musée archéologique** ⊘ (**FZ M³**) – *Entrance rue Voltaire.* The first floor of this archeological museum concentrates on Greek and Etruscan pottery and all that is Egyptian (sarcophagi, canopic vases – funerary urns, the covers of which are in the form of an animal or human head – bronze and painted statuettes).

The second floor concentrates on local civilizations covering prehistory to the invasion of the Norsemen, with displays of arms, tools, terracotta and bronze vases, jewellery, items from St-Nazaire dating from the neolithic to the Bronze Age, and Gallo-Roman objects excavated at Rezé (Loire-Atlantique).

ADDITIONAL SIGHTS

★**Ancienne île Feydeau** (**GZ**) – Between 1926 and 1938 the islet was linked to the mainland and a second island, the Île Gloriette, by filling in several arms of the Loire. The islet has retained its 18C appearance, especially between place de la Petite Hollande and cours Olivier-de-Clisson (no 4 was the birthplace of Jules Verne). It was here that rich shipowners used to build their vast mansions which stretch from the central street, rue Kervégan, right back to one of the outer avenues, Allées Turenne or Duguay-Trouin. Curved wrought-iron balconies and grotesque masks, probably the work of seafaring craftsmen, adorn the façades. The inner courtyards have staircases with remarkable vaulting.

Opposite, on the northern bank, there are also some fine 18C houses (nos 7 and 11) on **place de la Bourse** (**GZ 24**).

Quai de la Fosse (**EFZ**) – Several 18C mansions line this quay (nos 17, 54, 70), including no 86, Hôtel Durbé, whose outbuildings served as a warehouse for the India Company.

Musée de l'Imprimerie ⊘ (**AZ M⁴**) – Before entering the workshop, visit the gallery with its lithographs, illuminated manuscripts and engraved wood. In the workshop, composition and printing techniques are illustrated with machines – lithographic and typographic presses, copper-plate engraving press, type-setting and casting machines – all in perfect working order.

Maillé-Brézé ⊘ – Docked on the Loire, this escort ship (132.65m/434ft long and 12.70m/40ft wide) was launched in 1957 and served until 1988. The visit includes anti-submarine and anti-aircraft weapons and detection systems, the command post and the officers' and sailors' living quarters.

In the officers' quarters, a small museum evokes the life of French Admiral Jean Armand de Maillé (1619-46) through literature and various exhibits. There is an interesting tour of the machine room.

Église Notre-Dame-de-Bon-Port ⊘ (**FZ**) – Also known as the **Église St-Louis**, this unusual building overlooks place Sanitat. This great cubic mass (1846) is adorned by a fresco and a triangular pediment and topped by a majestic dome. Massive hexagonal pillars support the dome decorated alternatively with panels of stained glass and frescoes.

★**View from Ste-Anne Lookout point** – *Access via Quai E.-Renaud* (**EZ**) *and rue de l'Hermitage.*

From the terraced lookout point there is a good view of the port installations with cranes in the foreground and shipyards and Beaulieu Islet in the distance.

A viewing table *(table d'orientation)* helps the visitor pinpoint Nantes' main sights and its new buildings.

★**Musée Jules-Verne** ⊘ – *No 3 rue de l'Hermitage* (**EZ 94**). A 19C mansion houses the museum devoted to Jules Verne (1828-1905), one of the first to write science fiction novels such as *Five Weeks in a Balloon, A Journey to the Centre of the Earth* and *Around the World in Eighty Days.*

Musée Jules Verne, Nantes

Book cover of an original Hetzel edition

His life is retraced with the help of memorabilia: autographs, furniture, personal objects, portraits, busts, a planisphere showing his extraordinary journeys, and a collection of his works.

Near the Jules Verne Museum stands the statue of St Anne, blessing the port. Cross the shaded place des Garennes which is overlooked by the west front of the Église Ste-Anne and take rue des Garennes to reach square Maurice-Schwob.

Square Maurice-Schwob – *Access by boulevard Saint-Aignan* (**EZ**). Overlooking the Loire, this garden is dominated by an expressive statue of a Breton woman cursing the sea. One can make out part of the port, the tip of Beaulieu Islet and Rezé.

Planétarium ⊘ – *Access by Quai E.-Renaud* (**EZ**) *and rue de l'Hermitage* (**EZ 94**). *No 8 rue des Acadiens.* In the planetarium, the visitor discovers the mysteries of the universe: the sun, moon, stars and planets are projected onto the dome. Each show takes a different theme.

The 20 years that Jules Verne spent in Nantes from his birth on Feydeau Island in 1828 until he set up house in Paris in 1848, undoubtedly helped to strengthen his vocation as a writer of fiction, whose exceptional talent and boundless imagination successfully combined dream, scientific fact and adventure. The sight of the great port crowded with ships, their holds giving off all kinds of smells, or the equally fascinating scene of the steam-driven machines at the Indret factory, the tales of voyages he listened to from his uncle Prudent, once a privateer, lessons in reading and writing with Madame Sambin, the widow of the captain of an ocean-going vessel, or imaginary shipwrecks conjured up while playing among the little islands of the Loire, all played a part in inspiring the author's imaginative genius when he came to write *Voyages extraordinaires*, which earned him the acclaim of more than 25 million teenagers even before he was universally acknowledged to be a great writer.

Musée de la Poupée et des Jouets anciens ⊘ (**EZ M⁶**) – *No 39 boulevard St-Aignan.*
Tableaux with dolls, their furnishings, knick-knacks and accessories have been set up in display cabinets illustrating daily life (the first ball, grandmother's house, wedding celebration) and trades (laundress, seamstress, chimney sweep). One display case shows the evolution of the doll between 1830 and 1930; the different costumes reflect the changes in fashion of the times.
On the second floor old toys are exhibited: toy cars, soldiers, magic lantern, and also children's clothes.

Parc de Procé (**EY**) – It is a pleasure to stroll through this undulating park (16ha/40 acres) landscaped with perspectives and rhododendrons, azaleas, oaks etc.

Musée de la Poste ⊘ (**EY**) – *No 2 bis rue du Président-Herriot.*
Located in the post office's regional headquarters, the museum recounts the history of the postal system from the mounted couriers to the post office box to private messenger services. Displays include the model of a 19C relay post, uniforms worn by the postillion and postman, scales, stamp-making machines, telephones, calendars etc. An audio-visual show ends the visit.

★**Jardin des Plantes** (**HY**) – Opposite the station, decorated with brightly coloured mosaics, is this very fine garden which was created in 1805. It is beautifully landscaped and contains, in addition to the masses of white, pink, purple and yellow camellias, magnolias, rhododendrons and splendid trees, several fine ponds and wooden sculpture. A statue of Jules Verne is a reminder that Nantes was the writer's native town.

Chapelle de l'Immaculée ⊙ (**HY**) – The former Chapelle des Minimes is in an older area of Nantes where 17C porches adorn the houses, and streets narrow to alleys. It was built in the 15C Flamboyant style by Duke François II. The façade and aisles are 17C and the 19C pulpit has small columns intertwined with a vine and snake. Modern stained-glass windows light the interior.

Église St-Nicolas (**GY F**) – The basilica was built in 1854 in the Gothic style. There are fine views of the building and its tall spire (85m/279ft) from place Royale and of the east end from rue Cacault.

Île de Versailles (**GY**) – Once covered with marshland, the islet was landfilled during the building of the Nantes-Brest Canal. A charming Japanese garden has been landscaped with rock gardens, waterfalls, and lanterns.
The **Maison de l'Erdre** (House of the River Erdre) ⊙ (**M'**) displays the river's flora and fauna; the river, until the 19C, flowed into the canal.

★BOAT TRIP ON THE ERDRE ⊙

Landing stage: Quai de la Motte Rouge (Gare fluviale – GY).

This is a favourite trip for the Nantais in a pleasantly green countryside dotted with manor houses; the 16C Château de la Gascherie with its ornate windows is notable. The Erdre widens beyond Sucé to form Lake Mazerolles.

CHÂTEAU DE LA GOULAIN

13km/8mi southeast on N 149, then D 119 towards Haute-Goulaine.

The **château** ⊙, surrounded by vineyards, was built between 1480 and 1495 by Christophe de Goulaine, Groom of the Bedchamber to Louis XII and François I. He built it on the foundations of an old medieval fortress which, with those at Clisson and Nantes, had been used to defend the Duchy of Brittany against France.
Remains from this military past include a machicolated tower and a small castle in front of a bridge spanning a moat. This handsome residence consists of a Gothic 15C main building of calcareous tufa from the Saumur region, and two wings added in the early 17C.

Interior – A spiral staircase leads to the first floor, which opens into the **Great Hall**, in which the most striking feature is the richly sculpted, monumental Renaissance chimney-piece. A beautiful 16C Flemish tapestry depicting the Fall of Phaethon adorns the wall. The **Blue Room** still has its early-17C decor intact: blue and gold coffered ceiling, chimney-piece with Corinthian columns and caryatids, panelling decorated with pastel landscapes, and a large majestic Gobelins tapestry. The **Grey Room** has interesting panelling and mythological scenes on its piers.

Volière à papillons – An enormous greenhouse next to the castle's curtain wall contains tropical flowers and shrubs and is an aviary for butterflies.

Île d'OUESSANT★★

Ushant – Population 1 062
Michelin map 58 fold 2 or 230 fold 1

An excursion to the Île d'Ouessant by sea is of the greatest interest, since it enables you to see Brest Channel, Pointe de St-Mathieu, Four Channel, the famous Black Stones (Pierres Noires) reef and the Green Stones (Pierres Vertes) reef, the islands of Béniguet and Molène, and Fromveur Channel. The island itself is extremely curious. On the way to Ouessant the boat usually anchors off and sometimes calls at **Molène**. There the pastures on the rare patches of earth in this archipelago are so small that, according to a local jest, a Molène cow which has all four feet in one field grazes from another and manures a third.

Nature – Ouessant is 7km/4mi long and 4km/2.5mi wide and its highest point is 60m/197ft above sea level. It is famous in marine history for the danger of its waters due to frequent fog, strong currents (the Fromrust to the northwest and the Fromveur to the southeast) and countless reefs.
In winter the wind is master and hurls the waves against the broken and rocky shores with the utmost fury for as much as 10 days on end. The scene is often sinister when the fog comes down and the mournful howl of the foghorns mingles with the roar of the storm.
Few tourists know the island in this inhospitable guise, for the summer season brings calm and a quieter atmosphere, similar to that of the coasts of Brittany. The climate is mild. In January and February, Ushant has the highest mean temperature in France. The colonies of sea birds that nest on the island's cliff and on the neighbouring islets are particularly numerous in the autumn when the migrants from Northern Europe fly in, attracted by the beams of the two lighthouses.

The **Parc naturel régional d'Armorique** to which Ouessant has been attached since 1969, helps maintain its traditional character.

The men and their work – The majority of the island's population is made up of women and men who have retired from the Navy or the merchant marine. Their principle occupations are stock raising and food crops.

Vegetables and potatoes grow in beautifully maintained lots. The grain cultivated on larger parcels of land is used as feed for poultry and also as a supplementary fodder crop for the cattle's diet. The livestock (sheep, dairy cows, horses) consists mainly of sheep with brown wool, which graze on meagre tufts of salt grass; the result is meat with a splendid flavour, comparable to the famous *prés salés* of Mont-St-Michel Bay.

They live in the open and take shelter from northwesterly or southwesterly gales behind low dry-stone walls built in a star formation or wood shelters. Though from early February (first Wednesday: a great cattle fair) before lambing to late September they are tethered in twos to a stake; they wander freely the rest of the year, their owner's mark being nicked on their ears.

A few dairy cows are raised and two riding centres have reintroduced horse breeding.

The cultivation of algae and the raising of mussels have developed into very promising enterprises.

Coast of Ushant

The men of Ouessant work on the continent (Brest region), at sea (the Navy or merchant marine), fishing (coastal or in deeper oceans) or on oil platforms.

Tradition – The important part played by the women of Ouessant in family life was recognised by an old custom by which it was the girls who proposed marriage. Women's traditional dress is severe and not often worn; it is made of black cloth and consists of a short skirt and a small *coiffe*; the hair is combed back and falls on the shoulders. The character of the people is reflected in the customs, which were observed until 1962, for when a member of a family was lost at sea. The friends and relatives would meet at the man's home to pray and watch over a little wax cross that stood for him; the sad vigil would last all night. The next day at the funeral service, the cross would be deposited in a reliquary in the church. Later, at some major ceremony, it would be put in a mausoleum in the cemetery where the crosses of all the missing were assembled. These little wax crosses are called Proëlla crosses. The word means "the homecoming of souls".

TOUR *1 day*

Roads from Lampaul lead to the best sites but many paths and tracks enable the visitor to crisscross the island, to reach the fine cliffs, the pretty little creeks and to discover the flora as well as the marine fauna: herring gulls, cormorants, oyster catchers, puffins, terns etc.

Lampaul – This is the island's capital. Note the old houses kept in excellent repair; the shutters are painted in green or blue, the island's traditional colours. A small monument containing the Proëlla crosses *(see above)* stands in the cemetery.
The tiny port, west facing, is picturesque, while the sandy beach of Le Corz nearby extends to the south.

★★★ La Côte Sauvage – *Leave Lampaul west by an uphill road; after 500m/547yd, bear right.*

Écomusée de l'île d'Ouessant ⊘ – At the hamlet of **Niou Uhella**, two traditional houses have been restored and rearranged by the Parc naturel régional d'Armorique. Visitors will see in one of them furniture typical of the island built of wood from wrecked vessels, painted in blue, symbol of the Virgin's protection, and in the second a display of farm and domestic implements and costumes etc which depicts aspects of life on Ouessant; an exhibit on the island's geology and population is upstairs.

Lherpinière/CAMPAGNE CAMPAGNE

Carry on towards the coast.

Moulin de Karaes – This is the island's last mill (restored) with its round stone base. It was used to mill barley from which bread was still made at the beginning of the 20C.

Phare de Créac'h – This lighthouse, with that at Land's End, marks the entrance to the English Channel; it has two tiers of revolving beams. The light is cast by four lamps giving a total of 20 million candlepower and an average range of more than 60km/37mi.

In the old machine room, there is a small **Centre d'Interprétation des Phares et Balises** (Lighthouse Museum) ⊙ retracing their history from Antiquity to the present. It shows how the original lighthouse was a tower, with, at its summit, a light fuelled by burning coal, wood or oil. The exhibit includes turbines, lens, lamps, beams and recounts the life of the lighthouse keeper. An audio-visual show completes the tour.

Go round the lighthouse to the right to view the coast.

Its extraordinarily jagged **rocks★★★** *(rochers)* pounded by the sea are very impressive. A gangway in front of the lighthouse gives access to Pointe du Créac'h where the foghorn stands. Cargo boats and oil tankers can be seen on the horizon; some 300 ships pass daily in the area which is patrolled day and night by the French Navy.

Turn back and bear right towards Pointe de Pern.

Chapelle Notre-Dame-de-Bon-Voyage – Also known as the Chapelle St-Gildas after the English saint who came here in the 5C, it was built at the end of the 19C. The people of Ouessant come to the chapel every year for the island's *pardon* on the first or second Sunday in September.

★**Pointe de Pern** – This, the western-most point of the island, extends into the sea in a series of rocks and reefs lashed by the rollers. In the distance is the unmanned Nividic Lighthouse (Phare de Nividic).

Presqu'île de Feunteun Velen – *At Lampaul, take the road skirting the cemetery.* Pass near the small port of Lampaul, where the boat from Brest sometimes drops anchor. The jetty gives shelter to the fishing boats.

The road goes round the deep Lampaul Bay bounded by the Corz and Le Prat Beaches, with the Le Grand Truk and Youc'h Corz rocks in the centre, then descends gently towards the Pointe de Porz Doun. Note on the left the white pyramid of Le Runiou (Pyramide du Runiou), a landmark for shipping; on the right is the great cove of Porz Coret.

Getting there

Departing from Brest (regular line) on the Enez Eussa or the Fromveur, departures at 8.30am for Ouessant or Molène via Le Conquet. From Le Conquet (regular line), departures at 9.45am; Apr to end-Sept there are additional departures. From Brest or Camaret (summer line): mid-July to end-Aug on the André Colin, departing Brest at 7.45am, departing Ouessant at 6pm (except Sun); May and June, Wed. Bicycle rental at Stiff during school holidays; at Lampaul, all year. Information: Compagnie maritime Penn Ar Bed. ☎ 02 98 80 24 68. By plane leaving Brest-Guipavas. ☎ 02 98 84 64 87.

Hotels

OUR SELECTION

Hôtel Roc'h Ar Mor – *In Lampaul, 29242 – ☎ 02 98 48 80 19 – 15 rooms 280/350F – breakfast 40F – restaurant 90/180F.* On the outskirts of the village of Lampaul, this grand building facing the bay has been renovated and now offers quality comfort. The veranda and the majority of the rooms enjoy a sea view.

Eating out

BUDGET

Crêperie Ti A Dreuz – *In Lampaul, lower town, 29242 – ☎ 02 98 48 83 01 – closed Oct-Easter except during school holidays – 35/75F.* In this old house with a slanting façade, you can enjoy crêpes while listening to the unusual stories behind the decorations on the buffet in this white and blue dining room … Another dining room opens onto a pretty flower garden.

Pointe de Porz Doun – The cliff-lined point at the southern tip of the island affords a fine **view** over Lampaul, the Pointe de Pern and Jument Lighthouse (built from 1904-12; unmanned) which reaches a height of 42m/138ft and houses a foghorn.

Phare du Stiff – *Leave Lampaul by the road running along the north side of the church.*
The road rises gently to the island's highest point (alt 60m/197ft), the Pointe de Bac'haol. The lighthouse, built by the military architect Vauban in 1695, comprises two adjoining towers, one containing a spiral staircase (126 steps) and the other three small superposed rooms. The light has a range of 50km/31mi thanks to a lamp of 1 000W giving a total of 600 000 candlepower. From the top a vast **panorama**★★ unfolds over the islands and the mainland from Vierge Lighthouse to the Pointe du Raz.
Nearby stands the new radar-tower (height 140m/459ft) which controls the sea lane off the island.
Paths lead to the tip of the **Presqu'île de Cadoran** (Cadoran Peninsula) from which may be enjoyed a pretty view of Beninou Bay, sometimes frequented by a seal colony, and Keller Island, favoured by nesting birds.

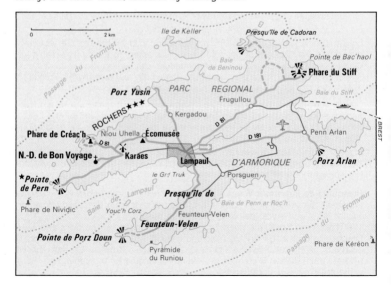

Crique de Porz Yusin – *Leave Lampaul north by a road running past the island's electricity generating plant.*

The road passes several hamlets with white houses adorned with brightly coloured shutters and surrounded by small gardens, on the way to Porz Yusin, one of the few sheltered spots on the north coast.

This pretty rocky setting is ideal for birdwatching. There are also very fine varieties of seaweed.

Crique de Porz Arlan – *Leave Lampaul by the road skirting the cemetery, then turn left.*

The road runs across the plateau, leaving on the right the 1863 Chapelle Notre-Dame-d'Espérance and on the left the airfield, before bearing right towards picturesque Porz Arlan.

In this creek nestle a tiny sandy beach and a small port sheltered by a jetty. From this charming site the beautiful **view** extends over the rocky coastline, Fromveur and Kéréon Lighthouse, and the Île de Bannec.

PAIMPOL

Population 7 856
Michelin map 59 fold 2 or 230 fold 8

Pierre Loti's novel *Pêcheur d'Islande* (Fisherman of Iceland, 1886) and Botrel's song *The Paimpolaise* (the cliff mentioned in the song is located near the town, towards the Pointe de Guilben) brought both literary fame and popularity to Paimpol. Life has changed a great deal, however, since those days when deep-sea fishing was done off the banks of Iceland. The fishermen now tend to fish along the coast; the port, large and impersonal, contains mostly pleasure boats. The town retains a certain prosperity as a market for early vegetables. Oyster farming has brought wealth to the region.

Place du Martray – In the centre of the town, the square retains fine 16C houses; note at the corner of rue de l'Église the house with a square corner turret where Loti used to stay and where Gaud, the heroine of *Pêcheur d'Islande*, lived.

Square Théodore-Botrel – In the square stands an isolated 18C bell-tower, all that remains of a former church, and a monument to the popular singer Théodore Botrel, who died in Pont-Aven in 1925.

Musée de la Mer ⊙ – *Rue de la Benne.* Paimpol's seafaring activity, from the time of the Icelandic fishing expeditions to the present day, is recalled by models, photographs and navigational instruments.

★★POINTE DE L'ARCOUEST

9km/5mi. Leave Paimpol north on D 789 and after 2km/1mi bear right on a dirt track.

Tour de Kerroc'h – This tower stands in a pretty wooded setting. From the first platform there is a fine **view**★ of Paimpol Bay.

Return to the road to the Pointe de l'Arcouest.

Ploubazlanec – In the cemetery is a wall on which the names of men lost at sea are recorded.

★★**Pointe de l'Arcouest** – On the way down to the creek of Arcouest there are remarkable **views** of the bay and of the Île de Bréhat at high tide. Each summer the place is invaded by a colony of artists and men of science and letters. A monument – two identical pink blocks of granite set side by side – has been erected to the memory of Frédéric and Irène Joliot-Curie, who were frequent visitors to Arcouest (below the car park, before the point's larger car park).

Loguivy-de-la-Mer – *5km/3mi north. Leave Paimpol towards the Pointe de l'Arcouest, then take D 15.*

This fishing port, the second in the Côtes d'Armor departement, is simply a creek in which boats are grounded at low tide.

Climb the promontory that encloses the creek on the left to get a view of the mouth of the River Trieux, Bréhat and the many islands.

★★**Île de Bréhat** – *From the Pointe de l'Arcouest allow 2-4hr to cross and visit Bréhat. See Île de BRÉHAT.*

★LA CÔTE DU GOËLO

Round tour of 47km/24mi – 4hr

Take D 786 south towards St-Quay-Portrieux and on leaving Paimpol, turn left.

Pointe de Guilben – This is the cliff mentioned in the song by Botrel. From the point which ends in a long spur cutting the cove of Paimpol in two, there is a lovely view of the coast.

After Kérity, a road to the left leads to the Abbaye de Beauport.

Hotels

BUDGET

Pension Bocher – *Rue P.-Loti, 22620 Ploubazlanec, 5km/3mi northeast of Paimpol –* ☎ *02 96 55 84 16 – closed 4 Nov-31 Mar –* 🅿 *– 15 rooms 160/300F – breakfast – 32F – restaurant 110/225F.* With its ivy covered façade, this little village hotel is unpretentious and has simple, well-kept rooms. The owners have been serving the same regional dishes in the dining room for years, and it has now acquired a pleasant familial air.

OUR SELECTIION

Relais Brenner – *Rue St-Julien, 5km/3mi on the route de Tréguier, at the Pont de Lézardrieux –* ☎ *02 96 22 29 95 – closed 1 Nov-14 Mar –* 🅿 *– 11 rooms 380/650F – breakfast 50F.* This inn amid a flower garden has been completely renovated, and is located close to the Trieux Bridge. From its panoramic salon, there is a beautiful view over the estuary. The spacious rooms have blonde parquet and lots of character.

Schooner outings

Le Vieux Copain – ☎ *02 96 20 59 30.* This wooden schooner takes up to 30 passengers for a sailing trip around the archipelago of Bréhat.

★**Abbaye de Beauport** ⊘ – Founded in the 13C by the Premonstratensians, the abbey was seen as an important spiritual and economic centre for the St-Brieuc diocese. Of the 13C and 14C church only the façade, open-air nave, north aisle and north arm of the transept remain. The long chapter-house with its polygonal apse, lying to the east of the cloisters, is an excellent example of the Anglo-Norman Gothic style, in the pure Mont-St-Michel tradition.

In the northwest corner of the cloisters, to the right of the three fine depressed arches, which stood above the lavabo, is the elegant entrance to the large refectory which looks out over the sea. Pass into the lower court overlooked by the Duc building, a huge hostelry for receiving the pilgrims, and the cellar underneath the refectory, whose groined vaulting rests on eight massive granite columns.

The tour ends with the almonership, the room in which the monks collected the tax on salt and cereals, and the visitor's hostel, with its two naves, where you can see an unusual box bed open on two sides.

The "*Conservatoire du Littoral*", a national body in charge of preserving France's coastal heritage, has acquired the abbey estate and implemented a programme aimed at protecting the premises and organising guided tours for visitors.

Return to the St-Quay road, turn left and past the pool, turn left again onto an uphill road.

Ste-Barbe – The sea can be seen from the small square of the chapel, the porch of which is decorated with a statue of St Barbara. A path *(car park)*, 250m/274yd further on takes you to a viewing table from where one can see beyond the meadow, Paimpol Bay and its nearby islands, the oyster beds, Port-Lazo and Mez du Goëlo Lighthouse.

At Plouézec, turn left and at St-Riom left again to Port-Lazo.

Port-Lazo – At the end of the road there is a view of Paimpol Bay.

Return to St-Riom; bear left.

★**Pointe de Bilfot** – From the viewing table, the **view** extends westwards to the Île de Bréhat and eastwards to Cap Fréhel. Between the small lighthouse at Mez du Goëlo nearby and Paon Lighthouse at Bréhat in the distance, the bay is studded with rocks.

Turn back and at the entrance to Plouézec, bear left.

★★**Pointe de Minard** – Make for this rocky platform which affords a wide **view** over St-Brieuc Bay and Cap d'Erquy, the Paimpol Cove and the Île de Bréhat.

After a picturesque run along the coast to Le Questel, bear left twice after the hamlet.

Pors Pin – A small creek with rocks curiously shaped by erosion.

Return to the first junction and make a left turn.

The road runs along the edge of the bare cliff offering glimpses of St-Brieuc Bay and leads to a **viewpoint** *(car park)*. The **view**★ extends over the site of Bréhec-en-Plouha, Pointe de la Tour, St-Quay rocks and the coast from Erquy to Le Val-André.

Bréhec-en-Plouha – A small harbour sheltered by a dike and a modest seaside resort at the bottom of a cove bounded by the Pointe de la Tour on the right and the Pointe de Berjule on the left. St Brieuc and the first emigrants from Britain landed at Bréhec in the 5C *(see Introduction: Historical table and notes)*.

Go up the green valley of the Kergolo stream.

Lanloup – The 15C-16C church has an interesting south porch *(see Introduction: Breton Art)* flanked by buttresses with niches and with St Lupus and St Giles standing on the pediment. The twelve Apostles, carved in granite, on ornate corbels precede the doorway topped by a 14C Virgin. In the cemetery are a cross (1758) and the tomb of the composer Guy Ropartz (1864-1955) in an alcove to the right of the porch.

Return to Paimpol via Plouézec.

Forêt de PAIMPONT★

Michelin map 59 fold 15 and 63 fold 5 or 230 folds 38 and 39

The Forest of Paimpont – the ancient "Brocéliande" where, according to the songs of the Middle Ages, the sorcerer Merlin and the fairy Viviane lived *(see Introduction: Tradition and Folklore)* – is all that remains in the east of the great forest which, in the early centuries of our era, still covered a large part of inner Brittany extending almost 140km/85mi. The cutting and clearing that went on for centuries have reduced the forest so that it now covers an area of only 7 067ha/27sq mi where 500ha/2sq mi belong to the state. Recently great areas have been replanted with conifers which will increase the industry of the massif.

A few charming corners remain, especially in the vicinity of the many pools.

BROCÉLIANDE, LAND OF LEGEND

This route leaves from St Léry and follows a round tour through the forest of Paimpont, past the best-known sites. In the wake of the great fire of September 1990, nature is gaining the upper hand, and, although some trees many centuries old have been lost forever, gorse, heather, broom and ferns are composing a new landscape, which clearly has its own charm. The reforestation of the areas destroyed by the fire will be completed this year.

St-Léry – On the south side of the 14C **church** is a Renaissance porch with two elegant basket-handle arched doors surmounted by delicately carved ogee mouldings. Sculpted figures frame the door on the right: the Virgin, the Angel Gabriel, St Michael slaying the dragon, and one of the damned. The leaves of the door are beautifully carved.

Inside, in the nave, is the 16C tomb of St Léry, and opposite it is a little bas-relief in sculpted wood depicting the life of the saint. The lovely Flamboyant chapel in the south side aisle is illuminated through a stained-glass window dating from 1493 which is dedicated to the Virgin Mary. Beneath the gallery, the clock can be seen through a glass door.

Near the church, note a 17C house decorated with three lovely dormer windows.

Château de Comper ○ – The Montforts, the Charettes, the Rieux, the Lavals, the Colignys, the La Trémoilles and the Rosmadecs are the great families who have at some point been the owners of this site where the fairy Viviane is supposed to have been born. This is also where she is said to have brought up Lancelot, the gallant Knight of the Round Table. The castle was destroyed twice, in the 14C and in the 18C, and all that now remains of it are two sections of curtain wall, the postern and a huge tower; the body of the main building was restored in the 19C. The castle is the headquarters of the Centre Arthurien, which organises exhibitions and events every year on the Celtic world, Arthurian legend or the Middle Ages.

Tombeau de Merlin – Merlin's tomb is indicated by two schist slabs and some holly.

Fontaine de Jouvence – Ordinary looking fountain said to have magic powers.

Étang du Pas-du-Houx – This lake, which is in a very pretty setting, is the largest in the forest (86ha/212 acres). Two châteaux were built on its shores in 1912: Brocéliande, in the Norman style, and Pas-du-Houx.

Paimpont – This market town, deep in the forest near a pool amid tall trees, dates back to the Revolution. It owes its origins to the founding of a monastery in the 7C which, raised to the status of abbey in the late 12C, survived until the Revolution. The 17C north wing houses the town hall and the presbytery.
The 13C abbey church was decorated in the 17C with richly ornate **woodwork**. Busts, carved medallions and festoons of fruit and flowers have been executed with remarkable skill. Note in particular the 15C and 16C statues, including one of St Judicaël, in stone, and a St Méen, in wood, the 16C high altar and some beautiful 17C woodwork. The **treasury** ⊘, in the sacristy, displays a statue of St Anne carrying the Virgin and Child (15C), an interesting arm reliquary of St Judicaël (15C) and, most importantly, a magnificent ivory Christ (18C).

Les Forges de Paimpont – This pretty hamlet, next to a lake, owes its name to the forges which were here between the 16C and late 19C. They were fuelled by iron ore and local wood and produced a highly valued metal.

Beignon – The church contains some beautiful 16C stained-glass windows. In the chancel, behind the altar, there are a representation of the Crucifixion of St Peter, and, in the north transept, that of the Tree of Jesse.

Château de Trécesson ⊘ – This castle, surrounded by a pool, was built at the end of the 14C in reddish schist and still has its original medieval appearance. A striking gatehouse flanked with corbelled turrets commands the entrance.

Tréhorenteuc – In the **church** ⊙ and sacristy, mosaics and pictures illustrate the legend of the Val sans retour and the Barenton fountain. In the chancel: stained-glass window of the Holy Grail; painting of the Knights of the Round Table.

Val sans retour – Known as the "Valley of No Return", this is one of the places most heavily steeped in legend in the Forêt de Paimpont. It can be found by taking the unsurfaced track, for pedestrians only, after the second car park. This leads to the Fairies' Mirror and False Lovers' Rock (Miroir des Fées et Rocher des Faux Amants). Legend has it that Morgana the witch, jealous of a knight who had been unfaithful to her, cast a spell over the valley preventing anyone who had done wrong from leaving it. Only Lancelot, who remained faithful to Guinevere, was able to break the spell. At the Fairies' Mirror, note the splendid **Golden Tree** (Arbre d'Or), the work of François Davin, which marks the furthest spot reached by the fire of 1990.

CANTON DE GUER-COËTQUIDAN

The Canton de Guer-Coëtquidan at the edge of the forest is home to the St-Cyr-Coëtquidan military academy and, further south, the Monteneuf megaliths.

École de St-Cyr-Coëtquidan – Coëtquidan military academy houses the training schools for elite officers of the land forces: the École Spéciale Militaire, founded in 1802 by Napoleon Bonaparte, commonly known as St-Cyr or Coët in military cir-

cles; the École Militaire Interarmes, founded in 1961 by Général de Gaulle; the École Militaire du Corps Technique et Administratif, founded in 1977 by President Giscard d'Estaing and the Bataillion des Élèves-Officiers en Réserve (EORs – Reserve Officers' Training Cadet Corps). A wide avenue, next to which, to the south of N 29, are statues of Bayard and Du Guesclin, leads to the modern buildings. On the lawns there are statues of the last four field marshals of France: Maréchal de Lattre de Tassigny, Maréchal Juin, Maréchal Koenig and Maréchal Leclerc.

★ **Musée du Souvenir** ⊙ – This museum, famed for its memorial ("France" by Antoine Bourdelle) in honour of 17 000 officers killed in action, is to the right of Cours Rivoli. It retraces the history of officer training from the Ancien Régime to the present and contains numerous documents, uniforms and military decorations connected with this elite.

P. Wysocki/EXPLORER

St-Cyriens

▣ **Site mégalithique de Monteneuf** ⊙ – Located on the moor lying between Guer and Monteneuf, this megalithic site is seen as one of the most important in central Brittany; it is currently being excavated and restored. More than 20 huge blocks of purple schist have been raised with the help of the Engineers from the nearby military college of Coëtquidan. A 9km/5.6mi long pedestrian itinerary takes you past the Loge Morinais (Morinais Hut – schist gallery graves), the Menhirs de Chomet, the Menhirs de Coëplan, the Bordoués (gallery grave) and Pierres Droites (Standing Stones – over 400 officially listed menhirs flanking the road D 776, thought to have been knocked down towards the end of the first millenium on the orders of the Church).

St-Méen-le-Grand – In the 6C, St Méen (Mewan), a monk from Great Britain, founded an abbey on this site, which was reconstructed several times from the 11C to the 18C. The abbey buildings now contain flats. The **church** retains a fine 12C square **tower**. Inside, note in the south aisle, the tombstone, and in the south transept, the statue and funerary monument of St Méen, all from the 15C. Some 13C and 14C frescoes recently discovered beneath the plasterwork are currently undergoing restoration.
In the cemetery, beside the church, are the saint's tomb, a basin, recumbent figures and tombstones.

Louison Bobet, the legendary cycling champion who won the famous Tour de France race several times in the early 1950s, was born in St-Méen, and a small museum is dedicated to his career.

PARISH CLOSES★★

See Les ENCLOS PAROISSIAUX

PERROS-GUIREC ♙♙

Population 7 497
Michelin map 59 fold 1 or 230 folds 6 and 7
Local map see CORNICHE BRETONNE

This much-frequented seaside resort (casino, seawater therapy centre), built in the form of an amphitheatre on the pink granite coast, overlooks the fishing and pleasure boat harbour, the anchorage and the two gently sloping, fine sand, sheltered beaches *(ideal for children)* of Trestraou and Trestignel.

Church ⊘ – A porch with delicate trefoil arches abuts onto the massive 14C belfry topped by a dome (1669) crowned by a spire. Go into the **Romanesque nave★**, all that remains of the first chapel built on the spot. Massive pillars, cylindrical on the left and with engaged columns on the right, support capitals which are either historiated or adorned with geometrical designs. It is separated by a diaphragm arch from the Gothic nave built in the 14C at the same time as the chancel. In this arch is a rood beam on which Christ is surrounded by the Virgin and St John. The church has a 12C granite stoup decorated with small figures and several old statues: an *Ecce Homo* (15C), St Lawrence and St Catherine (16C), St James, patron of the parish (17C). The round-arched south porch is richly ornamented.

Musée de Cire Chouannerie Bretonne ⊘ (**B M**) – This wax museum has reconstituted historical scenes with figures dating from La Chalotais to Auguste Renan. Note the collection of regional headdresses from Lower Brittany.

Pointe du Château – From this steep little viewpoint, there is a lovely **view★** over the site of Perros-Guirec, Sept-Îles, the Île Tomé and the coast as far as Port-L'Épine.

Viewing Table (Table d'orientation) (B E) – A splendid **view★** of the Pointe du Château, Trestignel Beach, Port-Blanc, Trélevern, Trévou, the Île de Tomé, Sept-Îles and of the rocks below.

EXCURSIONS

★★◪ **Le Sentier des Douaniers** – *3hr on foot there and back. The best time to go is in the morning, and if possible, at high tide.*
Follow the edge of the cliff as far as Pors-Rolland to reach the lighthouse via the Pointe de Squéouel, the Ploumanac'h lighthouse and the Maison du Littoral information centre.

Gaulle (R. Gén.-de)..... **A** 6
Joffre (R. du Mar.) ..... **B**
Le-Bihan (Bd J.) .... **A** 7
Leclerc (R. Gén.) .... **B** 9

Bons-Enfants (R.)....... **A** 2
Casino (Av. du).......... **A** 3
Foch (R. du Mar.)....... **A** 5
Le-Braz (R. A.) .... **B** 8
L'Héveder
(R. Sergent) .... **B** 10
Messe
(Chemin de la)........ **B** 12
Renan (R. Ernest)....... **B** 20
Rochellon (R. de) .... **A** 22

E Table d'orientation   **M** Musée de cire – Chouannerie bretonne

★★ Ploumanac'h – This little fishing port on the pink granite coast, belonging to the municipality of Perros-Guirec and well situated at the mouths of the two pictur-esque Traouiéros valleys, has become a well-known seaside resort, famous for its piles of **rocks★★**. You will get a good view of them by going to the lighthouse. The **Parc municipal★★** extends from Pors-Kamor, where the lifeboat is kept, to Pors-Rolland. It is a sort of reserve where the rocky site is kept in its original state. The most interesting feature is the Pointe de Squewel, formed of innumerable rocks separated by coves. The Devil's Castle (Château du Diable) also makes a fine picture.

The park is studded with curiously shaped rocks: note a turtle by the sea, and inland, a mushroom, a rabbit etc.

Hotels

BUDGET

Chambre d'hôte La Ferme de l'Étang – *22660 Tréleven, 9km/6mi from Perros-Guirec, route de Paimpol then D 73, towards Tréléven –* ☎ *02 96 91 70 44 – no credit cards – 4 rooms 250/300F*. Ducks frolic in the pond and strut around the lawn of this charming 19C rustic building. You will enjoy its tranquillity, its vast salon, its pleasant rooms, and its doll collection. Non-smokers only.

OUR SELECTION

Hôtel Europe – *In Ploumanac'h – 6km/4mi from Perros-Guirec on D 788 –* ☎ *02 96 91 40 76 – closed 4-17 Jan –* 🅿 *– 18 rooms 260/360F; breakfast 43F*. This hotel, flanked by a modern wing, is very close to the beach, and so allows you to take advantage of the particularly clear waters around Ploumanac'h. It is modern and functional. Attractive prices off-season.

TREAT YOURSELF!

Manoir du Sphinx – *67 chemin de la Messe –* ☎ *02 96 23 25 42 – closed 4 Jan-20 Feb –* 🅿 *– 20 rooms from 580F – breakfast 47F – restaurant 130/280F*. The garden of this elegant early-20C villa descends to the sea. Sea lovers will be absolutely delighted: all the modern and warmly decorated rooms as well as the restaurant have beautiful views of the sea and the nearby islands.

Eating out

BUDGET

Crémaillère – *Place de l'Église –* ☎ *02 96 23 22 08 – closed 15 Nov-2 Dec and Mon off-season – 98/189F*. In a 19C village house, this little restaurant spe-cialises in grilled meats, cooked in the fireplace in the dining room. The atmos-phere is warm with stone and wood walls. Children's menu.

Crêperie Les Vieux Gréements – *19 rue Anatole-Lebras, on the marina –* ☎ *02 96 91 14 99 – closed Mon Jan and Oct; Tues and Wed Nov-Mar – 40/80F*. Crêpes or mussels? In this 19C residence, you can choose dishes as well as decors. Downstairs, woodwork and portholes accentuate the maritime flavour; upstairs, wainscotting and a view of the port are good accompaniments for enjoying seafood.

Market

The **market** is held on place du Marché on Friday mornings.

Recreation

Beaches – There are two superb sheltered beaches: at Trestraou and at Trestrignel. Their fine sand and gentle slopes make them excellent beaches for children.

Scuba diving – *Perros-Plongée –* ☎ *02 96 23 22 13*. State-certified monitors will take you on scuba-diving outings.

Surfing – *Surf Club, 102 boulevard de la Corniche –* ☎ *02 96 91 46 20*. For novices or experts, at Trestraou beach.

Sailing – *Centre nautique –* ☎ *02 96 49 81 21*.

Schooner sailing - L'Argentilez – ☎ *02 96 23 25 62*. Sail along the Côte de Granit rose.

Casino – *9 boulevard Joseph-Le-Bihan –* ☎ *02 96 49 80 80*.

Municipal Park, Ploumanac'h

La Maison du Litoral ⊘ – This information centre has a variety of exhibits related to the formation of granite and the different methods for extracting and using this stone.

Beach – The beach lies in the bay of St-Guirec. At the far end on the left, on a rock washed by the sea at high tide, stands the oratory dedicated to St Guirec, who landed here in the 6C. A granite statue of the saint has taken the place of the original wooden effigy which had suffered from a disrespectful tradition: girls who wanted to get married stuck a pin into his nose.

Lighthouse – Go down to the beach, pass in front of the Hôtel St-Guirec and follow the uphill path to the lighthouse, passing among splendid **rocks★★**. Note the unusual shapes: a skull, a clog turned upside down, a foot. From the platform the view extends from Trégastel to the beach at Trestel and beyond it to the coast towards Port-Blanc, taking in Sept-Îles and the Presqu'île de Perros-Guirec.

La Clarté – *3km/2mi by ② on the town plan.*
The pretty rose granite **Chapelle Notre-Dame-de-la-Clarté★** stands 200m/219yd back from the road. In the 16C the lord of Barac'h, whose ship was in danger in fog off the coast, vowed to build a chapel to Our Lady at whatever spot on the coast that first emerged from the fog. The promised chapel was built on the height which enabled him to take his bearings; to commemorate the circumstances, it was called Our Lady of Light (Notre-Dame-de-la-Clarté). The south doorway is adorned with sculptures in low relief: on the lintel, an Annunciation and Pietà; two coats of arms and a Virgin and Child frame the mullioned window in the registry; under the porch are two 17C wood statues and 16C door panels. The tall nave includes three bays decorated with carved roses and foliage; the 15C stoup ornamented with three Moorish heads and the Stations of the Cross by Maurice Denis (1931) are noteworthy. A *pardon* is held every year *(see Calendar of events)*.

Take Rue du Tertre which starts on the north side of the chapel, leading to the top of a rocky knoll which affords a good **view★** over Pleumeur-Bodou and the Radôme and Planétarium, Ploumanach, Sept-Îles, Perros-Guirec and the Pointe du Château.

★★Signal Station (Sémaphore) – *3.5km/2.5mi west. Leave Perros-Guirec by ② on the town plan.*

Bellevue (Q. de) 2	Fournier (R. A.) 5
Centre (Pl. du) 3	Pointe (R. de la) 6
Centre (R. du) 4	Port (R. du) 7

From the roadside look-out point the **view**★ extends to the rocks of Ploumanach, seawards to Sept-Îles and behind to the beaches of Perros-Guirec, and in the distance along the Port-Blanc coastline.

BOAT TRIP

Sept-Îles ⊙ – *Boats tour the islands. The islands became a sea bird sanctuary in 1912.*

Rouzic – *Landing forbidden*. The boat goes near the island, also known as Bird Island, where a large **colony**★ of northern gannets, some 12 000 pairs, settle from February to September; they can be observed from Grande Island's ornithological centre (closed-circuit remote control television). One can see guillemots, razorbills, lesser and great black-backed gulls, puffins, crested cormorants, black-legged kittiwakes, oyster catchers and petrels all of which reproduce in March and leave at the end of July. Another interesting feature is the presence of a small colony of grey seals (around a dozen). The boat then skirts Malban and Bono Islands.

D'après photo Baranger /JACANA

Sept-Îles – A puffin

Île aux Moines – The boat stops at the island *(1hr)* where you may visit the old gunpowder factory, the **lighthouse** ⊙ (83 steps; range 40km/25mi) which offers a fine panorama of the islands and the coast, the ruined fort erected by Vauban on the far tip and below the former monastery with its tiny chapel and well. On the return journey, the curious pink granite rocks at the Pointe de Ploumanach come into view.

PLEYBEN★★

Population 3 446
Michelin map 58 folds 15 and 16 or 230 folds 18 and 19
Local map see Monts d'ARRÉE

The great feature of Pleyben is its magnificent parish close, built from the 15C to the 17C. *Pardon on the first Sunday in August.*

★★PARISH CLOSE *30min*

The monumental door was rebuilt in 1725.

★★**Calvary** – Built in 1555 near the church's side entrance, it was displaced in 1738 and given its present form in 1743. Since then new motifs and scenes have been added to the monument: the Last Supper and Washing of the Disciples' Feet date from 1650. The huge pedestal with triumphal arches enhances the figures on the platform.
To follow the life of Christ start at the corner with the Annunciation and move in an anticlockwise direction to discover the Nativity, the Adoration of the Shepherds etc.

★**Church** ⊙ – The church, dedicated to St Germanus of Auxerre, is dominated by two belfries, of which that on the right is the more remarkable. It is a Renaissance **tower**★★ crowned with a dome with small lantern turrets. The other tower has a Gothic spire linked to the corner turret at the balustrade level. Beyond the arm of the south transept is a curious quatrefoil sacristy, dating from 1719, with cupolas and lantern turrets.
Inside, the nave has 16C panelled **vaulting**★; the ribs and the remarkable **purlin** are carved and painted with mythological and religious scenes.
At the high altar is an altarpiece with turrets and a two storey tabernacle (17C). At the centre of the east end is a 16C **stained-glass window**★ depicting the Passion. Note the pulpit, the organ case (1688), the Baptism of Christ over the font and the many coloured statues including St Yves between the rich man and the pauper.

Chapelle funéraire – A former 16C ossuary where exhibitions are held. The façade of this funerary chapel is adorned with basket-handled twin arches.

Michelin's famous star ratings are allocated for various categories:
regions of scenic beauty with dramatic natural features
cities with an exceptional cultural heritage
elegant resorts and charming villages
ancient monuments and fine architecture
museums and galleries.

Presqu'île de PLOUGASTEL

Population 11 139

Michelin map 58 fold 4 or 230 fold 17

Lying away from main roads, Plougastel Peninsula is a corner of the Breton country-side, that may still be seen in its traditional guise.

Narrow, winding roads run between hedges through farming country, characteristi-cally cut up into squares. There are few houses apart from occasional hamlets grouped round their little chapels. Here everything seems hidden away; you are deep in the strawberry country, but you will not see the strawberries, which grow in open fields, unless you get out of your car and look through the gaps in the hedges. Vast glassed-in areas shelter vegetables and flowers.

In May and June, however, when the strawberries are picked, there is plenty of life on the roads; often you will come upon lorries fitted with open racks in which the little baskets of strawberries are carefully packed.

PLOUGASTEL-DAOULAS

★★**Calvary** – *See illustration p 39.* Built in 1602-4 to commemorate the end of the Plague of 1598, the Calvary is made of dark Kersanton granite and ochre stone from Logonna. It is more harmonious than the Guimiliau Calvary but the attitude of the 180 figures seems more stiff. On either side of the Cross, the two thieves (do not appear at Guimiliau) are surmounted by an angel and a devil respectively. On the Calvary base an altar is carved under a portico; above is a large statue of Christ leaving the tomb. The **church** ⊙ is built of granite and reinforced concrete; inside it is brilliant with blue, green, orange and violet, all used in its decoration. The furnishings include altars and wooden altarpieces.

Musée du Patrimoine et de la Fraise ⊙ – This museum of local history, traditions and ethnology contains various documents, objects, tools and items of furniture and clothing relating to everyday life from the 18C until the present. Displayed in more detail are the cultivation of linen and strawberries, and marine activities linked with exporting these two crops, as well as trawling for scallops in Brest Bay. The ground floor features the reconstruction of the inside of a late-19C peasant dwelling.

The first floor houses, in a glazed gallery, a beautiful collection of costumes, the oldest of which dates from 1820, and an interesting display window of the "*Breuriez*", a traditional ceremony which takes place every All Saints' Day, bringing together the members of a particular confraternity to honour their dead around an apple tree, the "*Gwezen an anaon*".

Chapelle St-Jean – *4.5km/3mi northeast on D 29 towards Landerneau and after crossing the Brest-Quimper expressway bear left then right.*
The 15C chapel, remodelled in the 17C, stands in a verdant **site**★ on the banks of the Élorn.

★PENINSULA

Round tour of 35km/22mi – 2hr

Leave Plougastel-Daoulas by a road to the right of the church; follow the signposts to Kernisi.

★**Panorama de Kernisi** – *At the entrance to the hamlet of Kernisi, leave the car and make for a knoll.* From here you will see a panorama of the Brest roadstead, the outer harbour and town of Brest, the Élorn estuary and the Pont Albert-Louppe.

Turn round and at the second main junction, bear right to-wards Langristin.

Chapelle Ste-Christine ⊙ – This 16C chapel possesses old statues in the north transept. There is a small Calvary dating from 1587.

Anse du Caro – From this pleas-ant setting, there is a view of Brest and Pointe des Espagnols, which forms the south shore of the Brest Sound.

Go back in the direction of Plougastel-Daoulas and after 3km/2mi, turn right.

★★Pointe de Kerdéniel – *15min on foot there and back. Leave the car at the bottom of Kerdéniel and after the houses turn right and take the lane on the left (signposts) to the blockhouse.* The view extends, from left to right, over Le Faou estuary, the mouth of the Aulne, Ménez-Hom, Île Longue, Presqu'île de Crozon's east coast to Pointe des Espagnols and Brest Sound.

Continue by car towards Pointe de l'Armorique to Porzmeur, a tiny fishing port in a pleasant setting.

Turn back and after 3km/2mi, bear right.

Lauberlach – A small fishing port and sailing centre in a pretty cove.

Take the road on the right towards St-Adrien.

From the hillside, the road gives fine glimpses of Lauberlach cove and passes the Chapelle St-Adrien (1549) on the right.

Then turn right towards St-Guénolé.

At Pennaster, go round Lauberlach cove. The Chapelle St-Guénolé (1514) stands in a wooded setting on the left side of the road.

At the first junction beyond St-Guenolé, take an uphill road on the right; turn right, then left onto a stony lane.

★Panorama de Keramenez – *Viewingtable.* An extensive panorama over the Presqu'île de Plougastel and the southern section of Brest roadstead.

Return to Plougastel-Daoulas by the fishing port of Tinduff, then Lestraouen and Lanriwaz.

PONT-AVEN★

Population 3 031
Michelin map 58 fold 11 or 230 fold 33

The town lies in a very pleasant setting at the point where the River Aven, after flowing between rocks, opens out into a tidal estuary. The Aven used to drive numerous mills, hence the saying: "Pont-Aven, a famous town; 14 mills, 15 houses". Today only one mill remains in operation. Pont-Aven is also famous for Galettes de Pont-Aven (butter cookies). It has been a favourite resort of painters; the Pont-Aven School, headed by Gauguin, was formed in about 1888. The poet and songwriter Théodore Botrel spent a great part of his life in Pont-Aven and is buried here. Botrel started the Festival of the Golden Gorse *(Fête des Fleurs d'Ajoncs – see Calendar of events).*

Pont-Aven School – Between 1886 and 1896 more than 20 painters (Charles Laval, Paul Sérusier, Charles Filiger, Maurice Denis...) grouped around Paul Gauguin seeking to invent new forms of artistic expression. The meeting between Paul Gauguin and Émile Bernard in 1888 was the beginning of the Synthetist group. Rejecting the Impressionist and Pointillist movements, their work was characterised by painting from memory, two-dimensional patterns, bright vivid colours and spiritual subjects.

Breton Women by Gauguin

Musée d'Orsay, Paris /RMN

PONT-AVEN

The Caisse Nationale des Monuments Historiques has set up **La Route des Peintres**, which includes five itineraries of one or two days each, described in a book of the same name *(available in English)*. The tours start in an art gallery, concentrating on the works of local and visiting artists in Cornouaille, 1850-1950, then take the visitor off to discover the landscapes which inspired the art.

SIGHTS

★ **Bois d'Amour** – *Access via Promenade Xavier-Grall.*
A footpath follows the meanders of the Aven and climbs the hillside. With the aid of maps produced by the tourist office, this pleasant walk unfolds to visitors the places which inspired the painters of the Pont-Aven School.

Promenade Xavier-Grall – *Access via rue Émile-Bernard.*
This promenade (named after the poet and reporter **Xavier Grall**, 1930-81), along the Aven, passes by the mill course and gates, which regulated the water to the mills, and old wash-houses scattered on either side of the river. Footbridges span the river, which winds between the Porche-Menu rocks.

The banks of the Aven – *30min on foot there and back. Walk to the right of the bridge towards the harbour.*
Follow the river bank lined with rocks and ruined watermills. On the river's east bank, there is an enormous rock called Gargantua's shoe *(soulier de Gargantua)*. In the square, beside the harbour, is a statue of Botrel and on the opposite bank, amid the greenery, stands the house where he lived. About 800m/875yd further on, there is a view of the fine stretch of water formed by the Aven. The once prosperous port (oysters, wine, salt and grain) is now used by pleasure boats.

Chapelle de Trémalo – *Access via rue Émile-Bernard and right on D 24, the Quimper road (signposted).*
This characteristic early-16C Breton country chapel is set amid fine trees. It has a lopsided roof, with one of the eaves nearly touching the ground. Inside is a 17C wooden Christ, which was the model for Gauguin's *Yellow* Christ where, painted in the background, is the village of Pont-Aven and Ste-Marguerite Hill.

Hotels

OUR SELECTION

Chambre d'hôte Château du Hénan – *Le Hénan, 29920 Névez, 4km/2.5mi route de Concarneau, then follow the indications on the route de Kerdruc –* ☎ *02 98 06 62 69 – no credit cards – 7 rooms 290/520F – breakfast 45F.* In its vast park, this 15C residence welcomes its guests in three beautiful rooms and several luxurious salons. The rooms in the caretaker's house are less luxurious, but still very pleasant.

Chambre d'hôte Kermentec – *1km/6mi route de Quimper, then by the Chapelle de Trémalo –* ☎ *02 98 06 07 60 – closed Dec-Jan – no credit cards – 3 rooms 260F.* Nestled in the upper reaches of Pont-Aven, this small ivy covered Breton house offers three spacious and comfortable rooms (to non-smokers only). The calm environment and the proximity to town make this a very enjoyable rustic stopover.

Eating out

BUDGET

Crêperie la Petite Tourte – *Rue de la Petite-Tourte –* ☎ *02 98 06 13 62 – closed Jan and Fri off-season – no credit cards – 40/80F.* You will feel perfectly at ease in this small *crêperie* located at the entrance to a narrow little street. Its intimate decor, pretty wooden tables, fireplace and stone walls full of paintings, evoke a family atmosphere.

OUR SELECTION

Moulin de Rosmadec – *Near the bridge in the centre of town –* ☎ *02 98 06 00 22 – closed 15-30 Nov, Feb, Sun evening off-season and Wed – 165/300F.* This mill is extremely popular! As much for its starred restaurant as for its four rooms which seem to be in constant demand. Everything about this place is charming: its beautifully preserved surroundings, its warm welcome, and its lovely location on the banks of the River Aven.

Shopping

Traou mad – An extensive choice of tinned goods and preserves. Among other things, La Boutique de Pont-Aven (place Gauguin) sells a delicious "bachelor's jam."

Museum (Musée) ⊘ – The modern wing is for temporary exhibits and the old wing recounts with photographs and documents the history of Pont-Aven: the town, port, Gorse-Bloom Festival, and the Pont-Aven painters and their lodgings (Pension Gloanec).

The first floor houses the permanent collection concentrating on the Pont-Aven School *(see above)*: Maurice Denis *(St John Bonfire at Loctudy)*, Émile Jourdan *(Trémalo Chapel)*, Rouillet *(The Port in Pont-Aven)*, Gustave Loiseau *(View of Pont-Aven)*, Henri Moret *(Seascape)*.

EXCURSIONS

Nizon – *3km/2mi northwest. Leave Pont-Aven by D 24 towards Rosporden.*
The small **church** (restored) with its squat pillars dates from the 15C and 16C and contains many old statues. The colours of the stained-glass windows by the master glazier Guével are remarkable. The Romanesque Calvary was used as a model by Gauguin for his *Green Christ.*

From Pont-Aven to Concarneau on the coast road – *45km/28mi – 1hr 30min. Leave Pont-Aven west on D 783, the Concarneau road and after 2.5km/1.5mi, turn left.*

Névez – In the **Chapelle Ste-Barbe** ⊘ there are some old wooden statues, in particular the large statue of St Barbara and her tower.

Beyond Névez, in the direction of Port-Manech, take the road on the left leading to Kerdruc.

Kerdruc – In a pretty **setting★** overlooking the Aven, this small port still has some old thatched cottages.

Port-Manech – Facilities. A charming resort with a well-sited beach on the Aven-Belon estuary. A path cut in the hillside links the port to the beach and offers fine views of the coast and islands.

Make for Rospico Cove via Kerangall. The rest of the excursion is described in the opposite direction see CONCARNEAU: Excursions.

PONT-L'ABBÉ

Population 7 374

Michelin map 58 folds 14 and 15 or 230 folds 31 and 32 – Local map see CORNOUAILLE

This town, which stands at the head of an estuary, owes its name to the first bridge *(pont)* built by the monks *(abbés)* of Loctudy between the harbour and the lake *(étang)*. It is the capital of the Bigouden district which is bounded by the estuary of the Odet, the coast of Penmarc'h and Audierne Bay. *Bigouden* costume is most original and is still worn, for example, during the Embroidery Festival *(Fête des Brodeuses)*, where it lends a picturesque note to the scene. Local specialities are embroidery and the making of dolls.

The shipyards (fishing and pleasure boats) also play a significant role in the town's activities.

SIGHTS

Église Notre-Dame-des-Carmes (B) – Former 14C chapel of the Carmelite monastery. On the right going in, stands an 18C font; the canopy comes from the Église de Lambour. Above the high altar is a 15C stained-glass window with a rose 7.7m/25ft in diameter. To the left, the Chapelle Ste-Anne is a modern processional banner; in the nave statues of the Virgin and St John, both of the 16C, flank Christ. As you come out, turn right to go round the church and look at the flat chevet crowned by an unusual domed belfry. *Pardon* on the Sunday after 15 July.

Château (B) – This 14C-18C fortress has a large oval tower or keep with a building attached. Go round the tower to see the turret overlooking rue du Château. Inside the keep you may visit the **musée Bigouden** ⊘ (taped commentary on each floor) housed on three floors *(79 steps)*, which has collections of Bigouden costumes, beautifully embroidered headdresses and 19C furniture (box beds, dressers, chests), models of boats, sailing equipment. The tour ends with a visit to a **Maison du Pays bigouden** *(see below)*.

Église de Lambour (B) – The ruined church retains a fine 16C façade and some bays of the 13C nave. The bell-tower was razed during a peasant revolt *(see below)*.

EXCURSIONS

Chapelle N.-D.-de-Tréminou ⊘ – *2km/1mi west on rue Jean-Moulin* **(A 19)**.
Standing in a shaded close this 14C and 16C chapel (restored) has a belfry which is set above the nave.

OUR SELECTION

Bretagne – *24 place de la République* – ☎ *02 98 87 17 22* – *closed 15 Jan-5 Feb* – *20 rooms 240/400F* – *breakfast* – *40F* – *restaurant 125/250F*. This attractive hotel in grey stone is located in the centre of town, on the market square. It is a pleasant stopover for families; the rooms may not be very big, but they are well kept, and the restaurant is warm and welcoming. Terrace in the summer.

BUDGET

Crêperie Bigoudène – *33 rue du Gén.-de-Gaulle* – ☎ *02 98 87 20 41* – *closed 15-30 Nov, 8-30 Jan, Sun and Mon except during school holidays* – *40/80F*. When you leave the château, take the commercial street to this rustic and pleasant crêperie.

Near this chapel, in 1675, the Cornouaille peasants in revolt adopted the "peasant code". Closely linked with the "stamped paper" revolt, this mass uprising was severely crushed and many bell-towers in the vicinity were razed to the ground in reprisal. A *pardon* takes place on the fourth Sunday in September.

Maison du Pays bigouden ⊙ – *2km/1mi on ② on the town plan, the road to Loctudy.*
A fine alley bordered by chestnut trees leads to the Ferme de Kervazégan. Built around the courtyard are the farmhouse and outbuildings (sheds, cowshed, pigsty, stable). The farmhouse is a solid squat building with dressed stone covered with lime; inside, the two rooms, which were lived in, are furnished with Bigouden furnishings (cupboards decorated with copper studs, box beds, longcase clock) and utensils (churn, creamer, salting tub).
In the outbuildings are the farm tools (apple crusher, press...).

★**Manoir de Kérazan** – The **manor house** ⊙ is situated in a large park full of tall trees and consists of a main building with large windows, which was rebuilt in the 18C, and a wing set at right-angles, dating from the 16C. The estate was bequeathed to the Institut de France by Joseph Astor in 1928. The rooms, richly decorated and furnished, bear witness to the luxurious setting the Astors aimed to create. Louis XV woodwork, both authentic and reconstructed, adorns the great hall, the billiards room, the corner room and the green hall. The dining room, decorated with painted panelling, contains a display of a number of works by **Alfred Beau** (1829-1907). This ceramic painter, who was associated with the Porquier de Quimper faience works (hence the well-known PB insignia), created many works of art from plates and trays, as well as by painting works on enamel which was then framed in either plain or carved wood, giving the impression that they were real paintings. The true masterpiece has to be the life-size cello made from polychrome faience, for which the manufacture process involved 15 different firings. The library is as it was arranged by Joseph Astor's father, mayor of Quimper and a great admirer of Beau; the furniture and the layout of the shelves have not been changed. As a whole, the rooms contain a collection of paintings and drawings in which Brittany and the Breton way of life in days gone by play an important role. Various Schools are represented, from the 16C to the 20C (Frans Francken, Charles Cotter, Lucien Simon, Maurice Denis). The tour ends in the blue hall, once a chapel, which houses the Astor family's memorabilia and a collection of 19C weapons.

Loctudy – Loctudy is a quiet little seaport and resort at the mouth of the River Pont-l'Abbé.
Port – An animated fishing port on weekday evenings, when the fishing fleet (prawns, burbot, sole and sea bass) comes sailing in.
A pretty view of the Île Chevalier, in Pont-l'Abbé estuary and Île-Tudy and its beach can be had from the quays.
Church – Dating from the beginning of the 12C and remodelled several times: the porch added in the 15C, its façade and belfry built in the 18C. In spite of the additions, the **interior**★ is elegant and well proportioned with its nave, chancel, ambulatory and radiating chapels in pure Romanesque style. Admire the capitals and column bases carved with small figures, animals, scrolls, foliage and crosses. In the cemetery to the left of the church, near the road, is the 15C Chapel of Pors-Bihan. Left of the lane leading to the church is a Gallic stele 2m/6ft high surmounted by a cross.

Boat trips ⊙ **to Île-Tudy** – From Loctudy, cyclists and pedestrians can sail to Île-Tudy, a fishing port which, despite its name, is not on an island, but a peninsula.

PORT-LOUIS★

Population 2 986
Michelin map 63 fold 1 or 230 fold 34

Port-Louis is a small fishing port and seaside resort where many of the inhabitants of Lorient may be found. It still has its 16C citadel, 17C ramparts, as well as several interesting old houses (rue de la Poste, rue des Dames, Petite Rue, rue du Driasker). Port-Louis was originally called Blavet. During the League, the Duke of Mercœur captured it with the help of the Spaniards. Forty young girls fled in a ship, but the Spaniards saw them and gave chase. Rather than be taken by the victorious enemy, all 40 girls joined hands and jumped into the sea.

It was under Louis XIII that Blavet took the name of Port-Louis in honour of the King. Richelieu made it a fortified port and the headquarters of the first India Company, which failed. When Colbert founded the second India Company, Lorient was built to receive it. From that time on, Port-Louis declined. Under Louis-Philippe the town found new life in sardine fishing and canning in oil.

The town has two **fishing harbours**: Locmalo in Gâvres cove and, opposite Lorient, La Point, a marina which has been equipped with 200 moorings for yachts.

★★CITADELLE *1hr 30min*

The citadel is at the entrance to the Lorient roadstead. Its construction occurred in different stages: in 1591, during the Spanish occupation by Juan del Aguila; continued in 1616-22, by Marshal Brissac and completed in 1636 under Richelieu. Built on a rectangular plan, the citadel is bastioned at the corners and sides; two bridges and a demilune protect the entrance. The citadel has always been a prison – among its "occupants" was Louis Napoleon, the future Emperor Napoleon III.

A signposted path directs you to the parapet walk (note the cannons facing the Île de Groix) which looks onto two courtyards and the different parts of the edifice of which some contain museums, the **Musées de la Citadelle** ⊘.

Musée du Port-Louis – In the entrance pavilion or keep. Exhibits trace the town's maritime past and the citadel's history.

★★**Musée de la Compagnie des Indes** – Housed in the new wing of the Lourmel barracks, this India Company Museum traces the history of this prestigious company from the founding of Lorient, its expansion in the 18C, its crews, cargoes, trading posts (in India, Africa, China), maps, furnishings and engravings.

One gallery concentrates on the theme of the India Company's fleet: shipbuilding, cargoes, models of *Comte d'Artois* (with cargo and passengers) and *Comte de Provence* (both built in the Lorient shipyards).

★**Salle de l'Arsenal** – Housed in the Arsenal, in a room which has fine woodwork, ship's models (corvettes, frigates, merchant ships, cruisers etc), portraits of seamen, paintings and documents pertaining to navigation on the Atlantic are on display. Reduced model of the *Napoleon's* (launched in Cherbourg in 1850) engine room.

Poudrière – The former Powder Factory contains 17C to 20C arms (torpedoes, mines, mortars, munitions etc) and documents on naval artillery.

Musée de la Compagnie des Indes, Port-Louis

Porcelain bowl

Musée de Bateaux – The Boat Museum focuses on a lifeboat, *Commandant Philippes de Kerhallet*, manned by 12 oarsmen, built in Le Havre in 1857 and used between 1897 and 1939 at Roscoff. Also on display are old and modern lifesaving equipment and several fishing boats.

Ramparts – Built between 1649 and 1653 by Marshal Meilleraye, these ramparts envelop the town on two sides. On Promenade des Pâtis, a door in the wall leads to a fine sandy beach from where there is a pleasant view onto the Pointe de Gâvres, Île de Groix, Larmor-Plage and the citadel's Groix bastion, named as such because it is across from the Île de Groix.

Presqu'île de QUIBERON★

Michelin map 63 folds 11 and 12 or 230 folds 35 and 49

This former island is now attached to the mainland by a narrow isthmus. This natural jetty acts as a breakwater for a great bay which is often used by warships for exercises and firing practice (Polygone de Gâvres).

The landscape of the peninsula varies; the sand dunes of the isthmus are fixed by maritime pines. The ocean coast, known as the "Wild Coast" (Côte Sauvage), is an impressive jumble of cliffs, rocks, caves and reefs; to the east and south are wide beaches and two lively fishing ports.

Hoche repels the exiles (July 1795) – Quiberon saw the rout of the Royalists in 1795. The French exiles in England and Germany had made great plans; 100 000 men, led by the princes, were to land in Brittany, join hands with the Chouans and drive out the "Blues". In fact, the British fleet which anchored in the Quiberon roadstead carried only 10 000 men, commanded by Puisaye, Hervilly and Sombreuil. The princes did not come. The landing began on the beach at Carnac on 27 June and continued for several days. Cadoudal's Chouans joined them. But the effect of surprise was lost; long preparations and talk among the exiles had warned the Convention; **General Hoche** was ready, and he drove the invaders back into the peninsula. Driven to the beach at Port-Haliguen, the exiles tried to re-embark. Unfortunately, the British ships were prevented by a heavy swell from getting near enough to land and the Royalists were captured. The Convention refused to pardon them. Some were shot at Quiberon and others were taken to Auray and Vannes and shot there.

TOUR

⌂ **Quiberon** – At the far end of the peninsula, Quiberon is a popular resort with its fine south-facing sandy beach and proximity to the Côte Sauvage. **Port-Maria**, which is the departure point for boat services to Belle-Île, Houat and Hœdic, is a busy harbour and a fishing port where a few sardine boats can still be seen. Some of the catch is marketed to be eaten fresh; the rest is canned in the local factories.

★★ 1 **ROUND TOUR OF LA CÔTE SAUVAGE**

18km/11mi – 2hr

Go to Port-Maria and bear right onto the coast road (signposted "route côtière").

This wild coast is a succession of jagged cliffs where caves, crevasses and inlets alternate with little sandy beaches with crashing rolling waves (bathing prohibited; ground swell).

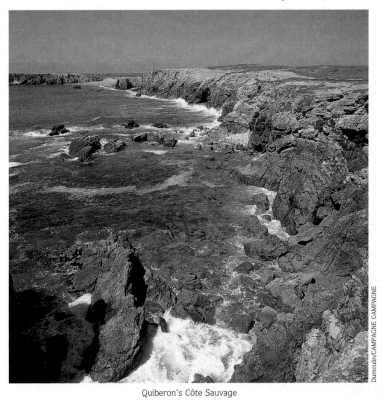

Quiberon's Côte Sauvage

Rocks of all shapes and sizes edge the coast, forming passages and labyrinths in which the sea boils and roars.

Small granite steles line the road on the left and mark the main sights: Port-Pilote, Trou du Souffleur, Pointe du Scouro, Grotte de Kerniscob etc which should be seen on foot.

Beg er Goalennec – Go around the Café Le Vivier and over the rocks to reach the tip of the promontory from where there is a pretty view over the whole length of the Côte Sauvage.

After Kroh-Kollé, bear left.

The road runs downhill towards **Port-Bara**, a cove prickling with rocks, before going inland. Surfaced roads lead to Port-Rhu and Port-Blanc; the latter has a nice white sandy beach.

★**Pointe du Percho** – *Go on foot to the tip of the point.* A lovely **view**★ opens out, on the left, to the Côte Sauvage, on the right, to the Isthme de Penthièvre, its fort and beach, and beyond the islands of Belle-Île and Groix.

The last stele indicates Beg en Aud, the furthest point on this coastline.

Cross Portivy and drive to St-Pierre-Quiberon.

St-Pierre-Quiberon – This resort has two beaches on either side of the small port of Orange. Take rue des Menhirs to see the St-Pierre lines made up of 22 menhirs on the right.

Beg-Rohu – Rocky home of the **École nationale de Voile** (National Sailing School).

Return to the main road and turn left for Quiberon.

② ROUND TOUR OF POINTE DU CONGUEL

6km/4mi – 1hr 30min

Leave Quiberon to the east by boulevard Chanard.

Drive round the **Institut de Thalassothérapie** – salt-water cures for arthrosis, rheumatism, over-exertion and the after-effects of injuries.

Pointe du Conguel – *Viewing table. 30min on foot there and back.* From the tip of the point there is a view of Belle-Île, Houat and Hœdic Islands, the Morbihan coast and Quiberon Bay. Teignouse Lighthouse, near which the battleship France, which sank in 1922 after striking a reef, can also be seen.

Go to Port-Haliguen.

Hotels

OUR SELECTION

Hôtel Petite Sirène – *15 boulevard R.-Cassin* – ☎ *02 97 50 17 34* – *closed 21 Oct-31 Mar* – ▣ – *14 rooms 342/533F* – *breakfast* – *42F* – *restaurant 100/320F*. This modern hotel, located between the centre of town and the thalassotherapy centre, faces the sea. Its neat and tidy rooms open their windows and small balconies onto sea views. Don't miss the restaurant, it is an important culinary stop in the area.

Eating out

BUDGET

Relax – *27 boulevard Castero, at the Plage de Kermorvan* – ☎ *02 97 50 12 84* *–closed 1 Jan-15 Feb, Sun evening Oct-Dec, and Mon except in summer* – *78/190F*. This recently opened seafood restaurant is located on the coast with sea views. All the tables on its two levels are turned towards the ocean and the terrace which is open in good weather.

Crêperie La Closerie St-Clément – *36 rue St-Clément* – ☎ *02 97 50 40 00* – *45/100F*. Behind the Palais des Congrès, This pretty traditional Breton establishment welcomes you into its half-pub, half-bistro ambience. Pleasantly seated in your armchair, you'll linger over the crêpes and seafood served at this congenial crêperie.

Le Vivier – *Beg er Groalennec (Côte sauvage)* – ☎ *02 97 50 12 60* – *closed Nov-Jan and Mon off-season* – *80/150F*. Perched on the rocky Côte Sauvage, this bar is for shellfish lovers. You can enjoy them on its veranda, while admiring the spectacular view of the ocean.

Thalassotherapy

Institut de Thalassothérapie – *Between Quiberon and la Pointe de Conguel* – ☎ *02 97 50 20 00*. This institute treats arthritis, rheumatism, and other health problems with sea-water therapy. You may also frequent it simply to enjoy its other offerings such as the dietetic, body tonic or beauty programs.

On the left there is an aerodrome with a runway for light aircraft. Beyond Fort-Neuf, note the bustle created on the beach by the various sailing clubs and schools. The view opens out over the bay and the Morbihan coastline. Pass on your right, an obelisk commemorating the surrender of the exiles in 1795.

Port-Haliguen – A small fishing and pleasure boat harbour (summer regattas). *Return to Quiberon by rue de Port-Haliguen.*

③ ISTHME DE PENTHIÈVRE

This provides road and rail links between the former island and the mainland.

Fort de Penthièvre – Rebuilt in the 19C, it commands the access to the peninsula. A monument and a crypt commemorate 59 members of the Resistance shot here in 1944.

Penthièvre – This small resort has two fine sandy beaches on either side of the isthmus.

Plouharnel – Located at the edge of Bego Cove, the **Galion de Plouharnel** ⊘ a modern replica of an 18C galleon, displays a collection of shells and shell pictures including the Piazza San Marco in Venice, a Japanese pagoda etc.
On the opposite side of the road, in an old blockhouse, is the **Musée de la Chouannerie** ⊘. The Chouannerie movement, a Breton Royalist revolt, is recounted with dioramas peopled with terracotta figures, depicting the movement's main antagonists and Chouan arms, costumes, guillotine etc.

The length of time given in this guide
  – for touring allows time to enjoy the views and the scenery;
  – for sightseeing is the average time required for a visit.

QUIMPER★★

Conurbation 59 437
Michelin map 58 fold 15 or 230 fold 18 – Local maps see CORNOUAILLE
and Excursions below

The town lies in a pretty little valley at the junction (*kemper* in Breton) of the River
Steir and River Odet. This used to be the capital of Cornouaille, and it is here, perhaps,
that the traditional atmosphere of the province can best be felt. The **Festival de
Cornouaille★** *(see Calendar of events)* is an important folk festival.

HISTORICAL NOTES

St Corentine's fish – For centuries the town was called Quimper-Corentin, after its
first bishop. According to legend, Corentine lived on the flesh of a single, miraculous
fish. Every morning he took half the fish to eat and threw the other half back into
the river. When he came back the next day the fish was whole once more and offered
itself to be eaten again. Corentine was the adviser and supporter of King Gradlon.

Four men of Quimper – The statue of **Laënnec** (1781-1826) commemorates the most
illustrious son of Quimper – the man who invented the stethoscope *(see
DOUARNENEZ: Ploaré)*.
Streets are named after Kerguelen, Fréron and Madec, three other famous men of
Quimper. **Yves de Kerguelen** (1734-97) was a South Seas explorer; a group of islands
bears his name. **Élie Fréron** (1718-76) was a critic, bitterly opposed to Voltaire and
other philosophers. **René Madec** (1738-84) was a hero of adventure. As a cabin boy in
a ship of the India Company, he jumped overboard and landed at Pondichéry. He
served a rajah and became a successful man. The British found a relentless enemy in
him. When he returned to France, enormously rich, the king gave him a title and the
Cross of St-Louis, with a colonel's commission.

QUIMPER FAÏENCE

Over the centuries, the evolution of Quimper faience has been enriched by numerous con-
tributions giving fresh impetus to its production and encouraging creativity, with the result
that it impossible to talk of any one particular style when discussing this art form.

A dynasty of faience makers – In 1690, a southerner, Jean-Baptiste Bousquet, a
faience maker from St-Zacharie near Marseilles, settled on the site which was to
become Locmaria, a suburb of Quimper on the banks of the Odet, where it has been
revealed that potters were active as early as the Gallo-Roman era. Bousquet founded
the first Quimper faïence works, where he adopted his favoured style from Moustiers
faience ware. His son Pierre succeeded him in 1708 and associated himself with a
faience maker from Nevers, Pierre Belleveaux, and later on with a faience maker from
Rouen, Pierre-Clément Caussy. Both were to play an important role in the evolution
of Quimper faience, one by enriching it with new shapes, colours (yellow) and Nevers
decorative motifs, the other by introducing rich iron red to the Quimper palette and
adding some 300 decorative designs (tracings). It is this blend of expertise and
working methods handed down to Quimper "painters" over the centuries which has
made Quimper, now a real guild centre for this craft, the seat of an artistic production distinguished by the diversity of style it encompasses. Two more faience works
were established in Quimper towards the end of the 18C, Porquier faience works,
founded by François Eloury c 1772 and with which the name of **Alfred Beau** is linked,
and Dumaine faience works, over which Jules Henriot assumed directorship in 1884.
It was c 1840 that faience ware decorated with Breton motifs appeared (such as the
"little Breton", a caricature character which was to usurp traditional motifs), and that
production began to be industrialised. The series of "Breton Scenes" created by A Beau
was inspired by tales and engravings, and his later series of "Breton Legends" met
with resounding success.
The techniques currently in use at Quimper are directed towards decoration entirely
done by hand, which demands considerable manual dexterity.

The Age of Artists – The creativity of artists, both associated with and independent from
the faience works, allied itself with spirit of enterprise and the faience makers' craft, giving
rise to unique works of art. Under the encouragement of Jules Verlingue, one of the last
great directors of the "Grande Maison" faience works, production took a new direction,
laying greater emphasis on inventiveness and attracting in this way a long succession of
artists from 1920 onwards. One of the first, **René Quillivic** (1879-1969), sculptor and
ceramic painter, produced some striking works with designs based on woodcuts.
The "*Ar Seiz Breur*" ("Seven Brothers" – a reference to seven Breton heros) movement was founded in 1923 by René-Yves Creston, Jeanne Malivel and Jorg Robin with
the aim of modernising traditional Breton folk art by combining it with Art Deco and
Cubism. Many of the works produced by the artists who were members of this movement can be seen in exhibitions on this period.
The Odetta trademark, registered in 1922, produced works in sandstone, in dark tones
made iridescent with enamel. Artists whose signatures adorn such work include Georges
Renaud, René Beauclair, one of the most prolific, Louis Garin, Paul Fouillen and Jacques
Nam, whose passion for cats earned him the task of illustrating Colette's *Dialogue de
bêtes* (conversations between Toby-chien the dog and Kiki-la-doucette the cat, 1904).

QUIMPER

B   Faïencerie de Quimper
    H.-B. Henriot
K   Jardin de l'évêché
M¹ Musée départemental breton

M² Musée de la faïence
M³ Musée des Beaux-Arts
N   Église N.-D. de Locmaria
Q   Église de Kerfeunteun

★★ CATHÉDRALE ST-CORENTIN ⊘ (BZ) *1hr 30min*

This fine Gothic cathedral was built from the 13C (chancel) to the 15C (transept and nave). The two steeples were only erected in 1856, being modelled on the Breton steeple of Pont-Croix. To pay for their building the bishop asked the diocese's 600 000 faithful to each subscribe one sou a year for five years. The sea air quickly toned down the new stone, and it is difficult to believe that the upper part of the façade was erected four centuries later than the lower part.

After seeing the north side of the building, look at the façade. Between the spires stands the statue of a man on horseback: this is King Gradlon. Until the 18C, on 26 July each year, a great festival was held in his honour. A man would climb up behind him, tie a napkin round his neck and offer him a glass of wine. Then he drank up the wine himself, carefully wiped the King's mouth with the napkin and threw the empty glass down on the square.

Any spectator who could catch the glass as it fell received a prize of 100 gold écus, if the glass was not broken. It used to be said that to save money the Town Council had a few sawcuts made in the stem of the glass.

Enter through the main door.

During the League, in the 16C, the nave was used as a place of refuge by the local people. Mass was said there among palliasses, boxes and hanging linen. Plague broke out there, killing 1 500 people.

The first thing that strikes you on entering the church is the fact that the choir is quite out of line with the nave due to the presence of a previous building. One theory is that in the early 13C, the cathedral craftsmen incorporated a small sanctuary, separated from the old Romanesque chancel by an alley and set off to the left, as the apsidal chapel. The new chancel linked this "chapel" to the nave.

The cathedral has a remarkable set of 15C **stained glass**★★ in the upper windows, mainly in the nave and transept, depicting canons, lords and ladies surrounded by their patron saints.

The tourist, going round the fine 92m/302ft long building, will see in the side chapels, tombs (15C), altars, frescoes, altarpieces, statues, old (St John the Baptist, 15C alabaster) and modern works of art, a 17C pulpit adorned with low-relief sculptures relating the life of St Corentine, and in the chapel beneath the south tower an Entombment copied from that in Bourges Cathedral and dating from the 18C.

★OLD QUIMPER *2hr 30min*

The old district stretches in front of the cathedral between the Odet and the Steir. Rue du Parc along the Odet leads to Quai du Steir. This small tributary has now been canalised and covered before its confluence with the Odet, to form a vast pedestrian precinct. Note on the right, the elegant covered market, rebuilt in 1979 after a fire.

Quimper – Rue Kéréon

From the bridge, there is a lovely view upstream of the Steir lined with flower-bedecked houses.

Place Terre-au-Duc (AY 54) – A picturesque square lined with old half-timbered houses. This was the lay town opposite the episcopal city and included the Law Courts, prison and the Duc de Bretagne market.

Take rue St-Mathieu (**AZ 47**) which has some fine houses, then cross the square diagonally. Bear right to cross the Steir by the bridge from which there is a lovely view with Mount Frugy in the distance.

★**Rue Kéréon (ABY)** – A busy shopping street. The cathedral and its spires between the two rows of old corbelled houses make a delightful picture.

Turn left into rue des Boucheries then right into rue du Sallé.

Rue du Sallé (BY 52) – Note the beautiful old house of the Mahault de Minuellou family.

Cross the tiny place au Beurre to reach **rue Élie-Fréron**; walk up to no 22 to admire a corbelled house with a slate roof, and a Renaissance porch at no 20.

Go down to the cathedral.

At the entrance to the square, on the right, opens **rue du Guéodet (BY 16)** where a house with caryatids and figures of men and women in 16C costume stands. On the left, in the square itself, stands the town hall, which houses the Musée des Beaux-Arts.

★★**Musée des Beaux-Arts ⊘ (BY M³)** – This Fine Arts Museum, housed behind an undamaged 19C façade, has been entirely rebuilt following categorically modern architectural principles, based on the idea of transparency. It contains a collection of paintings representing European painting from the 14C to the present. The museum has its own unique atmosphere, largely due to the mixing of natural and artificial lighting, in which it is possible to view the works in – quite literally – a new light. On the ground floor, two rooms are devoted to 19C Breton painting: *A Marriage in Brittany* by Leleux; *A Street in Morlaix* by Noël; *Potato Harvest* by Simon; *Widow on Sein Island* by Renouf; *Flight of King Gradlon* by Luminais and *Fouesnant Rebels* by Girardet. One room is devoted to **Max Jacob** (1876-1944), who was born and grew up in Quimper. His life and work are evoked through literature, memorabilia, drawings, gouaches, and in particular a series of portraits signed by his friends Picasso, Cocteau and others.

At the centre of the first floor, the architect **J-P Philippon** designed an area fitted in pale beech wood to set 23 paintings from the dining room of the Hôtel de l'Épée, executed by the painter **Lemordant** (1878-1968). The area around the edges displays the work of different European Schools up to the contemporary period: Flemish (**Rubens, Van Schriek**); Italian (**Bartolo di Fredi**); Spanish; and French. Note in particular works by **Boucher, Fragonard, Van Loo,** *View of the Château de Pierrefonds* by **Corot** and *View of Quimper Harbour* by **Boudin**.

★**Musée départemental breton ⊘ (BZ M¹)** – This museum, devoted to regional history (archeology, ethnology, economy), occupies what used to be the episcopal palace, a large edifice built from the 16C to the 19C adjoining the cathedral.

The rooms have been wonderfully restored and are now galleries arranged both chronologically and thematically.

After a brief display on prehistory, the visitor enters the first rooms devoted to the environment and way of life in one of the Gallo-Roman cities of the Osismes: coins, monumental mosaics, vases and funerary urns, silverware, figurines of Venus and mother-goddesses etc.

The medieval section displays, among other things, a stone likeness of King Marc'h, Romanesque capitals, and tomb stones, including the magnificently sculpted tomb-stone of Grallon de Kervaster.

The galleries of medieval and modern statues bring to mind the various religious cults which inspired this art form. The display includes two large 16C stained-glass windows.

Devoted to an exhibition on the theme "Ils ont des chapeaux ronds... Vêtements et costumes en Basse-Bretagne" (They have round hats... Clothing and costumes of Lower Brittany), the following galleries contain traditional folk dress worn every day and during festivals.

The galleries which contain furniture retrace the history (17C-20C) of the domestic space occupied by folk furniture and the use to which it was put, from the grain and linen chests of Léon to the "petits meubles" mementoes by Plovézet. It is particularly interesting to see the role played by the cupboard in both the marriage ritual and in the attempt to create a "modern Breton piece" between the World Wars.

The final section is devoted to Quimper faience and displays a rich collection of exhibits dating from the 18C to the present, illustrating the evolution of this decorative art form which reflects at once everyday life, creative spirit and perhaps even the dreams of an entire region.

Le Pardon de Kergoat by Jules Breton

The museum regularly houses temporary exhibitions.

The Rohan tower houses a remarkable large **spiral staircase**★ ending under a magnificent carved oak canopy.

Jardin de l'évêché (**BZ K**) – Situated between the cathedral and ramparts, the garden offers a good **view**★ of the cathedral chevet and spires, the Odet lined by the Préfecture with its ornate dormer windows, the former Ste-Catherine hospital and Mont Frugy.

Some vestiges of the old ramparts can be seen in boulevard de Kerguélen (**BZ 23**) and rue des Douves (**BY**).

ADDITIONAL SIGHTS

★ **Musée de la faïence** ⊘ (**AX M²**) – *Start your tour on the first floor.* This faience museum, located on the banks of the Odet, is in the old Maison Porquier dating from 1797. It contains a rich collection of almost 2 500 items which it displays in rotation, retracing on two floors several centuries of the history of Quimper and its faience. Passing the riot of shapes and colours as one room succeeds another enables the visitor to appreciate the diversity of style in the Quimper faience production, as well as to follow its evolution. The tour also explains the craft itself, giving details of techniques, artists and anonymous craftsmen (throwers, kiln-chargers and painters), to whom the museum pays homage in the form of a tall, colourful bas-relief.

The first two rooms are given over to the sequence of stages in the manufacturing process and to the tools and materials used. The marvellous works displayed in the following two rooms illustrate the blend of different styles: Rouen, with essentially floral motifs (floral basket is a particularly popular subject), vivid and varied colours (including the red unique to this area, which comes from a clay rich in iron oxide); Nevers, with biblical or mythological scenes, blue monochromes, two distinctive yellows (one from a lead antimony base, the other, stronger, from a uranium oxide base), the technique of decorating on fixed white (enamel), at a stroke (the paint brush produces both shape and colour in a single application).

Dish decorated with Breton figures, HB faience works (late 19C)

241

Hotels

BUDGET

Hôtel Coudraie – *Impasse du Stade, 29700 Pluguffan, 7km/4.2mi from Quimper, road to Pont-l'Abbé and D 40* – ☎ *02 98 94 03 69 – closed end Oct, mid-Feb, and Sun in winter* – 🅿 – *11 rooms 220/280F – breakfast 32F.* This small modern hotel in a garden seems like a family residence, and indeed the owners will give you a warm and friendly welcome. The rooms are simple and clean, and the prices are very reasonable.

OUR SELECTION

Hôtel Mascotte – *6 rue Th.-Le-Hars* – ☎ *02 98 53 37 37 – 63 rooms 345/490F – breakfast 42F – restaurant 80/95F.* The most recent hotel in the city centre. Well-designed and functional, all its rooms are large, but those in the front are more spacious and soundproof. A nice welcome and good quality for the price.

Eating out

BUDGET

Café de l'Epée – *14 rue du Parc* – ☎ *02 98 95 28 97 – 85/149F.* Many famous film and theatre actors, writers and politicians have frequented this local institution. The brasserie offers a variety of dishes: shellfish, fish, choucroutes and meats.

Crêperie du Guéodet – *6 rue du Guéodet* – ☎ *02 98 95 40 38 – closed 1-22 Oct, 8-23 Mar, Sun and Mon evening - no credit cards – 35/75F.* This tiny crêperie is very popular with the locals who enjoy the crêpes made with organic flour, and the simple and convivial atmosphere. If no tables are available, take a stroll around the old part of Quimper, and come back a little later.

Salon de thé Boule de Neige – *14 rue des Boucheries* – ☎ *02 98 95 88 22 – closed in the evening and on Mon off-season – 40/60F.* This establishment is famous for its pastries, made by one of the "best artisans in France". In addition to its tea salon offerings, a small section of savoury tarts and salads is available at lunchtime. Try the house speciality, "the Torchette."

Night-life

Le Ceili – *4 avenue Aristide-Briand* – ☎ *02 98 95 17 61 – daily 6pm-1am.* More Breton beer (850 hectolitres in 1998) is consumed in this bar than almost anywhere else! In fact, there's nothing extraordinary about this rather plain-looking spot... nothing except the legendary graciousness of its owners, who have been shaking hands with each and every customer for 20 years now.

Molly Malone – *8 rue de Falkirk* – ☎ *02 98 53 40 42 – daily 11am-1am.* This is definitely one of the most beautiful bars in Brittany. It was built by a Breton carpenter who was enamoured of the legend of Molly Malone, a 14C character

The ground floor is reserved for 20C production concentrating on that from the period between the World Wars, which was particularly varied and prolific: from the shapes, colours and complex motifs by Quillivic or **Mathurin Méheut** to the highly refined ones of René Beauclair, or even the very original works by Giovanni Leonardi, to name but four artists.

The final gallery houses exhibitions on various themes.

Faïenceries de Quimper HB Henriot ⊘ (**AX B**) – Tour of the faience workshops.

Église Notre-Dame-de-Locmaria (**AX N**) – This Romanesque church, rebuilt in the 15C and then later restored, is on the banks of the Odet. The plain interior contains, in the north side aisle, three tombstones dating from the 14C, 15C and 17C, and, on the rood beam, a robed Christ. In the south side aisle, a door leads to the garden of the old Benedictine priory (16C-17C) which has a cloistral gallery dating from 1669 and two 12C arches.

Mont Frugy (**ABZ**) – From place de la Résistance a path *(30min on foot there and back)* leads to the top of this wooded hill, 70m/22ft high. From the look-out point there is a good **view★** of the city.

Église St-Mathieu (**AY**) – This church, rebuilt in 1898, retains a fine 16C stained-glass window of the Passion halfway up the chancel.

EXCURSIONS

① From the banks of the Jet to the Odet
Round tour of 27km/17mi – 2hr 30min

*Leave Quimper on avenue de la Libération (**BX 25**), at the first major roundabout, turn left on the road to Brest and take the second road to the right to Coray. 700m/766yd further on, take the road towards Elliant.*

in Dublin who sold fish by day and her charms by night ("singing cockels and mussels, alive, alive-o"). Around 12.30am every night, the bar's last song is dedicated to her.

Manoir du Kinkiz – *Chemin du Quinquis* – ☏ *02 98 90 20 57* – *Tues-Sat 9am-12.30pm, 13pm-6.30pm.* This family run cider shop has existed for five generations. Tours of the orchard and the cider cellar are available, as well as free tasting of various apple juices and ciders.

Cultural Activities

Théâtre de Cornouaille – *4 place de la Tour-d'Auvergne* – ☏ *02 98 55 98 55* – *theatrequimper@eurobretagne.frwww.bagadoo.tm.fr/fr/culture/theatre* – tickets and information Tues-Sat 2pm-7pm. Quimper's new national stage theatre offers music and dance concerts and plays ...

Le Quartier – *10 parc du 137ᵉ-RI, opposite the Théâtre de Cornouaille.* Quimper's contemporary art centre organises very high quality changing exhibitions and cultural events. Program available from the tourist office or from Le Quartier.

Information about other cultural activities and events – Consult the newspapers, *Le Télégramme de Brest* (Wednesday edition) and *Ouest-France* (Quimper edition).

Urban transport

By bus – Individual tickets (6F) are valid for 1hr, and can be bought from the bus driver; daily ticket *("le ticket journée")* costs 18F and can also be bought from the bus driver, or from the Welcome Center QUB (2 quai de l'Odet).

Recreation

Aquarive – *Boulevard de Creac'h Gwen* – ☏ *02 98 52 00 15* – *outside of school holidays, Mon, Thur 1pm-8pm, Tues, Fri noon-10pm, Wed 10am-8pm, Sat 11am-8pm, Sun 9am-7pm; during school holidays, Mon, Wed, Thur, Sat 10am-8pm, Tues, Fri 10am-10pm, Sun. 9am-7pm.* A nautical complex with a wave machine, a 60m/195ft water slide, jacuzzis, saunas and solariums ...

Canoë-kayak – *Base nautique de Locmaria, 34 route de Bénodet* – ☏ *02 98 53 33 65.* Canoeing and kayaking on the River Odet and even in the city centre.

The festival of Cornouaille★ – ☏ *02 98 55 53 53.* This important and festive folkloric event takes place in July; its music and displays of popular traditions attract over 250 000 visitors a year.

Schooner outings: Gouelia – ☏ *02 98 65 10 00.* This association organises outings on its flotila of schooners, some of which sail to the Îles de Glénan.

The road runs beside the River Jet and offers views of the wooded countryside and pastureland.

Ergué-Gabéric – In the chancel of the early-16C church there is a stained-glass window depicting the Passion (1571) and a 17C group of the Trinity. The organ loft dates from 1680.

Bear right after the church towards the Chapelle de Kerdévot.

Chapelle de Kerdévot ⊙ – The 15C chapel stands in an attractive setting near a Calvary, which is of a later date and unfortunately somewhat damaged. Inside, a late-15C Flemish **altarpiece★** standing on the high altar depicts six scenes from the life of the Virgin. There is a 17C statue of Our Lady of Kerdévot in painted wood in the nave.

Leave Kerdévot by the road on the left of the chapel, then turn left towards Quimper. After 3km/2mi turn right towards the hamlet of Lestonan. Go through Quellénec, turn right onto a partly surfaced road 600m/656yd to the Griffonès car park.

★Site du Stangala – After crossing an arboretum (red oak, copper beech etc), bear left through woodland to reach two rocky platforms. The site is a remarkable one: the rocky ridge overlooks the Odet from a height of 70m/230ft as the river winds between wooded slopes. Opposite and slightly to the right, the hamlet of Tréouzon clings to the slopes. Ahead, in the distance, to the left of the television tower, Locronan Mountain, with its characteristic outline and the chapel perched on its summit, can be picked out easily.

On the way back to the car park, a road to the left leads down to the bank of the Odet *(30min there and back).*

To return to Quimper, bear right as you leave the narrow road.

② Chapels and calvaries

Round tour of 57km/35mi – 3hr

Leave Quimper on rue des Douves (BY). Shortly after a cemetery at the entrance of Kerfeunteun, turn right.

Église de Kerfeunteun (BV Q) – A small square belfry with a stone spire surmounts the west façade.

The church was built in the 16C and 17C but the transept and chancel were rebuilt in 1953. It has kept a beautiful stained-glass window (16C) above the high altar, depicting a Tree of Jesse with a Crucifixion above.

800m/875yd further on, turn right towards Brest, then left in the direction of Briec and at Ty-Sanquer, left again.

★Calvaire de Quilinen – Near the main road, hidden by the trees, stands the **Chapelle Notre-Dame-de-Quilinen** ⊙ with its unusual Calvary. Built c 1550 on two superposed triangular bases with the points opposite one another, the Calvary reveals a rough and naive style. As the Cross rises to the figure of Christ above the two thieves who are placed close together, the statues become more and more slender. The other side of the Cross represents Christ resurrected.

The south portal of the 15C chapel is decorated by a graceful Virgin between two angels.

Return to the main road and bear right; after 5km/3mi, turn right towards the nearby Chapelle de St-Venec.

Chapelle de St-Venec ⊙ – In front of this Gothic chapel is a Calvary (1556) on a triangular base similar to that of Quilinen and on the other side of the road stands a charming 16C fountain.

Take the chapel road, pass under the Quimper-Brest motorway and turn left towards the Chapelle Notre-Dame-des-Trois-Fontaines.

This large chapel was built in the 15C-16C; the Calvary is badly damaged.

Proceed to the Gouézec road and turn right.

★La Roche du Feu (Karreg an Tan) – *30min on foot there and back.* From the car park, take a path to the summit (28m/899ft) which affords an extensive **panorama★** over the Montagnes Noires, Ménez-Hom and the Aulne Valley.

Return to Quimper via Edern and Briec.

③ Along the banks of the Odet

Round tour of 48km/30mi – 2hr 30min

Leave Quimper on the boulevard de Poulguinan to Pont-l'Abbé. After the round-about, uphill, bear left.

Port du Corniguel – This is the port of Quimper from which wine, timber and sand are exported. Fine view of the Odet and the Baie de Kérogan.

Return to the Pont-l'Abbé road, and then turn left towards Plomelin. At the next junction, bear left towards the Cale de Rosulien.

Cale de Rosulien – *Road unsurfaced at the end.* A ruined mill stands on the right. From the dock, there is a good view of the **Vire-Court★★** *(see below).*

Return to the junction, turn left and after the entrance to Perennou Castle, bear left towards the Odet (signposts).

From the car park, take a path *(15min on foot there and back)* to the banks of the Odet with good views of the river. Before the Croissant junction where you bear left for Combrit, the road crosses the deep Combrit Cove, which presents a fine sight at high tide.

> **Crêperie la Misaine** – *Quai Jacques-de-Thézac – 29120 Ste-Marine – ☎ 02 98 51 90 45 – closed Oct-March except school holidays and weekends, Tues except in summer months – 40/80F.* Between the chapel and the port of Sainte-Marine, this little stone house has great views of the Odet and the resort town of Bénodet. Both the crêpes and the terrace make it worth-while to stop.

Combrit – The 16C church has a square domed belfry flanked by two turrets. In-side, note the carved purlins and beams; in the chapel to the right of the chancel, there is a fine alabaster group of the Trinity in an alcove; to the left of the chan-cel is a 16C altarpiece from Catalonia. An ossuary (17C) stands next to the south porch.

Proceed in the direction of Bénodet, then bear right for Ste-Marine.

Ste-Marine – This small resort on the west bank of the Odet has a good sandy beach with a fine view over Loctudy and Pointe de Lesconil, the Île aux Moutons and the Îles Glénan, and a small pleasure boat harbour, from which you can enjoy a lovely view of Bénodet and the Odet. There is a ferry for pedestrians crossing between Ste-Marine and Bénodet.

Go over the Pont de Cornouaille.

Bénodet – *See BÉNODET.*
The return road is further inland from the east bank of the Odet.

Le Drennec – Standing in front of the chapel, beside the road, is a charming 16C fountain. A trefoil niche beneath a crocketed gable contains a Pietà.

Pass through Moulin-du-Port to return to Quimper.

BOAT TRIPS

★★ Down the Odet ⊙ – The woods and castle parks, which lie along the river form a fine, green landscape. The **Port du Corniguel**, at the mouth of Kérogan Bay, adds a modern touch to the picture.

★ Baie de Kérogan – The estuary at this point looks like a lake.

★★ Les Vire-Court – The Odet here winds between high, wooded cliffs. This wild spot has its legends. Two rocks at the narrowest point of the gorge are called the Maiden's Leap (Saut de la Pucelle). Another rock is called the Bishop's Chair (Chaise de l'Evêque). Angels are said to have made it in the shape of a seat for the use of a saintly prelate of Quimper who liked to meditate in this lonely place. A little further on, the river bends so sharply that a Spanish fleet, coming up to attack Quimper, did not dare go through. Having taken on water at a fountain now called the Spaniards' Fountain, the ships turned back. On the west bank, before Le Perennou, ruins of Roman baths can be seen.

QUIMPERLÉ ★

Population 10 748
Michelin map 58 fold 12 or 230 fold 34

This little town is prettily situated at the confluence *(kemper)* of the River Ellé and River Isole, which join to form the Laïta. It consists of an upper town, dominated by the Église Notre-Dame-de-l'Assomption, and a lower town grouped about the former Abbaye of Ste-Croix and rue Dom-Morice. Quimperlé was once a fairly important harbour but today it is chiefly used for small pleasure craft which sail along the Laïta to discover the Forêt de Carnoët and Le Pouldu.

SIGHTS

★★**Église Ste-Croix** – The church, which is interesting archeologically, was built in the 12C, but had to be rebuilt in 1862, except for the apse and the crypt, when its bell-tower collapsed. The new bell-tower stands alone.

The plan is copied from that of the Holy Sepulchre at Jerusalem. It includes a rotunda with three small apsidal chapels opening into it and a porch, the whole forming a Greek cross.

The **apse**★★, with its blind arcades, columns, capitals and windows, is the finest specimen of Romanesque art in Brittany. A Renaissance stone **altarpiece**★ (part of an old rood screen) stands against the façade.

The **crypt**★★ has remarkable capitals and two 15C tombs with recumbent statues. In the gallery dividing the church and sacristy, there is a 16C Entombment carved in stone.

On leaving the church, take rue Ellé which skirts the north side and affords a good view of the east end and the bell-tower.

★**Rue Dom-Morice** (9) – This narrow alley is lined with 16C half-timbered and cor-belled houses; no 7, the **Maison des Archers** (1470) is noteworthy.

Museum ⊙ (**M**) – Located in the Maison des Archers, the museum traces the history of the house and of the archers who lived there. Two floors are devoted to Quimperlé, its activities, famous men and regional costumes.

Rue Brémond-d'Ars (4) – There are some half-timbered and old 17C houses at nos 8, 10, 11 and 12. At no 15 bis note the staircase of the Présidial, a former Law Court. Note, also, the ruins of the Église St Colomban.

Eating out

BUDGET

Crêperie le Préau – *3 rue des Plages, 29350 Moëlan-sur-Mer – ☎ 02 98 96 50 91 – closed 12-27 Nov, 11-22 Jan, and Mon except in July-Aug – 35/70F.* Next to the church, this former school now houses a small crêperie decorated in yellow and blue. Maps line the walls, the delicious aroma of crêpes fills the room as you watch them being made before your eyes.

OUR SELECTION

Chez Jacky – *At the Port de Bélon, 29340 Riec-sur-Bélon – ☎ 02 98 06 90 32 – closed Oct-Easter and Mon except holidays – 105/450F.* Situated on the River Bélon, this little restaurant serves its own "home-grown" oysters as well as other seafoods. A very popular spot, and from inside the nautical bistro decor, its bay windows offer a nice view of the river.

Night-life

Le Surcouf – *1 quai Surcouf – ☎ 02 98 39 25 28 – Oct-May, Sun-Thur noon-12am, Fri-Sat until 1am; June-Sept, daily noon-1am.* Quimperlé's oldest bar is on the banks of the Laïta, and is still attracting crowds after 20 years, despite its rather sparse decor. Its undeniable success is due to its remarkable and unique ambience.

La Cordée – *24 place St-Michel – ☎ 02 98 39 20 75 – outside of school holidays, Mon-Thur 9am-7pm, Fri 8am-noon, Sat 9am-1am, Sun 2pm-7pm; during school holidays, daily 9am-1am.* This bar which serves no alcohol was founded by an association for the prevention of alcoholism and for providing support to recovering alcoholics, but it also seeks out younger clients to show them that they can enjoy themselves without drinking. This friendly gathering place presents exhibitions, philosophical evenings and theatre, and has two computers connected to the Internet.

Église Notre-Dame-de-l'Assomption – This 13C and 15C church, surmounted by a large square tower, is also known as St-Michel. Pass under the archway on the right, built into one of the buttresses, to get a glimpse of the fine carved porch (1450). Inside, look at the oak-panelled vault with a sculpted cornice, magnificent Flamboyant piscinas and, near the north door, a 15C font. Among the more interesting wooden statues note that of Our Lady of Good Tidings (Notre-Dame-de-Bonne-Nouvelle) (16C).

EXCURSIONS

★Rochers du Diable

12km/7mi northeast, plus 30min on foot there and back. Leave Quimperlé on D 790 towards Le Faouët and after 4.5km/3mi turn right and go through Locunolé.

There is a pretty run as the road descends towards the Ellé. *Cross the bridge and turn left towards Meslan; after 400m/437yd, leave the car in the car park to the left.* Paths leading up to the top of the "Devil's Rocks" drop vertically to the fast-flowing waters of the Ellé.

Domaine de Clohars-Carnoët

Round tour of 43km/27mi – 2hr 30min. Leave Quimperlé via Quai Brizeux.

Forêt de Carnoët – Bordered by the River Laïta, the forest offers pretty sites and pleasant walks *(some paths are reserved for walking and riding).*
Some 500m/547yd beyond Toulfoën, turn left towards the Rocher Royal.

The road winds through the forest to the banks of the Laïta where the **Rocher Royal** can be seen, a rocky ridge towering above the river, and the ruins of the Château de Carnoët. This is the legendary dwelling of the Count of Commore, the Bluebeard of Cornouaille. After hearing a prediction that he would die by the hand of his son, he put his first four wives to death as soon as they conceived. The fifth wife, Triphine, before she died, was able to save her son, who became **St Trémeur**. Commore, on meeting the saint, was struck by his resemblance to his mother and immediately had him beheaded. Then, according to the legend, Trémeur picked up his own head, walked towards his father's castle and threw a handful of earth against the building which collapsed, burying Commore alive.
Return to the Le Pouldu road, turn left and at a major junction, left again.

Pont de St-Maurice – The bridge over the Laïta gives a fine **view★** of the river and its steep banks.
Turn round and after 700m/766yd, turn right.

St-Maurice – This stands in a green and pleasant **site★**: the Laïta is on the right with a lake on the left. Nearby are remains of the chapter-house of the former Abbaye St-Maurice, founded in the 12C.

Le Pouldu – This small port lies at the mouth of the River Laïta.

The **Chapelle Notre-Dame-de-la-Paix** ⊘ near Grands Sables Beach, stands in a grassy close, the entrance of which is flanked by a monument to Gauguin. The chapel escaped ruin by being transported 26km/16mi and rebuilt here. The bays have flame and lily shaped tracery with stained glass by Manessier and Le Moal. Below the timber roof, the rood beam carries a Christ with a red loincloth and a second group depicting a Pietà.
Drive along Grands Sables Beach then turn left towards Doëlan.

View of the Île de Groix and Pointe du Talut.

QUIMPERLÉ

M Musée (Maison des Archers)

Doëlan – A small fishing port commanding the entrance to a deep, sheltered estuary.

Return to Quimperlé via Clohars-Carnoët.

The Bélon region

Round tour of 37km/23mi – 1hr 30min. Leave Quimperlé to the southwest on D 16 and at Gare-de-la-Forêt, bear right.

Moëlan-sur-Mer – In the **church** ⊘, note the four 18C confessional boxes in the Italian style. Pass along the south side of the church and by the chevet, take the lane leading to the **Chapelle St-Philibert-et-St-Roch** ⊘ which is picturesquely placed near a 16C Calvary. Alongside is the St-Roch fountain. A *pardon* takes place on the second Sunday following 15 August.

Proceed to Brigneau.

A menhir stands on the left-hand side of the road. There is a fine view over Brigneau Bay.

Brigneau – A tiny fishing port where pleasure craft also find shelter.
The road follows the coastline. Thatched-roofed houses are found along the way.

At Kergroës, bear left.

Kerfany-les-Pins – On the River Bélon, this small seaside resort has a pretty site and a sandy beach. Fine view over Port-Manech and the Aven estuary.

Take the uphill road beyond the beach and at Lanriot, turn left.

Bélon – This locality, on the south bank of the Bélon, is famous as an oyster-farming centre. The oyster beds on the north bank can be seen at low tide.

Return to Quimperlé via Moëlan-sur-Mer.

QUINTIN

Population 2 602
Michelin map 59 folds 12 and 13 or 230 fold 22

In the past, Quintin was well known for its fine linen which was used for headdresses and collars. In the 17C and 18C the industry expanded to the manufacture of Brittany cloth which was exported to America but decline set in at the Revolution when there were 300 weavers in the town. The old houses of Quintin rise in terraces on a hill; the River Gouët forms a fine stretch of water below.

SIGHTS

Basilica (Basilique) ⊘ – Built on the site of a collegiate church in 1887. The relics of St Thuriau and a piece of the Virgin's girdle, brought from Jerusalem in the 13C by a lord of Quintin (Geoffroy Botrel or Botherel), are kept in the basilica. There are also four stoups made of shells from Java and the old crowned statue of Notre-Dame-de-Délivrance (Our Lady of Safe Delivery), which is venerated by expectant mothers in particular; a 14C font in the north transept and two 14C recumbent figures in the chancel. At the east end of the basilica stands the 15C New Gate (Porte Neuve), all that remains of the ramparts which surrounded the town. In rue Notre-Dame, beyond the parvis, is the 15C fountain of Notre-Dame-d'Entre-les-Portes with two former chapter-houses with decorated façades opposite, at nos 5 and 7.

Old houses – There are fine 16C-17C corbelled houses lining the picturesque place 1830, rue au Lait (nos 12, 13) and Grande Rue (nos 37 and 43). In place du Martray, the Hôtel du Martray, the town hall and the house at no 1 date from the 18C.

Château ⊘ – *Access via place 1830.* The château is made up of an older 17C building and a grand 18C building, flanked by a low-lying wing at a right angle, visible once through the entrance gate.
The **museum**, housed in the 18C part of the château, recounts Quintin's history and that of the chateau's previous owners. Displayed inside are: 18C-19C fans, hand-painted India Company plates, Meissen tableware, archives and Quintin linen. In the kitchens is an unusual piece: an 18C granite oven with seven holes (used for heating platters).
A succession of vaulted rooms are visited in the old part of the château and its cellars, which overlook the lake.
Every summer a variety of exhibitions is organised.

EXCURSION

Menhir de Roche-Longue – *800m/875yd further on by the road beyond the Calvary which skirts the pool.*
At the top of the hill, a menhir 4.70m/14ft high stands in a field to the left.

Château de Beaumanoir ⊙ – *6km/3.6mi north towards Châtelaudren, follow the signs.*

A long avenue of beech trees leads to the main courtyard. This residence was built in the 15C by Olive de Beaumanoir and modified in the 19C, using the most innovative technology and principles of hygiene of the age (running water, electricity, central heating). The château, outbuildings and park constitute a complete estate in the Victorian style – rare in France – as conceived by wealthy families, addicted to progress, at the end of the last century in Great Britain.

The rooms, open to the public, reconstitute the daily atmosphere of family life by means of 18C and 19C furniture and a collection of modern art.

Every year, the works of well-known contemporary artists are displayed and add extra interest to the visit.

The **outbuildings** bear a remarkable witness to the evolution of attitudes concerning the organisation of work in the late 19C and early 20C. Note in particular the **stables**, constructed of iron, glass, wood and bricks in an architectural style reflecting the taste of the time for combining these materials.

Beaumont was the setting for the films *Tess* (1979 by Roman Polanski) and *Je suis le Seigneur du château*, the French adaptation of Susan Hill's novel *I'm the King of the Castle* (1987 by Régis Wargnier).

Vallée de la RANCE★★

Michelin map 59 folds 5, 6, 15 and 16 or 230 folds 11 and 25

The Rance estuary, lying between St-Malo and Dinard, is among the places most frequented in Brittany. Upstream, Dinan is a typical old inland town.

The Rance is a perfect example of a Breton river. It forms a deep gulf between Dinan and the sea, flowing with many branches and inlets over a level plateau. This curious gulf is due to the flooding by the sea of an ordinary but steep-sided valley: the stream itself and the bottom of the valley have been "drowned" by a mass of tidal water. All that remains visible of the original valley is its steep sides, sloping into the sea. The Rance proper is a small river without much water, which winds along above Dinan.

★★BOAT TRIP ⊙

5hr there and back – not counting the stop and tour of Dinan

The boat follows the Noires breakwater (Môle des Noires) and crosses the Rance estuary for a brief stop at Dinard. It enters the Rance, leaving the Corniche d'Aleth on the left (St-Servan), passes in front of Pointe de la Vicomté and Rocher Bizeux and then enters the lock of the Rance dam. You will go up the river, between its great banks, through a series of narrow channels and wide pools. After Chatelier Lock (Écluse du Chatelier), the Rance gets narrower and narrower and becomes a mere canal just as you come within sight of Dinan, perched on its ridge.

★★ **Dinan** – *See DINAN.* Your boat will stop for a longer or shorter time according to the tide – from 8hr to only 15min.
The scenes on your way back will be changed by the difference in the direction of the light and its intensity.

★★ALONG THE BANKS OF THE RANCE

Round Tour Starting From St-Malo

87km/54mi – allow one day

St-Malo – *3hr 30min. See ST-MALO.*
Leave St-Malo by ③ on the town plan. Turn right by the aerodrome.

La Passagère – Fine view over the Rance.
Make for the Chapelle du Boscq and St-Jouan-des-Guérets to St-Suliac.
On the right notice the Boscher mill, once a tidal mill.

In St-Suliac, before the church, bear left in the direction of Mont Garrot. 1km/0.5mi further on leave the car near an old crenellated watchtower.

From the foot of the tower, there is a wide **panorama★** of St-Suliac Cove, St-Malo, the Dol countryside, the River Rance and Pont St-Hubert.

Mont Garrot – *15min on foot there and back.* A path to the right leads to the point, passing behind a farm. Notice the views of the Vallée de la Rance on the way.

From La Ville-ès-Nonais continue onto the Pont St-Hubert.

Pont St-Hubert – From this suspension bridge, there is a pleasant view of the Rance, the Port St-Jean slipway and, on the rocky bank opposite, the St-Hubert slipway.

Return to La Ville-ès-Nonais, bear right.

Pleudihen-sur-Rance – The farm's outbuildings house the **Musée de la Pomme et du Cidre** (Apple and Cider Museum) ⊙. Before visiting the museum stop by the orchard planted with different varieties of apple trees. Inside the museum, the apple, its origin, the different varieties, diseases, cultivation and picking are explained. A film illustrating the different apple-related trades (eg cooperage) and a tasting end the tour.

Cale de Mordreuc – From this lovely place there are good views of Pont St-Hubert downstream, the deepening valley upstream and just opposite a promontory on which lie the ruins of an old castle.

Lanvallay – A remarkable **view★** of the old town of Dinan, its ramparts and its belfries. Below flows the Rance, spanned by a long viaduct.

★★Dinan – See Dinan.

Take the road which passes under the Dinan viaduct and skirts the harbour.

🔢 **Taden** – When you cross the village, on your way to the slipway, glance at the porch and keep which is flanked by a 14C turret. The towpath, which used to link Dinan to the Écluse du Chatelier, is a favourite spot for fishermen and a pleasant place to stroll. Taden Plain is the home of a number of aquatic birds: black-headed gulls, herring gulls, coots etc.

Return to the road towards Dinard. As you leave La Hisse turn right before the level crossing.

Écluse du Chatelier – This lock regulates the Dinan basin.

Continue onto **Plouër-sur-Rance**. Inside the 18C church are carved tombstones.

After Plouër-sur-Rance and Le Minihic bear right and then 250m/273yd further on right again.

La Landriais – The port contains naval dockyards. The walk along Hures Promenade (on foot take Chemin de ronde des Douaniers) starts from the car park and skirts the Rance for 2km/1mi affording fine views.

On your way back after 1.2km/0.7mi turn right then after a further 1km/0.6mi turn right again.

Cale de la Jouvente – Across from La Passagère. There is a nice view of the Rance and the Île Chevret.

La Richardais – The church is dominated by its pierced tower and the Calvary surmounting it. On the walls of the nave runs a fresco (1955) depicting the Stations of the Cross by Xavier de Langlais. In the transept is a fresco illustrating the arrival of St Lunaire and St Malo on the Breton coast. From the fine wood vaulting resembling the upturned keel of a ship, four lamps in the form of wheels hang down. Five stained-glass windows are by Max Ingrand.

On leaving La Richardais by the north, you get a viewpoint of the tidal power scheme and the Rance estuary.

Usine marémotrice de la Rance ⊘ – The use of tidal power is nothing new to the Vallée de la Rance. As early as the 12C, riverside dwellers had thought up the idea of building little reservoirs which, as they emptied with the ebb tide, drove mill wheels. To double the output of a modern industrial plant, it was tempting to try to work out a means of using the flow as well as the ebb tide. The French electricity board (EDF), therefore, searched for new technical methods of producing electricity and successfully set up, between the headlands of La Briantais and La Brebis, a Usine hydro-électrique (hydroelectric power station) ⊘ operated by both the flow and ebb of the tide.

The **power station** is in a huge tunnel nearly 390m/400yd long in the very centre of the dam. In this room, are the 24 AC generators of a combined capacity of 240 000kW which can produce 600 million kWh per year (equal to the annual consumption of a city comparable to Rennes and its outskirts).

The **view★** from the platform atop the dam extends over the Rance estuary as far as Dinard and St-Malo. The dam lies between the power station and the right bank with its centre on the small island of Chalibert. There are six sluice-gates at the eastern end which regulate the emptying and filling of the reservoir, thus controlling the water supply to the power station.

Return to St-Malo by the direct route along the crest of the dam.

Pointe du RAZ★★★

Michelin map 58 fold 13 or 230 fold 16 – Local map see CORNOUAILLE

Pointe du Raz ⊘, at the tip of Cornouaille, is in a beautiful setting. Walk round the signal station in front of which stands a statue of Our Lady of the Shipwrecked (Notre-Dame-des-Naufragés) to enjoy a wide **panorama★★** of the horizon: straight ahead is the Île de Sein and beyond, in clear weather, the Ar Men Lighthouse. Between the Île de Sein and the mainland is the fearful Raz du Sein or tide race which, so an old saying has it, "no one passes without fear or sorrow"; to the northwest can be seen Tévennec Lighthouse (Phare de Tévennec) standing on an islet.

Recently, protective measures have been taken to preserve the site and its environment. A new visitors' centre has opened, the **Porte du Cap Sizun** *(information centre, exhibit area, restaurants and shops). To reach the end of the point, motorists must pay to leave their car in the parking area. It takes about 15min to follow the waymarked paths to the far end. A free shuttle provides transportation for those with difficulty walking.*

Pointe du Raz

Y. Arthus-Bertrand /ALTITUDE

*Michelin Maps are updated constantly.
Always travel with the latest edition.*

REDON

Population 9 260
Michelin map 63 fold 5 or 230 folds 38 and 39

Redon, the centre of an active region, is the meeting point of three departements (Ille-et-Vilaine, Loire-Atlantique and Morbihan) and two regions (Brittany and Pays de Loire). In Redon, the River Vilaine and the Nantes-Brest Canal converge at the pleasure boat harbour (tourism on inland waterways).

Traditions are still well implanted in the region around Redon; markets and fairs (the popular chestnut fair, Teillouse Fair, held the fourth Saturday in October) take place here. The town's industrial activities include the production of computers, automobile seats and bodies, children's clothes and lighters.

Église St-Sauveur (**Y**) – This former abbey church, founded in 832, was a great pilgrimage centre throughout the Middle Ages and until the 17C. This accounts for the impressive size of the building. In 1622 Richelieu was the commendatory abbot. It was cut off from its 14C Gothic bell-towers (**D**) by a fire in 1780. A remarkable Romanesque sandstone and granite **tower★** stands at the transept crossing. From the neighbouring **cloisters** (17C), occupied by the College of St Saviour, the superimposition of its arcades can be seen. From the esplanade planted with chestnut trees and overlooking rue Richelieu, one has a good view of the chevet with its buttresses.

The **interior** reveals a dimly lit low nave (11C) with wood vaulting separated from the side aisles by flat pillars. The 12C vaulting at the transept reveals remains of frescoes; note the carved pillars in the transept crossing. A 17C altarpiece in stone and marble takes the form of the chancel which, with the ambulatory, is 13C.

The old town – The old town contains elegant 15C-18C town houses. Leave from the Église St-Sauveur and walk along Grande Rue, noting nos 22, 25, 38, 44, 52 and 54; look down rue d'Enfer and rue Jeanne-d'Arc. Cross the flower-decorated bridge which spans the Nantes-Brest Canal. In rue du Port across from no 6, Hôtel Carmoy, are three corbelled houses. Go into rue du Jeu-de-Paume which has, at no 10, the old customs barracks, a 4-storey building with a severe façade and a wall with a scene of swineherds and fishmongers dressed in costumes of the past. Return to rue du Port where old salt houses (no 40) can be seen; occupying no 3 rue du Plessis is the Hôtel Richelieu. Quai Duguay-Trouin is lined with stately shipowners' homes of which nos 15, 7, 6 and 5 are particularly worth looking at. By way of Quai St-Jacques, where ramparts in ruins still stand, and rue de Richelieu, you return to the church.

REDON

D Clocher

EXCURSIONS

Rieux – *7km/4mi south on* ③ *on the town plan towards Vannes.* The **church** (1952) has a slim belfry built against the side of the main vessel. The groined brick vaulting springs from roughly hewn capitals supported by short columns. The unfaced stonework of the walls is interrupted only by the vividly coloured **stained-glass windows★** of unevenly cut glass by Job Guével.
On entering the village, in a bend, take the road to the left which leads you to a car park, from where there is a pleasant view of the Vilaine Valley and Redon; occupying the wooded promontory are castle ruins.

Île aux Pies – *12km/7mi northwest. Leave Redon by D 65 and then D 764 to Ploërmel* (Y), *at St-Vincent-sur-Oust, turn right.*
The road leads to the bank of the Oust, a peaceful river, partly canalised, flowing through verdant countryside. A path to the left gives a view of the Île aux Pies. This is a good place for climbing, canoeing and kayaking.

St-Just – *19km/11.5mi northeast. Leave Redon on* ① *on the town plan (D 177) towards Rennes and turn left to St-Just.*
This small town lies at the centre of an area rich in **megaliths**, especially in the **Cojoux Moor** (Landes de Cojoux signposted path). Lovely viewpoint on the Étang de Val (rock-climbing).

Take D 873 22mi/14mi north towards Guer.

Carentoir: La ferme du Monde ⊘ – The park around the Bois Brassu manor house is home to tame animals from around the world: 55 different species of pets come from the five continents. There is a petting zoo and a mini-golf course, all built and maintained by disabled workers from the Carentoir training centre.

Help us in our constant task of keeping up-to-date.
Send us your comments and suggestions to

Michelin
Travel Publications
38 Clarendon Road – WATFORD Herts WD1 1SX
Tel: (01923) 415000

thegreenguide-uk@uk.michelin.com

RENNES★★

Conurbation 245 065
Michelin map 59 fold 17 or 230 fold 26

Over the last few years Rennes, regional capital of Brittany, has been implementing a policy of restoration of its heritage; resurfacing of stonework, renovation work and the introduction of pedestrian zones have all played a part in highlighting the essentially dignified air of this city, also emanating from the Classical style buildings. Rennes, a city of artistic and historical interest, where good food is highly valued, exudes atmosphere from its narrow, winding medieval streets, lined with charming half-timbered houses with carved sills, which happily escaped the ravages of a huge fire in 1720. The public buildings and numerous private mansions on the two "royal" squares (place du Palais and place de l'Hôtel-de-Ville) give these an air of sober elegance. It is here, at the very heart of the city, delimited to the south by the lively quays along the Vilaine, that the people of Rennes come to do their shopping, watch a play or go for a drink with their friends.

South of the River Vilaine lie the residential suburbs and the industrial zone, which have been built to a modern urban plan (Le Colombier). West of boulevard de La Tour-d'Auvergne stand the glass Law Courts, a good example of contemporary architecture.

Three industrial zones have attracted many plants manufacturing cars, railway equipment, the building industry and public works and transportation etc.

Recently Rennes has become a centre of the electronics and communications industry (the French Telecom videotext service, MINITEL was conceived here). Rennes is also a university city: two universities, a medical school and several other specialised schools, with a total student enrolment of 38 000.

HISTORICAL NOTES

Du Guesclin's beginnings (14C) – Bertrand Du Guesclin was born in the castle of La Motte-Broons (now disappeared), southwest of Dinan. He was the eldest of 10 children and by no means handsome. On the other hand, he was bursting with energy and good sense. Bertrand spent his childhood among peasant boys whom he taught to fight. In this way he acquired strength, skill and cunning – and rough manners. His family was ashamed of him and kept him out of sight.

In 1337, when Du Guesclin was 17, all the local nobles met for a tournament at Rennes. Our hero went to it in peasant dress, mounted on a draught horse. He was kept out of the lists. His despair at this was such that one of his cousins from Rennes lent him his armour and charger. Without giving his name, Bertrand unseated several opponents. At last a lance thrust lifted his visor and his father recognised him. Delighted and proud, he exclaimed: "My fine son, I will no longer treat thee scurvily!"

The duchess's marriage (1491) – In 1489, when François II died, his heiress, Anne of Brittany, was only 12, but this did not prevent wooers from coming forward. Her choice fell on Maximilian of Austria, the future Emperor. The religious marriage was performed by proxy in 1490.

Charles VIII, who had an unconsummated marriage with Margaret of Austria, daughter of Maximilian, asked the Duchess's hand for himself; he was refused and laid siege to Rennes in August 1491. The starving people begged their sovereign to accept the marriage. She agreed and met Charles VIII. Anne was small and thin and slightly lame, but she had gaiety and charm; she knew Latin and Greek and took an interest in art and letters. Charles was short and ill-favoured, with large, pale eyes and thick lips always hanging open; he was slow-witted, too, but loved power and had a taste for pomp. Quite unexpectedly the two young people took a liking to each other, which grew into tender affection. Their engagement was celebrated at Rennes. There remained, however, the problem of freeing the fiancés. The Court of Rome agreed and the wedding took place in the royal Château de Langeais, in the Loire Valley, on 6 December 1491 (see The Green Guide Châteaux of the Loire). The marriage united Brittany to France.

The great fire of 1720 – At the beginning of the 18C the town still looked as it did in the Middle Ages, with narrow alleys and lath-and-plaster houses. There was no way of fighting fire, for there was no running water. In the evening of 22 December 1720, a drunken carpenter set fire to a heap of shavings with his lamp. The house burned like a torch and immediately others around it caught fire.

The ravaged areas were rebuilt to the plans of **Jacques Gabriel**, the descendant of a long line of architects and himself the father of the Gabriel who built the place de la Concorde in Paris. A large part of the town owes its fine rectangular street pattern and the uniform and rather severely distinguished granite houses to this event. In order that they might be inhabited more quickly, new houses were divided into apartments or flats which were sold separately. This was the beginning of co-ownership.

The La Chalotais affair – In 1762, the Duke of Aiguillon, Governor of Brittany, clashed with Parliament over the Jesuits. The Jansenist lawyers (robins) opposed the Society of Jesus, whose colleges made it very powerful in Brittany – that of Rennes had 2 800 pupils. La Chalotais, the Public Prosecutor, induced Parliament to vote for the dissolution of the Order. His report had a huge success: 12 000 copies were sold in a month. Voltaire wrote to the author: "This is the only work of philosophy that has ever come from the Bar."

Aiguillon, who defended the Jesuits, asked Parliament to reverse its vote. It refused. Louis XV summoned the Councillors to Versailles, scolded them and sent three into exile. On returning to Rennes the Members of Parliament resigned rather than submit. The King had La Chalotais arrested and sent him to Saintes; the other Councillors were scattered over various provinces, but the Paris Parliament took the side of the Rennes Parliament and Louis XV hesitated to go further. Aiguillon, lacking support, retired in 1768. The Assemblies had defeated the royal power. Revolution was on the march.

★★ OLD TOWN (VIEUX RENNES) (ABY) *1hr 30min*

This is the part of the old town which escaped the fire *(see above)*. It contains a maze of 15C and 16C houses with overhanging storeys and lordly mansions with sculpted façades which can be seen as you stroll in the cathedral district.

Basilique St-Sauveur (AY) – 17 and 18C. Inside this basilica are a fine gilded wooden **canopy** and an **organ loft** (17C). To the right is a chapel consecrated to Our Lady of Miracles who saved Rennes from the English during the siege of 1357. Note the numerous ex-votos which have been donated in gratitude to Our Lady.

Rue St-Sauveur (AY 75) – At no 6 stands a 16C canon's residence.

Rue St-Guillaume (AY 68) – At no 3, a beautiful medieval house, known as **Maison Du Guesclin**, contains the restaurant Ti Koz.

Rue de la Psalette (AY 60) – This street is lined with old houses.

Rue du Chapitre (AY 9) At no 22 is a Renaissance house; no 8 is the **Hôtel de Brie** (17C); at no 6 the 18C **Hôtel de Blossac** with a fine granite **staircase** (on left on entering) with marble columns and a wrought-iron handrail.

Rue St-Yves (AY 77) – At nos 6 and 8 are 16C houses.

Rue des Dames (AY 14) – No 10 is the Hôtel Freslon de la Freslonnière.

Cathédrale St-Pierre ⊘ **(AY)** – This, the third cathedral built on the site since the 6C, was finished in 1844 after 57 years' work. The previous building collapsed in 1762 except for the two towers in the Classical style flanking the façade.

The **interior**★ is very rich, its stucco facing covered with paintings and gilding. The cathedral contains a masterpiece: the gilded and carved wood **altarpiece**★★ in the chapel before the south transept. Both in size and in execution, this 16C Flemish work is one of the most important of its kind. The scenes represent the life of the Virgin.

Portes Mordelaises (AY B) – The city's main entrance, these gates are all that remain of the 15C ramparts. The dukes of Brittany passed through it on their way to the cathedral for their coronation. In 1598 the silver-gilt keys of the city were presented there to Henri IV. At this kind of ceremony the Béarnais made a statement which always went down well: "These are beautiful keys," he would say, "but I would rather have the keys to the hearts of your citizens".

Place des Lices (AY) – Jousts and tournaments were once held on this square. At no 34 stands a 17C stone mansion, the Hôtel de Molant, with a mansard roof; inside, there is a sumptuous oak staircase with trompe-l'œil

Cathédrale St-Pierre

H. Weller /EXPLORER

RENNES

A | B

ST-MALO
DINAN

0   300 m

paintings (a skyscape) and woodwork decorating the ceiling of its stairwell. At nos 26 and 28 the 17C mansions have wide staircases with hull-shaped roofs.

Rue St-Michel (AY 74) – This street is lined with half-timbered houses and still has the inns and taverns dating from the time when it was part of the city's suburbs.

Place Ste-Anne (AY) – The coloured half-timbered houses, Gothic and Renaissance in style, surround a 19C neo-Gothic church. The house formerly occupied by Mayor Leperdit is at no 19. This square is next to rue d'Échange, which contains the Jacobin Convent where Anne of Brittany was betrothed to the king of France.

Rue du Pont-aux-Foulons
(**AY 56**) – This is a shopping
street with 18C half-tim-
bered houses.

Rue du Champ-Jacquet
(**AY 8**) – This street leads
to an oddly shaped triangular square of the same
name. It is lined to the
north with tall half-tim-
bered 17C houses and is
overlooked by the stone
and wood façade of Hôtel
de Tizé (no 5).

The itinerary continues
along rue La Fayette and
rue Nationale into the Classical part of the city with its
majestic buildings.

★★**Palais de Justice** ⊘ (**BY**) –
Commonly known as the
"**Parlement de Bretagne**", it
was badly damaged by fire
in February 1994. While the
firefighters struggled
valiantly to save the building, tons of water were
poured over and into it,
resulting in damage which
required more than
400 000hr of work to
repair. The restoration was

Place du Champ-Jacquet

J.-D. Sudres /EXPLORER

completed in 1999 and the Court of Appeals of Rennes once again sits in this historic place; the ground floor gallery and the Court of Assises on the floor above,
as well as the French gardens in front have been restored to their original appearance. The Court stands on the place du Palaisa, which is surrounded by 17C and
18C buildings.

The architecture and decor of the mansion, which was the first stone building in
a town of wood, were to influence the whole of Haute-Bretagne. The design of
local architect Germain Gaultier was reworked for the façade by the Court architect of Marie de' Medici, Salomon de Brosse. Building went on from 1618 to 1655.
A tax of 1 sou per pitcher of wine and 3 deniers per pitcher of cider provided the
necessary funds for the building work (a journeyman earned between 7 and
12 sous a day).

Members of Parliament

Brittany's Parliament, one of the thirteen provincial parliaments which made
up the Kingdom of France, initially had its seat in Rennes for part of the
year and Nantes for the other, before finally the decision was taken in 1561
to establish a single Parliament seat in Rennes. It was the Supreme Court
of 2,300 Breton tribunals, as well as fulfilling a legislative and political function. It was not slow to restrict its recruitment catchment net; from 1678,
only noblemen or those "with the lifestyle of a nobleman" were admitted
as members. In the following century applicants had to prove that they had
at least four generations of noble blood in the family. The 100-120 councillors and presidents bought their seats, usually for a very high sum (about
100 000 **livres** by the mid 17C), and because these were hereditary this
meant that extremely young people were sometimes inheriting them, at
younger even than 20 years of age. There was an entry examination, but
the level of this was very low.

Salaries were very low, and the renowned "sweeteners" received from
clients, known as "**épices**" (spices) because they consisted mainly of sweetmeats, preserves and other such comestibles, were only really adequate for
magistrates of long-standing office. However, the members of Parliament
enjoyed many considerable privileges, not the least of which was undoubtedly exemption from payment of debts, and were acknowledged as the
ruling class of Rennes. They exercised power over thousands of lawyers. It
was traditional that they should have large families; the 33 children borne
to one president by his wife raised hardly the flicker of an eyelid.

In June 1995, Jean-Loup Roubert's project on the interior redesigning of the Palais de Justice was ratified by the French authorities. This project has restored the ground floor gallery to its former glory, as well as the Assizes Chamber on the first floor. Today, the Court of Appeal is once again housed on its original and historical premises.

Rue St-Georges (BY 67) – This animated street, lined with cafés and restaurants, has many old houses: nos 8, 10 and 12 form a remarkable group of 17C half-timbered houses. No 3, the 16C Hôtel de Moussaye, has a lovely Renaissance façade with sculptured pilasters.

Palais St-Georges (BY D) – Preceded by a beautiful garden, this former Benedictine abbey (1670) now houses administrative services.

Église St-Germain (BY) – This Flamboyant church (15C-16C) with its 17C gable (on the south side) retains certain characteristics typical of a Breton cathedral: wood vaulting and its beams with sculpted ends. In the south transept the beautiful 16C **stained-glass window** recounts the life of the Virgin and the Passion. The nave contains modern stained-glass windows by Max Ingrand.

Place de l'Hôtel de Ville (AY 24) – This regal square is the centre of the Classical district. On its west side stands the town hall (Hôtel de Ville) and on the east side, the theatre. To the south, beyond rue d'Orléans, the view is blocked by the **Palais du Commerce** (Trade Hall) (E), an imposing building decorated with monumental sculpture.

The **town hall** ⊘ (H) was built to the plans of Jacques Gabriel in 1734-43, after the fire of 1720. A central tower, standing back from the façade, carries the great clock – "le gros", as the townspeople call it – and is joined by two curved buildings to two large annexes. Inside are the former chapel and a lovely 17C Brussels tapestry. The right wing contains the Pantheon of Rennes, a hall dedicated to the memory of men who have died for France. Provided no official reception is being held, the public is admitted to the left wing of the building and can see the monumental staircase, the 18C Brussels tapestries and the hall where a wedding's civil ceremony is performed.

The **theatre** (T), joined by arcaded buildings, was built in 1832.

★★MUSÉE DE BRETAGNE AND MUSÉE DES BEAUX-ARTS
(BY M) *2hr 30min*

These two museums are housed, respectively, on the ground floor and first floor of the former university.

★★ **Musée de Bretagne** ⊘ – This museum recalls the history of Brittany. Through the exhibits (objects, models, carved figures) different eras are evoked: prehistory, Gallo-Roman Armorica, medieval Brittany and Brittany under the Ancien Régime. In the second-to-last gallery, concerned with modern Brittany (1789-1914), costumes, everyday objects, tools and furnishings, characteristic of Rennes, are displayed. An audio-visual programme presenting Brittany of today occurs in the last gallery.

★★ **Musée des Beaux-Arts** ⊘ – The Museum of Fine Arts contains an important collection of works covering the 14C to the present. Among the 16C masters are Veronese *(Perseus Rescuing Andromeda)* and Maerten van Heemskerk *(St Luke Painting the Portrait of the Virgin)*. The 17C is well represented (Rubens, Jordaens, and Champaigne); **The Newborn** by Georges de La Tour is a masterpiece.

The 18C is exemplified by the works of Chardin *(The Basket of Plums; Peaches and Grapes)* and Greuze *(Portrait of a Young Girl)*.

Among the 19C canvases are Jongkind, Corot, Boudin and Sisley. Works of the members of the Pont-Aven School are also on display: Bernard *(Yellow Tree)*, Gauguin *(Oranges)* and Sérusier *(Solitude, Argoat Landscape)*.

The last gallery, concerned with the 20C, displays works by Laurent, Picasso, Utrillo, Vlaminck, Tanguy and contemporary artists such as De Staël, Poliakoff and Asse. Old drawings, porcelain and fine Egyptian, Greek and Etruscan archeological artefacts are also on show.

A small room presents works by 19C and 20C Breton painters who painted Brittany, its landscapes and activities, such as Blin, Lemordant and Cottet.

★★JARDIN DU THABOR (BY) *1hr*

In the 16C the Benedictine abbey of St-Mélaine stood on an elevated site, beyond the city walls. The monks called the place Thabor in memory of the biblical Mount Tabor. The abbey's former orchards were transformed in the 19C to their present appearance by Bülher and Martenot and completed by the placing of Lenoir's

Hotels

BUDGET

Garden Hôtel – *3 rue Duhamel* – ☎ *02 99 65 45 06* – *24 rooms 245/320F* – *breakfast 34F*. Most of this hotel's rooms look onto an interior patio where you can eat your breakfast in nice weather. The building has been pleasantly renovated, and provides a good departure point for discovering the old part of the city.

OUR SELECTION

Hôtel Anne de Bretagne – *12 rue Tronjolly* – ☎ *02 99 31 49 49* – *43 rooms 435/560F* – *breakfast 43F*. Located in the heart of Rennes, this is a good address for those who want to mix business and tourism. The modern rooms are functional, air-conditioned, and even better, are all equipped with a jacuzzi … ideal for relaxing!

TREAT YOURSELF!

Hôtel Lecoq-Gadby – *156 rue Antrain* – ☎ *02 99 38 05 55* – ▣ – *11 rooms from 650F* – *breakfast 60F* – *restaurant 140/185F*. A cozy address: behind an old house with the reception area, the new wing houses the rooms, all carefully decorated with personal touches. Its pleasant dining room looks onto the garden where there is a terrace in the summer.

Eating out

BUDGET

Four à Ban – *4 rue St-Mélaine* – ☎ *02 99 38 72 85* – *closed 1-22 Aug, 15-22 Feb, Sat and Sun* – *98/275F*. Located in a 17C house, this restaurant is warmly decorated in red and green and has beautiful old ceiling beams and an impressive fireplace. Its refined cuisine and its very reasonable prices have made it quite a success. It's wise to reserve. Children's menu.

Brasserie Le Picadilly – *place de la Mairie* – ☎ *02 99 78 17 17* – *88/145F*. Fancy a choucroute at 4am? This local institution was founded in 1832, and welcomes its customers day and night on the comfortable banquettes in its beautiful woodwork-adorned dining room. Nice terrace.

Crêperie des Portes Mordelaises – *6 rue des Portes-Mordelaises* – ☎ *02 99 30 57 40* – *closed Sun lunch* – *40/80F*. This crêperie is beautifully situated at the foot of one of the old doors to the city, opposite Anne de Bretagne's house. A nice spot to enjoy traditional crêpes by the fireplace in a simple and familial ambience.

Thé au Fourneau – *6 rue du Capit.-Alfred-Dreyfus* – ☎ *02 99 78 25 36* – *closed Sun and evenings* – *no credit cards* – *60/80F*. Savoury or sweet? An assortment of tarts, salads, teas, but also breakfast offerings let you compose the meal to your own liking. This tea salon occupies a 17C house, and is very well-situated, near the Musée de Bretagne and Musée des Beaux-Arts.

OUR SELECTION

Des Souris et des Hommes – *6 rue Nationale* – ☎ *02 99 79 75 76* – *closed Sun* – *138/185F*. In a pedestrian street near the former Parlement de Bretagne, this fashionable bistro has been decorated with ochre walls, little curios and dried flowers, which make for a soft, warm atmosphere. Reasonable prices.

Night-life

Le Chatham – *5 rue de Montfort* – ☎ *02 99 79 55 48* – *Mon-Sat 6pm-3am*. One of the city's most attractive pubs. Its nautical decor of boat models, rudders and an enormous copper lantern will make you itch to get out to sea. Often frequented by well-heeled young professionals, the pub's atmosphere is warm and inviting. Mostly Irish music.

Le Zing – *3-5 place des Lices* – ☎ *02 99 79 64 60* – *daily 4pm-3am* – *closed New Year's Day*. This fashionable bar is located at the very heart of Rennes' night-life. In fact, there are no less than 25 cafés on the place and on the small pedestrian street, rue Saint-Michel. A pretty and calm terrace in the late afternoon sun. Very stylized aviation decor.

Le Dejazey – *54 rue de St-Malo* – ☎ *02 99 38 70 72* – *Tues-Sun 6pm-3am*. If you love rhythm and blues, this is the place for you. Jazz concerts every Sunday at 6pm. Salsa and other world music concerts on Wednesdays, Thursdays and/or Fridays.

Café Méliès – *13 quai Lamennais* – ☎ *02 99 79 61 40* – *Mon-Sat 10m-3am.* This café has many identities: it's a brasserie offering a wide variety of beers, a place for jazz concerts on Thursday and Friday evenings, and it also hosts philosophical evenings two Tuesdays a month. Caters mostly to young professionals 30-40 years old.

La Prison St-Michel – *Impasse Rallier-du-Baty.* The former prison now houses a *crêperie*, the pub L'Aventure, and the discotheque Delicatessen. The majestic building dates from the 15C; it's hard to imagine its previous use.

Café-Théâtre Le Bacchus – *23 rue de la Chalotais* – ☎ *02 99 78 39 93* – *Mon-Sat 11pm-1am.* Worth visiting for its wine list, served by the glass. The ambience is warm and friendly. Shows Wed-Sat at 9.30pm.

Guided Tours

Many thematic guided tours are offered. They are usually walking tours which last around 2hr. Information is available from the tourist office.

Theatres and concert halls

Théâtre de la ville/Opéra – *Place de la Mairie* – ☎ *02 99 28 55 87.*

Théâtre national de Bretagne – *1 rue St-Hélier* – ☎ *02 99 31 12 31.* Founded in 1990, this theatre presents plays and dance events.

Théâtre de l'ADEC – *45 rue Papu* – ☎ *02 99 33 20 01.*

Le Triangle – *30 boulevard de Yougoslavie* – ☎ *02 99 53 01 92.*

Espace instrumental du conservatoire – *26 rue Hoche* – ☎ *02 99 28 55 72.*

Péniche-Spectacle L'arbre d'eau – *Quai St-Cyr* – ☎ *02 99 59 35 38.*

Markets

One of the largest markets in France is held on Saturday mornings on place des Lices.

Festivals

"Transmusicales" de Rennes – ☎ *02 99 31 12 10.* A three-day music festival.

Tombées de la Nuit – Held during the last week in July, this summer festival presents street theatre, plays, concerts, opera, and pop music – all in the historic center of Rennes.

statues. The beauty of the different flowers (roses, dahlias, chrysanthemums, camellias, rhododendrons...) and trees (oak, beech, sequoia, cedar...), spread over more than 10ha/25 acres, composed of a French garden, botanical garden, rose garden, landscaped garden and an aviary, makes these gardens particularly pleasant whatever the season.

Église Notre-Dame-en-St-Mélaine (BY) – This church was rebuilt in the 14C and 17C. The tower and transept, both of the 11C, are all that remain of the former St-Mélaine Abbey's church.

In the south arm of the transept a 15C fresco represents the Baptism of Christ. The decoration inside the church is modern: stained-glass windows by Le Moal and a tapestry and a painting (1942) by Mériel-Bussy.

Go round the building, on the left, to see the 17C cloisters which have been restored, adjoining the north side of the church, with beautiful carvings and a well. To the left of the square is the former bishop's palace (17C-18C).

EXCURSIONS

★**Écomusée du pays de Rennes** ⊙ – *8km/5mi south of rue Maréchal-Joffre (signposted).*
Located between city and country, the **Ferme de la Bintinais** (Bintinais Farm) was for a long time one of the largest properties around Rennes. The museum illustrates by means of a remarkable collection of tools and farming equipment, reconstituted interiors, costumes etc the evolution of rural life on a farm, near an urban area – the city of Rennes – as from the 16C. There is also a display on earlier construction methods. Take a walk across the 15ha/37 acre estate and discover some of the many sights: gardens, beehives, orchards, and cultivated plots of land which illustrate the evolution of local farming techniques.

In November 1994, the botanical park was complemented by the presence of live-stock: 14 country breeds of endangered farm animals. All these races are characteristic of Brittany and its surrounding region: horses (Breton draught post-horses), cows (Pie Noire, Froment du Léon, Nantaise and Armoricaine), pigs (Blanc de l'Ouest and Bayeux), goats, sheep (from Ushant, Landes de Bretagne and the Avranchin) and poultry (La Flèche hens, the Coucou de Rennes and the famous Gauloise Dorée).

The commentaries on the notice boards provide scientific explanations, while at the same time recounting unusual tales and legends. This museum also organises demonstrations and other celebrations: lettuce competition, harnessing contest for Breton draught horses, feast of the swine etc... and many other festive events testifying to the vivacity of Rennes' long-standing traditions and customs.

La Chapelle-Thouarault – *7km/4mi east on D 30, then right on D 68 to Cintré.* At the place called "Basse-Vallée" the **Musée et Atelier d'art animalier** (animal art museum and workshop) ⊙ displays, in about 40 dioramas, 250 stuffed animals placed in a minutely detailed reconstruction of their natural habitat. Many examples of local fauna are on display, enabling visitors to observe at their leisure scenes of animals going about their daily way of life – underground as well as under water – which they would rarely so much as glimpse in the wild.

Châteaugiron – This old town, which was famous for its hemp sailcloth used for rated ships in the 17C, has preserved picturesque half-timbered houses (mainly in rue de la Madeleine) and an impressive fortified **castle**. The moat, 13C keep, which in the 14C was capped by a pepper-pot roof, and 15C clock tower next to the chapel are all that remain of the often-besieged castle. The living quarters, rebuilt in the 18C, house administrative offices. From boulevard du Château there is a full view of the castle and its site.

Montfort-sur-Meu – This charming small town, built of local red stone, is located at the confluence of the River Meu and River Garun.
It was founded by Raoul I who, in 1091 had a castle built on a hill, which he called Montfort.

Écomusée du pays de Montfort ⊙ – The regional museum is housed in the 14C **Tour de Pagegaut** (Papegaut Tower), all that remains of the medieval construction. It is named after a game of skill. A spiral staircase takes you up to the temporary and permanent exhibits held on the different floors, which present Montfort and its region (landscapes, folklore: collection of dolls in traditional costumes and head-dresses).

Maison natale de saint Louis-Marie Grignion de Montfort – *15 rue de la Saulnerie.* The missionary Louis-Marie Grignion de Montfort was born in this house in 1673 (d 1716; canonised in 1947). Several rooms (restored) with fine stonework are open to the public. The garden overlooks the Meu Valley.

VALLÉE DE LA VILAINE
Round tour of 36km/23mi – 1hr

Leave Rennes on D 177 towards Redon.

Cross the river at Pont-Réan in beautiful surroundings. As you leave the town, turn left.

Le Boël – You can enjoy a pleasant walk by the river, which runs between rocky hills in a verdant setting.
Return to Pont-Réan and after crossing the bridge over the Vilaine, turn right.

Bruz – This country town is an example of successful planning in rural surroundings with its tiny square on the north side of the church. The **church★** ⊙ (1950), which is built of pink veined schist, is beautiful. A pointed spire rises above the square tower that forms the porch at its base. The interior blends well; daylight enters on all sides through square panes of glass decorated with a picture of three fishes within a circle; in the apse through stained-glass windows depicting the Seven Sacraments and in the two arms of the transept through windows, to the south of the Crucifixion and to the north of the Virgin Mary. The organ is flanked on either side by the long, narrow stained-glass windows of unequal height that can be seen in the façade.

Parc ornithologique de Bretagne ⊙ – This small park contains an interesting collection of more than 1 000 birds from every continent.

From Bruz one can reach the old Boël mill (4km/2.5mi) by taking D 77 south and 3km/2mi further on bear right and then turn left before the level crossing.
Return to Rennes by Chartres-de-Bretagne.

La ROCHE-BERNARD

Population 766
Michelin map 63 fold 14 or 230 fold 52

This little old town, picturesquely sited on the spur of La Garenne, overlooks the River Vilaine. Its naval dockyards were famous in the 17C.

The port stands on a tributary of the river. It was very prosperous in the past due to its trade of wood, wheat, wine, salt and spices. It has now become a pleasure boat harbour (capacity for 300 boats).

A real Republican – The town of La Roche-Bernard welcomed the Revolution and opposed the Chouans. In 1793, 6 000 "Whites" (Royalists) easily defeated the 150 "Blues" (peasants) who were defending the town. Mayor Sauveur refused to flee; he was imprisoned. He was ordered to shout, "Long live the King!" and he replied, "Long live the Republic!" He was shot down. He became a hero of the Republic by decree; the town was named La Roche-Sauveur until 1802.

SIGHTS

★**Bridge (Pont)** – The suspension bridge, built in 1960, stands more than 50m/160ft above the river. Stop at either end or on the corniche roads upstream to see how it blends with the landscape.

★**Viewpoint** – From a bend in the road towards La Baule, a rocky viewpoint *(23 steps)* dominates the Vilaine Valley extending its views onto the wooded slopes, on the right the suspension bridge and on the left the pleasure boat harbour on the Rhodoir. On a rock, a commemorative plaque for the launching of *La Couronne* (1634), France's first battleship, has been placed.

Old district – Across from the viewpoint and on the other side of the road begins **Promenade du Ruicard**, which overlooks the port. It goes into rue du Ruicard and leads through a maze of small streets, some of which are stepped. Houses of the 16C and 17C follow: nos 6 and 8 are well restored, no 11 has an interesting doorway, no 12 has a turret.

Passage de la Quenelle, with its dormer windows surmounted by sculpted pediments, leads to **place Bouffay** where the guillotine stood in 1793. Situated on the square is the town hall, which is also known as the "House of the Cannon" (Maison du Canon) (1599) because of the cannon (from the *Inflexible* which sought refuge in the estuary after a sea battle) placed in the corner. On the left opens rue de la Saulnerie with a 15C house.

In rue Haute-Notre-Dame stands the small 11C Chapelle Notre-Dame, rebuilt in the 16C and 19C. The first church built in the city, it was converted into a Protestant church in 1561, and then during the Terror used to store fodder; it became Catholic once again in 1827.

Musée de la Vilaine maritime ⊘ – The 16C and 17C Château des Basses-Fosses, on a spur on the west bank of the Vilaine, houses this museum of rural and maritime life on and along the Vilaine.

The ground floor explains the intense maritime activity which the river once had. The diorama of the Vilaine recreates the atmosphere which reigned along it in the early 1900s. A reconstructed cabin shows how life was on board a coastal fishing vessel. Upstairs, rural life is shown with exhibits of houses and the different kinds of timber work, roofing, and dormers; the old trades through tools belonging to the carpenter, mason and roofer; local costumes and headdresses.

Boat Trip on the River Vilaine ⊘ – Boats go down the Vilaine to the Barrage d'Arzal (Arzal Dam) or up to Redon.

Auberge Bretonne – *Place Du-Guesclin* – ☎ *02 99 90 60 28 – closed 15 Nov-4 Dec, Mon lunch Sept-June except for holidays, Fri lunch and Thur – 210/650F*. This establishment is luxurious and refined. A well-tended vegetable and herb garden surrounds the patio; inside the decor is bright and elegant, a lovely setting for the excellent dishes prepared by the award-winning chef and served by an attentive staff. The rooms are of the same high caliber.

EXCURSIONS

Missillac – *13km/8mi southeast by N 165 – E 60 towards Pontchâteau*.
The 19C church, built in the Gothic style, contains in its north apsidal chapel a graceful 17C wood **altarpiece★** ornamented with angels and prophets.
Separated from the town by a small stretch of water beside the wood, the 15C **Château de la Bretesche** (Bretesche Castle), with its low crenellated ramparts and water-filled moat, stands in an outstanding **site★**.

Barrage d'Arzal – *Round tour of 19km/12mi. Take the road towards Vannes; after 2km/1mi bear left.*

This dam on the Vilaine forms a freshwater reservoir thus eliminating the effect of the tides and making the trip easier for the coasting vessels that ply upstream to Redon. It is also an attractive stretch for pleasure craft. A road follows the crest of the dam over the river.

Past the dam, turn left to return to La Roche-Bernard.

Le Guerno – The village, once a popular place of pilgrimage, has a 16C church built where a Templars' Chapel once stood. The church's exterior has on its south side a pulpit, stalls and bench (reserved for the clergy); the altar is backed against the Calvary (on the square). The round tower, on the west side, is capped by an 18C lantern turret.

The inside is decorated by 16C stained-glass windows and choir stalls; 22 carved panels, also 16C, ornament the loft. At the transept two cylindrical columns support the vaulting. The trunk of the column on the left is hollow to collect offerings.

Once outside Le Guerno bear right then left onto the avenue which goes to Château de Branféré.

On the way to Branféré, notice two 18C fountains (on the right side of the road), dedicated to St Anne and St Mary.

Parc zoologique de Branféré ⊘ – The château stands in 50ha/124 acres of parkland, where over 200 species of exotic animals and countless birds roam amid the trees and a series of lakes.

Moulin de Pen-Mur ⊘ – *17km/11mi west on N 165 – E 60; leave this road at Muzillac and follow the signs for "Site de Pen-Mur".*

The mill, prettily located near a lake, contains an exhibition on the production of paper by hand using traditional 18C methods, showing all the stages from cutting up rags to the drying process.

Château de Léhélec – *18km/11mi to the north via D 774. At Péaule, take D 20 in the direction of Redon and after 8km/5mi turn right.*

Foleux – The marina is located in a lovely site at the confluence of the River Vilaine and River Trévelo.

After Foleux skirt the Vilaine – from here there is a good view of the wide valley. Bear right then turn left three times before taking the road which leads to the château.

Château de Léhélec ⊘ – Surrounded by woodland, this manor house, built of ferruginous schist, offers on its south front an attractive perspective of the three courtyards bordered by the 16C and 18C outbuildings. One of these buildings houses a small rural museum containing regional furniture and everyday objects. Visitors are also admitted to two rooms lit by tall windows – the drawing room and dining room on the ground floor. In the entrance hall note the staircase with its 18C wrought-iron handrail.

ROCHEFORT-EN-TERRE★

Population 645
Michelin map 63 fold 4 or 230 fold 38

This charming small, old town occupies a picturesque **site★** on a promontory between deep dells. This landscape of rocks, woods, ravines, orchards and old houses bright with geraniums attracts many painters.

★**Old houses** – In the heart of the town stand 16C and 17C town houses which you can see as you stroll along rue du Porche, place des Halles and place du Puits. At place du Puits note the former law court, the entrance of which is surmounted by a set of scales.

Château ⊘ – The only features that remain of the castle, destroyed in 1793, are the imposing entrance fort, sections of the walls, the underground passages and the outbuildings. The latter were restored at the turn of the century by the American Alfred Klots with parts – most notably the dormer windows – from the 17C Kéralio manor house near Muzillac.

The four rooms open to visitors are a good example of the studied decor of enthusiastic collectors avid for knowledge, whose eclectic spirit is reflected in the variety of the furniture and objets d'art they have assembled. Note a beautiful collection of Madonnas in Quimper faience. A small museum of folk art adjoining the old workshop of the owners evokes one or two aspects of the way of life in Rochefort in days gone by (lovely collection of headdresses). Another room contains the doors from the old dining room of a mansion, which were painted c 1880.

From the terrace, behind the castle, there is a fine view of the Gueuzon Valley and the Grées schist plateau.

Rochefort-en-Terre – Old houses

J. Labbé /AZIMUT

Église Notre-Dame-de-la-Tronchaye – The 12C, 15C and 16C church has a façade embellished with four gables pierced with Flamboyant bays. Inside, the chancel contains 16C stalls and, left of the high altar, a white stone Renaissance altarpiece. In the south arm of the transept, a 17C altarpiece behind a fine 18C wrought-iron grille bears the venerated statue of Our Lady of La Tronchaye, which was found in the 12C in a hollow tree where it was hidden at the time of the Norsemen invasions. The statue is the object of a pilgrimage on the Sunday after 15 August. In the north arm of the transept is a wrought-iron baptismal font and white stone Renaissance altarpieces; one of the altarpieces is decorated with three niches, each of which contains a painted wood statue. At the back of the nave the magnificent gallery in finely carved wood comes from the old rood screen as does the canopy over the high altar.

On the square stands a small 16C Calvary with three tiers of carved figures: the scenes of the Passion, the Crucifixion and the Deposition (both at the top) are represented.

Hotels

OUR SELECTION

Chambre d'hôte Hélioscope – *Rue Candré, below the town hall* – ☎ *02 97 43 35 44 – no credit cards – 5 rooms 260/290F.* In the heart of the city's medieval district, this museum presents the work of regional artists in changing exhibitions. However, the building also houses a few modern, white, comfortable and calm rooms.

TREAT YOURSELF!

Chambre d'hôte Château de Talhouët – *6km/4mi from Rochefort-en-Terre, on the route de Malestroit, then follow the signs* – ☎ *02 97 43 34 72 – 8 rooms from 700F – meals 230F.* If you've been dreaming of château life, you can enjoy it here in this beautiful 16C and 17C Breton manor house. Its luxurious salons, antique furniture, the wonderful comfort of its rooms, and the absolute tranquillity of its vast park make for a truly unforgettable experience!

EXCURSION

Malansac: Parc de Préhistoire ⊘ – *3km/2mi east on D 21 towards Malansac then D 134 to St-Gravé.*
Gwenfol site, with its lakes and old slate quarries, is now an outdoor museum of prehistory. Different tableaux composed of people and animals (life-size models) accompanied by explanatory panels illustrate the Paleolithic to the Neolithic Ages with such scenes as the discovery of fire, flint knapping, hunting, family life and the erection of a menhir.

Bretagne – *Rue St-Michel in Questembert* – ☎ *02 97 26 11 12 – Closed 5-31 Jan, Tues lunch and Mon except in summer and on public holidays – 295/520F.* This is a very special place to stop and enjoy an exceptional meal and luxurious rooms. The panelled rooms of the restaurant create a warm ambience, while the rooms are spacious and modern. In fine weather, you can enjoy your meal in the garden.

Questembert – A small friendly town located in a verdant countryside. Around the market place stand elegant granite town houses (16C-17C) with carved pediments. In rue St-Michel, in a garden, is an odd-looking turret, the roof of which is held up by two carved busts of "Questembert and his wife". The impressive **market place** was built in 1552 and restored in 1675; the timber work covers the three alleys.

Chapelle St-Michel – This small 16C chapel stands in the cemetery. On the north side is a Calvary. This monument, as well as the one built on place du Monument, recalls the victory of Alain-le-Grand over the Norsemen in 888 at Coët-Bihan *(6.5km/4mi southeast of Questembert)*.

La Vraie-Croix – *8km/5mi west by D 1.* This charming village decked with flowers (awarded First Prize for the prettiest flowered village in 1994) still has its chapel resting on ribbed vaulting. In the old days, the road used to run underneath the vaulting. The lower part of the building appears to date back to the 13C. Two flights of steps carved in stone on the outside of the chapel lead to the upper section, which was rebuilt in 1611.
The building houses a gilded reliquary cross containing a fragment of the Cross of Our Lord.

ROSCOFF

Population 3 787
Michelin map 58 fold 6 or 230 fold 5

Roscoff is a much-frequented seaside resort and a medical centre using seawater treatment (thalassotherapy); it is also a fishing port for lobster and spiny lobster, a pleasure boat harbour and a great vegetable market and distribution centre to England. Fishing and pleasure boats dock behind two jetties near the town centre, beyond the old ramparts. A pier to the east of Pointe de Bloscon closes off the deep-water harbour from which car ferries sail to and from Plymouth and Cork.
The University of Paris and the scientific research body Centre National de la Recherche Scientifique (CNRS) have set up a laboratory in the town for oceanographic and biological research.

SIGHTS

★Église Notre-Dame-de-Croas-Batz (Y) – This Gothic church was completed in 1545, funded by the privateers and merchants of the town. For this reason the outside walls and tower feature sculpted ship's nails as ex-votos. The church has a remarkable Renaissance **belfry★** with lantern turrets, one of the finest examples of its type in Brittany. Inside, on the retable of the altar to the Sacré-Cœur (south aisle), there are four 16C **alabaster bas-relief sculptures★** from the Nottingham studio depicting the Flagellation, the Crucifixion, the Ascension and Pentecost. The **altar-**

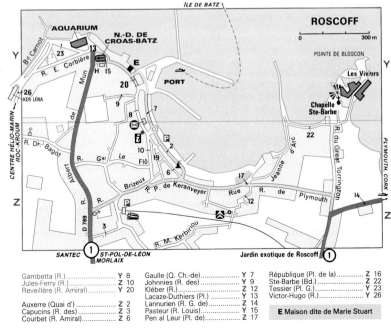

Gambetta (R.)	Y 8	Gaulle (Q. Ch.-de)	Y 7	République (Pl. de la)	Z 16
Jules-Ferry (R.)	Z 10	Johnnies (R. des)	Y 9	Ste-Barbe (Bd.)	Z 22
Reveillère (R. Amiral)	Y 20	Kléber (R.)	Z 12	Tessier (Pl. G.)	Y 23
		Lacaze-Duthiers (Pl.)	Y 13	Victor-Hugo (R.)	Y 26
Auxerre (Quai d')	Z 2	Lannurien (R. G. de)	Z 14		
Capucins (R. des)	Z 3	Pasteur (R. Louis)	Y 15		
Courbet (R. Amiral)	Z 6	Pen le Leur (Pl. de)	Z 17	**E Maison dite de Marie Stuart**	

piece of the 17C high altar has six wreathed columns and is richly decorated with statues of the Evangelists, cherubs and pampers. The organ case dates from the 17C. The font (1701) was restored in 1991.

In the church close are two chapel-ossuaries: that in the southwest corner dates from the 16C and has been dedicated to St Brigitte; that in the northwest corner (early 17C) did not originally have a door at all, as it was used purely to store bones.

★**Aquarium Charles-Pérez** ☉ **(Y)** – The aquarium has a central pool and several tanks in which most of the creatures to be found in the Channel are shown in their natural state. The first floor is devoted to the history of the biological centre and a maritime exhibition.

Chapelle Ste-Barbe (Y) – *It is best to visit this chapel at high tide. Go round the fishing port and leave the car in the car park on the left. Viewing table.*

In the centre of a pretty little garden sits the tiny chapel dedicated to St Barbara. Its white walls still serve as a landing mark to mariners. There is a beautiful view of the town, the port, the Île de Batz, Pointe de Primel and the deep-water harbour at Bloscon, which is the departure point for car ferries to Britain and Ireland.

Go round the hill on which the chapel stands.

Viviers ☉ **(Y)** – Footbridges lead visitors round the 5 200m²/55 972sq ft fish farm in which lobsters, crawfish and crabs are raised. Thanks to the renewal of the 32 000m³/1 130 070cu ft of water with every tide, the shellfish live in conditions which are almost identical with those found in their natural environment.

Go back along the rue de Great Torrington, then take the road to the deep-water harbour towards St-Pol. Turn left at Keraison.

★**Jardin exotique de Roscoff** ☉ – This extraordinary garden is wrapped around the Rocher de Roch-Hievec (or Rocher de Maison Rouge). Over 1 000 subtropical plant species thrive here, producing both blossom and fruit. The footpaths will take you past proteaceous shrubs from Australia, more than 50 varieties of eucalyptus tree, several other southern species and an amazing collection of "succulent plants", in other words, cactuses. A staircase leads to the summit, which commands a nice view of the bay of Morlaix, Roscoff, Carantec and the Château du Taureau.

EXCURSION

Île de Batz – The island of **Batz** ☉ (pronounced Ba), 4km/2.5mi long and 1km/0.6mi wide, is separated from the mainland by a narrow channel, notorious for its treacherous currents. The ferry arrives in Kernoc'h Bay, which is fringed by the village and the modern buildings of the rescue station. This treeless – with the exception of the village – island has sandy beaches. To the north, the island is fringed by offshore skerries. The mild climate is particularly suitable for market gardening. On Batz the men are either sailors or farmers, and the women help in the market gardens or gather seaweed.

> **Grand Hôtel** – *Île de Batz* – ☏ *02 98 61 78 06 – closed Dec-Feb – 34 rooms – half-board 240/280 – breakfast 30F – restaurant 85/130F.* From the terrace, the view over the harbour provides the perfect backdrop for savouring seafood and the family style dishes on the menu. In winter time, the dining room with its traditional Breton decor is attractive too. Though the rooms are very plain, the peace and quiet and the lovely view are a great advantage.

Church – The church in the centre of the village was built in 1873. Note in the choir the statues of the Virgin (14C-15C) and St Paul the Aurelian (in wood, 17C), the Celtic saint of British origin who died on the island in 573. In the north transept, there is a piece of oriental material dating from the 8C, reputed to be 'the stole of St Paul' *(details at the Trou du Serpent).*

Lighthouse – *On the island's west side. 210 steps.* The 44m/144ft tall lighthouse stands on the island's highest point (23m/75ft). View of the island and reef-fringed coast.

Trou du Serpent – *Go beyond the lighthouse and after the ruined house on the dune, take the path to the right.*

The low-lying rock offshore is said to mark the spot where St Paul the Aurelian, with the help of his stole, cast out the dragon who was terrorising the island.

Chapelle Ste-Anne – *On the island's east side.*

A ruined Romanesque chapel stands on the site of the monastery founded by St Paul. *Pardon on the Sunday nearest to 26 July.*

From the nearby sand dunes there are fine views of the coast and offshore islets.

ROSTRENEN

Population 3 664

Michelin map 59 fold 11 or 230 fold 21

This pretty little town is situated on a hillside.

Église Notre-Dame-du-Roncier – The church was once the castle chapel (set on fire during the League in 1572). It was built in the 14C and remodelled in the 18C and 19C, and has a beautiful transitional Gothic-Renaissance porch. Close by is an interesting 17C sacred fountain. A *pardon* is held on 15 August.

Le Miniou – Take the road towards Pontivy, then a road to the right and up the hill turn left to reach a weather centre *(station climatologique)* situated at an altitude of 263m/928ft. The panorama extends over Rostrenen and the area round Callac to the northwest and Loudéac to the east; from the terrace, there is a view over the Guéméné region to the south and the Montagnes Noires to the west.

EXCURSIONS

Round tour of 45km/28mi – 2hr 30min. Leave Rostrenen northeast by D 790, the St-Brieuc road.

St-Nicolas-du-Pélem – The town includes a 15C-16C church with two fine stained-glass windows depicting the Passion (1470) at the flat east end. Go round the north side of the church to see the 17C fountain of St-Nicolas which abuts onto a house.

Proceed to Lanrivain.

The road crosses the delightful Vallée du Faoudel.

Lanrivain – In the cemetery stands a 15C ossuary with trefoil arches. To the right of the church is a 16C Calvary adorned with huge granite figures.

Chapelle Notre-Dame-du-Guiaudet – *1.5km/1mi north by the road towards Bourbriac. At the entrance to the hamlet of Guiaudet take an alleyway marked by two granite pillars on the right.*
The chapel, which dates from the late 17C, has over the high altar a sculpted scene representing a recumbent Virgin holding the Infant Jesus in her arms. The bell-tower contains a carillon of 16 bells which plays two hymns dedicated to Our Lady.

Continue to Trémargat and after 1.5km/1mi bear left.

★**Gorges de Toul Goulic** – *15min on foot there and back.* At the far end of the car park overlooking the wooded valley of the Blavet, take the steep path leading downhill through the woods to the cleft in which the Blavet disappears. The river is still full at the beginning of the cleft (north side) but has completely vanished by the time you reach the middle of the cleft and flows, rumbling, beneath a mass of huge rocks.

Turn back and bear left.

Between Trémargat and Kergrist-Moëlou, the landscape is studded with great boulders.

Kergrist-Moëlou – On the church square, shaded by fine old yew trees, stands a Calvary (1578) with some 100 figures in Kersanton granite resting on its octagonal plinth. The figures were damaged during the Revolution and have been replaced haphazardly. The imposing 16C church has a twin transept and in the chancel the stained-glass windows are decorated with the coat of arms of the Rostrenen family, the church's founders. On the south side is a small ossuary with trefoil arches.

Via St-Lubin return to Rostrenen.

Nantes-Brest Canal – *Round tour of 20km/12mi – 2hr 30min. Leave Rostrenen on the road towards Carhaix-Plouguer and after 3.5km/2mi, turn left into the Gourin road.*
The road reaches the canal, built between 1823 and 1834, at the summit level (alt 184m/604ft). Walk along the towpath to the right of the bridge, leading to the canal cutting and affording a view of the 44 locks through which boats climb or descend 120m/384ft over 17km/11mi to Carhaix-Plouguer.

Proceed to Glomet and then turn right onto the road towards Paule; after 1.8km/1mi, bear right.
On the canal banks, the former lock-keeper's house stands in a pretty **site**★. It is a pleasant walk along the towpath upstream and downstream from the bridge.

Return to the main road and turn right back to Rostrenen.

To find the description of a town or an isolated tourist attraction, consult the index.

ST-BRIEUC ★

Conurbation 83 861

Michelin map 59 fold 3 or 230 folds 8 and 9

The town is built 3km/2mi from the sea on a plateau deeply cleft by two water courses: the Gouëdic and the Gouet. Bold viaducts span their valleys. The Gouet is canalised and leads to the commercial and fishing port of Légué.

St-Brieuc is the administrative, commercial and industrial centre of the departement (Côtes d'Armor). The markets and fairs of the town are much frequented, especially the Fair of St Michael (Foire de la St-Michel) on 29 September and another event in early September. On Saturdays, a market is held on the cathedral's parvis.

An industrial zone has been established southwest of the town. The *pardon* of Notre-Dame-d'Espérance takes place the last Sunday in May.

SIGHTS

★**Cathédrale St-Étienne** ⊙ (**AY**) – This great cathedral of the 13C and 14C has been reconstructed several times and restored in the 19C; its mass bears striking witness to its original role of church fortress. The front is framed by two great towers complete with loopholes and machicolations and supported by stout buttresses. The two arms of the transept jut far out and are protected by towers with pepper-pot roofs. The lofty nave with its seven bays was rebuilt in the 18C. The harmonious three-sided chancel has an elegant triforium with quatrefoil balustrade and trefoil arches above the great arcades.

In the south aisle, note the carved wooden altar by Corlay (c 1745) in the Chapel of the Holy Sacrament. The south arm of the transept is lit by fine 15C stained-glass windows and in the small chapel stands the tomb of St William (d 1234). The stained-glass windows represent the Glorification of Mary. The 16C organ loft, the 18C pulpit and the Stations of the Cross carved in granite by Saupique (1958) are also noteworthy.

★**Tertre Aubé** (**ABV**) – The hill commands a fine **view**★ of the Vallée du Gouet, crossed by the viaduct which carries the road to Paimpol; also of the partly hidden port of Légué, below, and, to the right, of St-Brieuc Bay. On a hill to the right is the ruined tower of Cesson.

Old houses (**AY**) – The area to the north of the cathedral still retains many 15C-16C half-timbered and corbelled houses.

Walk through place du Martray, rue Fardel (at the corner of place au Lin: the Ribeault mansion; at no 15, the house known as the "mansion of the dukes of Brittany"; nos 17, 19, 27, 29, 31, 32 and 34), rue Quinquaine (no 9) and rue de Gouet (nos 6, 16, 22).

Museum (**Musée**) ⊙ (**AZ M**) – Located in renovated rooms, the museum traces the history and development of the Côtes d'Armor departement (formerly Côtes-du-Nord) during the 19C, when traditional Brittany evolved into modern Brittany. Different themes – St-Brieuc Bay, heathland, cloth and linen trade, village life – accompanied by models, equipment and tools used for fishing, navigation and husbandry, as well as costumes and furnishings, are evoked.

Grandes Promenades (**BYZ**) – These walks encircle the Palais de Justice (Law Courts). Among the statues are a bust by Elie Le Goff senior of the writer Villiers de l'Isle-Adam, who was born at St-Brieuc, *Form Arising from Matter* by Paul Le Goff and *La Bretonne du Goëlo* by Francis Renaud.

Rond-Point Huguin (**BX**) – From the roundabout, on which stands a monument to the folklorist Anatole Le Braz, there is a view of the Vallée du Gouëdic and its two viaducts with the village and tower of Cesson perched high above, St-Brieuc Bay and the coast as far as Cap Fréhel.

Fontaine de St-Brieuc (**AY B**) – The fountain, which is sheltered by a lovely 15C porch, stands against the east end of the Chapelle of Notre-Dame-de-la-Fontaine, which was rebuilt in the 19C.

Tour du Saint-Esprit (**AY**) – This tower, an interesting Renaissance structure with a pepper-pot octagonal corner tower, was restored in 1962.

EXCURSION

Round tour of 25km/15mi – 2hr. Leave St-Brieuc north by Légué port, follow the quay on the north bank.

On the right, the ruined tower of Cesson is outlined amid the greenery; as the road climbs there is a good view over the Pointe des Guettes at the far end of the bay and the coast as far as Cap d'Erquy.

★**Pointe du Roselier** – Take a path on the right of the telescope to go round the point. Fine **views**★ extend over St-Quay-Portrieux and the coast; the path passes near an old oven used for turning cannon-balls red-hot, and skirts a villa. The view takes in the Pointe de Cesson, the far end of St-Brieuc Bay and the Pointe des Guettes with its mussel poles, and the coast towards Le Val-André. Paths cut in the cliffside lead back to the starting point.

Turn back and after 2km/1mi, bear right.

ST-BRIEUC

B Fontaine de St-Brieuc   **M** Musée

Martin-Plage – This pretty beach lies between Pointe du Roselier and the Tablettes Reef (Rocher des Tablettes).
The road then climbs steeply and at Ville-Fontaine, bear right onto a pleasant little road descending between wooded embankments.

Plage des Rosaires – The beach is framed by wooded cliffs some 100m/320ft high. The view includes the whole of St-Brieuc Bay from St-Quay Point to Cap d'Erquy.
The road leads straight back to St-Brieuc.

Marinarium de la Baie de St-Brieuc ⊘ – *10km/6mi east. Take ② on the town plan, then leave the expressway for Yffignac. Take D 80 to Hillion. Follow the signs to "Maison de la Baie".*

Rue du Gouët

OUR SELECTION

Hôtel Clisson – *36 rue Gouët* – ☎ *02 96 62 19 29* – *closed 27 Dec-9 Jan* – 🅿 – *24 rooms 270/430F* – *breakfast 38F*. In a calm street near the town centre, this is the most pleasant hotel in St-Brieuc. The rooms are recent and are of various sizes, but they have all been furnished with care. The rooms with bath are the most spacious.

Eating out

BUDGET

Crêperie les Druides – *1 bis rue des Trois-Frères-Le-Goff* – ☎ *02 96 33 53 00* – *closed 25 Oct-7 Nov, at lunch and Mon, except in summer* – *40/70F*. Located near the cathedral, this crêperie enjoys a good reputation and its *"galettes aux noix de St-Jacques"* (scallops) are quite popular. Don't hesitate to ask they will gladly cook your crêpes exactly to your liking. Despite the rather ordinary decor, the welcome is nonetheless attentive and pleasant.

OUR SELECTION

Aux Pesked – *59 rue du Légué* – ☎ *02 96 33 34 65* – *closed 22 Dec-15 Jan, Sat lunch, Sun evening, and Mon* – *115/495F*. "Pesked" (fish in Breton) have the starring role in this well-known restaurant. The regulars praise this cuisine and its accents on local specialities, prepared and served by a very competent team.

Shopping

Poterie du Légué – *Rue de la Poste* – *Mon-Fri 10am-1pm, 2pm-7pm, Sat-Sun 2pm-7pm*. Etienne Huck has installed his pottery studio in this splendid 16C house.

La Duchesse de Rohan – *2 rue Saint-Goueno* – ☎ *02 96 33 36 27* – *Tues-Sat 8.30am-1pm, 3pm-7pm, Sun 8.30am-1pm*. Immediately recognizable by its historic façade, this is one of the best pastry shops in St-Brieuc. Its simplicity is charming, and its owner was a gymnastics instructor before converting to a life in pastries.

Markets – St-Brieuc's markets and fairs are very popular, particularly the fair of St Michael (29 September), and the festival exhibition which is held at the beginning of September. On Saturdays, there is a very lively market in front of the cathedral.

Going out

Le Piano Bleu – *4 place Fardel* – ☎ *02 96 31 41 62* – *daily 5pm-3am*. An inimitable little bar which hosts memorable concerts of rock and well-known French music. Bistro decor.

La Passerelle – *Place de la Résistance* – ☎ *02 96 68 18 40* – information and performances Tues-Sat 10am-pm. National stage which hosts the majority of the city's cultural performances: theatre, music, opera, dance.

Recreation

Aéroclub des Côtes-d'Armor – *Aéroport de St-Brieuc, Le Plessis* – ☎ *02 96 94 97 04*. This flying club offers various kinds of flights (private planes, helicopters etc) starting at 120F per person (100F for children under 12).

Centre municipal de voile de Saint-Brieuc – *27 boulevard de Cornouaille, in Plerin* – ☎ *02 96 74 51 59* – *open year round, Mon-Sat 9am-noon, 2pm-6pm.* Sailing school which offers day sailors, catamarans, and sail-boarding.

Hotels

OUR SELECTION

Chambre d'hôte Château du Val d'Arguenon – *Route de St-Malo, 9km/6mi* – ☎ *02 96 41 07 03* – *closed Oct-Mar* – *no credit cards* – *5 rooms 450/610F.* This is a romantic spot where you can stroll around the park down to the sea, admire the architecture of the manor house which has belonged to the same family for two centuries, enjoy the beautiful antique salons, and sleep in a room with character and charm. Three simpler *gîtes* also available.

Eating out

BUDGET

Le Biniou – *Route de Dinard, 1.5km/1mi* – ☎ *02 96 41 94 53* – *closed 11 Nov-15 Dec, 5 Jan-18 Feb, Mon evening and Tues except during school holidays* – *98/220F.* Here, facing the beach, you can enjoy simple, fresh food. In the summer the bar offers a simplified menu. The restaurant serves salads at lunchtime and only on weekdays.

This visitor information centre for the marine environment displays about 100 species of animal and plant life collected exclusively from the Bay of St-Brieuc, between Plérin and Erquy. Each aquarium illustrates a different type of behaviour: mimicry (plaice and skate on the sandy sea floor); group life in shoals; interrelation of certain species (hermit crab and sea anemone). Regular excursions are organised in discovery of local bird life or the natural habitat.

ST-CAST-LE-GUILDO ≜≜

Population 3 093
Michelin map 59 fold 5 or 230 folds 10 and 11
Local map see CÔTE D'ÉMERAUDE – Facilities

This seaside resort is formed by three settlements: Le Bourg, L'Isle and Les Mielles. The port shelters a small fishing fleet which specialises in scallops and clams.

★★Pointe de St-Cast – There is a superb **view★★** of the Côte d'Emeraude from the point (viewing table – *table d'orientation* – beside the signal station). At the tip of the point a monument to the Escaped Prisoners of France (Monument aux Évadés) can be reached by a cliff path which follows the shore, passes another monument dedicated to the crew of the frigate *Laplace*, mined in 1950, and rejoins the St-Cast road at La Mare Beach (Plage de la Mare).

★★Pointe de la Garde – At the end of this point there is a very fine **view★★** of the beaches of St-Cast and Pen Guen and the coast as far as Pointe de la Garde; also a statue of Notre-Dame-de-la-Garde by Armel Beaufils. A scenic path goes round the point by way of the Corniche de la Plage near the Hôtel Ar Vro, passes beside the oratory, follows the cliff along the point and, on the south shore, joins the road leading to the slipway near the oratory.

Church – *At Le Bourg.* The modern church, built between 1897 and 1899, contains a 12C stoup and some 17C statues. In the north arm of the transept, a modern stained-glass window depicts the Battle of St-Cast *(see above)*.

Chapelle Ste-Blanche – *At L'Isle.* Above the high altar is an old statue of St Blanche – the mother of St Guénolé, St Jacut and St Venec – which is the object of great veneration.

The Green Guide France:
Designed to enhance your travels in France,
with suggested 5-day touring programmes,
Personalise your journey be taking advantage
of interesting options and combinations.

ST-MALO ★★★

Population 48 067

Michelin map 59 fold 6 or 230 fold 11 – Local maps see CÔTE D'ÉMERAUDE
and Vallée de la RANCE

St-Malo, St-Servan, Paramé and Rothéneuf have joined together to form the munici-pality of St-Malo. The **site★★★** is unique in France and makes it one of the great tourist centres of Brittany.

The port – Located in the centre of the large roadstead, which once divided the pri-vateer's encampment (St-Malo-de-l'Isle) from the continent (St-Servan, Paramé), the port is developing a wide range of activities. It has four wet docks (Vauban, Duguay-Trouin, Bouvet and Jacques-Cartier) sheltered by a lock, where handling of goods and fish are concentrated. Imported products hold an important position: fertilisers, timber and wood. Its outer harbour is equipped with two shipping terminals for car ferries and boat services; there are daily services between St-Malo and Portsmouth and St-Malo and the Channel Islands (Jersey and Guernesey).

Pleasure boating has not been forgotten: dockage is located at the foot of the ram-parts and especially at Bas-Sablons near the Corniche d'Aleth.

HISTORICAL NOTES

Origin – St Malo, returning from Wales in the 6C, converted the Gallo-Roman settle-ment Aleth (St-Servan) to Christianity and became its bishop. The neighbouring island, on which the present town of St-Malo is built, was then uninhabited. Later, people settled there because it was easy to defend from the Norsemen, and it became impor-tant enough for the Bishopric of Aleth to be transferred to it in 1144. It took the name of St Malo, while Aleth put itself under the protection of another local saint, St Servan.

The town belonged to its bishops, who built ramparts round it. It took no part in provincial rivalries. At the time of the League, St-Malo declared itself a republic and was able to keep its independence for four years. This principle was reflected in the device: *"Ni Français, ni Breton, Malouin suis"* (I am neither French nor Breton but a man of St-Malo).

Famous men of St-Malo – Few towns have had as many famous sons as St-Malo over the centuries.

Jacques Cartier left in 1534 to look for gold in Newfoundland and Labrador: instead he discovered the mouth of the River St Lawrence, which he took to be the estuary of a great Asian river. As the word *Canada*, which means "village" in the Huron lan-guage, was often used by the Indians he encountered, he used the word to name the country. Cartier took possession of the land in the name of the king of France in 1534, but it was only under Champlain that the colonisation of Canada began and that Quebec was founded (1608).

Porcon de la Bardinais, who had been charged in 1665 by the St-Malo shipowners to defend their ships agains the Barbary pirates, was captured and taken before the Dey of Algiers. The Dey sent him to Louis XIV with peace proposals on condition that if these were not accepted he would return to Algiers. The Dey's proposals were refused, whereupon Porcon went to St-Malo to put his affairs in order, said farewell to his family and returned to Africa, where he was executed.

Duguay-Trouin (1673-1736) and **Surcouf** (1773-1827) are the most famous of the St-Malo privateers. These bold seamen received "letters of marque" from the king which permitted them to attack warships or merchantmen without being treated as pirates, that is, hanged from the main yard. In the 17C and 18C, privateers inflicted heavy losses on the English, Dutch and Spanish.

Duguay was the son of a rich shipowner and had been destined for the priesthood; but by the time he was 16 the only way to put an end to his wild living was to send him to sea. His gifts were such that, at 24, he entered the so-called Great Corps of the French Navy as a commander and at 36 he was given a peerage. When he died, he was a Lieutenant General in the seagoing forces and a Commander of the Order of St Louis.

Surcouf's history is completely different, but just as outstanding. He answered the call of the sea when very young and soon began a prodigious career of fabulous exploits. First as slaver, then as privateer, he amassed an enormous fortune. At 36 he retired, but continued to make money by fitting out privateers and merchantmen.

Chateaubriand and Lamennais brought the flavour of the Romantic Movement to their native St-Malo.

François-René de Chateaubriand (1768-1848) was the tenth and last child of a very noble Breton family who had fallen on bad times. His father went to America in search of fortune and was able, on his return, to set up as a shipowner at St-Malo. In a room on the second floor of a modest town house (Maison Natale de Chateaubriand – it gives onto the courtyard of the Hôtel France et Chateaubriand and is near the Tour Quic-en-Groigne) René was born. From its window he could look out to sea beyond the ramparts and dream...

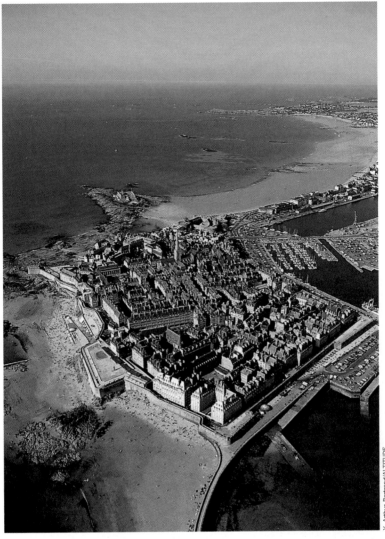

St-Malo

The future poet spent his early years in roaming about the port, then went in succession through schools at Dinan, Dol, Rennes and Brest, dreaming sometimes of the priesthood, sometimes of the sea.

He spent two years in exile at Combourg with his father, mother and sister Lucile. It was through the profession of arms that he began, in 1786, the adventurous career which ended in 1848 in the solitary grandeur of Grand Bé.

Lamennais (1782-1854), another St-Malo shipowner's son, also had a place in the Romantic Movement. He became an orphan early and was brought up by an uncle at the castle of Chesnaye, near Dinan. At 22 he taught mathematics in the College of St-Malo before entering the seminary of that town.

He was ordained a priest in 1816 and had a great influence on Lacordaire and Montalembert. His writings and violent quarrels got him into trouble with Rome which led him to renounce the Church.

He retired to Chesnay and published, in 1834, the famous *Paroles d'un croyant (Words of a Believer)*. Owing to his advanced political ideas, he was sentenced to a year's imprisonment in 1840 but won a seat in the National Assembly in 1848.

To the famous men of St-Malo, already mentioned, should be added **Mahé de la Bourdonnais** (1699-1753), a great colonist and the rival of Dupleix in the Indies; **Broussais** (1772-1838), who transformed the medical science of his time; **Gournay** (1712-59), the economist to whom the formula "*laissez faire, laissez passer*" (let it be, let it go) is attributed; and finally the saintly figure of **André Desilles**. In 1790 the garrison of Nancy, to which this 23-year-old lieutenant belonged, revolted against the National Assembly. Troops were sent to subdue it. To prevent the fratricidal struggle, Desilles threw himself in front of the guns and fell, mortally wounded.

Hotels

BUDGET

Chambre d'hôte La Gœlettrie – *20 rue Goëlettrie, quartier Quelmer, 7km/5mi from St-Malo, direction Dinard then Quelmer* – ☎ *02 99 81 92 64 – no credit cards – 5 rooms 240/300F – meals 100F*. The country side of St-Malo! An unusual spot in such a sea-centred city. This pretty farm, facing the River Rance, offers peace and tranquillity. Although the rooms lack character, the welcome is quite charming.

OUR SELECTION

Hôtel les Ajoncs d'Or – *10 rue des Forgeurs* – ☎ *02 99 40 85 03 – closed 15 Nov-24 Feb – 22 rooms 440/590F – breakfast 48F*. In the old section of the city, this cosy hotel recently modernised its rooms and bathrooms. Breakfast is served on bistro tables and chairs in its small bar area, where you can also have a drink at other times.

Hôtel Quic en Groigne – *8 rue d'Estrées* – ☎ *02 99 20 22 20 – 15 rooms 270/420F – breakfast 42F*. This old stone hotel is well run, and is a good address to have. Located in a narrow street, it offers understated rooms that are pleasant and light. Breakfast is served on the veranda.

Hôtel la Rance – *15 quai Sébastopol (Port Solidor)* – ☎ *02 99 81 78 63 – 11 rooms 415/515F – breakfast 49F*. At the foot of the Solidor Tower, this little hotel offers pretty views of the port and the bay. The salon is decorated with paintings, models and curios relating to the sea, and is furnished with the same care as the rooms. A few balconies look onto the sea.

TREAT YOURSELF!

Hôtel Valmarin – *7 rue Jean-XXIII* – ☎ *02 99 81 94 76 – closed 15 Nov-20 Dec and 3 Jan to mid-Feb* – ◪ – *12 rooms from 550F – breakfast 60F*. It's impossible not to be completely charmed by this elegant 18C building. Its beautiful salons that open onto the park and its spacious rooms, decorated with antiques, couple refinement with comfort.

Eating out

BUDGET

Chalut – *8 rue de la Corne-de-Cerf* – ☎ *02 99 56 71 58 – closed Sun evening and Mon Sept-June – 100/300F*. An indispensable stop for food-lovers! Run by a young and impassioned chef, this restaurant serves delicious seafood. It's a well-known fact that the quality is excellent for the price here, so it's best to reserve.

Crêperie Ti Nevez – *12 rue Broussais (intra-muros)* – ☎ *02 99 40 82 50 – closed Jan, 15 Nov-7 Dec, Wed except in summer and evening except on weekends – 45/80F*. Founded in 1959, this tiny crêperie is proud of its traditional aspects, as much in its decor of Breton furniture and old photographs, as in its cuisine. Try the famous *gâteau breton*.

La Corderie – *At St-Servan-sur-Mer, cité d'Aleth, chemin de la Corderie* – ☎ *02 99 81 62 38 – closed mid-Oct to mid-Mar and Mon except in summer – 98F*. This villa is superbly situated above the Solidor Tower, overlooking the River Rance and its dam. In nice weather, the terrace is quite popular, and in the winter, its two dining rooms are also charming, with their large bay windows, antique furniture and paintings.

OUR SELECTION

Clos du Chanoine – *6km/3.6mi route de Canacale, La Mettrie au Chanoine* – ☎ *02 99 82 84 57 – closed 21-30 June, 15-30 Nov, Thur lunch except in Aug, and on Wed – 130/280F*. In this charming 17C Breton house, you'll revel in a starred stopover. Already well-known locally, it will win you over as well by its up-to-date preparation of regional products, served in the garden in the summer.

Going out

Cunningham's Bar – *2 rue des Hauts-Sablons* – ☎ *02 99 81 48 08 – daily 5pm-3am*. With its beautiful nautical decor and its bay window facing the ocean, this high-class bar is one of the choice addresses in St-Malo. It has been in business for 25 years and is still thriving. You can relax with a beer while listening to the pianist or a musical group.

Le Cancalais – *1 quai Solidor* – ☎ *02 99 81 15 79* – *off-season, daily 10.30am-1pm; July-Aug, daily 9am-2am.* This little 100-year-old bistro on the Solidor port is known all over St-Malo. It has been run by the same family since the late 1980s, and provides an ideal spot to sip an aperitif on the terrace in the late afternoon. A clientele of regulars.

L'Aviso – *12 rue du Point-du-Jour* – ☎ *02 99 40 99 08* – *off-season, Tues-Sat; June-Sept, daily 6pm-3am.* This beer bar (300 on the menu) has been run by the same person for 20 years. His friends call him the "beer-therapist" since he always has the right beer for whatever ails you, and because he writes up your bar total on a doctor's prescription pad! To know more about the medicinal virtues of his brews, pay him a visit in this enjoyable establishment.

Saint-Patrick – *24 rue Ste-Barbe* – ☎ *02 99 56 66 90* – off-season, Sun-Thur 11am-1am, Fri-Sat 2pm-1am; summer, daily 2pm-2am. This pub is made of a succession of small rooms. Go straight up to the first floor and sit on the unusual, sunken, circular banquette. Specialises in beers and whiskies (40 are offered).

Shopping

La Droguerie de Marine – *66 rue Georges-Clémenceau, at St-Servan-sur-Mer.* This store houses a surprising universe of seafaring articles, such as the "pop-pop boat" which is sure to delight young children.

Recreation

Théâtre de St-Servan – *6 place Bouvet* – ☎ *02 99 81 62 61* – *information Tues-Sat 10am-12pm, 3pm-7pm.* This theatre presents the principal performances in St-Malo: plays, variety shows, classical music, ballet, cabaret...

Point Passion Plage – *Plage de Bonsecours* – ☎ *02 99 40 11 45* – *Spring-Autumn, daily 1.30pm-5.30pm; summer, daily 10am-6pm.* Located just behind the Intra-Muros, this sailing centre offers classes and rentals for day sailors and sailboards.

Surf School – *2 avenue de la Hoguette* – ☎ *02 99 40 07 47* – *off-season, daily 9am-noon, 1.30pm-6pm; July-Aug, Mon-Sat until 7pm, Sun 2pm-6pm.* This club organises classes and rentals for sailboards, funboards, sandsurfers, kitesurfers, speed sail, and surfboards.

Sailing on a schooner

La Renard – *Association Cotre Corsaire* – ☎ *02 99 40 53 10.* Originally built for "Brest 92," this schooner sails 27 passengers towards Cap Fréhel, or 12 passengers towards the Îles Chausey.

Association Étoile marine – ☎ *02 99 40 48 72.* This association organises day and weekend trips out to sea on its schooners: Étoile Molène, Le Popoff et Fleur de Mai.

Boat trips

The Émeraude Lines company organises excursions on the bay of St-Malo (1hr), to l'Île Cézembre (15min), to cap Fréhel (2hr 45min), to Dinan by the Rance River (2hr 30min), to the Îles Chausey (1hr 45min). July-Aug to go directly from St-Malo to Dinard, without taking the car, take the "sea bus" (15min), 7h30am-10.40pm; Sept-June every hour. Gare maritime de la Bourse, B.P. 16, 35401 St-Malo Cedex. ☎ *02 23 18 15 15.*

Dinard★★★ – *See this name.*

Croisière du cap Fréhel★★★ – *See this name.*

Vallée de la Rance★★ – *See this name.*

Île de Cézembre – *See Dinard.*

Îles Chausey★ – *The sights and curiosities are described in the Michelin Green Guide to Normandy-Cotentin-Îles anglo-normandes.*

Îles anglo-normandes – *The sights and curiosities are described in the Michelin Green Guide to Normandy-Cotentin-Îles anglo-normandes. To go to Jersey, Guernesey, Sark and Aurigny, boats (catamaran hydrojet, catamaran waver) and car-ferries depart regularly from St-Malo. Mar to beginning Nov: the Condor Ferries company runs daily links to the Îles anglo-normandes (Jersey, Guernesey) and to Great Britain (Weymouth et Poole) by rapid stabilised car-ferries.* ☎ *02 99 20 03 00.*

ST-MALO
PARAMÉ-ST-SERVAN

0 ———— 500 m

E Quic-en-Groigne   **M¹** Musée de la Poupée et du Jouet ancien

---

As Chateaubriand commented of his home town: "It's not a bad record for an area smaller than the Tuileries Gardens."

Destruction and renaissance of St-Malo – St-Malo and the surrounding area were turned into an entrenched camp by the Germans and became the prize for which a merciless battle raged from 1-14 August 1944. The town was left in ruins. With a great sense of history, its restorers were determined to bring the old city back to life. They have been completely successful in their quest.

★★★ ST MALO'S WALLED CITY (The Ramparts) *2hr*

*Leave your car on Esplanade St-Vincent (**DZ**).*

The statue near the esplanade, at the entrance to the Casino garden, portrays Chateaubriand by Armel Beaufils. It was erected in 1948 on the centenary of his death. Pass under Porte St-Vincent which consists of twin gates; then take the staircase to the right leading to the ramparts.

The ramparts, started in the 12C, were enlarged and altered up to the 18C and survived the wartime destruction. The rampart walk commands magnificent views, especially at high tide, of the coast and islands.

From Porte St-Vincent to Bastion St-Louis – Directly after Grande Porte (Great Gate), which is crowned with machicolations, the view opens out over the narrow isthmus which joins the old town to its suburbs, the harbour basins and, in the distance, St-Servan.

276

M² Musée d'Histoire de la ville et d'Ethnographie du pays malouin

From Bastion St-Louis to Bastion St-Philippe – The rampart skirts the houses where the rich shipowners of St-Malo lived; two, near the Bastion St-Louis, are still intact but the following walls and façades are reconstructions of carefully dismantled buildings. This fine group of houses with its high roofs, surmounted by monumental chimneys rising from the ramparts, once more gives this part of town its old look. The view extends over the outer harbour; to Rocher d'Aleth, crowned by Fort de la Cité, and the mouth of the Rance estuary; to Dinard, with Prieuré Beach and Pointe de Vicomté.

From Bastion St-Philippe to Tour Bidouane – A very fine view of the Côte d'Émeraude west of Dinard, and of the islands off St-Malo. To the right of Pointe du Moulinet, you can see part of the great beach at Dinard, Pointe des Étêtés separating Dinard from St-Lunaire, Pointe du Décollé, the Hébihens Archipelago, Pointe de St-Cast and Cap Fréhel; nearer, on the right, are the Île Harbour and, further to the right, Grand Bé and Petit Bé Islands; then, in the background, Île de Cézembre and Fort de la Conchée. Near Tour Bidouane stands a statue of Surcouf.

From Tour Bidouane to Porte St-Vincent – Having skirted the École nationale de la Marine marchande, you can see the Fort National and the great curve which joins St-Malo to Pointe de la Varde, passing through the beaches of Paramé, Rochebonne and Le Minihic.

At the end of the ramparts take the stairway going down near St-Thomas Gate (Porte St-Thomas) – this gate opens onto the immense Paramé Beach.

Cathedral St-Vincent ⊘ (**DZ**) – The building, started in the 11C and completed in the 18C, was topped by a pierced spire in the 19C, replacing the quadrangular roof. The nave is roofed with quadripartite vaulting typical of the Angevin style; dark and massive it contrasts with the slender 13C chancel. Lit by magnificent **stained-glass windows★** by Jean Le Moal, the chancel becomes a kaleidoscope of colours. In the transept, restored in the 17C style, the stained-glass windows are muted in colour while in the side aisles the windows by Max Ingrand are brighter (Chapel of the Holy Sacrament). The north side aisle has preserved its original vaulting. A 16C Virgin, Notre-Dame-de-la-Croix-du-Fief, which comes from a medieval house, is kept in the second chapel north of the ambulatory together with the remains of Duguay-Trouin. The neighbouring chapel houses the head reliquary of Jacques Cartier.

★★CASTLE (**DZ**) *1hr 30min*

You can enter the courtyard and see the façades of the former 17C-18C barracks (now the town hall), the well, the keep and the gatehouse.
The little keep was built as part of the ramparts in 1395. The great keep (1424) dominates the castle while the corner towers were constructed in the 15C and 16C. The chapel and the galley date from the 17C.

★**Musée d'Histoire de la ville et d'Ethnographie du pays malouin** ⊘ (**M²**) – The museum, which is installed in the great keep and gatehouse, records the development of the city of St-Malo and its celebrities (Jacques Cartier, Duguay-Trouin, La Bourdonnais, Surcouf, Chateaubriand, Lamennais and the mathematician Maupertuis). Documents, ship models, paintings and arms trace St-Malo's sea-faring tradition.
To end the visit climb up to the keep's watchtowers, from where you will admire an impressive **panorama★★** of the town, harbour, coast and sea.
A passage leads from the old chapel to the Tour Générale. This tower contains an exhibition laid out on three floors devoted to the economy (commercial fishing, shipbuilding), way of life (headdresses, furniture) and significant historical events in the St-Malo region.

★**Tour Quic-en-Groigne** (**E**) – This tower *(65 steps)*, which is located in the left wing of the castle, bears the name Quic-en-Groigne from an inscription Queen Anne had carved on it in defiance of the bishops of St-Malo: "*Qui-qu'en-groigne, ainsi sera, car tel est mon bon plaisir*" (Thus it shall be, whoever may complain, for that is my wish).

ADDITIONAL SIGHTS

Aquarium Intra-Muros ⊘ – Built inside a curtain wall of the ramparts, the aquarium, formerly a weapons store, has 35 tanks where colourful tropical fish swim.

★**Fort National** (**AX** – *town plan below*) ⊘ – *Access by Plage de l'Éventail at low tide, 15min on foot there and back.*
Built by Vauban in 1689, the Royal Fort became the National Fort after the Revolution (1789), and then private property. Built on the rock, this stronghold assured the protection of the city. The **view★★** from the ramparts is remarkable. The fort commands extensive views of the coast and the islands: St-Malo, St-Servan, the Rance estuary, Dinard, the île du Grand Bé, Île du Petit Bé, Île Harbour, the Grand Jardin Lighthouse, the Fort de la Conchée and in the distance the Îles Chausey.
During the tour, one of the events recorded is the fort's resistance in 1692 against the English and Dutch fleet, and Surcouf's memorable duel in which he defended the honour of France against 12 opponents, of whom he spared the last to testify to his exploit. The visit to the dungeon is interesting.

Île du Grand Bé (**AX** – *town plan below*) – *45min on foot there and back. Only at low tide. Leave St-Malo by Porte des Champs-Vauverts and cross the beach diagonally to the causeway. Follow the road that skirts the right side of the island.*
Chateaubriand's tomb is on the seaward side; it is a plain, unnamed flagstone surmounted by a heavy granite cross.
From the highest point on the island there is a beautiful **panorama★★** of the entire Côte d'Émeraude.
Cross the open space, go down a few steps and turn left along a road leading back to the causeway by which you came.

★ST-SERVAN-SUR-MER

The resort of St-Servan-sur-Mer is cheerful with its many gardens, in striking contrast to the walled town of St-Malo. Its main beach is formed by Sablons Bay, although there are also smaller beaches along the Rance. The town has three ports: the Bouvet dock, a trading and a fishing port, linked with that of St-Malo, the Solidor, a former naval base, and that of Saint-Père.

The *Renard* sailing past St-Malo

The name of **Jeanne Jugan** (1792-1879) is revered here. A humble servant, she managed to buy an old house with three friends, which they opened as a hospice for the aged. The spiritual association was the beginning of the order which would later become the Little Sisters of the Poor.

★★Corniche d'Aleth – This walk offers magnificent **views★★**. Leave your car in place St-Pierre, where the ruins of the former cathedral of Aleth stand in a garden.

Take rue St-Pierre at the east end of the church and follow on the left the coastal pathway.

First comes a remarkable view of St-Malo. Further to the left can be distinguished the Petit Bé, the Grand Bé and Cézembre Islands. Bear left and skirt the seashore. Go round the fort *(see below)*. The whole harbour is now visible: to the right of the Île de Cézembre, in the distance, is the fortified Île de la Grande Conchée; on the left, the Grand Jardin Lighthouse, Île Harbour and its fort and, in the distance, Cap Fréhel and Pointe du Décollé, followed by a maze of reefs. Finally take a steep downhill path to the right to enjoy a very fine view of the Rance estuary, barred by the Rocher Bizeux, on which stands a statue of the Virgin, and beyond, of the Usine marémotrice de la Rance.

★Tour Solidor – This tower (27m/88.5ft high), which commands the Rance estuary, was built in 1382 and restored in the 17C. It now houses the **Musée international du Long Cours Cap-Hornier★** ⊘, a museum devoted to Cape Horn Vessels. Visitors can study the exhibits on their way up to enjoy the view from the the top of the tower, making the climb easier.

Parc des Corbières – It is a wooded park with trees of different species. Bear right, follow the cliff path which goes round Pointe des Corbières, affording fine **glimpses★** of the Rance estuary and the tidal power scheme.

Fort de la Cité – The City Fort was built in 1759 on the orders of the Duke of Aiguillon. Around the inner courtyard is a chain of blockhouses joined by over 2km/1mi of underground passages, which also serve the barracks, the hospital and all the offices of this little town, laid out on several storeys.

ST-SERVAN-SUR-MER

Église Ste-Croix – The church is in the Greco-Roman style. The interior is decorated with frescoes (1854) and stained-glass windows (1962).

★**Belvédère du Rosais** (**BZ** – *town plan p 268*) – The viewpoint is near the little marine cemetery on the side of a cliff overlooking the Rance which contains the tomb of the Count and Countess of Chateaubriand, the writer's parents. **View**★ of Rance Dam, the Rocher Bizeux with a statue of the Virgin on top of it, Pointe de la Vicomté and Dinard.

⌂ PARAMÉ

Paramé, a much-frequented seaside resort, possesses a salt-water thermal establishment. It has two magnificent beaches extending for 2km/1.5mi: Casino Beach, which continues that of St-Malo, and Rochebonne Beach. The splendid seafront promenade, 3km/2mi long, is the chief attraction for the passing tourist.

ROTHÉNEUF *on ① on the town plan on p 269*

This seaside resort has two beaches, which differ widely. That of Le Val is wide open to the sea. That of Le Havre lies on an almost landlocked bay like a large lake surrounded with dunes, cliffs and pines.
Near Rothéneuf is **Le Minihic**, with its own beach and villas.

★**Manoir de Jacques Cartier** ⊘ – *Rue David Macdonald Stewart.*
After his expeditions to Canada, the explorer, Jacques Cartier, bought a farm which he extended and called "*Limoëlou*" (bald hillock). This 15C-16C house and its 19C extension have been restored and furnished in the style of the period. The tour includes an audio-visual presentation on the explorer's expeditions and of the colony "Nouvelle France" otherwise known as Canada.

Rochers sculptés ⊘ – From 1870 onwards, some rocks along the coast were patiently sculpted by a priest, the Abbé Fouré, who spent 25 years of his life on the task. There are almost 300 little granite characters.

Aquarium marin – This has interesting specimens of live salt-water creatures from the Channel and a large collection of shells.

OTHER EXCURSIONS

★★**Grand Aquarium** ⊘ – *Leave St-Malo by T on the map, and the follow the signs.* This is one of the region's most popular attractions, with eight large rooms on two storeys, much of the space devoted to the great navigators from St-Malo.
The aquariums include a hands-on area which is a miniature reproduction of Brittany; the "sunken ship" gives visitors the strange sensation of being at the bottom of the sea; the **Anneau** is a ring-shaped basin which puts you right in the middle of the action.

Château du Bos ⊘ – *5km/3mi. Leave St-Malo on ③ on the town plan then bear right on D 5.*
The château, built in granite from the Îles Chausey, is a perfect example of a *malouinière*. These 18C mansions were constructed by wealthy shipowners, merchants or privateers, who sought the peace of the countryside.
The estate covers 10ha/24.5 acres and overlooks the Rance. The château's interior, with its great chimneys, typical of the region, can be visited.

ST-NAZAIRE
Population 64 812
Michelin map 63 fold 15 or 230 fold 52

A visit to St-Nazaire, which is above all a great shipbuilding centre, is particularly interesting. Originally a small fishing port in the 15C, the town developed rapidly in 1856, when large ships, finding it difficult to sail up to Nantes, stopped at its deep-water port.

St-Nazaire during the war – The Allied forces landed here during the First World War; during the Second World War the town became a German submarine base. On 27-28 March 1942, a British commando caught the enemy by surprise, while the destroyer *Campbeltown* knocked down the Louis-Joubert entrance lock and the following day neutralised the lock by blowing itself up. A stele, reminding us of this heroic act, faces the sea on boulevard de Verdun.
An obvious target for aerial bombardment between 1940 and 1945, the town got caught up in the fighting for the St-Nazaire Pocket and consequently was a desolate site when finally liberated.
A monument to commemorate the Surrender of the St-Nazaire Pocket (May 1945) stands west of Bouvron, on the road between Savenay and Blain, 36km/22mi from St-Nazaire.

St-Nazaire restored – Rebuilt after the war, the town is now divided into two distinct districts: to the east is the **harbour and industrial zone** and to the west the **residential area** opened with wide avenues following the plans of the architect, Lemaresquier. In the town centre, the town hall (1969) stands amid a fine square decorated with fountains; the rectangular basin faces avenue de la République.

Further west Avenue Léo-Lagrange separates the **park**, 50ha/124 acres of green space enhanced by a lake, from the **sports ground**. Beyond are the hospital centre and schools. Near the coast, modern buildings have been set up in the Kerledé district.

To the east of St-Nazaire, near the mouth of the Brivet, the **Pont-routier St-Nazaire-St-Brévin★** spans the Loire, a distance of more than 3 356m/2mi; it stands 61m/200ft above mean high water at midpoint. It provides a link between the town of St-Nazaire and the Retz country, the Vendée and the Charentes and promotes industrial development on both banks of the Loire.

THE PORT *1hr 30min*

★Panorama ⊘ (**BZ B**) – On the submarine exit *(see below)*. This terrace offers a remarkable overall view of the harbour, the Loire estuary, and St-Brévin-les-Pins. Suspension Bridge on the other side of the river.

Harbour installations (**BYZ**) – The **Bassin de St-Nazaire** (St-Nazaire Basin), 10.5ha/26 acres and reduced to 9ha/22 acres after the submarine base was built, was established in 1856, when St-Nazaire was only an annexe of Nantes. The port became autonomous in 1879. Two years later **Bassin de Penhoët** (Penhoët Basin: 22ha/54 acres), one of the largest in Europe with three types of dry dock (the largest measures 226 x 32m/741 x 105ft), was opened. The port is governed jointly with that of Nantes by the Autonomous Port Authority of Nantes-St-Nazaire.

Three works deserve attention: the entrance lock, the submarine base and the submarine exit.

The **Louis-Joubert entrance lock** (Forme-écluse Louis Joubert), was built between 1929 and 1932, to allow for the increase in tonnage of great Atlantic liners. The lock is 350x50x15m/1 148x164x49ft. It has three functions: first a dry dock for the repair and careenage of very large ships; second as a lock allowing ships drawing not more than 8.50m/28ft to pass from the Penhoët dock directly to the Loire estuary at high tide; finally the lock can also serve as a loading and unloading berth. This lock (measurements: 211x30m/692x96ft) supplements, for the larger ships, the lock at the southern entrance to the port.

The **submarine base★** *(base de sous-marins)*, which was built during the Occupation, was a very large reinforced concrete structure covering an area of 37 500m²/44 830sq yd and measuring 300x125m/960x400ft. It had 14 bays, which together could take some 20 submarines. Machine shops were installed at the back of the bays. In spite of much bombing, the base came through the war undamaged and is now the site of various industries.

The **submarine exit** (**BZ B**), opposite the base, is a covered lock. This was to provide shelter from air attack and to allow the German submarines to enter and leave the base in secret (it is no longer used). It adjoins the port's former entrance, 53m/170ft long by 13m/42ft wide, now used for traffic on the River Loire and for fishing craft. It presently houses the submarine Espadon, part of the St-Nazaire Maritime Museum.

Sous-marin Espadon ⊘ – From the Augustin Normand Shipyards in Le Havre, the *Espadon*, launched in 1957, was the first French submarine to cruise the polar ice caps. Seventy men lived on board; the torpedo room, engine room, sleeping area and control room can be visited.

Not far from the Espadon is a gallery, which presents temporary exhibitions on St-Nazaire's history.

Écomusée de St-Nazaire ⊘ (**BZ**) – On the banks of the Loire, at the heart of the port, a bright yellow building houses exhibits concerned with the St-Nazaire shipyards and the port's development: models of the shipyards, ocean liners *(Normandie, Île de France, France)*, battleships *(Jean Bart)*, dockers' old tools, portraits of people who contributed to the city's development...

The shipyards – Between the Bassin de Penhoët (**BY**) and the Loire lies the Atlantic Dockyard (Chantiers de l'Atlantique), made up of the former Loire workshops and dockyard and the Penhoët Dockyard; these were linked together in 1956 and since 1976 have been incorporated into Alsthom, now forming a subsidiary of the GEC Alsthom group. Among the ships which have come from the Atlantic Dockyard are the battleship *Jean Bart*, and the ocean liners *Normandie* and *France*. Cargo boats, container ships, ore carrying ships and tankers (550 000t capacity) and passenger transport ships for French and foreign use are also built in the yards. Since 1987, the year in which *Sovereign of the Seas* (capacity 2 600) was delivered, the Chantiers de l'Atlantique have built a total of 11 cruise liners, including the largest in the world: *Monarch of the Seas, Majesty of the Seas* (capacity 2 770).

The Atlantic Shipyards are equipped to build several ships simultaneously. This method substitutes for the conventional slipway, a huge dry dock divided into sections in which the ships under construction stand. Launching the completed ship is achieved by filling the section with water and floating her out. A new dock enables ships of 500 000t to be built. Near the naval repair dock is a 450x95m/1 476x312ft dock for battleships.

ADDITIONAL SIGHTS

Lighthouse (Phare) (BZ D) – Standing on the old pier, the lighthouse commands a view of the shipyards and the Loire estuary.

Dolmen (BY E) – In a square in the town centre, not far from the port, stand a dolmen and menhir, a reminder of St-Nazaire's prehistoric past.

Église Ste-Anne ⊙ – The church (1957) stands between rue du Soleil-Levant and boulevard Jean-Mermoz, which you reach via ③ on the town plan. The belfry stands separately to the left of the façade. The entrance is surrounded by great mosaics by Paul Colin depicting work in the St-Nazaire naval dockyard. Inside, the stained-glass windows contrast vividly with the bare concrete walls; to the left, the chapel with blue stained-glass windows contains a statue of St Anne.

B Sortie sous-marine du port et terrasse panoramique
D Phare
E Dolmen

Hotels

BUDGET

Hôtel Touraine – *4 avenue de la République* – ☎ *02 40 22 47 56* – *18 rooms 130/215F* – *breakfast 25F*. A very useful hotel address for small budgets. The rooms are very simple, but are well-kept, neat and tidy.

Recreation

Beaches – The sand beaches of Grand and Petit Traict stretch over almost 2km/1.2mi, between the outer harbour jetty and the Point of Ville-ès-Martin. Farther on, towards Pornichet, the St-Marc and St-Marguerite beaches are also very attractive.

Tours of the Atlantic maritime construction yards – The tourist office has exclusive rights to give tours of the "Chantiers Atlantique": in season, each Tues and Fri (guided tour by bus, 2hr), reservations and information: ☎ 02 40 22 40 65.

Église St-Nazaire (**BZ**) – This vast 19C Gothic style church with its slate-topped belfry, was restored in 1945. Sculpted round the side aisles is a Stations of the Cross with a series of expressive figures. The transept is lit through fine rose windows with modern stained glass. In the transept crossing is a fine modern granite altar. In the chancel is an elegant 18C gilt wooden altarpiece adorned with scenes of the Gospel and statues of the Prophets.

Beaches (Plages) – The Grand and Petit Traict Beaches extend for over 2km/1mi between the outer harbour *(avant-port)* jetty, bristling with lift nets, and Pointe de la Ville-ès-Martin. They are skirted by Président-Wilson and Albert I Boulevards. The view from the beach extends over the Loire estuary to the south as far as Pointe St-Gildas.

Jardin des Plantes (**AZ**) – Across from the Loire Estuary the gardens with their shaded alleys and colourful flower beds offer a pleasant resting spot near Grand Traict Beach.

Église Notre-Dame-d'Espérance ⊘ – Standing to the south of place Pierre-Bourdan, near Rue de Pornichet (via ② on the town plan), this 1965 church has a white façade with oblique buttresses and a bare interior showing stonework.

EXCURSIONS

★★ La Grande Brière – *Round tour of 83km/51.5mi. See LA GRANDE BRIÈRE.*

Tumulus de Dissignac ⊘ – *7km/4mi west on N 171, the road to Escoublac.* Built on a hill, surrounded by drystone walls, this tumulus, with two covered burial chambers, dates from 5C BC; two narrow passageways lead to these chambers.

ST-POL-DE-LÉON★

Population 7 261
Michelin map 58 fold 6 or 230 fold 5

This little town, which St Paul, known as the Aurelian, made the first bishopric in Lower Brittany, offers the tourist two of the finest buildings in Brittany: the former cathedral (the bishopric did not survive the Concordat passed under Napoleon in 1802) and the Kreisker belfry.

From January to September, during the season of cauliflowers, artichokes, onions and potatoes, St-Pol is extremely busy. Numerous lorries, vans and tractors with trailers arrive, bringing these famous Breton products to the market for many transporters and agricultural cooperatives.

★CHAPELLE DU KREISKER ⊘ *30min*

This 14C-15C chapel used to be where the town council met; it is now the college chapel. What makes it famous is its magnificent **belfry★★**, 77m/246ft high. It was inspired by the spire of St Peter's at Caen (destroyed during the war – *see The Green Guide Normandy*) but the Breton building in granite surpasses the original. The Kreisker belfry has served as a model for many Breton towers.

The upper part of the spire is Norman in style, while the lower part with the squaring of its mullions and railing of the overhanging balcony recalls the English Perpendicular style.

The chapel aisles are formed of a series of gables over fine, tall windows. The west front and the flat east end are pierced with very large bays.

Enter through the north porch.

The 15C gable is surmounted by a statue of Our Lady of Kreisker (11C). The church is roofed with wooden barrel vaulting. The only stone vault joins the four huge uprights which support the belfry at the transept crossing. In the south aisle is a vast 17C carved wood altarpiece (from the Chapelle des Minimes, no longer standing) depicting the Visitation.

You may climb the tower *(169 steps)*. From the platform you will get a superb circular **view**★★ of the town, Batz, the coast as far as the Corniche Bretonne and the Monts d'Arrée inland.

ST-POL-DE-LÉON

	Colombe (Pl. M.).... 3
	Croix-au-Lin (R.)...... 4
Leclerc (R. Gén.) 6	Minimes (R. des).... 7
Guébriant (pl. A. de). 5	Psalette (R. de la)... 10

D Maison prébendale

ADDITIONAL SIGHTS

★**Cathedral (Ancienne Cathédrale)** – Built on the 12C foundations, the former cathedral was erected in the 13C and 14C (nave, aisles, façade and towers) and in the 15C and 16C the side chapels, chancel, apse and remodelling of the transept. The architects were inspired by the cathedral at Coutances and used Norman limestone to build the nave; the traditional granite was used for the façade, transept and chancel. The Breton influence can be found in the bell-turrets on the transept crossing and also in the porches *(see Introduction: Breton Art)*.

Exterior – From a small public garden, on the north side between the church and the former bishop's palace (now the town hall), is a view of the north transept wall with Romanesque characteristics. The south side, which faces Place Budès-de-Guébriant, has a fine porch. The transept contains a remarkable rose window with above it a sort of pulpit from which sentences of excommunication used to be read.

The façade is dominated by two towers each 50m/160ft high. The terrace which surmounts the porch was used by the bishop to bless the people; the small door under the right tower was reserved for lepers.

Interior – To the left is a Roman sarcophagus which serves as a stoup. Starting the tour from the right, note a Renaissance stained-glass window (1560) and in the transept the 15C rose window. Around the chancel there are tombs of local bishops and two 17C altarpieces. The carved **stalls**★ of the chancel date from the 16C. Over the high altar, a palm tree in carved wood, bent in the shape of a crozier, contains a ciborium for the Host.

In wall niches against the chancel to the right of the ambulatory, 34 wooden reliquaries contain skulls. In a chapel, left of the chancel, kept in a gilded bronze shrine, is the chief reliquary of St Paul the Aurelian.

Rue Général-Leclerc (6) – There are interesting old houses in this street: note the slate-faced wooden façade at no 9; a Renaissance house with a corbelled turret at no 12; a mansion with a fine porch and ornate dormer windows (1680) at no 30.

Maison prébendale (D) – This was the 16C residence of the canons of Léon. The façade is emblazoned.

Champ de la Rive – *Access by rue de la Rive.*
A pleasant shaded walk. Take the surfaced path on the right to reach the top of a hillock crowned by a modern Calvary. From the viewing table there is a fine view of Morlaix Bay.

Rocher Ste-Anne – *Access by rue de la Rive and rue de l'Abbé-Tanguy.*
As the road descends, there is a **view**★ over Morlaix Bay and its islands. A dike leads to the Rocher Ste-Anne and the Groux pleasure boat harbour. From the rock, which forms a remarkable viewpoint (benches), the **view** extends from Roscoff as far as Pointe de Primel.

Cemetery (Cimetière) – Small arched ossuaries are built into the walls. In one corner is the Chapelle St-Pierre in the Flamboyant style lit by modern stained-glass windows. Opposite the south porch, at the end of an alleyway, is a war memorial by the sculptor Quillivic, backed by a semicircular wall adorned with low-relief sculptures.

EXCURSIONS

★**Château de Kérouzéré** ⊘ – *8km/5mi to the west. Leave St-Pol-de-Léon via D 788 towards Lesneven, then the road to the right to Plouescat. At Sibiril, turn right towards Moguériec and after 500m/547yd left towards the castle.*
This granite feudal castle is an interesting specimen of early-15C military architecture. Three of the massive machicolated corner towers remain standing, the fourth having been demolished in 1590 after a siege. A central stone staircase gives access to the three floors which were used by soldiers and include large bare rooms with deep window recesses and stone seats, a wall walk and a guard tower. The castle also retains pepper-pot roofs, oratory frescoes, some tapestries and fine Breton furniture, all dating from the 17C.

Berven – The triumphal arch through which you enter the parish close is a fine specimen of Renaissance art with its three semicircular arches and its pilasters with capitals.
The 16C **church**★ has a façade surmounted by a square tower crowned with a dome with small lanterns and ornamented by balustrades; it was the first of its kind in Brittany (1573) and served as a model for many others.
A wooden rood screen stands before the very fine chancel **enclosure**★, ornamented on the front with small fluted granite columns and at the sides with wooden ones. In the chancel are 17C stalls with armrests in the form of winged caryatids.

Ferme-musée du Léon ⊘ – *200m/220yd after leaving Berven on D 788 towards Lesneven, take the little road towards Quéran.* The buildings of an old family farmhouse, in which the original furniture has been kept on display, house this small museum of agricultural tools and equipment and horsedrawn carts, which evokes the evolution over the course of a century of country life in Léon.

Kerjean Castle ⊘ – Half-fortress, half-Renaissance mansion, stands in the midst of a huge park. Towards the mid 16C Louis Barbier inherited a fortune from his uncle, a rich abbot of St-Mathieu, and decided to build a castle which would be the finest residence in Léon. In 1710 part of the building burned down, later the castle was sacked. However, the castle, which has belonged to the State since 1911, has since been restored except for the right wing. The buildings are guarded by a moat and ramparts; enter the main courtyard via the old drawbridge.
A main building with two wings and a large portico enclose the main courtyard, which is adorned with a fine Corinthian-columned Renaissance well. The dwelling house contains a museum of Breton art with fine 17C and 18C **furnishings**: box beds, chests, grain chests.
The kitchen, a vast room with a ceiling 6m/20ft high, has two monumental chimneys facing each other, one of which was used as the bread oven, and a large copperware collection. The stairs lead down to the food stores.
On the courtyard's other side is the chapel. Inside it is decorated with a wooden vault in the shape of a ship's keel and carved beams and purlins. The coach house wing, which once housed the stores, a forge and the servants' quarters, has been restored. There is a slide show on the history of Kerjean. A door leads to an alley supported on a gallery with eight arches, which give a good overall view of the main courtyard and the buildings around it.

Harvesting artichokes

The park contains a charming Renaissance fountain, consisting of a niche surrounded by four colonnettes, set into a little stone wall. The noise of the spring, mingled with the warbling of the birds, makes a pleasant background in which to meditate. On leaving, to the left of the central avenue, note the dovecot, a stone tower 9m/29.5ft in diameter.

Every year, there are temporary exhibitions held, devoted to contemporary art in spring, and the history of Brittany in summer. During July and August, evening theatre performances are on offer.

ST-QUAY-PORTRIEUX ⚓

Population 3 018
Michelin map 59 fold 3 or 230 folds 8 and 9

St-Quay-Portrieux, a popular seaside resort, owes its name to an Irish monk – St Ké – who, legend has it, landed on this coast c 472. Its beautiful beaches – Casino, Châtelet and Comtesse – are sheltered by a rocky fringe known as the Roches de St-Quay.

The ports – The tidal port at Portrieux used to equip fleets bound for Newfoundland. Nowadays, it is the lively home of a fishing fleet which fishes for mackerel, pollack, bass and, from November to April in particular, scallops and shellfish. The new deep sea harbour, inaugurated in 1990, contains 950 berths for pleasure boats and 100 for fishing boats. There is a regular crossing to the Channel Islands during the summer, and also the opportunity to take a boat out to Île de Bréhat.

Chemin de ronde – *1hr 30min on foot there and back, preferably at high tide.*
This former customs officers' path starts at Portrieux port, beyond the town hall, skirts Comtesse Beach, passes in front of the Viking stele and the signal station, affording a fine **view★** of St-Brieuc Bay, from Bréhat to Cap Fréhel. It then continues along the terrace overlooking Plage du Châtelet *(viewing table)*, round the sea-water pool and reaches Casino Beach. The walk may be extended as far as the Grève St-Marc *(add on about 2hr on foot there and back)*.

EXCURSIONS

Étables-sur-Mer – *5km/3mi south. Leave St-Quay-Portrieux on D 786 in the direction of St-Brieuc.*
The road goes towards the coast which it finally overlooks and follows closely. The town, built on a plateau and possessing a fine public park, overlooks the quiet family resort on the coast. The two parts of the town are linked by an avenue lined with villas. The two fine sandy beaches, Godelins and Le Moulin, are separated by the Pointe du Vau Burel.

Chapelle Notre-Dame-de-l'Espérance ⊙ – Built after the cholera epidemic of 1850, the restored Chapel of Our Lady of Hope, decorated with stained-glass windows in blue tones, two paintings by Jean Michau and a tapestry depicting the Virgin and Child by Toffoli, stands on Étables cliff, overlooking St-Brieuc Bay.

⌂ **Binic** – *7.5km/4.5mi south.* Binic is a delightful resort whose port, in the past, sheltered fishing schooners in winter. It is now used by pleasure craft and a few coastal fishing boats.

Hotels

BUDGET

Hôtel Gerbot d'Avoine – *Boulevard du Littoral* – ☎ *02 96 70 40 09 – closed in mid-Feb, 2-19 Nov, Sun evening and Mon, off-season* – ▣ *– 20 rooms 210/365F – breakfast 45F – restaurant 88/230F.* This establishment cultivates the atmosphere of seaside resorts of days past: in a garden not far from the sea, this rather amusing house appears slightly out-of-date. Its clean rooms are being progressively renovated as is the restaurant.

OUR SELECTION

Benhuyc – *1 quai J.-Bart – 22520 Binic* – ☎ *02 96 73 39 00 – 25 rooms 365/450F – breakfast – 35F – restaurant 95/210F.* Located on the port, this Breton house has been renovated into a modern hotel. Its light-filled rooms, with their white textured walls, pretty stylish chairs and pale fabrics are very pleasant. Good quality for the price in the restaurant.

Beaches

The beautiful beaches – Casino, Châtelet, La Comtesse, and La Grève Noire are sheltered by a rocky fringe called the "Roches de St-Quay."

Museum ⊘ – This little museum of "Brittany in days gone by", in a completely restored setting, evokes daily life in Binic a century ago with a display of head-dresses, Breton costumes and various objects related to marine life and deep-sea fishing. The visit is completed by several reconstructed scenes (classroom, forge, carpenter's workshop).

Jetée Penthièvre – The pier, closing off the outer harbour, is reached by Quais Jean-Bart and Surcouf. From a belvedere on the jetty there is a pleasant view of the beach with its raised huts dominated by a pine-topped knoll and the port.

From Binic, take the road to St-Quay-Portrieux and, after a short distance, turn left towards Lantic. After 3km/1.8mi, turn left towards Trégomeur and, 5km/3mi further on, take a steep road to the right.

Jardin zoologique de Bretagne ⊘ – At **Trégomeur**. The zoo consists of an undulating park of 12ha/30 acres which contains animals such as lions, tigers, lynxes, African and Asian antelopes and kangaroos roaming in vast enclosures. Islands recreate a natural habitat for chimpanzees. Madagascar lemurs and numerous birds complete the collection. Several of these animals are part of a European breeding and con-servation programme directed towards species in danger of extinction. A small train takes people for rides round the zoo in afternoons during the tourist season.

Le Palus-Plage – *11km/6.6kmi north.* A lovely cove. To the left of the beach, a stairway cut in the rock leads to an upper path from which there are good views of St-Brieuc Bay.

Plage Bonaparte – *13km/8mi north.* From this beach at the bottom of Cohat Bay, reached by a tunnel cut through the cliff, Allied pilots, brought down on French soil, were taken back to Great Britain. To reach the commemorative monument, take the stairway to the right of the beach car park, then the path up to the top of the cliff or, by car, drive along the road leading off to the right before the beach.

★**Chapelle de Kermaria-an-Iskuit** – *11km/6.6mi north via D 786; turn left on D 21.* The **Chapelle de Kermaria-an-Iskuit**★ (House of Mary who preserves and restores health) is a popular scene of pilgrimage (third Sunday in September). This former baronial chapel, in which a few of the bays of the nave are 13C, was enlarged in the 15C and 18C. Above the south porch, in the archives, is the former 16C court-room, with a small balcony. The inside of the porch is adorned with statues of the Apostles.
The walls over the arcades are decorated with 15C **frescoes**★. The best preserved, in the nave, depict a striking dance of death: Death, in the shape of jumping and dancing skeletons and corpses, drags the living into a dance; those depicted include pope, emperor, cardinal, king, constable, bourgeois, usurer, lover, lord, ploughman, monk etc. Above the high altar is a great 14C Christ. In the south transept are five alabaster **low-relief sculptures**★ of scenes from the life of the Virgin. There are numerous wooden statues, including, in the transept, a curious 16C figure of the Virgin suckling her unwilling Child and a Virgin in Majesty (13C).

★**Lanleff** – *5.5km/3mi. Leave Kermaria west on D 21 to the left and after Pléhédel, bear left.*
In the village, away from the road, stands the **temple**★, a circular building, a former chapel or baptistery built by the Templars in the 11C on the model of the Holy Sepulchre in Jerusalem. Twelve round-arched arcades connect the rotunda with an aisle set at an angle with three oven-vaulted apsidal chapels to the east. Note the simple decoration of the capitals: small figures, animals, geometrical figures, foliage.

ST-THÉGONNEC★★

Population 2 139
Michelin map 58 fold 6 or 230 fold 5 – Local map see Les ENCLOS PAROISSIAUX

This village has a magnificent parish close, the ossuary and the church being the key features of this rich 16C-17C Renaissance group.

★★PARISH CLOSE

(ENCLOS PAROISSIAL) *45min.*
Enter the parish close via the place de l'Église to the south.

★**Triumphal Arch (Porte triomphale)** – A rounded arch surmounted by small lantern turrets (1587).

Auberge St-Thégonnec – ☎ *02 98 79 61 18 – closed 20 Dec-5 Jan –* ▣ *– 19 rooms – 370/450F – breakfast 40F – restaurant 100F.* Across from the church, this traditional inn has a nice terrace to the front. Behind the rustic stone façade, the modern decor comes as a pleasant surprise. The big windows in the guest rooms open onto the gardens.

Parish close, St-Thégonnec

★**Funerary Chapel** (**Chapelle funéraire**) ⊙ – The chapel was built from 1676 to 1682. Inside is a 17C altarpiece (restored) with spiral columns. In the crypt, under the altar, is a **Holy Sepulchre**★ with figures carved in oak and painted (1699-1702), the work of a Breton sculptor, Jacques Lespaignol.
The treasury which contains gold and silver plate is situated in the ossuary.

★★**Calvaire** – The Calvary was erected in 1610. On the base are groups of figures depicting the Passion. Below, a small niche shelters St Thégonnec with the wolf he harnessed to his cart after his donkey had been devoured by wolves.
The platform is surmounted by a double-armed cross bearing figures and two simple crosses for the thieves.

★**Church** – The church has been remodelled several times. The only trace of the old building is the gable belfry (1563) on the left of the tower. The Renaissance tower is crowned with a dome with lantern and corner turrets. A fire in June 1998 caused the roof to collapse and severely damaged the five chapels on the north side. Ten fire companies and local volunteers were able to keep the flames from damaging rood screens, the windows, the organ and the pulpit.
Over the porch is a statue of St Thégonnec; in niches in the corner buttresses there are statues of the Annunciation, St John and St Nicholas; inside the porch, four statues of Apostles.
Inside, the **pulpit**★★ is one of the masterpieces (1683) of Breton sculpture. The corners are adorned with the four Cardinal Virtues, while the Evangelists are depicted on the four panels. On the medallion at the back, God is giving the Tablets of the Law to Moses. The sounding board (1732) decorated with angels and roses, is surmounted by the Angel of Judgement blowing a trumpet.
In the entrance of the Apostles' porch is a statue of the Virgin carrying the Child Jesus, framed in a Tree of Jesse.
The apse and both arms of the transept are covered with **woodwork**★ dating from the 17C and 18C, which has been restored. The panels of the **Rosary altarpiece**★, on the left, represent below and in the centre, the Virgin and the Child, Jesus giving a rosary to St Dominic and St Catherine; above, the Virgin and St Lawrence give Christ a soul saved from the flames of Purgatory.
The organ (1670-6) was restored in the 19C.

Île de SEIN

Population 348
Michelin map 58 fold 12 or 230 folds 15 and 16

Sein Island makes a picturesque excursion. Off Pointe du Raz, it is less than 0.5sq mi in area and is very low-lying; the sea sometimes covers it, as it did in 1868 and 1896. The island is bare: there are no trees or even bushes; old fields are enclosed by low, drystone walls.

Men and their work – For centuries the island was the object of superstitious dread. In the 18C, its few inhabitants lived in almost total isolation. The islanders were shipwreck looters. Now they are among the most active lifesavers. The women do all the manual labour, the men are sailors or fishermen. Fishing is the island's only means of livelihood.

A fine page of history (1940-44) – Immediately after General de Gaulle's appeal of 18 June 1940, the men of the Île de Sein (altogether 130 sailors and fishermen) put to sea and joined the troops of Free French Forces in England. Moreover, nearly 3 000 French soldiers and sailors also reached the island and embarked for England. When the Germans arrived on Sein they found only women, children, old men, the mayor and the priest. For several months fishing boats brought or embarked Allied officers. Of the sailors from the island who went to England 29 were killed on the battlefields. A commemorative monument stands to the right of the road to the lighthouse. General de Gaulle came in person in 1946 to award the Liberation Cross to the Island.

TOUR

Port – The port provides a good shelter for pleasure craft.

Village – Its small white houses with brightly painted shutters stand along alleys barely 90cm/1yd wide for protection from the wind. On a hillock near the church, two menhirs rise side by side, hence known as "The Talkers". Beyond the church, the Nifran Calvary is a simple granite cross resting on a tiered plinth. Behind it is the only dolmen on the island.

The **museum** ⊘ commemorates the events of the Second World War by means of photographs, explanatory panels and diagrams: the departure of the men of the Île de Sein for England; the activities of the marine Free French Forces; the campaigns in which the activists of the Liberation took part; the losses of the Merchant Navy (45 000 missing, 5 150 ships sunk); and the anti-submarine struggle.

Lighthouse – The lighthouse, on the island's western tip, is equipped with a 6kW light which has an average range of 50km/31mi. Left of the lighthouse stands the tiny Chapelle St-Corentin, an old hermitage. Beyond the point lies Sein Reef (Chaussée de Sein), submerged or visible, it prolongs the island some 20km/12mi towards the open sea.

On one of these rocks, which is constantly pounded by the sea, the **Phare d'Ar Men** (Ar Men Lighthouse), which took 14 years of superhuman effort to build, was erected in 1881. Its light, with a range of 55km/34mi, warns seamen off the rocks.

C. Chevalier

Île de Sein

SIZUN★

Population 1 728

Michelin map 58 fold 5 or 230 fold 18 – Local map see Les ENCLOS PAROISSIAUX

Sizun, a village in the Léon region, has an interesting parish close.

★**Parish Close (Enclos paroissial)** – The most interesting parts of the close are the triple **triumphal arch★**, decorated with Corinthian capitals and topped by a Calvary, and the twin-arched **ossuary-chapel★**; both date from 1585 to 1588.

The ossuary-chapel houses a small local museum with box bed, dresser, head-dresses, costumes and sacred art objects. The 16C **church**, remodelled in the 17C and 18C, is joined by a passage to the sacristy (late 17C) which stands alone. Inside, the decoration of the panelled vaulting is remarkable: a sculpted purlin with, in the transept and chancel, angels presenting the instruments of the Passion, crocodile-headed tie-beams, keystones and fluting. The organ loft, high altar, altarpieces and font canopy are all 17C.

Labbé /PIX

Sizun: small town, great arch

EXCURSIONS

Maison de la Rivière, de l'Eau et de la Pêche ⏱ – *1km/0.6mi west.*
Located in Vergraon Mill, water and its importance, fish and their habitat and angling (fishing tackle, flies used in salmon fishing etc) are the themes evoked in this
small museum. The exhibits are complemented by aquariums containing freshwater fish, explanatory panels, models and films.

Its annexe, the **Maison du Lac**
(Fish-Breeding Centre) ⏱, located at the foot of the Drennec dam *(6km/4mi east)*, is
an information centre on the
worldwide exploitation of
rivers, lakes etc.
Both these places aim to
help the public understand
the importance of pre-
serving the quality of water
sources.

> **Hôtel des Voyageurs** – ☎ *02 98 68 80 35
> – closed 10 Sept-3 Oct, Sat evening and Sun
> evening Oct-Easter –* 🅿 *– 27 rooms
> 200/270F – breakfast 36F –* restaurant
> *80/155F.* Near the church, this is a modest
> family run hotel which is a pleasant place to
> stop. For those on a tight budget, the hotel
> has smaller rooms in another building.

Locmélar – *5km/3mi north of Sizun.* The 16C and 17C **church** houses imposing
altarpieces consecrated to St Mélar and St Hervé and two 16C and 17C **banners★**
embroidered in gold and silver.
Purlins and beams adorn the vault.
In the churchyard stands an interesting Calvary (1560), with two crossbars peopled
with figures; the sacristy has a keel-shaped roof.

TRÉGASTEL-PLAGE ♨♨

Population 2 201
Michelin map 59 fold 1 or 230 fold 6 – Local map see CORNICHE BRETONNE

The resort of Trégastel rivals the neighbouring locality of Ploumanach for the beauty
and strangeness of its **rocks★★**, which are characteristic of the Corniche Bretonne.

SIGHTS

Aquarium marin ⏱ – This sea-water aquarium is located in caves, which housed
a church in the 19C (*Coz Ilis* means the old church) under a mass of enormous
rocks, known as the Turtles. In three rooms varieties of fish from Breton waters
and tropical seas are exhibited, along with stuffed birds including puffins, herring
gulls, guillemots, penguins and gannets, all from Sept-Îles.
At the exit, a stairway *(28 steps)* leads up to a **statue of the Eternal Father** (Père
Éternel). From the look-out point, there is a good **view** of the mass of rocks and
the pink granite coastline.

Plage de Coz-Porz – This sandy beach is lined with rocks bearing descriptive
names: the Turtles, the Witch. At the north end of the beach, beyond the jetty,
make for a small beach near two rocks, the Death's Head (Tête de Mort) and the

Pile of Pancakes (Tas de Crêpes), both on the right. This last rock, which appears to lie in folds, is a good example of wind erosion. Beyond a sandbank there is a mass of rocks, among which is the Thimble (Dé).

★**Grève Blanche** – *1hr on foot there and back.* Rock enthusiasts will go there from Coz-Porz. The path, which starts from the left end of this beach (Plage de Coz-Porz), follows the cliff edge around a promontory from the end of which can be seen the White Shore, Rabbits' Island (Île aux Lapins) and, out at sea, the Triagoz Islands. The path continues near the foot of a rock called the Corkscrew (Tire-Bouchon) and reaches the end of the White Shore, dominated by a great rock known as King Gradlon (Roi Gradlon) on account of its resemblance to a crowned head.

Viewing table – *Telescope.* This gives a circular **view**★ of the coast: the White Shore, Île Grande, the Triagoz Lighthouse, Sept-Îles and the hinterland (when weather permits): Clarté, Pleumeur-Bodou (with its distinctive Radôme) and Trébeurden villages.

★★**Île Renote** – *Northeast.* Leaving the sand bar you will find opposite you Renote Island, formed of huge blocks of granite and now connected with the mainland. *Follow the road that crosses the island.*

You pass Plage de Touldrez on your left and approach the Chasm (Le Gouffre), a cavity in the middle of a mass of rocks which can be reached at low tide. As you walk amid the rocks to the very tip of the peninsula, you get good views of the horizon out to sea and of the Sept-Îles looking north; of the Ploumanach coast to the east and the Baie de Ste-Anne to the south.

Trégastel-Bourg – *3km/2mi south towards Lannion.* The 13C church was remodelled in the 14C and 18C. To the right of the south porch stands a semicircular 17C ossuary adorned with balusters and crowned with a domed turret. At the nave is an unusual 14C stoup, a former grain measure. In the cemetery are a small Calvary, an altar for offerings and the tomb of the Breton author, Charles le Goffic. Situated just beyond the village to the south, a modern Calvary rises on a knoll. Steps lead to the top from which there is a fine **view** of the pink granite coastline.

Hotels

OUR SELECTION

Belle Vue – ☎ *02 96 23 88 18 – closed 1 Oct-2 Apr, and Mon lunch* – 🅿 – *31rooms 400/570F – breakfast – 55F – restaurant 95/260F.* Practically right on the Côte de Granit rose (Pink Granite Coast), this 1930s house and its garden have lots of charm. The rooms' furnishings may be slightly out-of-date, but they are impeccably maintained and they all offer views over the islands.

Eating out

BUDGET

Les Triagoz – *Forum de Trégastel, Plage du Coz-Pors* – ☎ *02 96 15 34 10 – closed Dec and Jan – 78/210F.* Whether you are seated on its terrace on the beach facing the famous coastal boulders, or in its dining room with large bay windows, this is a wonderful place to admire the sunset. And of course, it specialises in seafood.

TRÉGUIER★★

Population 2 799
Michelin map 59 fold 2 or 230 fold 7

The town (evangelized in the 6C by St Tugdual), a former episcopal city, was built in terraces on the side of a hill overlooking the wide estuary of the River Jaudy and River Guindy. The port, which provides a magnificent anchorage for yachts, can receive big ships.

One of the great Breton pardons takes place in the town of St Yves on the third Sunday in May. This is the "*pardon* of the poor", as well as that of advocates and lawyers. The procession goes from the cathedral to Minihy-Tréguier.

SIGHTS

*Leave the car in the harbour car park and enter the town along rue Ernest-Renan, which is lined with tall half-timbered houses. The two great square towers (**D**) once framed the town gate.*

Maison de Renan ⊙ (**M**) – This 16C half-timbered house contains memorabilia of Ernest Renan (1823-92). It displays manuscripts and portraits, and one room contains a video presentation on the life of the writer and the places he used to frequent. Visitors can see the room in which he was born, a reconstruction of his study and library at the Collège de France and, on the top floor, the two tiny rooms in which, as a child, he liked to shut himself away to work (lovely view of the town).

★★**Cathédrale St-Tugdual** ⊙ – The cathedral, which dates from the 14C-15C, is one of the finest in Brittany. The transept is surmounted by three towers: the tower of the south arm, topped by an 18C pierced spire, rises 63m/202ft. At its base is a porch (1438) under a fine Flamboyant **window**★. The Gothic tower of the sanctuary, uncompleted, rises above the crossing. The Romanesque Hastings Tower is all that is left of the 12C church.

Enter through the main porch.

Steps lead down towards the luminous nave with its Gothic arches worked delicately in granite. A sculpted frieze runs under the triforium. The ribbed vaulting in the Tudor style is lit by clerestory windows. The modern stained-glass windows, the work of the master glazier Hubert de Sainte-Marie, portray biblical themes (to the left scenes from the Old Testament, to the right scenes from the Gospels).

Start from the north aisle.

The tomb of St Yves is an 1890 copy of the monument built by Jean V, Duke of Brittany, in the 15C. The recumbent figure of Jean V, sculpted in 1945, is located in the Duke's Chapel, lit by stained glass donated in 1937 by American, Belgian and French lawyers. The north arm of the transept is cut off by the Hastings Tower. The doors of the sacristy and cloisters open under handsome Romanesque arches which rise above a heavy pillar, coupled by columns with sculpted capitals and surmounted by an arcature.

In the ambulatory, the third chapel houses a 13C Christ carved in wood. The chancel with slender columns has 15C painted vaulting. It holds 46 Renaissance **stalls**★.

The **stained-glass window**★ brightens the south transept. It recounts the story of the Vine (symbol of the Church) which winds round the founders of the seven Breton bishoprics (among them St Tugdual), around the saints of the land and around the Breton trades. Near the south doorway an interesting 15C **carved wooden group** represents St Yves between the Rich and the Poor. In the south aisle, note the 15C recesses sculpted with knights in armour.

TRÉGUIER

B Calvaire de la protestation
D Tours carrées
M Maison de Renan

Treasury ⊙ – The sacristy contains the treasure, which includes the head reliquary (19C) of St Yves in gilded bronze placed against the foundation wall of the Hastings Tower (c 11C). Also of interest are a cupboard reliquary, a vestiary with revolving drawers (1650), old statues and a 15C manuscript.

★**Cloisters** ⊙ – The 15C cloisters abut the former bishop's palace and the cathedral chevet cuts across the north gallery. The Flamboyant arches in Breton granite, roofed with slate, frame a cross rising on a lawn. Under the wooden vaulting with its sculpted purlin, there are 15C to 17C recumbent figures in the ambulatory.

Place du Martray – The shaded square, in the heart of the town, still features picturesque old houses. It contains a **statue** of Ernest Renan, commemorating the writer's birth in Tréguier and his attendance at the local college.

Rue St-Yves (12) – A small tower in this pedestrian street gives a view of La Psalette, a residence for young singers, which was built in 1447.

Monuments aux Morts – *North of the cathedral.*
This war memorial is a sober and moving work by F Renaud, depicting a grieving Breton woman wearing a cape of mourning.
Take rue Colvestre, almost opposite, which features some lovely old houses and, more particularly, Duke Jean V's house, the Hôtel de Kermorvan and the Hôtel de Coetivy. Turn back and go down, beneath the old bishop's palace, to the Bois du Poète.

Bois du Poète – The wood overlooks the River Guindy and contains a monument to the writer Anatole Le Braz. Pleasant walk.
Notice also the **Calvaire de la Protestation** (Calvary of Protest) (**B**) by the sculptor Yves Hernot, put up in 1904 to reflect the Catholics' objections to the erection of the statue in honour of Ernest Renan in the place du Martray.

EXCURSIONS

Minihy-Tréguier – *1km/0.6mi south. Leave Tréguier towards La Roche-Derrien. On leaving the built-up area, turn left.*
The birthplace of St Yves is the scene of a *pardon* on the third Sunday in May. This is called locally "going to St-Yves"; the local priest is even known as the Rector of St-Yves. The 15C church is built on the site of the former chapel of the manor of Ker-Martin, where Yves Helori was born and died (1253-1303). His will is written in Latin on a painted canvas kept in the chapel. A 13C manuscript kept in the pres-bytery is called the *Breviary of St Yves* (Bréviaire de Saint Yves). In the cemetery is a 13C monument pierced in the middle by a very low archway, under which the pilgrims pass on their knees. This is called the "tomb of St Yves" (Tombeau de Saint Yves), but is probably an altar belonging to the original chapel.

★**Château de la Roche-Jagu** – *13km/8mi southeast via D 786 and D 787.*

Hotels

OUR SELECTION

Kastell Dinec'h – *2km/1.3mi on D 786 route de Lannion, then take a sec-ondary road –* ☎ *02 96 92 49 39 – closed 9-24 Oct, 1 Jan-21 Mar, Tues and Wed off-season –* ▣ *– 15 rooms 450/550F – breakfast 65F – restaurant 130/320F.* This farm is truly a delightful stop! Amid its pretty and lush garden, it looks a little like a cute guesthouse. Its understated rooms are small, but pleasantly intimate, and its dining room is warm and inviting. The owners dine there every night.

Chambre d'hôte Troézel Vras – *22610 Kerbors, 9km/6mi from Tréguier on the route de Paimpol, towards Pleumeur-Gautier then Kerbors –* ☎ *02 96 22 89 68 – closed Nov-Mar – no credit cards – 6 rooms 260/300F – meals 100F.* The delightful rooms in his 17C manor house are all eclectically decorated with baked clay tiles underfoot, white-washed walls, regional engravings, antique armoires and more recent furnishings. The unex-pected combinations are quite successful and charming.

Eating out

BUDGET

Café Pesked – *22220 Plouguiel – At the port la Roche-Jaune, 6km/4mi, route de Plougrescant and follow the indications –* ☎ *02 96 92 01 82 – closed Oct-Mar – 60/110F.* A pretty little Breton house whose white façade contrasts nicely with the blue of the port. You can enjoy oysters, mussels and smoked trout in a simple and pleasant café ambience. Good choice of rums.

Travellers' addresses Trav

The **castle** ⊘ was built in the 15C at the top of the steep wooded slopes which form the west bank of the River Trieux. It was restored in 1968. Together with other fortresses, no longer extant, it commanded the river and thus retains its defensive aspect. On the west façade, note the corbels which supported the former wall-walk and its five doors. The tour includes several rooms with French-style ceilings and large chimneys, the small chapel and its two oratories. There is a magnificent view of the **setting**★ of the Trieux from the covered wall-walk in front of the east wall. The river forms a steep-sided loop at the foot of the castle which can be reached by a footpath to the right. Notice the ornate chimneys.

During the summer, exhibits and displays take place in the castle.

Runan – *13km/8mi south via D 8.*

Runan, which stands on a plateau in the Tréguier region, has a large church which belonged to the Knights Templar and then to the Hospitallers of St John of Jerusalem.

★**Church** – The 14C-15C church is richly decorated. The south side has four gables pierced with broad windows and emblazoned façades. The porch gable is adorned with a sculpted lintel depicting the Annunciation and a Descent from the Cross. The superimposed figures of the twelve Apostles join to form the keystone of the vaulting. The ossuary adjoining the church dates from 1552; the outdoor pulpit from the time of St Vincent Ferrier.

Inside, the building is roofed with panelled vaults resting on multicoloured purlins: signs of the Zodiac to the left of the nave, animals on the right. The Commandery Chapel (right) contains slim sculpted pillars. The furnishings are remarkable: the great stained-glass window depicting the Crucifixion in the east end (1423) is beautifully designed. The old altarpiece of the font chapel of the same period includes exceptionally delicate figures (five scenes from the lives of Christ and the Virgin) made of bluish Tournai stone, Christ and a Pietà.

★① Jaudy estuary to Port-Blanc

Round tour of 37km/23mi – about 2hr.

Leave Tréguier on D 8 to the north and at Plouguiel, bear right.

La Roche-Jaune – A small port on the Jaudy Estuary. Oyster farms.

On leaving La Roche-Jaune in the direction of St-Gonéry, you will enjoy a good view of the Jaudy estuary, the oyster-beds and the islands.

★**Chapelle St-Gonéry** ⊘ – The chapel has a curiously leaning lead steeple (1612) on a 10C tower.

Inside, the painted wood vaulting depicts scenes from the Old and New Testaments; these **paintings**, which date from the late 15C, were restored in the 18C and 19C. In the chapel on the right of the chancel, there is a 16C **reliquary cupboard**★, a finely carved canopied type of chest. The left chapel contains the 16C **mausoleum**★ of a bishop of Tréguier; the recumbent figure rests on a great marble slab decorated with mouldings and supported on four lions. A 15C Virgin in alabaster stands in the nave. Under the belfry-porch are the sarcophagus and tomb (1614) of St Gonery, a hermit who preached in the region in the 6C. An opening in the tomb's arches enabled sailors and soldiers leaving for a long journey to remove a handful of earth which they promised to restore on their return.

A small Calvary and an octagonal 16C pulpit stand in the cemetery.

At St-Gonéry, take the road to Pors-Hir.

Pors-Hir – A small harbour built between great rocks near a little cove.

The road follows the coastline in a beautiful setting; houses built against huge rocks or nestling between tall boulders add a fairy like touch.

Pointe du Château – From the tip of the headland, there are beautiful views over the Îles d'Er, the Heaux Lighthouse and Sept-Îles.

★**Le Gouffre** – *15min on foot there and back.* A deep cleft in a mass of rocks into which the sea roars furiously.

Turn back and follow the road along the bays, then bear right three times.

From Le Roudour, you can make for **Anse de Pors Scaff** bristling with islands.

After Le Roudour the coastal road affords lovely views.

Buguélès – A small resort fringed by islands, all inhabited. From the harbour there is a good view of Pointe du Château; inland the Plougrescant belfry stands out on the horizon.

⌂**Port-Blanc** – A small fishing port and seaside resort. Under the dunes of the main beach are traces of memorial stones (now covered) which suggest the existence, at one time, of a necropolis.

To reach the **Chapelle Notre-Dame-de-Port-Blanc** ⊘, go to the great esplanade by the sea, turn left before a group of houses built on the rocks *(car park)*. At the left corner, take an uphill path and a stairway *(35 steps)*. The 16C chapel has a roof that comes down to the ground. Inside, to the right of the chancel, note a group showing St Yves between a rich man and a pauper. There is a Calvary in the close. A *pardon* is held on 15 August. Every year, the small **Île St-Gildas** hosts the *pardon aux chevaux*, also known as *pardon de St-Gildas*.

Return to Tréguier by Penvénan.

② Presqu'île Sauvage – *Round tour of 49km/30mi – 3hr*

Leave Tréguier towards Paimpol.

After crossing the bridge over the Jaudy, you will see a glass-blower's workshop on the left.

Lézardrieux – The town is built on the west bank of the Trieux, which is spanned by a suspension bridge. The 18C church has an elegant gabled belfry flanked by two turrets and topped by a pinnacle pierced with arcades containing the bells. This particular type of belfry is to be found throughout the peninsula.

Make for the Talbert Spit (Sillon de Talbert), skirting the large marina on the Trieux. After 3km/2mi bear right onto a downhill road.

Ancien moulin de marée – The ruined mill was driven by water from a small reservoir upstream. From the dike, there is a good view over the mouth of the Trieux.

Return to Talbert Spit and turn right.

Phare du Bodic – This small lighthouse commands the mouth of the Trieux. A path on the left leads through fields to a look-out point from which the **view**★ extends over the Trieux estuary and the Île à Bois in the foreground and the Île de Bréhat in the distance.

The road then passes near Pommelin Bay, crosses Lanmodez and Larmor-Pleubian.

This stretch of coast (Port-Blanc – Paimpol) can also be explored on foot along the long-distance footpath GR 34.

Sillon de Talbert – This long (3km/2mi), narrow tongue of land, surrounded by reefs, consists of sand and shingle washed by the currents of the Trieux and the Jaudy; it is possible to go round on foot. Seaweed is collected (the annual local production is estimated at 8 to 10 000t of algae) and dried on the spot and then sent to a factory nearby for processing. The Sillon de Talbert is now a national preserved site, placed under the protection of the Conservatoire du Littoral.

Return to Larmor-Pleubian and bear right towards Pors-Rand Beach.

Créac'h Maout viewing table – From the viewing table in front of the war memorial and the signal station, there is a wide **panorama**★ over Pointe de l'Arcouest, Île de Bréhat, Sillon de Talbert, Heaux Lighthouse (built in 1836-9, 56m/184ft high, average range 35km/22mi), Pointe du Château and the Jaudy estuary.

Go through St-Antoine to the entrance of Pleubian and bear right.

Plage de Kermagen – This faces Pointe du Château and the Îles d'Er.

Pleubian – On the north side of the church with its characteristic belfry, is a fine 16C round **pulpit**★ surmounted by a cross and decorated with a frieze depicting the Last Supper and scenes from the Passion: Judas's Kiss, the Flagellation, Christ bearing the Cross.

At Pleubian, take the direction of Kerbors by the coast road.

The road passes near the covered alleyway at Men-ar-Rompet, partly hidden in the greenery, and by the Île à la Poule.

At Kerbors, turn right before the church.

Bellevue – It is located on the bank of the Jaudy. On the right the view extends over the Jaudy estuary, on the left over the valley and site of Tréguier dominated by the cathedral towers; opposite, La Roche-Jaune rises in terraces. There are trout and salmon farms along the Jaudy, which is tidal, as fish farming develops in the region.

The road winds through fields growing early vegetables and descends towards the Jaudy Valley and Tréguier.

La TRINITÉ-SUR-MER ⚓

Population 1 433

Michelin map 63 fold 12 or 230 folds 35 and 49

The village, built on a height, now extends down the slope to the harbour and beaches on the River Crach estuary, which is lined with oyster-beds. A small fishing port, a busy pleasure boat harbour and shipyards add to the activity of this resort which has fine beaches along the Presqu'île de Kerbihan.

The marina can accommodate 1 200 yachts. La Trinité is a popular meeting place for sailing buffs, whether they prefer sleek competition models or lovingly restored old schooners. There are regattas and races held here all year long, including the *Spi Ouest-France*, where the competition is open to both amateurs and champions.

Pont de Kerisper – From this great bridge over the River Crach, there is a good **view★** of the estuary, the town and the port installations.

Hotels

BUDGET

Chambre d'hôte Mme Gouzer – *17 route de Quéhan (C 203), 56470 St-Philibert, 2km/1.3mi route d'Auray and turn left at the first light after the Kérisper bridge* – ☎ *02 97 55 17 78* – *no credit cards* – *3 rooms 250/400F*. Bordered by 100-year-old pine trees, this oyster-farmer's house is magnificently situated above the River Crach. It offers three white rooms, each with a beautiful view out to sea. Sea-lovers will be delighted!

TREAT YOURSELF!

Le Petit Hôtel des Hortensias – *Place de la Mairie* – ☎ *02 97 30 10 30* – *closed 1-10 Dec and 8-30 Jan* – *5 rooms 750F* – *breakfast* – *58F*. Overlooking the famous marina, this 1880 villa hosts five magnificent rooms, named for Breton islands. The ivory coloured pine and wicker furnishings, sailboat models, and the salon-library create an extremely pleasant atmosphere.

Eating out

OUR SELECTION

L'Arrosoir – *Place de la Mairie – 56470 La Trinité-sur-Mer* – ☎ *02 97 30 13 58* – *closed 1-20 Dec and 8-30 Jan, Sat in winter except during school holidays, Mon evening and Tues in Apr, May and Sept* – *130/200F*. The restaurant of the Petit Hôtel des Hortensias sets up its beautiful terrace with a view over the River Crach as soon as the weather permits. In the winter, you can enjoy the shellfish and seafood in the small bistro-style dining room, decorated with boat models and other maritime items.

Sports

Boat rentals – Here, there are no less than eight boat rental companies! List available from the tourist office. You can rent anything from a small motor boat with no license required to a 40ft yacht.

Lessons in sailboats and catamarans – *Société nautique, cours des Quais* – ☎ *02 97 55 73 48.*

Water-skiing – *Triniloc, 35 cours des Quais* – ☎ *02 97 30 10 00.* For novices or experts.

Beach clubs for children – There are two beach clubs for children: the Club Plein Air (Men-Dû beach), and the Olympic Club Mickey (Kervillen Beach).

USHANT★★

See Île d'OUESSANT.

Le VAL-ANDRÉ ⌂⌂

Population 3 600

Michelin map 59 fold 4 or 230 fold 9 – Local map see CÔTE D'ÉMERAUDE

The resort, known officially as Pléneuf-Val-André, has one of the finest sandy beaches on the north coast of Brittany.

★🚶 **Pointe de Pléneuf** – *15min on foot there and back. From the car park at the port of Piégu starts this walk at the foot of the cliff.*
It leads to a small viewpoint *(bench)* facing the Île du Verdelet, a bird sanctuary. Certain spring tides permit access on foot *(apply for information at the Poste des Sauveteurs on the pier or at the tourist office).*
By skirting Pointe de Pléneuf it is possible to reach Plage des Vallées *(allow 30min on foot).*

Leave from the port of Piégu and go up the steps which end in Rue de la Corniche.
This very pretty walk, on a cliff path overlooking the sea, affords superb **views★★** of St-Brieuc Bay and the beach and resort of Le Val-André. It is possible to continue to Plage de la Ville Berneuf *(45min on foot).*

★🚶 **Promenade de la Guette** – *1hr on foot there and back. At the southwest end of the quay at the juncture with rue des Sablons, two arrows point the way to the Guette pathway (Chemin de la Guette), the Corps de Garde and the Batterie.*
Go round the stairs (Anse du Pissot), which go down to the beach, and along the Corps de Garde, which has recently been restored. Soon after, there is an extensive **view★** of St-Brieuc Bay. From the statue of Our Lady of the Watch go down to **Dahouët**, a fishing port and pleasure boat harbour.

Follow Quai des Terre-Neuvas and take, across from the pool, after the bridge, Mocquelet Path to Val-André Quay.

Hotels

OUR SELECTION

Grand Hôtel du Val André – *Rue Amiral-Charner, 22370 Le Val-André –* ☎ *02 96 72 20 56 – closed 15 Nov-12 Mar –* 🅿 *– 39 rooms 295/440F – breakfast 47F – restaurant 90/155F.* A seaside hotel from the turn of the century. The modern rooms look out onto the beach with far-reaching sea views, as does its vast panoramic restaurant. Ideal for vacations, with competitive prices.

Eating out

BUDGET

Au Biniou – *121 rue Clémenceau, 22370 Le Val-André –* ☎ *02 96 72 24 35 – closed 2-31 Jan, Tues evening and Wed except in summer – 95/200F.* In a small house in the centre of town, this restaurant serves tasty food in its small dining rooms. It specialises in seafood, and some of the prices are very reasonable.

Recreation

Casino de la Rotonde – *Promenade de la Digue –* ☎ *02 96 72 85 06.* Open every day frm 5pm on.

Sailing sports – Le Val-André has been a sailing centre since 1987 and is magnificently equipped. It is open all year for sailboarding and renting a catamaran, but you can also enjoy sand-sailing at Saint-Pabu Beach *(*☎ *02 96 72 95 28).*

Golf du Val – *Plage des Vallées –* ☎ *02 96 63 01 12.* A splendid 18-hole course with a sea view.

Schooner sailing – La Pauline – *Office du tourisme de Pléneuf-Val-André –* ☎ *96 72 20 55.* This beautiful black-and-red skiff will take you along the Côte d'Émeraude.

Festivals – There are many festive events throughout the summer: from the festival of torches to the café waiters' race, from yacht races to concerts. Information available from the tourist office. You are sure to find the festival for you!

EXCURSION

Round tour of 19km/12mi – 1hr 30min. Leave Le Val-André via D 786 east towards Erquy. After 5km/3mi, turn right.

Château de Bienassis ⊘ – At the park entrance take the main tree-lined avenue to the château. Go through an opening in the crenellated wall, all that remains of the 15C enclosure; its corner towers and turrets were added in the 17C, when the château was rebuilt. The ground floor includes a grand drawing room, the former guardroom and the dining room adorned with porcelain from China, Japan and Bayeux, and furniture in the Louis XIV and Breton Renaissance styles. The north façade overlooking the garden retains two 15C towers.

On leaving the park, bear left in the direction of St-Brieux and after 3km/2mi, turn left towards St-Jacques-le-Majeur.

Chapelle St-Jacques-le-Majeur ⊘ – The 13C chapel, restored in the 16C, stands at the crossroads. Its elegant doorway is adorned with clustered columns crowned with carved capitals.

The bare interior, lit by modern stained-glass windows, contains a charming statue of a Virgin and Child (14C) known locally as Our Lady of Safe Return (Notre-Dame-du-Bon-Voyage) and a Stations of the Cross carved in granite by Saupique, a contemporary sculptor from Rennes.

Take the direct road back to Le Val-André.

VANNES★★

Population 45 576

Michelin map 63 fold 3 or 230 folds 36 and 37 – Local map see Golfe du MORBIHAN

Vannes, built in the shape of an amphitheatre at the head of the Golfe du Morbihan, is a pleasant city, very popular in season. It is also a good departure point for boat trips. The old city, enclosed in its ramparts and grouped around the cathedral, is picturesque. It is a pedestrian zone where elegant shops have established themselves in old half-timbered town houses.

HISTORICAL NOTES

During the period of the Veneti, the original settlement was called Darioritum and seems to have prospered well, at least until the Barbarian invasions of the 3C and 4C. In the 4C, Waroc'h, leading the Bretons from the other side of the Channel, took possession of the town.

Nominoé, founder of Breton unity (9C) – Nominoé, a Breton of modest origin, was discovered by Charlemagne, who made him Count of Vannes. Becoming Duke of Brittany (826) under Louis the Pious, he had decided to unite all the Bretons in an independent kingdom. When Louis died, he went into action. In 10 years unity was achieved: the duchy reached the boundaries which were to be those of the Province until January 1790. From the first, Vannes was the capital of the new Breton kingdom, which reverted later to the status of a duchy.

The union with France (16C) – Anne of Brittany, who married successively Charles VIII and Louis XII, remained the sovereign of her duchy.

When she died in 1514 at the age of 37 without leaving a male heir, Claude of France, one of her daughters, inherited Brittany. A few months later Claude married the heir to the throne of France, François of Angoulême, and after a few months, on 1 January 1515, became Queen of France. The King easily persuaded her to yield her duchy to their son, the Dauphin. Thus Brittany and France would be reunited in the person of the future king.

The last step was taken in August 1532. The States (councils), meeting at Vannes, proclaimed "the perpetual union of the Country and Duchy of Brittany with the Kingdom and Crown of France". The rights and privileges of the duchy were maintained: taxes had to be approved by the States; the Breton Parliament kept its judicial sovereignty and the province could maintain an army.

★★THE OLD TOWN *allow half a day*

Start from place Gambetta.

This semicircular square, built in the 19C, frames **Porte Saint-Vincent** (St Vincent Gateway), which leads into the old town along a road of this name, lined with beautiful 17C mansions. At the entrance to the road, the most remarkable of these, the Hôtel Dondel, was the headquarters of Général Hoche in 1795.

Take the little alley on the right and join rue A.-Le-Pontois via the Calmont tower bridge.

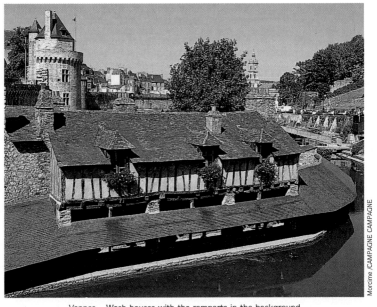

Vannes – Wash-houses with the ramparts in the background

From here there is a very pleasant view of the old Hermine Ducal Castle (rebuilt around 1800) with a pretty flower garden in front of it. The castle houses the Law School.

★**Ramparts** – After crossing a small bridge, go to the left-hand parapet, which overlooks some old **wash-houses★** with very unusual roofing. From Allée des Frères-Jolivet in the Promenade de la Garenne you will get a **view★★** of the most picturesque corner of Vannes, with the stream (the Marle) that flows at the foot of the ramparts (built in the 13C on top of Gallo-Roman ruins and remodelled repeatedly until the 17C), the formal gardens and the cathedral in the background.

When you reach the end of the promenade, follow rue F.-Decker, bordered by the Préfecture's gardens (Jardin de la Préfecture), which leads to the 15C **Porte Prison** (Prison Gate), flanked by a machicolated tower.

On the other side of the gate, the east end of the cathedral comes into view. Going into rue St-Guenhaël, to the left, the rue des Vierges and a little passage lead to a section of the ramparts which gives a pretty view of the gardens.

Retrace your steps.

Rue St-Guenhaël, lined with old houses, leads to place St-Pierre.

★**La Cohue** – This term (literally, a bustling crowd) is commonly used in Brittany to designate the market place, the area where traders and the courts of law were found. In the 13C, the market was held in the lower part of the building; the upper floor was reserved for legal affairs. Beginning in 1675, the exiled Parliament of Brittany held its meetings there. Under the French Revolution, the building became a theatre, and functioned as such until the 1950s.

Now, the **musée de la Cohue** ⊘ is located in the beautifully restored building, and offers visitors a permanent collection of paintings.

Galerie des Beaux-Arts – On the first floor, the courtroom (1550), with its fine oak timber ceiling, was the seat of the Presidial court of justice. It has now become a museum, which houses, for the most part, 19C-20C works of art by local painters (Jules Noël, Henri Moret, Flavien Peslin, Félix Bouchor), who were inspired by Brittany and its folklore.

Folk art is represented by a collection of polychrome wood statues – note the 16C Christ at the Column.

★**Cathédrale St-Pierre** ⊘ – Men worked on this cathedral from the 13C to the 19C. The only trace of the 13C construction is the north tower of the façade (on place St-Pierre), which is surmounted by a modern steeple. In the garden next to the north side of the cathedral are the remains of some 16C cloisters. The rotunda chapel, which juts out, was built in 1537 in the Italian Renaissance style, rarely found in Brittany. Enter the church by the fine transept door (Flamboyant Gothic, with Renaissance niches). In the entrance, on the left, a painting describes the death of **St Vincent Ferrier**, with the Duchess of Brittany present. This Spanish monk, who was a great preacher, died at Vannes in 1419 and was canonised in 1455. On the right is

St Vincent preaching at Granada. In the second chapel of the north aisle, a rotunda chapel, is the tomb of the saint. On the walls, a fine tapestry (1615) depicts the miraculous cures made by Vincent and his canonisation.

In the apsidal chapel or Chapel of the Holy Sacrament and nave chapels, you will see altars, altarpieces, tombs and statues of the 17C and 18C. In the Baptismal Chapel there is an altar frontal (16C) in stone depicting the Last Supper. The 15C nave has lost some of its original character as the heavy 18C vaulting has reduced its height and masked the panelled woodwork.

The cathedral **treasure** ⓥ is exhibited in the old chapter-house, which is ornamented with 18C woodwork. It includes a remarkable 12C-13C painted chest, a 12C reliquary cross, an ivory cross and pyx, chalices and other vessels.

★**Place Henri-IV** – The picturesque square is lined with 16C gabled houses. Glimpse down rue des Chanoines.

Walk along rue St-Salomon with its old town houses then turn into rue des Halles, where La Cohue's other entrance is situated.

Musée archéologique de Morbihan ⓥ – This museum occupies three floors of Château Gaillard (15C), which once contained the House of Parliament (Parlement de Bretagne).

The museum is rich in prehistoric specimens, most of which come from the first megalithic excavations made in the Morbihan region: Carnac, Locmariaquer and the Presqu'île de Rhuys. Exhibited are a remarkable collection of **necklaces**, bracelets, **polished axes**, swords etc; another gallery contains a variety of objets d'art (13C-18C). On the second floor, there is an unusual display case of 17C paintings, on the theme of "Fathers of the Desert". Collection of weapons used in hand-to-hand combat.

Maison de Saint Vincent-Ferrier (**E**) – *No 17 place Valencia.*

VANNES

D Maison de Vannes	**E** Maison de St-Vincent Ferrier	**H** Hôtel-de-Ville

Hotels

OUR SELECTION

Hôtel Roof – *At Conleau, 4.5km/3mi southwest of Vannes –* ☎ *02 97 63 47 47 –* ▣ *– 42 rooms 385/675F – breakfast 52F – restaurant 100F*. This modern hotel is remarkably situated in a lush enclave at the tip of the Presqu'île de Conleau, overlooking the Golfe du Morbihan. Choose the rooms facing the marina, the others overlook the car park.

Hôtel Vénètes – *At the Point d'Arradon, 56610 Arradon, 9km/6mi from Vannes on D 101 and D 127 –* ☎ *02 97 44 03 11 – 12 rooms 350/550F – breakfast 46F –restaurant 120/320F*. Right on the water, this 1960s hotel is beautifully located: its view over the gulf and the islands is worth making a detour. In addition, it is secluded and offers absolute calm. Here, you can enjoy sunsets over the gulf in utter tranquillity.

Eating out

BUDGET

Crêperie Dan Ewen – *3 place du Gén.-de-Gaulle –* ☎ *02 97 42 44 34 – 55F*. The owners of this *crêperie*, located in a beautiful half-timbered house, passionately defend traditional Breton culture. Their crêpes are made in the old style, the furniture is authentic Breton, and the music is Celtic A bastion of Breton culture!

OUR SELECTION

Pavé des Halles – *17 rue des Halles –* ☎ *02 97 47 15 96 – closed 15 Jan-7 Feb, Mon except July-Sept, and Sun evening Oct-June – 109/210F*. It's almost surprising to find such a good address in this touristic street in the old section of Vannes. This restaurant, located in a half-timbered house, is almost always full of customers enjoying its delicious food in the attractive bistro atmosphere. Reservations advised.

Table des Gourmets – *6 rue A.-Le-Pontois –* ☎ *02 97 47 52 44 – closed 28 June-7 July, 27 Dec-5 Jan, evenings off-season, Mon lunch and Wed – 115/320F*. This discreet little restaurant, run by a dedicated young couple, is quite popular with the locals. In the modern and warmly decorated dining room, you can enjoy fresh cuisine pleasantly served.

Afghan' Café – *12 rue Fontaine –* ☎ *02 97 42 77 77 – closed Sun – 110/160F*. If you want a change from crêpes and seafood, this restaurant offers the mild spices and subtle mixtures of Afghan cuisine. You can enjoy its unusual offerings in the tiny colourful dining room, with Afghan music in the background and photos of Afghanistan and its people on the walls. Best to reserve.

TREAT YOURSELF!

Pressoir – *7 rue de Hôpital, 56890 St-Avé, 6km/4mi north of Vannes on D 767 –* ☎ *02 97 60 87 63 – closed 2-17 Mar, 29 June-8 Aug, 1-24 Oct, Tues Nov-Apr, Sun evening and Mon – 220/430F*. An enticing starred restaurant slightly outside of the city. The owner will receive you in the warm decor that mixes classic furnishings with contemporary paintings for an original and delicious meal.

Night-life

Le Glasgow – *10 avenue de Verdun –* ☎ *02 97 54 39 17 – Mon-Sat 6pm-2am*. This very Scottish bar is particularly popular with the military. Here, the specialty is beer, and drinking is considered to be an art form. Scottish music.

L'Océan – *4 place Gambetta –* ☎ *02 97 47 22 81 – daily 7am-1am*. This café-restaurant belongs to "Le Marina" hotel, facing Vanne's little port. The locals come here for lunch or to have a drink after work on its magnificent terrace on place Gambetta.

H. Dewynter/MICHELIN

Le Roof – *Presqu'île de Conleau* – ☎ *02 97 63 47 47*. This hôtel-restaurant occupies an exceptional site bordering the beach on the Presqu'île de Conleau. The bar occasionally hosts pianists or other musical entertainment, and has a beautiful terrace.

The Ballyshannon – *Kergrippe* – ☎ *02 97 66 93 72* – *Tues-Thur 10pm-4am, Fri and Sat until 5am*. An Irish pub run by two interesting women who organise rock, folk and blues concerts on Friday and Saturday evenings. Small "techno" discotheque nearby.

Le Master – *Parc du Golf* – ☎ *02 97 46 09 00* – *Mon-Fri noon-2am, Sat and Sun from 2pm*. This establishment offers eight bowling lanes, 23 billiard tables (pool, snookers, French billards), and a karaoke evening every two weeks on Thursdays. Other performances (hypnosis, fakirs, drag-queens...) once a month. Bar and meals also available.

Schooner sailing

Notre-Dame-de-Becquerel – ☎ *02 97 47 24 34*. This "pirate ship" embarks eight passengers for a tour around the islands of the gulf.

In this house, remodelled in the 16C, Vincent Ferrier died in 1419. A fine example of a timber framed house with a ground floor in stone.

Maison de Vannes (D) – An old dwelling adorned with two carved wood busts of jovial peasants known as "Vannes and his wife".

Go down rue Rogue.

Place des Lices – This square used to be the tilt-yard, where tilts and tournaments were held in 1532, the year France and Brittany were united under one crown. At one end of the square, set in the niche of a turreted house, is a statue of St Vincent-Ferrier. The saint preached here in 1418.

Returning via the ramparts, you will pass by the Constable's Tower (Tour du Connétable), the Postern (Porte Poterne), and cross the small bridge over the Mairle.

ADDITIONAL SIGHTS

Parc du Golfe – This park is located by the exit to the marina, and is the departure point for boat trips.

★**Aquarium océanographique et tropical** ⊘ – This large building constitutes a "link between the sea and mankind". More than 50 pools, in which the relevant natural environment has been reconstructed, house about 1 000 fish from all over the world (cold seas, warm seas, freshwater), which make up an incredible kaleidoscope of colour. In one 35 000l/7 700gal tank, a coral reef has been recreated and is home to numerous species of fish which habitually frequent this environment. A huge aquarium contains several varieties of shark and an exceptional sight: a huge sawfish 2.5m/8.5ft long!

Palais des Automates ⊘ – This display includes about 200 automated characters, from the valuable collectors' items from the last century to those used in department store window displays.

Le Jardin aux Papillons ⊘ – Visitors are free to stroll around at will among the many varieties of vibrantly coloured butterfly that are housed in this environment of tropical trees and floral shrubs. Glass hatching cases illustrate the various stages of development of the chrysalis.

Hôtel de Limur – A late-17C town house with a fine stone staircase.

Town hall (Hôtel de Ville) (H) – This building in the Renaissance style, erected at the end of the 19C, stands in place Maurice-Marchais, which is adorned with the equestrian statue of the Constable de Richemont, one of the great figures of the 15C, for it was he who created and commanded the French army which defeated the English at the end of the Hundred Years War. He became Duke of Brittany, succeeding his brother in 1457, but died the following year.

Promenade de la Garenne – The park of the former ducal castle of Vannes was arranged as a public promenade in the 17C. The view of the ramparts, especially of the Constable's Tower, is attractive. In the upper part of the garden, on a wall, to the left of the War Memorial, a marble tablet recalls the shooting of the Royalists in 1795.

EXCURSIONS

★**Presqu'île de Conleau** – *5km/3mi – plus 30min on foot there and back. Leave Vannes by Promenade de la Rabine*. After 2km/1mi a good view of the Golfe du Morbihan unfolds before you.

Cross the estuary of the Vincin on a causeway to reach Presqu'île de Conleau. Leave your car (car park). Turn right in the woods onto the path skirting the Vincin.

Conleau – A small port well placed at the mouth of the Vincin; landing-stage for boat trip to the Île d'Arz. From the beach there is a good view over the Île de Boëdic between Pointe de Langle, on the left, and Pointe de Kerguen on the right.

Presqu'île de Séné – *10km/6mi south – about 45min. Leave Vannes by rue Ferdinand-le-Dressay which skirts the harbour's left shore, then bear left towards Séné.*

Séné – Formerly known for its typical fishing boats, the **sinagots**, the village maintains its maritime tradition.

On leaving Séné, bear right towards Bellevue and Port-Anna.

The old salt-marshes (almost 220ha/544 acres) have recently become a haven of peace for thousands of migratory or nesting birds of the region. The **Réserve naturelle de la Falguérec-en-Séné** (Falguérec-en-Séné Nature Reserve) ⊙ organises nature rambles and the opportunity to observe (through binoculars) birds such as the black-winged stilt, the elegant avocet or the redshank.

Port-Anna – This little port, frequented by fishing boats and pleasure craft, commands the narrow channel though which boats sail heading for Vannes.

Return to Bellevue and bear right towards the wharf.

Wharf (Embarcadère) – It is used for goods dispatched to the Île d'Arz. From the car park, the **view**★ extends over the River Vannes with Presqu'île de Conleau to the left and Séné, at the end of a creek, to the right.

Château du Plessis-Josso ⊙ – *15km/9mi east. Leave Vannes on N 165 towards Nantes. 3km/2mi after Theix, turn left on D 183 towards Sulniac.*
This charming castle, set in a verdant spot near a lake, is made up of three distinct parts added at three different periods: a 14C fortified manor house, a 15C main building with a polygonal staircase tower and a Louis XIII-style pavilion.
The visit inside enables you to follow the evolution of the castle's construction. It is easy to imagine how life was in the past, as you walk through the different rooms: the low reception room, the state rooms and the kitchen (fireplace with counterweight roasting spit, a granite stove with holes used for heating platters). Temporary exhibits are held in the outbuildings.

Grand-Champ - *19km/12mi north. Leave Vannes on rue Hoche and take D 779.*
In the nave of the church there are two carved wooden panels which come from Notre-Dame-de-Burgo, a ruined chapel in a pretty woodland setting, 2km/1mi east of the town.

ROUND TOUR OF LES LANDES DE LANVAUX

55km/34mi – 3hr
Leave Vannes by rue du Maréchal-Leclerc and take N 166. After 14km/9mi turn left to the castle.

★**Forteresse de Largoët** – These imposing feudal ruins, also known as **Tours d'Elven** (Elven Towers) ⊙, stand in the middle of a park. The road (Vannes to Ploërmel road) to the towers branches off left between two pillars.
The Forteresse de Largoët belonged to Marshal de Rieux, who was first a councillor of Duke François II and then tutor to his daughter, Anne of Brittany. When the troops of the king of France, Charles VIII, invaded Brittany in 1488, all the Marshal's strongholds, including Largoët, were burnt down or razed to the ground. Pass through the 15C entrance fort built against the first entrance gate (13C). Of the castle there remains an impressive 14C keep, 44m/144ft high, with walls 6-9m/19-29ft thick. Near the keep is a smaller tower flanked by a lantern tower.

After Elven turn left.

Landes de Lanvaux – Contrary to what the name landes – moors – implies, this long crest of flaking rock land, which was not even cultivated last century, is now a fertile region. There remain, however, many megalithic monuments.
On entering **Trédion**, turning left, you go along the banks of a pool which surrounds a most attractive Breton manor house.

Across from it turn right and cross the built-up area, then left, above the square.
The road drops into the rural valley of the Claie and its tributary, the Callac stream.

Callac – On the left of the road before a crossroads is a man-made grotto, a copy of the one at Lourdes. To the left of the grotto a path climbs steeply; on either side are Stations of the Cross consisting of groups of figures carved in granite. The path leads to a Calvary from where there is a view on the Landes de Lanvaux. The descent is by another path, which passes near the chapel. On the other side of the road, a stream flows swiftly at the foot of a hillock at the top of which stands a cross; it is a pleasant spot.

Take the left-hand road. When it reaches the Plumelec road, turn left, and 600m/656yd later bear right. After 2km/1mi take the road on the left back to Vannes.

St-Avé – The **Chapelle Notre-Dame-du-Loc** ⊙ rises by the old lie of the Vannes road. A Calvary and a fountain stand before the 15C building. Inside, note the carvings on the purlins and tie-beams which depict angels, grotesques and animals; in the centre of the nave stands a Calvary with figures, surmounted by a wooden canopy. There are alabaster panels on the high altar and 15C granite altarpieces at the right and left-hand altars. The statues, which date from the 15C, 16C and 18C, include a 15C Virgin in white stone.

VITRÉ★★

Population 14 486
Michelin map 59 fold 18 or 230 fold 28

This is the best-preserved "old world" town in Brittany; its fortified castle *(see photograph p 48)*, its ramparts and its small streets have remained just as they were 400 or 500 years ago and make a picturesque and evocative picture which is long remembered.

The old town is built on a spur commanding the deep valley of the Vilaine on one side and a railway cutting on the other. The castle stands proudly on the extreme point. From the 15C to the 17C, Vitré was one of the most prosperous of Breton cities; it made hemp, woollen cloth and cotton stockings which were sold not only in France but in England, Germany, Spain and even America and the Indies. Gathered together to form the powerful brotherhood known as "Marchands d'Outre-Mer", the Vitré tradesmen of this period commissioned the building of the highly distinctive houses with half-timbering, many of which can still be seen today.

CHÂTEAU DE VITRÉ

★★Arrival at Vitré – Vitré Castle and the houses at its foot are a fine sight. Motorists should pause before going into the town.

Coming from Fougères: magnificent view of the town on the road coming down the hill.

Coming from Rennes: view of the castle from the bend in the road from Brest.

★★CASTLE ⊙ *45min*

The castle, rebuilt from the 13C to the 15C, was bought in 1820 by the town from the La Trémoille family.

The present square used to be the castle forecourt where the stables and outbuildings were. The fortress is triangular in plan. The entrance is guarded by a drawbridge and entrance fort (Châtelet) flanked by two big machicolated towers. At the south corner stands the main keep or Tour St-Laurent; at the northeast corner stands the Madeleine Tower, and at the northwest corner, the Montafilant Tower. These various works are linked by a wall, reinforced by other towers. As you enter the courtyard you will see, on the right, a Romanesque porch (1) with archstones alternating in colour (red granite and black schist), the town hall (1913) abutting on the north front, and before you, the Oratoire Tower with an elegant Renaissance chapel (2).

From the platform of the Montafilant Tower *(82 steps)* there is a fine view★ of the town, the Tertres Noires and Moines Quarters, the River Vilaine and the old tannery.

Via the curtain wall you arrive at the Oratoire Tower. In its chapel is a beautiful 16C triptych★ decorated with 32 Limoges enamels.

The Argenterie Tower presents exhibits of the region's natural history. The St-Laurent Tower houses the **Musée St-Nicolas** ⊙ containing 15C and 16C sculpture, which comes from the houses of Vitré (a beautiful chimney has been remounted), the 15C tomb of Gui X (a local lord), a 17C chest, 16C Flemish and 17C Aubusson tapestries and engravings of old Vitré.

★ **THE TOWN** *1hr 15min*

Starting from place du Château, take rue Notre-Dame and turn right.

★★ **Rue de la Baudrairie** (**A** 5) – This, the most curious street in Vitré, gets its name from baudroyeurs meaning leather craftsmen. Each house is worth looking at.

Rue d'En Bas (**A** 8) – This street used to lead to the gate (partly destroyed in 1846) of the same name. It is lined with half-timbered houses; note no 10, Hôtel de la Botte Dorée (1513).
Continue along Promenade St-Yves from where a tower, remaining from the ramparts, can be seen.
At place du Général-de-Gaulle (B 13) take rue Garangeot.
Cross Rue Sévigné: note no 9, a 17C mansion known as "Tour de Sévigné", home to the famous writer.
Turn right.

Rue Poterie (**B**) – Picturesque houses: some half-timbered, some with porches.
Turn right into rue Notre-Dame.

★ **Ramparts** (**B**) – From place de la République you will see one of the old rampart towers, the 15C Bridolle Tower (machicolations) (**B B**).
On the south side of the town the walls follow the line, at a little distance, of the present rue de la Borderie and place St-Yves and then join the castle. Only fragments remain, built into private properties. On the north and east sides the ramparts are still intact.
Old houses line rue de Paris, which leads into place de la République.
Go through the gate in Promenade du Val to circle the ramparts. At the end of the alley, after passing a gate, take the ramp to the left which passes under the St-Pierre postern; follow rue du Bas-Val uphill and turn right in the square, then left into rue Notre-Dame.

★ **Église Notre-Dame** – The church is 15C-16C. Outside, the most curious part is the south side, with its seven gables decorated with pinnacles and its pulpit from which preachers addressed the congregation assembled on the small square and its two finely-carved doors.
Inside, you will see many altarpieces and a fine Renaissance stained-glass window in the south aisle (third bay) depicting Christ's Entry into Jerusalem.
At no 27 rue Notre-Dame is the former Hôtel Hardy or de la Troussanais (16C) with its finely carved porches and dormer windows.
Turn round and go to place du Château.

ADDITIONAL SIGHTS

★★ **Tertres Noirs** – *Access by Rue de Brest and Chemin des Tertres Noirs, to the right after the bridge over the Vilaine.*
There is a fine **view**★★ of Vitré, its site and its castle from this shaded terrace.

Hotels

OUR SELECTION

Hôtel Ar Milin' – *35220 Châteaubourg, 15km/10mi from Vitré, towards Rennes on D 857 –* ☎ *02 99 00 30 91 – closed 20 Dec-4 Jan, and Sun Oct-Mar –* 🅿 *– 30 rooms 360/590F – breakfast 50F – restaurant 110/200F.* Ar Milin' means "The Mill" in Breton. This one is located in a bucolic park along the River Vilaine. Its two old granite buildings have been renovated and mix antique wood, beautiful fireplaces and modern furnishings to create a cosy decor.

Eating out

BUDGET

Rest. Petit Billot – *5 place du Gén.-Leclerc –* ☎ *02 99 74 68 88 – closed Fri evening and Sat Sept-June except on holidays, Sat and Sun evenings in summer – 85/205F.* Here's a very enticing restaurant! Its delicious menus are created around fresh market ingredients, and are truly inexpensive. Served in two Breton-style dining rooms, the cuisine emphasizes regional specialities.

Crêperie La Gavotte – *7 rue des Augustins –* ☎ *02 99 74 47 74 – closed end-Sept to early-Oct, 1 week in early-Feb, and Mon and Sat lunch in winter – 40/80F.* In this restaurant, with typical Breton decor, located in a narrow street next to the château, you can enjoy traditional Breton crêpes made with dark flour and various regional ciders.

Au Vieux Vitré – *1 rue d'En-Bas –* ☎ *02 99 75 02 52 – Mon-Sat 10am-1am.* This is the only private residence in Vitré to be classed as an historic monument; its façade and fireplace date from the 16C. Today, it houses a bar-pizzeria-crêperie, run by a friendly and dynamic couple.

Bar du château des Rochers-Sévigné – *Route d'Argentré-du-Plessis –* ☎ *02 99 96 52 52 – Mon-Fri 9.30am-7pm, Sat. 9.30am-8pm, Sun 8.30am-8pm.* You don't have to be a golf pro to enjoy this charming golf course bar located in the former stables of the château des Rochers, where Madame de Sévigné was a frequent guest. From the terrace, you can admire this magnificent residence while sipping a refreshment.

Le Café du Marché – *Place Notre-Dame – Mon-Sat 8am-8pm, Sun 8am-noon, 6pm-8pm.* This *"café-épicerie"* has been run by the same woman for almost 40 years. After Mass, the city elders gather here, and after school, children come to buy their candy or cookies, while the owner continues doing her crossword puzzles.

Nightlife

Rue d'en-Bas – The rue d'En-Bas is the bar and restaurant street. Many nocturnal bars there, such as Aston Bar or le Nain Jaune, are very popular with Vitré's young population.

Sports

ANCPV – *Bassin de haute Vilaine –* ☎ *02 99 76 74 46 – outside school holidays, Wed and Sat 2pm-5pm; during school holidays, daily 9am-5pm.* At this nautical centre, you can enjoy small sailboats, sail boards and rowboats. Rentals available.

★**Public garden** (Jardin public) – *Via ③ of the town plan.* A pleasant, well-kept garden.

Faubourg du Rachapt (A) – During the Hundred Years War, this suburb was occupied for several years by the English, while the town and the castle resisted all their attacks. The people of Vitré paid the invaders to go away: hence the name of the suburb *(Rachapt means rachat or repurchase)*.

This suburb, lying at the foot of the castle, crosses the Vilaine Valley and rises on the north slope. Rue Pasteur, which affords picturesque views of the town and river, leads to the 15C **Chapelle St-Nicolas** which is the museum annexe (in season).

Enter by the little door on the left and skirt the chapel.

At the end, on the right, go through a pretty basket-handle arched door into the chapel where there is an 18C wooden gilded high altar. On the right is St Augustine, on the left St Nicholas and the three children (18C); 16C frescoes have been discovered.

Rue du Rachapt is lined with old houses. Lovely view of the castle.

EXCURSIONS

Château des Rochers-Sévigné ⊘ – *6.5km/4mi southeast. Leave Vitré via* ② *on the town plan. 6km/4mi from the town, on coming out of a wood, take the château drive on the left.*

The Rochers-Sévigné Château, which was the home of the Marquise de Sévigné (1626-96), is a place of literary interest. Admirers of the famous *Letters* will enjoy visiting the castle and park.

The château was built in the 15C and remodelled in the 17C. It consists of two wings set at right angles. Besides the chapel built in 1671 for the "exemplary" abbot of Coulanges, the marquise's maternal uncle, two rooms in the large north tower are open to visitors. That on the ground floor was the "Green Room" ("Cabinet Vert"). It still contains some of Mme de Sévigné's personal possessions, family pictures and her portrait; there is a collection of autographs and documents in a glass case. The 16C chimney-piece is adorned with the Marquise's initials (Marie de Rabutin-Chantal – MRC).

Garden and park – In the French-style garden, rearranged following designs by Le Nôtre, is the semicircular wall that Mme de Sévigné called "that little wall that repeats words right into your ear" because of its double echo (stones mark the places where the two conversationalists should stand). Beyond the garden lies the large, wooded park, which is crossed by avenues, the names of which recall the Marquise and her literary environment: the Mall, the Lone Wolf, Infinity, the Holy Horror, My Mother's Whim, My Daughter's Whim, Royal Avenue.

★**Champeaux** – *9km/5.5mi west. Leave Vitré via* ④ *on the town plan. 2km/1mi from the town turn right.*

The **village square**★ composes a harmonious scene with its collegiate church, its small town hall with a large hipped roof, and the few houses, former canons' residences, standing around an old well.

Collégiale – This 14C and 15C collegiate church, with a single nave, has some fine Renaissance canopied **stalls**★ and an elegant door, of the same period, which opens onto the sacristy, the former chapter-house. To the left of the high altar and in a chapel to the left of the chancel are two stone and marble mausolea (1551-4) belonging to the d'Espinay family, who founded the church.

The two handsome Renaissance **stained-glass windows**★, made in Rennes, are note-worthy: depicted in the apse is the Passion of Christ and in the sacristy the sacrifice of Abraham. In the nave, the south chapel contains a 17C altarpiece recounting scenes of the Passion and the north chapel is adorned with a 14C Virgin – both of these works are in polychrome wood.

Half-timbered houses in Quimper

A. Le Bot/DIAF

Practical
Information

Planning your trip

Formalities

Passport – Nationals of countries within the European Union entering France need only a national identity card (or in the case of the British, a passport or a Visitor's Passport). Nationals of other countries must be in possession of a valid national **passport**. In case of loss or theft report to the embassy or consulate and the local police.

Visa – An **entry visa** is required for Canadian and US citizens (for a stay of more than three months) and for Australian and New Zealand citizens. Apply to the French Consulate (visa issued same day; delay if request submitted by mail).
US citizens should obtain the booklet *Safe Trip Abroad* ($1), which provides useful information on visa requirements, customs regulations, medical care etc for international travellers. Published by the Government Printing Office, it can be ordered by phone – ☎ (202) 512-1800 – or consulted on-line (www. access.gpo.gov).

Customs – Apply to the Customs Office (UK) for a leaflet on customs regulations and the full range of "duty free" allowances; available from HM Customs and Excise, Dorset House, Stamford Street, London SE1 9PS, ☎ 0171 928 3344. The US Customs Service offers a publication *Know before you go* for US citizens: for the office nearest you, consult the phone book, Federal Government, US Treasury (www.customs.ustreas.gov).
There are no customs formalities for holidaymakers bringing their caravans into France for a stay of less than six months. No customs document is necessary for pleasure boats and outboard motors for a stay of less than six months but the registration certificate should be kept on board.
Americans can bring home, tax-free, up to US$400 worth of goods; Canadians up to CND$300; Australians up to AUS$400 and New Zealanders up to NZ$700. Persons living in a Member State of the European Union are not restricted in regard to purchasing goods for private use, but the recommended allowances for alcoholic beverages and tobacco are as follows:

Spirits (whisky, gin, vodka etc)	10l	Cigarettes	800
Fortified wines (vermouth, ports etc)	20l	Cigarillos	400
Wine (not more than 60 sparkling)	90l	Cigars	200
Beer	110l	Smoking tobacco	1kg

French tourist offices abroad

For information, brochures, maps and assistance in planning a trip to France travellers should apply to the official French Tourist Office in their own country:

Australia – New Zealand
Sydney – BNP Building, 12 Castlereagh Street
Sydney, New South Wales 2000
☎ (61) 2 231 52 44; Fax (61) 2 221 86 82.

Canada
Montreal – College Suite 490
Montreal PQ H3A 2W9
☎ (514) 288-4264; Fax (514) 845 48 68.

Eire
Dublin – 38 Lower Abbey St, Dublin 1
☎ (1) 703 40 46; Fax (1) 874 73 24.

United Kingdom
London – 179 Piccadilly, London WI
☎ (0891) 244 123; Fax (0171) 493 6594.

United States
East Coast: New York – 444 Madison Avenue, NY 10022
☎ 212-838-7800 – Fax (212) 838 7855.
Mid west: Chicago – 676 North Michigan Avenue, Suite 3360
Chicago, IL 60611
☎ (312) 751 7800; Fax (312) 337 6339.

West Coast: Los Angeles – 9454 Wilshire Boulevard, Suite 715 Beverly Hills, CA 90212.
☎ (310) 271 2693; Fax (310) 276 2835.

Cyberspace

www.info.france-usa.org
The French Embassy's Web site provides basic information (geography, demographics, history), a news digest and business-related information. It offers special pages for children, and pages devoted to culture, language study and travel, and you can reach other selected French sites (regions, cities, ministries) with a hyper-text link.

www.ottowa.ambafrance.org
The Cultural Service of the French Embassy in Ottawa has a bright and varied site with many links to other sites for French literature, news updates, E-texts in both French and English.

www.fr-holidaystore.co.uk
The new Travel Centre in London has gone on-line with this service, providing information on all of the regions of France, including updated special travel offers and details on available accommodation.

www.visiteurope.com
The European Travel Commission provides useful information on travelling to and around 27 European countries, and includes links to some commercial booking services (ie vehicle hire), rail schedules, weather reports and more.

Local tourist offices

Regional Tourist Offices – Comité Régional de Tourisme de Bretagne, 1 rue Raoul-Ponchon, 35069 Rennes Cedex. ☎ 02 99 36 25 25; Fax 02 99 28 44 40. www.brittanytourism.com

Departmental Tourist Offices (CDT) – Fédération Nationale des Comités Départmentaux de Tourisme, 2 rueLinois, 75015 Paris. ☎ 01 45 75 62 16.
Ille-et-Villaine: 4 rue Jean-Jaurès, BP 6046, 35000 Rennes Cedex. ☎ 02 99 78 47 47; Fax 02 99 78 33 24.
Loire-Atlantique: 2 allée Baco, 44000 Nantes. ☎ 02 51 72 95 30; Fax 02 40 20 44 54.
Côtes-d'Armor: 29 rue des Promenades, BP 4620, 22406 Saint-Brieuc Cedex 2. ☎ 02 96 62 72 00; Fax 02 96 33 59 10. www.cotes-darmor.com
Finistère: 11 rue Théodore-Le-Hars, 29104 Quimper Cedex, BP 1419. ☎ 02 98 76 20 70; Fax 02 98 52 19 19.
Morbihan: PIBS-Kerino, allée Nicolas-Le-Blanc, BP 408, 56010 Vannes Cedex. ☎ 02 97 54 06 56; Fax 02 97 42 71. www.morbihan.com

Tourist Information Centres (🛈) – See the Admission times and charges for the addresses and telephone numbers of the local tourist offices *(Syndicats d'Initiative)*; they provide information on craft courses and itineraries with special themes – wine tours, history tours, artistic tours.

Tourist Pass: 100 sights for 280F

This pass gives unrestricted access to more than 100 historic buildings managed by the Caisse Nationale des Monuments Historiques et des Sites (CNMHS). It is valid for one year throughout France as of the date of purchase. It is for sale at the entrance to major historic buildings, monuments and musuems.

When to go

Brittany has a reputation for rainy weather and heavy fog which rolls in from the sea, but it is rarely very cold. The climate is mild, thanks to the surrounding ocean waters and the tides, which keep the clouds moving and allow the sun to shine through regularly. The flora is a unique blend of Mediterranean and northern species. In the summer months, the weather is generally pleasant, never too hot.

Getting there

By air

The various national and other independent airlines operate services to **Paris** (Charles de Gaulle-Roissy airport 27km/14mi north, and Orly airport 16km/10mi south). There are also package tour flights with a rail or coach link-up as well as fly-drive schemes. Information, brochures and timetables are available from the airlines and from travel agents.

You may also find direct flights from the UK to the airports in Nantes and Brest; other regional airports are located in Rennes, Lorient, Quimper and Lannion.

Arriving by sea from the UK or Ireland

There are numerous **cross-Channel services** (passenger and car ferries, hovercraft) from the United Kingdom and Ireland and also the rail Shuttle through the Channel Tunnel. For details apply to travel agencies or to:

Stena Line	Charter House, Park Street, Ashford, Kent TN 24 8EX. ☎ 0990 707070
P &O Stena Line (Ferries)	Channel House, Channel View Road, Dover CT17 9JT. ☎ 0990 980 980 or 01304 863 000 (Switchboard)
Hoverspeed	International Hoverport, Marine Parade, Dover, Kent CT17 9TG. ☎ 0990 240 241
Brittany Ferries	The Brittany Centre Wharf Road Portsmouth, Hampshire PO2 8RU. ☎ 0990 360 360
Portsmouth Commercial Port	George Byng Way, Portsmouth, Hampshire PO2 8SP. ☎ 01705 297391

By rail

Eurostar runs via the Channel Tunnel between **London** (Waterloo) and **Paris** (Gare du Nord) in 3hr (bookings and information ☎ 0345 303 030 in the UK; ☎ 1-888-EUROSTAR in the US). From Paris-Gare Montparnasse, the TGV Atlantique (high-speed rail service) leaves for Le Mans, Rennes, Nantes, Quimper and Brest. The Paris-Le Croisic line stops at Nantes, St-Nazaire and La Baule. Paris-Quimper serves Rennes, Redon, Vannes, Auray, Lorient, Wuimperlé, Rosporden. The Paris-Brest line stops at Rennes and St-Brieuc.

Eurailpass, Flexipass and **Saverpass** are travel passes which may be purchased in the US. Contact your travel agent or: **Rail Europe** 2100 Central Ave. Boulder, CO, 80301, ☎ 1-800-4-EURAIL; **Europrail International** ☎ 1-888-667-9731. Information on schedules can be obtained on web sites for these agencies and the **SNCF**, respectively (www.raileurop.com.us or www.eurail.on.ca, www.sncf.fr).

Tickets bought in France must be validated (composter) by using the orange automatic date-stamping machines at the platform entrance (failure to do so may result in a fine).

The French railway company SNCF operates a telephone information, reservation and prepayment service in English from 7am to 10pm (French time). In France call ☎ 08 36 35 35 39 (when calling from outside France, drop the initial 0).

By coach

Regular coach services are operated from London to Paris and to large provincial towns:

Euroways/Eurolines, 52 Grosvenor Gardens, Victoria, **London** SWI OA4. ☎ 0171 730 8235.

28 avenue du Général-de-Gaulle, 93547 Bagnolet (Paris Region). ☎ 01 49 72 51 51.

Travellers with special needs

The sights described in this guide which are easily accessible to people of reduced mobility are indicated in the Admission times and charges section by the symbol &.

Useful information on transportation, holidaymaking and sports associations for the disabled is available from the Comité National Français de Liaison pour la Réadaptation des Handicapés (CNRH), 236 bisrue de Tolbiac, 75013 Paris. Call their international information number ☎ 01 53 80 66 44, or write to request a catalogue of publications. Web-surfers can find information for slow walkers, mature travellers and others with special needs at www.access-able.com and www.handitel.org. For information on museum access for the disabled contact La Direction, Les Musées de France, Service Accueil des Publics Spécifiques, 6 rue des Pyramides, 75041 Paris Cedex 1, ☎ 01 40 15 35 88.

Michelin publishes **The Red Guide France** and the **Michelin Camping Caravaning France** which indicate hotels and camp sites with facilities suitable for physically handicapped people.

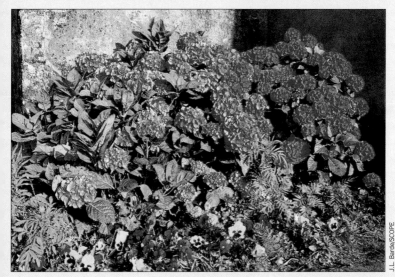

Hydrangeas

Motoring in France

Planning your route – The area covered in this guide is easily reached by main motorways and national routes. **Michelin map 911** indicates the main itineraries as well as alternate routes for avoiding heavy traffic during busy holiday periods, and gives estimated travel times. **Michelin map 914** is a detailed atlas of French motorways, indicating tolls, rest areas and services along the route; it includes a table for calculating distances and times. The latest Michelin route-planning service is available on Internet, **www.michelin-travel.com.** Travellers can calculate a precise route using such options as shortest route, route avoiding toll roads, Michelin-recommended route and gain access to tourist information (hotels, restaurants, attractions). The service is available on a pay-per-route basis or by subscription.

Documents – Travellers from other European Union countries and North America can drive in France with a valid national or home-state **driving licence**. An **international driving licence** is useful because the information on it appears in nine languages (keep in mind that traffic officers are empowered to fine motorists). A permit is available (US$10) from the National Auto Club, Touring Department, 188 The Embarcadero, Suite 300, San Francisco CA 94105; or contact your local branch of the American Automobile Association. For the vehicle it is necessary to have the registration papers (logbook) and a nationality plate of the approved size.

Insurance – Certain motoring organisations (AAA, AA, RAC) offer accident insurance and breakdown service schemes for members. Check with your current insurance company in regard to coverage while abroad. If you plan to hire a car using your credit card, check with the company, which may provide liability insurance automatically (and thus save you having to pay the cost for optimum coverage).

Highway Code – The minimum driving age is 18. Traffic drives on the right. It is compulsory for the front-seat passengers to wear **seat belts** and it is also compulsory for the back-seat passengers when the car is fitted with them. Children under the age of 10 must travel on the back seat of the vehicle. Full or dipped headlights must be switched on in poor visibility and at night; use side-lights only when the vehicle is stationary.

In the case of a **breakdown** a red warning triangle or hazard warning lights are obligatory. In the absence of stop signs at intersections, cars must **yield to the right**. Traffic on main roads outside built-up areas (priority indicated by a yellow diamond sign) and on roundabouts has right of way. Vehicles must stop when the lights turn red at road junctions and may filter to the right only when indicated by an amber arrow.

The regulations on **drinking and driving** (limited to 0.50g/l) and **speeding** are strictly enforced – usually by an on-the-spot fine and/or confiscation of the vehicle.

Speed limits – Although liable to modification, these are as follows:
– toll motorways *(péage)* 130kph/80mph (110kph/68mph when raining);
– dual carriageways and motorways without tolls 110kph/68mph (100kph/62mph when raining);

– other roads 90kph/56mph (80kph/50mph when raining) and in towns 50kph/31mph;
– outside lane on motorways during daylight, on level ground and with good visibility – minimum speed limit of 80kph/50mph.

Parking Regulations – In town there are zones where parking is either restricted or subject to a fee; tickets should be obtained from the ticket machines (*horodateurs* – small change necessary) and displayed inside the windscreen on the driver's side; failure to display may result in a fine, or towing and impoundment. In some towns you may find blue parking zones *(zone bleue)* marked by a blue line on the pavement or road and a blue signpost with a P and a small square underneath. In this case you have to display a cardboard disc with various times indicated on it. This will enable you to stay for 1hr 30min (2hr 30min over lunch time) free. Discs are available in supermarkets or petrol stations (ask for a *disque de stationnement*); they are sometimes given away free.

Tolls – In France, most motorway sections are subject to a toll (péage). You can pay in cash or with a credit card (Visa, Mastercard).

Car Rental

There are car rental agencies at airports, railway stations and in all large towns throughout France. European cars have manual transmission; automatic cars are available in larger cities only if an advance reservation is made. Drivers must be over 21; between ages 21 and 25, drivers are required to pay an extra daily fee of 50-100F; some companies allow drivers under 23 only if the reservation has been made through a travel agent. It is relatively expensive to hire a car in France; Americans in particular will notice the difference and should make arrangements before leaving, take advantage of fly-drive offers, or seek advice from a travel agent, specifying requirements.

Central Reservation in France:

Avis: 01 46 10 60 60   **Europcar:** 01 30 43 82 82
Budget France: 08 00 10 00 01   **Hertz France:** 01 39 38 38 38
SIXT-Eurorent: 01 44 38 55 55   **National-CITER:** 01 44 38 61 61
Baron's Limousine and Driver: 01 45 30 21 21

Global Motorhome Travel rents fully equipped recreational vehicles in a range of sizes; Paris pick-up. The toll-free US number is 800-468-3876, Fax 310-456-9292. **Overseas Motorhome Tours, Inc** organises escorted tours and individual rental of recreational vehicles: in the US ☎ 800-322-2127; outside the US ☎ 1-310-543-2590; Internet www.omtinc.com.

Petrol (US: gas) – French service stations dispense: *sans plomb 98* (super unleaded 98), *sans plomb 95* (super unleaded 95) and *diesel/gazole* (diesel). Petrol is considerably more expensive in France than in the USA, and also more expensive than in the UK. Prices are listed on signboards on the motorways; it is usually cheaper to fill up after leaving the motorway, check the large hypermarkets on the outskirts of town.

Accommodation

Places to stay – The **Places to stay map** *(see p 18)* indicates recommended places for overnight stops and can be used in conjunction with the Michelin's current edition of **The Red Guide France**, which lists a selection of hotels and restaurants.
In this guide, we have listed suggestions for places to stay and places to enjoy local cuisine or a have a drink. In the **Budget** category, you will find camp sites, guest-houses, hotels generally under 250F and restaurants where a good meal costs 100F or less. In the category **Our selection**, you will find a list of quite comfortable hotels, often in charming locations, as well as restaurants with special flair. This selection also includes bed and breakfast establishments and more traditional restaurants. And if you are in the mood, **Treat yourself** to a hotel or restaurant from this category, which includes châteaux and luxury hotels, as well as highly rated restaurants serving excellent meals in impeccable surroundings.
For further information, **Loisirs Accueil** (280 boulevard St-Germain, 75007 Paris, ☎ 01 44 11 10 44) is a booking service that has offices in most French départements: contact the tourist offices listed above for further information (www.resinfrance.com for internet booking). Or contact local offices directly:
Côtes-d'Armor Tourisme, service réservation, 29 rue des Promenades, BP 4620, 22046 Saint-Brieuc Cedex 02. ☎ 02 96 62 72 15.

Ille-et-Vilaine, 8 rue de Coëtquen, BP 5093, 35061 Rennes Cedex. ☎ 02 99 78 47 57.
Morbihan RESA, hôtel du Département, rue de St.-Tropez, BP 400, 56000 Vannes Cedex. ☎ 02 97 42 61 60.
Loire-Atlantique, 2 allée Baco, 44000 Nantes. ☎ 02 51 72 95 30.

Economy Chain Hotels – If you need a place to stop en route, these can be useful, as they are inexpensive (under 200F for a double room) and generally located near the main road. While breakfast is available, there may not be a restaurant; rooms are small, with a television and bathroom. Central reservation numbers:
– **Akena** ☎ 01 69 84 85 17
– **B&B** ☎ 0 803 00 29 29
– **Etap Hôtel** ☎ 08 36 68 89 00 (2.23F per minute, from France)
– **Mister Bed** ☎ 01 46 14 38 00
– **Villages Hôtel** ☎ 03 80 60 92 70
The hotels listed below are slightly more expensive (from 300F), and offer a few more amenities and services. Central reservation numbers:
– **Campanile** ☎ 01 64 62 46 46
– **Climat de France** ☎ 01 64 46 01 23
– **Ibis** ☎ 0 803 88 22 22
A guide to good-value, family-run hotels, **Logis et Auberges de France**, is available from the French Tourist Office, as are lists of other kinds of accommodation such as hotel-châteaux, bed and breakfasts etc. **Relais et châteaux** provides information on booking in luxury hotels with character: 15 rue Galvani, 75017 Paris, ☎ 01 45 72 90 00.

Self-catering accommodation – The **Maison des Gîtes de France** is an information service on self-catering accommodation in the regions of France. Gîtes usually take the form of a cottage or apartment decorated in the local style where visitors can make themselves at home.
Contact the Gîtes de France office in Paris: 59 rue St-Lazare, 75439 Paris Cedex 09, ☎ 01 49 70 75 75, or their representative, in the UK, **Brittany Ferries** *(address above)*. The web site is quite complete and has an excellent English version (www.gites-de-france.fr).
Gîtes de France, Springfield Books Ltd and FHG Publications/World Leisure Marketing all publish listings of gîtes in France with details of how to book. Try contacting the local tourist offices as they also publish lists of available properties.

Bed and Breakfast – Gîtes de France *(see above)* publishes a booklet on bed and breakfast accommodation *(chambres d'hôtes)* which include a room and breakfast at a reasonable price. You can also contact:
Bed & Breakfast (France), International reservations centre, PO Box 66, Henley-on-Thames, Oxon RG9 1XS. ☎ (01491) 578 803; Fax (01491) 410 806.

Youth Hostels

There are two main youth hostel *(auberge de jeunesse)* associations in France.
– **Ligue Française pour les Auberges de Jeunesse,** 38 boulevard Raspail, 75007 Paris. ☎ 01 45 48 69 84; Fax 01 45 44 57 47
– **Fédération Unie des Auberges de Jeunesse,** 27 rue Pajol, 75012 Paris. ☎ 01 44 89 87 27; Fax 01 44 89 87 10; Internet: www.Fuaj.org.
Holders of an International Youth Hostel Federation card should contact the IYHF in their own country for information and membership applications (US ☎ 202 783 6161; UK ☎ 1727 855215; Canada ☎ 613-273 7884; Australia ☎ 61-2-9565-1669; internet www.iyhf.org).

Camping

There are numerous officially graded sites with varying standards of facilities throughout Brittany; the **Michelin Guide Camping Caravaning France** lists a selection of the best camp sites. An International Camping Carnet for caravans is useful but not compulsory; it can be obtained from the motoring organisations or the Camping and Caravanning Club (Greenfield House, Westwood Way, Coventry CV4 8JH, ☎ (01203) 694-995).

The Fédération Française des Stations Vertes de Vacances, Hôtel du Département de la Côte d'Or, BP 1601, 21035 Dijon Cedex, ☎ 03 80 49 97 80, publishes two guides (no charge), *Guide des stations vertes de vacances* and *Guide des villages de neige,* which list accommodation, leisure facilities and natural attractions in rural locations.

Basic information

Medical treatment

First aid, medical advice and chemists' night service rota are available from chemists (*pharmacie* – green cross sign). Prescription drugs should be clearly labelled and tourists are advised to carry a copy of prescriptions.

It is advisable to take out comprehensive insurance cover as medical treatment in French hospitals or clinics must be paid for by the recipient. Nationals of non-EU countries should check with their insurance companies about policy limitations. Reimbursement can then be negotiated with the insurance company according to the terms of the policy held.

American Express offers a service, *Global Assist*, for any medical, legal or personal emergency.

British citizens should apply to the Department of Health and Social Security for **Form E 111**, which entitles the holder to urgent treatment for accident or unexpected illness in EU countries. A refund of part of the costs of treatment can be obtained on application in person or by post to the local Social Security Offices (Caisse Primaire d'Assurance Maladie).

Currency

There are no restrictions on the amount of currency visitors can take into France, however, the amount of cash you may take out of France is subject to a limit, so visitors carrying a lot of cash should complete a currency declaration form on arrival.

French francs *(see illustration following)* are subdivided into 100 centimes. European currency units known as **euros** are being printed, and in January 1999 the banking and finance industries began making the changeover. Banknotes are scheduled to go into circulation in January 2002, with national instruments phased out by July of that year. In the meantime, both euro and franc values (1 euro is about 6 francs 50 centimes) are given in more and more instances (store and restaurant receipts, bank documents etc).

Banks

Banks are usually open from 9am to noon and 2pm to 4pm and are closed on Mondays or Saturdays (except on market days); some branches open for limited transactions on Saturdays. Banks close early on the day before a bank holiday.

A passport is necessary as identification when cashing cheques in banks. Commission charges vary and hotels usually charge more than banks for cashing cheques for non-residents.

Most banks have **cash dispensers** (ATM) which accept international credit or debit cards and are easily recognised by the logo showing a hand holding a card. American Express cards can be used only in dispensers operated by the Crédit Lyonnais Bank or by American Express.

Credit cards – American Express, Visa (Carte Bleue), Mastercard/Eurocard and Diners Club are widely accepted in shops, hotels and restaurants and petrol stations. In the case of a lost or stolen credit card, ring one of the following 24-hour numbers:

American Express	☎ 01 47 77 72 00	**Visa**	☎ 08 36 69 08 80
Mastercard/Eurocard	☎ 01 45 67 84 84	**Diners Club**	☎ 01 49 06 17 50

Such loss or theft must also be reported to the local police who will issue a certificate to show to the credit card company.

Post and telephone

Post offices open Mondays to Fridays, 8am to 7pm, Saturdays, 8am to noon. Smaller branch post offices often close at lunchtime between noon and 2pm and in the afternoon at 4pm.

Postage via air mail to
- UK letter (20g) 3F
- US letter (20g) 4.40F
- US postcard 4.10F
- Australia and New Zealand letter (20g) 5.20F

Stamps are also available from newsagents and tobacconists.

Stamp collectors should ask for timbres de collection in any post office.

Poste Restante (General Delivery) mail should be addressed as follows: Name, Poste Restante, Poste Centrale, postal code of the département followed by town name, France.

Public Telephones – Most public phones in France use prepaid phone cards *(télé-cartes)*, rather than coins. Some telephone booths accept credit cards (Visa, Mastercard/Eurocard: minimum monthly charge 20F). *Télécartes* (50 or 120 units) can be bought in post offices, branches of France Télécom, *bureaux de tabac* (cafés that sell cigarettes) and newsagents and can be used to make calls in France and abroad. Calls can be received at phone boxes where the blue bell sign is shown; the phone will not ring, so keep your eye on the little message screen.

National calls – French telephone numbers have 10 digits. Paris and Paris region numbers begin with 01; 02 in northwest France; 03 in northeast France; 04 in southeast France and Corsica; 05 in southwest France.

International calls – To call France from abroad, dial the country code (33) + 9-digit number (omit the initial 0). When calling abroad from France dial 00, then dial the country code followed by the area code and number of your correspondent.

International dialling codes (00 + code):

Australia	☎ 61		New Zealand	☎ 64
Canada	☎ 1		United Kingdom	☎ 44
Eire	☎ 353		United States	☎ 1

To use your **personal calling card** dial:

AT&T........☎ 0-800 99 00 11	Sprint...........................☎ 0-800 99 00 87
MCI ....☎ 0-800 99 00 19	Canada Direct..............☎ 0-800 99 00 16

International Information, US/Canada: 00 33 12 11
International operator: 00 33 12 + country code
Local directory assistance: 12
Toll-free numbers in France begin with 0 800.

Minitel – France Télécom operates a system offering directory enquiries (free of charge up to 3min), travel and entertainment reservations, and other services (cost varies between 0.37F – 5.57F/min). These small computer-like terminals can be found in some post offices, hotels and France Télécom agencies and in many French homes. 3614 PAGES E is the code for **directory assistance in English** (turn on the unit, dial 3614, hit the *connexion* button when you get the tone, type in "PAGES E", and follow the instructions on the screen).

Cellular phones in France have numbers which begin with 06. Two-watt (lighter, shorter reach) and eight-watt models are on the market, using the Itinéris (France Télécom) or SFR network. *Mobicartes* are prepaid phone cards that fit into mobile units. Cell phone rentals (delivery or airport pickup provided):

Ellinas Phone Rental
☎ 01 48 01 63 33; Fax 01 48 01 62 13
Rent a Cell Express
☎ 01 53 93 78 00; Fax 01 53 93 78 09

Emergency numbers:	
Police:	17
Fire *(Pompiers)*:	18
"SAMU" (Paramedics):	15

Notes and coins

500 Francs featuring
scientists
Pierre and Marie Curie
(1858-1906), (1867-1934)

200 Francs featuring
engineer Gustave Eiffel
(1832-1923)

100 Francs featuring
Post-Impressionist painter
Paul Cézanne
(1839-1906)

50 Francs featuring
pilot and writer
Antoine de Saint-Exupéry
(1900-1944)

20 Francs

10 Francs

5 Francs

2 Francs

1 Franc

50 Centimes

20 Centimes

10 Centimes

5 Centimes

Conversion tables

Weights and measures

1 kilogram (kg)	2.2 pounds (lb)	2.2 pounds
1 metric ton (tn)	1.1 tons	1.1 tons

to convert kilograms to pounds, multiply by 2.2

1 litre (l)	2.1 pints (pt)	1.8 pints
1 litre	0.3 gallon (gal)	0.2 gallon

to convert litres to gallons, multiply by 0.26 (US) or 0.22 (UK)

1 hectare (ha)	2.5 acres	2.5 acres
1 square kilometre (km²)	0.4 square miles (sq mi)	0.4 square miles

to convert hectares to acres, multiply by 2.4

1 centimetre (cm)	0.4 inches (in)	0.4 inches
1 metre (m)	3.3 feet (ft) - 39.4 inches - 1.1 yards (yd)	
1 kilometre (km)	0.6 miles (mi)	0.6 miles

to convert metres to feet, multiply by 3.28. kilometres to miles, multiply by 0.6

Clothing

Women	🇪🇺	🇺🇸	🇬🇧		🇪🇺	🇺🇸	🇬🇧	Men
	35	4	2½		40	7½	7	
	36	5	3½		41	8½	8	
	37	6	4½		42	9½	9	
Shoes	38	7	5½		43	10½	10	**Shoes**
	39	8	6½		44	11½	11	
	40	9	7½		45	12½	12	
	41	10	8½		46	13½	13	
	36	4	8		46	36	36	
	38	6	10		48	38	38	
Dresses &	40	8	12		50	40	40	**Suits**
Suits	42	12	14		52	42	42	
	44	14	16		54	44	44	
	46	16	18		56	46	48	
	36	08	30		37	14½	14,5	
	38	10	32		38	15	15	
Blouses &	40	12	14		39	15½	15½	**Shirts**
sweaters	42	14	36		40	15¾	15¾	
	44	16	38		41	16	16	
	46	18	40		42	16½	16½	

Sizes often vary depending on the designer. These equivalents are given for guidance only.

Speed

kph	10	30	50	70	80	90	100	110	120	130
mph	6	19	31	43	50	56	62	68	75	81

Temperature

Celsius (°C)	0°	5°	10°	15°	20°	25°	30°	40°	60°	80°	100°
Fahrenheit (°F)	32°	41°	50°	59°	68°	77°	86°	104°	140°	176°	212°

To convert Celsius into Fahrenheit, multiply °C by 9, divide by 5, and add 32.
To convert Fahrenheit into Celsius, subtract 32 from °F, multiply by 5, and divide by 9.

Electricity

The electric current is 220 volts. Circular two pin plugs are the rule – an electrical adaptor may be necessary. US appliances (hairdryers, shavers) will not work without one. Adapters are on sale in electrical stores and also at international airports.

Time

France is 1hr ahead of Greenwich Mean Time (GMT).

When it is **noon in France**, it is

3am	in Los Angeles
6am	in New York
11am	in Dublin
11am	in London
7pm	in Perth
9pm	in Sydney
11pm	in Auckland

In France "am" and "pm" are not used but the 24-hour clock is widely applied.

Public holidays

Museums and other monuments may be closed or may vary their hours of admission on the following public holidays:

1	January	New Year's Day *(Jour de l'An)*
		Easter Day and Easter Monday *(Pâques)*
1	May	May Day
8	May	VE Day
40 days after Easter		Ascension Day *(Ascension)*
7th Sun after Easter		Whitsun *(Pentecôte)*
14	July	France's National Day (Bastille Day)
15	August	Assumption *(Assomption)*
1	November	All Saint's Day *(Toussaint)*
11	November	Armistice Day
25	December	Christmas Day (Noël)

National museums and art galleries are closed on Tuesdays; municipal museums are generally closed on Mondays. In addition to the usual school holidays at Christmas and in the spring and summer, there are long mid-term breaks (10 days to a fortnight) in February and early November.

Shopping

Opening hours

Department stores and chain stores are open Monday to Saturday, 9am to 6.30pm or 7.30pm. Smaller, more specialised shops may close during the lunch hour. Food stores (grocers, wine merchants and bakeries) are open from 7am to 6.30pm or 7.30pm. Some open on Sunday mornings. Many food stores close between noon and 2pm and on Mondays. Hypermarkets are usually open until 9pm or 10pm.

What to take home

Oysters from Cancale, charcuterie such as *rillettes* or *boudin noir*, globe artichokes, chestnuts, cider, Muscadet and Gros Plant wine, Breton mead (hydromel), Breton butter biscuits. Local crafts such as carved wood, lace, Quimper pottery.
Travellers from America should note that they are not allowed to take food and plant products home, so this rules out French cheeses and fruit, for example.
Americans are allowed to take home, tax-free, up to US$400 worth of goods, Canadians up to CND$300, British up to £136, Australians up to AUS$400 and New Zealanders up to NZ$700.

Recreation

Weather

For any outdoor activity, on sea or land, it is useful to have reliable weather forecasts. The French weather reporting service, **Météo-France**, can be consulted by telephone: for coastal weather reports, dial ☎ 08 36 68 02 followed by the number of the département in question (for the Morbihan, for example, you would dial 08 36 68 02 56); for beach weather reports and five day forecasts, ☎ 08 36 68 08 followed by the number of the département; for weather conditions at sea and five day forecasts for the Channel (Manche), Atlantic or Mediterranean dial ☎ 08 36 68 08 08.

BEAUFORT NUMBER	WIND NAME	WIND SPEED		CONDITIONS	
		knots	mph	Land	Sea
0	calm	1	1	smoke rises vertically	sea like a mirror
1	light air	1-3	1-3	smoke curves slightly upwards	small ripples
2	slight breeze	4-6	4-7	leaves rustle	small wavelets
3	gentle breeze	7-10	8-12	leaves move constantly	large wavelets, some white horses
4	moderate breeze	11-16	13-18	dust and sand rise	small waves lengthening, frequent white horses
5	fresh breeze	17-21	19-24	shrubs sway	moderate waves, many white horses and some spray
6	strong breeze	22-27	25-31	electric cables hum	large waves, white foam crests and spray
7	moderate gale	28-33	32-38	trees sway, walking is difficult	white foam blown in streaks
8	fresh gale	34-40	39-46	walking into the wind impossible	fairly high waves, spindrift, foam blown in marked streaks
9	strong gale	41-47	47-54	damage to buildings	high waves, spray affects visibility
10	whole gale	48-55	55-63	trees uprooted	heavy rolling sea with very high waves and dense spray
11	storm	56-63	64-72	extensive damage	huge waves, sea covered with spindrift
12	hurri-cane	>64	>73	very rare inland	air and sea filled with foam and spray, visibility almost nil

Boating – The Channel and Atlantic coasts lend themselves particularly well to exploration by boat, be it under sail or motor-powered. The main marinas are indicated on the Places to stay map at the beginning of the guide; criteria dictating their selection include number of berths available and range of facilites offered (fuel, fresh water and electricity on the quayside, toilets and washing facilities, elevators or cranes for loading, repair workshops, security guards).

Cycling – For information contact the Fédération Française de Cyclotourisme, 8, rue Jean-Marie-Jégo, 75013 Paris, ☎ 01 44 16 88 88, which will give you the details of its local representatives. Tourist Information Centres have lists of places to hire bicycles.
Main railway stations (Auray, Brest, Châteaulin, Combourg, Concarneau, Dinan, Dol, Guingamp, Lamballe, Lannion, Lorient, Morlaix, Quiberon, Quimper, Rennes, Roscoff, St-Brieuc, St-Malo, St-Nazaire, Vannes) offer three types of bicycle for hire (drop-off can be at a different station).

Deep-sea fishing – From Mont-St-Michel Bay to the River Loire estuary, Breton coastal waters offer infinite possibilities to amateur deep-sea fishermen. Contact the local marine authorities (Service des Affaires Maritimes) to find out about regulations governing fishing from boats or underwater. Fishing from the shore is not subject to any formal regulations, apart from the use of nets, which requires permission from the marine authorities. Different areas may however have particular coastal rules; it is advisable to find out what these are from the appropriate local authority.

Freshwater angling – Obey national and local laws. You may have to become a member (for the year in progress) of an affiliated angling association in the departement of your choice, pay the annual angling tax or buy a day card, and obtain permission from the landowner if you wish to fish on private land. Special two-week holiday fishing permits are also available.

A leaflet with a map and information called *Pêche en France* (Fishing in France) is available from Conseil Supérieur de la Pêche, 134 avenue de Malakoff, 75116 Paris, ☎ 01 45 02 20 20.

Rambling – A number of long-distance footpaths (sentiers de Grande Randonnée – GR) cover the region described in this guide. Walking holidays and rambles are organised by La Maison du Tourisme, 29 rue des Promenades, BP 620, 22011 St-Brieuc, ☎ 02 96 62 72 00 and France Randonnée, 9 rue des Portes-Mordelaises, 35200 Rennes, ☎ 02 99 67 42 21; Fax 02 99 67 42 23.

Argoat is crisscrossed by the **GR footpaths 34, 37, 38, 341 and 380**, which offer a range of pleasant rambles to walkers of all abilities.

The Topo-Guides, published by the Fédération Française de la Randonnée Pédestre, give detailed maps of the paths and offer valuable information to ramblers. You can find these and other guides and maps to local short-distance footpaths in local Tourist Information Centres and sports shops.

Riding – The possibilities for riding holidays in Brittany are numerous and open to riders of all abilities. For details, contact the following organisations:

Confédération nationale des usagers des loisirs équestres (FREF) – 16 rue des Apennins, 75017 Paris. ☎ 01 56 09 01 93.

Formules Bretagne – 17 rue de l'Arrivée, centre commercial Maine-Montparnasse, 75737 Paris Cedex 15. ☎ 01 42 79 07 07.

Association Régionale pour le Tourisme Équestre en Bretagne (ARTEB) – 33 rue Laënnec, 29710 Plonéis. ☎ 02 98 91 02 02.

Comités départementaux de tourisme équestre.

CDTE des **Côtes-d'Armor** – Association des cavaliers d'extérieur des Côtes-d'Armor (ACECA), 5 bois l'Abbé, 22970 Ploumagoar. ☎ 02 96 74 68 05.

CDTE du **Finistère** – Siège à l'ARTEB de Plogastel-St-Germain.

CDTE de l'**Ille-et-Vilaine** – Siège à l'ARTEB de Plogastel-St-Germain.

CDTE de la **Loire-Atlantique** – Le Clos de la Vigne, 44460 Fegréac. ☎ 02 40 91 21 47.

ADTE du **Morbihan** – 4 rue Georges-Cadoudal, 56390 Grandchamp. ☎ 02 97 66 40 46.

Sailing and windsurfing – The rugged Breton coastline shelters numerous bays which make an ideal setting for sailing enthusiasts to practise their sport. Many of the Breton yacht clubs have a sailing school attached to them, for example the centre at Glénan.

Sailing school

Fish auction at Concarneau

Windsurfing is possible from many beaches, although it is subject to certain rules; contact the yacht clubs for details. Windsurfers can be hired at all the major beaches, as can boats, with or without a crew, in season. For further information, contact the Fédération Française de Voile, 55 avenue Kléber, 75784 Paris Cedex 16, ☎ 01 45 53 68 00, or France Station-Voile, La Corderie royale, BP 108, 17303 Rochefort Cedex, ☎ 02 46 82 07 47.

Regattas are organised throughout the season in all the major resorts.

Skin-diving – This activity is becoming increasingly popular in Brittany. The clear waters of the inlets along Brittany's south coast (Port-Manech, Port-Goulphar to Belle-Ile) are rich in fish and marine plantlife, providing interest for underwater anglers and admirers of underwater landscapes alike. The Îles de Glénan diving centre attracts deep-sea divers, who can practise in the swimming pool during the winter.

Further information can be obtained from the Comité interrégional Bretagne-Pays de Loire de la Fédération Française d'Études et de Sports Sous-Marins (39 rue de la Villeneuve, 56100 Lorient, ☎ 02 97 37 51 51).

Holidays on a theme

ARTISTIC AND HISTORICAL CENTRES

Breton towns designated by the CNMHS as "Villes d'Art et d'Histoire" A (Towns of Art and History) have been regrouped as a special unit in Brittany since 1984. Similarly, smaller towns of particular local character – "Petites Cités de Caractère" – have been administered as a regional association since 1977. These towns regularly hold medieval pageants, *son et lumière shows*, and traditional and modern festivals in their historic town centres. Guided tours accompanied by CNMHS-approved guides are also available *(see the Admission times and charges section)*. Tourists can obtain relevant literature from tourist offices, rest places alongside main roads and motorways, or from the town hall of the town in question.

Eight Breton towns have been designated as "Villes d'Art et d'Histoire":

Auray (☎ 02 97 24 09 75)	**Dinan** (☎ 02 96 39 75 40)
Fougères (☎ 02 99 94 12 20)	**Quimper** (☎ 02 98 53 04 05)
Rennes (☎ 02 99 79 01 98)	**St-Malo** (☎ 02 99 56 64 48)
Vannes (☎ 02 97 47 24 34)	**Vitré** (☎ 02 99 75 04 46).

There are 19 "Petites Cités de Caractère": Bécherel, Châteaugiron, Châtelaudren, Combourg, Le Faou, Guerlesquin, Josselin, Jugon-les-Lacs, Lizio, Locronan, Malestroit, Moncontour, Pont-Croix, Pontrieux, Quintin, La Roche-Bernard, Rochefort-en-Terre, Roscoff and Tréguier.

For details on the above, contact the *Associations régionales des Villes d'Art et d'Histoire et des Petites Cités de Caractère de Bretagne*, 11 rue St-Yves, CS no. 26410, 35064 Rennes Cedex, ☎ 02 99 67 11 11; Fax 02 99 67 11 10.

CRUISING ON INLAND WATERWAYS

A 600km/380mi network of rivers and canals offers the opportunity of discovering inland Brittany by boat. The Channel and Atlantic coasts are linked by the Ille-et-Rance canal and the River Vilaine, passing through Dinan, Rennes and Redon.

Leaving from Lorient, a pleasant cruise along the Blavet, the east stretch of the Nantes-Brest canal, and the River Erdre takes visitors through Josselin and Redon before arriving in Nantes.

From the Brest roadstead, the River Aulne and the west stretch of the Nantes-Brest canal lead to Châteaulin and Carhaix-Plouguer.

The main companies handling river cruises are based at Blain, La Chapelle-aux-Filzméens, Châteauneuf-du-Faou, Dinan, Josselin, Messac, Redon, Rohan and Sucé-sur-Erdre.

Helpful publications include the brochures *Tourisme fluvial en Bretagne* (Comité de Promotion Touristique des Canaux Bretons et des Voies Navigables de l'Ouest Bretagne-Pays de la Loire, place du Parlement, 35600 Redon, ☎ 02 99 71 06 04) and *Formules Fluvial* (203 boulevard St Germain 75007 Paris, ☎ 01 53 63 11 53; Fax 01 53 63 11 57.)

Grafocarte (125 rue Jean-Jacques Rousseau, 92132 Issy-les-Moulineaux, ☎ 01 41 09 19 00) publish nautical maps and guides, also available in English (of particular interest: no 12, which covers from St-Malo to the Arzal dam and from Lorient to Nantes).

HISTORICAL ROUTES

Having been set up in 1975 by the organisations Demeure Historique and Caisse Nationale des Monuments Historiques et des Sites (CNMHS), there are now over 80 historical routes covering France. They explore architectural, archeological, botanical or geological heritage within a historical context: the Dukes of Brittany, the Painters of Cornouaille etc. These routes are signposted.

Five historical routes run through Brittany, on: Châteaubriand, the regions of Léon and Tréguier, the Painters of Cornouaille, the Dukes of Brittany and the Breton Marches.

M. Guillard/SCOPE

LIGHTHOUSES AND BEACONS

The Breton coast has the highest concentration of lighthouses and beacons on the whole French coast. A route running along the north Finistère coast leads past some of the most important lighthouses in Europe. For details contact Les Pays de Brest, BP 24, 29266 Brest Cedex, ☎ 02 98 44 24 96.

SET SAIL ON A HISTORICAL SHIP

The last sailing ships (coastal or fishing vessels) were taken out of active service towards the end of the 1960s. But thanks to restoration efforts, visitors can now enjoy cruises for the space of an afternoon or for as long as week. See the Practical information pages for specific towns on the coast for further details.

THALASSOTHERAPY CENTRES

A seaside setting (with the attendant healthy sea air, seaweed etc) is well known as an excellent natural restorative for those suffering from fatigue or stress. Thalassotherapy (medical sea treatment, from the Greek *thalassa*, or sea) involves various techniques which maximise the beneficial effects of a seaside climate: algo-therapy (seaweed and sea mud baths), hydrotherapy (spray-jets, sea-water showers or baths), kinesitherapy (massages, gymnastics), saunas, sea-water spray treatments etc. The average length of a treatment (recognised as being effective) at one of these thalassotherapy centres is around 7-10 days.

Brittany's major thalassotherapy centres are at La Baule, Belle-Île-en-Mer, Carnac, Le Crouesty, Dinard, Perros-Guirec, Quiberon, Roscoff and St-Malo. For information and bookings, contact *Formules Thalasso*, 203 boulevard St- Germain 75007 Paris Cedex, ☎ 01 53 63 11 53; Fax 01 53 63 11 57.

Further reading

Brittany by K Spence (George Philip)

Megalithic Brittany: A Guide by Aubrey Burl (Thames and Hudson)

Oysters of Locmariaquer by E Clark (University of Chicago Press)

Pierre Deux's Brittany by L Dannenberg, P Le Vec and P Moulin (Crown)

The Celts by TDE Powell (Thames and Hudson, Ancient Peoples and Places series)

La Route des Peintres en Cornouaille (Groupement Touristique de Cornouaille) – available in English

Le Blé en Herbe (Ripening Seed) by Colette

La Bretagne by J Markale (Sun coll "Voir en France")

Le Recteur de l'Ile de Sein by H Queffélec (Presses de la Cité)

Les Chouans by H de Balzac (Livre de Poche)

Memoirs by F-R de Chateaubriand (trans R Baldick)

Pêcheur d'Islande (Iceland Fisherman) by P Loti (Livre de Poche)

SOME CYBER-RESOURCES

A wealth of information on travel to Brittany, history, Celtic legends and local events can be found at: **www.bretagne.com**, which provides many links to other sites as well. Another good site with information in English is devoted to the Rhuys peninsula (south Brittany): **www.rhuys.com**. Other French sites: **www.tourisme.fr/ www.inet-bretagne.fr**

Regional Nature Parks

Regional nature parks play a different role from national parks, in that they are populated areas which have been selected for development with a threefold aim: promotion of local economy (creation of cooperatives, fostering of local crafts etc); protection of the natural and cultural heritage of the region (museums, architecture etc); and education (introduction to the natural environment for visitors). Regional nature parks are administered by an official body (syndicate, association etc) composed of local councillors, landowners and representatives of various local associations. A charter is set up in agreement with local residents to define the nature and extent of the park's projects.

PARC NATUREL RÉGIONAL D'ARMORIQUE

Parc naturel régional d'Armorique – This park was founded in September 1969 and encompasses 39 communes, covering an area of 172 000ha/425 021 acres (of which roughly two-thirds is on land and one-third is at sea). The park comprises three zones: the Monts d'Arrée (east and west sections); the Aulne estuary; and the capes and islands (Roscanvel and Camaret peninsulas and Ushant archipelago). The aims of the park are to preserve local countryside, flora and fauna, to improve the economy by fostering local industry (cooperatives, crafts), and to safeguard the traditional lifestyle of the region. Major innovations so far include the setting up of an information centre at Ménez-Meur (29460 Hanvec, ☎ 02 98 21 90 69), the opening of museums in traditional houses (in Brasparts, Kérouat, St-Rivoal, Trégarvan and on Ushant), the waymarking of footpaths and the founding of open-air museums (écomusées) on Ushant and in the Monts d'Arrée (which include exhibitions on the Breton horse and minerals).

Parc naturel régional de Brière – See La GRANDE BRIÈRE.

Calendar of events

PARDONS

Palm Sunday
Callac .... Stations of the Cross

Second Sunday in May
Quintin .... Pardon of Notre-Dame-de-Délivrance, ☎ 02 96 74 92 17

Ascension Day
St-Herbot .... Pardon of St-Herbot

Third Sunday in May
Tréguier .... Pardon of St-Yves, ☎ 02 96 92 30 51
Bubry 230 fold 35 *(1)* ... Pardon of St-Yves

Whit Saturday and Sunday
Moncontour .... Pardon of St-Mathurin, ☎ 02 96 73 41 54
St-Gildas Island .... Blessing of the horses

Whit Monday
Carantec .... Pardon of Notre-Dame-de-Callot

Sunday after Whit Sunday
Rumengol Le Faou .... Pardon of the Trinity

Trinity Sunday and eve
Notre-Dame-du-Crann ... Pardon, ☎ 02 98 93 84 78
Chapel
Rumengol .... Pardon, ☎ 02 98 81 93 45

Saturday evening and Sunday before the feast of St John the Baptist (24 June)
St-Tugen .... Pardon, ☎ 02 98 74 80 28

Last Sunday in June
St-Jean-du-Doigt .... Pardon of St John the Baptist, ☎ 02 98 67 30 40
Plouguerneau .... Pardon of St Peter and St Paul, ☎ 02 98 04 71 02
Le Faouët .... Summer Pardon of St Barbara

First Sunday in July (and preceding Friday and Saturday)
Guingamp .... Pardon of Notre-Dame-de-Bon-Secours, ☎ 02 96 43 73 59

Second Sunday in July
Locronan .... Petite Troménie (the Grande Troménie takes place every 6 years; the next one will be on the second and third Sundays in July 2001), ☎ 02 98 91 70 14

Third Sunday in July
Carantec .... St-Carantec Pardon, ☎ 02 98 67 02 72

25 and 26 July (Feast of St Anne)
Ste-Anne-d'Auray .... Grand Pardon of St Anne, ☎ 02 97 57 68 80

26 July (Feast of St Anne) and following Sunday
Fouesnant .... Grand and Petit Pardons of St Anne, ☎ 02 98 56 00 91

Fourth weekend in July
Le Vieux Marché .... Islamic-Christian pilgrimage to the Chapelle des Sept-
230 fold 6 (1) Saints, ☎ 02 96 38 91 73

Fourth Sunday in July
Le Releg Pardon of St Anne – Breton mass (11am) – Festival of Celtic Music (3.30pm)
Bubry 230 fold 35 (1) .... Pardon of Ste-Hélène, ☎ 02 97 51 70 38

First Sunday in August
Persquen 230 fold 21 (1) Pardon of Notre-Dame-de-Pénéty

15 August (Feast of the Assumption) and eve
Perros-Guirec .... Pardon of Notre-Dame-de-Clarté
Quelven .... Pardon of Notre-Dame
Rumengol .... Pardon of Notre-Dame-de-Rumengol
Porcaro .... Pardon of the "Madone des Motards" (Our Lady of Bikers)
Bécherel .... Haute-Bretagne Troménie
Pont-Croix .... Pardon of Notre-Dame-de-Roscudon

Rochefort-en-Terre .... Pardon of Notre-Dame-de-la-Tronchaye
Carantec.......................... Pardon of Notre-Dame-de-Callot, ☎ 02 98 67 07 88
Ploërdut .... Pardon of Notre-Dame-de-Crénenan
Le Releg.......................... Pardon of Notre-Dame-du-Releg

Ste-Anne-la-Palud .... Grand Pardon, ☎ 02 98 92 50 17
Le Faouët........................ Pardon of St-Fiacre

Camaret .... Pardon of Notre-Dame-de-Rocamadour – Blessing of the sea
Le Folgoët .... Grand Pardon of Notre-Dame, ☎ 02 98 83 00 67
Lamballe .... Pardon of Notre-Dame-de-la-Grande-Puissance
Pouldreuzic..................... Pardon of Notre-Dame-de-Penhors, ☎ 02 98 54 42 44

Carnac............................. Pardon of St-Cornély, ☎ 02 97 52 08 08

Josselin........................... Pardon of Notre-Dame-du-Roncier, ☎ 02 97 22 20 18

Notre-Dame-de-Tronoën . Pardon, ☎ 02 98 87 02 80
Pontivy............................. Pardon of Notre-Dame-de-la-Joie

Hennebont .... Pardon of Notre-Dame-du-Vœu, ☎ 02 97 36 24 52
Plouguerneau................... Pardon of St-Michel

Mont-St-Michel............... Feast of the Archangel St Michael
Gourin............................. Bellringers' Pardon

Le Faouët........................ Winter Pardon of St Barbara

Carantec.......................... Pardon of Notre-Dame-de-Callot, ☎ 02 98 67 07 88

FESTIVALS AND SPORTING EVENTS

Nantes .... La Folle Journée music festival, ☎ 02 51 88 20 00

La Trinité-sur-Mer .... Spi Ouest-France sailing event (1st week of April)
Vannes .... Café-Théâtre Festival, ☎ 02 97 47 24 34
Nantes .... Carnival, ☎ 02 40 35 75 52

La Baule .... International horse jumping competition
St-Malo .... "Étonnants Voyageurs" (Astonishing Explorers), ☎ 02 99 30 07 47
Mont St-Michel .... Folk Festival

Rennes .... Les "tombées de la nuit" (Breton art festival), ☎ 02 99 30 38 01
Carhaix-Plouger .... Popular Music Festival (mid-July), ☎ 02 98 99 29 18; www.vieilles-charues.com
Nantes .... International Summer Festival (music, song and dance), ☎ 02 40 08 01 00
Quimperlé .... Musiques Mosaïques" Festival, ☎ 02 98 96 04 32
Concarneau .... Maritime book fair (mid-July), ☎ 02 97 01 81 00.
Guer-Coëtquidan .... "Triomphe des Écoles de St-Cry-Coëtiquidan"
Quimper .... Cornouaille festival (week before 4th Sunday in July) ☎ 02 98 55 53 53
Vannes .... Jazz Festival, ☎ 02 97 01 81 00
Medieval Festival (before July 14), ☎ 02 97 01 81 21
Rennes .... Les "tombées de la nuit" (Breton art festival), ☎ 02 99 30 38 01

Dinan	Fête des remparts (every other year, in 2000, on 22 and 23 July)
Paimpol	Festival of sea chanties (last weekend of July in 2001), ☎ 02 96 20 83 16

Erquy	Festival of the Sea, ☎ 02 96 72 30 12
Pont-Aven	Gorse Festival, ☎ 02 98 06 12 33
St-Malo	Jazz Festival

Dinard	International horse jumping event, ☎ 02 99 46 19 35
Guingamp	Festivals of Breton Dance and of St-Loup, ☎ 02 96 43 73 89
Lorient	Interceltic Festival, ☎ 02 97 21 24 29
Plomodiern	Ménez-Hom Folklore Festival, ☎ 02 98 81 57 94 230 fold 18 (1)
Île de Fédrun	Festival of the Brière Region – Boat Race
Guérand	Celtic Festival, ☎ 02 40 24 93 13
St-Lyphard-en-Brière	Peat Festival
Vannes	Grand Festival of Arvor, ☎ 02 97 47 24 34

Carnac	Menhir Festival
Concarneau	Festival of the Blue Nets, ☎ 02 98 97 09 09
Lizio	Craft Festival
Moncontour	Medieval Festival
Perros-Guirec	Hydrangea Festival

Dol-de-Bretagne	Fête du cheval breton (local horse breeds)
Dinard	British Film Festival, ☎ 02 99 88 19 01

St-Malo	Quai des Bulles (Comic-Strip Festival), ☎ 02 99 40 39 63
Redon	"La Teillouse" chestnut festival, ☎ 02 99 71 06 04.

Nantes	"3 Continents" film festival, ☎ 02 40 69 74 14

MAIN MARKETS

Market day is an important event in the life of local communities, and provides visitors also with an opportunity to meet people, exchange news and views, and find out a bit about the region and local produce from those who live and work there.

MONDAY	Auray, Châtelaudren, Combourg, Concarneau, Guerlesquin, Moncontour, Pontivy, Pontrieux, Redon, Vitré
TUESDAY	Le Croisic, Landerneau, Quintin, St-Malo, St-Pol-de-Léon
WEDNESDAY	Châteaubriant, Guérande, Nantes, Quimper, Roscoff, Tréguier, Vannes
THURSDAY	Châteaugiron, Le Croisic, Dinan, Hennebont, Lannion, Malestroit, Pont-Croix, La Roche-Bernard
FRIDAY	Concarneau, Guingamp, Jugon-les-Lacs, Landerneau, Quimperlé, St-Malo
SATURDAY	Bécherel, Le Croisic, Dol-de-Bretagne, Fougères, Guérande, Guingamp, Josselin, Landerneau, Morlaix, Nantes, Port-Louis, Quimper, Redon, Rennes, Vannes, Vitré

For markets on slightly more unusual themes, try: the **Book Market** at *Bécherel* on the first Sunday of every month; the *Flea Market* at *Dinan* every Wednesday during July and August, otherwise the first Wednesday of the month; the largest **Cattle Market** in the west of France at **Fougères** opens every Friday morning at 5.30am.

FRESH FISH AUCTIONS

The fresh fish auctions which take place on the return of the fishing fleets are certainly lively and colourful affairs. They are generally held every day of the week 30min after the boats come in, and they last for about 2hr. The major ones are to be found at Audierne, Concarneau, Douarnenez, Erquy, Le Guilvinec, Loctudy and Lorient.

---

(1) Map references are given here for places not described in the main text of the guide

Admission times and charges

As admission times and charges are liable to alteration, the information below is given for guidance only. In cases where it has not been possible to obtain up-to-date information, the admission times and charges from the previous edition of the guide have been given in italics.

The information applies to individual adults. Special conditions for groups are common but arrangements should be made in advance. In some cases there is no charge for admission on certain days (Wednesdays, Sundays or public holidays).

Churches are usually closed from noon to 2pm; they should not be visited during services, other than to worship. Admission times are indicated if the interior is of special interest. Visitors to chapels are usually accompanied by the key-holder; a donation is welcome.

*Most tours are conducted by French-speaking guides but in some cases the term "guided tours" may cover group visiting with recorded commentaries. Some of the larger and more frequented sights may offer guided tours in other languages. The symbol ▲ indicates that tours are given by lecturers from the Historic Monuments Association (Caisse Nationale des Monuments Historiques et Sites). Enquire at the ticket office or book stall. Other aids for foreign visitors are notes, pamphlets or audio guides. Enquire at the tourist office, **🖪**, for local religious holidays, market days etc.*

Every sight for which there are times and charges is indicated by the symbol ⊘ in the alphabetical section of the guide. The entries are listed in the order under which they are to be found in the alphabetical section of the guide.

Sights which have comprehensive facilities for the disabled are indicated by the symbol 🚶 below.

A

ABERS

Gouesnou, Church – Guided tours Wed and Thur, 10am-noon; apply to the Town hall. ☎ 02 98 07 86 90.

Chapelle St-Jaoua – To visit the chapel, apply to Mr Roux, ☎ 02 98 40 91 27.

St-Jean-Balanant, Chapel – To visit the chapel, apply to Mr Paugam, ☎ 02 98 40 98 12.

Ruines d'Iliz Koz – Open mid-Jun to mid-Sept, daily, 2.30-6.30pm; rest of the year, Sun and holidays 2.30-5pm. 15F. ☎ 02 98 04 70 93.

Phare de l'Île Vierge – *Open July and Aug, daily, 11am-noon and 3-6pm; June, Sun same times; May, Sun and holidays same times. No charge.* ☎ 02 98 04 78 01.

Château de Kergroadès – *Guided tours (30min) by appointment only. 20F.* ☎ 02 98 84 21 73.

Monts d'ARRÉE

Lannédern, Church – Guided tours July and August. Apply to the Tourist Information Office in Pleyben. ☎ 02 98 26 71 05

Domaine de Menez-Meur – Open June to Sept, daily, 10am-7pm; during May Sun-Fri 1.30-5.30pm; rest of the year open Wed, Sun and holidays 10am-noon and 1pm to 6pm. Closed January. 20F. ☎ 02 98 68 81 71.

St-Rivoal, Maison Cornec – Open July and Aug, daily, 11am-7pm; in June and September 2-6pm (closed Sat in Sept). 15F. ☎ 02 98 68 87 76.

Maison des Artisans (North of Brasparts) – Open Apr to Dec, daily, 10am-7pm; Jan to Mar, Sat-Sun and holidays 1-7pm. Closed 1 Jan and 25 Dec.2-6.30pm

Brennilis, Church – *To visit, apply to the presbytery.*

AURAY   🖪 Place de la République, 56400 – ☎ 02 97 24 09 75

Guided tours of the town – Contact the tourist office.

Goélette St-Sauveur – Open Apr to Sept, daily, 10am-7pm. Late closing July and Aug. 20F. ☎ 02 97 56 63 38.

Chartreuse d'Auray – Guided tours (30min) Apr to Oct, daily (except Tues), 2.30-5pm (last admission at 4.30pm). Closed end of Aug to early Sept. No charge. ☎ 02 97 24 27 02.

St-Degan, Écomusée – Open July and Aug, daily 10am-7pm; Apr to June and Sept 2-5.30pm; rest of the year, Sat-Sun 2-5.30pm. 26F. ☎ 02 97 57 66 00.

Ste-Anne d'Auray:

Basilica Treasury – ♿ Open Mar to early Oct, daily, 10am-noon and 2.30-6pm, Sun and holidays 2.30-6pm. Closed rest of the year. 10F. ☎ 02 97 57 68 80.

Historial de Sainte Anne – ♿ Open daily 8am-7pm. 20F. ☎ 02 97 57 64 05.

Musée du costume breton – Open Mar to Oct, daily, 10am-noon and 2-6pm. Closed rest of the year. 10F. ☎ 02 97 57 68 80.

Maison de Nicolazic – Open Easter to Oct, daily, 9am-7pm. No charge. ☎ 02 97 57 68 80.

Ste-Avoye, Chapel – Guided tours daily except Monday mornings 10am-noon and 3-5.30pm ☎ 02 97 24 02 94.

B

La BAULE

Le Pouliguen: Chapelle Ste-Anne-et-St-Julien – Open July to Sept, daily, 10am -noon and 2-7pm.

BÉCHEREL

Château de Caradeuc:

Park – ♿ Open end of Mar to mid-Sept, daily, 10am-7pm; mid-September to Oct, 2-6pm; rest of the year, open Sat-Sun 2-6pm. 15F. ☎ 02 99 66 77 76.

Excursion

Château de Hac – Guided tours (40min) in July and Aug, daily (except Sat), 2-7pm; in June and Sept, Sun only, 2-7pm. Closed holidays. 20F. ☎ 02 96 83 43 06.

Tinténiac: Musée de l'outil et des métiers – Open July to Sept, daily, 10.30am-noon and 3-6pm, Sun and holidays 3-6pm. 10F. ☎ 02 99 68 02 03.

BELLE-ÎLE   🛈 Quai Bonnelle, Le Palais, 56360 – ☎ 02 97 31 81 93

From Le Palais it is possible to hire cars (without a driver), bicycles, tandems and mopeds.

Citadelle Vauban – Open July and Aug, daily, 9am-7pm; Apr to June, Sept and Oct, 9.30am-6pm; rest of the year, open 9.30am-noon and 2-5pm. 35F (adult), 15F (child). ☎ 02 97 31 84 17.

Grand Phare – Open July to mid-Sept, daily, 10.30am-noon and 2-5.30pm.

Le Palais

🅸 29, avenue de la Mer, 29950 – ☎ 02 98 57 00 14

Excursions

Boat trips up the Odet River – Aprto Sept, up to 10 daily guided trips are organised by the "Vedettes de l'Odet"; luncheon-cruises daily (except Monday). ☎ 02 98 57 00 58.

BLAIN

Le Gâvre, Maison Benoist – Open May to mid-Nov, daily, 2.30-6.30pm; in Apr, Sat-Sun and holidays at the same hours. Closed mid-Nov to end of Mar. 15F. ☎ 02 40 51 25 14.

Vallée du BLAVET

Pontivy: Château – Open July to mid-Sept, daily, 10.30am-7pm; rest of the year, open 10am-noon and 2-6pm. Closed 1 Jan, 1 Nov, 25 Dec, Mon and Tues from Oct to May. 8F; 25F including summer exhibition. ☎ 02 97 25 12 93.

Bieuzy: Church – Closed except for services.

Melrand: Ferme archéologique – ♿ Open May to August, daily, 10am-7pm; Sept to Apr 11am-5pm (6pm Sat-Sun). Closed mid(Dec to mid-Jan and 1 Nov. 20F. ☎ 02 97 39 57 89.

Baud: Vénus de Quinipily – Open Apr to Oct, daily, 10am-7pm; rest of the year, 11am-6pm. 10F. ☎ 02 97 51 14 93.

Poul Fetan: a typical Breton village of the past – Open June to mid-Sept, daily 10am-7pm (guided tours only in the morning); Apr, May and mid-Sept to Oct, 2-6pm (2-7pm on Sun); the rest of the year, open Sund, holidays and school holidays, 2-6pm. Closed 1 Jan and 25 Dec. 30F high season; 20F off season. ☎ 02 97 39 72 82.

Écomusée industriel de Inzinzac-Lochrist – Open July and Aug, daily, 10am-6.30pm, Sat-Sun 2-6.30pm; June and Sept, daily, 10am-noon and 2-6pm, Sat-Sun 2.6pm; rest of the year, daily (except Sat), 10am-noon and 2-6pm, Sun 2-6pm. Closed 1 January, 1 May, 1November and 25 December. 25F. ☎ 02 97 36 98 21.

Île de BRÉHAT 🅸 22870 – ☎ 02 96 20 04 15

Tour – Bicycles can be hired in Port-Clos.

Boat trips – There are regular ferry services (10min) all year round leaving from the Pointe de l'Arcouest. It is also possible to tour the island by boat (6 or 7 departures daily from-Apr to Oct). There are day excursions leaving from Binic, St-Quay-Portrieux and Erquy in July and Aug. Estuaire de Trieux: 4hr. For further information apply to "Les Vedettes de Bréhat". ☎ 02 96 55 73 47 or 02 96 55 79 50.

BREST 🅸 Place de la Liberté, 29200 – ☎ 02 98 44 24 96

Guided tour of the town – Contact the tourist office.

Musée de la Marine – Open Apr to Sept, daily 10am-6.30pm, Tues 1.30-6.30pm; rest of the year, daily (except Tues), 1.30-6pm. Closed Nov to mid-Dec, 1 Jan, 1 May and 25 Dec. 29F. ☎ 02 98 22 12 39.

Tour of the Dockyard – Guided tours (90 min) on foot are open to French nationals only. July to mid-Sept, daily, 9-11am and 2-4pm; mid-June to end of June, 9-10am and 2-3pm; in Apr, at 10am and 2.30pm. Report to the Police Station (Poste de Gendarmerie) at the Porte de la Grande Rivière (on Route de la Corniche). No charge (donations are welcome for the volunteer guides). ☎ 02 98 22 07 56.

Musée des Beaux-Arts – Open daily (except Sun morning and Tues), 10-11.45am and 2-6pm. Closed public holidays. 25F. ☎ 02 98 00 87 96.

Tour Tanguy – Open June to Sept, daily, 10am-noon and 2-7pm; Oct to May, open Wed and Thur 2-5pm, Sat-Sun 2-6pm. Closed 1 Jan, 1 May and 25 Dec. No charge. ☎ 02 98 00 88 60.

Océanopolis – ♿ Open Apr to early Sept, daily, 9.30am-6pm (last admission 1hr before closing), Sat-Sun 9.30am-7pm. 50F (adult), 30F (child). ☎ 02 98 34 40 40.

Conservatoire botanique national de Brest – Open in spring and summer 9am-8pm (the exhibition pavilion is open July to mid-Sept, Sun to Thur 2-5pm); in fall and winter open 9am-6pm (the exhibition pavilion is open mid-Sept to June, Wed and Sun only 2-5pm). Audio-guided tours of the greenhouses July to mid-Sept, Sun to Thur 2-5pm; rest of the year, Sun at 4.30pm. No charge for the garden and information centre; 22F for the greenhouses. ☎ 02 98 02 46 00.

Boat trips – Tours are organised to the naval port and the roadstead (90min) Apr to Sept, 5 times a day. For the Presqu'île de Crozon (45min), there are 3 return trips a day mid-Mar to mid-Oct. One may also travel upstream and downstream the rivers Aulne and Elorn, depending on the tides. Apply to the "Compagnie des Vedettes armor-icaines", 1er bassin, Port de Commerce. ☎ 02 98 44 44 04.

Brest roadstead – Compagnie maritime Azénor: military port (90min); dining cruise (lunch or dinner – 3hr15min), reservation required; Brest-Crozon on a speed boat. ☎ 02 98 41 46 23

Fort Montbarey, Mémorial du Finistère – Open Mon to Sun 2-6pm. Closed public holidays. 20F. ☎ 02 98 05 39 46.

Fort de Bertheaume – Open June to Aug and Easter school holidays, daily, 1.30-6.30pm; May, Sept and Oct, Sat-Sun and holidays only 1.30-6.30pm. Closed Nov to Mar. 22F (adult), 12F (child). Sound and light show (1hr) from Apr to Oct at 9pm. 44F (adult), 25F (child). ☎ 02 98 48 30 18.

Pointe de St-Mathieu: Lighthouse – Temporarily closed. ☎ 02 98 89 00 17.

C

🛈 5, quai Kléber, 29570 – ☎ 02 98 27 93 60

Boat trip – Trips to the Ouessant and Sein islands in July and Aug. May to October, trip on the "Belle Étoile", a lobster skiff. Information from the Tourist office.

🛈 44, rue du Port, 35260 – ☎ 02 99 89 63 72

Église St-Méen: Ascent to the Tower – Apply to the tourist office. 5F.

Musée des Bois sculptés – Open July and Aug, daily (except Sun and Mon), 2.30-6pm. 8F40. ☎ 02 99 89 60 15.

La Ferme Marine Musée de l'Huître et du Coquillage – ♿ There are guided tours (1 hour) from 16 June to 15 September at 11am, 3pm and 5pm; from 15 February to 15 June and 16 September to 1 November at 3pm. Closed weekends except for school holiday periods. 38F. ☎ 02 99 89 69 99.

Musée des Arts et Traditions populaires – ♿ Open July and Aug, daily, 10am-noon (except Mon morning) and 2.30-6.30pm, Thur night 8.30-10pm; June and Sept, Thur to Sun 2.30-6.30pm. 20F. ☎ 02 99 89 79 32.

Maison de Jeanne Jugan – On request only. Apply to Mme Rey. No charge. ☎ 02 99 89 62 73.

Musée d'Ethnographie locale (Maison du Sénéchal) – Open July and Aug, daily, 9am-12.30pm and 1.30-7pm (Sun10am-1pm); rest of the year, open daily (except Sun and holidays), 10am-noon and 2-6pm. No charge. ☎ 02 98 93 04 42.

Locarn, Church – Guided tours daily 10am-noon and 2-5pm. ☎ 02 96 36 66 11.

🛈 Avenue des Druides, 56340 – ☎ 02 97 52 13 52

Musée de Préhistoire J.-Miln-Z.-Le-Rouzic – ♿ Open July and Aug, daily (except Tues), 10am-6.30pm, (Sat-Sun 10am-noon and 2-6.30pm); rest of the year, 10am-noon and 2-5pm (6pm in June and Sept). Closed 1 Jan, 1 May and 25 Dec. 25F (30F in summer). ☎ 02 97 52 22 04.

Alignements de Kermario – Guided tours organised in July and August, reservations required. 25F. ☎ 02 97 52 29 81.

Tumulus de Kercado – Open Apr to Oct, daily 9am-7pm (5pm rest of the year). 4F. Information at the crêperie nearby.

Castle – Guided tour (1hr) mid-June to mid-Sept, daily (except Tues), 10.30am-5pm, Sun and holidays 2-5pm. ☎ 02 40 28 20 90.

Castle and Park – Guided tours (1hr) July and Aug, daily 11am-12.30pm and 1.30-5.30pm, park open 10am-12.30pm and 1.30-6pm; Apr to June and Sept, daily (except Tues), 2-5.30pm, park open 10am-12.30pm and 2-6pm; Oct, daily (except Tues), 2-4.30pm, park open 10am-noon and 2-4.30pm. Closed Dec to Feb. 28F (castle and park). ☎ 02 99 73 22 95.

Château de Lanrigan – Open July and Aug (château exterior only), Wed to Fri, 9am-noon and 2-6pm. No charge.

Cobac Parc, Country Park – ♿ Open July and Aug, daily, 10am-7pm; Apr to June and first fortnight in Sept, 10.30am-6.30pm. Closed mid-Sept to Easter. 60F. ☎ 02 99 73 80 16.

Antrain: Château de Bonne-Fontaine – Park open Easter to All Saints' Day, daily, 2-6pm. 15F. Maze open mid-July to mid-Sept, daily 11am-7pm. 35F (adult), 25F (child). Musée des Fables de La Fontaine and Musée de l'illusionisme open mid-June to mid-Sept, 11am-7pm. Each museum: 35F (adult), 25F (child). ☎ 02 99 98 31 13.

CONCARNEAU
🛈 Quai d'Aiguillon, 29900 – ☎ 02 98 97 01 44

Fresh fish auction – The fish are unloaded Sun to Thur nights, 11pm-5am. Fresh fish auction Mon to Friday, 6.30-9am (depending on the day's catch). No charge to attend, 30F for a guided tour. ☎ 02 98 97 01 44.

Musée de la Pêche – ♿ Open early July to early Sept, daily, 9am-8pm; rest of the year, open 9am -noon and 2-6pm. Closed last three weeks of January, 1 Jan and 25 Dec. 36F. ☎ 02 98 97 10 20.

Walk round the ramparts – Mid-June to mid-Sept, daily, 10am-8pm; rest of the year, 10am-5pm. Closed during school holidays in Feb and Nov. Access to the ramparts may be forbidden in adverse weather conditions or during the Blue Nets Festival. 5F; no charge off season.

Marinarium – ♿ Open July and August, daily, 10am-noon and 2-6.30pm; Apr to June and Sept, 2-6.30pm. 20F. ☎ 02 98 97 06 59.

CORNICHE BRETONNE

Pleumeur-Bodou: Musée des Télécommunications and Radôme – ♿ Open July and Aug, daily, 10am-7pm; May and June, 10am-6pm, Sept, 10am-6pm, Sat 2-6pm; Apr daily (except Sat), 10am-6pm; Nov and Jan, Mon to Fri, 1.30-5.30pm; Feb and Dec, daily (except Sat), 1.30-5.30pm; Mar and Oct, daily (except Sat), 1.30-5.30pm, Sun 2-5pm. Closed 1 Jan, 11 Nov, 5 and 12 Dec. 45F; combined ticket for Musée/Radôme + Planétarium: 65F; family ticket (2 adults + 2 children) for Musée/Radôme: 100F + 10F for each extra child. Family ticket available. ☎ 02 96 46 63 80.

Planétarium du Trégor – ♿ Astronomy presentations (1hr) July and Aug, daily at 11am, noon, 2pm, 3pm, 4pm, 5pm and 6pm; rest of the year by appointment (at least one presentation in the afternoon at around 4pm). 40F (adult), 30F (child); combined ticket for Musée/Radôme + Planétarium: 65F; family ticket available. ☎ 02 96 15 80 30.

Île Grande : Station ornithologique – Open June to Sept, daily 10am-noon and 2-6pm, Sat-Sun 2.30-6pm; during school holidays, daily, 10am-noon and 2-6pm, Sat-Sun 2-6pm; rest of the year, open Sat-Sun only 2-6pm. No charge. ☎ 02 96 91 91 40.

CORNICHE DE L'ARMORIQUE

St-Jean-du-Doigt: Church Treasury – The treasury is visible only on the day of the Saint-Jean pardon (last Sun in June). No charge. ☎ 02 98 67 30 40.

Château de Rosanbo – Guided tours (45min) July and Aug, daily, 11am-6pm; Apr to June, 2-5pm; Sept and Oct, Sun and holidays 2-5pm. Closed the rest of the year. 30F. ☎ 02 96 35 18 77.

CORNOUAILLE

Réserve du Cap Sizun – 10am-6pm Apply to the Maison de la Réserve, Chemin de Kérisit, 29770 Goulien. ☎ 02 98 70 13 53.

Audierne:

Grands Viviers – Open July and Aug, Mon-Fri, 9am-noon and 3-5pm; rest of the year, Mon-Fri, 3-5pm. No charge. ☎ 02 98 70 10 04.

La Chaumière – ♿ Guided tours (30min) Apr to mid-Oct, daily, 10am-1pm and 2-7pm. Closed the rest of the year. 15F. ☎ 02 98 70 13 20.

Chapelle de Languivoa – Open July and Aug, daily, 2.30-6.30pm. ☎ 02 40 40 47 01.

St-Guénolé, Musée préhistorique finistérien – ♿ Open June to mid-Sept, daily (except Tues), 11am-12.30pm and 2.30-6.30pm; rest of the year by appointment. 20F. ☎ 02 98 58 60 35.

Phare d'Eckmühl – Tours of the lighthouse depend on the availability of the keepers. ☎ 02 98 58 61 17.

Penmarch, Église St-Nonna – Guided tours mid-July to mid-Aug, daily, 10am-noon and 3-6pm. ☎ 02 98 58 60 30.

Sea trips – Apply to the tourist office.

Océarium – ♿ Open June to mid-Sept, daily, 10am-7pm; rest of the year, open 10am-noon and 2-6pm. Closed for three weeks in Jan. 48F (adult), 29F (child). ☎ 02 40 23 02 44.

Musée des Marais salants – ♿ Open June-Sept and school holidays, 10am-noon and 3-7pm; Oct-May Sat-Sun 3-7 pm; closed 1 Jan., 25 dec, 21F . ☎ 02 40 23 82 79.

Presqu'île de CROZON

Les Grandes Grottes – Boat trips (45min) May to Sept. Departures all day depending on the tide, leaving from the port. 45F (adult), 33F (child). Armement Rosmeur ☎ 02 98 27 10 71 or Vedettes Sirènes ☎ 02 98 96 20 10.

D

DAOULAS

Abbey: Cloître et Centre culturel – Opening times vary. Closed 1 January and 25 Dec. 15F to 45F, depending on temporary exhibitions. ☎ 02 98 25 84 39.

DINAN

Guided tour of the town 🅰 – Contact the tourist office. Tour de l'Horloge – Open June to Sept, daily, 10am-6pm; Apr and May, 2-6pm. Closed the rest of the year. 16F. ☎ 02 96 39 22 43.

Castle – Open June to mid-Oct, daily, 10am-6.30pm; mid-Mar to May and mid-Oct to mid-Nov, daily (except Tues), 10am-noon and 2-6pm; mid-Nov to Dec and early February to mid-Mar, daily (except Tues), 1.30-5.30pm. Closed Jan and 25 Dec. 25F. ☎ 02 96 39 45 20.

Ancien Couvent des Cordeliers – Open July and Aug, daily 10am-6pm. No charge.

Maison d'Artiste de la Grande Vigne – Open June to mid-Sept, 10am-6pm; in May, 2-6pm. 16F. Dinan Town Hall. ☎ 02 96 39 22 43.

Excursions

Léhon: Monastery buildings, Cloisters, Museum and Gardens – Open July and Aug, daily (except Sun), 10am-noon and 3-6pm. 15F. ☎ 02 96 39 07 19.

Corseul : Musée de la Société archéologique de Corseul – Open July and Aug, daily (except Sat afternoon and Sun), 8.30am-noon and 2-6pm; rest of the year, daily (except Sat afternoon and Sunday), 8.30am-noon and 2-5.30pm. Closed on public holidays. 5F (No charge off season). ☎ 02 99 27 90 17.

Château de la Bourbansais:

Parc zoologique et jardin – ♿ Open Apr to Sept, daily, 10am-7pm; the rest of the year open 2-6pm. 68F (garden, zoo and château; child 40F), 55F (garden and zoo; child 35F), ☎ 02 99 69 40 07.

Château interior – Guided tours (45min) Apr to Sept, daily at 11am, then every hour from 2-5pm; rest of the year, Sun at 3.30pm and holidays at 3pm and 4pm. 55F (château only; child 35F), 68F (garden, zoo and château; child 40F). ☎ 02 99 69 40 07.

DINARD

Promenade du Clair de Lune – Floodlit musical performances June to Sept, daily.

Musée du Site Balnéaire – The museum is temporarily closed. ☎ 02 99 46 81 05.

Aquarium et Musée de la Mer – ♿ Open mid-May to mid-Sept, daily, 10.30am-12.30pm and 3.30-7.30pm, Sun 10.30am-12.30pm and 2.30-7.30pm. 15F. ☎ 02 99 46 13 90.

Excursions

St-Lunaire: Vieille église St-Lunaire – Open Easter to Sept. ☎ 02 99 46 30 51 (Town Hall).

DOL-DE-BRETAGNE

Cathédraloscope – Open May to Sept, daily, 9am-7pm; rest of the year, 10am-6pm. Closed early Jan to early Feb. 40F. ☎ 02 99 48 35 30.

Museum – Open June to Sept, daily (except Mon), 9am-12.30pm and 2-6.30pm; rest of the year, holidays only at the same times. 20F. ☎ 02 99 48 33 46.

DOL-DE-BRETAGNE

Excursion

Baguer-Morvan : Musée de la Paysannerie – ♿ Open May to Sept, daily, 10am-7pm. 24F. ☎ 02 99 48 04 04.

DOUARNENEZ
🛈 2, rue Docteur-Mevel, 29100 – ☎ 02 98 92 13 35

Port-Musée – ♿ Open mid-June to Sept, daily, 10am-7pm; rest of the year, daily (except Mon) 10am-12.30pm and 2-6pm. Closed Jan and 25 Dec. 30F. ☎ 02 98 92 65 20.

Chapelle St-Michel – If the chapel is closed, apply to the presbytery at 10, rue Ernest-Renan. ☎ 02 98 92 03 17.

Ploaré : Church – Open July and Aug, daily, 10am-noon.

Pouldavid : Church – To visit the church, apply to the presbytery. ☎ 02 98 92 09 41.

Excursions

Le Juch : Church – If the church is closed, apply to Mme Pennanéac'h. ☎ 02 98 74 73 21 and ☎ 02 98 74 71 38.

E

ENCLOS PAROISSIAUX

Moulins de Kerouat – Open July and Aug, daily, 11am-7pm; in June, 10am-noon and 2-6pm, Sat-Sun afternoons only; mid-Mar to May and Sept to Oct, daily (except Sat), 10am-noon and 2-6pm, Sun and holidays afternoons only. 18F. ☎ 02 98 68 87 76.

F

Le FAOUËT

Excursions

Chapelle St-Fiacre – April to mid-Nov, 10am-noon, 2pm-6pm; mid-Nov to March, Sat-Mon 2pm-5pm. ☎ 02 97 23 23 23.

Chapelle Ste-Barbe – April to mid-Nov, 10am-noon, 2pm-6pm; mid-Nov to March, Sat-Mon 2pm-5pm. ☎ 02 97 23 23 23.

Le FOLGOËT

Museum – ♿ Open mid-June to mid-Sept, daily (except Sun and public holidays in the morning), 10am-12.30pm and 2.30-6.30pm. 10F. ☎ 02 98 83 03 78.

FOUGÈRES
🛈 1, place Aristide-Briand, 35300 – ☎ 02 99 94 12 20

Guided tour of the town 🅰 – Apply to the Service du Patrimoine.

Castle: Inner Tour – Open mid-June to mid-Sept, daily, 9am-7pm; Apr to mid-June and last two weeks of Sept, open 9.30am-noon and 2-6pm; rest of the year, open 10am-noon and 2-5pm. Closed Jan and 25 Dec. 30F (adult), 11F (child). ☎ 02 99 99 79 59.

Musée Emmanuel de la Villéon – Open mid-June to mid-Sept, daily, 10am-12.30pm and 2.30-6pm; rest of the year, Wed to Sunday, 10am-noon and 2-5pm. Closed Jan, 1 May and 25 Dec. No charge. ☎ 02 99 99 19 98 or ☎ 02 99 94 88 60.

Cap FRÉHEL

Access to the Site – June to Sept: 10F for private cars; no charge the rest of the year.

Lighthouse – Guided tours July to mid-Sept, daily, 2.30-6pm. ☎ 02 96 41 40 03.

Boat trips – Departures from Dinard and St-Malo (2hr45min). For all information apply to "Emeraude Lines" in St-Malo. ☎ 02 23 18 15 15.

G

La GRANDE BRIÈRE

Parc naturel régional de Brière:

Maison de l'Éclusier – Guided tours (1hr) Apr and June to Sept, daily, 10.30am-1pm and 2.30-6.30pm; Feb and Nov school holidays, open 2.30-6.30pm; 8 and 9 May, Ascension Day, Whitsun and Oct to Dec, Sat-Sun and holidays, 2.30-6.30pm. Closed Jan and 25 Dec. 18F; combine ticket with parc animalier 22F. ☎ 02 40 66 85 01.

Parc animalier – Open July and Aug, daily 9am-7pm; June and Sept to the end of the Nov school holiday, 9am-6pm. 18F. Combine ticket with the Maison de l'éclusier 22F. ☎ 02 40 66 85 01.

Île de Fédrun : Maison de la Mariée – Guided tours (1hr) June to Sept and Easter school holiday, daily, 10.30am-1pm and 2.30-6.30pm; Oct to Dec, Sun and holidays, 2.30-6.30pm; 8 May, Ascension Day and Whitsun, 2.30-6.30pm. Closed Jan and 25 Dec. 14F. ☎ 02 40 66 85 01.

Château de Ranrouët – Open July and Aug, daily, 10am-7pm; Apr to June and Sept, Tues to Sat, 2.30-6.30pm, Sun and holidays 2-7pm. Closed Oct to Mar and 1 May. 15F. ☎ 02 40 88 96 17.

St-Lyphard : Church Belfry – Guided tours (30min) July and Aug, daily, 10am-noon and 1.30-6pm (Sat 5.30pm), Sun 10.30am-noon and 1.30-5pm; Feb to June and Sept, 10.30am-noon and 1.30-5pm; Oct to Jan, Wed, Fri and Sat only, 11am-noon and 2-5pm. Closed 1 May and Christmas school holiday. 10F. ☎ 02 40 91 41 34.

Kerhinet : Musée du Chaume – Guided tours (1hr) Apr and June to Sept, daily, 10.30am-1pm and 2.30-6.30pm; Feb and Nov school holidays, 2.30-6.30pm; 8 and 9 May, Ascension Day, Whitsun, Sun and holidays from Oct to Dec, 2.30-6.30pm. 12F. ☎ 02 40 66 85 01.

Île de GROIX

Tour – Bicycles, scooters and cars can be hired in Port-Tudy.

Access – Year-round, daily departures from Lorient (45min, 4 to 8 return trips a day depending on the time of year). High season, 110F there and back, off season 105F. Contact Compagnie Morbihannaise et Nantaise de Navigation (Lorient). ☎ 02 97 64 77 64.

Écomusée de l'Île de Groix – Open June to Sept, daily, 9.30am-12.30pm and 3-7pm; mid-Apr to May, 10am-12.30pm and 2-5pm; Oct to mid-Apr, daily (except Mon), 10am-12.30pm and 2-5pm. Closed 1 Jan, 24 Dec (afternoon) and 25 Dec. 24F. ☎ 02 97 86 84 60.

Presqu'île de GUÉRANDE

Saillé: Maison des Paludiers – ♿ Open Mar to Oct, daily, 10am-12.30pm and 2-6pm. 19F. Guided tours (2hr) of a salt marsh July and August, daily at 4.30pm (except in rainy weather). 40F. ☎ 02 40 62 21 96.

Guided tour of the town of Guérande – Contact the tourist office: Tour St-Michel, 44350 – ☎ 02 40 24 96 71.

Porte St-Michel ("**Château-musée**") – Open Apr to Sept, daily, 10am-12.30pm (noon in Oct) and 2.30-7pm (6pm in Oct). Nov to Mar, by appointment. 20F. ☎ 02 40 42 96 52.

Château de Careil – Guided tours (30min) June to Aug, daily, 10.30am-noon and 2.30-7pm. In July and Aug, guided tours by candlelight Wed and Sat at 9.30pm. 25F, tour by candlelight 30F. ☎ 02 40 60 22 99.

La GUERCHE-DE-BRETAGNE

Excursions

Lac des Mottes – Fishing is permitted on Thur, Sun and public holidays.

Lac de GUERLÉDAN

In July and August, canoes and kayaks can be hired from the Rond-Point du Lac in Mur-de-Bretagne.

Boat trips – July and Aug, daily trips (90min), departures at 2.30pm, 3pm and 4pm; Apr to June and Sept to Oct, inquire. 40F (adult), 22F (child). Luncheon cruise (3hr), reservations required; also cruise along the Nantes-Brest canal. ☎ 02 96 28 52 64.

St-Aignan : Electrothèque – By appointment only. 20F. ☎ 02 97 27 51 39.

Les Forges des Salles – Guided tours (1hr) July to August, daily, 2-6.30pm; Easter to June and Sept to Nov, Sat-Sun 2-6.30pm. 25F. ☎ 02 96 24 90 12.

Abbaye de Bon-Repos – Open Easter to Sept, daily; rest of the year, daily (except Sat). 15F. ☎ 02 96 24 82 20.

GUINGAMP

Hôtel de Ville – The town hall is open daily (except Sat afternoon and Sun), 8.30am-noon and 1.30-5.30pm. No charge. ☎ 02 96 40 64 40.

Excursions

Chapelle Notre-Dame-de-Restudo – By appointment, preferably in the afternoon. Apply to Mme Melou next door. ☎ 02 96 21 43 01.

Chapelle d'Avaugour – By appointment. Apply to Mme Mallégol. ☎ 02 96 43 48 08.

H

Île de HŒDIC and Île d'HOUAT

Access to the Islands: Boat Service – July to mid-Sept, one to four daily trips (90min) leaving from Quiberon; rest of the year, daily trips (except Thur). Off season 105F there and back, high season 110F there and back. For information apply to the Société Morbihannaise et Nantaise de Navigation. ☎ 02 97 50 06 90.

J

JOSSELIN   🄸 Place de la Congrégation, 56120 – ☎ 02 97 22 36 43

Château – Guided tours (45min) daily July and Aug, daily, 10am-6pm; June and Sept 2-6pm; Apr, May and Oct, Wed, Sat-Sun, public holidays and during school holidays 2-6pm. 32F (adult), 23F (child) or combined ticket for the Castle and the Musée de Poupées 59F (adult), 42F (child). ☎ 02 97 22 36 45.

Musée de Poupées – Open July and Aug, daily, 10am-6pm; June and Sept 2-6pm; Apr, May and Oct, Wed, Sat-Sun, public holidays and during school holidays 2-6pm. 30F (adult), 23F (child). Combined ticket for the Castle and the Musée de Poupées 59F (adult), 42F (child). ☎ 02 97 22 36 45.

Basilique Notre-Dame-du-Roncier – Guided tours available. ☎ 02 97 22 20 18.

Ascent to the Tower – July and Aug, daily, 10.30am-12.30pm and 2.30-6pm; rest of the year, apply to the Café de la Mairie. No charge. ☎ 02 97 22 20 18.

Chapelle Ste-Croix – Open in summer, during exhibitions. ☎ 02 97 22 24 17.

Ploërmel: Musée du Père Jean-Marie de la Mennais – ♿ Open mid-Apr to Oct, daily, 9am-noon and 2-6pm, Sun and holidays 10am-noon and 2-6pm; rest of the year, Sun and holidays, 10am-noon and 2-6pm. No charge. ☎ 02 97 74 06 67.

Château du Crévy – Guided tours (1hr15min) July and Aug, daily, 10am-6pm; Easter school holiday, June and Sept, 2-6pm; May, Sat-Sun when public holidays, 2-6pm. 30F. ☎ 02 97 74 91 95.

St-Marcel: Musée de la Résistance bretonne – ♿ Open mid-June to mid-Sept, daily, 10am-7pm; rest of the year, daily (except Tues), 10am-noon and 2-6pm. Closed 1 Jan and 25 Dec. 35F. ☎ 02 97 75 16 90.

JUGON-LES-LACS

Excursion

Ferme d'antan de St-Esprit-des-Bois en Plédéliac – Open June to Aug, daily (except Mon morning), 10am-12.30pm and 2-6.30pm; Apr, May and Sept, Sun and holidays only 2-6.30pm. Closed during Christmas school holiday. 22F. ☎ 02 96 34 14 67.

K

Domaine de KERGUÉHENNEC

Contemporary Art Centre, Park and Sculptures – ♿ Open mid-Jan to mid-Dec, daily (except Monday), 10am-6pm (7pm mid-June to mid-Sept). Closed mid-Dec to mid-Jan. 25F. ☎ 02 97 60 44 44.

KERNASCLÉDEN

Excursion

Château de Pont-Calleck – Park only open all day. Closed in Aug. No charge. ☎ 02 97 51 61 17.

L

LAMBALLE   🄸 Place du Martray, 22400 – ☎ 02 96 31 05 38

Haras national – ♿ Guided tours of the stables mid-June to mid-Sept, daily, 10.30am-12.30pm and 2-6pm; school holidays (except Christmas), at 2.30pm, 3.30pm and 4.30pm; rest of the year, Wed and Sat-Sun, 2-6pm. 25F. ☎ 02 96 50 06 98.

Musée du Pays de Lamballe – Open July and Aug, daily, 9.30am-6.30pm, Sun 10am-noon; Apr to June and Sept, daily (except Sun) 10am-12.30pm and 2-6pm (5pm the rest of the year). Closed Jan, 1 and 8 May, 14 July, 15 Aug. 10F. ☎ 02 96 34 77 63.

Musée Mathurin-Méheut – Open June to Sept, daily (except Sun), 10am-noon and 2.30-6pm; spring school holiday, 10am-noon and 2.30-5pm; rest of the year, Tues, Fri and Sat, 2.30-5pm. Closed January and all public holidays. 15F. ☎ 02 96 31 19 99.

Collégiale Notre-Dame – Guided tours July and Aug, daily (except Sun), 10am-noon and 2-6pm; rest of the year, apply to the tourist office or the presbytery. ☎ 02 96 31 02 55.

Excursions

Château de la Hunaudaye (**ruins**) – Tours with guides in period costume July and Aug, daily, 11am-12.30pm and 2.30-6pm, onSat-Sun 2.30-6pm; in June, Sun 2.30-6pm. 30F (adult), 15F (child). Guided tours July and Aug, Sat 2.30-6pm; Apr, May and Sept, Sun and public holidays 2.30-6pm; Easter school holiday, daily (except Mon), 2-5.30pm. 15F. ☎ 02 96 34 82 10.

Château de la Touche-Trébry – Guided tours (45min) July and Aug, daily, 2-7pm. 18F. ☎ 02 96 42 78 55.

LANDERNEAU
🚹 Pavillon Pont-de-Rohan, 29800 – ☎ 02 98 85 13 09

Église St-Thomas-de-Cantorbéry – Guided tours mid-July to mid-Aug, Mon to Fri, 9.30am-noon and 2-6pm.

LANDÉVENNEC

Ruines de l'ancienne Abbaye – Open mid-June to Sept, daily, 10am-7pm, Sun and holidays 2-7pm; rest of the year, Sat-Sun and school holidays 2-6pm. 25F. ☎ 02 98 27 35 90.

Abbey Museum – Same times and charges as for the Ruines de l'ancienne Abbaye.

LANNION

Église St-Jean-du-Baly – Closed Sun afternoons.

Castles and chapels

Chapelle de Kerfons – Open July to Sept, daily, 10am–noon and 2-6pm; rest of the year, apply to the Town hall (Mairie) in Ploubezre. ☎ 02 96 47 15 51.

Château de Tonquédec – Open June to Aug, daily, 10am-7pm; Easter to May and 1 to 30 Sept, 3-7pm. 20F; ☎ 02 96 47 18 63 or ☎ 02 96 47 15 47.

Château de Kergrist – Open June to Sept, daily, 11am-6.30pm; spring school holidays and public holidays in May, 2-6pm. Combined ticket château and gardens 30F, gardens only 20F. ☎ 02 96 38 91 44.

Chapelle des Sept-Saints – To visit the chapel during the off season, apply to the Town Hall (Mairie) in Vieux-Marché or to the address on the chapel door. ☎ 02 96 38 91 13.

Caouënnec-Lanvézéac: Church – Guided tours by appointment, 9–11.30am and 1.30-5pm. Apply to Mme Mayou, route de Lanvézéac. ☎ 02 96 35 89 96.

Locquémeau: Church – Guided tours July and Aug, daily, 10am-noon and 3-6pm.

Ploumilliau: Church – Guided tours during the high season, daily, 2-6pm; off season, apply to M. Maurice L'Escop. ☎ 02 96 35 44 44.

LOCMARIAQUER
🚹 Place de la Mairie, 56740 – ☎ 02 97 57 33 05

Ensemble mégalithique – Open June to Sept, daily, 10am-7pm (last admission 30min before closing); Apr and May 10am-1pm and 2-6pm; rest of the year 2-5pm. Closed mid-Dec to mid-Feb. High season 32F, low season 25F. ☎ 02 97 57 37 59.

LOCRONAN
🚹 Place de la Mairie, 29180 – ☎ 02 98 91 70 14

Église St-Ronan and Chapelle du Penity – Guided tours are available by appointment.

Chapelle Notre-Dame-de-Bonne-Nouvelle – Open Easter to All Saints' Day, daily, 10am-7pm.

Museum – Open mid-June to mid-Sept, daily, 10am-7pm; Easter to mid-June and mid-Sept to 1 Nov 10am-noon and 2-6pm; 1 Nov to Easter, 2-6pm. Closed Jan and Feb. 20F. ☎ 02 98 91 70 14.

Conservatoire de l'Affiche en Bretagne – Open late June to late Aug, daily, 10am-6pm; Apr, May and Sept to mid-Oct, daily (except Sat), 10am-1pm and 2-6pm. Closed holidays off season. 20F. ☎ 02 98 51 80 59.

Excursions

Montagne de Locronan: Chapel – Open only during the "Troménies': the "Petites Troménies" are held every year on the 2nd Sun in July; the "Grandes Troménies" are held every six years from the 1st to the 2nd Sun in July (the next one will take place in the year 2001). ☎ 02 98 91 70 93.

Ste-Anne-la-Palud: Chapel – Open Easter to All Saints' Day, daily, 9am-7pm. ☎ 02 98 92 50 17.

LOHÉAC

Manoir de l'Automobile – Open daily (except Mon), 10am-noon and 2-7pm. 38F. ☎ 02 99 34 02 32.

LORIENT
🛈 6, quai de Rohan, 56100 – ☎ 02 97 21 07 84

Guided tour of the town – Contact the tourist office.

Enclos du Port (dockyards) – Open mid-May to mid-Sept. Apply to the public relations officer, Comar Lorient BP1, 56998 Lorient-naval. ☎ 02 97 12 17 22 or ☎ 02 97 12 17 55.

"Ingénieur-Général-Stosskopf" Submarine Base – Guided tours (1hr15min) July and Aug, daily, 9.30am-6.15pm; mid-June to end of June and beginning of Sept to mid-Sept, daily (except Mon), 10am-5pm. 25F (A tour), 35F (B tour). ☎ 02 97 21 07 84.

The Victor Pleven – June to Aug, daily, 9am-7pm; Sept to May, 9am-12.30pm and 1.30-6pm. Closed 1 Jan and 25 Dec. 50F (adult), 35F (child). ☎ 02 97 88 15 12.

Zoo de Pont-Scorff – Open Apr to mid-July and mid-Aug to end of Sept, daily, 9.30am-6pm (last admission 1hr before closing; mid-July to mid-Aug, 9.30am-10pm; the rest of the year 9.30am-5pm. 57F (adult), 32F (child). ☎ 02 97 32 60 86.

LOUDÉAC

Race meetings – Daily (except Sat-Sun). No charge. ☎ 02 96 28 08 42. Excursion

La Chèze: Musée régional des Métiers de Bretagne – Open July and Aug, daily, 10am-noon and 2-6pm; in May, June and Sept, 2-6pm; Oct, Sat-Sun and holidays, 2-6pm. Closed Nov to Apr. 19F. ☎ 02 96 26 63 16.

M

MONTAGNES NOIRES

Chapelle Notre-Dame du Crann – Guided tours May to Sept, daily, 1.30-6.30pm; rest of the year, apply to M. Unvoas. ☎ 02 98 93 86 03.

Park and Château de Trévarez – Open July and Aug, daily, 11am-6.30pm; Apr to June and September 1-6pm; rest of the year, Wed, Sat-Sun and public holidays, 2-5.30pm; Christmas school holiday 1.30-5.30pm. 25F (adult), no charge (child). ☎ 02 98 26 82 79.

MONT-ST-MICHEL
🛈 Corps-de-Garde-des-Bourgeois, 50116 – ☎ 02 33 60 14 30

Car Park – Notice boards, updated on a daily basis, give the times of high tides and warn visitors of possible dangers. These instructions should be followed closely. 15F.

Abbey – Open May to Sept, daily, 9am-5.30pm; rest of the year 9.30am-4.30pm (5pm during school holidays). Guided tours also available at the same dates and times. Closed 1 Jan, 1 May, 1 and 11 Nov, and 25 Dec. 40F (guided tour included), 65F (visit-conference by appointment): ☎ 02 33 60 14 14.

Abbey Gardens – Open to the public in summer only (ask at the abbey entrance).

Archéoscope – Early Feb to mid-Nov, 9am-6pm (15min show, last admission 5.30pm). 45F (adult), 30F (child). ☎ 02 33 48 09 37.

Logis Tiphaine – Open July and Aug, daily, 9.30am-10pm or 11pm; Feb school holiday to June, Sept to mid-Nov, Christmas school holiday, daily 9.30-6pm; school holidays and public holidays, 9am-7pm. 25F. ☎ 02 33 60 23 34.

Golfe du MORBIHAN

The Gulf by boat: Île aux Moines – Departures every 30 min (time: 5 min) in July and Aug, 7am-10pm; rest of the year, 7am-7.30pm.. 20F there and back. ☎ 02 97 57 23 24.

St-Gildas-de-Rhuys: Church: Open daily (except Mon morning, Sat afternoon and Sun). Guided tours available. Apply to the presbytery. ☎ 02 97 45 24 71.

Treasury – Open July and Aug, daily, 10am-noon and 4-6pm, Sun, Mon and holidays 4-6pm, Sat 10am-noon. No charge. ☎ 02 97 45 23 10.

Château de Suscinio – Open Apr to Sept, daily 10am-noon and 2-7pm (June to Sept, 10am-7pm); rest of the year, daily (except Tues), 2-5pm, Sat-Sun and holidays 10am-noon and 2-5pm. Closed 20 Dec to 10 Jan. 30F (adult), 10F (child). ☎ Sagemor 02 97 41 91 91.

MORLAIX
🚩 Place des Otages, 29600 – ☎ 02 98 62 14 94

Guided tour of the town – Contact the tourist office.

Église St-Mélaine – Daily except Sat-Sun.

Maison de la Reine Anne – Open July and Aug, daily (except Sun), 10am-6.30pm; May and June, 10am-noon and 2-6pm; Sept, 10am-noon and 2.30-5pm; Apr, daily (except Sun and Mon), 10am-noon and 2.30-5.30pm. Closed Oct to Mar and public holidays. 10F. ☎ 02 98 88 23 26.

Musée des Jacobins – ♿ Open July and Aug, daily, 10am-12.30pm and 2-6.30pm; Easter to June, Sept and Oct, daily (except Sat morning and Tues), 10am-noon and 2-6pm; rest of the year, daily (except Sat morning and Tues), 10am-noon and 2-5pm, Sun 10am-noon and 2-6pm. Closed 1 Jan, 1 May and 25 Dec. 26F. ☎ 02 98 88 68 88.

Église St-Mathieu – Open Mon to Fri.

Excursions

Carantec: Musée maritime – Open Apr and mid-June to early Sept, daily (except Thur), 10am-noon and 3-6pm. 12F. ☎ 02 98 67 00 43.

Île Callot: Chapelle Notre-Dame – Visiting the chapel or attending religious services depends largely on the tides (times and tidal ranges). If the chapel is closed, apply to M. L'Hour, who lives in the next-door house. ☎ 02 98 67 07 88.

N

NANTES
🚩 Place du Commerce, 44000 – ☎ 02 40 20 60 00

Every day from April to September, as of 10.15am, a miniature train carries visitors around the centre of town. Departures from place St-Pierre, in front of the Cathedral. ☎ 02 40 62 06 22.

Guided tour of the town 🅰 – Contact the tourist office.

Musée du château des ducs de Bretagne – Open July and Aug, exhibition 9am-6pm, courtyard and ramparts 9am-7pm; Sept to June, daily (except Tues), 9am-noon and 2-6pm. Closed 1 Jan, Easter, 1 and 8 May, 1 and 11 Nov, 25 Dec. 20F, no charge on 2nd Sun of every month. ☎ 02 40 41 56 56.

Musée des Beaux-Arts – ♿ Open daily (except Tues), 10am-6pm, Fri 10am-9pm, Sun 11am-6pm. Closed all public holidays. 20F (free no charge on Fri 4.30-9pm). ☎ 02 40 41 65 65.

Muséum d'Histoire naturelle – ♿ Open daily (except Sun morning and Mon), 10am-noon and 2-6pm. Closed public holidays. 20F, no charge on 3rd Sun of every month. ☎ 02 40 99 26 20.

Palais Dobrée – Open daily (except Mon), 10am-noon and 1.30-5.30pm. Closed public holidays. 20F (combined ticket giving access to the Manoir de la Touche and Musée archéologique). ☎ 02 40 71 03 50.

Manoir de la Touche – Open daily (except Mon), 10am-noon and 1.30-5.30pm. Closed public holidays. 20F (combined ticket giving access to the Musée archéologique and the Palais Dobrée). ☎ 02 40 71 03 50.

Musée archéologique – Open daily (except Mon), 10am-noon and 1.30-5.30pm. Closed public holidays. 20F (combined ticket giving access to the Manoir de la Touche and the Palais Dobrée). ☎ 02 40 71 03 50.

Musée de l'Imprimerie – ♿ Open Mar to July, Mon to Fri 2-5pm; Sept to Feb, Tues to Sat 2-6pm, Sat 10am-noon and 2-5pm. Closed August and all public holidays. 30F. ☎ 02 40 73 26 55.

Maillé-Brézé – Guided tours (1hr or 90min including machinery) June to Sept, daily, 2-6pm; rest of the year, Wed, Sat-Sun, school holidays and public holidays 2-5pm. 30F (45F including machinery). ☎ 02 40 69 56 82.

Église Notre-Dame-de-Bon-Port – Open Mon to Fri.

Musée Jules-Verne – ♿ Open daily (except Sun morning and Tues), 10am-noon and 2-5pm. Closed public holidays. 8F. ☎ 02 40 69 72 52.

Old LU biscuit advertisement

H. Gyssels/DIAF

Planétarium – ♿ Shows (1hr), daily (except Sat) at 10.30am, 2.15pm, 3.45pm; Sun at 3pm and 4.30pm. Closed public holidays. 28F (adult), 14F (child). ☎ 02 40 73 99 23.

Musée de la Poupée et des Jouets anciens – This museum had closed at press time and may not open again.

Musée de la Poste – Open daily (except Sat afternoon and Sun), 8am-7pm. Closed public holidays. No charge. ☎ 02 51 83 39 39.

Chapelle de l'Immaculée – For reasons of security, the chapel is temporarily closed during major restoration work.

Maison de l'Erdre – Open daily (except tues), 11.30am to 6pm, Sat-Sun and holidays, 10am-noon and 3pm to 6pm. No charge. ☎ 02 40 29 41 11.

Boat Trip on the Erdre – Cruises at various times depending on the season; July and August, daily at 3pm and 5pm. 55F (adult),25F (child). Luncheon cruise (noon-3pm) year-round, 255F; dinner cruise (8pm-11pm) year-round, 295F. Reservations required. For information apply to the "Bateaux Nantais." ☎ 02 40 14 51 14.

Excursion

Château de Goulaine – Guided tours (1hr) mid-June to mid-Sept, daily (except Tues), 2-6pm; late Mar to mid-June and mid-Sept to end of Oct, Sat-Sun and public holidays 2-6pm. Closed Nov to Mar. 30F. ☎ 02 40 54 91 42.

Île d'OUESSANT

Écomusée de l'Île d'Ouessant – Open June to Sept and school holidays, daily 10.30am-6.30pm; Apr and May, daily (except Mon), 2-6.30pm; rest of the year, daily (except Mon), 2-4pm. Price not given. ☎ 02 98 48 86 37.

Centre d'Interprétation des Phares et Balises – ♿ Open May to Sept and during school holidays, daily, 10.30am-6.30pm; Apr, daily (except Mon), 2-6.30pm; rest of the year, daily (except Mon), 2-4pm. 25F. ☎ 02 98 48 80 70.

Océarium du Croisic – Sfenico

Océarium du Croisic

P

PAIMPOL

Musée de la Mer – Open mid-June to mid-Sept, daily 10.30am-1pm and 3-7pm; Easter school holiday and mid-May to mid-June, 3-6pm. Closed the rest of the year. 21,50F. ☎ 02 96 22 02 19.

La Côte du Goëlo

Abbaye de Beauport – Open mid-June to mid-Sept, daily, 10am-7pm; rest of the year open 10am-noon and 2-5pm. Closed 1 January and Christmas. 25F. ☎ 02 96 55 18 58.

Forêt de PAIMPONT

Château de Comper – Open June to Aug, daily (except Tues), 10am-7pm; Apr, May and Sept, daily (except Tues and Fri), 10am-7pm. . 25F. ☎ 02 97 22 79 96.

Paimpont, Abbey Church – Open late June to early Sept. Guided tours available; apply to M. Rebour, Abbaye, 35380 Paimpont. ☎ 02 99 07 81 37.

Treasury – ♿ Open July and Aug, daily, 10am-noon and 3-6.30pm; Easter to June and Sept, Sat-Sun and holidays, 10am-noon and 3-6.30pm. No charge. ☎ 02 99 07 81 37.

Château de Trécesson – Access is limited to the interior courtyard.

Tréhorenteuc, Church – Open daily (except Sun morning), 9.30am-noon and 2-5.30pm. ☎ 02 97 93 05 12.

Canton de Guer-Coëtquidan

École de St-Cyr-Coëtquidan, Musée du Souvenir – Open daily (except Mon), 10am-noon and 2-6pm. Closed 1 May and mid-Dec to mid-Feb. 22F. ☎ 02 97 73 53 06.

Site mégalithique de Monteneuf – Open July and Aug, daily, 10.30am-6.30pm; Apr to June, Sept and Oct, Sat-Sun and holidays, 2.30-6pm. 10F. ☎ 02 97 22 04 78.

PERROS-GUIREC   🖪 21, place de l'Hôtel-de-Ville, 22700 – ☎ 02 96 23 21 15

Church – Open Mon to Fri, 9.30-noon and 2.30pm-5.30pm. Presbytère de Perros-Guirec ☎ 02 96 23 21 64.

Musée de Cire-Chouannerie Bretonne – Open mid-June to mid-Sept, daily, 10am-6pm; Feb school holiday, from Easter school holiday to mid-June and from mid-Sept to end of Oct, 2-6pm. Closed the rest of the year. 18F. ☎ 02 96 91 23 45.

Ploumanac'h: Maison du littoral – ♿ Mid-June to mid-Sept, 10.30am-7pm; school hoidays: daily except Mon 2.30pm-5.30pm. No charge. ☎ 02 96 91 62 77.

Boat trips

Sept-Îles: Tour of the Islands – Four companies use a central reservation service at the Trestaou Gare Maritime. Some boats are "glass bottomed". Excursions (1hr30min to 3hr30min) round various islands (with or without stopovers of variable length) from Feb to early Nov. ☎ 02 96 91 10 00.

Île aux Moines: Lighthouse – Guided tours (30min) June to Sept, daily, depending on arrival time of the boats. ☎ 02 96 23 92 10.

PLEYBEN

Church – Guided tours available July and August by appointment; guided tours of the seven chapels in Pleyben once a week. ☎ 02 98 26 60 11.

Presqu'île de PLOUGASTEL-DAOULAS   🖪 BP 27, 29470 – ☎ 02 98 40 34 98

Church – Open July and Aug, daily, 9am-noon and 2-6pm; rest of the year 9am-noon.

Musée du Patrimoine et de la Fraise – ♿ Open June to Sept, daily (except Sat and Sun mornings), 10am-noon and 2-6.30pm; Apr and May, Oct and school holidays, daily (except Tues), 2-6pm. Closed public holidays. 25F. ☎ 02 98 40 21 18.

Excursion

Chapelle Ste-Christine – Apply to Mme Le Gall at the next-door house.

PONT-AVEN   🖪 Place de l'Hôtel-de-Ville, 29930 – ☎ 02 98 06 04 70

Museum – ♿ Open July and Aug, daily, 10am-7pm; Apr to June, Sept and Oct, 10am-12.30pm and 2-6.30pm; Feb, Mar, and Nov and Dec, 10am-12.30pm and 2-6pm. The museum closes for four days between temporary exhibitions. 25F (20F off-season). ☎ 02 98 06 14 43.

Névez, Chapelle Ste-Barbe – Guided tours daily (except Sat-Sun), apply to the tourist office. ☎ 02 98 06 87 90.

PONT-L'ABBÉ
🛈 3, rue du Château, 29120 – ☎ 02 98 82 37 99

Musée Bigouden – Open June to Sept, daily 10am-noon, 2-6pm. April and May, daily (except Sun), 10am-noon, 2-5pm. Closed Oct to March, 1 May. 20F. ☎ 02 98 66 09 09.

Excursions

Chapelle Notre-Dame-de-Tréminou – Open July to early Sept, daily, 2-6pm. Presbytery. ☎ 02 98 82 00 76.

Maison du Pays Bigouden – Open June to Sept, daily (except Sun), 10am-noon and 2-6pm. Closed public holidays. 15F ☎ 02 98 87 35 63 or ☎ 02 98 66 09 09.

Manoir de Kérazan – Open mid-June to Aug, daily 10.30am- 7pm; Easter to mid-June and Sept, daily (except Mon) 2-6pm. 32F. ☎ 02 98 87 40 40.

Boat trips to Île Tudy – The peninsula can be reached by CD 144 or by sea, with departures from Loctudy. There are several two-way trips a day (except Sun mid-Sept to mid-June). 10F there and back.

PORT-LOUIS

Musées de la Citadelle – Open June to Sept, daily, 10am-6.30pm; Apr to May, daily (except Tues), 10am-6.30pm; Jan to Mar, Oct and Nov, 1.30-6pm. Closed December, 1 Jan and 1 May. 29F. ☎ 02 97 12 10 37.

Q

Presqu'île de QUIBERON

Isthme de Penthièvre, Galion de Plouharnel – Open July and Aug, daily, 9.30am-7pm (last admission 30min before closing); Apr to June and Sept, 10am-noon and 2-6pm. Closed the rest of the year. 20F. ☎ 02 97 52 39 56.

Musée de la Chouannerie – ৬ Open April to Sept, daily, 10am-noon and 2-6pm; rest of the year, apply three days in advance to M. Halna du Fretay. 25F. ☎ 02 97 52 31 31.

QUIMPER
🛈 Place de la Résistance, 29000 – ☎ 02 98 53 04 05

Guided tour of the town – Contact the tourist office.

Cathédrale St-Corentin – Guided tours July and Aug, daily, 10am-noon and 2-6pm. SPREV (Sauvegarde du Patrimoine Religieux en Vie). ☎ 02 98 95 06 19.

Musée des Beaux-Arts – ৬ Open July and Aug, daily, 10am-7pm; Apr to June, Sept and Oct, daily (except Tues), 10am-noon and 2-6pm; rest of the year, daily (except Sun morning and Tues), 10am-noon and 2-6pm. Closed 1 Jan, 1 May, 1 and 11 Nov and 25 Dec. 25F. ☎ 02 98 95 45 20.

Musée départemental breton – Open June to Sept, daily, 9am-6pm; rest of the year, daily (except Sun morning, Mon and holidays), 9am-noon and 2-5pm. 25F. ☎ 02 98 95 21 60.

Musée de la Faïence – ৬ Open mid-April to Oct, daily (except Sun), 10am-6pm. Closed public holidays. 26F. ☎ 02 98 90 12 72.

Faïenceries de Quimper HB Henriot – ৬ Guided tours (45min) July and Aug, Mon to Fri, 9-11.15am and 2-4.45pm (3.45pm Fri); rest of the year Mon to Fri 9-11.15am and 2-4.15pm (3pm Fri). Closed mid-Dec to end of Dec. 20F. ☎ 02 98 90 09 36.

Excursions

Chapelle de Kerdévot – Open July to Aug, daily, 2-6pm; May, June and Sept, Sun only 2-6pm.

Chapelle Notre-Dame-de-Quilinen – Guided tours available, apply to the Landrévarzec Town hall. ☎ 02 98 57 90 44.

Chapelle de St-Venec – Visit by appointment, apply to the tourist office. ☎ 02 98 57 70 73.

Boat trips

Down the Odet – Aprto Sept, up to 5 cruises a day (2hr30min). Luncheon cruises Tuesday to Sunday. Stopover in Bénodet, depending on tides, or longer trips out to the Îles Glénan. For information apply to the tourist office in Quimper or to "Les Vedettes de l'Odet". ☎ 02 98 57 00 58.

🛈 Le Bourgneuf, 29391 – ☏ 02 98 96 04 32

Maison des Archers: Museum – Open July and Aug; daily (except Tues), 11am-7m; rest of the year open depending on temporary exhibitions or events. Guided tours (1hr) available. 10F. ☏ 02 98 96 04 32.

Excursions

Le Pouldu: Chapelle Notre-Dame-de-la-Paix – Open July and August, daily, 10-11.30am, when volunteers are available.

Moëlan-sur-Mer:

Chapelle St-Philibert-et-St-Roch – Open July and Aug, daily, 10am-noon and 3.30-7pm. Tourist office. ☏ 02 98 39 67 28.

Church – Open daily (except Sat-Sun), 9am-6pm.

QUINTIN 🛈 Place 1830, 22800 – ☏ 02 96 74 01 51

Basilica – Open daily (except Wed afternoon). ☏ 02 96 74 92 17

Château – ♿ Guided tours (1hr15min, last admission 30min before closing) mid-June to mid-Sept, daily, 10.30am-12.30pm and 1.30-6.30pm; May to mid-June and mid-Sept to end of Sept, Easter and Nov school holidays, 2-5pm; Apr and Oct, Sat-Sun 2.30-5pm. Closed the rest of the year. 30F (adult), 15F (child). ☏ 02 96 74 94 79.

Excursions

Château de Beaumanoir – ♿ Open end of June to mid-Sept, daily, 2-7pm. 30F (adult), 15F (child). ☏ 02 96 74 90 82 or ☏ 01 47 55 19 46.

R

Vallée de la RANCE

Boat trip – For all information, apply to the tourist offices of St-Malo, Dinard, Dinan or the offices of Emeraude Lines, Naye Ferry Terminal, B.P. 16, 35401 St-Malo cedex, ☏ 02 23 18 01 80.

Croisière Gourmande – Mid-May to mid-Oct, dining cruise (3hr) on board the *Châteaubriand*, leaving from Port de la Richardais – ☏ 02 99 16 35 30.

Pleudihen-sur-Rance, Musée de la Pomme et du Cidre – ♿ Open June to Aug, daily, 10am-7pm; Apri, May and Sept, daily (except Sund), 2-7pm. 20F. ☏ 02 96 83 20 78.

Usine marémotrice de la Rance (Hydro-Electric Power Station) – Guided tours mid-June to mid-Sept, Tues and Thur at 2pm and 4pm; apply a few days in advance. No charge. ☏ 02 99 16 37 14.

Pointe du RAZ

Cars must be left in the car park (fee: 20F) 800m away from the point. Allow 1hr for the visit. Free shuttle service available. Information centre (Maison de la Pointe du Raz et du Cap Sizun) open July and Aug, daily, 9.30am-7.30pm; Apr, June and Sept, 10.30am-6pm. Guided walk round the site, 25F per adult, minimum 4 persons. ☏ 02 98 70 67 18.

REDON 🛈 Place de la République 35600 – ☏ 02 99 71 06 04

Carentoir: La Ferme du Monde – ♿ April to mid-Nov, 9 am-7pm (last entrance 5.30pm). 40F (adult), 25F (child). ☏ 02 99 93 70 70.

RENNES 🛈 11, rue St-Yves, 35064 – ☏ 02 99 67 11 11

Guided tour of the town 🅰 – Contact the "Rennes Ville d'Art et d'Histoire" department of the tourist office.

Cathédrale St-Pierre – Guided tours available, apply to the tourist office.

Palais de Justice – The fire that ravaged the Palais de Justice (Breton Parliament) during the night of 4 to 5 February 1994 makes it impossible to visit the building for the time being.

Town Hall – ♿ Open daily (except Sun), 8.30am-5.30pm, Sat 9.30am-noon). Closed public holidays. No charge. ☏ 02 99 28 55 55, extension 3339.

Musée de Bretagne – ♿ Open daily (except Tues), 10am-noon and 2-6pm. Closed public holidays. 15F. ☏ 02 99 28 55 84.

Musée des Beaux-Arts 🅰 – Open daily (except Tues), 10am-noon and 2-6pm. Closed public holidays. 20F. ☏ 02 99 28 55 85.

Écomusée du Pays de Rennes – Open daily (except Sat-Sun mornings and Tues), 9am-noon and 2-6pm (7pm on Sun). Closed mid-Jan to end of Jan and public holidays. 30F (adult), 15F (child). ☎ 02 99 51 38 15.

Écomusée du pays de Montfort – Open Sat 10am-noom, 2-6pm and Sun 2-6pm. Closed 1 Jan, 25 Dec. 20F. ☎ 02 99 09 15 35.

Bruz:

Church – Open daily (except Sat-Sun), 9-11.30am, apply in advance to the presbytery. ☎ 02 99 05 56 56.

Parc ornithologique de Bretagne – ♿ Open July and Aug, daily, 10am-noon and 2-7pm; 1Apr to June and Sept, 2-7pm; rest of the year, open Sun and holidays 2-6pm. Closed 25 Dec. 38F (adult), 22F (child). ☎ 02 99 52 68 57.

La ROCHE-BERNARD

Musée de la Vilaine maritime – Open mid-June to mid-Sept, daily, 10.30am-12.30pm and 2.30-6.30pm; Easter school holidays, beginning of June to mid-June and mid-Sept to end of Sept, 2.30-6.30pm; Oct to Dec and Mar to May, Sat-Sun and public holidays 2.30-6.30pm. Closed Jan, Feb and 25 Dec. 20F. ☎ 02 99 90 83 47.

Boat Trip on the River Vilaine – Boat trips (1hr30min) are available July and Aug, leaving every hour 2-6pm from the Arzal dam or La Roche-Bernard. 47F (adult), 30F (child). Lunch/dinner cruises May to Sept departing from the Arzal dam daily at 12.30pm, Fri and Sat at 8pm; rest of the year at 12.30pm. Meal and boat, about 185F (lunch) or 263F (dinner). ☎ 02 97 45 02 81.

Crowned cranes at Branféré zoo

Parc zoologique de Branféré – ♿ Open Apr to Sept, daily, 9am-8pm; Oct to Mar, 1.30-6.30pm. Closed 1 Jan and 25 Dec. 45F (adult), 25F (child). ☎ 02 97 42 94 66.

Moulin de Pen-Mur – Guided tours (30min) July to Sept, daily, 10am-12.30pm and 2-7pm; Apr to June and school holidays, daily (except Sun morning), 10am-12.30pm and 2-6pm; rest of the year, Sat and holidays, 10am-12.30pm and 2-6pm, Sun 2-6pm. 25F. ☎ 02 97 41 43 79.

Château de Léhélec – ♿ Guided tours (30min) mid-June to early Sept, daily (except Tues), 2-7pm; early Sept to early Oct, Sat-Sun 2-7pm. 20F. ☎ 02 99 91 84 33.

ROCHEFORT-EN-TERRE   🛈 Town Hall, 56220 – ☎ 02 97 43 33 57

Château – Guided tours (1hr) July and Aug, daily, 10am-6.30pm; June and Sept, 10am-noon and 2-6.30pm; May and Oct, daily, 2-6pm, Sat-Sun and public holidays 10am-noon and 2-6pm; during the school holidays, daily, 10am-noon and 2-6pm. 20F. ☎ 02 97 43 31 56.

Malansac: Parc de Préhistoire de Bretagne – ♿ Open Apr to mid-Oct, daily, 10am-6pm; mid-Oct to 11 Nov, Sun and Nov school holiday 1.30pm to 6pm; during late October-early November school holidays open daily 1.30-6pm. Closed 12 November to end of March. 44F (adult), 22F (child). ☎ 02 97 43 34 17.

ROSCOFF   🛈 46, rue Gambetta, 29680 – ☎ 02 98 61 12 13

Aquarium Charles-Pérez – Open June to Aug, daily, 10am-noon and 2-6pm; Apr, May, Sept, daily, Sat-Sun in Oct, Nov school holiday, 2-6pm. 26F. ☎ 02 98 29 23 25.

Viviers – Open Monday to Friday 9am-noon and 2-5pm, Sat 9-11am. Closed public holidays. No charge. ☎ 02 98 61 19 61.

Jardin exotique de Roscoff – Open July and Aug, daily, 10am-7pm; Apr to June, Sept and Oct, 10.30am-12.30pm and 2-6pm; Nov to Dec and Feb to Mar, daily (except Tues), 2-5pm. Closed Jan. 25F (adult), child free. ☎ 02 98 61 29 19.

Excursion

Île de Batz: Boat trips – You can take the Roscoff/Île de Batz crossing from from late June to mid-Sept, daily, 7.45am-8.15pm (every 30min); 8 departures daily the rest of the year. Tour the island or else visit the Baie de Morlaix: "Compagnie Finistérienne de Transports Maritimes", BP 10, Le Rhû, 29253 Île de Batz. ☎ 02 98 61 76 61 or ☎ 02 98 61 78 87 or "Armeïn excursions" ☎ 02 98 61 77 75.

S

ST-BRIEUC
🖪 7, rue Goueno, 22000 – ☎ 02 96 33 32 50

Guided tour of the town – Contact the tourist office.

Cathédrale St-Étienne – Guided tours July and Aug by appointment. Apply to the tourist office.

Musée – Open daily (except Sun morning and Mon), 9.30-11.45am and 1.30-5.45pm. 21F, no charge from Oct to Mar.

Marinarium de la Baie de St-Brieuc – Open July and Aug, daily (except Sat-Sun mornings), 9am-noon and 2-6pm; rest of the year, daily (except Sun morning and Sat), 9am-noon and 2-6pm. 10F. ☎ 02 96 32 27 98.

ST-MALO
🖪 Esplanade St-Vincent, 35400 – ☎ 02 99 56 64 48

Guided tour of the town 🅰 – Apply to the Musée d'Histoire de la Ville set up in the great keep of the castle. ☎ 02 99 40 71 57.

Cathédrale St-Vincent – Guided tours July and Aug, daily, 9am-6.30pm.

Musée d'Histoire de la Ville et d'Ethnographie du pays malouin – Open Apr to Sept, daily, 10am-noon and 2-6pm; rest of the year, daily (except Mon and holidays), 10am-noon and 2-6pm. Closed 1 May,1. 26,50F. ☎ 02 99 40 71 57.

Aquarium Intra-Muros – Open mid-July to Aug, daily, 10am-1pm and 2-10pm, Sun 10am-1pm and 2.30-6.30pm; Apr to mid-July, Sept and school holidays, 10am-1pm and 2-6.30pm; rest of the year, Sat-Sun and holidays, 10am-1pm and 2-6pm. 30F (adult), 20F (child). ☎ 02 99 56 94 77.

Fort National – Guided tours (30min) June to Sept, daily at low tide (variable times). Closed during high tide. 20F.

St-Servan-sur-Mer: Musée international du Long Cours Cap-Hornier – Open Apr to Sept, daily, 10am-noon and 2-6pm; rest of the year, daily (except Mon and holidays), 10am-noon and 2-6pm. Closed 1 May. 26,50F. ☎ 02 99 40 71 58.

Saint-Malo

ST-MALO

Rothéneuf:

Musée-Manoir de Jacques Cartier – Guided tours (30min) July and Aug, daily, 10-11.30am and 2.30-6pm; June and Sept, daily (except Sat-Sun), 10-11.30am and 2.30-6pm; Oct to May, daily (except Sat-Sun) at 10am and 3pm. Closed Apr and holidays. 25F. ☎ 02 99 40 97 73.

Rochers sculptés – Open daily 10am-6pm. Closed Jan and during violent storms. 15F. ☎ 02 99 56 97 64.

Excursions

Grand Aquarium – ♿ Mid-July to Aug, Mon-Sat 9am-10.30pm (last entrance 1hr before closing); first half of July, 9am-10pm; Sept to June, 9.30am-7pm. Closed 1 Jan and 25 Dec (mornings). 52F (adult), 36F (child); 64F (aquarium and 3-D movie). ☎ 02 99 81 40 11.

Château du Bos – ♿ Guided tours (2hr) of the "malouinière", a typical St-Malo mansion, July and Aug, daily at 3.30pm. 30F. ☎ 02 99 81 40 11.

ST-NAZAIRE   🛈 Place François-Blancho, 44600 – ☎ 02 40 22 40 65

Guided tour of the town – Contact the tourist office.

Panorama – Same opening times as for the Sous-Marin Espadon.

Écomusée and Sous-Marin Espadon – Open mid-June to mid-Sept, daily, 10am-8pm (10pm-midnight in July and Aug); early Feb to mid-June and mid-Sept to early Nov, 10am-and 6pm; early Nov to early Jan, daily (except Mon and Tues), 10am-noon and 2-6pm. Closed early Jan to early Feb, 1 Jan, 11 Nov, 24-25 and 31 Dec. 20F (Écomusée only), 45F (Écomusée and submarine). ☎ 08 00 44 10 00.

Église Ste-Anne – To visit the church, apply to the presbytery, 28 bd Mermoz. ☎ 02 40 53 31 95.

Église Notre-Dame-d'Espérance – To visit the church, apply to the presbytery, 2, rue Léon-Jouhaux. ☎ 02 40 70 17 43.

Tumulus de Dissignac – Open July and Aug, daily (except Tues), 10am-12.30pm and 2-6.30pm. 16F. ☎ 02 40 70 70 21.

ST-POL-DE-LÉON

Chapelle du Kreisker – Guided tours available in July and Aug.

Excursion

Château de Kérouzéré – Guided tours (1hr) mid-July to Aug, once every afternoon; 1 to 14 July and 1 to 15 September, Wed and Sundays at 5pm; mid-May to June and mid-Sept to Oct, Wed at 5pm. 18F. ☎ 02 98 29 96 05.

Ferme-Musée du Léon – Open May to Sept, daily, 10am-noon and 2-7pm; rest of the year, Sat-Sun and holidays, 2-7pm. 25F. ☎ 02 98 29 53 07.

Kerjean Castle – Open July and Aug, daily, 10am-7pm; June and Sept, daily (except Tues), 10am-6pm; Apr and May, daily (except Tues), 2-6pm; Oct, daily (except Tues), 2-5pm; rest of the year, Wed and Sun only 2-5pm. High season 25F; off season 18F. ☎ 02 98 69 93 69.

ST-QUAY-PORTRIEUX

Excursions

Étables-sur-Mer: Chapelle Notre-Dame-de-l'Espérance – Open July and Aug, daily, 2-6.30pm; rest of the year, Sun 2-6.30pm. ☎ 02 96 70 61 51.

Binic: Museum – ♿ Open July and Aug, daily, 2.30-6pm; Apr to June and Sept, daily (except Tues), 2.30-6pm. Closed the rest of the year. 18F. ☎ 02 96 73 37 95.

Trégomeur: Jardin zoologique de Bretagne – ♿ Open June to Aug, daily, 10am-6pm; in Apr, May and Sept, 2-6pm; Jan to Mar Oct and Dec, Wed and Sun, 2-6pm. Closed 1 Jan and 25 Dec. 50F (adult), 30F (child). ☎ 02 96 79 01 07.

ST-THÉGONNEC

Chapelle funéraire – Open Apr to Sept, daily, 9am-6pm (7pm June to Aug). No charge. ☎ 02 98 79 47 64.

Île de SEIN

Access to the Island by Boat – There are daily crossings from Audierne (Sainte-Evette) year-round aboard the *Enez Sun III*; July and Aug at 9am, 11.30am and 4.50pm, return journey at 10.20am, 3.30pm and 6.15pm; Sept to June at 9.30am, return journey at 4pm. Penn ar bed. ☎ 02 98 70 70 70.

Mid-July to mid-Aug, crossings from Camaret (aboard the André Colin, 196 passengers) at 8.45am, return journey Sun only at 5pm. Penn ar bed. ☎ 02 98 27 88 22.

Museum – Open late June to late Sept, daily, 10am-6pm. 15F. ☎ 02 98 70 90 35.

SIZUN

Excursion

Maison de la Rivière, de l'Eau et de la Pêche – Open mid-June to mid-Sept, daily 11am-6.30pm; rest of the year, by appointment. 25F. ☎ 02 98 68 86 33.

T

TRÉGASTEL-PLAGE

Aquarium marin – &. Open Jmid-June to mid-Sept, daily, 10am-6pm; Apr to mid-June and mid-Sept to end of Sept, 10am-noon and 2-6pm; in Oct, 2-5pm; Nov to Mar, 2-5pm during school holidays. 28F. ☎ 02 96 15 38 38.

TRÉGUIER   🖪 Hôtel de Ville – 22222 – ☎ 02 96 92 30 19

Maison de Renan – Open July and Aug, daily, 10am-1pm and 2.30-6.30pm; Apr to June, Sept, Oct and school holidays, daily (except Mon and Tues), 10am-noon and 2-6pm. 25F. ☎ 02 96 92 45 63.

Cathédrale St-Tugdual – Guided tours available July and Aug, daily (except Sun and holidays), 10am-noon and 2.30-6pm.

Treasury – Open July and Aug, daily 10am-6.30pm, Sat 10am-noon, Sun and holidays, 12.30-6.30pm; mid-June to end of June and beginning of Sept to mid-Sept, 10am-noon and 2-6pm, Sat 10am-noon, Sun and holidays 2-6pm. 4F. ☎ 02 96 92 30 51 or ☎ 02 96 92 30 19.

Cloisters – Open July and Aug, daily, 9.30am-6.30pm, Sun and holidays, 12.30-6.30pm; May, June and Sept, 10am-noon and 2-6pm, Sun and holidays 2-6pm. 14F (Cloisters and Treasury). ☎ 02 96 92 22 33.

Excursions

Château de la Roche-Jagu – Open July and Aug, daily, 10am-7pm; mid-Feb to June, 10.30am-12.30pm and 2-6pm; Sept to mid-Nov, 10.30am-12.30pm and 2-7pm. Closed the rest of the year. 25F. ☎ 02 96 95 62 35.

St-Gonéry: Chapelle St-Gonéry – Guided tour by appointment. Apply to Mme Richard. ☎ 02 96 92 50 00.

Port-Blanc: Chapelle Notre-Dame-de-Port-Blanc – Open July and Aug, daily, 10.30am-12.30pm and 3-6pm.

U – V

USHANT – See île d'OUESSANT

Le VAL-ANDRÉ

Excursions

Château de Bienassis – Guided tours (45 min) mid-June to mid-Sept, daily, 10.30am-12.30pm and 2-6.30pm, Sun and holidays 2-6.30pm. 24F. ☎ 02 96 72 22 03.

Chapelle St-Jacques-le-Majeur – To visit the chapel, apply to the next-door farm.

VANNES   🖪 1, rue Thiers, 56000 – ☎ 02 97 47 24 34

Guided tour of the town 🅰 – Contact the tourist office.

Musée de la Cohue – Open mid-June to Sept, daily, 10am-6pm; rest of the year, daily (except Tues), 10am-noon and 2-6pm. Closed public holidays off season. 26F. ☎ 02 97 47 35 86.

Cathédrale St-Pierre: Treasury – Open May to Oct, daily (except Sun), 10.30am-6pm; rest of the year, during school holidays daily (except Sun), 2-6pm. 15F. ☎ 02 97 42 40 55.

Musée archéologique de Morbihan – Open April to 31 Oct, daily (except Sun), 9.30am-noon and 2-6pm (July and Aug, 9.30am-6pm); rest of the year, daily (except Sun), 2-6pm. Closed public holidays. 20F. ☎ 02 97 42 59 80.

Aquarium océanographique et tropical – ♿ Open June to Aug, daily, 9am-7pm; rest of the year, 9am-12.30pm and 1.30-6pm. Closed mornings of 1 Jan and 25 Dec. 50F (adult), 30F (child). ☎ 02 97 40 67 40.

Palais des Automates – ♿ Open July and Aug, daily, 10am-7pm; Apr to June and 1 Sept to mid-Sept, 10am-noon and 2-6pm; mid-Feb to Mar and mid-Sept to Oct, 2-6pm. Closed Nov and Dec. 30F. ☎ 02 97 40 40 39.

Le Jardin aux Papillons – Open June to Aug, daily, 10am-7pm; Apr, May and Sept, 10am-12.30pm and 2-6pm. 37F (adult), 28F (child). ☎ 02 97 46 01 02.

Excursions

Presqu'île de Séné: Réserve naturelle des marais de Séné – Guided tours (1hr30min) July and Aug, daily 10am-1pm and 2-7pm; May and June, Sat-Sun and holidays 2-7pm; Apr, daily, 2-7pm; Feb, Tues and Fri at 2.30pm, Sun 2-6pm. 25F. Nature trail (3hr) July and Aug, 3 times a week; Jan to Sept, twice a month. 40F. ☎ 02 97 66 92 76.

Château du Plessis-Josso – Guided tours (30 min) July to early Sept, daily, 2-7pm. 25F. ☎ 02 97 43 16 16.

Forteresse de Largoët: Tours d'Elven – Open June to Sept and school holidays, daily, 10.30am-6.30pm; mid-March to May and Oct, Sat-Sun and holidays, 2-6.30pm. 20F. ☎ 02 97 53 35 96.

St-Avé: Chapelle Notre-Dame-du-Loc – Open July and Aug, daily (except Sun), 10am-12.30pm and 2-6.30pm; rest of the year apply to the Town hall (Mairie). ☎ 02 97 60 70 10.

VITRÉ
🛈 Promenade St-Yves, 35500 – ☎ 02 99 75 04 46

Guided tour of the town 🅰 – Contact the tourist office.

Castle – Open July-Sept daily, 10am-6pm; Apr to June, 10am-noon and 2pm-5.30pm; rest of the year, daily (except Sat-Mon mornings and Tues), 10am-noon and 2-5.30pm. Closed 1 Jan, Easter Sun, 1 November and 25 Dec. 26F. ☎ 02 99 75 04 54.

Musée St-Nicolas – Same times and charges as for the Castle. ☎ 02 99 75 04 54.

Excursion

Château des Rochers-Sévigné – Guided tours (1hr) July to Sept, daily, 10am-6pm; Apr to June, 10am-noon and 2-5.30pm; rest of the year, daily (except Sat-Sun and Mon mornings, and Tues), 10am-noon and 2-5.30pm. Closed 1 Jan, Easter Sun, 1 Nov and 25 Dec. 18F (Dec to Mar, 3 museums) or 26F (4 museums). ☎ 02 99 75 04 54.

Herring gulls

Index

A

B

C

O – P

Q

R